Teaching Language Arts In Middle Schools

Connecting and Communicating

Teaching Language Arts In Middle Schools

Connecting and Communicating

Sharon Kingen
Ball State University

2000

LAWRENCE ERLBAUM ASSOCIATES, PUBLISHERS
Mahwah, New Jersey   London

Lawrence Erlbaum Associates, Inc., Publishers
10 Industrial Avenue
Mahwah, NJ 07430

Cover design by Kathryn Houghtaling Lacey

Library of Congress Cataloging-in-Publication Data

Kingen, Sharon.
Teaching language arts in middle schools : connecting and communicating
/ by Sharon Kingen.
        p.   cm.
Includes bibliographical references and index.
ISBN 0-8058-3055-3 (pbk : alk. paper)
1. Language arts (Middle school)—United States Handbooks, manuals, etc.
2. Middle school teaching—United States Handbooks, manuals, etc.
I. Title.
LB1631.K493   2000
428'.0071'2—dc21   99-42074
                                                                        CIP

Books published by Lawrence Erlbaum Associates are printed on acid-free paper, and their bindings are chosen for strength and durability.

Printed in the United States of America
10 9 8 7 6 5 4 3 2 1

Contents

Chapter 5   Teaching Writing   144

Chapter 6   Teaching Speaking and Performing   216

Chapter 7   Teaching Listening   260

Chapter 8   Teaching Visual Literacy   289

Part III   Teaching the Content of Language Arts   345

Chapter 9   Teaching Literature   347

Chapter 10   Teaching Language   418

Chapter 11   Teaching Media   469

PART IV   Connecting Teaching and Learning   503

Chapter 12   Integrating the Language Arts   505

Note
to the Reader

Congratulations! You are one of the special people who has discovered that the introduction to a book often unlocks some of its mysteries, such as Who is this writer anyway? and What makes her think she knows anything about teaching middle school? You already know my name, but that tells you little. If you check the first pages, you will discover that I am affiliated with Ball State University, which may not mean much unless you are from the Midwest. Ball State is a public university in Muncie, Indiana, with a long history and distinguished reputation in teacher education. It is also my alma mater. However, I have spent most of my career teaching in middle schools, 17 years, in fact. After spending some additional time supervising student teachers throughout Indiana, I finally settled into my current position which centers around teaching language arts methods, especially those associated with middle schools.

Although this book will be useful to a broad range of language arts educators, I designed it primarily for people who are much like my students: preservice teachers who have had little experience working in middle school classrooms. Those who enroll in my class are English majors seeking a license to teach at the secondary level. To most of them, middle school is a question mark, unexplored territory about which they have mixed feelings. Part of my task each semester is to erase some stereotypes and misconceptions while sharing the realities and rewards of middle grades instruction, so that they can decide for themselves whether they can find satisfaction in teaching young adolescents.

I have created this book to meet the needs of preservice students who are just coming to understand the challenges of teaching well. Three ideas are central to this book:

- Teaching language arts at the middle level is a complex activity. Connecting a wide range of students with the intertwined communication of language arts demands expertise in the use of a variety of strategies.
- Reading and writing are key processes of language arts study, but so are speaking, listening, and viewing and visually representing.
- Although teaching the processes of effective communication is crucial, middle school students must also begin to learn the content of the field—literature, language, and media.

This book presents balanced attention to various teaching strategies, processes, and content, demonstrating how all of these connect to improve students' abilities to communicate.

Research and theory are summarized and applied to practice. Throughout the book, useful theories and recent research findings that have practical implications for the classroom are highlighted. To make well-informed decisions, beginning teachers need to know what language arts professionals currently believe about how to teach effectively.

A nonprescriptive approach is integrated with practical information. Although relevant research and theory are included, I have avoided prescriptions. Effective teaching is far more a matter of making the best choices than of following instructions. The definition of *best choices* depends on who you are, who the students are, and the environment in which teaching and learning occur. This book challenges you to think about what you know and what you believe. It asks you to stretch your ability to interpret, apply, analyze, synthesize, and evaluate. On the other hand, you probably want straight talk about how to teach. Therefore, I have included many illustrations and examples that clarify concepts, as well as practical activities that have succeeded in middle level classrooms. But you, as the reader, will still have to make many decisions about your teaching philosophy and style.

Debates in the field are acknowledged. No single teaching style, approach, or method is consistently superior to all the rest, but some classroom practices are far better than others in producing certain kinds of positive results. Some familiar strategies are more controversial than you may think, and experts consider some commonly accepted methods to be detrimental. Nonetheless, many of these persist. These controversies are briefly sketched so that you will be aware of the different viewpoints. These debatable issues need to be considered thoughtfully, even if your prior experiences have led you to particular conclusions. For example, your own experiences as a student may have led you to believe that teaching is primarily about transferring information from your head to the heads of your students. The fact is, however, that many of the characteristics that mark this teaching style and philosophical viewpoint are at odds with the current research and recommendations of expert teachers concerning what is most appropriate for middle level students. The decision of whether to accept or reject this information is yours to make, but you need to know what is most strongly supported and encouraged by the profession before you make that choice.

Additional reading and research are emphasized. The information presented in this text is drawn from many sources. To make the text more readable, I have used in-text citations sparingly. Instead, each chapter contains a selected list of Recommended Readings. You should explore as many as you can and locate more recently published ones that may be useful. This additional reading will reassure you that the information here presents best practices as defined by a broad array of professional language arts educators, and it will aid you in keeping abreast of new developments in the field. This book represents the current status of our knowledge about teaching language arts effectively, but we all have much to learn.

The author's voice and point of view are explicit. Although most of the material in this book is a synthesis of information, occasionally I, as the author, do speak as an individual, especially to relate a personal experience that illustrates a point or clarifies a concept. When I do so, I have tried to label this perspective as mine alone. Furthermore, a useful book should tell readers what they do not already know. Now and then you will read a statement or recommendation and wonder to yourself why it was included. "Everybody knows that already. It's common sense," you may think. However, I have learned that what is logical and obvious to one reader may not be all that reasonable and apparent to another. In choosing what to include and what to omit, I have relied on my experiences with student teachers and preservice methods students. Their questions and concerns formed the original foundation of this book. When you read suggestions that you find to be obviously true, I hope you will accept these not as condescending statements, but as reinforcements of what you have already learned from your course work or your personal experiences. Most importantly, I hope that this book provides the basis for exchanging ideas, views, and perspectives with others so that you can create meaningful content that you can apply effectively in the classroom as soon as you have the opportunity to do so.

ACKNOWLEDGMENTS

As with most books, this one has been both a labor of love and just plain labor. Fortunately, many individuals have helped to ease the burden. My sincerest gratitude must first go to Naomi Silverman, Senior Editor at Lawrence Erlbaum Associates, who never faltered in her support for this project. But what I appreciated most was that she cared about me as a person. I also wish to thank the staff at Lawrence Erlbaum Associates, who provided invaluable assistance in numerous ways. I would also like to extend appreciation to the English Department at Ball State for providing time so that I could continue writing even though it inconvenienced others. To those who reviewed the early drafts of this work—Josephine P. Young, Judith L. Irvin, Carol A. Pope, and Nancy B. Mizelle—my apologies for the weaknesses in the drafts that made your task more difficult. But more importantly, my heartfelt thanks for the thoroughness of your constructive criticism and the encouragement of your praise. The finished piece, with whatever shortcomings it may have, is mine, and I take full responsibility for it, but your assistance was invaluable. To my friends, thanks for your support. To Mom, all my love—I could never have made it through without you. And to Dad, I'm sorry you missed the finale, but without you the journey would not have been possible. Thank you for all the wonderful memories.

I

Foundations and Principles

1

Centering on Students

Overview

- Consider These Questions
- The Best Starting Point
- Developmental Characteristics
- Motivation
- Special Student Populations
- The Gender Issue
- Recommended Readings

CONSIDER THESE QUESTIONS ABOUT MIDDLE SCHOOL STUDENTS

1. What stands out in your memory about your own middle school experiences? Which teachers do you remember most vividly? Do you recall any peers, friends, or social activities?
2. Middle school students always seem to be on the move. Are there any physical reasons for this perpetual motion?
3. The center of life for many middle school students seems to be friends. Is this a characteristic that has to be curbed, or is it an attribute that a language arts teacher can use to enhance learning? How?

4. Middle school students are riding an emotional roller coaster. As a language arts teacher, what can you do to help students climb aboard with confidence? How can you make their ride smoother?

5. Is it typical for middle school students to be interested in issues such as world hunger or environmental protection? Are they capable of making moral decisions for themselves?

6. Some teachers believe that middle school students need to concentrate on basic skills. Other teachers believe that these students need more challenging and complex learning experiences. Which of these two positions more closely matches your own? Why?

7. What motivates you to learn? Are middle school students motivated by the same things?

8. What kinds of classroom experiences are best suited to the developmental needs of middle school students?

9. Who are some of the special groups of students who may need special attention in a language arts classroom? What assistance may be necessary?

10. How can you create and adapt instruction to meet the diverse needs of middle school students?

THE BEST STARTING POINT

As a preservice teacher, you are probably anxious to get into the classroom on a full-time basis and apply what you have already learned. At the same time, you may have many questions and concerns about your ability to teach well. Perhaps you feel confident about your knowledge of the content, but you are wondering whether you can explain it clearly to others. You may consider yourself well prepared to teach some elements of language arts but less ready to tackle other aspects. For example, you may feel sure of your ability to provide literature instruction but insecure about teaching composition or language. You may also have some concerns about how the students will perceive you. Will they like you as a person? Will they respond well to your teaching style? Will they enjoy your classes? And you may have serious questions about managing a classroom and disciplining students. All of these insecurities are normal; most preservice teachers have self-doubts as they move closer to graduating and beginning their careers. The material in this text should help to alleviate some of these worries and provide answers to some of your most bothersome questions. For the moment, however, you need to put these questions aside, because effective middle school language arts instruction cannot start with the teacher's concerns.

The middle school teacher must first look to the students. If someone says to you, "Oh, you're a teacher; what do you teach?" how will you answer? If you say, "students," you are well on your way to thinking as an effective middle level teacher. Of course, you will probably want to say something about the content area, too, but if that comes first on your priority list, then middle school teaching is apt to be an attitude-adjusting experience. According to the Carnegie Council on Adolescent Development (1989), whose report has become the driving force behind recent efforts to restructure middle schools, there is ample evidence to verify that failing to focus on the needs, interests, aptitudes, concerns, and abilities of young adolescents places them at risk of academic failure. However, many are at risk of even worse fates—drug addiction, teen pregnancy, sexually transmitted diseases, homelessness, suicide, and abject poverty. It is at the middle level that students begin seriously contemplating dropping out of school, running away from home, joining gangs, and committing violent crimes. To help them avoid such destructive behaviors, teachers must be prepared specifically for teaching at this level. A significant aspect of that preparation must be acquiring knowledge about the characteristics of middle level students and understanding the educational implications of those characteristics.

DEVELOPMENTAL CHARACTERISTICS

There is no such thing as a typical middle school student. Each is a unique human being. However, some general characteristics are important for you to know (Manning, 1993; National Middle School Association, 1995). These features can be divided into at least five categories of attributes: physical, emotional, social, moral, and cognitive.

Physical Attributes

In general, middle level students range in age from approximately 10 to 14, depending on a variety of factors such as whether the school includes Grades 5 or 9 and whether the school district tends to retain students in grade. Both sexes usually experience a growth spurt during the middle grades. This often happens earlier for girls than for boys, such that middle level girls tend to be more fully developed physically than boys until about age 14, when boys begin to catch up. However, the rate of development between sexes varies drastically from one individual to the next. Because of these physical changes, middle level students can be uncoordinated and clumsy. Rapid growth also creates bodily discomfort, making it physically painful to sit or stand in any one position for more than a short period of time. Appetite often increases. Both sexes begin to develop secondary sexual features. Girls begin menstruation. Their breasts expand and their hips widen. Boys begin to show facial hair, and their voices deepen. Body odor becomes more pronounced. All of these factors can be sources of embarrassment and self-consciousness, and they can also be sources of distraction. Young adolescents find it difficult to ignore such obvious marks of developing sexuality, both in themselves and in their peers.

Emotional Attributes

Middle level students are on an emotional roller coaster—up one minute and down the next. They can be very impatient, quick to anger, and extremely sensitive to any perceived slight. They may pout or weep or shout hurtful insults. Moments later, they are full of giggles, confidence, and compassion. They may make disparaging remarks about others but display extreme offense when they are the target of retribution. Some withdraw into shyness; others cover insecurity in showy displays of arrogance and loud expressions of vulgarity. Others are mature, outgoing, thoroughly enjoyable people. Most are trapped in contradictions. They want to break free from adult restrictions, especially those imposed by parents, teachers, and other authority figures; at the same time, they long for the security of structure and dependence. They need many opportunities to try on the mantle of adult responsibility and autonomy, but at the same time they need the safety net of supportive adults to catch them when they fall. The self-esteem of middle level students is rather fragile. Emotional tension can produce the need to expend energy, but it can also result in periods of lethargy.

Social Attributes

Despite all of the concerns they have about their physical and emotional selves, the realm of socialization is the center of the universe for middle level students. They are worried about who they are, but they are even more concerned about how others see them. In the social order of the class and the school, where do they fit? How can they be popular? How can they make friends? This is the time of cliques and gangs, the time when peer pressure exerts a tremendous influence on attitudes and behavior. It is also a time of striving for independence while expecting unconditional support from parents, teachers, and other adults.

Moral Attributes

Although some still view the world as if there are only two perspectives—right and wrong, good and bad—many students at the middle level begin to develop the ability to make reasoned moral and ethical choices. They start to see situations as more complex and view actions from a less egocentric perspective. This is often a time of testing the meaning of fairness, justice, equality, rights, and morality. As a result, many middle level students are hypersensitive about their possessions and their "space." They are also easily offended by what they perceive as prejudicial, unjust, and unethical behavior. Although middle grades students may be hypercritical of others, they may not see their own flaws. They want to develop their own set of standards and values, but they rely heavily on adults and peers for advice. Furthermore, they are often quite aware of double standards that exist around them.

Cognitive Attributes

Given what has been described, it should come as little surprise that for many, if not most, middle level students, intellectual pursuits attract about as much interest as carrying out the garbage. When one is wearing a bra for the first time, it is difficult to pay attention to a lecture on the use of commas in a series. When a best friend, in a sudden fit of abandonment, has just told personal secrets to one's worst enemy, all the definitions of the words so carefully memorized for the vocabulary test vanish. And when one is afraid to face the nightly abuse of a parent, the symbolism in a poem just does not seem to matter much. Middle level students must work hard to focus their attention on anything for very long. In fact, the general consensus is that the attention span of the average young adolescent is about 10 minutes. Many middle grades students are still linked very closely to concrete knowledge; abstract concepts are puzzling and difficult to grasp. They have a preference for active rather than passive learning activities, and they usually respond well to a variety of stimuli. Although some teachers behave as if middle level students are so overwhelmed with other aspects of their development that they cannot learn new material, that is not the case. Most young adolescents want school to be intellectually stimulating and they want to learn. They also want teachers who respect their ability to think. Once motivated, they can be very tenacious. A teacher who can tap into the individual interests of these students and who is willing to go the extra mile to persuade them that the topic at hand is absolutely fascinating (even when it really isn't) will find that middle level students are capable of significant learning gains.

Implications

Stevenson, in *Teaching Ten to Fourteen Year Olds* (1998) summed up these characteristics by stating five generalizations that he believed to be universal:

- Youngsters want physical exercise and freedom to move.
- Children want to believe in themselves as successful people.
- All youngsters want to be liked and respected.
- Youngsters want life to be just.
- Youngsters want to do and learn things that are worthwhile.

Physically, emotionally, socially, morally, and intellectually, middle level students are diverse and in flux. Although all of the shifting and changing—almost on a moment-to-moment basis—is disconcerting to teachers, it is even more perplexing to the students. A few middle level students are truly disruptive, disturbed, and even violent, but the vast majority are just desperately trying to discover a self with whom they can live for the rest of their lives. Middle level teachers, through caring and reaching beyond the insecurity, bravado, shyness, or pseudosophistication, can have a significant impact on this journey of self-discovery and creation.

If you are to develop a positive rapport with students, you must be aware of all of these developmental factors. Whenever possible, you should use this information about students to plan language arts instruction. For example, you can choose literature that explores the motivation and values of adolescent characters. To address their need for independence, you can give them some choices about when and how to complete tasks. You can plan cooperative learning activities wherein students share ideas and responsibilities with their peers. And students can be given some opportunities to move around in the classroom while they work. When their needs are addressed appropriately, middle school students are more readily motivated to learn.

MOTIVATION

All people are motivated—some by greed, some by envy, some by fear, and some by more positive factors. One of the basic theories related to motivation comes from the work of Maslow (1943), who identified a hierarchy of factors that influence motivation. According to the theory, people cannot attend to the higher levels of consideration until the more basic levels of need are satisfied. Food, shelter, and clothing are at the bottom rung of the ladder. Once these needs are met, people become conscious of their need for belonging and being valued by others. The need for learning, however, does not become evident until these physical and emotional needs are satisfied.

More recent research, however, indicates that human beings are innately motivated to learn. Were this not the case, infants probably would not learn to talk. Babbling is a kind of trial-and-error learning, as is child's play. On the other hand, students do not seem to be innately motivated to learn in the classroom.

Academic Motivation

Student motivation for academic learning is intriguing, puzzling, and frustrating. Educators do not yet know enough about what turns some students on to school, but they do know that what works for some has the reverse effect on others. If teachers reached the point of truly valuing human diversity, they might better appreciate this fact; but until this happens, educators are probably going to continue to struggle with the "problem" of motivating students.

Although the research on motivation is far from definitive, Frymier (1985) stated that when children start school, boys and girls have about the same level of motivation for learning, but during the elementary grades and into middle school, motivation among girls rises, whereas that of boys declines. During the high school years the trend reverses; motivation among boys rises; and it declines among girls. Factors such as socioeconomic status (SES) and education of family members influence motivation. Although there certainly are exceptions, the lower the SES, the lower the motivation; the less education completed by the parents, the lower the motivation. However, many young people born into poverty do succeed, and supportive parents can positively enhance motivation. Anxiety is another factor that influences motivation. A certain amount of tension generally enhances performance, but when the anxiety level reaches an intolerable point, performance declines swiftly.

The source of motivation varies. Some people are motivated extrinsically. They almost exclusively rely on factors outside themselves for motivation (e.g., teacher praise, grades, reactions of peers). They tend to feel that any success (or failure) is the result of luck, chance, or other people. No matter what the outcome, the responsibility rests outside themselves, and they cannot accept personal credit for success. Intrinsically motivated people, on the other hand, tend to take the credit (or accept the blame) for the outcome. Although they may find external rewards pleasing, they are much more strongly influenced by personal satisfaction or dissatisfaction. In effect, they motivate themselves.

Although most educators agree that teachers should strive to increase students' intrinsic motivation, most young people are extrinsically motivated. Commonly used reward systems—gold stars, smiley face stickers, special passes, food prizes, verbal praise, and even grades—reinforce extrinsic motivation. This is also true of various forms of classroom competition. A great deal of research evidence shows that such rewards work in the sense that the desired performance occurs (e.g., attendance improves, test scores go up, students report more positive attitudes, etc.). Other researchers argue that although extrinsic rewards produce short-term results, they actually reduce motivation. There is evidence to suggest, for example, that praising self-confident students for completing easy tasks causes performance to decline. Other studies show that if the value or quantity of the reward does not continually increase, performance declines. (If this is a topic that interests you, you might enjoy reading *Punished by Rewards* by Kohn, 1993.)

Whether you agree or disagree about the necessity of rewards, and whether you see competition as an asset or detriment, one thing that is very clear in the classroom is that grades do not motivate some students. Students who ordinarily get high grades tend to be motivated by them. Those who do not are not motivated much by them nor are they motivated by the threat of low grades. There is even a theory that some students feel so powerless over much of their own lives that they actually choose to fail because it is something they can control.

Strategies for Motivating

With such a mixture of factors affecting motivation, enticing recalcitrant students into learning may seem impossible. You have little, if any, control over some factors related to motivation, but you can manipulate other factors so as to produce conditions that make learning more inviting. Frymier (1985) visualized motivation as a jigsaw puzzle made up of six interlocking factors. Three of these, unfortunately, are somewhat beyond your direct control. The first is the *characteristics of the learner*. You cannot magically give students the skills or abilities they lack nor instantly shift to positive attitudes the negative ones that students have already developed. Some students come to school without breakfast. Some have no friends. And some are abused and terrified. All of these are factors that you may be able to overcome if you first accept the idea that they do have a negative effect on learning. You should not use them to excuse students from learning, but ignoring them will not make them go away, either.

The second factor is *interest in a topic*. Some students come anxious to learn more about language arts; others come to the class detesting the thought of more reading and writing. You may not be able to change that fact on the first day, but you can broaden your curriculum to include whatever students are interested in, use examples with which they can connect, select more relevant reading materials, create meaningful writing assignments, and show them other aspects of the discipline that they have not yet explored.

Third, there is the issue of the *influence of others*. Some students come from home environments and communities where learning is not highly regarded. School may be viewed as a waste of time or even an evil force bent on teaching unacceptable values. Some students come from positive environments, but when they arrive in school they associate with peers who have negative attitudes toward school. Programs that involve parents, classroom activities that include community members, and teaching methods that address students' social needs in positive ways can change attitudes and offset negative influences.

These three forces are the most challenging to change. The other three factors are ones over which you have some, if not a great deal, of control—*curriculum materials, teaching methods,* and *your own characteristics*. You can choose curriculum materials and activities that engage even the most reluctant of learners, and you can use a wide variety of instructional methods that are designed to motivate as well as educate. At the very least, you can certainly demonstrate personal enthusiasm for the subject matter and for the students.

Using What Is Known

General information on what tends to increase motivation can lead teachers to the best options. To motivate students, you must first get their *attention*. The following items tend to attract attention and, thereby, encourage motivation:

1. Activity or movement
2. Reality (real situations, objects, or events, not abstractions or examples)
3. Proximity (close to students in space and time)
4. Familiarity
5. Novelty (old topics presented in new ways)
6. Suspense
7. Conflict
8. Humor
9. The vital (what the individual sees as important)

These are qualities that can be built into units and lesson plans, especially at the beginning of each year, unit of study, and even class period. If you can grab student attention initially, you have a chance of keeping it, at least for a while. You can maintain it by structuring for success: providing various learning aids, such as graphic organizers, and modeling how to proceed—techniques described as *scaffolding*. You can use examples that students recognize, interests they may have, and experiences to which they can relate. You can let them know what is expected and build their self-confidence. You can focus energy on developing intrinsic motivation and reduce reliance on extrinsic rewards. Also, you can make your classroom a place where risk taking is valued, where making a mistake is viewed as an opportunity to learn rather than a source of embarrassment, and where everyone is a potential contributor to the learning of everyone else. Most of all, you can retain positive thinking even when the student's own sense of self-worth begins to falter.

Motivating Middle Level Learners

Although some middle level students seem devoid of motivation, they are not. However, they may well have little interest in learning what you want to teach. Young adolescents do not usually make conscious decisions to fail; nevertheless, some behave in ways that they know, at least subconsciously, will lead to failure. Often they have tried before and been unsuccessful. It is far easier for them to choose to fail and much less damaging to the ego. "I could if I tried," they rationalize, but beneath it all, they are afraid. Trying is simply too risky. Others refuse to acknowledge that consequences exist. They act as if they believe that somehow, in some way—through good luck, personal charm, parental intervention or teacher sympathy—negative consequences will not happen, not to them. When one considers that young people engage in even riskier behaviors (e.g., experimentation with addictive drugs, delinquency, unprotected sex, etc.) in the belief that bad things only happen to other people, it certainly is no surprise that they can believe that poor performance in school will not necessarily lead to failing grades.

Research shows that students are motivated to achieve academically by five needs (Raffini, 1996):

- autonomy
- competence
- belonging and relatedness
- self-esteem
- involvement and enjoyment

As is true of most students, young adolescents appreciate the chance to exercise some autonomy or control over the situation. They prefer those classes in which they feel competent. They have a strong desire to belong socially, and they want instruction that relates to them personally. Many middle school students have overwhelming insecurities about themselves, so they especially value opportunities to enhance their sense of self-worth. They also demand to be actively involved in enjoyable, worthwhile experiences. If you, as the teacher, do not provide these opportunities and experiences, middle level students will create them, sometimes in social and behavioral ways that interfere with the teaching and learning you have in mind.

Recent research on brain function and motivation has produced some interesting and useful information about ways to enhance learning at the middle level. These data indicate that teachers can address student needs and encourage engagement in learning more fully by thoughtfully manipulating the six factors in Fig. 1.1, which form the acronym TARGET (Epstein, 1988, 1989; see also Ames, 1992):

To motivate, hit the

T-task
A-authority
R-reward
G-grouping
E-evaluation
T-time

FIG. 1.1

Tasks may be intrinsically interesting, at least to some students. Those who enjoy reading, for instance, will respond positively to a reading assignment. Those who do not must be enticed. The task itself can be modified to be more appealing. For example, requiring that students read but giving them some choice about what to read or when to read may encourage more to take part.

Authority in this context is directly related to autonomy. Giving students the chance to control some aspect of the learning process allows them to develop their sense of mastery. Viewed from another perspective, classroom activities can be designed such that students become authorities in some content or skill. For example, excellent spellers might assist other students in proofreading their written work. Acting as an authority enhances self-esteem and validates competence.

Rewards do motivate students. Some middle level students will work very hard for high grades. A few seek teacher praise. Most desire peer recognition. Others rely almost exclusively on the personal sense of satisfaction that accompanies achievement. Teachers can create a variety of rewards that will appeal to the range of student preferences. They can strive to ensure that all students are appropriately acclaimed for their achievements. An unexpected note to parents about good effort, positive attitude, helpfulness, cooperative spirit, or regular attendance can make students feel very good about themselves.

Grouping can be varied to increase interest. At times, students need to work independently. Indeed, some students find this situation preferable. However, many middle level students like to work in groups of various sizes—pairs, triads, or larger groups. The most capable students may respond positively to whole-class activities because they have a chance to demonstrate their knowledge to all of their classmates. Some students who rarely participate in whole-class instruction become leaders when small groups are created. A student who is unsure of his or her competence can bloom when given the chance to share ideas and information with a confused peer. Flexible grouping can help students feel as if they belong, and smaller group sizes increase the likelihood of active involvement.

Evaluation, too, can be a motivating force. How a teacher responds to student work and the content of that feedback can enhance a student's desire to perform well. Conversely, destructive criticism, biased grading, and sarcastic comments can decrease a student's self-esteem and sense of competence. A teacher must provide constructive criticism and accurate feedback, but how and when these responses are given can alter motivation. When students see the evaluation plan as reasonable and fair, they are more likely to strive to achieve.

Time allotment can influence motivation. Too much time may encourage some students to procrastinate; too little time may encourage students to rush. Either way, the end product is apt to be of lesser quality. Demanding that everyone finish at the same time sends the message that the teacher is more concerned with schedules than students. How time is allotted in the classroom tells much about what a teacher values.

It is important to note that the need for enjoyment is only one of several associated with academic achievement. At times it may seem as if the only criterion that middle level students use for judging a class is whether or not it is fun. They do want learning experiences to be enjoyable, but in the final analysis, they also want to learn. In considering how to motivate middle level students, balance is probably a key element. Just as it is necessary to consider all aspects of adolescent development—social, emotional, physical, moral, and intellectual—it is also necessary to consider all of the needs that motivate students toward academic excellence. Fun alone will not suffice. Similarly, it is necessary to recognize that all six factors of TARGET need to be orchestrated to enhance motivation. For example, giving students more time to work on a purposeless, irrelevant task will probably not encourage better performance. For additional information about using TARGET to improve middle school language arts instruction, the Mizelle (1997) article in the list of Recommended Readings at the end of this chapter is an excellent source.

Finally, whether for the sake of maintaining a positive learning environment or motivating students to do their best, you need to know the students by name as quickly as possible. As long as you cannot call a student by his or her name, that student will feel that you cannot possibly care about him or her. Once you know their names, students begin to feel that you know them as individuals.

SPECIAL STUDENT POPULATIONS

Because of the manner in which school programs are designed and external funds are allocated, certain groups of students have been identified as being of special concern. However, you should be aware that labels are often relative, fuzzy, inaccurate, and deceptive. What's more, students in the middle of the middle level population are often overlooked. Among the so-called "average" students will be ones who deserve special attention but do not match the criteria set by the schools or outside agencies for providing extra services. Some will have unrealized talents, potential gifts, and experiential knowledge that teachers have yet to tap. Others will have learning gaps that have escaped attention. And others will be coping with problems or undetected disabilities that they have learned to hide quite well from teachers, school officials, and peers. But the vast majority of these students will be hard-working, curious, humorous, attentive, cooperative, and generally delightful. Because they often attract little attention to themselves, they can easily be overlooked in the bustle of a hectic middle school environment. Even though they wear no special label, they deserve just as much attention as those who have received special designations.

Gifted and Talented Students

One of the most important things to remember about gifted and talented (G/T) students is that the labels are inconsistent. Students who qualify for these designations in one school district might not be identified as such in another. The theory of multiple intelligences (Gardner, 1983) has added yet another dimension to the categorization. In some schools, young people who have outstanding talents in the performing and fine arts are included in special programs for G/T students. However, the tendency is to continue to focus on cognitive facets of performance (verbal and mathematical) when identifying G/T students.

Although many G/T students are exceptionally able in many different areas, they are as diverse as all other students. Many G/T students at the middle level enjoy the challenge of verbally exploring abstract thinking, but they may not yet have all of the skills necessary to express these ideas well in writing. High ability in one area of the curriculum does not necessarily mean equally high productivity in others. As is true of most students, motivation and interest affect performance.

Educators and researchers tend to agree that G/T students need to be challenged. Boredom is a common complaint among this group of students. They need opportunities to investigate significant and personally interesting topics in depth. There is less agreement, however, about how to make this instruction a reality. Many experts in the field of gifted education argue that these students need special programs in which they are homogeneously grouped with peers. Other educators point out that segregating students by ability negatively affects less able students and denies G/T students the opportunity to develop socially and emotionally within a natural environment that includes people of varied abilities. Although the research indicates that G/T students can benefit somewhat from special programs and opportunities to interact with others of similar abilities, the research does not clarify what is best for all G/T students.

You may find yourself in a school or district where G/T students receive no special instruction, or you may find yourself in a place where such students are pulled out of your class for special programs daily or weekly. Another possibility is that students will be grouped by ability such that you have a class composed almost entirely of G/T students. Each of these structures necessitates a different approach. You may need to plan an individual program for just one student, create special tasks for a small number of students, differentiate instruction to allow for pull-out absences, or devise a significantly different curriculum for a G/T class.

When working with G/T students, you need to be aware of some potential problems. First, merely tinkering with tasks and curriculum may not engage G/T learners. They often need very different kinds of assignments, not just modifications of the typical one. Tasks that require synthesizing material, hypothesizing about possibilities, and forming complex webs of connections among ideas are appropriate for G/T students, as are those that ask them to explore unfamiliar territory—unusual discourse modes, varied forms of communication, creative modes of expression. Second, quantity should not substitute for quality. Adding more pages of exercises to the workload of G/T students is not an effective way to provide instruction, nor is requiring that they write longer papers and read thicker books. Instead, G/T students need opportunities to explore ideas in more depth, choose their own materials, design their own tasks, and work on challenging projects. Third, if you use a cooperative learning approach, you must ensure that the G/T students are not forced to carry more than their fair share of the work. Be aware, too, that although some gifted and talented students are effective tutors who enjoy helping classmates, others find this responsibility burdensome, especially when it prevents them from pursuing their own learning. Although G/T students do need opportunities to work with others, they also need to engage independently in research and projects. Fourth, keep in mind that G/T students are still middle level learners. They, too, are developing socially, emotionally, physically, morally, as well as intellectually. They can be just as insecure, shy, arrogant, opinionated, or uncoordinated as other students. Furthermore, if they have not previously been asked to make full use of their potential, they may resist being moved in this direction. If their talents have not been developed in their elementary school experiences, they may lack some of the skills they need to participate in higher level learning. These learners will probably need some scaffolded activities at first, but they will usually pick up speed quickly.

Mainstreamed and Inclusion Students

Whether your classroom will include students who are mentally and/or physically challenged depends on the policies and procedures of the school system. Federal law states that students are to be educated in the least restrictive environment. In some schools, this takes the form of *inclusion*, where these students participate fully as members of regular classes. In other schools, *mainstreaming* is used: Students who are mentally and/or physically challenged attend some classes with other students, but spend part of their time in a special program. Another possibility is that these students spend nearly all of their time in one classroom or area of the building, mixing with the rest of the school population only during lunch or special activities. The particular approach is supposed to be adjusted to meet the needs of each individual.

In considering mainstreamed and inclusion students, it is worth noting that many different subcategories of special needs exist. One group that presents special challenges for the language arts teacher are those who have been diagnosed as dyslexic (having significant difficulties in processing language). Although many varieties of dyslexia exist, most of these students struggle with decoding and comprehending text and with expressing their ideas in writing. They may do reasonably well in mathematics and performance classes such as art and physical education, but they may dread language arts class because that is where they must confront their frustrations.

Students who have been diagnosed with attention deficient disorder may have a similar response. They may do well in classes in which they can be physically active, but in those classes in which they must sit for an extended period of time, they are likely to have difficulty maintaining focus. Although the needs of these students often necessitate some changes in behaviors and expectations among all teachers, the language arts teacher may well be the one who must adapt the most.

If mainstreamed or inclusion students are a part of the classes you meet with regularly, you will probably be given some information about goals and expectations, usually in the form of an individualized education plan (IEP) that has been specifically tailored for each student. If you have an opportunity to be involved in the development of this plan, you may have the chance to blend your curriculum with the students' goals. Otherwise, you may find yourself having to provide a special curriculum for each of these students.

Although you may prefer to use a great deal of whole-class instruction, you may find that this does not adequately address the needs of students who are mentally challenged, physically challenged, or both. You will probably need to find ways to differentiate your instruction. Using cooperative learning, independent study, reading and writing workshops, inquiry learning, flexible pacing, and interdisciplinary units that incorporate some choices of tasks are some of the ways to accommodate the needs of mainstreamed and inclusion students.

In most instances, you will have access to some educational specialist who can give you helpful information about how to work with individuals with special needs. At times you will need to provide activities that are designed especially for students who are mentally challenged, physically challenged, or both; however, as much as possible, these students should be fully included in the class activities as often as possible. Some of the adaptations that you may need to consider include extending time limits, reducing quantities, simplifying tasks, relying more on verbal than on print communication (or more on print than on verbal in the case of hearing impairment), providing quick feedback that focuses primarily on strengths and improvement, using tape-recording and other kinds of technology that compensate for student differences, and substituting one activity within a unit for another. Of course, giving students choices allows them to select those tasks that best suit their individual capabilities.

Students who are mentally challenged, physically challenged, or both will be very vulnerable to abuse from peers. Some will not be socially aware. Some will be unbelievably patient, whereas others will have no emotional control. Many students who are physically challenged or those who have endured extensive medical treatment may have a world of knowledge and experience that far exceeds their physical maturity. As much as possible, each of these students needs the opportunity to develop his or her potential to its fullest. Each of these students will have unique combinations of strengths, weaknesses, interests, fears, joys, and concerns. Your task will be to discover the individuality that lies within each of them and provide an environment that nurtures this diversity.

Culturally Diverse Students

Meeting a classroom filled with culturally diverse students should be cause for celebration. Unfortunately, too many teachers see such classrooms as problematic. To some extent, this reaction is understandable because teachers tend to adhere to a model of education in which moving students along through the material at approximately the same rate is important. The more diverse the student population, the more difficult this appears to be. On the other hand, in the old one-room schoolhouse, teachers successfully coped with several grade levels at once. Surely, this was no more challenging than the diversity in a single middle level classroom.

Only in recent years have educators begun to study the effects that culture has on the learning styles of students. What we are discovering is a brilliant array of differences in communication modes, patterns of thinking, and learning preferences. Students who come from diverse cultures bring to the classroom a variety of experiences, familial structures, values, and lifestyles. This variety provides a grand opportunity for all to learn from each other, if educators provide the environment for the sharing of personal knowledge. Multicultural literature comes to life when students in the classroom can talk about their similar experiences. Multilanguages provide concrete examples of comparison that may not exist in monolingual classrooms. Differences become interesting rather than frightening. Awareness evolves into familiarity and respect. Used advantageously in the classroom, diversity becomes the foundation of civility.

It is overly simplistic advice, yet it is valuable: know the cultures of your students. Use the presence of cultural diversity as an opportunity to learn more about other people—their beliefs, their values, their customs, and their behaviors. Learn some of their languages. Be aware of some significant differences in communication styles, especially nonverbal expressions. Do not assume that certain behaviors are misbehaviors simply because they are different from your expectations. Some cultures rely on storytelling and circular verbal paths to make a point. Others consider literal level questions to be rhetorical; students will not respond when the answer is obvious. In some cultures, looking directly at the teacher is a sign of disrespect, and some cultures are based on cooperation instead of competition. Classroom instruction can be tailored not only to accommodate but also to enhance the potential value of each of these differences. Used in this way, diversity becomes a source of instructional strength.

On the other hand, overemphasizing differences can be somewhat dangerous. Diversity in the classroom ought not be used as the single reason for including multicultural literature, for example. Such literature belongs in every classroom, not just in those members of a particular ethnic, racial, or religious group are physically present. Similarly, students of varied cultures ought not be considered spokespersons unless they wish to take this role. Not every Asian-American student comes to the classroom with a wealth of knowledge about Japanese culture, for instance. Not every African-American student knows the history of the struggle for civil rights. Be very careful about allowing your own hidden prejudices and biases to creep into your instruction.

Linguistically Diverse Students

You may encounter middle level students who speak English as their native language, but who also speak one or more other languages. Although these students certainly have something unique to contribute to a language arts classroom, especially when the class focuses on the study of language or on multicultural topics, these students usually fare well without special attention when the instruction is high in quality.

However, students for whom English is a second or even a third language are of concern, particularly in the language arts classroom. You may find such students identified as bilingual, multilingual, English as a second language (ESL), or limited English proficient (LEP). The central controversy surrounding bilingual education focuses on whether it is better to teach students the language first and then try to help them catch up in the other subject areas or to teach subject matter in their native language while they also study English.

Three distinct approaches have been used for instructing these students. *English-only* or *immersion* programs are those in which the students receive instruction primarily or only in English. Often these are intensive language programs that are designed to last for only 1 or 2 years until students are supposedly proficient enough to perform satisfactorily in regular classrooms. In some schools, these students meet in a resource room staffed by a teacher who has special preparation in teaching ESL. In other schools, the students receive some intensive tutoring during a portion of the day, but during the remaining periods they are immersed in the regular schedule. As might be expected, some students flourish in immersion programs but others flounder. Currently, most bilingual programs are designed to be *transitional*. In this approach students receive some instruction in their native language while they learn English. The intention of these programs is to ensure that students continue to learn appropriate subject matter similar to what their peers are learning, while also developing their English skills. Most of these programs are meant to provide support for a limited period of time until students can succeed in regular classrooms. Unfortunately, in many of these programs students fail to develop English skills rapidly. Instead of moving out into the regular classrooms, many students continue to receive bilingual instruction for several years (Hill, 1998). The third approach, which is relatively rare, is best described as *bilingual development*. The intention of this program is to produce students who are equally adept in both their native language and English. Although transitional programs use the student's native language for communication, that language is not a subject of study. In bilingual development programs, both the native language and English are studied and perfected as students also learn other subject matter.

No matter which approach you encounter, you must be prepared to provide a supportive environment for the student who is linguistically diverse. Furthermore, you may need to simplify your language and use visual aids and familiar situations to illustrate abstract concepts. At times you may need to use the student's native language to explain ideas. If you cannot do so yourself, another student may be able to provide the explanation. Most importantly, students need to hear and see English, but they also need to produce it when writing and speaking. To do so, they must feel safe to make mistakes. If students can take part in meaningful, purposeful activities in which language is used naturally as a means of communication among peers, linguistically diverse students will improve their ability to use English well.

In terms of linguistic diversity, another group of students must be considered although they may not be identified as a special population within the school. These are the students who speak one of several dialects of English, all of which are often labeled as substandard. Those dialects you are most apt to encounter are Black English (sometimes labeled *Ebonics*), Appalachian, and French Creole. Linguistically, each of these dialects has a grammar of its own, and speakers follow these grammatical patterns unconsciously. Children who are born into families in which a dialect predominates learn those patterns intuitively. Furthermore, the dialect is often the major means of communication in the family or community where the child resides. Many dialects are vibrant, colorful, and expressive means of communication. They often reflect the values and central concerns of the speech community from which they evolved. The teacher must be sensitive to dialects and knowledgeable about the ones that are most common in the school. Students have a right to their own language, especially when that language allows them to live in harmony with their neighbors. Socially and economically, however, regional and ethnic dialects present problems. Delpit (1995) argued that dialect speakers are often judged as being poorly educated and possibly less intelligent simply on the basis of their speech. She contended that failing to assist young people in mastering Standard English is nothing short of discrimination. Standard English is the language of power in the United States and, to some extent, around the world; those who hold influential positions in business, politics, entertainment, and the media speak Standard English. If students are to compete successfully for those positions of strength, they must know Standard English. As a teacher, you can acknowledge the students' home dialect as a legitimate means of communication, particularly in their own speech community. You can even encourage students to use their knowledge of dialect to produce some forceful writing, especially in narration and poetry. However, you also need to teach students how, when, and why to use Standard English.

Students in Poverty

For a number of years, researcher Martin Haberman has been studying characteristics of teachers who work with children and youth in large urban districts. He has focused especially on what differentiates teachers who quit or fail from those he describes as "stars," teachers whose students score higher on achievement tests and who are identified by parents and other educators as being successful. His findings appear in a slim but powerful volume titled *Star Teachers of Children in Poverty* (Haberman, 1995).

There is not enough space here to include all of the characteristics of the stars, but the following comments will provide a sense of how these teachers create a learning environment that works. Star teachers design tasks that engage students so fully in learning that inappropriate behavior ceases to be of concern. They avoid approaches that focus on rewards, reinforcements, and punishment. Their homework assignments are not typical drill and practice, but suitably challenging tasks that are of interest to students. They focus on learning, not on tests and grades, and they involve students in projects rather than provide direct instruction to the whole class. Most importantly, they believe that students can learn, and they persist in their efforts to make this a reality. They do not let interruptions interfere with learning, and they convince students that learning is important, enjoyable, and intrinsically satisfying. Furthermore, they reject the notion that learning is limited by ability; instead, they focus on effort as the determining factor. They believe that students are supposed to need instruction and that it is the teacher's responsibility to provide that instruction, not just assign work. They do not expect students to come into the classroom with all the skills and knowledge necessary for immediate success. They know students well. They care about their students, respect them as human beings, and trust them. Star teachers work hard to develop a positive, productive rapport with their students, but they are careful not to allow their own emotional or social needs to come before the needs of their students.

Teachers who do not have these combinations of qualities can succeed in other settings, but this list seems to describe what might be considered as preferred characteristics of effective teachers almost anywhere. In essence, what works for children in poverty is apt to work for other student populations as well.

Underachieving Students

Chall and Curtis (1991) stated that although there are important differences among students who are "at risk," all share two characteristics: "Their performance in school lags behind that expected for their age ... and their school performance lags behind their potential for achievement" (p. 349). What is nearly impossible to determine is whether they are at risk because they fail to achieve or whether they are failing to achieve because other factors in their environment place them at risk.

Whatever the cause of their underachievement, the research, as summarized by Chall and Curtis (1991), indicates that at-risk students benefit from a number of strategies. They need instruction that stems from well-defined objectives. New content must be linked to what they already know, and new skills must build on ones they already use with confidence. They need the opportunity to apply new knowledge and skills in meaningful ways and to evaluate the results of these attempts. At-risk students often benefit from direct instruction that supports the development of reading comprehension, vocabulary, and spelling skills, but they also need access to a wide range of reading materials. Furthermore, they need to engage in a variety of activities that build their experiential understanding, such as field trips and community action projects.

There are certainly environmental, physical, emotional, and intellectual factors that hamper some students. Many of these factors have already been addressed in this chapter. However, some students, for no apparent reason, perform at a much lower level than might be expected. This includes, for instance, the student who is identified as G/T but who is satisfied with mediocre work and the above-average student who just slides along, earning C grades without being concerned about improving. These are the students who seem to know precisely how little they can do and still get by. To many middle school teachers, these students are the most puzzling and frustrating. No matter what the teachers try, these students remain unmoved and disengaged.

Unfortunately, there is little research that provides clear direction for coping with this kind of underachieving student. Nevertheless, these students deserve some special attention (Rimm, 1986). One of the first considerations must be to investigate whether this behavior is new or whether it is a pattern that has existed for some time. If it is new, there is probably some direct cause. It may be related to some change in the family resulting from death, divorce, economic woes, medical difficulties, or other changes that have created instability. Or the change may be related to peer pressure. You may be able to assist, but the student may be in need of some professional guidance that could help him or her find support and develop coping skills. You should also consider the possibility that your personality or behaviors are in conflict with the student. A private conference with the student or with the student and his or her parents may solve the problem. If not, you need to contemplate either changing your behavior or switching the student into another teacher's class.

However, if the behavior is ongoing and long-term, the cause may be much more difficult to unearth. Underachievement may be a coping mechanism the student has perfected. Sometimes an appearance of unconcern masks a serious weakness in skills. Struggling readers, for example, may hide their problem by demonstrating an outward contempt for the subject matter, the tasks, or the teacher. These students may even say that they could do the work if they wanted to but prefer not to waste their time. Other students may have a more serious problem, such as being the victims of abuse. Their performance, minimal though it may be, is really all they can muster. On the other hand, underachievement may actually represent overachievement if the student has an undiagnosed learning disability for which she or he has learned to compensate. An underachiever who complains of boredom may be an unidentified G/T student who is not being sufficiently challenged. Or the teacher may be using methods that do not engage this individual's interests or allow the use of a preferred learning style. In today's fast-paced world filled with media that assault the senses from all sides, some students may find the slower-paced, less media-oriented classroom unstimulating.

You may have to try a number of approaches when working with underachieving students. You will need to confer with the student to try to obtain some insight, but you should also confer with former teachers and with the parents. Find out what has already been attempted and avoid repeating those unsuccessful strategies. This is the time to be creative and to reach beyond the usual.

Immature or Precocious Students

As noted, middle level students develop at vastly different rates. You may find yourself facing a classroom that contains boys who are quite small in stature seated beside those who have begun to shave. Some of the students will whine and pout or tattle on their peers, whereas others come to school wearing provocative clothing. At times you will find yourself wanting to say to one student, "Grow up," and to another, "Slow down." What complicates the situation even further is that physical appearance can be very deceptive at this age. The smallest student in your class may actually be the most adept socially or the most advanced intellectually. The tallest and heaviest person who appears far older than the rest may be functioning well below grade level emotionally. There is no consistency.

The middle level teacher must be self-aware in order to avoid treating students differently just on the basis of outward physical appearance. At the same time, the teacher needs to make appropriate adjustments for individuals. To some extent, this means orchestrating circumstances to avoid potential embarrassment and enhance successful performance. Tall podiums may call attention to a student's shortness. Full-sized desks may leave a student's legs dangling in air. High shelves may be inaccessible. Students who are going to give presentations before the class may need to be reminded about the kinds of clothing they should and should not wear.

More importantly, students need to see each other as human beings and treat each other with respect. Often the immature or precocious students are the brunt of much teasing and harassment. They are especially vulnerable because they stand out. As the teacher, your responsibility is to ensure that they do not become targets of ostracism or abuse. All students must be taught that such behavior is not acceptable. It may even be illegal.

THE GENDER ISSUE

What students read and write influences how they perceive themselves. Feminist theory points out that school activities and assignments often reinforce stereotypical male and female roles. Through your choice of literature and writing tasks and through the content of discussions, you can engage students in an exploration of these stereotypes and the cultural factors that ingrain them.

Studies of discussions in middle level language arts classrooms reveal that boys often dominate the conversations while girls assume a subservient role. Oral discourse patterns of male and female students differ, and these differences are associated with perceptions of power (Bonvillain, 1997). For example, boys use a register that is more direct, informative, and assertive. Classroom interactions may include remarks that are self-deprecating, discriminatory, or exclusionary. These remarks reveal, to some extent, how the individual sees him or herself. What's more, these patterns of discourse subconsciously affect how others perceive the speaker (i.e., powerful or subordinate, credible or unreliable, knowledgeable or insecure). In some small groups, boys tend to dominate (Benjamin & Irwin-Devitis, 1998), but in others, girls take the lead (Styslinger, 1999). Students who are excluded or marginalized in the classroom have less chance of using oral participation as a means of developing their knowledge. As a language arts teacher, you can assist students in examining how they use language to present themselves and control others, especially when their statements effectively eliminate other students from the instructional conversation or when their hesitancy and imprecision cause others to ignore them. You can also vary the composition of small groups to determine whether gender issues are hampering the conversation.

Recent research indicates that teachers tend to respond differently to student behaviors on the basis of gender. Boys often receive more response from teachers. Also, they are permitted to speak out in class without being reprimanded. Girls may not be encouraged to think critically and expand on their answers. Researchers speculate that these differences result in unequal learning. In general, teachers are not consciously aware that they are behaving differently according to student gender. Once they realize that this is occurring, they can change their behavior. As a beginning teacher, you have the opportunity to avoid developing habits that might be detrimental. One effective way to examine yourself is to videotape your teaching and then view the results. Look for any evidence of differences in your responses that seem to differentiate boys and girls. If you want more information about this research, you should read *Failing at Fairness* (Sadker & Sadker, 1994), *Just Girls* (Finders, 1997), or *Gender Gaps* (American Association of University Women Education Foundation, 1999). Not everyone agrees with these conclusions, however, so you do need to explore other points of view, too (e.g., see Schmidt, 1994).

RECOMMENDED READINGS

Alvermann, D., Hinchman, D., Moore, D., Phelps, S., & Waff, D. (1998). *Reconceptualizing the literacies in adolescents' lives.* Mahwah, NJ: Lawrence Erlbaum Associates.

American Association of University Women Education Foundation (1999). *Gender gaps: Where schools still fail our children.* New York: Marlowe.

August, D., & Hakuta, K. (Eds.). (1998). *Educating language-minority children.* Washington, DC: National Academy Press.

Benjamin, B., & Irwin-Devitis, L. (1998). Censoring girls' choices: Continued gender bias in English language arts classrooms. *English Journal, 87*(2), 64–71.

Carnegie Council on Adolescent Development. (1989). *Turning points: Preparing American youth for the 21st century.* New York: Carnegie Corporation of New York.

Delpit, L. (1995). *Other people's children: Cultural conflict in the classroom.* New York: The New Press.

Feldhusen, J. (1998). Programs for the gifted few or talent development for the many? *Phi Delta Kappan, 79,* 735–738.

Finders, M. (1997). *Just girls.* New York: Teachers College Press.

Haberman, M. (1995). *Star teachers of children in poverty.* West Lafayette, IN: Kappa Delta Pi.

Hill, D. (1988, January 14). On assignment: English spoken here. *Education Week, 17*(18), 42–46.

Kohn, A. (1993). *Punished by rewards: The trouble with gold stars, incentive plans, A's, praise, and other bribes.* Boston, MA: Houghton Mifflin.

Manning, M. (1993). *Developmentally appropriate middle level schools.* Wheaton, MD: Association for Childhood Education International.

Manning, M. (1998). Selected resources for multicultural education. *Focus on Middle School, 10*(3), 1, 3, 6.

McCracken, N., & Appleby, B. (Eds.). (1992). *Gender issues in the teaching of English.* Portsmouth, NH: Boynton/Cook-Heinemann.

Mizelle, N. (1997). Enhancing young adolescents' motivation for literacy learning. *Middle School Journal, 28*(3), 16–25.

Monseau, V. (Ed.) (1999). Genderizing the curriculum [themed issue]. *English Journal, 88*(3).

National Middle School Association. (1995). *This we believe.* Columbus, OH: National Middle School Association.

Raffini, J. (1996). *150 ways to increase intrinsic motivation in the classroom.* Boston: Allyn & Bacon.

Rigg, P., & Allen, V. (Eds.). (1989). *When they don't all speak English: Integrating the ESL student into the regular classroom.* Urbana, IL: National Council of Teachers of English.

Roller, C. (1996). *Variability not disability: Struggling readers in a workshop classroom.* Newark, DE: International Reading Association.

Sadker, M., & Sadker, D. (1994). *Failing at fairness: How America's schools cheat girls.* New York: Scribner's.

Schmidt, P. (1994, September 28). Idea of "gender gap" in schools under attack. *Education Week 14*(4), 1, 16.

Stevenson, C. (1998). *Teaching ten to fourteen year olds* (2nd ed.). New York: Longman.

Styslinger, M. (1999). Mars and Venus in my classroom: Men go to their caves and women talk during peer revision. *English Journal, 88*(3), 50–56.

VanNess, J., & Irvin, J. (1997). What research says: Linguistic minority students in middle schools. *Middle School Journal, 29*(1), 57–58.

Villa, R., & Thousand, J. (Eds.). (1995). *Creating an inclusive school.* Alexandria, VA: Association for Supervision and Curriculum Development.

Winebrenner, S. (1992). *Teaching gifted kids in the regular classroom: Strategies and techniques every teacher can use to meet the academic needs of the gifted and talented.* Minneapolis, MN: Free Spirit.

2

Teaching Middle School

Overview

- Consider These Questions
- Becoming a Middle Level Teacher
- The Middle School Philosophy
- Middle School Curriculum
- Classroom Organization and Management
- Discipline at the Middle Level
- Teaching Strategies
- Tracking, Immersion, and Grouping
- Assessment and Evaluation
- Deciding Whether Middle School Is for You
- Recommended Readings

CONSIDER THESE QUESTIONS ABOUT TEACHING MIDDLE SCHOOL

1. Of the middle school teachers you have known, which ones were the most effective? Did these teachers seem to have any qualities in common?

2. Some schools are identified as junior high schools whereas others are labeled middle schools. Is there any difference between the two?

3. Examine some language arts textbooks designed for middle school. How would you characterize them? Is there any consistency among the books?

4. Is there a curriculum guide for the middle grades in your state? What are the goals for language arts instruction? What skills must middle school students have in order to score well on standardized tests? Are test scores important?

5. Visualize your ideal classroom. How is it organized? What materials are available? How will you manage to keep everything running smoothly?

6. What have you learned from classes or personal experience about discipline? What would you consider to be a "bad" school or classroom rule?

7. How many different teaching strategies can you name? Which ones do you think you will use most often? Which ones match the needs of students?

8. Is tracking middle school students by ability a good idea? Are there any other approaches that might be equally good or better? What are they?

9. When you assess and evaluate students, for what will you be looking? What do you think will be the most difficult part of determining grades?

10. What is your level of commitment to teaching middle school students? How will you know whether you are well suited for teaching middle school?

BECOMING A MIDDLE LEVEL TEACHER

Your success as a middle level teacher to a large extent depends on whether or not you enjoy working with middle level students. If you do not like young adolescents, you will probably not find much satisfaction in teaching this age group.

Successful middle level teachers are different. Some people are cut out to be kindergarten teachers, and some have the natural aptitude to be coaches. Defining exactly what differentiates one group from the other is difficult, if not impossible; they are just different. The same is true of middle level teachers. Although there are many exceptions and variations, successful middle level teachers seem to have certain personality traits that set them apart. Among these is *energy*. High school and elementary school teachers often have to lead their students; middle level teachers have to scurry to keep up with theirs. Middle level students are very active. *Calmness* and *patience* in the midst of all this motion are positive attributes as well. Another characteristic is *enthusiasm* for both students and subject matter, and in that order. The best middle level teachers walk into classrooms every day knowing that they have to "sell" their subject matter or the activities of the day. No matter how interested students were yesterday, they may not be as interested tomorrow. Middle level teachers need *flexibility*. A good teacher will make on-the-spot decisions, change lesson plans entirely at a moment's notice, and find an innovative way to deal successfully with a problem, all without skipping a beat, making it look as if it were planned that way. *Ingenuity* is another valuable asset. Successful middle level teachers are creative problem solvers who adapt as necessary. The best are innovators and experimenters who are not afraid to take calculated risks.

Effective middle level teachers are very serious about what they do, but they generally do not take themselves too seriously. The best ones seem to have an inexhaustible supply of *positive self-esteem, but little arrogance*. Teachers who come into the middle school believing they know it all will soon find out from their students that they do not. Middle level students can be openly receptive, but they can also be tactless and insensitive. A thick skin is beneficial, but a positive *sense of humor* is a must. Humor can defuse a conflict, relieve tension, and focus attention. Some of the best middle level teachers seem to have *a soft hand inside an iron glove*. Middle level students need structure, firm guidelines, and high expectations that are clearly understood, but they also need a gentle touch, genuine concern, and the sure sense that they are in the care of an adult who knows them individually and respects each as a worthwhile human being.

Many other characteristics are assets. A middle level teacher has to know when to attend to distractions and when to ignore them, how to distinguish honest criticism from hostile accusation, and why the most innocent of statements can create ill will. Some teachers will tell you that all you need is the ability to wield a whip and a chair. Others will say all you need is the knack for repeating directions 500 times without becoming annoyed. There are probably as many desirable traits as there are successful middle level teachers.

Teaching middle school is not an effortless task, but then no teaching assignment is easy. Every level of education has its plus points and its drawbacks. Although many people wonder why anyone would choose to work with middle level students, you may find that you genuinely appreciate their spontaneity. Though they are not easily motivated, once you get them started on a project that interests them, you often cannot get them to stop. You may find that the energy of these students just makes you dizzy, or you might discover that this involvement challenges you to do more, think more, try harder, and learn. Working with middle level students keeps you active and alert. You can never become complacent when you work in a middle school.

THE MIDDLE SCHOOL PHILOSOPHY

Just what is a middle school anyway? Are middle schools and junior highs the same thing? No, they are not, at least they should not be. Junior high schools were originally developed to fulfill the role that the name implies. They were meant to be places in which students were prepared for the rigors of high school. During junior high school the students were supposed to move from the student-centered environment that generally characterizes elementary schools to the content-centered focus of high school. Over the years, junior highs took on more and more of the features of high schools—departments, multiple teachers, tracking by ability, competitive grades, greater content coverage, and less attention to the needs of individual students. In addition, junior highs increased in size, such that enrollments of 1,000 or more were not uncommon.

However, junior highs have always been arenas of debate, especially because people who prepared to become elementary and secondary teachers have both been eligible for employment in them. Philosophical differences over teaching and learning goals often divided faculties. Some junior highs maintained a focus on students; others concentrated more on content. The National Middle School Association (NMSA) evolved out of this vacuum of clarity over the purpose and function of those schools. As the members of this organization shared successful practices, and researchers produced more information about effective instruction, professional middle level educators began to develop an image of a school of a different sort, one designed especially to meet the unique needs of young adolescents.

Recent research has verified that the middle years are extraordinarily crucial. The Carnegie Council on Adolescent Development (1989) pointed out that decisions many young adolescents make determine how they will spend their adult lives. After surveying the situation, the panel of experts recommended significant changes in middle level education, most of which strongly supported the middle school philosophy envisioned by the NMSA. Their report called for more close-knit communities of learning (e.g., teaming or schools-within-schools); core and exploratory curricula; success for all students; advisor–advisee groups, wherein one teacher comes to know a small group of students personally; more attention to health issues; and better home–school cooperation. The report also reiterated the need for special teacher preparation for middle school educators.

Both junior highs and middle schools vary significantly. Few junior highs have all of the characteristics shown in Fig. 2.1. Similarly, few middle schools have implemented all of the recommended and suggested features. Whether the school is identified as a middle school or a junior high is relatively uninformative. The key difference is in the view the faculty hold about teaching and learning and how that view is realized in the policies, methodology, and curriculum of the school. Although schools vary significantly, middle schools focus on all the needs of their students, not only their intellectual needs, but their physical, emotional, moral, and social needs

Comparison of Characteristics	
Junior High School	*Middle School*
• Retention in grade	• Multiage grouping, remediation, varied expectations
• Strict discipline policies; suspension and expulsion	• Humane discipline policies; in-school suspension, Saturday school
• Large buildings (e.g., 1,000 or more students)	• Schools-within-schools, smaller schools
• Impersonal climate	• Positive, supportive climate; advisor–advisee programs
• Many different teachers and classmates, classes held throughout the building	• Students divided into teams assigned to one part of the building
• Departmentalized, 40–50 min classes	• Interdisciplinary, block-scheduled classes
• Singular focus on intellectual development, little attention given to building positive self-esteem	• Attention given to physical, social, moral, emotional, and cognitive, growth through health, social, and guidance services
• Teaching through rote learning, lecture, drill, and review, focusing on basic skills	• Teaching through concrete experiences, inquiry, exploratory learning, focusing on higher order thinking
• Homogeneous groups or tracks, with emphasis on competition	• Heterogeneous, flexible grouping with emphasis on cooperation
• Expectations and assignments determined solely by teachers	• Opportunities for student decision making and empowerment
• Isolated from the community and parents; limited communication	• Involved with community; parents and other adults welcomed and encouraged to participate in school functions
• Teacher-centered, passive instruction	• Student- and learning-centered active engagement
• Teachers prepared to teach in elementary or high school	• Teachers who have received special preparation in teaching ages 10–14

FIG. 2.1

as well. Experts have some conflicting opinions about what practices define the middle school philosophy, but most middle schools either have adopted or are moving toward adopting advisor–advisee programs, interdisciplinary teams of teachers who plan collaboratively and who share a group of students, programs to involve parents, and curricula that center on the interests and skills of students. Research has shown that when schools implement most or all of the aspects recommended by the Carnegie Council on Adolescent Development (1989), student achievement and attitudes improve; however, piecemeal programs that include only a smattering of recommended practices have little or no effect (Lipsitz, Jackson, & Austin, 1997). Middle schools are often distinguished by their attention to engaging students actively in learning and using approaches that give students more choices and responsibilities. Cooperative learning, social action projects, in-depth research activities, and inquiry learning are often associated with middle schools, more so than with junior highs.

There is little agreement over the grade levels, however. Some middle schools include fifth graders, but many do not. Some include ninth graders, but most do not. Many middle schools span Grades 6 to 8 whereas others include only Grades 7 and 8. What is most significant is that a middle school is designed not as a place to prepare students for high school, but as a place that provides the most appropriate education for the students it enrolls, an education that is specifically designed for the early adolescent.

MIDDLE SCHOOL CURRICULUM

The course of study provided in a school is called the curriculum. A curriculum generally includes

- the content to be learned
- the skills to be mastered
- the dispositions to be developed

Some states provide curriculum guides, but most of these guides are rather vague. They establish goals for public instruction, but they often do little more than outline what the state expects students to focus on at various grade levels. Currently many state and national efforts are under way to establish standards that will influence what is taught at all grade levels. Eventually, these may form a national curriculum of some sort, but this is a very controversial notion, to which many people object. Certainly this is a debate about which you, as an educator, should be informed. Here is another opportunity for you to explore the current literature in order to understand the arguments on both sides of this issue.

Most school districts have curriculum guides, although these guides vary in their usefulness. Some give teachers a great deal of latitude; others are very constraining. Whether the guide is flexible or prescriptive, you, as a teacher, will be responsible for ensuring that students achieve the goals that are set. Even if no one else in the school pays much attention to it, as a beginning teacher, you may find a curriculum guide helpful.

The factor that has been most influential over the years in determining the taught curriculum is the textbook. Despite the fact that publishers and education experts recommend that textbooks should only be used as one of several instructional tools, teachers tend to rely very heavily on texts, often to the point of starting on page 1 and moving students through the book chapter by chapter. However, there is no guarantee that progressing through the book exactly as it was designed will produce learning.

However, compared with the impact of the teacher, curricula and texts are of less importance. The teacher is the determining factor in whether learning happens.

At present, a great deal of diversity exists in what is taught at the middle level. Experts tend to agree that middle level students need to further develop basic skills. However, some research suggests that too often the curriculum at the middle level is narrow, restrictive, and repetitive to the extent that it fails to challenge and engage students (Scales, 1996). Middle level students need to explore new educational territory, contemplate ideas they have not encountered before, and attempt activities they have not yet tried. They also need to examine some familiar ideas in more depth.

As much as possible, the content, skills, and dispositions that are taught at the middle level ought to build on what students already know and can do. Including curriculum that reflects some of their existing interests is helpful, but students should also be introduced to new areas that may intrigue them. Integrative curriculum and challenging and exploratory instruction seem to have positive effects on student achievement and attitudes toward learning (Vars, 1997). Curriculum that takes into consideration the physical, emotional, social, moral, and intellectual development of students is more likely to succeed than curriculum that focuses only on the cognitive content that adults think students should study at this age (Brazee, 1997). The curriculum, no matter how important or well planned, will not have much effect if students remain uninterested and detached.

Much of the rest of this book focuses on language arts curricula for the middle grades, but as you read and study this material, keep in mind that the most highly recommended approach integrates subject matter in the form of interdisciplinary or integrative units and projects (Beane, 1997; NMSA, 1995). When these are well designed, students learn to apply basic skills in meaningful and authentic ways. No matter what you are asked to teach or what you choose to teach, middle school students need to be engaged fully in the learning. Authentic tasks are more enthralling. Projects that combine hands-on experiences with content learning are inherently more interesting. *New* grabs more attention than *review*.

CLASSROOM ORGANIZATION AND MANAGEMENT

Arranging the Room

How the furniture and materials in a classroom are arranged tells a great deal about the class climate. When you enter a classroom in which the desks are in a circle, you expect a discussion. Desks in clusters indicate small group work. A large lecture hall with seats bolted to the floor sends a very different message. Teachers have to live in the classroom environments they create; students only visit there for short periods of time. You need to make the classroom a place in which you will be comfortable all day, but it also needs to be a place that welcomes students. Podiums, big desks, or full-sized tables in the front of the room can send negative messages to students. Student work displayed all over the room will speak eloquently about what you value.

No matter what messages you choose to send through the arrangement of furniture, try to avoid traffic jams. Spread things out around the room so that students do not have to cluster in specific places. A table in the center of the room that contains all of the supplies for a unit may seem like a good idea until it is surrounded by 25 or so middle school students jostling for position. Your desk can become the worst roadblock of all. A long line of students waiting for your assistance invites trouble.

Also, try to make sure that you can see almost everyone from most of your vantage points, especially early in the year. Carrels and dividers may seem like good visual barriers to keep students from distracting each other, but they can obstruct your view. If you are to know what students are up to (and you must), you have to be able to see them without moving around excessively. Putting your desk at the far back corner of the room has some advantages. Of course, the arrangement needs to vary depending on the activities, too.

If you can, make books and materials readily accessible to students. If students can get portfolios, reference books, and other supplies for themselves, you will not have to waste energy and attention serving as a supply sergeant, and students will have to take some responsibility for maintaining the learning environment. Overall, this saves time, and the class may run more smoothly. Of course, whether or not you can do this will depend in part on your ability to help the students learn to accept responsibility for taking care of these materials.

Management

Classroom management refers primarily to the things you need to do to help ensure that learning takes place efficiently and effectively. A great deal has been written about this topic, and you should investigate some of these sources for more details and suggestions. However, in a nutshell, the recommendations in Fig. 2.2 summarize much of the literature (and highlight what I learned through experience).

DISCIPLINE AT THE MIDDLE LEVEL

For beginning teachers, the matter of classroom discipline is often an overwhelming concern. In fact, many novice teachers live in terror of the day that a class will "get out of hand." Although it may not help to alleviate your fear, it may be useful to keep in mind that most middle level students have as much to learn about self-control, conflict resolution, and just getting along with others as they have to learn about language, literature, and the rest of the curriculum. Teachers have a role to play in helping students learn about themselves and how to become self-regulated (Ridley, McCombs, & Taylor, 1994). Many discipline problems are directly related to power. No one likes to feel powerless, yet many students see themselves as powerless. Creating a disruption in the classroom may be an attempt to gain some personal sense of influence, but the usual teacher response is to exert even more control. Logic indicates that this probably is not the most effective way to cope with the cause of the problem. When it comes to discipline, your first instinct may not be the best response. Discipline is not so much about control as it is about learning how to live well with oneself and others. In its best form, discipline is instructive, not punitive.

Preventing Discipline Problems

As indicated earlier in this chapter, in the section on classroom management, the most effective tactic is to do as much as you can to prevent problems. Here are some suggestions for additional ways to prevent difficulties:

1. Begin the first minute of the first day with a clear plan for managing the class. A well-organized first day sets the tone for the rest of the year. Know exactly what you are going to do and exactly how you are going to do it. Have something ready for students to do the first day, something that is interesting and challenging, but easy for you to direct. If possible, make it something that leaves them begging for more and looking forward to the next day's class.
2. Monitor what is going on from the moment students come into class until the last student leaves. Observe closely. Let students know that you know what is happening.
3. Move, don't sit. A roving teacher is much more difficult to track. You need to see your own classroom from students' vantage points. Also, you need to be able to move close to potential trouble.
4. Maintain a quick pace. Start with energy and keep it going. If things start to drag, change the strategy.
5. Be alert. You will know you've achieved this goal when students think that you have eyes in the back of your head.
6. Organize the environment so that you and students can find things quickly. Label containers and shelves.
7. Plan for active learning that keeps students so involved that they have neither the time nor the inclination to get into mischief. While this is good advice, watch out for the pitfall of assigning busywork just to keep the students occupied. In the long run, it won't. Challenging, engaging tasks are far more enduring.
8. Keep on-task. If you let students distract you, they will. Short deviations are fine, and you need to pursue lines of interest when they are expressed, but students also need to know that you will quickly go back to where you left off.

Most importantly—

9. Prevent problems. As you plan lessons, think about the ideal scenario: How do you want the lesson to go in the best of all possible worlds? Then consider all of the things a problematic student might do to make the lesson go awry. Revise your plan accordingly. If a problem does occur, do something different next time to make sure that the same thing does not happen.

FIG. 2.2

1. Know the school discipline policy, district discipline policy, or both. Do your best to follow the policy, even if you do not personally agree with it.
2. Set some general classroom rules and inform students of these from the beginning. Keep the list short and positive. Be sure that these are rules you can and will enforce. Be consistently firm but fair.
3. Set specific expectations for activities, especially the first time you have students do them. Teach students how to meet your goals.

4. Act rather than react. If you see a potential problem, do something before it happens, but avoid creating a confrontation. If you can act at a low level initially, escalation, if it occurs at all, may be more gradual.

5. Listen actively. You may have to ask a student to wait until a more appropriate time, but students need to know that you will listen to their concerns and complaints.

6. Watch for gender, racial, or cultural biases in your own behavior. Videotape yourself and check for unequal patterns of response.

7. Watch out for uncontrolled anger, humiliation, and sarcasm. If you use verbal abuse or even physical abuse, what behaviors are you modeling, and what can you expect from students? Put-downs eventually take their toll on self-esteem.

8. Humor can defuse many tense situations. If you can use it without making the student feel small, do. Take a step back from the situation. How would it look to an outsider? Are you behaving as a mature adult or a petulant child?

9. When the situation warrants, take immediate action to prevent harm to students and to yourself. If a fight breaks out and you can stop it, do so. If you cannot stop it, get help from anyone you can without putting other students at risk.

About Discipline Theories and Programs

Many different discipline theories and implementation programs are described in the professional literature. One of the most popular programs is *assertive discipline*, based on the work of Canter and Canter (1976). Their approach accords power to the teacher. The teacher sets the rules and establishes rewards and punishments as enforcement. It is similar to the approach known generally as *behavior modification*, in which goals are set for individual students. Through a system of rewards, punishments, and increased expectations, a student's behavior is changed. You may find these systems to be very effective, especially in the short run, but they may conflict with the teacher-as-equal-learner atmosphere that you want to achieve in your language arts classroom. Alternatives that might be more compatible with a student-centered environment include the approach described in *Discipline with Dignity* (Curwin & Mendler, 1988), which focuses on shared decisionma king and conflict resolution. In this approach, students know what is expected, but when a problem occurs, the teacher attempts to work out a solution that avoids embarrassing the student. Another program to consider is something called *transactional analysis*, featured in *T. E. T. (Teacher Effectiveness*

Training) by Gordon (1974). If you want a more practical and succinct version, refer to *Games Students Play* (Ernst, 1972), where you will find descriptions of just about every kind of misbehavior you can think of as well as advice about how to deal with the problem. Keystones of this approach are maintaining an objective adult stance and listening actively. The significance of listening in this program complements language arts instruction nicely. Another possibility is *choice theory*, as described by Glasser (1990, 1997). This approach is based on the idea that students and teachers should share power, rather than teachers coercing students into behaving appropriately. This approach is quite compatible with learner-centered workshops, which are often used in language arts classrooms.

Numerous articles in professional journals explain how to handle discipline problems. You can take courses and attend workshops that focus on discipline, too. The more you know, the more options you will have for coping with problems when they arise, even if no single approach seems best to you.

What you must consider is that the discipline approach you choose has to be consistent with your beliefs about how students learn. If you hope to establish a community of learners in which you share both the teaching and learning roles with students, and if you prefer to create an environment in which students feel secure in taking educational risks and assuming some responsibility for their own learning, then you need to select a discipline approach that mirrors this intent. However, if you believe that students must be controlled and managed and if your style is one of dominating the classroom, then you will probably be better satisfied with a discipline approach in which you retain the power.

No matter which philosophy guides your decision, you need to remain true to it as long as it is working well for students. If you give some control to students one day and take it away the next, students will see you as inconsistent and untrustworthy. Once that happens, you will not be able to maintain order.

Keys to Effective Discipline

Teachers must create an orderly environment. Some experienced teachers will offer the advice "Don't smile until Christmas." They may also tell you that at the first hint of trouble you should take strong action (e.g., assign detentions or send the student to the principal). The implication is that, in the beginning, you have to be a tough, strict disciplinarian. Students who come to school believing that teachers are supposed to be rigid authoritarians will take advantage of teachers who do not behave accordingly. However, if students are accustomed to less punitive approaches, they will rebel against policies they view as overly strict. Thus, the discipline approach you use must fit the school climate and student expectations.

As a new teacher, you ought to know the school policies and adhere to them. If possible, try to find out the general tone of discipline before school begins so that you have some sense of what students will expect. As much as you may want to present yourself as a warm, compassionate, friendly person, you should first establish yourself as an adult—firm but fair, decisive but thoughtful, consistent but not unbending, friendly but businesslike. Once you earn student respect, you can adjust your discipline policies. Start the school year by setting clear limits and enforcing them. Teach students the routines you expect them to follow, conduct more whole-class activities, and monitor student behavior closely.

If you are of the opinion that the more frightened students are of you the better, you need to recognize that fear, tension, and anxiety tend to depress learning. Students who are afraid of their teachers or who fear that they will fail may be too tense to learn. Fear breeds anxiety and rule testing. Those who learn in fear are unlikely to find the experience enjoyable. On the other hand, students will not feel safe in a classroom where chaos prevails. Students need to feel safe in your classroom, and they need to feel confident that they can learn in the environment you create.

I consider the keys to effective discipline in the middle level language arts classroom to be curriculum and methods. When middle level students are disinterested, inactive, and unengaged in learning, they find ways to entertain themselves and others. What they consider entertaining, the teacher may well see as misbehavior. When students see the work as relevant, useful, important, and interesting, and when they are actively taking part, they do not misbehave. Moreover, they do not tolerate the distracting antics of classmates. Middle level students who do not gain attention and/or approval from their peers by misbehaving usually stop those behaviors.

Nevertheless, despite an effective curriculum and exemplary methods, students will act inappropriately. All people are motivated to behave as they do. Middle level students, however, act out for reasons that they themselves often do not understand. Sometimes they do so just to explore their need for autonomy and to test the reactions of peers and adults. Some problems occur because students feel unnoticed. They may unconsciously prefer to be recognized in a negative way than to go through the day as if they are invisible. Middle level students are often so preoccupied with creating a niche for themselves within a peer group that they are willing to do almost anything. At the middle level, resistance to authority is related to the struggle for independence.

Trying to control student behavior may not only be impossible, it may be unwise; instead, teachers need to aid students in learning how to control their own behavior. Many discipline strategies may alter behavior without influencing the causes. Discipline, at the middle school level, often needs to be a personalized search for reasons as well as a guided exploration of more positive reactions to situations. As the teacher, you can use discipline problems as opportunities for teaching. In this regard you have a distinct advantage; you can, for example, incorporate literature that looks at self-discipline, and you can engage students in other language activities that focus on coping with social pressures.

Middle level students are especially sensitive to inconsistency. Although they tend to demand preferential treatment, they expect you, as the teacher, to treat everyone else equally. Of course, they do not see this as inconsistent. You will find this a very narrow path filled with potholes. Remember that the trail you choose to follow today with the thorn-in-your-side student may be the track you must follow tomorrow with your best student. Also, if you overreact or make a mistake, admit it. Saving face is not likely to be worth losing the respect of the class.

Discipline plans at the middle level must take into account the physical need for movement, unpredictable emotions, experimentation with social roles, and other behaviors associated with typical changes in young adolescents. Rigid, repressive systems that demand consistent subservience to rules can conflict with positive growth in independence and in understanding moral and ethical issues. An approach that involves the students in planning expectations and setting rules seems better matched to young adolescent needs, especially in a learner-centered language arts classroom.

TEACHING STRATEGIES

One way to prevent discipline problems is to choose strategies that address the needs of young adolescents. You have many choices of teaching strategies (see Fig. 2.3). Using a variety of methods attracts student attention and enhances motivation. Of course, too much variety can be confusing to students. Although they look forward to changes of pace, they also need the security of structure. It is a delicate balancing act.

Although you have many instructional options from which to choose, the amount of freedom you may have to use them varies from school to school. Furthermore, some students may not respond well to certain strategies, parents may object to some, and you may not feel comfortable using a few. Some strategies produce certain kinds of learning more effectively than others. In the best of all possible worlds, you should use the strategies that match your goals and

Teaching Options

- Direct instruction
- Demonstration/modeling
- Higher-order questioning
- Oral reports and readings
- Learning centers
- Student–teacher conferences
- Games and puzzles
- Mastery learning
- Portfolios
- Project work
- Cognitive learning styles options
- Intelligences and brain-based teaching
- In-class homogeneous grouping
- Adult, peer, or cross-age tutoring
- Audiovisual presentation
- Data collection (observations, surveys, interviews, etc.)
- Lecture
- Recitation
- Discussion
- Debates
- Skills mini-lessons

- Computer-aided instruction
- Independent study
- Self-directed learning
- Creative dramatics
- Literature-based study
- Programmed instruction
- Field trips or field study
- Guest speakers
- Simulations
- Paper-and-pencil exercises
- Peer response groups
- Contract learning
- Role playing
- Storytelling
- Listening stations
- Workshops
- Textbook study
- Team teaching
- Coaching/facilitating
- Library research
- Laboratory experiments
- Interdisciplinary units/projects
- Cooperative learning/collaborative group work

FIG. 2.3

objectives, and you should use a variety of strategies in order to keep students actively involved in learning.

When considering your teaching options, you need to keep several things in mind. First, each of these strategies can be successful, but each can fail. The difference is not in the strategy itself, but in whether or not it is appropriate for the situation and how well it is planned and executed. Second, each of these strategies has some strengths, but each also has some drawbacks. No strategy is superior, and all of them require effort and forethought. None is easy. Third, although you should develop some proficiency in using several different strategies, you need not feel that you ought to be equally competent in using all of them. Some of these are ones that will suit you and your students well; you may prefer to disregard others. However, if your preferences are not working, you should feel a professional obligation to broaden your repertoire and develop the expertise to use other strategies. Fourth, some of these strategies work in harmony with others, but some are contradictory. For example, some of these strategies empower students by giving them more responsibility, whereas others make students dependent on the teacher. Going back and forth between teacher-directed and student-centered strategies will make students feel that you are inconsistent. They will be confused, and they will not know where they stand. They may come to resent this feeling of insecurity.

Some Cognitive Learning Styles Options

Several teaching strategies that are of particular value in the language arts classroom will be addressed in later chapters of this book. However, a few of these options deserve attention here because they sometimes form the basis of school programs at the middle level. Several of these are highlighted in the March 1997 issue of *Educational Leadership*. Cognitive learning styles teaching is one possible option. Entire books have been devoted to the topic of various learning styles, and you should consult several for additional information, especially if the school in which you teach uses a particular system.

Differences in learning styles can be defined or described in many different ways. Probably the most comprehensive system of classification is that developed by Dunn and Dunn (1999) which identifies five stimuli that subdivide into 21 elements that influence student learning and combine in various configurations to form each person's style. The chart shown in Fig. 2.4 illustrates these various classes and elements.

Another system for describing and teaching to cognitive styles is called 4 MAT, developed by McCarthy (1987). This system is based on

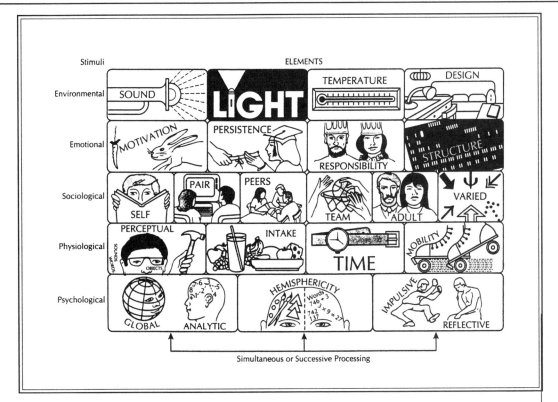

FIG. 2.4   From R. Dunn & K. Dunn, *The Complete Guide to LearningStyles* (p. 12). Copyright © 1999 by Allyn & Bacon. Reprinted with permission.

the theorized differences in functioning between the right and left hemispheres of the brain. The original theory behind this was that people tended to be dominated by either the left or the right hemisphere. Left-brained people were thought to be rational, controlled, organized people, whereas right-brained people were thought to be more holistic, artistic, subjective people. The idea was to provide all students with experiences in four categories—sensing/feeling (concrete experience), watching (reflective observation), thinking (abstract conceptualization), and doing (active experimentation) —which would appeal to and develop the skills of both left-brained analyzers (convergent thinkers) and right-brained synthesizers (divergent thinkers). Although the research on 4 MAT is rather inconclusive, the approach does encourage teachers to modify instruction in systematic ways so that student differences are addressed.

Another way to look at learning styles emanates from research surrounding the Myers–Briggs Type Indicator (Myers, 1962), which classifies people according to various learning preferences. This test identifies an individual's location on continua that measure preferences for concrete thinking versus abstract thought and sequential patterns versus random ones. Concrete-sequentials are thought to need authentic experiences to learn and are most comfortable when ideas are presented in a step-by-step fashion. At the opposite end of these continua from concrete-sequentials are abstract-randoms, holistic learners who can deal readily with hypothetical situations and theories; they presumably prefer to be immersed in the middle of everything all at once.

Each of these cognitive learning styles systems has its advocates and detractors. Some school programs are designed around one of these systems; other schools encourage teachers to consider differences but do not identify a particular system to apply; many ignore the whole matter. There is no consensus about which, if any, of these systems is the best foundation for planning a curriculum or designing instruction.

But what do you do if you discover that the class is a great mix of styles? Much of the time, that is precisely what happens. Most people are mixtures of various ways of learning. Also, we have little information about whether learning styles shift over time and change with subject matter. Thus, when you think of learning styles, some caution is in order. Learning styles systems have a tendency to label students. These labels can generate stereotypes that may inhibit learning if a teacher focuses too strongly on one type of instruction and excludes most others simply because the majority of students seem to learn best in one way. Identifying the preferred learning style is most useful when you have a student who is having some difficulty in your class. Information about an individual's learning style is especially helpful in one-on-one tutoring and individualized instruction.

The important fact is that students are different. They learn in different ways and at different rates. They find different topics and activities appealing, and they can demonstrate learning in a variety of ways. The specific system is far less important than the recognition of these differences and adaptation of instruction to address diversity. In a nutshell, students need learning options, and teachers need to use a variety of teaching strategies. Moreover, teachers need to see this variation of cognitive styles as an interesting challenge rather than an insurmountable hindrance. Educators need to welcome this variety rather than ignore it or wish that it would go away.

Intelligences Teaching and Brain Research

One recent theory that has evolved from cognitive science research is influencing instructional decisions in many middle level schools. This is the theory of multiple intelligences proposed by Gardner (1983) and explained initially in *Frames of Mind*. Gardner has now identified eight distinct intelligences (see Fig. 2.5). He contended that all of them have value in our culture, but only a few are nurtured

Gardner's Multiple Intelligences

- **Verbal–Linguistic**: Special aptitude for comprehending and using language, usually revealed through reading, writing, speaking, and listening. Students may have a special capacity for rhetorical persuasion, recalling verbal or printed information, explaining through language, and/or using language to reflect on language (i.e., metalinguistic awareness).

- **Logical–Mathematical**: Special aptitude for scientific and mathematical thinking, usually revealed through calculating, estimating, classifying, hypothesizing, and problem solving. Students may have a special capacity for calculating rapidly, reasoning logically, identifying relationships, estimating quantities, recognizing visible patterns, observing closely, and/or identifying and solving problems.

- **Visual–Spatial**: Special aptitude for perceiving the visual world accurately, transforming or modifying visual perceptions, and re-creating aspects of visual experience, usually revealed through drawing, painting, sculpting, drafting, illustrating, and mapping. Students may have a special capacity for recognizing and manipulating shapes, visualizing objects and events, reproducing visual images, creating innovative ways to use space, and/or creating original interpretations of objects.

- **Musical–Rhythmic**: Special aptitude for performing, composing, or appreciating music, usually revealed through such activities as playing an instrument, singing, composing scores, and/or critiquing musical performances astutely. Students may have a special capacity for identifying pitch and rhythm, recognizing audible patterns, using music to communicate, reproducing music once heard, and/or creating original music.

- **Bodily–Kinesthetic**: Special aptitude for using the body for functional or expressive purposes, usually revealed through participation in gross motor activities such as athletics, dance, pantomime, drama, and construction and/or fine motor activities such as tying flies and stitchery. Students may have a special capacity for moving with coordination, agility, and quickness; constructing objects with skill and dexterity; repairing mechanical equipment, using tools, and/or inventing devices.

- **Interpersonal**: Special aptitude for noticing and understanding the behavior, feelings, and motivation of others, usually revealed through effective leadership, persuasiveness, working cooperatively in groups, forging strong ties to social groups and friends, expressing sympathy and empathy, and providing psychological support and understanding to others. Students may have a special capacity for analyzing the needs of an audience, demonstrating selflessness, understanding the motivation of others, and creating a sense of community among people.

- **Intrapersonal**: Special aptitude for self-awareness and reflecting on one's own behavior, attitudes, values, and emotions, usually revealed through such behaviors as decisiveness, independence, self-assurance, and individualism. Students may have a special capacity for analyzing and expressing personal feelings, setting personal goals, judging their own performance, working alone, and reflecting introspectively.

continued on next page

• **Naturalistic**: Special aptitude for observing, exploring, and understanding the natural world and man-made phenomena which impact the environment, usually revealed through keen awareness of surroundings, discriminating among various categories of flora and fauna, and/or noting patterns in nature. Students may have a special capacity for sorting and classifying, observing nature, caring for plants and animals, and/or understanding and explaining natural systems, relationships, and patterns of cause and effect.

FIG. 2.5

in schools, primarily logical–mathematical and linguistic, although musical and spatial are partially developed through fine arts programs and kinesthetic is developed through physical education. He also contended that many students feel alienated from school because their particular intelligences are not valued. He believed that if teachers create situations in which students can learn material and demonstrate proficiency in ways that are compatible with their intelligence strengths, students will learn more, learn more readily, and find school a much more exciting place to be (Gardner, 1991).

The theory of multiple intelligences has a growing body of followers among educators, and some schools are developing programs around this theory. Giving students choices about how they demonstrate learning is one of the most common ways in which this theory is being implemented. Recently, several books have become available to give teachers ideas for activities that focus on those intelligences that are often overlooked. If you find this theory to be of interest, you should examine some of the sourcebooks that describe the theory in more detail and suggest activities associated with various intelligences. One source of these references is Zephyr Press, which has published several practical guidebooks for teachers at many grade levels. Another is IRI/Skylight. You may also check for workshops on this subject, which are offered periodically in many locations across the nation.

Of increasing interest are theories evolving from neuroscientific investigations of brain functioning. These include studies of what is commonly referred to as *emotional intelligence* (see Goleman, 1995). Some of the implications that have been suggested include the need for social interaction among learners; the use of thematic, integrative, and cooperative units; the value of individual projects; and the merit of delegating more responsibility for learning to students (Caine & Caine, 1994). Although these data are interesting and provocative, the classroom implications are still unclear. Nevertheless, this is a promising area of research about which you should remain well informed. One of the best introductions to this research base is Jensen's (1998) *Teaching with the Brain in Mind*. The November 1998 issue of *Educational Leadership* also contains several articles focusing on how the brain learns.

TRACKING, IMMERSION, AND GROUPING

Curricula, classroom organization and management, discipline policies, and teaching strategies must blend with and support what is developmentally appropriate for middle level students. However, the material in chapter 1 of this book demonstrates that accommodating the diversity of students in a middle school is challenging. This raises the issues of how to group students in order to reduce the range and whether or not such grouping is effective. How your school groups students for instruction can have a major impact on how you teach language arts.

Middle school educators have three primary options for creating classroom groups of students. One is **tracking by ability**. On the basis of factors such as test scores, previous grades, and teacher recommendations, students are grouped by ability, and they remain throughout the day with peers who are thought to perform at a similar academic level. The second option is **immersion**, which means that students are heterogeneously grouped throughout the day although some students may be pulled out for special instruction at times. The third option is **flexible grouping**. One version of flexible grouping is *class grouping*. In this approach students are grouped by ability in some classes but not in others. For instance, they may be scheduled into low, middle, and high level classes in math and social studies, but not assigned to special sections in other classes. However, when students are grouped in one or more subject areas, the groupings tend to overlap into other classes as well, creating more homogeneous groups than intended. Another possibility is the use of *in-class grouping*. For example, in a language arts class, students may be temporarily grouped by ability in order to complete a unit of work, but during the remaining time, students may be mixed heterogeneously or regrouped periodically on the basis of interest, topic choice, or assignment. Sometimes these groups are created by the teacher so as to include a mix of various factors—gender, verbal skills, leadership, motivation, and quality of study skills. At other times, students may choose their own groups.

Middle school experts tend to support both immersion and flexible grouping. However, the NMSA (1995) is opposed to tracking. There is strong research evidence to support that tracks and inflexible ability groups are detrimental to many students, especially those the approaches are intended to help the most—students in the lowest ability groups. In part because of their placement in low tracks, students in these groups tend to be unmotivated and disruptive. They lack positive self-esteem and confidence, and they see themselves as failures with no hope of improving. Worse yet, teachers tend to see these students in similarly negative lights. They expect little from them, and they get what they expect. Year after year, students in these tracks fall farther and farther behind, trapped in the downward spiral of a self-fulfilling prophecy.

Teachers say that ability grouping and tracking are designed to allow them to provide instruction that is more closely aligned with the needs of students. They also say that the intent of low ability classes is remediation, an attempt to fill in gaps so that these students can catch up with their peers. But the fact is that students in the lowest track often receive the least stimulating kind of education. Rather than bringing students up to speed, this instruction tends to leave them farther behind. Once students are assigned to a track, movement to another, especially a higher one, is rare. Of equally grave concern is that the lower track classes often contain high percentages of the neediest students—physically or mentally challenged, culturally diverse, multilingual, poor, underachieving, or immature. Often these classes are taught by the least experienced teachers on the faculty. Furthermore, the curriculum to which these students are exposed is radically different from the content taught in other tracks. These students, who are in desperate need of engaging content that actively involves them in learning, are far more likely to encounter workbooks, drills, low level questions, and simplistic tasks meant to keep them busy and under control. For more information about specific findings associated with tracking, you should consult either *Keeping Track* by Oakes (1985) or *Crossing the Tracks* by Wheelock (1992).

ASSESSMENT AND EVALUATION

There is no perfect system for assessing and evaluating student work and assigning grades. Most school systems have some established grading policies. Some systems provide handbooks, checklists, criteria sheets, rubrics, and other kinds of aids to teachers; others do not. Report card formats vary. Computers have altered the ways in which grades are recorded and calculated. Scales also vary; an A in one school ranges from 90% to 100%, but in another school, an A ranges from 94% to 100%. The difficulty of tests can be adjusted to match any grading scale, and an A in one teacher's class may be a lower grade in another teacher's class. In short, grades are not the objective, consistent measures of performance that some people believe them to be.

As a new teacher, you will need to find out how grading is handled in your school or district before the school year begins. Most school districts provide some orientation sessions in which policies and procedures are explained. You will need to talk with other teachers to make sure that your grading policies are generally in line with theirs, even if this may be uncomfortable or even disagreeable at first. If your grades are significantly different from the grades students have received in the past, either higher or lower, you are apt to find yourself in a parental or administrative spotlight that you would rather have avoided. You may gradually raise or lower your standards during the year or over a period of years without attracting much attention, or you may volunteer to work on school or district committees that revise grading and reporting policies in order to bring about change, but first you need to establish yourself and develop a solid reputation with students, parents, other teachers, and administrators.

Additionally, you need to find out if grades carry special weights in the school or district. In some locations students cannot participate in sports and other extracurricular activities if their grades are not satisfactory. In some schools, earning low grades may relegate students to a lower track of classes. This does not mean that you should lower your standards, but you must be cognizant of the fact that the grades you give can have outcomes that stretch beyond your classroom. For instance, some parents may provide substantial rewards to their children for high grades, whereas low grades may result in punishment, even physical abuse. A student complaint about a grade may reflect a deeper concern. You may not be able to change the outcome, but you do need to be aware of these possibilities. Use questions about grades as opportunities both to teach students how to better assess themselves and to learn for yourself how to better assess. If you cannot, in good conscience, change a grade, consider giving the student credit for knowledge exhibited during a grade conference.

Assessment Versus Evaluation

The terms *assessment* and *evaluation* tend to be used synonymously. However, a somewhat technical difference separates these two. Assessment refers to collecting data on student performance. Assessment usually includes observations of work in class, conference notes, anecdotal records, checklists, rubrics, work logs, and other such data that provide a sketch of the student's performance. These data may also include test and quiz scores and grades on various tasks. Collectively, this information can be used to help you decide what else to teach. Furthermore, assessment is what you do while the learning is taking place. It tells students how they are doing. In psychometric terms, assessment is diagnostic and formative.

Evaluation, on the other hand, is summative. It is the interpretation of the assessment data for the purpose of judging the learning that has occurred. When you assign a grade at the end of a unit or grading period based on the assessment data you have collected, you are evaluating. Evaluation results tell students and other interested parties how the learners have performed.

What Is Authentic Assessment?

Authentic or performance assessment is currently a hot topic in education. Although the reality of it is much more complicated, the concept itself is relatively simple. The idea of authentic assessment is that teachers should grade on the basis of how well students achieve the goals of instruction. Whatever the goals are, assessment should match. If students are supposed to learn to write better, for example, teachers should have students write and then assess how they perform.

You may ask what the big deal is. The big deal is that for many years student performance has been evaluated on the basis of paper-and-pencil tests that produce objective scores. To measure how well students write, for instance, standardized tests ask students to identify misspelled words, correct punctuation errors, and locate usage mistakes, as if these indirect but objective measures were equivalent to effective writing. Language arts teachers often give literature quizzes that focus on basic comprehension, and they consider these scores as accurate measures of literary understanding.

Given that information, you may readily conclude that authentic assessment is far superior to the standardized approach, but there are problems. For example, there is actually little difference between classroom activities and authentic assessment. At the extreme, everything students do is evidence and is therefore subject to assessment. It would even be possible to give students daily grades on their performance. That, of course, is not a practice that proponents of authentic assessment advocate. In fact, they tend to support much the opposite: an accumulation of data over time that shows growth and change in learning rather than isolated glimpses of student development.

However, authentic assessment creates other challenging problems. Statisticians point out that tests that are reliable (i.e., produce the same score over and over) and valid (i.e., actually measure what is supposed to be measured) can be and have been created. Authentic assessment performances, such as portfolios of written work or videotapes of students presenting speeches, may be more valid tools, but they are much more difficult to judge reliably. For good or for ill, standardized tests can, for instance, pinpoint whether a student is in the 10th or 20th percentile. Furthermore, these results tend to be consistent; no matter what version of the test the student takes, the results will be relatively the same. Authentic assessment is far less precise, and the results can vary, depending on a number of factors, such as who is doing the judging. Consider, for example, the variation in composition work that you produce. One paper may be excellent, but the next mediocre, depending on your skills and interest in the tasks, among other things. What accurate conclusion can be drawn from this variation of performance?

Educators are struggling with these problems, attempting to find ways to standardize the evaluation of authentic assessment results. They are developing rubrics, checklists, and other tools that can make the judgments more consistent. Authentic assessment certainly makes sense and appears to be more valid, but it is not without its weaknesses, nor is it without its critics (Ellis & Fouts, 1997). At this point, you need to read more about this issue, know both sides of the controversy, and consider your options wisely. It is probably best to strike some kind of balance between authentic and traditional assessment, at least until you have enough experience to judge student performance with consistency. Meanwhile, talk with other teachers who use authentic assessment, compare strategies, and work to develop a plan that benefits students the most. See Fig. 2.6 for some suggestions. No matter what the assessment technique, if students

---

Suggestions for Assessing and Evaluating

- Keep accurate, thorough records
- Plan in advance what you are going to assess and how
- Involve students in the assessment and grading process
- Observe carefully, looking for both strengths and weaknesses
- Use a variety of methods and tools for assessing
- Focus on learning rather than grades and help students do the same
- Avoid grading practices which create inaccurate averages, such as giving zeros for missing assignments
- Try to be objective, but recognize that you can and probably will make some mistakes and misjudge
- Try not to grade when you are too tired, preoccupied, upset, or rushed. Allow plenty of time for grading
- Return papers promptly

FIG. 2.6

do not learn more as a result, the approach does not have much worth, no matter how reliable and valid it may be.

You can keep student records in any number of ways. No matter how you set up your record-keeping system, you should keep two points in mind. First, keep accurate records. This is time-consuming, but if you get sloppy, you will not be able to verify your evaluations should you need to do so. Second, from a legal standpoint, any records that anyone knows that you keep are public documents. They can be called into court. Do not write anything in these records that you would not want the child or parents or other people to read. If you keep any private records, keep them absolutely private (i.e., do not even mention their existence). Be very careful about what you record. When you assess, record what you observe. This is not the time for making judgments. You may want to note some questions or formulate a hypothesis, but for the most part you should just make accurate notes of what happened and what was said or done.

A Checklist of Work Habits

Figure 2.7 is a checklist of some items that you may want to include when you observe and assess how students work in the classroom. It is unlikely that you would want to use all of these items, however. This kind of checklist can be used as a guide for observing, or it can be included in a student's portfolio. It can also be used as the basis for periodic student self-assessment. You need to create a meaningful code that you use consistently (e.g., plus, check, minus; U [usually], S [sometimes], N [never]; or P [proficient], M [making progress], N [not yet]). Another option is to use these items but to create a form on which comments could be written.

DECIDING WHETHER MIDDLE SCHOOL IS FOR YOU

At this point in your professional career, try to keep an open mind about teaching at the middle level, at least until you have had an opportunity to work with these students in a classroom setting. Some of the tales of terror about working with middle school students are true, but most are the result of inappropriate teaching. Those who enjoy working with middle level students will tell you that the stories are exaggerations. And those who are dedicated to educating middle level students will tell you that no other age group is more exciting, challenging, and rewarding.

There are, however, some additional factors that need to be thrown into the decision-making process. First, if the present trend continues, middle level teachers will need to develop the ability to

Work Behaviors	Grading Period 1	Grading Period 2
• Begins work promptly.		
• Stays on-task.		
• Persists until tasks are completed.		
• Shows organization.		
• Completes tasks on time (or in a timely fashion).		
• Shows pride in work.		
• Speaks and behaves courteously.		
• Monitors voice volume.		
• Follows directions.		
• Uses classroom resources when needed.		
• Works independently when appropriate.		
• Returns materials & books to proper places.		
• Respects rights and property of other students.		
• Works effectively with others.		
• Shares and takes turns.		
• Encourages and assists other students.		
• Resolves conflicts peacefully.		
• Assumes responsibility.		
• Collaborates when appropriate.		
• Takes a leadership role when appropriate.		
• Takes learning risks.		
• Is self-motivated.		
• Self-assesses thoughtfully and accurately.		
• Contributes positively to maintaining the community of learners in the classroom.		

FIG. 2.7

integrate multiple subject areas. This is much easier to do if the teachers are well informed about more than one content field. More and more, middle school teachers are going to be asked to broaden their knowledge beyond a single discipline. Second, working in the middle school means working with a variety of other people besides students. Teaching on a team will require skills in planning instruction cooperatively. Greater parental involvement necessitates more interaction with other adults. Third, middle school teachers need to develop expertise in active learning strategies, which involve cooperative learning, concrete experiences, project work, and student choice. Fourth, middle school teachers must be comfortable acting as student advisors who are ready, willing, and able to help students with a wide range of physical, emotional, moral, and social problems. Those individuals who love only their subject will probably find the middle school a less than ideal environment.

RECOMMENDED READINGS

Anthony, R., Johnson, T., Mickelson, N., & Preece, A. (1991). *Evaluating literacy: A perspective for change*. Portsmouth, NH: Heinemann.

Arth, A., Lounsbury, J., McEwin, K., Swaim, J., & 83 Successful Middle Level Educators (1995). *Middle level teachers: Portraits of excellence*. Columbus, OH: National Middle School Association and National Association of Secondary School Principals.

Beane, J. (1993). *A middle school curriculum: From rhetoric to reality* (rev. ed.). Columbus, OH: National Middle School Association.

Burke, K. (1994). *The mindful school: How to assess authentic learning*. Palatine, IL: IRI/Skylight.

Caine, R., & Caine, G. (1994). *Making connections: Teaching and the human brain*. Menlo Park, CA: Addison-Wesley.

Curwin, R., & Mendler, A. (1988). *Discipline with dignity*. Alexandria, VA: Association for Supervision and Curriculum Development.

Emmer, E., Evertson, C., Sanford, J., Clements, B., & Worsham, M. (1984). *Classroom management for secondary teachers*. Englewood Cliffs, NJ: Prentice-Hall.

Ernst, K. (1972). *Games students play (and what to do about them)*. Millbrae, CA: Celestial Arts.

Gardner, H. (1991). *The unschooled mind: How children think and how schools should teach*. New York: Basic Books.

Gardner, H. (1993). *Multiple intelligences: The theory in practice*. New York: Basic Books.

Glasser, W. (1997). A new look at school failure and school success. *Phi Delta Kappan, 78*(8), 597–602.

Herman, J., Aschbacher, P., & Winters, L. (1992). *A practical guide to alternative assessment*. Alexandria, VA: Association for Supervision and Curriculum Development.

Irvin, J. (Ed.) (1997). *What current research says to the middle level practitioner.* Columbus, OH: National Middle School Association.

Jensen, E. (1998). *Teaching with the brain in mind.* Alexandria, VA: Association for Supervision and Curriculum Development.

Kellough, R., & Kellough, N. (1996). *Middle school teaching: A guide to methods and resources* (2nd ed.). Columbus, OH: Merrill.

Lipsitz, J., Jackson, A., & Austin, L. (1997). What works in middle-grades school reform. *Phi Delta Kappan, 78*(7), 517–556.

McDaniel, T. (1981). Power in the classroom. *Educational Forum, 46*(1), 31–44.

Oakes, J. (1985). *Keeping track: How schools structure inequality.* New Haven, CT: Yale University Press.

Pardini, P. (1998). Shoring up the middle: Middle school movement responds to national criticism with calls for reflection, resurgence, renewal. *Middle Ground, 2*(1), 11–39.

Scales, P. (1996). *Boxed in and bored: How middle schools continue to fail young adolescents—and what good middle schools do right.* Minneapolis, MN: Search Institute.

Scherer, M. (Ed.) (1997). How children learn. *Educational Leadership* [themed issue], *54*(6).

Scherer, M. (Ed.) (1998). How the brain learns. *Educational Leadership* [themed issue], *56*(3).

Schurr, S., Thomason, J., & Thompson, M. (1995). *Teaching at the middle level: A professional's handbook.* Lexington, MA: Heath.

Wheelock, A. (1992). *Crossing the tracks: How "untracking" can save America's schools.* New York: New Press.

Wood, G. (1992). *Schools that work: America's most innovative public education programs.* New York, NY: Plume (Penguin Books).

OTHER RESOURCES

IRI/Skylight Training and Publishing, Inc.
2626 S. Clearbrook Dr.
Arlington Heights, IL 60005–5310
1–800–348–4474
www.skylightedu.com

Zephyr Press
P.O. Box 66006–G
Tucson, AZ 85728–6006
1–800–232–2187
www.zephyrpress.com

3

Literacy Learning and Teaching

Overview

- Consider These Questions
- Becoming a Language Arts Teacher
- Defining the Language Arts
- Literacy Learning From a Natural Perspective
- From Natural Learning to Classroom Instruction
- Best Practices in Language Arts Instruction
- Philosophies of Middle School Language Arts Teachers
- Characteristics of Effective Middle School Language Arts Teachers
- Some Patterns of Language Arts Practice
- Language Arts Teaching Strategies
- Planning
- Recommended Readings

CONSIDER THESE QUESTIONS ABOUT LITERACY LEARNING AND TEACHING

1. What are the language arts? Do you feel adequately prepared to teach all of them? Which of the language arts are your strengths? Your weaknesses?
2. What are students likely to know about language and literacy when they begin middle school? How can you use this knowledge in your classroom?
3. What can you do to make language learning easier and more effective in your classroom? Why do you think these conditions might enhance learning?
4. Have you ever experienced a workshop environment in a language arts class? If so, what was your reaction?
5. Do you see language as a dynamic, ever-changing entity or something that must be preserved for posterity in its best form? Can language improve society?
6. Besides knowing content and methods, what other skills will you need when you begin teaching? Other than students, with whom will you need to communicate?
7. In your classroom, will all students complete the same tasks? Will students study in small groups? Will you work with teachers in other disciplines to create units?
8. What do you find most helpful when a teacher gives directions and provides information? How will you know your students are listening and understanding?
9. What are some strengths and weaknesses of working in small groups? How can you, as the teacher, ensure that these groups function effectively?
10. What do you already know about long- and short-term planning? What are some important components of effective lesson plans?

BECOMING A LANGUAGE ARTS TEACHER

Chapter 1 centered on the kaleidoscope of middle level students. The second chapter focused more specifically on the philosophy of middle level education and what it takes to be a middle school teacher. Now it is time to consider what you need to know and be able to do in order to teach language arts well at the middle level. Much of what you have studied during your college education has helped you to understand the discipline of English. Additionally, your course of study most likely has taught you to read, write, speak, listen, and view well. What you may lack is the knowledge of how to use what you know to aid others in learning, particularly young adolescents. That is what methods courses are supposed to help you to learn. On the surface, this might seem to be a simple concept: You have learned literature, language, and composition, and now you need to know how to teach that knowledge to others. However, the content that you know may not be the content that your students need to learn or are capable of learning. Your favorite poem, for example, may be incomprehensible to younger students. In addition, although you may be a successful user of language, you may be unaware of how you make decisions. You may, for instance, recognize errors in your own writing and be quite capable of repairing them, but you may have difficulty explaining the problems you find in the work of students in terms they can understand.

Being a teacher is not the same as being a conduit through which the information you have learned is passed along to the students you teach. Much of the knowledge you have gained must be sorted, transformed, modified, and adjusted to meet the needs of your students. Furthermore, if learning is a process of making meaning for one's self, then you have to find ways to help your students create their own meanings, not reproductions of your knowledge. Although you may learn best by simply listening to someone explain a concept, your students may need illustrations and examples. You may prefer to be told exactly what is expected of you, but your students may find learning more meaningful and exciting if they have a chance to explore the topic and determine their own goals. Your cultural background may be very different from that of your students.

Even the best college education may not have prepared you to teach some concepts and information that are useful at the middle level. Rarely is there time in a college course of study to take classes in creative dramatics, puppetry, film techniques, science fiction literature, advertising, comic strip creation, television viewing, and a multitude of other topics that may appeal to middle level students.

You will be able to use some of your literary and linguistic knowledge in the middle level classroom, but what you will find invaluable is your knowledge of processes, your grasp of general concepts, and your enthusiasm for the subject. What, for example, are the qualities of good literature? What makes literature worth the time it takes to read it? What makes a reader successful? How does a person begin to write a piece of discourse, and how does he or she adapt a piece of writing to suit an audience? If language use goes awry, what can a writer do to fix it? Why should people be concerned about the impression that speech makes? What are the relationships among linguistics, literature, and composition? What is enjoyable and satisfying about reading, writing, and speaking well? These are a few of the things that are important for your students to understand.

The fact is that you have a lot of useful information at your disposal, but this is only the beginning of the knowledge base you will need to develop while you teach. Be assured that no one expects you to know all of this now. Being a teacher of language arts demands a lifelong commitment to learning.

DEFINING THE LANGUAGE ARTS

Preservice teachers often come into a methods class believing that they will learn strategies for teaching literature. Literature is certainly important, but it is only one part of what we call language arts. In the 1950s, English was said to consist of a triad of literature, language, and composition. Over the years, the definition has expanded. Baines (1998) reported that contemporary curriculum includes not only the triad, but also speech and drama, critical thinking, technology, media literacy, and interdisciplinary studies. Not only has the definition stretched to include additional areas of study, but it has shifted focus toward language arts processes. According to *Standards for the English Language Arts* (1996), cooperatively published by the National Council of Teachers of English and the International Reading Association, the language arts include the following: reading, writing, speaking, listening, viewing, and visually representing. In addition, they highlighted both critical and creative thinking. Many curriculum guides include library and research skills as part of language arts. In some middle schools, the language arts teacher is responsible for journalism in the form of a school newspaper, yearbook, or literary magazine.

There is no way that any college program, methods courses, or even this book can fully prepare you for the variety of responsibilities you may encounter in the schools. Rather than attempt to cover everything superficially, I have only focused on what might be considered the basics. At present, most resource books tend to agree that the language arts consist of **reading, writing, speaking,** and **listening**. New standards call for adding **viewing** and **visually representing** to that list. These are essential **Processes** that students need to learn. However, through these processes, students should also learn language arts **Content**. That usually means teaching **literature** and **language**, but in order to understand viewing and envisioning, students will also need some knowledge of **media** as well.

Although defining the territory is tricky, we also have to add to this equation the idea of purpose. To what end are students supposed to learn language arts? The NCTE and IRA (1996) standards suggest that knowing content and understanding the processes is not sufficient; students must be able to use language well for:

- obtaining and communicating information
- literary response and expression
- learning and reflection
- problem solving and application

Furthermore, competency should be measured by assessing the extent to which students can use language in the following ways:

- clearly
- strategically
- critically
- creatively

Many of these aims will be considered indirectly in this book, but for additional details and examples, you are urged to peruse a copy of *Standards for the English Language Arts* (NCTE & IRA, 1996), as well as other publications associated with these standards, so that you can join the professional conversation about these recommended goals.

LITERACY LEARNING FROM A NATURAL PERSPECTIVE

Literacy can be defined as the ability to create meaning by speaking, reading, writing, listening, viewing, and visually representing. Content knowledge of literature, language, and the media actually goes beyond what is generally considered to be basic literacy, although the notion does exist that a literate person not only reads but reads widely and not only writes but writes well. Nevertheless, most of the American public would be pleased if students graduated from high school able to communicate by successfully using the language arts processes.

What do we know about conditions that make the learning of these processes possible? We know that some people develop literacy without formal schooling. Some adults truly are self-educated. Young children are effective language learners, too. Nearly all children come to school having already mastered the complexities of speaking and the grammatical system that underlies language. Some children come to school already reading. How does this happen?

Figure 3.1 is the result of major research conducted in New Zealand by Cambourne (1988). One reason this research is worth attending to is that New Zealand has one of the highest literacy rates in the world. There may be a variety of other factors that influence this outcome, but Cambourne's work was an attempt to identify the most significant factors that make literary learning possible.

Although the diagram does not emphasize this point, Cambourne (1988) was convinced that the single factor that prompts students to

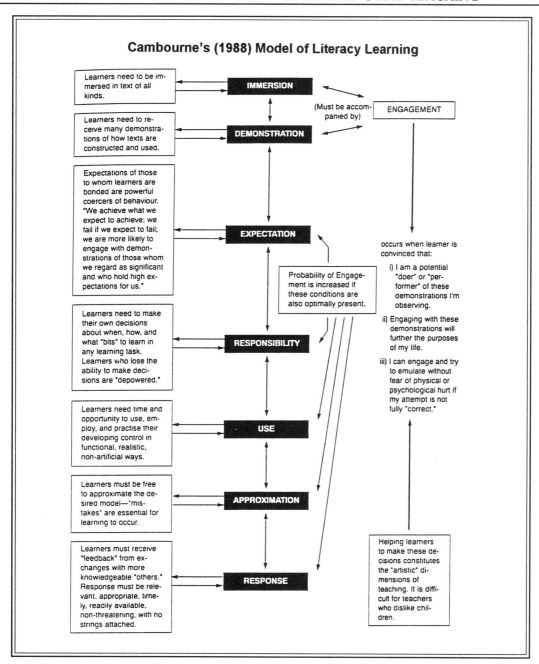

Cambourne's (1988) Model of Literacy Learning

Learners need to be immersed in text of all kinds.

IMMERSION

(Must be accompanied by)   ENGAGEMENT

Learners need to receive many demonstrations of how texts are constructed and used.

DEMONSTRATION

Expectations of those to whom learners are bonded are powerful coercers of behaviour. "We achieve what we expect to achieve; we fail if we expect to fail; we are more likely to engage with demonstrations of those whom we regard as significant and who hold high expectations for us."

EXPECTATION

occurs when learner is convinced that:

i) I am a potential "doer" or "performer" of these demonstrations I'm observing.

Probability of Engagement is increased if these conditions are also optimally present.

ii) Engaging with these demonstrations will further the purposes of my life.

Learners need to make their own decisions about when, how, and what "bits" to learn in any learning task. Learners who lose the ability to make decisions are "depowered."

RESPONSIBILITY

iii) I can engage and try to emulate without fear of physical or psychological hurt if my attempt is not fully "correct."

Learners need time and opportunity to use, employ, and practise their developing control in functional, realistic, non-artificial ways.

USE

Learners must be free to approximate the desired model—"mistakes" are essential for learning to occur.

APPROXIMATION

Learners must receive "feedback" from exchanges with more knowledgeable "others." Response must be relevant, appropriate, timely, readily available, non-threatening, with no strings attached.

RESPONSE

Helping learners to make these decisions constitutes the "artistic" dimensions of teaching. It is difficult for teachers who dislike children.

FIG. 3.1   From *The Whole Story: Natural Learning and the Acquisition of Literacy in the Classroom*, by B. Cambourne, published at Ashton Scholastic Ltd., Auckland, New Zealand, 1988, p. 33. Reproduced with permission.

become literate is **Engagement**. Students must be fully engaged in language learning for progress to occur. He concluded that in order for engagement to occur, two preconditions were necessary: **Immersion** and **Demonstration**. In other words, if students are to engage in language learning, they must be immersed in what is often described as a print-rich environment. However, print may not be sufficient; perhaps a better description would be a *communication*-rich environment, one where language in all forms—print, visual, and oral—surround the child from morning to night, day in and day out. As for demonstration, young children must also be surrounded by language users who model literate behaviors: people who read, write, speak, listen, view, and visually represent as a part of their everyday existence. Although special demonstrations can be helpful (e.g., reading aloud to a child, correcting an error in speech, or showing the child how to write letters of the alphabet), living a literate life probably carries greater significance.

The remaining conditions—**Expectation, Responsibility, Use, Approximation**, and **Response**—enhance the likelihood that engagement will occur, although they are not essential. *Expectation* has to do with those surrounding the learner expecting that learning will occur. Parents of young children expect their children to speak. In fact, they become rather frantic if this ability does not appear early in the child's life.

Children become literate by being in a position to accept *responsibility* for using language. They make choices for themselves and have some control over their literacy development. For example, they may choose which story will be read to them and when. They also have the opportunity to write for themselves when they choose to do so in a way that pleases them. They are not coerced into performing. Rather, they take the initiative to engage in literacy activities.

Use concerns opportunity. Children who become literate have the time and the opportunity to read, write, speak, listen, view, and visually represent. They have access to books, paper, writing implements, verbal sources, and an environment that is language-rich, and they use these materials extensively.

Humans learn by making mistakes. If you have ever tried to learn to play a sport, you know that you must repeat certain actions over and over before you begin to get them right. If it is tennis, you serve and serve and serve again. At first, you do everything wrong. Eventually you begin to get the hang of some of the motion. Gradually the parts begin to come together until you can serve over and over without making too many more mistakes. This is learning by *approximation*. Children learn to be literate by approximating literate behavior, observing the results, adjusting their performance, and approximating again.

It would be possible for a child to become literate alone, but if the child receives *response* or feedback, the process of learning is easier. Response, however, need not be formal in the sense of written comments on papers or corrections of errors when one reads aloud. Response can be a natural part of communicating. If you speak and someone asks a question, you may quickly realize that you have not made an idea clear or you have used a term that has been misinterpreted. The question is a response that provides feedback.

FROM NATURAL LEARNING TO CLASSROOM INSTRUCTION

Cambourne's (1988) research tells us a great deal about the conditions that make it possible for young children to become literate in a natural setting. It also tells us much about why some children are more advanced learners by the time they start school. Children who have the advantage of growing up in a literate environment where all or most of these conditions are present are certainly a giant step ahead of children coming from a language-deprived environment, a gap that can widen during the elementary grades and persist into the middle level.

Prior experience may explain some of the variations in student performance in middle school, but what, you may ask, does this research have to do with teaching literacy at this level? The theory is that if teachers can reproduce these natural learning conditions in the classroom, literacy should be easier to foster. Students should be able to apply the language learning abilities they have developed naturally so as to learn additional literacy processes.

The question of whether or not this natural learning process can or should be replicated within the classroom is as yet unanswered, but current research points to this as a strong possibility. Many experienced elementary teachers see this as a way of improving how we currently go about teaching young children to read and write. They argue strongly in favor of what is commonly called *whole language* instruction, a philosophy that supports the idea that children should learn language by using it in natural ways—purposefully, and in authentic contexts, just as people do in the world outside of school. Some cognitive psychologists support the value of learning in natural contexts as opposed to using simplified, linear systems of instruction that contradict the complexity of natural learning situations. Also, some researchers note that applying natural learning concepts produces success in what are currently labeled *brain-compatible* classrooms. However, opponents argue that although learning to speak develops naturally, learning to read and write well must be taught. They point out that a significant number of young learners do not benefit from immersion, and they argue adamantly that children need direct instruction in word attack skills, particularly systematic phonics or alphabetic decoding, to learn to read. Others advocate a combination in beginning reading known as *balanced instruction*, an approach that includes both isolated skill building and natural literacy events.

The extent to which natural learning theory can be applied successfully at the middle level has not been systematically studied. However, experience and related research tend to indicate some positive correlations between what we know about learning to read and write and this list of natural conditions. Experienced middle level teachers and researchers such as Allen and Gonzalez (1998), Atwell (1998), Butler and Liner (1995), Krogness (1995), and Rief (1992) demonstrated that effective literacy learning at the middle level demands time, choice, student responsibility, high expectations, a supportive classroom climate, a language-permeated setting, effective feedback during the learning process, the opportunity to make mistakes and learn from the experience, and hands-on activities. In essence, students must be fully engaged in purposeful tasks that they view as worthwhile. However, all of these authors described ways in which they or the teachers they studied incorporate direct instruction within these student-centered frameworks.

All the same, the idea of applying natural learning in the classroom is just a theory. Some research shows that the use of this theory produces desirable results, but other studies indicate that it is no better than a traditional, skills-based approach. Some advocates note that results may be directly related to teacher competence and attitude toward the approach; those who believe in whole language and have the necessary pedagogical skills can make it work, but those who do not, cannot. Some critics point out that this kind of classroom demands superteachers, ones who far outstrip the typical teacher's capabilities.

Advocates often note that the standardized tests commonly used to measure outcomes do not satisfactorily assess the improvement in performance and positive attitude that natural learning fosters. If you refer back to the list of communication goals from the NCTE and IRA (1996) standards, you may quickly see a problem. How do we measure the degree to which students use language clearly? Strategically? Critically? Creatively? Standardized tests that measure a student's ability to identify which of four words is spelled incorrectly or that ask students to identify language usages not considered to be Standard English do not begin to measure what professionals in the field believe to be important. They may not measure what you believe to be important either. However, the American public is convinced that test scores truly reflect the quality of learning in the schools. This is one of the major conundrums that language arts teachers face today. Without more agreement about the purposes of education and how to best measure the outcomes, controversy will continue. The usefulness of Cambourne's (1988) theory to you as a classroom teacher depends, at least in part, on what you want to achieve in your classroom and what others believe you should achieve.

BEST PRACTICES IN LANGUAGE ARTS INSTRUCTION

As previously discussed, there is controversy over which are the best practices in teaching language arts. Some would say that the best practices are the ones that produce higher standardized test scores. Others would contend that the best practices are those recommended by professionals and experts. Others still would argue that the best practices are those used by ordinary teachers who work hard in the classroom every day to help students to do their best. To complicate the matter further, some state legislatures have recently enacted laws in support of the use of certain instructional practices, particularly the systematic teaching of phonics in the early elementary grades. To some extent, proposed reforms in teacher licensing and national board certification through the National Board for Professional Teaching Standards implicitly support certain practices. And national, state, and local standards often hint at what modes of instruction are considered best. If the world were a perfect place, all of these would match, but they do not.

It would be wonderful if you could rely on the typical classroom teacher as the ultimate determiner of what is and what is not best practice. Thousands of exemplary teachers do extraordinarily good teaching every day, all across the country. Unfortunately, others are poorly prepared to teach at the middle level and poorly motivated to do anything more than a mediocre job. Between those extremes are many more who simply do what they have always done, achieving much with some students and little with others. To be fair, many of these individuals are hamstrung by legislative mandates, bureaucratic systems, unsupportive administrators, and disinterested parents. Many are overworked and underpaid. And many have few, if any, opportunities to take part in meaningful staff development programs, even though they would like to improve their skills. If students were coming out of schools well-prepared for college or work, if these students had the skills they needed, and if they were positive about their learning, then best practice could be defined as what is done by today's teachers. That, however, is not the case. Therefore, we have to look elsewhere for the definition.

One useful source is a recent publication by Daniels and Bizar (1998) entitled *Methods That Matter: Six Structures for Best Practice*

Classrooms. These include integrative units, small group activities, representing-to-learn, classroom workshops, authentic experiences, and reflective assessment. You will find information about all of these, as well as a variety of other effective techniques drawn from research findings, recommendations from the profession, and classroom experiences of expert teachers, in various sections of this book. However, you should read much more of the professional literature for details. Use the Recommended Readings at the end of this chapter as initial sources, particularly those from NCTE, but look also at more current articles in journals, and watch for new sources from various publishers. One particularly thought-provoking source is Mayher's *Uncommon Sense* (1990). It is not easy to read, but it is filled with information about why common teaching practices are not necessarily the best. In addition, you might want to review the chapters pertaining to language arts instruction in Zemelman, Daniels, and Hyde's (1998) *Best Practice: New Standards for Teaching and Learning in America's Schools.* Further, you might find it interesting to peruse descriptions of nationally recognized Blue Ribbon Schools (Ogden & Germinario, 1994). To find examples of middle schools, you will need to look at both volumes, however. These sources support a student-centered approach that actively engages learners in constructing meaning through social interaction, inquiry, and reflective thinking. Although you will find much agreement among these resources about what constitutes best practices, keep in mind that public opinions on this topic differ. Even experienced teachers do not necessarily agree on the matter, in part because they have varied philosophical viewpoints about the goals of instruction and how students learn best.

PHILOSOPHIES OF MIDDLE SCHOOL LANGUAGE ARTS TEACHERS

According to *Language and Reflection* (Gere, Fairbanks, Howes, Roop, and Schaafsma, 1992), four philosophies guide language arts instruction, depending on how the teacher views language: language as artifact, language as development, language as expression, or language as social action. Basically, the *language-as-artifact* teacher believes in the transmission of knowledge so that cultural values will be preserved. For the most part, this is the traditional approach to language arts instruction in which the teacher controls the curriculum, methods, and materials in the belief that he or she knows what students must learn. The focus is generally on content knowledge and skill acquisition. This approach is often described as a behavioristic approach or skill-based instruction. The *language-as-development* teacher believes in teaching students the cognitive processes that are necessary for using language effectively. This is the teacher who uses scaffolding techniques, graphic organizers, and process writing strategies to enhance student learning. In some sources, this approach is described as brain-compatible learning or strategic teaching. The *language-as-expression* teacher believes that students need to use language in order to understand themselves and their world. This is the teacher who gives students some control over their own learning and uses students' interests, needs, and strengths to develop the curriculum. This is also the teacher who focuses on individual growth. This approach is often associated with the whole-language approach or constructivist teaching. The *language-as-social-action* teacher believes that learning should be used to make the community and the world a better place in which to live. This is the teacher who guides students to engage both in authentic projects and in service learning activities that involve the use of language to improve society so that it is more just, equitable, humane, and peaceful. Respect for the dignity of others is a central focus of this instruction. In some sources, this approach is labeled *critical pedagogy*, but in others it is associated with democratic schools. See Fig. 3.2 for a summary of these approaches.

Each of these approaches can be effective. No one approach is better than all of the others. Indeed, most teachers see themselves as a combination of two or more. How you will teach language arts will depend, in part, on which of these philosophies you support.

CHARACTERISTICS OF EFFECTIVE MIDDLE SCHOOL LANGUAGE ARTS TEACHERS

Through various standards-setting activities, many states are in the process of determining the knowledge, performances, and dispositions that *beginning* teachers of language arts must be able to demonstrate. Although these lists are incomplete, standards do exist for what *exemplary experienced* teachers should know and be able to do. These are the goals a teacher must meet in order to be certified by the National Board for Professional Teaching Standards. Figure 3.3 summarizes expectations for exemplary early adolescent/English language arts teachers.

Language-as-artifact teachers put the content first.
Language-as-development teachers put learning to think first.
Language-as-expression teachers put students first.
Language-as-social action teachers put society and the world first.

FIG. 3.2

Standards Overview: From Early Adolescence/English Language Arts

The following standards are presented as facets of the art and science of teaching English language arts to young adolescents. They are an analytical construct, created to provide a closer accounting of the critical aspects of accomplished practice. However, in real time these segments of teaching occur concurrently because teaching is a seamless activity with many disparate purposes being served in the classroom at any given moment.

Preparing the way for productive student learning

I. Knowledge of Students

Accomplished EA/ELA teachers systematically acquire a sense of their students as individual language learners.

II. Curricular choices

Accomplished EA/ELA teachers set attainable and worthwhile learning goals for students and develop meaningful learning opportunities while extending to students an increasing measure of control over how those goals are pursued.

III. Engagement

Accomplished EA/ELA teachers elicit a concerted effort in language learning from each of their students.

IV. Learning environment

Accomplished EA/ELA teachers create a caring, inclusive and challenging environment in which students actively learn.

V. Instructional resources

Accomplished EA/ELA teachers select, adapt and create curricular resources that support active student exploration of literature and language processes.

Advancing student learning in the classroom

VI. Reading

Accomplished EA/ELA teachers engage their students in reading and responding to literature, and in interpreting and thinking deeply about literature and other texts.

VII. Writing

Accomplished EA/ELA teachers immerse their students in the art of writing.

VIII. Discourse

Accomplished EA/ELA teachers foster thoughtful classroom discourse that provides opportunities for students to listen and speak in many ways for many purposes.

IX. Language study

Accomplished EA/ELA teachers strengthen student sensitivity to and proficiency in the appropriate uses of language.

continued on next page

X. Integrated instruction

Accomplished EA/ELA teachers integrate reading, writing, speaking, and listening opportunities in the creation and interpretation of meaningful texts.

XI. Assessment

Accomplished EA/ELA teachers use a range of formal and informal assessment methods to monitor student progress, encourage student self-assessment, plan instruction, and report to various audiences.

Supporting student learning through long-range initiatives

XII. Self-reflection

Accomplished EA/ELA teachers constantly analyze and strengthen the effectiveness and quality of their teaching.

XIII. Professional community

Accomplished EA/ELA teachers contribute to the improvement of instructional programs, advancement of knowledge, and practice of colleagues.

XIV. Family outreach

FIG. 3.3.   Reprinted with permission of the National Board for Professional Teaching Standards, from Early Adolescence/ English Language Arts Standards for National Board Certification, 1994. All rights reserved.

What you may find most interesting about this list is what is not included. For example, there is nothing here about discipline or planning. There is also nothing about personal characteristics such as warmth, energy, or enthusiasm. Furthermore, there is nothing specific about the formal teaching of literature or grammar. What you will find are implications about the use of selected practices. For example, board-certified teachers encourage self-directed learning in their classrooms, and they integrate instruction thematically. They also include literature from a variety of cultures and encourage readers to respond personally to text. They appreciate and encourage effective uses of dialects and provide opportunities for students to converse informally. These teachers also use cooperative learning groups, and emphasize active engagement in learning. Referring back to the various philosophies previously described, the vision of an exemplary middle level language arts teacher by NBPTS standards does not seem to include the language-as-artifact model, but aspects of the other three stances are incorporated.

For additional information, examine the *Early Adolescence/English Language Arts Standards* published by the NBPTS (1994). Preparing for this certification is a lengthy, expensive, and time-consuming process, but striving to achieve these lofty expectations raises teaching to a much higher and more professional level. In some states and districts, teachers who are completing the requirements to apply for certification receive monetary support (Archer, 1998) or a temporary reduction in duties. Those who earn certification may be rewarded with a substantial increase in salary. One of the best things you can do for yourself is to begin now to work toward eventually obtaining NBPTS certification. Whether or not you achieve this goal, you will become a better teacher by completing the necessary tasks, which include the creation of a portfolio that contains videotapes of your teaching and written analyses of your performance and student work, as well as successful completion of a battery of standardized tests that focus on both pedagogy and language arts content.

SOME PATTERNS OF LANGUAGE ARTS PRACTICE

The stance a teacher takes toward the subject will determine, to some extent, how that teacher will organize instruction in general. There are many different patterns of language arts instruction. Teachers tend to rely on one or two of these patterns, although they may use others for shorter periods of time during the year for particular units or activities.

Whole-Class, Skills-Based Instruction

In this pattern, the teacher generally controls the curriculum. All students are given the same tasks to complete, usually independently. These tasks focus mainly on the development of separate language arts skills. For example, all students are expected to work through a spelling book by studying one chapter each week. During 1 or 2 days of the week, students work on exercises from the language textbook. The teacher explains the concept, such as how to identify nouns or how to use commas in a series, and then students complete one or more practice exercises. When students complete the chapter, they take a test. During the remaining class time, students read assigned stories, participate in class discussions, and complete related writing assignments that often focus on comprehension of the reading.

One modified version of this approach that you may encounter in schools is known as mastery learning. This approach focuses on skills in isolation, but it is an individualized program. Students work through the prescribed lessons, but they do so at their own pace. They cannot move to the next lesson until they demonstrate sufficient mastery of the current lesson. Thus, if all students begin on the first lesson on the first day of school, that will be the only time they all study exactly the same lesson at the same time. Some computer learning systems are based on this pattern of instruction.

Integrated Language Arts

This pattern of instruction is designed to bring together skills and content in meaningful ways. Students learn skills, but they learn them while engaging in activities wherein the skills are used. At the simplest level, students study quotation marks at the same time that they read text containing quotation marks and write some piece of discourse using quotation marks. More complex ways of integrating the language arts include units of study that focus on (a) a language arts discipline (e.g., a speech unit or a descriptive writing unit), (b) a topic (e.g., history of language or thinking through metaphors), (c) a theme (e.g., benefits of a just society or exploring fantasy and myth), (d) a single piece of literature or a collection of related works, (e) a genre, or (f) an author. No matter what the focus, the unit is designed to incorporate reading, writing, speaking, listening, and viewing and visually representing. In these units, students are taught the skills they need to complete the tasks that are assigned or chosen. Although some integrated units are designed so that the whole class moves from one activity to the next as a group, some of these units incorporate the use of small groups. Others are set up to include individual tasks.

Another popular version of integrated language arts instruction is known as the reading–writing workshop approach. In this instructional format, students generally choose their own reading material, read it both in class and outside of class, discuss it with peers, and complete some related activities. During the time set aside for the writing workshop, students complete writings that they have selected, some of which are related to their reading. They also participate in peer groups to share their own work and respond to the work of others. Depending on the needs and interests of the students, the teacher provides instruction in the form of mini-lessons and one-on-one conferences. In the reading–writing workshop approach, the focus is on those two language arts areas, but students also engage in speaking, listening, and viewing and visually representing as they discuss their work and complete literature response tasks, some of which they choose and some of which may be assigned by the teacher. Integrated language arts, particularly the reading–writing workshop approach, is the pattern most strongly advocated by expert middle school language arts practitioners and researchers.

Interdisciplinary/Integrative Instruction

This form of instruction is generally set up in units. However, these units stretch beyond language arts into at least one other subject area. Instruction is planned by a team of teachers from at least two and usually several subject areas, all of whom share the same students. Many of these units focus on a topic drawn from one curricular area, such as the Civil War (social studies), mammals (science), or drugs and alcohol (health). However, the best units focus on broader topics, such as peace and justice, courage, living in communities, or patterns in life. Interdisciplinary instruction can be carried out in several different ways. Some of these are explored later in this book, but one of the most common methods is a parallel structure in which a teaching team selects a topic or theme and then each teacher determines what to teach within the boundaries of his or her own discipline. Students learn the related language arts skills, concepts, and dispositions while they are learning about the topic or theme. However, the more the lines between disciplines blur, the better the approach. If the divisions between disciplines disappear, then the unit is considered *integrative*. This is the form most strongly advocated by the National Middle School Association (1995). However, not many schools have been able to move this far yet. Interdisciplinary instruction is more common. In both cases, instruction is planned by a team of teachers from a variety of subject areas, all of whom share the same students.

One form of interdisciplinary instruction that is gaining attention is inquiry process instruction. In this approach, students identify a question they wish to investigate, a problem they wish to solve, or a project they wish to complete. Students then determine how they will conduct their inquiry. In effect, they plan the curriculum, the assignments, and the requirements, working in conjunction with the teacher. Although inquiry process instruction can be limited to language arts topics only (e.g., How do other countries study English? What are the social effects of dialect in our community? How are books published, and who makes the decisions? What can we do to eliminate illiteracy in our town?), once students begin their investigations, they often cross disciplinary boundaries.

Cooperative Group Instruction

Another pattern of instruction is commonly known as cooperative or collaborative learning. Cooperative learning, when carefully structured according to specific guidelines (e.g., see Johnson, Johnson, Holubec, & Roy, 1991), is strongly supported by research. Less formal versions are supported by theory, experienced teachers, and several professional organizations. For example, composition teachers have repeatedly demonstrated the value of peer response groups, and literature teachers have verified the learning gains associated with literature circles. Small group activities can be included within any of the previously described patterns of instruction. However, these activities are usually short-term; students move into groups, achieve a goal, and then the group disbands. However, a teacher can design integrated language arts units for small groups that remain together for the duration of the unit. When cooperative or collaborative learning is the pattern of instruction, small groups remain together for several weeks, months, or possibly the entire school year.

Individualized Instruction

Although there are many different versions of it, individualized instruction is another pattern of instruction worth summarizing at this point. The key similarity among the different versions is that instruction is matched to individual students. In its purest form, no two students in a school experience the same curriculum. Each learns the same basic language arts skills, concepts, and dispositions, but in different ways, through different activities, and at varying paces. Each student learns different advanced skills and concepts as a result of their experiences. One common way in which individualized instruction is conducted is through independent study. Each student meets with an advisor and plans a course of study, sets goals and objectives, and identifies tasks to be completed. This information is usually recorded in the form of a contract. The plan generally calls for regular meetings between the student and the advisor to monitor progress. Although individualized instruction is not often used in public middle schools except among G/T students or students in special education programs, it is the basic approach in some private schools. Individualized instruction is also used in some alternative schools, and it is the basic approach used in home schooling. It is also relatively common when student populations are different from those in the typical school setting, such as children of migrant workers, adolescents who are medically incapacitated, and youth who are incarcerated.

Choosing a Pattern

These are sketchy descriptions, but they should be helpful in making the point that you have several choices of instructional patterns. Which one or ones you select will depend in part on your philosophy. Teachers who focus on subject matter and content learning tend to rely more heavily on whole-class instruction. This is the pattern of instruction often associated with the language-as-artifact teacher. The language-as-development teacher may also rely quite heavily on whole-class instruction, but he or she is likely to use a wider variety of materials and activities as well as some flexible grouping of students. Language-as-expression teachers are more student-centered and more concerned about the learning of processes and the application of skills. They tend to rely more heavily on the use of integrated language arts units or interdisciplinary/integrative units. They also use more cooperative group activities. Language-as-social-action teachers tend to rely on interdisciplinary or integrative units that focus on themes that raise consciousness about societal problems. However, they often structure these units as rather open-ended inquiries. Students may work in groups, but they may also work individually as they pursue their own projects associated with investigating the situation or solving the problem.

As you begin to think about how you will design instruction, you also need to begin thinking about which of these patterns you will probably want to rely on most heavily and which you might wish to use occasionally, if at all. One important factor to keep in mind is how familiar your students are with the pattern you wish to use. Students may need a gradual introduction to your pattern. You may consider using the whole-class pattern at the start of each year if it is familiar to students, even though you plan to have students working in small groups during much of the rest of the year. Changes in the pattern of instruction mean that students must learn new roles, and you will have to help them learn how to handle these responsibilities. Do not just expect students to know intuitively how to behave when the pattern changes.

LANGUAGE ARTS TEACHING STRATEGIES

Within these patterns of instruction, you will want to use a variety of teaching strategies. As was pointed out in chapter 2, you have a wide range of choices. Many of these are particularly appropriate when studying certain language arts processes and content. Some will be described later in this book. However, two strategies are very closely associated with the material presented earlier in this chapter, so they will be addressed now.

Direct Whole-Class Instruction

Direct whole-class instruction has dominated public education for a long time. This is the preferred form of instruction associated with the language-as-artifact philosophy. Many novice teachers use this strategy because it is familiar and because it is what other teachers commonly do. The research rather consistently shows that if one wants to improve student scores on standardized tests of basic skills, the best method seems to be teacher-directed instruction in which the whole class basically does the same thing at the same time. However, this form of instruction has its problems, especially in the middle school. Students may expect the teacher to act as an entertainer. Also, students can become dependent on the teacher. Students wait for the teacher to start class, give directions, distribute papers, and provide assistance. All this waiting creates opportunities for discipline problems to occur. Worse yet, direct whole-class instruction hampers efforts to adapt instruction to meet the needs of individuals.

Although this form of instruction tends to increase test scores, just what form of instruction is best when the measuring stick is another kind of performance (e.g., composing of discourse, appreciation of literature, problem-solving ability, etc.) is a much different question, and, based on the research to date, it has a decidedly different answer. This is especially pertinent in the language arts classroom where the learning of processes more than the accumulation of large quantities of factual information or the automatic performance of rote behaviors is the major focus.

When considering whether to use direct, whole-class instruction, you should consider several factors besides your personal preference and familiarity with this strategy. Student needs and characteristics must be first on the list. In many schools students are accustomed to this form of instruction and may even expect it. On the other hand, they may not particularly enjoy it or learn from it. Do not be fooled by what appears to be attention. If you talk for more than 10 minutes straight, you have probably lost most of the class. Observe the wiggle worms carefully; they are restless for a reason. Long lectures, tedious discussions, and complex explanations are generally too much for them to bear. At the very least, give them some papers to shuffle, show a visual, or write something on the board. Even a pregnant pause in the verbiage, a whispered statement, or a pantomimed action can be enough to rekindle interest. The goals of instruction must be next on the list of considerations. At times, this mode of instruction is the most efficient means of reaching a desired outcome, but at other times it may produce only superficial understanding. If the material is complex, students will probably need more than a verbal introduction in order to understand it.

Despite the drawbacks, you will probably need to use direct whole-class instruction at times, such as at the beginning of a new unit of study. Sometimes you may want to discuss literature with the whole class. At other times you may decide that it is necessary to present a sharply focused mini-lesson that concentrates on a specific skill or process that students need to know in order to begin or continue an activity, or you may want to present a brief lecture to introduce a new genre or author or explain a classroom procedure. If you decide that direct whole-class instruction will be the most efficient and effective means, you may find the suggestions in Fig. 3.4 helpful. For additional information, *Inspiring Active Learning: A Handbook for Teachers* by Harmin (1994) contains many useful ideas.

Suggestions for Improving Direct, Whole Class Instruction

1. Use a variety of strategies within the framework of whole-class instruction. Be innovative. Give students a chance to lead the discussion or use some of their questions. If you want them to complete a workbook, vary the way you check the answers—collect them and check them yourself, correct them orally, check the work of the first student done and have that student check the work of the next and so on.

2. Be well prepared so that you can maintain a good pace and avoid having to go back to something you forgot.

3. Get the students' attention before beginning and move on immediately. If you often get their attention and then get sidetracked, they will stop giving their attention in the first place.

4. Use physical and verbal cues to signal what is next (e.g., you need everyone's attention, note-taking is expected, listening is paramount, questions are welcome, students should take their seats, you are ready to take attendance, papers are to be passed forward, etc.).

5. Keep everyone involved and on task. If the activity is verbal, call on a variety of people not just volunteers (forewarn students that you will do this). In a discussion, have students respond to each other rather than directing their comments to you or through you. Monitor students as they work at their desks; walk around and look over shoulders, quietly ask questions, give them verbal praise, and so on.

6. Announce and post expectations for what students should do while they wait for classmates to finish their work (e.g., silent reading, using a computer, homework, choosing a book to read, revising a paper, completing a journal entry, helping an assigned peer, etc.)

7. Circulate and provide assistance during work periods as you see fit rather than having students come to your desk. If students make the decision, the same ones will come every time, and you will not see the ones you really need to see.

8. Teach students routines such as how to hand in papers and request to leave the room so that they will not interrupt during verbal instruction.

9. Plan short, well-structured lectures. Use some scaffolding to help students—an outline on the board or overhead, signaling that you are moving on to a new part, diagramming ideas as you go, lots of examples, metaphors that refer to familiar objects or activities, graphic organizers students complete as the lecture progresses, calling for summary statements periodically, and asking students to rephrase ideas in their own words.

10. Build from the known to the new, start with easier questions directed to individuals, move on to higher-order questions that students can volunteer to answer, occasionally ask students to rephrase a classmate's answer, request clarification and elaboration, and allow wait time when you ask higher-order questions. Provide chances for students to summarize the key points that have been made.

FIG. 3.4

Cooperative/Collaborative Learning

Direct whole-class instruction has a place in the middle school language arts classroom, but student-centered instruction must form the nucleus around which other strategies cluster. Small-group work is one learner-focused teaching strategy that can be very successful, particularly in the language arts classroom where learning to speak and listen well are primary goals. However, some clarification is in order. Simply seating students together in small groups does not necessarily constitute either cooperative or collaborative learning. In cooperative and collaborative learning, students work together to achieve a common goal. They teach each other, they produce one product, they jointly solve one or a set of problems, they plan together and give a group presentation, or in some other way they share in each other's learning.

Technically, *cooperative learning* is a carefully structured situation in which students assist each other in learning material and then are tested individually. Slavin (1983) reported that all three of the most common team structures (i.e., teams–games–tournament, student teams–achievement divisions, and jigsaw II) improved student achievement. The students also showed promise for improving individual self-esteem and interpersonal relations among students.

On the other hand, *collaborative learning* is simply a small group of students working together to complete a task. Although teachers and students confirm that collaborative groups "work," there is not sufficient data to verify that such groups increase test scores. This may, however, be due to the fact that collaborative group work, in its best form, asks students to engage in higher order thinking, problem solving, and creative and critical thought, which standardized tests generally do not measure. Most middle level students like to work in groups, so they tend to enjoy school more when they have an opportunity to do so. Collaborative group work addresses the social needs of middle school students. It also helps students develop interpersonal and leadership skills. Varying groups is one effective way to provide differentiated instruction, too. Language arts educators verify that this kind of experience, in the form of both literature circles (Daniels, 1994) and revising–editing groups (Spear, 1987), enhances literacy learning. In addition, the evidence is mounting that collaborative discourse about subject matter is a powerful tool for student construction of meaning that leads to depth of understanding (Almasi, 1996; Paratore & McCormack, 1997).

Preservice teachers often worry that students will waste time in groups. A certain amount of socializing is to be expected; it is a necessary part of effective group work, even among adults (Cohen, 1986). Students may socialize a bit more in small groups, but when they are on-task, everyone in the group is usually fully engaged. Long-term group work may be much more productive than the casual and occasional use of groups that teachers often try, but it does demand redesigning the curriculum and activities to fit the cooperative or collaborative group mode.

Orientation to Group Work.   One common mistake teachers make is to assume that students can readily work in small groups without any preparation. If you want this approach to work well in your classroom, you have to teach students how you expect them to work together. Furthermore, students need to know that everyone in the group is to contribute a fair share even though the specific type of contribution may differ according to the strengths each person brings to the group.

If you intend to use groups early in the year, start with some get-acquainted or ice breaker activities. Activities for pairs ease students into working with peers. The 5-Squares Game (Weitzman, 1974), with follow-up discussion of the importance of sharing with others, is an excellent activity. Collaboratively solving puzzles, such as those which appear in *Games* magazine or *Teaching PreK–8*, with a follow-up discussion of two heads being better than one, also prepares students for working in groups. Once students have developed some trust in their peers, a carefully structured task such as the one shown in Fig. 3.5 can be introduced.

When you prepare students to work in groups, one useful strategy is to spend at least a day at the start of the year brainstorming what to do if group members do not cooperate. You may want to try using the fishbowl discussion ideas that appear in Fig. 3.6 to illustrate potential difficulties. Suggestions for solving problems can be recorded on art paper and posted on the walls for reference throughout the year. Fishbowl discussions can be used repeatedly to model new expectations and discuss problems that groups encounter as the year progresses.

An Initial Group Task

1. The class reads a short story silently.
2. Students are assigned to groups. Each group is given one copy of a form that is to be completed in about 10 minutes. The task is to make a story map of the plot.
3. Each member of the group signs a statement at the bottom of the sheet indicating that he/she agrees with the list.
4. At the end of the time, lists are shared orally to produce a single class list, which is then written on the board or overhead.
5. Signed lists are collected.

FIG. 3.5

Demonstrating Discussions

Fishbowl 1
- Select students to sit in the center of the room and discuss a topic of interest. They are "in the fishbowl."
- Everyone else sits around the outside and observes.
- Discuss what behaviors help the group begin and progress and which ones hinder the group.

Fishbowl 2
- Select students to be "in the fishbowl," but assign a student a role to play (e.g., dominator, rejecter, nonattender, diverter, nonparticipant, etc.). The group tries to carry on a discussion.
- The rest of the class observes to determine the problem.
- Discuss the effect of the problem behavior and solutions.

FIG. 3.6

Organizing the Groups. Successful groups can be organized in a number of ways, depending on the instructional goals. Sometimes it is best to allow students to choose group members, but if groups are to work together for long periods of time, you may find that assigning students to groups is more effective. If students have a choice of reading material, you may want to use their choices as the basis for establishing groups. When the focus is on teaching a skill or strategy or introducing a new concept or genre, you may wish to bring together a group of students who are in need of or ready for this instruction. Teachers disagree over the optimum size of groups, but most would agree that between three and six students is appropriate. Some teachers intentionally mix male and female students, but others avoid doing so in order to enhance the chances of females taking leadership roles. Some teachers find that the group work progresses more smoothly if students are assigned specific roles within the group (e.g., leader, recorder, summarizer, questioner, and so on), although most teachers rotate these roles regularly. You will need to experiment to find the most successful combination. However, try to avoid placing the strongest and weakest students in the same group. Also, create groups that are large enough to function despite the absence of one or two members.

Designing Group Tasks. Another common pitfall is having students work together when they see no reason to do so. Group tasks must be activities that cannot be accomplished individually. Figure 3.7 contains an example of a successful collaborative project. The following guidelines for designing tasks may prove helpful:

Collaborative Group Work—An Example

Oral literature unit

1. Having been introduced to a wide variety of oral tales and sourcebooks, students selected one tale to read individually outside of class. They were also to prepare to tell their tale to a small group.

2. During the intervening class time, the class as a whole read, both silently and aloud, and discussed several other tales. The focus in these discussions was on comparing and describing different kinds of tales. Some class time was also devoted to considering effective storytelling techniques and a guest storyteller came to class to present a story and answer students' questions.

3. On the basis of the tales each selected, students were assigned to groups. On the prescheduled presentation days, students retold their tales to their small group. (Several students came in costume and had props, although neither was required.)

4. At the conclusion of each presentation, each group member had to write down whether the tale was a fairy tale, myth, legend, or fable and briefly explain why he or she considered it to be this kind of tale.

5. When all of the presentations in the group were done (in groups of five, this took about three class periods), the identifications and reasons were shared and discussed. Each group was required to reach consensus about each tale.

6. The teacher then selected one member from each group to retell his or her tale for the class (by carefully observing, the teacher spotted different types of tales being told so that the examples were varied).

7. Following each of these presentations, one member of the storyteller's group stated what kind of tale had been told and the reasons the group had generated. The class then agreed or disagreed. Further discussion followed.

8. Each group chose a particular kind of tale and wrote one as a group story of that sort. (Students who wished to write as individuals were allowed to do so, but they had to write the same kind of story selected by their group.)

9. Groups then either read their stories aloud or acted them out for the class.

FIG. 3.7

- The first task must be very specific, and students should know exactly what is expected of them.
- There must be an end product that the group produces together.
- A time limit must be specified.
- There must be printed directions for the task, one per group.

Assessing and Grading. Teachers must observe groups carefully, monitor their work, participate occasionally, listen carefully, keep anecdotal records, challenge groups to reach beyond the superficial, and help groups solve problems. One way to monitor work is to have students fill out schedules that show what the group plans to do the next day (eventually, the next week) and check these nightly, making suggestions and occasionally assigning particular tasks.

Although group members must be held accountable for the functioning of the group, individuals must be responsible for their own learning and that of other members of the group. Include group processes (e.g., ability to solve group conflicts or problems, effective use of time, participation, etc.) in the grades. Have students assess what they are learning in their groups, as well as how well the group is functioning as a whole. Give some group grades, but also give individual grades. In some instances, these grades can be based on the progress made by the group members as a whole.

PLANNING

Now that you have examined a number of factors related to teaching language arts effectively, you should be ready to begin to think about how to plan instruction for middle level students. Whether you use a curriculum guide, a textbook, student needs and interests, or personal judgment as the starting point for determining the curriculum that you will teach, planning for learning is necessary. Sometimes this planning is done in concert with a teaching team, but often the teacher must work out the details independently. The type of planning depends, in part, on the instructional approach you want to use; the more student-centered the instruction, the more individualized the planning, for example. Planning is also related to teaching experience. The more experienced the teacher, the less visible the planning tends to be. Although they may not record details on paper, the most effective teachers do think ahead about what they intend to do, how, and why. As a novice, you need to make rather thorough written plans. Having a prepared plan will give you confidence and help you remain focused on your instructional objectives.

Long-Term Planning

Long-term planning concerns the whole semester or year. Teachers look at the school calendar and make some tentative decisions about when they will teach which concepts. Sometimes this is as simple as deciding that they will cover one chapter per week in the textbook. Other teachers subdivide the year into grading periods and determine what they will try to achieve by the end of each segment. Others tend to divide the year into units of study and then schedule these according to difficulty. A long-term plan for a year subdivided into 9-week grading periods may look something like this if the teacher chooses to use a units approach:

Weeks 1 and 2: Introductions, diagnostics, and orientation to procedures.
Weeks 3–8: Short story unit.
Week 9: Grammar review.
Weeks 10–12: Novel unit.
Weeks 13–17: Persuasive language unit.
Week 18: Mechanics review.
Weeks 19–21: Research/speech unit.
Weeks 22–24: Descriptive writing unit.
Weeks 25–26: Grammar review.
Weeks 27–29: Drama unit.
Weeks 30–35: Poetry unit.
Week 36: Windup, class evaluation.

A teacher using a reading–writing workshop approach, which is more student-centered, may produce a very different kind of schedule, such as the following:

Week 1: Workshop and portfolio introduction.
Weeks 2–8: Reading–writing workshop.
Weeks 9–12: Whole-class novel study.
Weeks 13–19: Reading–writing workshop.
Weeks 20–25: Thematic unit.
Weeks 26–32: Reading–writing workshop.
Weeks 33–36: Portfolio polishing and reflection.

Other examples of long-term plans for workshops can be found in *Seeking Diversity* (Rief, 1992) and *In the Middle* (Atwell, 1998).

Any good long-term plan should be educationally logical. That is to say that it should take into consideration the skills and prior knowledge that students must have before they begin each unit. Easier, more intrinsically interesting units should be scheduled before more difficult and less obviously relevant ones. If students develop a high level of involvement and confidence initially, this may help them work through more challenging content later. A well-conceived long-term plan will ensure that all of the language arts processes and content are incorporated.

Another factor that teachers must consider when they create long-term plans is interruptions. Lots of these occur every school year—testing days, vacation breaks, holidays, convocations, field trips, and special programs. Introducing a new unit on the day before a lengthy vacation is not a good idea. All new teachers make some mistakes when they first create long-term plans. Including a buffer or catch-up day now and then allows for the unexpected, such as snow days, power failures, and broken water mains. No matter how carefully you plan, though, the schedule will never work exactly as you hope or intend.

Short-Term Planning

Once the long-term planning is done, teachers focus on each of the units or subdivisions of the year. This is one type of short-term planning. Part of this short-term planning is deciding which of the year's goals each unit or subsection should help to achieve. The choice of goals should lead to the development of more precise objectives. Identification of these objectives will help the teacher choose more specifically what can and will be included in each unit or portion.

Another part of short-term planning is the sequencing of activities that fit within the schedule. In general, this means looking at the concepts to be taught and the possible activities and then choosing the ones that best meet the needs of students and match the goals and objectives and also fit within the available time frame. A 5-week unit, for example, might be divided into the following parts:

- One day for introducing the unit.
- Two days for viewing a videotape introducing the concepts.
- Fifteen days of activities to explore and research the concepts.
- Five days for student presentations.
- Two days for reviewing and concluding the learning.

The other part of short-term planning is "daily" lesson planning. Effective teachers think ahead and prepare plans for each class. Many teachers see these lesson plans as one-period designs (e.g., "What I plan to do tomorrow in my 4th-hour class"); but some teachers see these as plans that cover the amount of time necessary to complete a subportion of a unit (e.g., "What I plan to do for the 3 days it will take to show this videotape"). Whether these plans cover single or multiple days, these are the plans that teachers develop to keep them on track during each class period. Every lesson should address goals and fit into the total scheme of instruction planned for the year. However, each lesson should be designed to achieve some specific objectives and provide a kind of road map for how the teacher expects the class period to proceed. If the teacher chooses to use a workshop approach, these daily plans are apt to include class announcements, outlines of mini-lessons, and lists of conferences the teacher needs to hold, as well as special events that must be preplanned (e.g., student presentations of projects, revising group meetings, or guest speakers).

A Plan for Teaching Processes

Lesson plans can be based on many different designs. One that is commonly used begins with a review of the previous day's work, followed by an introduction to the new material. Students then practice the skill or complete some exercise. The lesson usually concludes with a homework assignment in which students are to complete even more practice. This plan serves well in a teacher-dominated classroom in which students are studying rather rote material. However, when you are focusing on teaching various language arts processes and strategies, a different design may be needed, one that provides some support for the learner, but which also gives students a bit more freedom to work at their own pace and assume more responsibility. One such design, based on research by Holdaway (1979), is composed of the following four steps:

- Demonstration
- Participation
- Practice
- Performance

Demonstration is usually done by the teacher, but it could be done by a guest speaker or a student. This is not an explanation of what students are supposed to do; it is an illustration. If you want students to write journal entries, for example, you can write one on an overhead transparency while students watch and listen as you share your thoughts. This is known as a *think aloud*.

Participation is the step that is often excluded from instruction. This is an opportunity for students to begin to try the process with assistance, especially from peers. When beginning a writing task, for example, students may work with a peer to generate topics.

Practice is the time when students take the information and work with it primarily on their own, although they can still obtain assistance and feedback from others. Practice can also be thought of as rehearsal. It is the time to find out what one understands and what is still unclear. It is also the time for trial and error, discovery, and experimentation.

The final step is performance. However, this does not have to refer to drama or public speaking. Performance may be something as basic as reading a book independently. It can also refer to making work public in some way—displaying it on the bulletin board or reading it aloud to a small audience.

This is a very flexible sequence. It can be used for mini-lessons that last only a few minutes or it can serve as the foundation for a much longer lesson, possibly lasting for several days.

A Generic Plan

In some school districts, teachers are required to use a particular format for their lesson plans. You may even be required to submit plans to a mentor, team leader, or administrator. If you are not given a form to use, you can devise one that works for you, but it is helpful to include the items listed in Fig. 3.8.

Class, Topic, and Date. The class may be an identification of the period the class meets, a section number, or a description of the student population (e.g., grade level, team name, or a small group studying a particular novel). The topic of the lesson should fit what has occurred the previous day and what is planned for the next. Except for rare occasions, a lesson plan should be a "slice of the whole pie," not some isolated activity that is unrelated to the unit or subsection and the plan for the year.

Objectives. As much as possible, lesson objectives should be stated behaviorally (what students will know or be able to do or value by the end of the lesson) and should include action verbs that point to observable and possibly measurable behaviors (e.g., "students will *know*" is not observable; "students will *list*" is observable). If you are more comfortable with the constructivist perspective, which views learning as personal construction of meaning that may not be accurately predictable, you should still be able to identify the thinking or the learning processes in which you expect students to engage. The list of objectives for a single lesson should be short, but

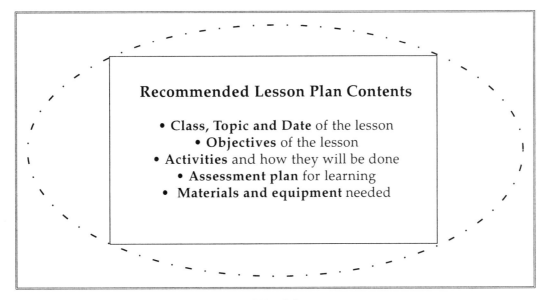

Recommended Lesson Plan Contents

- **Class, Topic and Date** of the lesson
- **Objectives** of the lesson
- **Activities** and how they will be done
- **Assessment plan** for learning
- **Materials and equipment** needed

FIG. 3.8

it should contain more than just the facts that you want students to accumulate. Think, too, about the processes, skills, and dispositions you want students to acquire.

Activities. As the example in Fig. 3.9 shows, the *activities* part of the plan will be the longest and most detailed section. It should include, in step-by-step fashion, what you plan to have students do during the class period. Also, state how this will occur (e.g., lecture, recitation, small group work, video, etc.). This section of the plan should include titles of books and page numbers, titles of videotapes, and other such specifics. To decide how much detail to include, consider this question: If you were absent and a substitute had to take your place, what would your stand-in need to know in order to conduct the lesson very much as you would if you were there?

The sequence of activities will depend on what you want to achieve, but as much as possible, the opening should be something that catches student attention and provides reasons for taking part. It is also a good idea to review or link to known information at the beginning of the lesson.

The central part of the activities usually should include a variety of things to be done. Variety helps hold attention. Plan to guide students along and help them see the relationships between one activity and the next; otherwise, the class period can seem to be a series of disconnected events. This formation of connections is one kind of scaffolding. Also, transitions from one task to the next must be designed to build understanding and avoid wasted time.

At the end of the lesson there should be some activity that signals closure, such as a brief review or summary. If you intend to assign homework, be sure to allow time for giving the directions and permitting students to ask questions. If possible, students should begin working on the task so they have a chance to discover any confusion while you are still available to clarify.

Assessment Plan. How you assess or evaluate student progress toward the objectives will depend on what those aims are. You must plan a means of assessment that reveals what you really want to know about what students have learned. A quick two-question quiz may be the best means of determining whether students have learned factual information. However, if you are trying to teach students a process, then observing them while they work may be a much better way of gauging what they are learning. No matter what type of assessment you select, you need to think about it in advance in order to be prepared to collect the data.

Materials and Equipment. The *materials and equipment* section of your lesson plan is a list of the books, supplies, handouts, videos,

A Sample Lesson Plan

Topic and Date   Introduction to poetry unit
                     January 15, 2000

Materials Needed
Visual puzzles transparency from *Games*
Transparency of hink pinks
Overhead projector and screen
Transparency markers
Answer keys
Literature anthologies

Objectives
1. Students will participate verbally in solving visual puzzles.
2. Students will identify poems by viewing appearance only.
3. Students will summarize, in writing, what they know about poetry.
4. Students will write hink pinks and suitable definitions.
5. Students will solve hink pink puzzles created by others.
6. Students will demonstrate enthusiasm by creating more hink pinks than required.

Activities
1. Prior to class, put up a hink pink bulletin board with a few examples (definitions on the outside of a folded piece of paper and answers hidden under the fold).
2. Before class begins, prepare the projector and transparency. Dim the lights and turn on the projector to begin class.
3. Ask students to look carefully at these puzzles to see if they can solve one. Point out the identification coding. If necessary, give students a solution or two.
4. Allow the solving to continue until attention wanes.
5. Ask students if they can see any similarities between these puzzles and poetry (e.g., looking from a new perspective, word arrangement on the page, meaningful white space, reader has to think about meaning).
6. Ask students to skim through the literature anthology and find poems just by glancing at the text. How could they recognize these as poems?
7. Have students take out a sheet of paper and jot down what they know about poetry. Share responses. Note the frequency of rhyming.
8. Have students write pairs of words that rhyme.
9. Show transparency of hink pinks to solve. Note definitions and syllable counts.
10. Have students write definitions for their own hink pinks.
11. Model how to put a puzzle on the chalkboard. Select students to put their puzzles on the board.
12. Have students write in answers and put their own puzzles on the board. Continue until enthusiasm lags or time grows short.
13. Have students file the papers in their portfolios for use the next day. Challenge students to think of more and better hink pinks to add to the bulletin board.

continued on next page

Assessment

1. Observe and note on participation record which students offer solutions to visual puzzles, keeping in mind that this requires both visual and verbal abilities (good opportunities for noticing viewing and visual representation talents?).
2. Observe and note which students successfully recognize poetry by format.
3. Monitor writing to determine which students can create rhymed pairs and definitions and who has difficulty with one or both tasks.
4. Examine written material later as part of poetry portfolio work.
5. Observe and note which students go to the board eagerly and confidently as well as those who are reluctant.
6. On portfolio checklist, record which students add new hink pinks to display.

FIG. 3.9

equipment, and whatever else you and your students will need in order to carry out the plan. These are listed last because you really cannot decide what you must have ready until the rest of the lesson is designed. Nevertheless, you may consider putting this list at the top of your own lesson plans. That way you can quickly check before class to make sure that you have everything prepared. Some teachers write these lists on Post-It notes and put them in their plan books for quick reference.

Other Kinds of Plans

A representative sample of other planning formats appears in Fig. 3.10. If you use collaborative or cooperative group work, your plans will need to reflect your expectations for each group. If the groups complete and submit a daily schedule of their work, the notations you make on these schedules may substitute for more formal lesson plans. These schedules can include space for recording goals and objectives as well as plans for assessment developed cooperatively with the group members.

If you use a workshop approach, your planning will revolve around individuals. The daily records you make of student activities can also serve as the basis for your planning. You may want to create a form for jotting reminders about the kinds of interactions you need to have with students during the week. Your plan can include a writing conference with one student, a portfolio check of another, a book discussion with another, and so on. In some ways, this plan may resemble a daily appointment book. You can write goals and objectives for individuals in a spiral notebook, one student per page, or they can be recorded on a form that each student keeps in his or her portfolio.

LESSON PLAN SAMPLE 1

Name _____ Date _____ Class _____ Unit _____

Period _____ School _____ Supervisor _____

activity	time	equipment	objective	organization

Evaluation:

FIG. 3.10   Sample 1.

LESSON PLAN SAMPLE 2

Day or number: _____

Unit Title: _____

Objective(s): _____

_____

Procedures: [estimated time, content, student/teacher activities, notes,

questions, closure.]

_____

_____

_____

_____

_____

_____

_____

_____

_____

_____

_____

_____

_____

_____

_____

Instructional Materials: [Textbooks, films, passouts, etc. {give page numbers}]

_____

_____

Assignment (be specific): _____

_____

FIG. 3.10 Sample 2.

LESSON PLAN SAMPLE 3

Name_____Date_____

Subject or setting_____Grade_____

Linking today's lesson with previous work: _____

_____

_____

Aims and objectives:

   Knowledge _____

   Skills _____

   Attitudes _____

<u>Content</u>   <u>Methods</u>

FIG. 3.10   Sample 3.

LESSON PLAN SAMPLE 4 (collaborative groups)

Week of _____   Class _____   Unit: _____

Observation Notes:	Instruction Plan
MONDAY	
Group 1:	Group 1:
Group 2:	Group 2:
Group 3:	Group 3:
Group 4:	Group 4:
Group 5:	Group 5:
TUESDAY	
Group 1:	Group 1:
Group 2:	Group 2:
Group 3:	Group 3:
Group 4:	Group 4:
Group 5:	Group 5:
WEDNESDAY	
Group 1:	Group 1:
Group 2:	Group 2:
Group 3:	Group 3:
Group 4:	Group 4:
Group 5:	Group 5:
THURSDAY	
Group 1:	Group 1:
Group 2:	Group 2:
Group 3:	Group 3:
Group 4:	Group 4:
Group 5:	Group 5:
FRIDAY	
Group 1:	Group 1:
Group 2:	Group 2:
Group 3:	Group 3:
Group 4:	Group 4:
Group 5:	Group 5:

FIG. 3.10.   Sample 4.

Figure 3.11 includes additional hints for creating better lesson plans. Although you want a planning system that makes it easier for you to orchestrate student activity, keep in mind that the form is less important than the quality. What you plan to have students do is much more significant than the format you choose for recording that plan.

Finally, any educational plan is only a guide. It is not a set of directions that can or should be followed slavishly. Plans should always be considered tentative.

---

12 Hints for Better Lesson Plans

- Plan thoroughly at first. As you gain experience, you will become adept at knowing which parts of the lesson you need to record on paper and which parts you can do somewhat automatically.
- Visualize the period as you hope it will evolve. Record what you will need to do and say in order to insure that events happen the way you want them to happen.
- Choose a lesson format that is easy to use. Lists and outlines are often more beneficial than paragraphs of description or scripts of lectures.
- Highlighting markers are handy tools for emphasizing reminders on plans.
- For small-group and workshop planning, create a system that gives you a quick overview of the class that you can scan at the start of the period.
- Beg and borrow as well as invent good teaching activities, but choose carefully. Many activities in commercial sources are little more than gimmicks and tricks, fun for students to do, but not instructive. Teaching well is much more than keeping students happily busy.
- If you plan to conduct a discussion, write down some questions that you intend to ask. Good higher-order questions are very difficult to create on the spot.
- Write the directions for any activity that is new. Write the instructions you intend to give students about participating and how you expect them to behave.
- Predicting pace will be difficult at first. Writing and reading assignments often take longer than you think they will; worksheets and drill exercises generally take far less time than you estimate. Discussions are unpredictable. Plan for more than you think can be done, even as much as twice the amount, but don't try to push students through it all.
- If it is helpful to you, add other information to your plans, such as a rationale for the lesson or goals for improving your teaching.
- Be prepared. Have a plan B and even a plan C in mind just in case plan A isn't working. Rarely will a lesson go exactly as planned.
- Keep your lesson plans. Having something in writing helps you reflect on what went well and what didn't, what to save and what to discard. Plans are useful for reminding you of what the class did when a student was absent, and they make good references when you are constructing exams and grading papers.

FIG. 3.11

RECOMMENDED READINGS

Allen, J., & Gonzalez, K. (1998). *There's room for me here: Literacy workshop in the middle school.* York, ME: Stenhouse.

Archer, J. (1998, November 18). States anteing up supplements to teachers certified by Board. *Education Week, 18*(12), 1, 12.

Atwell, N. (1998). *In the middle: New understandings about writing, reading, and learning* (2nd Ed.). Portsmouth, NH: Heinemann.

Burkhart, R. (1994). *The inquiry process: Student-centered learning.* Logan, IA: Perfection Learning.

Butler, D., & Liner, T. (1995). *Rooms to grow: Natural language arts in the middle school.* Durham, NC: Carolina Academic Press.

Cambourne, B. (1988). *The whole story: Natural learning and the acquisition of literacy in the classroom.* Auckland, New Zealand: Ashton Scholastic.

Cohen, E. (1986). *Designing groupwork: Strategies for the heterogeneous classroom.* New York: Teachers College Press.

Daniels, H. (1994). *Literature circles: Voice and choice in the student-centered classroom.* York, ME: Stenhouse.

Daniels, H., & Bizar, M. (1998). *Methods that matter: Six structures for best practice classrooms.* York, ME: Stenhouse Publishers.

Gere, A., Fairbanks, C., Howes, A., Roop, L., & Schaafsma, D. (1992). *Language and reflection: An integrated approach to teaching English.* New York: Macmillan.

Harmin, M. (1994). *Inspiring active learning: A handbook for teachers.* Alexandria, VA: Association for Supervision and Curriculum Development.

Hunter, M. (1984). Knowing, teaching, and supervising. In P. Hosford (Ed.) *Using what we know about teaching* (pp. 169–192). Alexandria, VA: Association for Supervision and Curriculum Development.

Johnson, D., Johnson, R., Holubec, E., & Roy, P. (1984). *Circles of learning: Co-operation in the classroom.* Alexandria, VA: Association for Supervision and Curriculum Development.

Johnson, D., Johnson, R., Holubec, E., & Roy, P. (1991). *Cooperation in the classroom.* Edina, MN: Interaction Book Company.

Krogness, M. (1995). *Just teach me, Mrs. K: Talking, reading, and writing with resistant adolescent learners.* Portsmouth, NH: Heinemann.

Lloyd-Jones, R., & Lunsford, A. (Eds.). (1989). *The English Coalition Conference: Democracy through language.* Urbana, IL: National Council of Teachers of English.

Mayher, J. (1990). *Uncommon sense: Theoretical practice in language education.* Portsmouth, NH: Boynton/Cook–Heinemann.

Myers, M., & Spalding, E. (Eds.). (1997). *Standards exemplar series: Assessing student performance grades 6–8.* Urbana, IL: National Council of Teachers of English.

National Board for Professional Teaching Standards (1994). *Early adolescence/English language arts standards.* Detroit, MI: Author.

National Council of Teachers of English and International Reading Association (1996). *Standards for the English language arts.* Urbana, IL, and Newark, DE: Authors.

National Middle School Association (1995). *This we believe: Developmentally responsive middle level schools.* Columbus, OH: Author.

Ogden, E., & Germinario, V. (1994). *The nation's best schools, blueprint for excellence* (vols. 1–2). Lancaster, PA: Technomic.

Paratore, J., & McCormack (Eds.) (1997). *Peer talk in the classroom: Learning from research.* Newark, DE: International Reading Association.

Rief, L. (1992). *Seeking diversity: Language arts with adolescents.* Portsmouth, NH: Heinemann.

Stone, J. (1994). *Cooperative learning and language arts: A multi-structural approach.* San Juan Capistrano, CA: Kagan Cooperative Learning.

Weitzman, D. (1974). Break the ice with 5 squares. *Learning, 2*(9), 32–37.

Wilhelm, J. (1996). *Standards in practice, Grades 6–8.* Urbana, IL: National Council of Teachers of English.

Zemelman, S., Daniels, H., & Hyde, A. (1998). *Best practice: New standards for teaching and learning in America's schools.* (2nd Ed.). Portsmouth, NH: Heinemann.

OTHER RESOURCES

Games magazine
P.O. Box 2031
Marion, OH 43305-2031
1-800-426-3768

Teaching Pre K–8
40 Richards Ave.
Norwalk, CT 06854
1-800-249-9363
www.TeachingK-8.com

National Board for Professional Teaching Standards
300 River Place
Suite 3600
Detroit, MI 48207
313-259-0830
www.nbpts.org

Part II

Teaching the Processes of Language Arts

4

Teaching Reading

Overview

CONSIDER THESE QUESTIONS ABOUT TEACHING READING

1. Must you, as an English teacher, teach reading? Should this be someone else's responsibility? Or should students already know how to read by middle school?

2. What should be the primary goal of teaching reading? Is assigning reading the same as teaching reading? Is teaching literature the same as teaching reading?

3. What behaviors do fluent readers exhibit? Nonfluent readers?

4. Is reading ever mastered?

5. Should you read aloud to students? Should they read aloud? Is round-robin reading an effective strategy to use in the classroom?

6. Should vocabulary be taught, or is it best learned from reading? If it should be taught, what are the best ways to teach it?

7. What do students need to know about reading narrative prose? Poetry? Drama? What do students need to know in order to read well various kinds of nonfiction?

8. How can you assess reading? Should students' use of reading processes be a part of their evaluation?

9. Must you be an avid reader to be an effective reading teacher? What skills and knowledge about reading do you possess that students need to know?

10. What are some activities that are likely to be most effective in teaching reading at the middle school level?

RETHINKING READING

Language arts teachers generally agree that they want students to comprehend what they read, but they also want them to enjoy and appreciate literature. Is it possible to have one without the other? The number of students who can read with understanding yet choose never to read or even resist reading indicates that the answer must be *Yes*. On the other hand, young children who are unable to read a single word are often entranced when someone reads to them. They know good stories when they hear them even if they have not yet grasped the significance of print. Having the ability to read does not guarantee that a person will enjoy literature, yet people can appreciate literature without having the skill to read. Most teachers (along with the general population) want students who not only *can* but *do* read—not just with comprehension, but with eagerness and appreciation as well.

People once believed that reading could be taught and mastered at a relatively early age. After reading was mastered, it was simply a matter of practicing to increase speed and vocabulary. The study of literature was generally considered to be the next step in the process and, to some extent, the goal of reading instruction itself, at least among language arts teachers. Thus, English majors preparing to teach at the middle and high school levels received no preparation for teaching reading because students were supposed to know how to read by the time they finished the elementary grades.

However, circumstances have forced people to rethink that notion. In the past, people were able to live reasonably well even if their reading skills were limited, but today people must be able to read reasonably well just to survive. Unfortunately, a sizable portion of students reach middle school without the reading skills they need, and even more arrive with negative attitudes. Students with various learning disabilities populate regular classrooms, and the number of students for whom English is a second language continues to grow. As students progress through school, they must learn to cope with text that gets increasingly more challenging. Even able college readers sometimes find their textbooks and assignments difficult to comprehend. Ordinary citizens must be able to read and understand material that is specialized and technical. Reading is not a set of skills mastered in the primary grades; readers need continued assistance in developing their ability to read well.

WHAT CURRENT RESEARCH INDICATES ABOUT READING

Research into the effective teaching of reading has been extensive for several decades (e.g., see Pearson, 1984), but during the past 20 years or so, the focus has shifted toward what cognitive science can reveal about how the brain works. What does the human brain do in order to process print? How do people make sense of what they read? There is an even more basic question: What is reading? Researchers have also been looking at the social context that surrounds reading. To what extent are readers influenced by the attitudes and expectations of other people?

We still do not know all of the answers. In fact, we still do not even know all of the questions. There are those who continue to believe that learning to decode the letters and sounds of English is the most important goal of reading instruction and marks the difference between the nonreader and the reader. Others point out that many students who can decode flawlessly (i.e., read aloud without error) do not understand what they are reading.

Experts in the field of emergent literacy (i.e., beginning reading and writing) tend to agree that students need to learn letter–sound correspondences. However, there is a great deal of disagreement over how much of this learning is enough. One group believes that every child should master phonics and that this systematic instruction should continue for several years in the elementary schools; others believe that students should move away as rapidly as possible from this kind of instruction and into reading children's trade books and other whole pieces of discourse. One way of thinking about this difference of opinion is to consider the first approach as a part-to-whole or bottom-up idea in which students first learn the small parts (i.e., letters and sounds) and gradually move on to wholes (i.e., words, sentences, etc.). The second approach is a kind of whole-first or top-down idea in which students are encouraged to move as swiftly as they can into reading whole words, phrases, sentences, and even books. Once students are reading with adequate fluency, the parts (including phonics skills) that give individuals difficulty are taught on an as-needed basis.

This whole-first or whole-language philosophy is supported by the knowledge that infants learn language in a holistic way. They babble sounds, but they quickly learn to speak whole words, two-word "sentences," and full sentences. They do not learn to pronounce every sound in the language before they begin talking. Furthermore, they learn to speak in a natural way without formal lessons. Parents do not sit children down for a specified period of time and teach speaking. It is an ongoing process that happens throughout the day simply as a part of living. We also know that some children learn to read without any formal instruction. These are the children who have benefited from Cambourne's (1988) list of natural learning conditions, which appeared in chapter 3. Others, however, seem to need more structured approaches. For a much more in-depth look at some of these aspects of reading, you may find the books by Adams (1990) and Coles (1998) very informative; they are listed in the Recommended Readings for this chapter.

READING AS A TRANSACTIONAL PROCESS OF THOUGHT

There is mounting research evidence in support of the idea that people should change their perceptions of how reading takes place and what it involves. Much of this evidence comes from the field of psycholinguistics, which studies the interactions between the mind and language (e.g., Smith, 1997; Weaver, 1994). People once thought that the meaning of the text was in the material alone. To comprehend well, all the reader had to do was extract the meaning that was already there. More recent research indicates that readers actually construct meaning for themselves as they read. To do so, they rely heavily on what they already unconsciously understand about how spoken language works. Research indicates that readers rely on three kinds of cues that exist in print and that their brains can process. When faced with an unfamiliar word, effective readers use a combination of *semantic*, *syntactic*, and *graphophonic* cues to create meaning from text. In simpler terms, they consider what makes sense in a sentence, what part of speech fits the context, and what the word looks and sounds like.

However, reading is not just a matter of decoding and understanding words. It also involves the development of concepts. When you read the word *tree*, what image comes to mind? Do you think of a sugar maple or a cedar? Do you think of a forest or a sapling you planted when you were a child? Maybe you recall a spindly seedling struggling through a sidewalk crack. Perhaps you associate the word with an experience, such as a violent storm that destroyed a park near your home or a holiday celebration at the foot of a decorated pine. Perhaps you think of the rain forest and ecological threats to the environment. The meaning you give to the word *tree*, as well as the intricate web of connections associated with the word, is known as a *schema*. Effective reading helps people develop more complex schemata. On the other hand, absence of a schema can inhibit understanding. If, for example, an author writes about Alpine skiing and the reader has little knowledge of the sport, creation of meaning may be difficult. Another reader who has a rich schema surrounding the topic will probably find the reading task easier and more pleasurable. Engaging in reading will help readers build their knowledge of concepts, but teachers need to provide means for aiding students both in developing a rich store of background knowledge about many concepts through other learning activities and in connecting new ideas to familiar ones.

Creating meaning demands thinking. Readers have to access their memories in order to retrieve relevant information. They have to decide which cueing system to use, and they have to recognize when the material no longer makes sense to them. They must be metacognitively aware of their thinking processes, and they must actively monitor comprehension as it develops or ceases to develop. Although comprehending what we read may seem to be an automatic process, we have all had the experience of reading something without understanding a word of it. The minute we flip on the "automatic pilot" when we read, we risk losing comprehension.

Failing to engage the brain before and during reading causes a breakdown in comprehension. Comprehension can also break down if one or more of the cueing systems is poorly developed or if a reader relies too heavily on one without cross-checking with the others. Comprehension is also difficult if the reader lacks a relevant schema. However, even if all of these systems are "go," comprehension can still be impeded because of other factors. Though we often blame failure to comprehend on the reader's lack of skill or concentration, the cause may be neither of these.

This is not really a new concept, though. In the 1930s, Rosenblatt (1938) proposed that reading should be viewed as a transaction between the reader and the text, rather than a one-way extraction of meaning. Her theory was that what the reader brought to the act of reading significantly influenced the meaning that would be derived. This certainly makes a great deal of sense. Middle level students, or any students for that matter, who are generally reading below grade level can comprehend more difficult text if it concerns a subject they know well. Rosenblatt (1978) proposed that the result of this interaction was what she called the "poem." She was not proposing that the meaning created was a poem in the typical sense of a piece of discourse containing rhyme, rhythm, and so on, but rather a creative product of thought and understanding, unique to the reader–creator. Although her theory was largely ignored for many years, it resurfaced recently as one of the best descriptions of what transpires in the reading process. It serves to explain why it is that two people can read the same piece of discourse and construct significantly different meanings, why two readers pinpoint different statements as the main idea of a passage, and why people do not always agree on the quality of what they read.

EFFECTS OF TEXT- AND READER-BASED FACTORS

The text itself can affect comprehension. If the print is too light or too small or if the graphics distract from the meaning, for example, comprehension may be inhibited. However, these shortcomings are usually visible to everyone, so a lack of understanding comes as no surprise. Furthermore, effective readers can often compensate for these text inadequacies. Some texts, though, are so poorly written as to be "reader-unfriendly." Such texts may be badly organized or conceptually dense. The vocabulary may be needlessly technical. Sentences may be inordinately long or so choppy as to lack coherence.

Although these textual features can be hindrances, there are also several reader-based factors that influence what "poem" a reader constructs. Readers themselves may be unaware that these factors are affecting meaning. Indeed, some of these factors are so much a part of personality or emotional makeup that readers would have great difficulty controlling them even if the readers were aware of their existence. Although these factors are quite complex and interrelated, there are five, as shown in Fig. 4.1, that researchers and theorists contend are prominent.

One factor that influences comprehension is the *reader's knowledge of textual conventions*. Whether or not a reader understands how text works affects meaning. This may be as simple as understanding how writers use punctuation, for example, or as complex as knowing how flashbacks function in narratives.

Another factor is the *reader's prior experiences* both with reading and with the topic. When a reader does not understand that printed

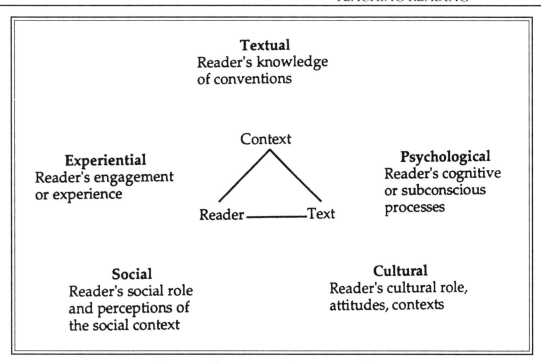

FIG. 4.1   From A *Teacher's Introduction to Reader-Response Theories* (p. 8), by R. Beach, 1993. Urbana, IL: National Council of Teachers of English. Copyright 1993 by National Council of Teachers of English. Reprinted with permission.

material is supposed to make sense or that it is organized in some logical fashion, that reader is at a disadvantage. Similarly, a reader who is unfamiliar with the concepts may struggle to create meaning. For instance, a reader from a small midwestern town may find a story that takes place in Harlem far less understandable than will a resident of New York.

A third factor that can influence comprehension is the *reader's cognitive processes*. The development of thinking skills has much to do with how readers create meaning from what they read. If the reader cannot or does not monitor his or her own comprehension, understanding can break down. Comprehension may also be inhibited if the reader does not predict well, fails to set a purpose for reading or chooses an inappropriate purpose, or does not question during the reading.

A fourth factor that can affect comprehension is the *reader's perception of social context*. Readers may not see themselves as capable of reading or may not see reading as personally worthwhile and valuable. These personal perceptions can affect the reader's attitude. If a reader's peers do not value reading, this further decreases motivation. However, if the reader sees him- or herself as part of a community of readers (i.e., a supportive group of individuals who share positive attitudes about reading and each other) in the classroom, the climate for successful reading is much more positive.

The fifth factor is the *reader's cultural situation*. If the culture from which the reader comes does not value reading, the individual may have little reason to participate or to see reading as useful. In some cases, the student's culture may set different expectations on the basis of gender—for example, by expecting girls to read but denigrating boys for doing so. Whether the culture and community which surrounds the student supports or discourages reading may have a powerful effect on performance.

Although Fig. 4.1 does not include them, certain situational factors have also been found to affect reading (Weaver, 1994). These include, for instance, the availability of appealing and appropriate reading material, an environment that is conducive to reading (e.g., sufficient lighting, comfortable seating, absence of distractions, etc.), and adequate time for reading and reflecting.

Summary of the Reading Process

1. Reading is an act of construction rather than extraction (making meaning rather than getting meaning).
2. Effective readers use 3 cueing systems:
   - semantic information (Does it make sense?)
   - syntactic information (Does it fit the sentence structure?)
   - graphophonic information (How is the word pronounced?)
3. Reading is an interaction of print with the brain in which the reader
   - decides which system to use
   - knows when comprehension stops
4. Reading is a transaction between the reader and the text
5. Reading is affected by
   - the text itself
   - reader's use of cueing systems
   - reader's thinking activities
   - reader's background knowledge
   - social factors
   - cultural influences
   - situational factors

FIG. 4.2

IMPLICATIONS FOR THE CLASSROOM

People once thought of reading as a rather solitary activity: just the reader alone with the text. What researchers are discovering about reading comprehension is that the interaction between the reader and the text is strongly influenced by many peripheral factors

(Alvermann, Hinchman, Moore, Phelps, & Waff, 1998; Coles, 1998). How the reader sees him- or herself in relation to others can have a bearing on the act of reading. A student's interactions with other people about reading can affect how the student comprehends.

Although educators have learned a great deal about how these influences help or hamper readers, they know far less about how to alter the factors. What can be done when students come from communities where reading is not valued or where adults do not expect their children to read critically? What should be done when students come to school believing that reading is either not personally significant or not a skill they will ever learn?

Attitudes About Teaching Reading

These are difficult questions without easy answers, but you have to begin somewhere, and the best place to start is with your own attitudes toward readers. Although you may wish it to be otherwise, students will arrive in your classroom with a wide range of reading skills and diverse attitudes toward the act of reading. The first thing that you have to acknowledge is that you must be a teacher of reading. You cannot expect someone else to have already taught students all they need to know about how to read.

On the other hand, teaching reading is not your job alone. Although many colleagues may think that this is your responsibility entirely, it is not. They, too, must teach reading. Learning to read literature does not require the same skills as learning to read social studies, math, or science materials. Most language arts teachers, schooled in literary forms, have little knowledge of the ways in which technical writing is structured, and many have little experience in reading field notes, political and legal tracts, or even mathematical formulas. The responsibility for teaching the reading skills that are closely associated with different subjects should be shared among the faculty. However, the language arts teacher is often the one to whom other faculty look for guidance. Regardless of whether you think it is fair, you will probably have to assume a leadership role in this regard.

If you are lucky, you will have had some special training in the teaching of reading. If not, this is an area of professional development that you will probably want to investigate. Two excellent resources are the books by Irvin (1998) and Beers and Samuels (1998), both of which are listed in the Recommended Readings for this chapter. Furthermore, you should maintain an independent study program, which should include perusing journals that focus on teaching reading, such as the *Journal of Adolescent & Adult Literacy*, published by the International Reading Association. Whether through courses or through independent reading, you should develop a collection of ideas about the most effective ways to approach the teaching of reading, which you can then test in your own classroom.

Creating a Supportive Climate

The more students are surrounded with quality print in a variety of forms and the more they work with written discourse, the easier reading becomes. They need far more than a literature anthology; they need ready access to books, newspapers, computer databases, student writing, and much more. As much as possible, your classroom needs to be a place where reading is accepted, expected, and valued. You need to be an avid reader, and you need to assume that students are or can become equally enthused. As much as possible, you need to know the social and cultural circumstances of your students, and you need to build on whatever positive influences you find there. Sharing information about the public library, adult reading or literacy groups, local authors, newspaper reporters and publishers, supportive parents, and so on may convince students that reading is valued within the community.

Building on Student Knowledge

Most language arts teachers want students to believe that reading is a lifelong, meaningful act and that they will develop a love of reading. You can achieve this by starting with students rather than with content. Although you may see the classics as the only material worth studying, you have to face the reality that middle school students may not yet be able to share that judgment. Most of the canon contains material that was intended for an adult audience. Middle school students have a long way to go before they develop the maturity needed to read this material with enthusiasm. Rushing them ahead into material you cherish may produce such distaste for both reading and literature that students will never visit that territory on their own. There are thousands of books, poems, plays, and other works that people probably ought to read; you can only teach a few. During their lifetimes, many more pieces of worthwhile reading material will be published. If you don't "turn students on" to reading and literature, they will never have the desire to discover all that you could not bring into the classroom.

In general, you want to facilitate whatever effective reading processes students have already developed. You want to help students use what they already understand about making meaning with language as they attempt to read more complex material. When that material is unusual in some way, as is the case with poetry and script forms of drama, you will probably need to help them discover reading strategies. They will also need assistance in developing skills for reading nonfiction texts. They may need both reminders about monitoring their own comprehension and assistance in finding ways to cope when their understanding falters. The more they know about a topic, situation, or setting, the easier reading will be, so you may need to build their background knowledge before they engage in reading a story or poem.

Choosing Appropriate Material

You have to make reading material accessible to students. You can begin by considering the reading levels of the students and whether the material you wish to teach matches those levels. Reading levels improve rather slowly: A student is not likely to improve more than a grade level or two in a single year except under unusual circumstances. There are several factors that influence readability of text, but at the very least you should have a general sense of the reading level of the material you assign.

Although literature anthologies are said to contain material that is close to the grade level for which it was chosen, the selection usually targets some mythical average. A literature anthology may not match any of the real people who sit in your classroom. Some works will be more difficult than others for students because of the reader factors described earlier. Furthermore, many students will not be reading at grade level, so the material will be either too difficult or too easy for them. You can use formulas to determine the reading level of material, but here again the calculated grade level may not coincide with the interests, experiences, and needs of your students.

As shown in Fig. 4.3, three reading levels describe how challenging a text may be. Students themselves are often the best gauge of what reading material matches them. When students select their own reading matter, they will usually choose material that they can read independently or with minimal instruction. They know what frustrates them, and they will avoid it. When they select material they can read independently, they will be building reading speed as well as topic and discourse structure knowledge. However, if you intend to assign reading to small groups and the whole class, you will want to select text that is at the instructional level for most students, rather than at the independent or frustration level.

Another way to think of this is that you want to select material that is in what Russian psychologist Vygotsky termed the *zone of proximal development* (Vygotsky, 1978; see also Dixon-Krauss, 1996). No matter how much a person learns or how effective he or she becomes as a reader, there is always an area beyond the individual's current level of understanding. For you that may be the area of theoretical physics or criminal law. For middle school students that area is likely to contain Shakespeare and Joyce. On the other hand, each person has a central core of knowledge and skills, things one already knows and can do well. Maybe it is how to survive on the street or how to find a book in the library, or perhaps it is the batting average of every major league baseball player, but each person knows certain information and has certain skills. This core, however, is different for each individual. Between those two regions is the zone of proximal development (see Fig. 4.4). It is just beyond the area of what one knows and can do, but it is accessible with some assistance and practice. In terms of reading material at the middle school level, the zone contains a lot of what is considered early adolescent literature. As a person learns, the central core expands to include what is learned, but the zone itself continues to exist. Its content changes, but it is always there. That is the area you want to keep trying to hit as you select reading material and make judgments about instruction.

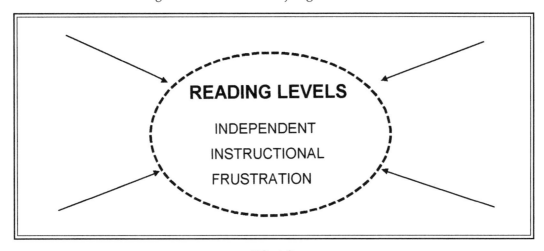

FIG. 4.3

INSTRUCTIONAL OPTIONS

Reading should be an active process, not a passive enterprise. The more you can engage students in reading, from start to finish, the more likely they are not only to comprehend what they read but also to enjoy and appreciate it, which will in turn lead to more reading. That is the ultimate goal. It will not happen overnight, but you can make reading for pleasure a reality for your students. One way to do that is to vary reading instruction through the use of many different strategies and activities. Mooney (1990) recommends a balance of ac-

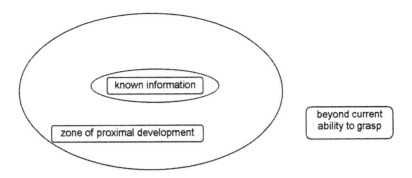

FIG. 4.4   Vygotsky's Zone of Proximal Development

tivities including reading to students, students reading with each other, and students reading independently to themselves.

As you plan units and lessons, in addition to selecting appropriate, relevant, and interesting reading matter, you need to consider some of the options you have in relation to helping students read the material more effectively. The content is important, but the methods you use to teach this material also deserve serious consideration.

Silently or Aloud?

When considering reading methodology at the most basic level, you have the choice of having students read aloud or silently. Fluent readers generally read silently. If students are to learn good reading habits, then silent reading should probably be the ultimate goal.

However, oral reading also has important values, and at times it is a better option. For example, having students read aloud examples or passages that support their statements during discussion and encouraging oral reading of puzzling or ambiguous segments of text can stimulate conversation about the reading material. Some teachers feel that if they have students read whole texts aloud, they are ensuring that comprehension is taking place; however, the research shows that oral reading of a text is no guarantee that comprehension will occur. In general, round-robin reading (students taking turns reading aloud) is not a good strategy (Optiz & Rasinski, 1998; Vacca & Vacca, 1989). It appears to control the class (i.e., keep students on-task), but during this kind of reading activity, students do not pay much attention to comprehension; they are so worried about not making fools of themselves in front of their peers that all they can do is read ahead so they will be prepared when they are called on. If you want students to read aloud in class, have them read the material beforehand so they first read for comprehension. Besides, if they have some understanding of what the material is about, they are more apt to read aloud smoothly and with meaningful expression.

One alternative to whole-class round-robin reading is to have students participate in shared reading—reading aloud in pairs or small groups. This is noisy, but less tense. It also allows groups to discuss the meaning as they go. Occasionally, choral reading, in which everyone reads aloud at the same time, is an effective choice. Some poems written for two voices and some plays that have parts for a chorus are especially effective for this. It is even possible to allow students to read aloud to themselves on occasion if the material is especially difficult. No matter how accomplished readers are, most will still revert to oral reading when the printed discourse is unusually challenging and comprehension is breaking down. Other useful alternatives can be found in *Good-bye Round Robin* by Optiz & Rasinski (1998).

Who Will Read?

If you opt for oral reading, you also have the opportunity to decide who will read aloud. Middle school students need to know that oral reading is not something that only little kids do. No matter the age of the student, most like to be read to, especially if the material is melodious and needs to be heard or is too difficult to understand otherwise. You need to read aloud to them often so that they internalize discourse modes and language patterns. Effectively reading selected material aloud is quite enjoyable and gives students a chance to listen appreciatively. Reading an excerpt aloud can motivate students to read on. However, most people are offended when something is rad to them that they have already read and understood without difficulty or that they are quite capable of reading independently. Reading material to capable students while they follow along in their own books may discourage them from assuming responsibility for reading. Although it may be motivational to read a segment of new text to students and beneficial during discussion to highlight an excerpt by reading it aloud, in general, if readers have copies in hand and the skills to read the material, it is best not to read it to them.

Of course, students can voluntarily select material to read orally, or you may choose someone who is prepared to do so to read a portion before silent reading begins. A guest speaker, librarian, or parent can also include some oral reading as part of a presentation to the class. Students can also tape-record their reading of text so that other students can listen to it.

Length of Time?

Whether the reading is to be oral or silent, you also have to choose how much time is to be spent reading. You may want students to read a portion aloud and the rest silently, for example. Alternatively, you may want them to read silently to a specific point and stop so that the next segment can be read aloud. The point is that the length of time is something that you can choose.

Figure 4.5 summarizes some of the instructional options you will have to think about in terms of teaching reading.

Summary of Basic Options

How is reading done?
- Silently
- Aloud

Who reads aloud?
- The teacher or a guest
- Students, chorally
- Students, individually

How much is read?
- The whole text
- Selected sections
- Excerpts

Who is the audience?
- Only the reader
- A partner
- A small group
- The whole class

FIG. 4.5

READING ACTIVITIES

The activities you choose and design for your classroom should aid students in preparing to read, comprehending what they are reading, and connecting their reading to other experiences. These activities should provide a temporary scaffolding that supports students while they learn. However, as much as possible, these should be activities that students can learn to do independently. In effect, you want to teach students strategies that they can apply whenever they need them.

Before-Reading Activities

As you plan, you need to give some thought to how you will introduce the reading task so that students will engage in it with eagerness. These are called before-reading or prereading activities. In general, they are designed to do one of the following: **build or activate background knowledge**, **stimulate curiosity**, or **set a purpose for reading**. There are any number of things that you can do to introduce a reading task. The list in Fig. 4.6 is a sample of ideas, although in several cases the teacher would have to give students the topic by posing questions, providing a scenario, or introducing a focus for discussion prior to reading.

By the time the introduction is done, students should be prepared to engage in the reading. With proper preparation, they will bring to the reading conscious knowledge of what they already understand about the subject matter, some curiosity as to what lies in store, and some reason for taking part in the reading. This prereading may be brief and simple, or it may be quite lengthy and elaborate. It probably is not a good idea to spend more time on the prereading than students will spend reading the text, but the better the preparation, the more likely students are to participate fully in the task and comprehend the material.

During-Reading Activities

Many activities can be a part of or an accompaniment to the reading itself. These are often identified as during-reading activities. The type of during-reading activity that is selected should be determined by the difficulty of the material. If most students can read without assistance, then the during-reading activities should be kept to a minimum. Having to take time away from the reading itself in order to complete some other task may discourage effective and enthusiastic reading. Answering questions in writing or filling out worksheets when such activities do not help readers comprehend are bothersome. Students' negative responses to these assignments often translate into negative attitudes toward reading. In an attempt to help students become better readers, teachers should not make reading more difficult or less enjoyable!

In general, there are two types of during-reading activities. One collection of these could be described as teacher-directed strategies. These are usually whole class activities that the teacher conducts and in which everyone participates, although some of these approaches can be used equally well with small groups. Most of the structured approaches are too involved to explain here, but you need to know that these exist. For the specifics, you should consult a professional refer-

---

Before-Reading Activities

- Read a much shorter and easier piece of written material.
- Read the first few paragraphs of the discourse.
- Read the bold print throughout the discourse.
- Read the captions and view the pictures.
- Read any blurbs or pre- or postreading questions.
- Write what they know about the topic of the discourse.
- Write their predictions of what the discourse will be about.
- Write questions that they hope the discourse will answer.
- Write original work in the same mode as the discourse they will read.
- Write a personal experience related to something they will read about.
- Speak about a personal experience related to something in the text.
- Speak about (discuss) current knowledge of the topic.
- Speak about possible answers to questions posed.
- Speak about predictions of what the text will include after previewing it.
- Speak to others about ideas that will be read (e.g., interview people).
- Listen to a related piece of written material.
- Listen to a tape of the material or related material.
- Listen to music that is related to the material.
- Listen to conflicting opinions and determine which is better supported.
- Listen to a guest speaker talking about a related topic.
- View real activities that are related to the reading material.
- View a film, video, or filmstrip of the material or related material.
- View pictures that are related to the material.
- View a stage performance of similar or related material.
- View objects brought in by classmates or the teacher that are related.
- Perform a short segment of text in script form.
- Perform a role-play about the topic or a related topic.
- Perform a pantomime about the topic or a related incident.
- Perform by using a musical instrument.
- Perform a task according to directions.

FIG. 4.6

ence that focuses on teaching reading or reading in the content areas (e.g., Vacca & Vacca, 1989). Others are described in journal articles. Figure 4.7 is a list of some of the most common strategies.

Teacher-directed During-reading Activities

Directed Reading Activity (Betts, 1946)

Directed Reading-Thinking Activity (Stauffer, 1980)

Guided Reading Procedure (Manzo, 1975)

Intra-Act (Hoffman, 1979)

Radio Reading (Vacca & Vacca, 1989)

Reciprocal Teaching (Palinscar and Brown, 1985)

Pairs or Shared Reading (Topping & Whiteley, 1990)

FIG. 4.7

Each of these approaches works best with certain kinds of reading material, so it is a good idea to match the strategy with the content. Also, some of these are very involved and can significantly slow reading down. This may be very beneficial to students when the reading material is quite difficult, but it can be frustrating when students feel that they would like to move ahead more rapidly. Therefore, it is not a good idea to choose one strategy and use it over and over.

The other category of during-reading activities may be considered supplementary. These are the kinds of activities that students can do more independently or at their own pace. Also, these activities can and should become the student's responsibility; you may need to teach the strategy, but you should not be the one who always controls its use.

One during-reading strategy is quite common in classrooms, namely, **discussion**. Of course, discussion can occur after the reading is finished, but it often takes place while the reading is in progress, particularly when the material is divided into segments or chapters or when the material is a whole book. The most important factor to keep in mind when planning discussion is to create higher-order questions that challenge students to grasp inferences, read more deeply, and relate the material to their own lives. Although it is necessary to ask some literal level questions, these should be kept to a minimum and used as stepping stones or scaffolds to higher levels of thought. Another factor to keep in mind is avoidance of unnecessary interruptions. Too much discussion scheduled too frequently can hinder reading enjoyment. After participating in effective discussions with the whole class, students can and should learn to conduct their own discussions (Almasi, 1996; Eeds & Wells, 1989; Strickland, Dillon, Funkhouser, Glick, & Rogers, 1989).

In addition to discussion, there are several other during-reading activities that can be very useful for students. Some of these are listed in Fig. 4.8. The book by Yopp and Yopp (1996) listed in the Recommended Readings for this chapter is a handy and concise source of during-reading activities (See also Activities 4.1 and 4.2 at the end of this chapter).

Supplementary During-reading Activities

- Journal responses to reading
- Writing questions as they occur to reader
- Creating character lists
- Drawing semantic maps
- Sketching story lines or time lines
- Diagramming the organization
- Highlighting or copying text
- Finding pictures that match the material
- Selecting music to accompany text
- Checking and updating predictions
- Creating a comparison chart of contrasting characters, points of view, or opinions

---

FIG. 4.8

Another useful during-reading activity is the completion of a **study guide**. Unfortunately, through overuse, study guides have earned a terrible reputation. If the use of study guides is reserved for those instances in which the material is quite difficult, and if answering the questions helps students understand it, then the guides will seem more worthwhile. There are many different kinds of study guides. Some are meant to be used after the reading is done, but one version is coded to the order in which the material is printed. To use this guide, students answer questions as they go through the text. There are other versions that do not require students to answer questions. Instead, students complete checklists or answer true–false questions as they go along. The book by Wood, Lapp, and Flood (1992), which is listed in the Recommended Readings for this chapter, is an outstanding source of samples of different kinds of study guides. Using a variety of guides helps prevent boredom.

Finally, one activity that may be very useful as a during-reading task is some kind of **vocabulary investigation**. Sometimes, it is necessary to introduce a few key terms to students before the reading begins, but the number should be kept to a minimum, and the list should contain only those words that are so important that comprehension is impossible without some prior knowledge of the meanings. The main problem with introducing vocabulary before the reading begins is that the words are out of context. This makes understanding them more difficult initially and does not help students retain the meanings. As much as possible, words should be studied in their natural context so that readers can use many signals in the text to help them grasp the meaning and use of the words. If possible, vocabulary words should be studied as collections of related words so that students are not looking at isolates. It is much easier to recall the general meaning of a word if that word is remembered as part of a set, group, or family of related words.

Vocabulary activities that are intended to be used as during-reading tasks should be created with the text as a background. For example, students can create personal word lists with definitions they express in their own words, or they can label illustrations using specific adjectives drawn from the reading material. They can add selected words to a vocabulary bulletin board or choose the list of words that the class will study more closely. They can also create puzzles and games that incorporate words from the texts they have read. They can be asked to search for particular kinds of words, such as descriptive phrases that best summarize a character's behavior or rhythmic words that can be substituted for other rhythmic words in poems. Other specific suggestions for linking vocabulary study with reading material can be found in *Words, Words, Words* (Allen, 1999) and *Effective Vocabulary Instruction* (Adams & Cerqui, 1989), as well as many professional journal articles (see also Activity 4.3).

After-Reading Activities

Finally, there are after-reading activities. Actually, there is no end to the responses that can follow reading. Although some comprehension tasks cannot be done until the reading is finished, these are still basically during-reading activities because they focus directly on understanding the text. In contrast, the best after-reading tasks ask students to extend their understanding of the material and relate it to other reading or other knowledge. Furthermore, these tasks ask them to think more deeply, broadly, critically, or creatively. Also, these tasks ask them to make use of other abilities or talents they have already acquired and with which they feel relatively comfortable. This is a good chance, for example, to incorporate tasks that focus on multiple intelligences or different learning styles.

Almost any kind of **written discourse** can be adapted to fit as an after-reading writing activity. Many suggestions are included in the next chapter of this book. Some students may want to do **additional reading**, and because this should be the main purpose of reading in the first place, you should find ways to encourage this. Students may want to read more material by the same author, read more about the topic or theme, or read more of the genre they have studied. There are numerous possibilities for **dramatic and formal speaking** as a follow-up to reading. Selecting excerpts for dramatic performance causes students to dig much more deeply into the work and see it from a different point of view. There are also some possible **listening activities**, such as listening to a tape of a professional speaker reading the text. Some other kinds of responses should be considered. Students may choose to create **games or puzzles**, for example (see Activity 4.4). Some may find **artistic or musical ways to respond**. Others may prefer to **lead a group project** that they design. This is the time to look to all sorts of **media** as possibilities—tape recorders, videocameras, still cameras, overhead and slide projectors, and even computers. As **multimedia** production becomes easier to do, more and more students will find creative ways to use the computer for literary responses. Fig. 4.9 provides additional examples.

After-reading activities should serve as models of what actual readers do in response to texts. Outside the classroom, real readers use text for other purposes (e.g., to build their personal knowledge or for pleasure), they share what they read and their responses with other people in book clubs and literary societies, they correspond with authors and other readers, and they select other books for further reading. They also use the material to create original print and nonprint texts (e.g., scripts of musicals, television versions of material, book jackets, etc.) to express themselves and to entertain others. As much as possible, after-reading activities ought to mimic what mature adults do with text.

After-reading tasks should do more than test student comprehension. Assignments that do nothing more than measure literal understanding often discourage enjoyment. In many instances, students have no interest in the tasks themselves, or they find them so difficult that they cannot demonstrate what they have learned. Asking middle school students to write a formal essay after reading, a very common assignment, is one such activity. It is little wonder that students come to dislike reading if it is associated with purposeless, inordinately difficult writing assignments when there are far more interesting discourse forms through which to respond (see Activity 4.5).

Although most reading activities require teacher direction initially, the more students can learn to use these or similar kinds of strategies on their own the better. They can be taught to conduct their own discussions, design their own study guides, and create their own forms of response. Indeed, all of the before-, during-, and after-reading strategies presented here should be just temporary scaffolds to help students become better independent readers.

A Sampling of After-reading Activities based on Frost's "The Road Not Taken"

1. Write a personal experience paper describing a time in your life when you had to make a decision. What were your choices? Which did you choose? What difference has this made in your life? Share your work with others who chose this task. Discuss the similarities among your experiences.

2. Find and read several poems by Frost. Choose one you like. Read it aloud to a small group of peers. Tell them why you chose this poem.

3. Using the computer, find some information about Frost and/or this poem. Create a new file and download the information. Then add your own thought about how this information relates to the poem or what new understandings you have as a result of reading this information. Save your finished work so you can share it with others.

4. Create a dramatic role-play that focuses on a dilemma. Show the possible outcomes of the two choices. Try to illustrate that both choices may have positive and negative consequences. Perform your role play for the class. Lead a discussion about the choices and consequences.

5. Find a partner who is interested in this activity. Experiment by reading each phrase and line of the poem aloud with emphasis on different words. Try pausing at different places, too. Listen closely as your partner reads. Discuss how shifts in emphasis and placement of pauses alter meaning. Decide which version is best. Rehearse together carefully and then make a tape recording of your choral reading of the poem.

6. Make a game or a collage that focuses on choices or making decisions. Your finished piece could also show consequences.

7. Create a musical composition that can be played as background for the poem. Make a tape recording of this while someone reads the poem aloud.

FIG. 4.9

STRUCTURE OF TEXT

One behavior that fluent readers exhibit is the ability to predict what is coming next in the text. They predict the next word on the basis of what they have read so far. They also predict the next phrase or the next sentence. They may not be able to predict the specific content, but they expect that a certain type of material (e.g., a definition of a term, an illustration, a narrative example, etc.) will follow. They are not taken by surprise by dialogue or even a flashback. Nonfluent readers just try to follow the words; they often do not see any kind of organization in what they read, and they do not recognize that authors structure material consciously. In essence, they do not see patterns in discourse (Pappas & Pettegrew, 1998).

As the teacher, you can help students at the middle level become better readers by assisting them in recognizing these discourse patterns. You can describe different patterns and have students read examples and discuss how each is structured. You can ask students to draw diagrams that show text patterns. You can give students portions of text and ask them to predict what will happen or what information the author is likely to provide next. However, you need to keep in mind that the accuracy of their drawings and their predictions is less important at first than learning how to look for patterns and acquiring the habit of predicting. As they read more, their accuracy should improve, but they must first be aware of these reading strategies and how to use them.

Middle school students are often delighted to learn that narrative fiction has structure. Once they know the typical pattern, they search for exceptions. They find it interesting to discover that mysteries and detective fiction follow different plans. They also like to explore patterns in poetry and compare poetic forms. However, gaining an understanding of how expository prose is arranged is difficult. Middle school students need to be introduced to some of the most common patterns (see Activity 4.6), and they need to compare texts and discuss structures. Initially, they will make lots of mistakes when they do this, though. Middle school is a good time to introduce students to a self-questioning reading–study strategy such as the one commonly called SQ3R (survey, question, read, recite, and review). One question they can ask is, "How is this piece structured?"

ASSESSING READING

There are many standardized tests for assessing reading, as well as informal reading inventories, checklists, and diagnostic tools such as miscue analysis (Goodman, Watson, & Burke, 1987). Many of these can be very helpful, especially when the teacher is trying to determine why a particular student is having difficulty comprehending or what to include in a program of remediation for an individual. Knowing in advance that a class has low reading skills can be useful in planning the year's program.

But the most important data about a student often come from observation (see Activity 4.7). Given the opportunity, does the student read or not? All too often, reading attention becomes focused on the remedial reader. The students who can read but do not are ignored. The assumption is that these students will read eventually, although they are reluctant to do so at the moment. Although this may be true, the student who resists reading is falling behind and wasting potential in the meantime. Reading speed can decline, making reading less appealing and more of a chore. The reluctant reader must be of concern even if standardized test scores are high and the student evidently comprehends well. One question that you will have to ask yourself is whether your plan for assessment reflects the student's progress or whether it reflects skills and attitudes that were present before the student entered your class. Should you give an A to the student who entered the class with above-average reading ability and who scores well on tests but who reads no more than the minimum?

Reading evaluation in the classroom often has two shapes—objective tests of comprehension and written papers based on reading (e.g., essay tests, book reports, compositions based on themes of literary works, poetry explications, critical reviews of material, etc.). Sometimes these products do little more than show that some students are better test takers or writers than others. Even when these data tell something about the results of reading (i.e., how well students comprehended the material), they do not tell much about the student's reading processes. Is the student using efficient and effective strategies? Does the individual know how to predict and use text to support opinions? Can the student use knowledge of discourse structures as an aid to understanding? Does the reader monitor comprehension so he or she knows when meaning breaks down? Does the student know what to do when that happens? Does the student know himself or herself well as a reader, recognizing his or her own strengths and weaknesses?

Assessing reading processes requires observation and conversation. You need to watch students read and take note of what you see them doing. You need to listen to students as they discuss what they have read. More than that, you need to ask them questions about how they tackle reading and listen for answers that indicate changes and improvement. You should encourage students to write periodically about how they read, what they do when they have a reading problem, and how they would evaluate their reading progress. Asking students to think about how they read and how their reading changes over time helps them develop metalinguistic awareness (i.e., the conscious awareness of how one uses language), which leads to a better understanding of how to use language in the future. If a reader is to improve, he or she must first be able to assess the current situation. You do have to assess student performance in order to instruct, but the more you can help students measure their own performance, the more likely you are to produce independent learners.

RECOMMENDED READINGS

Adams, D., & Cerqui, C. (1989). *Effective vocabulary instruction.* Kirkland, WA: Reading Resources.

Adams, M. (1990). *Beginning to read: Thinking and learning about print.* Cambridge, MA: MIT Press.

Allen, J. (1999). *Words, words, words: Teaching vocabulary in grades 4–12.* York, ME: Stenhouse.

Almasi, J. (1996). A new view of discussion. In L. Gambrell & J. Almasi (Eds.), *Lively discussions! Fostering engaged reading* (pp. 2–24). Newark, DE: International Reading Association.

Beers, K., & Samuels, B. (Eds.). (1998). *Into focus: Understanding and creating middle school readers.* Norwood, MA: Christopher-Gordon.

Braunger, J., & Lewis, J. (1997). *Building a knowledge base in reading.* Portland, OR: Northwest Regional Educational Laboratory's Curriculum and Instruction Services.

Brozo, W. (1990). Hiding out in secondary content classrooms: Coping strategies of unsuccessful readers. *Journal of Reading, 33,* 324–328.

Coles, G. (1998). *Reading lessons: The debate over literacy.* New York: Hill & Wang.

Dixon-Krauss, L. (1996). *Vygotsky in the classroom: Mediated literacy instruction and assessment.* White Plains, NY: Longman.

Francis, C. (1996). Notable novels in the classroom: Helping students to increase their knowledge of language and literature. In A. McClure & J. Kristo (Eds.) *Books that invite talk, wonder, and play* (pp. 78–91) Urbana, IL: National Council of Teachers of English.

Guthrie, J., & Wigfield, A. (Eds.) (1997). *Reading engagement: Motivating readers through integrated instruction.* Newark, DE: International Reading Association.

Hyerle, D. (1996). *Visual tools for constructing knowledge.* Alexandria, VA: Association for Supervision and Curriculum Development.

Irvin, J. (1998). *Reading and the middle school student: Strategies to enhance literacy* (2nd ed.). Boston: Allyn & Bacon.

Ivey, G. (1998). Discovering readers in the middle grades: A few helpful clues. *NASSP Bulletin, 82*(600), 48–56.

Ivey, G. (1999). Reflections on teaching struggling middle school readers. *Journal of Adolescent & Adult Literacy, 42,* 372–381.

Johnson, A., & Rasmussen, J. (1998). Classifying and super word web: Two strategies to improve productive vocabulary. *Journal of Adolescent & Adult Literacy, 42,* 204–206.

Opitz, M., & Rasinski, T. (1998). *Good-bye round robin: 25 effective oral reading strategies.* Portsmouth, NH: Heinemann.

Overturf, B. (1997). Reading portfolios reveal new dimensions of students. *Middle School Journal, 28*(3), 45–50.

Palinscar, A., & Brown, A. (1985). Reciprocal teaching: Activities to promote "reading with your mind." In T. Harris & E. Cooper (Eds.), *Reading, thinking, and concept development*, (pp. 147–159). New York: The College Board.

Pappas, C., & Pettegrew, B. (1998). The role of genre in the psycholinguistic guessing game of reading. *Language Arts, 75,* 36–44.

Rosenblatt, L. (1978). *The reader, the text, and the poem: The transactional theory of the literary work.* Carbondale, IL: Southern Illinois University Press.

Rupley, W., Logan, J., & Nichols, W. (1998/1999). Vocabulary instruction in a balanced reading program. *The Reading Teacher, 52,* 336–346.

Smith, F. (1997). *Reading without nonsense* (3rd ed.). New York: Teachers College Columbia University.

Swaim, S. (1999). Reading and writing in content areas. *Middle Ground, 2*(3), 34–36.

Towell, J. (1997/1998). Fun with vocabulary. *The Reading Teacher, 51*(4), 356–358.

Watts, S., & Graves, M. (1997). Fostering students' understanding of challenging texts. *Middle School Journal, 29*(1), 45–51.

Weaver, C. (1994). *Reading process and practice: From socio-psycholinguistics to whole language* (2nd ed.). Portsmouth, NH: Heinemann.

Wood, K., Lapp, D, & Flood, J. (1992). *Guiding readers through text: A review of study guides.* Newark, DE: International Reading Association.

Yopp, H., & Yopp, R. (1996). *Literature-based reading activities* (2nd Ed.). Boston, MA: Allyn & Bacon.

OTHER RESOURCES

Journal of Adolescent & Adult Literacy
International Reading Association
   800 Barksdale Road,
   P.O. Box 8139
   Newark, DE 19714–8139
   302–731–1600
   Www.reading.org

Cogix Corporation (Software)
   P.O. Box 2953
   San Anselmo, CA 94979–2953
   1–800-634-5682
   Http://cogix.com

The Horn Book, Inc.
   11 Beacon St., Suite 1000
   Boston, MA 02108
   1–800–325–1170

Book Links
   434 W. Downer
   Aurora, IL 60506
   630–892–7465
   Www.ala.org/BookLinks

Reading Activities and Suggestions

- 4.1 Useful Graphic Organizers
- 4.2 Additional Reading Activities
- 4.3 Vocabulary Activities
- 4.4 Reading Games
- 4.5 Book Report Alternatives
- 4.6 Expository Text Structures
- 4.7 Checklist to Assess Reading Processes

Activity 4.1:
Useful Graphic Organizers

Venn Diagrams

Venn diagrams are usually overlapping circles that show comparisons. One circle contains features related to one topic and the other circle contains features related to another topic. The overlapping section shows the features that both topics share (see Fig. 4.10). This kind of diagram can be used to illustrate, for example, how two main characters are both different and similar. It can also be used to summarize the similarities and differences between two short stories or novels. Venn diagrams can contain more than two circles to illustrate comparisons involving more than two items.

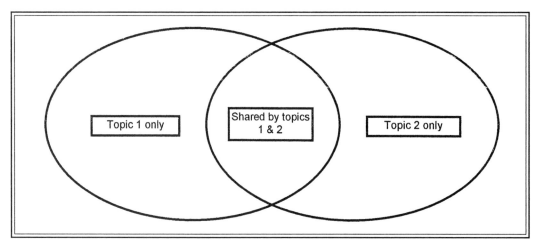

FIG. 4.10

T Charts

T charts are simply charts that contain two columns. These can be quickly created in the classroom by having students fold their papers lengthwise, dividing the page into two equal columns. In its simplest form, a T chart can be used to show comparisons between two topics. For example, one column can contain the positive qualities of a poem, and the other column can include a list of the negatives. T charts can be used not only to show contrasts but also to show similarities. For example, a T chart can be used to compare one short story with another. A simple comparison would show the positive qualities of one versus the positive qualities of the other. However, a more in-depth comparison would reveal some categories of comparison. For instance, the two stories could be compared on the basis of characters, plot, and author style. This should produce a more complex picture of both the positive and negative aspects of both stories. T charts can also be used to summarize fallacies in arguments when the speaker's ideas are examined for direct comparisons. These charts can also be used to illustrate relationships, such as cause-and-effect chains of events. Students can be asked, for instance, to find several examples of cause-and-effect links, with causes in one column and effects in the other. They could also be encouraged to find some instances in which the effect becomes the cause of another effect. T charts are excellent devices for summarizing and reviewing material, too.

Attribute Charts

Attribute charts are visual representations of qualities or characteristics. These can be used to guide research that is conducted in just a few days or developed over several months to show how topics compare and contrast. Students can, for example, create an attribute chart of qualities they prefer in short stories. They can rate each selection they read during a short story unit using minuses, checks, and pluses. The class can create a bulletin board display of comments pertaining to short stories they have all read. Such a chart may be similar to the illustration in Fig. 4.11.

Attribute	"To Build a Fire"	"The Most Dangerous Game"	"Raymond's Run"
Realistic Characters			
Natural dialogue			
Set in the present			
Vivid action			
Prompts strong reader response			
Satisfying conclusion			

FIG. 4.11

Attribute charts can also be used to guide research. Before students begin their search for information, they can identify certain facts that they think they should seek. These can be listed in chart form and summarized as students locate the data or find answers to their questions. Suppose, for example, that students are to locate information about young adult authors, and each student is responsible for one author. Students can begin by creating a list of categories of information that they should read to discover. That may include some of the following: date and place of birth, present age, current residence, marital status, family members, number of books written, awards won, most recent publication, and a quote about effective writing. Students can fill in the class chart as they locate the information. A wall chart can easily be seen and shared, but a similar version on computer would introduce students to the concept of creating a database. With added information, this database can be used to help students locate interesting books, access relevant websites, and correspond with authors.

One common form of an attribute chart is known as a K-W-L (know–want–learned) chart (Ogle, 1986). When a new topic is introduced, students begin by recording what they already *Know* or think they know about the topic. This information is written in the first column of the chart. The second column contains questions or what students *Want* to know about the topic. The final column is filled in after the students study the topic and contains a summary of what they have *Learned*. K-W-L charts can be adapted to include other columns of information, such as *Where* to search for facts and *Questions* that remain after the initial research is done.

Activity 4.2:
Additional Reading Activities

Think–Pair–Share

This is a flexible idea that can be used in many situations. Basically, it requires that students first think about a concept or an answer to a question. Then they talk about their thinking with one other person. Finally, they share their ideas with the class. This can be done during a lecture or class discussion in order to make sure that everyone is on track and participating. It can also be done while students are progressing through a lengthy reading task or after the reading is finished. For example, students who have finished reading *Number the Stars* (Lowry, 1989) can be asked to think–pair–share about why Lowry chose this title for the book. Each person first considers the question and formulates at least one conclusion. Then each person shares his or her idea(s) with a partner. Finally, each pair or those who volunteer shares their conclusions with the class.

How Do They Rate?

Likert-type scale rating is another strategy that can be used in many ways. In general, a Likert-type scale is a continuum that contains a descriptor at one end and its antonym at the other. The user places a mark on the continuum to show where the item to be rated falls. Such a scale can be used to ask students to make judgments about a book, characters, or some feature of the text. For example, given the following scale–

cowardly ———————————————————————— courageous

students can rate the characters in a story they just read or they can compare characters from different stories. To do this, they can write the names or titles in the proper locations or use a coding system to show the placement of each. Many other qualities can be rated similarly (e.g., honest–dishonest, mature–immature, peaceful–warlike, adventurous–timid). Students can also suggest the qualities, and this will help them understand antonyms. Different pieces of discourse can be compared on the basis of descriptors such as realistic versus unrealistic, interesting versus boring, simple versus complex, easy to read versus difficult to read, and so on. The value of this activity is in the discussion it generates, not in the accuracy of ratings.

Novel Tracings

Students can be asked to trace certain changes as a novel progresses. For example, certain moods may come and go in a novel. In Peck's *A Day No Pigs Would Die* (1972), humor appears recurrently. Students can be given graph paper for this task. Each square represents a book chapter. They start their graph at a point they choose. Then they plot the level of humor of each chapter. A graph showing the level of tension in a novel may look something like the one shown in Fig. 4.12.

Students can trace a variety of qualities such as sadness, action, pace of story, or even the importance of the chapters. For certain novels, other diagram shapes may be more appropriate. For example, the plot of Borland's (1963) *When the Legends Die* can be diagrammed as a circle. Cooney's (1990) *The Face on the Milk Carton* can resemble a flow chart showing the decisions the main character makes.

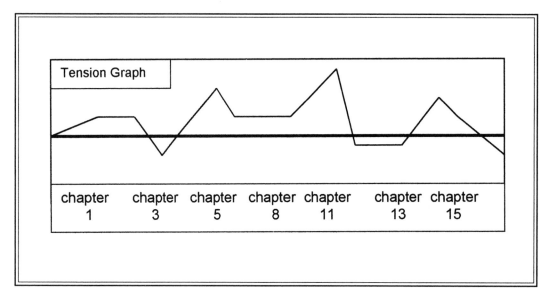

FIG. 4.12

Activity 4.3:
Vocabulary Activities

1. Using a list of words taken from a novel, short story, or long poem, have students create categories into which all of the words fit. Students may come up with traditional grammar categories (e.g., naming words, action words, etc.) or other kinds of groupings, such as happy words, hard-to-pronounce words, puzzling words, and so on. The actual categories will be much less important than the discussion in which students engage as they try to place all the words. It is also possible to give students categories—such as precise words, double meaning words, and words formed from other words—and ask students to choose the three best examples from either the list or the text itself.

2. Have students work independently or in pairs to create sentence stumpers. They have to find five sentences from the text that contain difficult words. They copy the sentences, leaving a blank for each difficult word. They then exchange papers with someone else or with another pair. They must figure out the missing word, but they must also think of a synonym that fits. They write both in the space. Papers are returned for checking. Disagreements over the suitability of synonyms are discussed.

3. Students are each given three words taken from a novel they have read. Working in groups of 3, they create sentences about the novel that use as many of their nine words as possible. Groups get 1 point for each sentence containing one word, 4 points for each sentence containing two words, 9 points for each containing three words, 16 points for four words, 25 points for five words, and so on. To earn the points, they must convince the rest of the class (and the teacher) that their sentences make sense and accurately reflect the content of the novel.

4. Students are given a rather lengthy list of words from a novel they have read. Working in groups of four, students must rate the significance of each word (i.e., how important the word is to the story). Ratings are shared with the class. Significant differences in ratings are discussed so that groups must share their reasoning. The goal is to identify the most important words. (The real goal, of course, is to learn the meanings of the words and review the story.)

5. Write the names of characters across the top of the chalkboard. Students are to search the text to find words that best describe each character. When they find one, they put it on the board in the proper category. Definitions of words are discussed. If possible, the words are subdivided into meaningful groups. Each student then selects a character and writes a brief character sketch, incorporating some of the words from the board into their own discourse.

Activity 4.4:
Reading Games

Middle school students enjoy the challenge of game playing. However, it is difficult in today's world of Nintendo and virtual reality to create classroom games that match the complexity, sophistication, and action to which students may be accustomed. Furthermore, creating games is very time-consuming, and much of the learning occurs during the creation rather than the play of the game. One option is to have students create their own games related to the reading they are doing. Computerized crossword puzzle programs, such as *Crossword Wizard* by Cogix, allow the user to input the words and definitions; the program then generates the puzzle. If you do not have access to this software, all that students really need to create these puzzles is graph paper and some experience with crossword puzzle formats. Students can create their own paper-and-pencil version of Where in the (Literary) World Is Carmen Sandiego? They can also create modified versions of Jeopardy, Trivial Pursuit, and Bingo using material drawn from their reading. They can devise adaptations of various board games to accompany their reading. For example, Clue can be used as the basis for a game based on mystery stories. Sorry, Life, or Monopoly can be re-created with material drawn from various human interest stories. Charades and Twenty Questions can be revised to fit reading selections.

There are many commercial sources of literary games. Although some of these are rather clever, many are little more than skill worksheets that many students will not find entertaining. On the other hand, commercial puzzles and games can support vocabulary development in an entertaining way. Although vocabulary study outside the context of reading is generally not very productive, frequent engagement in various vocabulary games seems to be of some value. Certainly, involvement in such games is a real-world activity. Solving various paper-and-pencil word puzzles is a popular pastime in which many adults participate voluntarily. The following commercial games can be used successfully with middle level students:

Scrabble	Scruples
Boggle	Scategories
Once ... : The Storytelling Game	Word Nerd Game
Clue	Spill and Spell
Trivial Pursuit	The Sentence Cube Game
The Charade Game	

Activity 4.5:
Book Report Alternatives

Typically a book report is a means of determining whether or not a student has read a book. Some teachers also consider these reports as a major part of their composition program. However, there are several problems associated with book reports. First, students can generally find out enough about a book to write a report without actually reading it. Second, book reports tend to be boring to write and boring to read. The writing is usually uninspired because students have no ownership of the task and no commitment to it. Furthermore, book reports are not real-world writing tasks. Only students write book reports.

What are some alternatives that both verify that students have read the material and challenge them to create a real (or at least realistic) piece of written discourse? Consider these alternatives:

1. Write a book review similar to those found in *The Horn Book, Book Links*, or a newspaper. Combine yours with ones written before or ones written by other students, and publish them as a newsletter for the library.
2. Create a poster or bookmark similar to those displayed in stores advertising the book.
3. Create a book jacket, front and back, for the book. Laminate it for bulletin board display.
4. Have students assist in creating the fields for a class database of books. When students are ready to use it, they must answer the questions they created and give the book a quality rating on the criteria they developed. These data are stored. Other students use the database for reference. This can be extended to an Internet website, and students from elsewhere can respond to the entries.
5. Write a letter to the author asking appropriate questions and offering comments.
6. Write fictional letters between or among characters.
7. Write a letter to one character expressing your feelings about actions or events.
8. Write a letter to a movie executive explaining why you think this book should be made into a movie.

9. Write a realistic news article about an event in the book. These can be combined with similar ones written by other students and published as a newspaper front page.
10. Write a poem based on the book. Explain how the poem relates to it.
11. Write a fictional interview with one of the main characters. The writer can pretend to be a news reporter or a talk show host.
12. Create a collage that revisits the main events or captures the theme. Write an explanation of the collage.
13. Create a diorama of a significant scene. Include a written explanation of why this scene was chosen.
14. Create a map or 3-D layout of the setting if it was a crucial element in the story. Be sure to include labels, captions, and a legend as needed.
15. Recreate the key scene in the book as a script. Have a narrator summarize the incidents that occurred before this scene takes place and how the book ends.
16. Create a game based on characters and events in the book. Write the directions for playing the game and create question/clue/drawing cards, if necessary.

This list concentrates primarily on written tasks that demonstrate comprehension. However, many oral possibilities exist, such as book talks, debates, dramatic readings, readers' theater versions, storytelling, and so on. Also, the best responses to literature ask students to do more than report comprehension. Although these alternatives are generally better than book reports, they are not as challenging as activities that ask students to extend beyond the book. Students need to do those kinds of tasks, too.

Activity 4.6:
Expository Text Structures

Figure 4.13 highlights 5 common expository text structures. The patterns are labeled and described. Some cue words that students should recognize are noted. Each structure can be diagrammed using the graphic organizer as shown. A sample passage is included to further clarify each structure.

One major expository structure that is not illustrated is *classification*. Material arranged by classification is divided into several equal groups. Usually, each group is described sufficiently to distinguish it from the other groups. This structure often contains cue words such as *part, factors,* or *qualities*. Numbers or words signifying additions may also be used to mark each group—*one, second, another, in addition, furthermore*, and so on. The graphic organizer that best matches this structure is what is sometimes referred to as a *tree diagram*. Figure 4.14 shows a diagram for a topic that is subdivided into four classes or groups.

As students encounter various expository structures, they can be asked to create their own diagrams of the parts. They can also be introduced to the cue words or asked to locate similar ones in the text. Once students have explored the structures using authentic texts, they can create their own charts which they can use for future reference.

As students explore these discourse forms, they may find that some are more complicated than the simple designs indicate. For example, comparisons are often written in a sort of seesaw arrangement. The writer points out a quality of one topic, then a comparable quality of the other, then another quality of the original, and continues the comparison. Another factor that is likely to become more obvious is that pieces of expository discourse are often composed of several different patterns. A single paragraph within a text may be organized chronologically, but another may be cause and effect, and the whole discourse may actually be a problem–solution piece.

One of the best ways to introduce text structure is to have students create diagrams of their own written work. In so doing, they may discover missing parts or imbalances of coverage. Once they identify these organizational problems, they can refer to published works to see how professional writers organize ideas.

Expository Text Structures

Pattern	Description	Cue Words	Graphic Organizer	Sample Passage
Description	The author describes a topic by listing characteristics, features, and examples.	*for example* *characteristics are*		The Olympic symbol consists of five interlocking rings. The rings represent the five continents—Africa, Asia, Europe, North America, and South America—from which athletes come to compete in the games. The rings are colored black, blue, green, red, and yellow. At least one of these colors is found in the flag of every country sending athletes to compete in the Olympic games.
Sequence	The author lists items or events in numerical or chronological order.	*first, second, third* *next* *then* *finally*	1. _____ 2. _____ 3. _____ 4. _____ 5. _____	The Olympic games began as athletic festivals to honor the Greek gods. The most important festival was held in the valley of Olympia to honor Zeus, the king of the gods. It was this festival that became the Olympic games in 776 B.C. These games were ended in A.D. 394 by the Roman Emperor who ruled Greece. No Olympic games were held for more than 1,500 years. Then the modern Olympics began in 1896. Almost 300 male athletes competed in the first modern Olympics. In the games held in 1900, female athletes were allowed to compete. The games have continued every four years since 1896 except during World War II, and they will most likely continue for many years to come.
Comparison	The author explains how two or more things are alike and how they are different.	*different* *in contrast* *alike* *same as* *on the other hand*		The modern Olympics is very unlike the ancient Olympic games. Individual events are different. While there were no swimming races in the ancient games, for example, there were chariot races. There were no female contestants and all athletes competed in the nude. Of course, the ancient and modern Olympics are also alike in many ways. Some events, such as the javelin and discus throws, are the same. Some people say that cheating, professionalism, and nationalism in the modern games are a disgrace to the Olympic tradition. But according to the ancient Greek writers, there were many cases of cheating, nationalism, and professionalism in their Olympics, too.

continued on next page

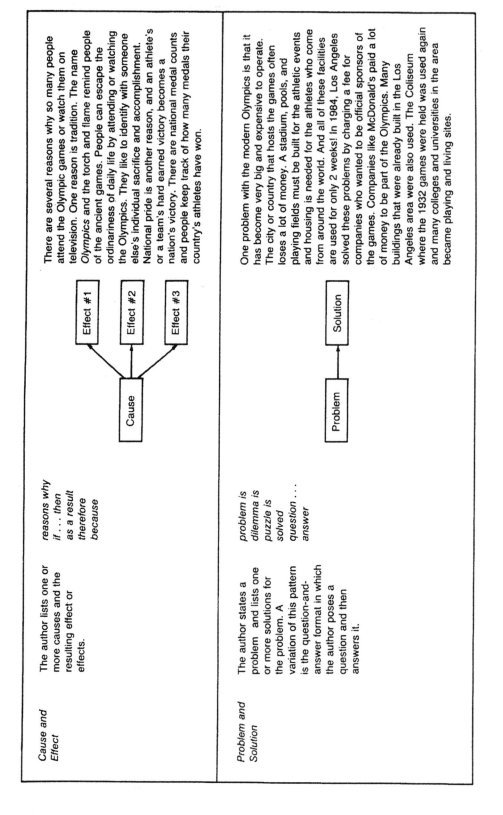

Cause and Effect

The author lists one or more causes and the resulting effect or effects.

reasons why
if . . . then
as a result
therefore
because

There are several reasons why so many people attend the Olympic games or watch them on television. One reason is tradition. The name *Olympics* and the torch and flame remind people of the ancient games. People can escape the ordinariness of daily life by attending or watching the Olympics. They like to identify with someone else's individual sacrifice and accomplishment. National pride is another reason, and an athlete's or a team's hard earned victory becomes a nation's victory. There are national medal counts and people keep track of how many medals their country's athletes have won.

Cause → Effect #1
Cause → Effect #2
Cause → Effect #3

Problem and Solution

The author states a problem and lists one or more solutions for the problem. A variation of this pattern is the question-and-answer format in which the author poses a question and then answers it.

problem is
dilemma is
puzzle is
solved
question . . .
answer

One problem with the modern Olympics is that it has become very big and expensive to operate. The city or country that hosts the games often loses a lot of money. A stadium, pools, and playing fields must be built for the athletic events and housing is needed for the athletes who come from around the world. And all of these facilities are used for only 2 weeks! In 1984, Los Angeles solved these problems by charging a fee for companies who wanted to be official sponsors of the games. Companies like McDonald's paid a lot of money to be part of the Olympics. Many buildings that were already built in the Los Angeles area were also used. The Coliseum where the 1932 games were held was used again and many colleges and universities in the area became playing and living sites.

Problem → Solution

FIG. 4.13 From *Language Arts: Content and Teaching Strategies*, 4/E by Tompkins, 1987. Reprinted by permission of Prentice-Hall, Inc., Upper Saddle River, NJ.

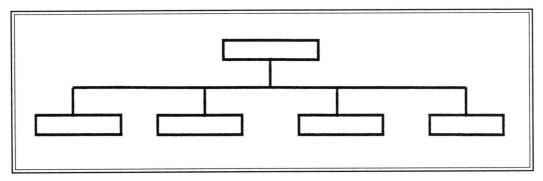

FIG. 4.14

Activity 4.7:
Checklist to Assess Reading

The following list illustrates the variety of behaviors that can be assessed as a means of measuring students' reading performance. Of course, others may be substituted.

1. Chooses appropriate books.
2. Reads for pleasure.
3. Reads to gather information.
4. Effectively uses print material for research.
5. Accurately interprets graphs, charts, and other visuals.
6. Makes predictions.
7. Checks and adjusts predictions.
8. Begins reading promptly.
9. Reads a variety of discourse.
10. Uses reference books readily and well when needed.
11. Skims and scans when appropriate.
12. Justifies or supports interpretations by referring to text.
13. Justifies or supports interpretations by connecting to experience.
14. Justifies or supports interpretations by comparing with other texts.
15. Uses context clues.
16. Reads fluently, at an appropriate pace for text.
17. Sets an appropriate purpose for reading.
18. Questions author, self, and other interpretations.
19. Reads silently for sustained periods of time.
20. Examines new books.
21. Listens to book talks.
22. Shares books with others on own initiative.
23. Asks others for book recommendations.
24. Monitors own comprehension
25. Reads orally with expression.
26. Uses varied strategies to construct meaning.
27. Reads orally at a satisfactory pace.
28. Takes note of punctuation when reading aloud.
29. Identifies unfamiliar words and searches for definitions.
30. Discusses reading strategies with others.
31. Applies learned strategies to new situations on own initiative.
32. Sees self as an able or potentially able reader.

33. Self-assesses reading skills and attitudes accurately.
34. Recognizes text structures.
35. Uses knowledge of text structures and features to aid in comprehension.
36. Compares and contrasts pieces of discourse.
37. Distinguishes fact from opinion.
38. Distinguishes nonfiction from fiction.
39. Responds appropriately to text's purpose.
40. Discusses reading eagerly.
41. Expresses a desire to read and enjoys reading.
42. Can follow plot sequence even when flashbacks occur.
43. Copes effectively with special features of literary texts.
44. Recognizes and understands cause-and-effect sequences.
45. Accurately describes character motivation.
46. Uses library resources successfully.

5

Teaching Writing

Overview

- Consider These Questions
- Composition Instruction—A Look Back?
- The Rhetorical Problem
- What Research Says About Writing as a Process
- The Teacher and the Teaching of Writing
- Specifics of Teaching Writing
- A Writing Instruction Dilemma
- Designing a Composition Curriculum
- Student-Selected Writing
- A Closer Look at Journals
- Ungraded Writing
- Mini-Lessons
- Writing Portfolios
- Rethinking Errors
- Response, Assessment, and Evaluation of Writing
- A Final Comment
- Recommended Readings
- Writing Activities and Suggestions

CONSIDER THESE QUESTIONS ABOUT TEACHING WRITING

1. When is composition instruction most beneficial to writers?
2. What should be the goals for teaching composing?
3. What are the five primary activities that comprise the writing process? What are some strategies related to each activity that students need to know?
4. Should students select their own writing tasks? Why or why not?
5. Should all student writing be graded? What is the value of journal writing?
6. Are peer response groups worthwhile? How can they be more effective?
7. How many discourse modes can you name? How many purposes for writing can you think of? Should you be the intended audience for student writing?
8. How can you evaluate student writing? Do errors ever signal growth? Which is more important—composing processes or the written product?
9. What writing skills and knowledge do you have that students need to know?
10. What are some activities that are likely to be most effective in teaching composing at the middle school level?

COMPOSITION INSTRUCTION—A LOOK BACK?

Traditionally teachers have employed the AWE method of composition instruction. Perhaps you have experienced this approach:

You were **A**ssigned to write something,
    you **W**rote it without much assistance, and
the teacher **E**valuated it (gave you a grade).

Does this sound familiar? Consider this question: If this is composition instruction, where is the instruction?

Some of you probably recall that there was not any instruction, just a grade. Perhaps you received feedback in the form of mechanical corrections, but little information about how to compose more effectively. If you were lucky, your teachers wrote some beneficial comments on your papers before returning them, although you may have discovered that few of those suggestions helped you the next time you wrote. If you were luckier, your teachers provided some instruction in the form of directions or gave you some models to examine before you wrote. Only if you were extraordinarily lucky did you have a teacher who gave you assistance when you needed it most—while you were in the process of writing the paper.

Most students who succeed under the AWE method are primarily self-taught. They somehow manage to figure out for themselves what makes writing work, at least for the teachers who grade their papers. Some students come to believe that there are two kinds of writing: school and personal (Emig, 1971). They do what is necessary to get by on the tasks that are assigned in school, but "real" writing is what they do on their own, the personal writing they do primarily to please themselves or some other interested audience. Personal writing matters.

Although the AWE method is fairly common, there are better ways to teach students to compose. Many teachers across the country are using more effective strategies to help their students learn to write confidently and well. The material in this chapter will examine some of the highlights of how you can provide better instruction. Many professional resource books focus exclusively on the teaching of writing, and some of the best are listed in the Recommended Readings for this chapter. You are encouraged to examine several of these.

THE RHETORICAL PROBLEM

Teachers often edit student writing so closely that learners come to believe that only the mechanics of writing matter. Students miss the truly important features of composing, the ones that have to do with content and communication.

What do effective writers consider when they compose? Studies show that both effective and ineffective writers consider many of the same factors when they write. Better writers, however, control their writing processes. They think more deeply, make better choices, set goals for themselves, and focus on only certain aspects of the writing at certain times (Flower & Hayes, 1980). Less able writers seem to understand what they need to do, but they cannot use this information effectively. More often than not, they get bogged down worrying over mechanics and ignoring some of the more important considerations (Pianko, 1979).

Many factors enter into the process of putting words on paper (see Fig. 5.1). One factor that effective writers take into consideration is the *writer* him- or herself. Writers think about what they know and what they are able to do. Effective writers are able to make the most of their own abilities. Less able writers sometimes see themselves as a limiting factor. For example, student writers may avoid new formats because they lack confidence.

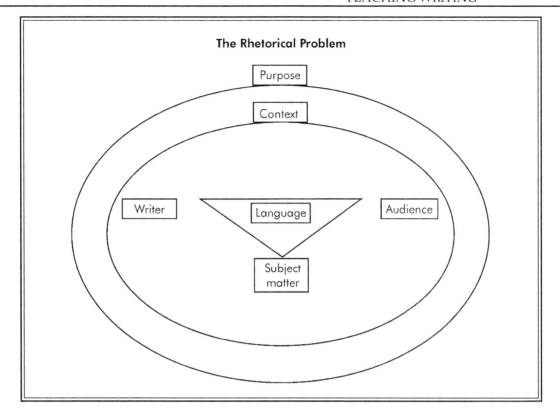

FIG. 5.1

Good writers consider the **audience**. They think about who will read the work and what that person or those people will expect. They set goals for themselves based on what effect they hope the discourse will have on the audience. Then, throughout the writing, they use this goal as a guide to make choices about their writing. For example, they may decide what content to include and what to omit on the basis of audience. Less effective writers often get so tangled in the production of text that they lose sight of audience needs.

The **subject matter** also has to be considered. How much is enough? What perspective is most important? What should be presented first? What needs further explanation and what can stand by itself? Better writers select; less able writers often include anything that comes to mind.

As writers consider themselves, their audience, and the subject matter, they also must consider **language**. What words will best express this idea? Should dialogue be used or not? Should the tone be informal or more objective? Is technical language best or would layman's terms be better? Are lengthy sentences okay, or will these confuse the reader?

Surrounding the entire decision-making process are sets of constraints the writer must also consider. One of these sets can be labeled **context**. The situation in which the writing takes place affects the outcome. One factor of context is time. A journalist meeting a deadline will make certain choices that a novelist who has no specific time line will not make. Another factor is space. For example, magazine articles have word limits, and advertisers have space limits. On the other hand, publishers of computer manuals talk about "shelf presence"; to sell well, certain books must be thick enough to give the appearance of having substantial content. Students often want to know how long a paper must be. This is a frustrating question to many teachers, but in the real world of writing, it is a part of knowing the context. Yet another important factor is the setting in which writing occurs. Does it permit deep thought or are there so many distractions and interruptions that the writer cannot reflect on the issue thoughtfully? On-the-spot reporting in the midst of a battle is affected by the setting and the writer has to adjust accordingly. Another context factor is resources. Does the writer have access to reference materials? Library facilities? The person about whom he or she is writing? Contextual factors may inhibit or support writers, but writers do make decisions based on the situation in which the writing takes place. In fact, many writers try to control the context, going off somewhere to be undisturbed when they work or setting aside specific times of the day for writing when they know they are most productive.

The other set of constraints that surrounds the entire writing process can be labeled **purpose**. Why is the writer writing this piece? What goal does he or she hope to achieve? Is this paper meant to entertain, inform, or persuade? The answers to these questions should guide the entire writing process and influence all of the other decisions that must be made.

Collectively, this mass of problem solving, decision making, and goal setting is described as **the rhetorical problem**. Good writers recognize the complexity of the problem they face each time they write, and they actively seek to make the best decisions that address all aspects of the problem. Less able or less experienced writers may not see writing as a problem-solving endeavor. They may fail to recognize certain aspects of the problem. All too often, students write for pragmatic purposes—to get the assignment done, to earn a high grade, to satisfy the teacher or parents, and so forth. When student writing serves only these purposes, the quality is apt to suffer.

Research into the composing processes of middle school students (Kingen, 1994) indicated that although students are aware of some of the factors that comprise the rhetorical problem, they are unable to maintain a focus on the issues. They may, for example, think about the needs of the audience at first, but make few decisions on that basis as the writing progresses. Even when they are given a purpose for writing, such as persuading an audience, they often slip off to other goals, such as conveying information or narrating an experience. The overall impression is that the activity of writing controls middle school writers much more than the writers control the process.

WHAT RESEARCH SAYS ABOUT WRITING AS A PROCESS

People once thought that good writing could be achieved by following a step-by-step process (e.g., find a topic, narrow it, and write an introduction, a body, and finally a conclusion) and that all writers basically followed the same pattern of steps. People also used to think that the best way to teach students to write was to give them a formula, such as a five-paragraph theme, which they could fill. Although giving students a formula seems to make sense in that it reduces a very difficult task to a manageable one, formulas also produce writing that is intolerably bad—purposeless, voiceless, and boring. They also produce writing that has been described as "academic," because it only exists in the world of schooling. Professional writers do not use these formulas.

Over 30 years ago, researchers (Braddock, Lloyd-Jones, & Schoer, 1963) searched diligently through studies of composing in an attempt to isolate evidence of how to teach writing well. They found that very little was known. Research to that point had been poorly done and had produced little conclusive data about what form of instruction helped students learn to write more effectively. Even more revealing was the finding that almost nothing was known about how people compose.

Research during the intervening years has revealed much about how people go about writing. For example, paragraphs written by professionals do not begin with topic sentences nor end with clinchers. Longer pieces of discourse are not strings of paragraphs each of which is neatly organized unto itself. Rather, paragraphs are intricately linked through the use of myriad forms of connectors (Halliday & Hasan, 1976). Classroom instruction has gradually shifted to incorporate some of this knowledge. Research indicates that encouraging students to engage in various process activities does produce better writing (Goldstein & Carr, 1996). However, many teachers now require that students complete a linear series of steps (i.e., first prewrite, then draft, then revise, and finally edit), a rigid sequence that does not reflect the flexibility exhibited by professional writers (Dahl & Farnan, 1998). Teachers have taken some recommendations to heart, but they continue to use other less effective practices, some of which negate the positive effects of the newer approaches.

Improving the teaching of writing means altering some attitudes about the activity of composing. Writing cannot be successfully simplified; it is a complex process involving many activities and strategies. Various researchers describe aspects of the writing process differently, but most would agree that writing involves at least five activities: prewriting, drafting, revising, editing, and publishing.

Prewriting refers to generating ideas and content. Often this is a mental activity that occurs before the first words are set to paper. Among students, this kind of incubation may be rapid, but professional writers often think about a piece of discourse for many months before beginning to write. Some writers use various strategies to generate ideas, such as clustering or brainstorming or some other kind of structuring activity to get them started. Other writers, especially those who are extensive revisers, simply sit down and start drafting. Prewriting is also the time when good writers consider all aspects of the rhetorical problem and set some tentative goals. These may change as the writing progresses, but the authors often have a sense of direction when they begin.

Drafting is the act of putting text on paper in some semblance of the form that the writer sees as the most likely outcome. This form may change drastically before the writing is complete, but during drafting the discourse becomes visible.

Revising is that portion of the process in which the writer reconsiders and reshapes the content. Paragraphs are reordered, new ones are added, and some are discarded. What looks like a poem is re-visioned as the first act of a play. The tone is shifted from lightly humorous to heavily sarcastic. What was first believed to be a diary entry develops into a personal narrative intended for publication.

Editing is the activity during which the writer searches for ways to make the work match the expectations of an audience. Once the content is generally secure, the writer must seek ways to guide the reader through the text and provide all of the language cues that will make the text understandable. It is during editing that the writer pays close attention to the social conventions that readers are apt to expect, and the writer proofreads the material for accuracy.

Publishing is the part of the writing process in which the polished work is presented, shared, or in some way made accessible to the audience. For students, that may be as simple as handing in the completed work or reading it aloud to classmates, but professional writers often have to deal with illustrations, graphics, font sizes, selecting colors of print, creating tables, layout, and other related issues.

Although it would be easy to assume that writing proceeds neatly from one activity to the next, these activities are actually intertwined. Researchers describe the writing process as *recursive* (Emig, 1971). That is to say that writers leap ahead and go back again and again to different activities. Writers often make several false starts before they find an opening that suits them. In effect, they begin revising almost before they begin drafting. They may have only a few words on the page before they recognize and correct a spelling error. Thus, editing may interrupt drafting. They may write the body of a paper before they write either the opening or the closing. They may create text to fit some visual image of the work as they think it should appear in the published version. Given the task to create a booklet of some sort, middle school students are likely to begin by creating a cover long before they have anything to go inside it. All in all, composing is a messy, difficult, and frustrating business. Although the end result may be very satisfying, the process itself is labor-intensive.

THE TEACHER AND THE TEACHING OF WRITING

In considering what is involved in learning to compose, it is easy to wonder how anyone ever learns to do it at all, let alone do it well. Whether the text is an informative article or a poem, writing is a creative endeavor. Although the taxpayers do not expect the art teacher to turn every student into a capable sculptor, they do expect language arts teachers to turn every student into an able writer. Whether or not that expectation is realistic, it exists. You have a professional responsibility to do your best to achieve that aim.

Let me begin with some of the hardest facts of life about teaching writing. If you want to teach writing well, you must be an avid writer yourself. You need not be a published author or even a publishable one, but if picking up a pen or sitting down at a keyboard prompts waves of anxiety rather than a positive sense of anticipation, you still have some learning to do. You probably agree that enthusiasm for reading is necessary for teaching language arts well. The same must hold true for composing. To help students learn to write well, you have to understand both the agony and ecstasy of it yourself. It is even better if you can bring yourself to share what you write with your students, at least on occasion. In some situations, a mediocre attempt may be better than what you find to be outstanding. If it is too good, middle level students can be intimidated by it or misled into thinking that you expect the same quality from them.

Another hard fact is that writing deserves at least as much classroom time as literature study. Teachers tend to think little of spending 2 weeks studying a play or an entire class period discussing a single poem, but they often relegate writing to homework. In doing so, they miss the opportunity to give students the kind of assistance they need when they need it most—while the writing is in progress. They ask students to write without assistance and then wonder why the papers are so disappointing. They look at a page of writing and conclude that the student did not put much effort into this work, but if the teacher had been there as the text developed, he or she might have seen just how much the writer had to struggle to get started, bring the piece to a satisfying conclusion, or locate and correct spelling errors.

Writing is a process. Learning to write means learning how to perform that process. Composition instruction, then, has to be about more than finished products. "Fixing" the effects will not help the writer; teachers need to examine the causes of the successes and failures. The causes, however, remain invisible unless you, as the teacher, observe writers as they initiate and participate in the various activities associated with writing. Not everything needs to be written in class, but more should be done there than is typical.

SPECIFICS OF TEACHING WRITING

Of all that can be said about teaching composing more effectively, three pieces of advice are most important. The first is to do the most you can to encourage students to read—widely and deeply. The research indicates that reading and writing are complementary processes, each supports and enhances the other (Irwin & Doyle, 1992). However, one cannot become an effective writer simply by reading. Second, students must be encouraged to discuss language, be it their own or that of professional writers. Language is a tool that students must learn to use well, but unless conversations about the mysteries and interesting aspects of language are a part of the classroom, students may not develop the language sense that will help them become effective writers (Langer, 1998). Third, and perhaps most important, students must write more often than has been typical. Frequency of writing increases fluency. Many middle school students have had little experience in composing. They may have spent a lot of classroom time studying language, especially grammar, usage, and spelling, but little time putting connected sentences on paper or screen. If that is the case among your students, they need to develop fluency first. They need to generate ideas and text. They need to write in journals and do lots of drafting that may never be turned into polished pieces. They need to experience and explore writing before they can begin to learn to control it. Fluent writers need many opportunities to experiment with written language. Like reading, writing is never fully mastered. There is always more to learn, skills to hone, processes to develop, new modes to attempt, and so on.

Whether you decide to teach students as a whole class or work more with small groups and individuals, you must plan to provide the instruction that students will need if they are to become more confident, successful writers. Moving students through a grammar/composition textbook is not apt to achieve this goal. Instead, you need to think seriously about the kinds of knowledge that students must develop, given their present levels of skills. More than likely, you will need to teach some writing process strategies. You will also need to help students examine the outstanding features of various discourse modes. In addition, you will need to provide some information about language conventions. As much as possible, you should choose the content of instruction on the basis of student writing. That is to say, you need to observe students while they write, talk with them about their writing, and look carefully at the material they produce. On that basis you should decide what to teach. You must plan to do more than just assign writing; you must have a system for providing the assistance and information that students need to become more proficient.

Teaching Process Strategies

Students need to learn a variety of strategies to use while they engage in the activities associated with the various processes of writing (see Activity 5.2). Good writers have many options at their disposal so if one fails, they can try another. Less able writers tend to rely on only one or two strategies. When these fail, they are paralyzed. For example, many writers seem to be doing nothing for several moments after they have been given a writing assignment. They will tell you, however, that they are trying to think of something to write about. In effect, they are waiting for some inspiration. If it does not happen, they are frustrated and unproductive. They can be taught some prewriting alternatives to use in case inspiration does not strike. They can, for example, learn clustering, brainstorming, free writing, jotting a list of ideas, and so forth. And you can help students choose a strategy that is likely to work for the type of discourse they are thinking of writing. Clustering or brainstorming may work best for exposition; free writing or making a list of who, what, when, where, why, and how may work better for narration. Students can teach each other strategies they discover. You can help them be inventive by encouraging them to look for new ways to generate ideas.

When students are engaged in drafting, the focus should be on fluency. Encourage them to get the words on paper in any way they can. If they cannot write fast enough, they should jot ideas in the margins or tape-record. Encourage them to write the middle first if it is shaping up more easily than the opening. Various kinds of drafting tools need to be available—paper, pencils, pens, word processors, computers, and so forth, whatever helps students get their ideas onto the page.

Revising is often the most difficult activity to teach, but many professional writers attest that it is the most important part of writing.

During revising, students must focus on the content and how it is developed and arranged (see Fig. 5.2). Teach them to use symbols to mark rearrangements or to number paragraphs as they try different sequences. They can be encouraged to outline expository material they have already written to see if it is balanced or if some part is too short. If they are using a computer, they can easily move parts around to see what arrangement of ideas works best. Students need to accept the idea that revising is natural and necessary. You must help them move beyond the one-draft-only mentality.

For editing, teach students to use all of the resources available to them—human, print, computer, and self. They can ask other people for assistance, use a personal or commercial checklist and reference books, run spelling and grammar checkers, and develop their own editing skills.

When the task is preparing a manuscript for publication, help students consider their options for illustrating, using special layout techniques, incorporating graphics, following instructions for entering contests, and so forth. As much as possible, provide them with a real audience and a means by which that real audience can communicate with the writer to provide authentic feedback.

Teaching Discourse Modes

In the elementary grades, students may write stories and poems, but starting there and continuing through most of the rest of their school years, students spend most of their composing time preparing reports and writing expository essays. Often these pieces are what can best be described as "academic writing," discourse that is rarely seen outside the school walls. Book reports and term papers are two examples of academic writing.

Student writers need the opportunity to learn to write many different discourse modes. There are far too many for students to learn all of

---

Good revision is in the cards

Combine
Add
Rearrange
Delete
Substitute

FIG 5.2

them, but they do need to encounter a wide variety. Consider trying to incorporate all of the eight modes identified by Moffett & Wagner (1976): labels and captions, wordplay, monologues and dialogues, invented stories, true stories, directions, information, and ideas and opinions. One of the most effective ways to teach modes is to surround students with all sorts of printed material that they have time to examine, read, and discuss. When they have questions about how to write a script or a poem, refer them to the works of professional writers to see how they handled it. Create folders labeled by mode that contain examples that students can study (Atwell, 1987). Read excerpts aloud occasionally. Teach mini-lessons about modes. In literature discussions, take some time to talk about how the work is structured and ask students to think about how they can use this method of organization in their own writing. Most importantly, give students the opportunity to try a variety of modes when they respond to literature and when they are focusing on learning to compose.

Teaching Purposes

Real-world writing serves many purposes. However, teachers tend to assign tasks that inform the teacher of what the students have learned. In effect, these writing assignments are disguised tests of reading comprehension or assessments of research and study skills. Students are frequently asked to compose on topics about which they know little or are still learning. Not surprisingly, students writing often reflects their fuzzy understanding.

In many cases, assigned topics are ones that students find boring. It is a struggle for anyone to write about topics that they do not care about and that do not interest them. Writing tends to be better when writers are curious about topics and have some personal commitment to the task. It is also better when the task is at least similar to real-world writing. It is better still when it will actually be read by an intended audience other than the teacher, someone who really wants or needs to know what the writer has to say.

Having students experiment with a variety of modes will naturally lead to an exploration of purposes, as Fig. 5.3 illustrates. However, the connection between purpose and form may have to be brought to students' attention. "What is the purpose of this piece of writing?" is a question you need to keep asking and students need to ask each other. This is also a question that needs to be asked about the literature and printed material that students encounter. Here again, it is important to have a variety of material available that represents different purposes so that students can compare. For middle level students, the more obvious the contrasts, the better. It is sometimes useful to have students look at parts of their own writing to ex-

Purposes and Forms of Writing	
Purpose	*Forms*
Amuse, entertain	Jokes, riddles, stories, comics, graffiti, plays, bumper stickers, anecdotes
Command, direct, request	Directions, warnings, rules, memos, signs, posters
Record events	Diaries, research notes, semantic maps, lists, reports, histories, chronicles
Predict, speculate, hypothesize	Forecasts, predictions, theories, horoscopes
Inform, advise	Announcements, invitations, pamphlets, catalogs, lists, graphs, broadcasts
Persuade	Editorials, graffiti, signs, advertisements, arguments
Explain	Textbooks, handbooks, recipes, captions, rules, excuses, brochures, newspaper articles
Narrate	Stories of all genres, both fiction and nonfiction
Create	Plays, jokes, commercials, poems, stories, songs, puzzles
Discover, find out, explore	Interviews, questionnaires, surveys, business letters, observations
Invite reflection	Quotations, questions, learning logs, journals, memoirs

Adapted from *New Connections: An Integrated Approach to Literacy* (2nd ed., p. 33) by Kathy Pike, Rita Compain, & Jean Mumper. Copyright 1997 by permission of Addison-Wesley Educational Publishers, Inc. Reprinted with permission.

FIG. 5.3

amine the purpose that each paragraph serves in the work. This can help them see that in a well-structured piece, each paragraph contributes to the whole, but in a poorly organized piece, the purposes of some paragraphs cannot be determined or fail to contribute to achieving the general aim of the whole discourse.

Teaching Audience Awareness

In the real world, writing is meant for an interested but uninformed audience. In school, however, much student writing is read only by the teacher, who is often better informed about the subject matter than is the writer. Aren't you intimidated by the thought of submitting your writing to someone you consider to be an expert? Surely middle school students are likely to feel a similar sense of insecurity. Successful composition students are often those who most quickly learn what pleases and distresses the teacher. However, the teacher's standards may not equate with those of other teachers. This inconsistency is very confusing to students. More importantly, though, the teacher's standards may not match those of other kinds of readers. Middle school students commonly submit work to the teacher that they readily admit they do not want peers to see, not because the content is personal but because they do not want their classmates to know the quality of their work. When students know that their writing will be seen and read by peers, the papers are often better. As much as possible, students need to write authentic papers that are read by a variety of real audiences. These may be people within the school, but they may also be people in the community (parents, politicians and policy-makers, newspaper readers, businesspeople, etc.) or others outside the immediate locale if students write letters, submit manuscripts for possible publication in periodicals, compete in writing contests, publish their own collections of stories or poems, and so on.

A WRITING INSTRUCTION DILEMMA

Although students do need to learn to use a broad range of writing strategies to cope with various modes, purposes, and audiences, precisely how to achieve that goal is problematic. There is a great deal of disagreement over the issue of whether writing tasks should be student-selected or teacher-assigned, particularly at the middle school level (see Fig. 5.4).

Composition experts tend to agree that at the elementary school level, students should make many of their own decisions about what, when, and how to write (Calkins, 1986; Graves, 1994). There are many advantages to this approach. One of the most significant is that elementary school students need a great deal of writing practice to develop fluency. If they choose their own topics and modes, they will write more. However, allowing students to make these choices also presents some problems, most of which have to do with making the teacher's job more complicated. When students choose their own topics and modes, the teacher must maintain better records in order to ensure that students are engaging in varied experiences. Also, student choice complicates the assessment and evaluation processes. It is somewhat easier to feel that grades on papers are equitable when every student writes a similar piece. New teachers who have not seen much student writing and have a limited base of comparison of-

---

A Writing Dilemma

Student-selected writing	Teacher-assigned writing
Advantages	
• Personal commitment	• Better control over skill & concept coverage
• Stronger voice	• Provides basis for discussion & evaluation
• Higher motivation	• Writing across curricula
• Natural adjustment for ability/skills	
Disadvantages	
• Imbalance of practice	• Difficult to find topics that appeal to all
• Inappropriate subject matter	• Can force students to try to stretch too far
• Difficult to schedule skill lessons	• Writing seen as artificial exercise
• Complicates peer response and editing	• May discourage fluency
• Complicates evaluation	

FIG. 5.4

ten have difficulty responding to, assessing, and evaluating writing. When students write all kinds of papers by choice, this task is even more complex.

On the other hand, research indicates that at the high school level, teacher-assigned writing, particularly that which requires students to engage in certain kinds of inquiry leading to specified writing outcomes, produces more effective writers (Hillocks, 1986). As usual, the middle school level remains unstudied, so we do not know if either method is preferable. The best guess is that a balance between the two is advisable. Students probably do need to complete some teacher-assigned tasks, but they also need to do some writing that is self-selected. This advice seems to match what we know about the middle school student's need to have personal control and the student's desire for imposed structure.

One way to approach the conflict between teacher-assigned versus student-selected tasks is to make use of a writing practice journal in which students experiment with different discourse modes, audiences, and purposes at the teacher's direction and then select the most promising pieces for further development. Another strategy is to implement a portfolio system, which includes the use of a working portfolio that contains all the student's writing, some assigned and some self-generated. From this collection, the student chooses the pieces to be revised, edited, and polished for evaluation. These finished pieces become part of a showcase portfolio. Either of these approaches allows for the inclusion of both student-selected and teacher-assigned tasks.

DESIGNING A COMPOSITION CURRICULUM

If you want students to learn to model the behavior of effective writers, they will need to explore the facets of the rhetorical problem from as many angles as possible, whether they choose their own tasks or complete those you assign. Assuming that you choose to have students complete some assignments that you design, how can you decide what to have students write and what task sequence is developmentally appropriate for middle level writers?

Sequencing Assignments

Some teachers rely very heavily on whatever sequence is recommended in the textbook. However, there is no guarantee that any sequence of assignments found in a literature anthology, for example, has been carefully thought through in terms of considering what skills students need for success. Assignments may conveniently match the literature, but the overall sequence may have serious weaknesses. For example, students may not encounter a variety of discourse modes, or they may encounter challenging tasks before easier ones. Creating your own tasks to accompany the literature you teach can work well, but here again the difficulty of assignments may be erratic unless you consider these carefully when you create a long-term plan for the year.

Unfortunately, sequences presented in composition textbooks and handbooks may not be carefully designed. They may match the skill being taught at the moment, but the overall design may have serious weaknesses. Often these texts follow a behavioral psychology viewpoint that writers have to start with isolated words and work their way up (what is known as the part-to-whole approach), or they divide discourse into the four traditional modes—narration, description, exposition, and argument/persuasion—and provide instruction on each one in turn (see Fig. 5.5). The major difficulty with both of these approaches is that neither reflects how effective writers write. Composing is not just one word strung after another, and the traditional modes are rarely found in isolation; rather, they are used harmoniously to form a whole discourse that is none of these four.

Both of these sequences pay scant attention to some of the crucial factors that we associate with effective writing—coherence, cohesion, unity of purpose, consistency of tone, and so on.

You may consider designing a sequence based on some concepts drawn from educational psychology, as shown in Fig. 5.6. We know, for example, that learning occurs best when we start with the simple and move to the complex, from the familiar to the unfamiliar, from the concrete to the abstract, and from the subjective (what I think) to the objective (what people in general think). Any one of these progressions, or even some combination of two or more, may work well.

Another possibility is to simulate the sequence in which oral language is learned (see Fig.5.6). Much of what we hear as young children is narrative. By the time children enter school, they already have a grasp of story grammar or how a story is structured. They can tell stories themselves and predict what is likely to come next in a story. Thus, it seems natural to consider beginning a composition sequence with narratives and then work toward the less familiar forms. Whether the next logical step is explaining or persuading, though, is difficult to determine because the data indicate that middle level students struggle with both expository and persuasive tasks (Pikulski, 1991).

On the other hand, there are some data that explain why exposition is more difficult than narration. Put simply, exposition is more difficult for most students because it is less frequently heard. Young people may have had few opportunities to hear others describe a

---

Common Sequences in Composition Textbooks and Handbooks

- Word, phrase, clause, sentence, paragraph, short discourse, long discourse

- Traditional modes (narration, description, exposition, argumentation/persuasion)

FIG. 5.5

Possible Sequences Based on Educational Psychology	Possible Sequence Based on Oral Language Development
• Simple to complex	1. Narrating
• Familiar to unfamiliar	2. Explaining
• Concrete to abstract	3. Persuading
• Subjective to objective	(With attention to grammatical structures not used in oral language)

FIG. 5.6

process or explain a topic factually. When they tell a story, young people know that they are supposed to keep moving ahead to tell what happened next. They do not need to be prompted by the audience to do this. However, in normal conversation, when they are providing an explanation or even trying to persuade, they tend to rely on responses from the listeners to aid them in determining what else to include. Questions, oral responses, and even nonverbal gestures and facial expressions give clues about what else needs to be said. When students try to write exposition, they do not have these audience prompts. They often provide only the barest essentials, in part because they have not been exposed to enough oral modeling of sustained exposition. For further information about why exposition may be especially difficult for middle school writers, see Bereiter and Scardamalia's (1987) *The Psychology of Written Composition*. If you choose this oral language sequence, you would probably want to link the teaching of composition with many speaking activities. Doing so will help students come to understand some of the differences between the spoken word and the written word. Related to that, you will probably want to focus some attention on developing sentence constructions such as appositives and introductory adverbial clauses, which are not often used in oral language, and conventions such as punctuation and spelling, which are not visible in speech.

Research-Based Sequences

Basing a sequence of assignments on either educational psychology or the development of oral language may make sense, but neither approach has any research to verify that it will work. Rather than make guesses, it may be useful to consider what some experts have proposed and why.

James Britton. Britton (Britton, Burgess, Martin, McLeod, and Rosen, 1975) spent most of his life studying language and how it was taught in England. His work led him to believe that spoken language and writing are closely connected, and he became a strong advocate of teaching in ways that create bridges between speech and composing. He believed that the best writing begins as a personal expression of what people, particularly young students, know best. He also believed that the best writing begins as material written primarily for the writer him- or herself. What he proposed was that writing instruction should begin with what he labeled as **expressive writing**, defined as personal writing done primarily for the writer's own satisfaction. Expressive writing is basically rough draft work; it is usually not meant to be shared with an audience and certainly is not meant to be evaluated or graded. It grows out of the writer's experiences, interests, needs, and concerns. When it is reshaped to fit an audience, it changes. According to Britton's theory, expressive writing, when adapted for an audience, may become either *transactional writing*, which he defined as writing that gets the work of the world done (i.e., exposition and information), or *poetic writing*, which he defined as artistic writing, commonly identified as the traditional forms of literature—short stories, drama, poems, and so forth (see Fig. 5.7). However, in some of his later work, he came to realize that some expressive writing can be polished for an audience, yet never actually be transformed into either of the two categories. He called this *transitional writing*. A personal diary that is edited for publication would fall into this category.

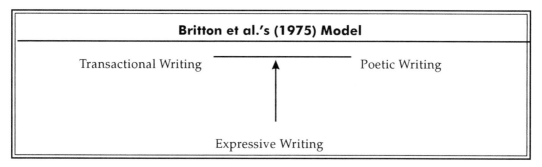

FIG. 5.7

The value of Britton's work lies in considering the necessity of having students engage in expressive writing as the starting point. Although this form should probably be used frequently at the elementary level, it should probably also be used, at least at the start of the school year, in most classes, including those at the middle level. Britton's work strongly supports the use of journals in the composition classroom, although the concept of journaling has now expanded far beyond purely expressive writing. Another value of Britton's work comes from his consideration of audience. He believed that students should be encouraged to write first for themselves, then for the teacher, then for a wider audience, and finally for an unknown audience (see Fig. 5.8).

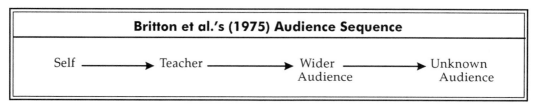

FIG. 5.8

James Moffett. Moffett was a highly respected discourse theorist and educator. His seminal work, *Teaching the Universe of Discourse* (Moffett, 1968), has served as the model for many curriculum plans in composition. He is also well-known for the multitude of books he wrote or coauthored about teaching, including four editions of *Student-Centered Language Arts and Reading* (e.g., see Moffett & Wagner, 1976), which focused on integrating the language arts and using collaborative group work in instruction. Over the years, Moffett made several recommendations concerning the sequencing of composition tasks (see Fig. 5.9). One of those sequences was based on audience and looks very similar to that of Britton *et al.* (1975), moving from the self to known individuals, then to unknown persons, and finally to the masses.

However, he proposed different sequences, depending on the mode involved. For the fictional mode, he proposed that young children be permitted to express themselves in something he called a *fictive essay*, which is a relatively familiar form for them anyway. A

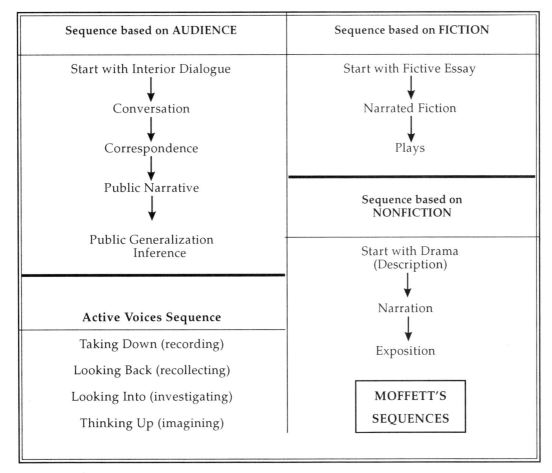

FIG. 5.9

fictive essay sounds like fact, but it is not. Young children often draw imaginary creatures or characters and then explain them (e.g., "This is Mr. Robot. He likes green beans. He's crazy."). Next comes narrated fiction, which begin as chains of events but eventually develop into stories with plot lines. Finally, students are ready to create plays. My own experience with middle school writers verifies that script writing is quite difficult for young people. Although they like the idea of creating a script for a commercial or a puppet show, the actual production of text moves quite slowly, and the results are little more than mediocre. Transforming an existing short story into a play is a challenge; creating a play with strong dialogue and plot is extremely difficult, even when students base the work on familiar characters (e.g., those in a television drama series).

According to Moffett (1968), nonfiction develops in somewhat of a reverse order. His observations showed that young children begin with what he called *drama*. These are actually descriptions of what exists around the children (i.e., observations similar to on-the-spot reports), but they are dramatic in the sense that they are immediate, much as stage plays are immediate. Nonfiction then moves to narrated forms—personal experiences, autobiographies, and biographies—all of which are organized chronologically and may cover a broad span of time. Finally, students move to the standard expository forms that are much more generalized and may move around through both time and space using an organizational scheme that is not chronological (e.g., problem–solution, classification, order of importance, etc.).

Active Voices (e.g., see Moffett with Tashlik, 1987), a series of books designed for classroom use based on Moffett's theories, illustrates a coordinated sequence that intermixes fiction and nonfiction. Students begin by *recording* what they see, hear, taste, touch, smell, read, notice, and so on. These recordings can be further developed, of course, into personal experience papers, science field notes, and so forth. The second stage is that of *recalling* or looking back. This would include narrating any kind of memory of any significant or trivial event. The next step is *investigating* or doing research, whether this be library or field research. *Imagining* comes next, which includes all of the forms of creative expression that would accompany fictional writing. Finally, students should engage in *reflecting* or thinking over, much as students are asked to do at the end of a semester or year when they examine work in their portfolios and write a description of what they have learned. *Active Voices II: A Writer's Reader for Grades 7–9* (Moffett with Tashlik, 1987) contains numerous examples of student work that can be used as writing models regardless of whether you wish to follow Moffett's sequence.

Although Moffett was thinking about curriculum as spanning a student's entire precollegiate schooling, he did not recommend that these five writing forms be delegated by grade levels (e.g., students in primary grades only record, students in upper elementary only recall, etc.) Rather, Moffett believed that students should progress through this sequence several times during their school years. He did not see this as a yearly sequence, but as a framework spanning two or three grade levels. Furthermore, each time students proceed through the cycle, the tasks should increase in abstractness. Young children should write about concrete experiences; high school students should be able to write about hypothesized experiences. Middle school students still need to rely on concrete links, but they should be stretching toward the abstract. Nevertheless, all students, at whatever level, should engage in all five types of writing.

Adapted from Tchudi's (Judy, 1981) Recommended Sequence

1. Opening up (personal to public writing)

2. Exploring the self

3. Writing about others and the world

4. Investigating / probing / researching

5. Exploring causes, problems, issues, and values

FIG. 5.10

Stephen Tchudi. Tchudi is another familiar name to language arts educators. He has been involved in looking at and writing about methods of instruction for many years. He proposed a sequence (Judy, 1981) that is similar to Moffett's (1968) in some ways but picks up a bit more of Britton *et al.'s* (1975) focus on self at the start. The version that appears in Fig. 5.10 is adapted for middle school writers.
No matter which sequence you choose or design for yourself, Tchudi (Judy, 1981) offers this caution:

> Under no circumstances should any sequence ... be allowed to create a lockstep curriculum. The point, after all, is to take the students at their present developmental level and to help them move forward, not to ensure that they have followed a prescribed pattern created by either textbook writer or teacher. (p. 201)

Assignment Cues

No matter how you decide to sequence writing tasks, you still must consider how to design these tasks so as to help students learn the most from the experience. Many teachers spend their careers searching for the magic writing assignment, the one that will motivate every student to produce excellent results. Some tasks are certainly more stimulating than others, but no single assignment will turn every student into an exceptional writer. What you can do is provide a variety of tasks so that students have a chance to discover those to which they respond best. There are several cues you can manipulate in order to challenge students. A list of these appears in Fig. 5.11 along with a sample task that includes all of the cues.

Some cautions are in order, though. Simply changing one cue can alter an assignment drastically, making it far more difficult or much easier. It probably is not wise to use all of the cues in most assignments; balance over time is probably better. The more cues you give to students, the more the task becomes yours, not theirs. They lose ownership of the writing, and the results are apt to reflect this. When too many cues are involved, you may find yourself grading papers

---

Assignment Cues

1. Subject matter (general or specific)

2. Organization of content

3. Audience

4. Purpose or aim

5. Mode

6. Speaker's role or point of view

7. Context of task

8. Tone

9. Mood

10. Style

Sample: You are the education reporter for the local newspaper. Write a front-page story about yesterday's class which informs readers about what occurred. Remember to be objective. Use traditional news style, format, tone, and organization. Your deadline is one hour from now.

FIG. 5.11

more on the basis of whether or not students followed the directions than on how well they wrote. Students will quickly come to sense that the quality of writing matters less than following the directions.

A Helpful Hint

When designing assignments, try to create ones that will produce writing that you will find interesting to read. Uninteresting assignments, no matter how much skill students develop in the process, produce mediocre writing that is often, at best, boring to read. When you first begin teaching, you will find much that students write to be somewhat interesting, but the more reports and papers you read, the less interesting the papers will be to you. In effect, you will become a more critical judge. This is particularly true if all students are asked to write on the same topic using the same discourse mode. The first 5 or 10 analyses of a short story you read may be rather informative, but by the time you read the 100th or the 150th, you may not be very impressed, even if the paper is truly above average. Often the more you know about a topic yourself, the more critical you are of student work. You may actually be a better judge about the information presented in an expository paper or the persuasive quality of an argument if you know little or nothing about the topic; you will be reading these more as a typical reader than as an expert. This does not mean that students should be deprived of the opportunity to write about a topic that is of interest to them simply because you have no interest in it, however. Students should not suffer because they happen to choose a topic that runs counter to your personal views or fails to pique your curiosity.

STUDENT-SELECTED WRITING

When students select their own writing tasks, they generally have more commitment to the task and feel a greater sense of ownership. As a result, they are apt to write more and to be more concerned about the quality of the product. Teachers who use instructional programs that give students the opportunity to choose what they will write throughout most of the year, as is the case in a reading–writing workshop, find that student writing is substantially better and shows dramatic improvement. If students generally have control over what they write, a chance to see and hear what other students write, and the opportunity to explore a wide range of printed material, they will compose a variety of discourse. During the course of a year they will cope with different purposes, audiences, and a range of other constraints. A teacher can enhance this breadth through mini-lessons introducing various stylistic options, modes, and techniques. The teacher can also enhance this exploration through careful record keeping and suggestions given during conferences.

Nevertheless, there are some problems associated with self-selection of writing tasks. Students who have never before in their schooling had the chance to select their own tasks may initially find it difficult to choose a topic. Often these students do not really believe that they have a choice; they will still think that they need to please the teacher, and so they will ask, "What do you want me to write about?" Choosing a topic is risky business: Get the right one and the writing progresses smoothly; pick the wrong one and the writing is drudgery. Students must be taught how to select a topic, and they should be encouraged to create a list of possibilities that continues to grow during the year.

If students are only given the opportunity to choose for themselves occasionally, they may tend to write the same kind of discourse over and over—poem after poem, nothing but sports stories, or one more chapter in their great American novel. If students must also complete a variety of assigned tasks throughout the year, then this repetition in self-selected topics or genre may not be a problem, but it can be bothersome. One alternative is to maintain a checklist of minimums—a limited number of discourse modes that students must attempt by the end of the grading period or the year. These need not be finished pieces that are graded, but students must submit a sample of each by the deadline. Another option is the practice journal previously described, in which students experiment with various modes, purposes, audiences, styles, and so forth.

When students self-select their writing, you will have to do much more one-on-one work with writers. This, of course, has significant advantages, but it can be confusing to both you and the writer. Consider that you have just finished a conference with a student who is deep into a research report on a rather technical topic that he or she hopes to submit to a magazine for publication. In the blink of an eye, you must be prepared to meet with a student who is thinking about writing a humorous piece about a typical event that happens in the school. It is just a piece of fluff that the student thinks will entertain classmates. Being able to respond effectively to both writers will challenge your flexibility. When students self-select writing, you must have a good record-keeping system, too. Without it you can reach the end of a grading period without realizing that some students have not submitted a single piece of finished work during the whole term.

Grading self-selected writing also presents challenges. You have to know what the student was trying to achieve and be able to judge the work, at least in part, on how well that purpose was fulfilled. You will not face a stack of papers, all addressing the same topic or written in the same discourse mode, which may be a plus from your point of view; instead, you will face a mixture of papers, each of which demands that you assume a slightly different mindset if you are to evaluate it effectively. On the other hand, you may find the diversity refreshing. You may also find that the higher quality of the products is enough to offset the complexity of grading.

If you decide that you want students to self-select topics, at least part of the time, be advised that students still need to create their own assignments in the sense that they need to be aware of the cues that they have chosen for themselves. They certainly do not need to write out their own assignment, but they do need to consider the purpose of the task, the audience, their own limitations, the subject matter they want to include, and perhaps other factors as well. Middle school students are not very good judges of context, particularly time. Whatever they choose to do tends to take far longer than they expect. The more experiences they have with self-selected writing, the better they will become at making these estimations, but at first they will have difficulty designing tasks that they can accomplish in the time they have.

A CLOSER LOOK AT JOURNALS

Whether you assign writing, or students self-select their tasks, authenticity is an asset. Students need to be authors of real pieces of discourse. Journals, logs, and diaries have been a significant part of real-world writing for centuries. Indeed, much of what we know about world and American history is drawn from the personal and public records maintained by individuals in these forms. Although journal keeping has enormous possibilities as an effective tool for teaching writing, it, too, is not without its problems, some of which have been created by language arts teachers themselves.

Initially, journals were considered to be the answer to a dilemma that all language arts teachers face—How can I have students write more without having to grade more? In general, journals, if they are graded at all, are usually evaluated on the basis of quantity of writing rather than quality. The concept is that journals contain prewriting material and help to develop fluency. Because prewriting is not meant to be final copy work and because worrying over mechanics tends to slow fluency, grading journals for polished quality contradicts their purposes. Language arts teachers quickly latched onto the idea of journal writing in the classroom as a way to solve the dilemma. They could, indeed, have students write more without increasing their grading load.

Journals can certainly increase writing fluency, and they can serve as a repository for ideas under development. In fact, they can serve many other purposes as well. However, in all too many classrooms, journals are just more of the same "dry run" writing, a busywork assignment that does not seem to serve a useful purpose, at least in the eyes of the students. Students are given prompts to which they must respond. Often, these are topics about which students care very little. They write in their journals in a perfunctory manner with little attention to either content or mechanics. Under the circumstances, it is little wonder that some students come to detest journaling. Journals can be wonderful tools, but they must be used wisely. They are only one part of a total composition program. Students need to see them as being valuable in some way. Journals need to be means to achieving some other goals, not ends in themselves. You need to vary the journal assignment so that it does not become stale and routine. Fortunately, as Fig. 5.12 shows, there are enough different types of journals to ensure that the task never becomes boring.

Students need to do some required writing in journals and logs, but they also need the opportunity to write about their own topics sometimes. When journal writing first hit the educational scene, some teachers encouraged students to create diaries in the belief that good writing springs only from personal experiences that are deeply meaningful. However, having students write about themselves and their personal lives created some unexpected problems. Language arts teachers found themselves confronted with revelations of sexual abuse, contemplation of suicide, eating disorders, and a host of personal problems and even criminal behaviors. More recently, conservative parents have spoken out vehemently against teachers requiring that students record personal information about themselves and their families in journals. They consider this to be an invasion of privacy, none of the teacher's business, and unrelated to the primary function of schooling, which they see as the acquisition of basic skills. Further, they abhor the notion that any teacher would accept writing that is not mechanically perfect. Be aware that the mere mention of the word *journal* sends up red flags among some parents and community residents. To some individuals, journals are automatically equated with diaries, and no amount of explanation will alter the mindset. One option is to use a term that more precisely describes what you are asking students to do. For example, you might identify the task as a writer's notebook or a reading log rather than a journal or diary.

You may want students to write from the heart about topics that matter to them, but you are required by law to report known or suspected abuse and the wise teacher reports various kinds of threats to appropriate officials. A few teachers have been sued for failing to report information that was recorded in student journals. You should inform students that if they confide certain information, you are bound by law and professional judgment to report it. You can also

---

Journal Writing: Some Possible Versions

DIARY—
personal accounts of events, people, and emotions.

WRITER'S NOTEBOOK—
jotted records of observations, quotes, comments, and so forth.

WRITING PRACTICE OR REHEARSAL JOURNAL—
guided experiments with rhetorical factors.

DISCOVER OR FREEWRITING JOURNAL—
entries to discover topics or generate ideas.

PROJECT RECORD OR LOG—
records of work being done, often by a group working independently.

LEARNING LOG OR CONTENT JOURNAL—
reflections or summaries of content learning or reactions to content.

DIALOGUE JOURNAL—
written conversations between student and teacher and/or between students.

TEXTBOOK JOURNAL—
responses to a text, often including evaluations of style and biases
as well as content.

TWO-COLUMN JOURNAL—
one column for summaries of content; the other column
for responses to content.

SUMMARY JOURNAL—
summaries of content to review daily classwork.

SIMULATED JOURNAL—
fictional accounts, often of literary characters.

LITERARY RESPONSE JOURNAL—
personal responses to reading material.

FIG. 5.12

tell them that if they disclose such information in their journals, you must assume that they are indirectly asking you to take action. If they do not wish you to do so, they should not include this material in their journals. As an alternative, encourage them to keep a personal diary that no one ever sees. Occasionally a student will still feel compelled to include an entry that he or she does not want you to read. Although it may not protect you from litigation, you can direct students to fold the page over, staple it shut, and write a note on the outside indicating that you are not to read it. When you check the journal, write a note indicating that you did not read the entry, and then sign and date the note.

To avoid other problems, provide printed instructions for maintaining journals, and require that students staple these to the inside back cover of their notebooks. Post a copy in the classroom. When you meet with parents, call attention to the bulletin board where these instructions, along with other sheets of information, are on display. Journals, logs, notebooks, and even diaries can be terrific tools when used appropriately as part of a composition program, but if you are to garner parental support for them, you must help parents understand their value.

UNGRADED WRITING

Students need to do far more writing than you can possibly grade. However, in today's grade-conscious society, students often do not take seriously any assignment that they know will not be graded. How can you cope with this dilemma? The trick is to find some writing tasks that have high pay value to students but do not require grading. The most obvious example of this concept is a year-end course evaluation. At the end of the year, you can ask students to spend some time looking back through everything in their portfolios and reviewing the major units studied during the year. You can then ask them to write an evaluation of the class and of you. Middle level students are always anxious to offer an opinion, so this task is strongly appealing. They will not ask if you are going to grade them and they will not ask how long these have to be.

This task works as an ungraded writing assignment; however, one cannot go around asking students to assess the class all the time. What are some other ungraded tasks that students will want to complete? Questions that students use as springboards in literary response groups appeal strongly to some students. They like the idea of being in control of the discussion by choosing what questions will be addressed. If you are trying to explain something that obviously puzzles students, you can ask them to take a few minutes to write down what they thought you meant, share this with a partner, and then ask you some questions. Occasionally, students will arrive at your classroom door all in a frenzy over something that has occurred the previous period, between classes, or outside of school. If you have the time and feel that this is something that you are willing to listen to them complain about, you may want to open the floor for discussion. However, at other times you may find it advantageous to ask students to freely write about what is bothering them. For the most part, the opportunity to record their feelings will be enough, and by the end of the writing time, they will be settled and ready to move ahead with the day's work.

MINI-LESSONS

No matter how you structure your composition program and whether or not you choose to use journals in your classroom, you must still provide instruction. In general, there are three common ways in which writing instruction is provided: peer response groups, student–teacher conferences, and mini-lessons. The first two will be considered later in this chapter. Mini-lessons are one of the most effective ways to provide direct instruction. These are brief explanations, demonstrations, and practices that focus on specific goals. If, for example, students will be or already are writing scripts, you can present a 10-minute lesson on script format and content. This may be a lesson that you teach to the entire class or just a small group. It may even be a lesson that you teach to an individual in a conference. If you want students to write summaries of short stories, you can take a few minutes to write one on an overhead transparency as you describe for the class the thinking processes that take place. If you have noticed that several students are having difficulty using quotation marks correctly, you can put some of the sentences on the board and review the punctuation. For additional ideas about teaching mini-lessons, you will find in Atwell's (1998) *In the Middle* a wealth of suggestions. Another excellent resource is Fletcher & Portalupi's (1998) *Craft Lessons*.

WRITING PORTFOLIOS

One of the hottest topics in language arts education today is portfolios, but the concept of a portfolio as a collection of work that is used to demonstrate one's proficiency has been around for a long time. For example, artists, photographers, and models have, for many years, used material collected in portfolios to convince employers of their talents.

There are several books about using portfolios in the language arts classroom. A few are listed in the Recommended Readings for this chapter. What you will find in these resources is that there are many different concepts of what a portfolio is or should be and how it can be used to enhance composition instruction. In fact, there are not only writing portfolios but also reading portfolios, mathematics portfolios, cross-curricular portfolios, and so on.

Language arts teachers are still exploring the possibilities that portfolios offer. When I taught middle school, students kept all of their work in what I called class folders. These remained in the room in boxes marked by the class hour. Every day when students arrived, they got their folders from the box before they started working. Every graded or checked piece of work completed during a grading period stayed in the folder until grades were out and conferences were done. Then we had a folder clean. Students removed everything except what they wanted to save and all final copies of compositions. At the end of the year they took their folders home.

At the present time, educators would call my simple system a version of a *working portfolio*. More than anything else, it was a storage area. Occasionally, it saved me when I forgot to write a grade in my grade book, and more than once the existence of the folders cooled an upset parent who stopped by for an unscheduled conference. I could hand the parent the folder and he or she could look at the child's work while I collected whatever records and data I needed. Often by the time I sat down, the parent would look at me and say with chagrin, "I don't need to talk to you. I need to talk to my child!"

Working folders, however, do not make the most of portfolios as instructional tools. Educators tend to talk now about four other kinds of writing portfolios. One is a *total collection portfolio*. This contains all of the work that a student does in relation to writing during a specified period of time, usually a year. Students are required to keep all rough drafts, revisions, versions produced during editing, and final copies. Everything—good, bad, and ugly—stays in.

The other three kinds of portfolios all involve some selection on the basis of certain criteria. The first of these is a *process writing portfolio*. The contents of this portfolio are chosen to illustrate the student's proficiency in engaging in all of the writing process activities—prewriting, drafting, revising, editing, and publishing. Often this portfolio contains all documents related to the production of one particular paper and additional samples collected during the writing of other papers—prewriting for one, a before-and-after revision of another, and so on.

When the term *portfolio* is used, the image that many people have is of what is sometimes called a *showcase portfolio*. This kind of portfolio usually contains only polished copies of the student's best work. Sometimes the selection is made by the student alone, but often the teacher and student confer and jointly decide which pieces will be included.

The last one that appears frequently in the literature is a *required contents portfolio*. Students are given a list of what must be included in the portfolio, and they must follow these instructions. This list often identifies specific discourse modes that must be included (e.g., one personal experience narrative, one piece of expository writing, one personal response to a novel, and one example of any type of creative writing). Some lists specify the general quality that is required (e.g., one example of your best work, one example of your worst work, and one example of a task that you learned much from doing). Some lists also require that the student include all of the prewriting, rough drafts, and final copy of one piece of writing. Thus, the required contents portfolio sometimes overlaps both the process writing and the showcase portfolio.

When you read about portfolios, you will find differences of opinion about the length of time that the portfolio should be maintained and who should select the material. Most portfolios cover only 1 year. Some portfolios are kept throughout the elementary grades, but a new one is started at middle school. That lasts until the student moves on to high school. However, in some school districts, portfolios are started as soon as the child enters the school system. They move along with the youngster as he or she progresses from elementary to middle to high school. This idea has a great deal of appeal; most students would love to have such evidence of progress. However, there are some difficulties with this concept, not the least of which is mobility. Students transfer from school to school, switch from one district to another, and move to other states. How can the system keep each portfolio where it needs to be? Another difficulty is space. Where does a middle level teacher find space to store and make accessible over 100 portfolios containing 6 or more years of material? The solution may lie in electronic portfolios stored on disks or CD-ROMs, which are already being used in pilot programs (Wiedmer, 1998).

Who should choose the material for the portfolio? Many portfolio advocates are adamant that students must make the choices. They see this as a reflective learning activity that is just too good to ignore. Some teachers, however, disagree, particularly those who live in states or districts where large-scale portfolio assessment is practiced. They argue that young children (and older ones, too) do not always make good choices. When the effectiveness of a school district's curriculum or a state's writing program is being measured, teachers are reluctant to leave the choices to children. Most teachers do agree, however, that selecting material is an excellent learning experience for students. There is also general agreement that having students write reflective pieces about the contents of their portfolios is valuable. These reflections may introduce the portfolio to parents or whoever else might see it, explain why particular pieces were chosen, or record the student's perceptions of strengths, weaknesses, and what he or she has learned.

Although it may be easier to implement the use of portfolios if others in the school also use them, you can still use this approach when others do not. One of the outstanding advantages of a writing portfolios is that you will have several samples to examine. This should give you a much better picture of each student's strengths and weaknesses. Thus, portfolios are wonderful assessment tools for diagnosing students and for planning activities that address student needs. Portfolios are also excellent databases for setting goals for an upcoming grading period and for self-reflection during the year and at the end of the year. If you grade each paper a student submits, you end up with a sequence of grades that tells you nothing. It is just a collection of disconnected snapshots of student work—this one looked good, that one was awful, this one was not bad, that one should have been thrown out. In contrast, a portfolio, like a photo album, shows change over time. When you look only at separate pictures, you see the details, but you may miss the important patterns of growth and change that an album captures.

Theoretically, portfolios have great potential. However, grading portfolios is a very complicated business. There are also the practical matters of feedback and reporting progress intermittently. As a general rule, portfolios do not receive a grade until the end of each grading term or even the end of the year. Unless you are very careful to monitor students closely and confer often, a student can slip through the cracks and accomplish little without being discovered until it is too late. It is also possible to work along with a struggling student, being as supportive as possible and building his or her self-esteem only to be forced to issue a low grade at the end of the term. This may shock the student and destroy the positive rapport you have nurtured.

Preservice teachers often wonder just how practicing teachers grade portfolios. Unfortunately, you probably will not like the answer—they rely on their professional judgment and grade the work holistically. They look at the whole collection and they see quantity, quality, changes, and so on. Then they consider this in relation to what they know about the student and about students in general. From that, they determine a grade. Some add checklists of attempted and completed work. Some have students keep lists of tasks. Some establish minimums that are necessary in order to earn various grades. Most of these devices can measure quantity, but they cannot measure quality or progress or creativity or effort or many of the other factors that mark effective writing and growth in learning. When it all shakes out, the final grade on a portfolio is likely to be more subjective than objective. That may not be a very appealing notion to you, but when it comes to compositions, the more objective the grading system, the less likely it is to measure what distinguishes the mediocre from the superb.

RETHINKING ERRORS

Many teachers feel that the goal of writing instruction is the elimination of errors. However, approximation, one of the conditions of literacy learning identified by Cambourne (1988), involves making mistakes. Even professional writers make errors. Everyone does when writing. The more complex the writing task, the more students are apt to make errors. When you encourage students to take risks in their writing in order to learn to manage new discourse modes, achieve different purposes, and address the needs of varied audiences, you increase the likelihood of error. Furthermore, when students become engrossed in meeting one part of a writing challenge, they often backslide in some other areas.

Although students will not be able to eradicate all their mistakes, you do need to help them learn strategies for finding the errors that fall into their range of known concepts. Teachers often look at these as careless mistakes, ones that students seem to make because they are not thinking or paying attention. At the middle school level, the most ordinary varieties are the misuse of common homonyms and the misspelling of frequently used words. Inappropriate end punctuation is another. The frequency of common error in student work should decline as writers become more proficient, but other kinds of mistakes are likely to be present in most pieces of writing. Reducing error is a worthwhile goal; expecting students to eliminate all errors, however, can prompt students to take evasive action that actually hinders their development as writers. They may, for example, write short but complete sentences in order to avoid writing fragments or run-ons, or they may use only the words they are sure they can spell correctly even though other word choices would be more appropriate and clear.

Defining Errors

In considering error, you have to think about whether the problems you see are the result of lack of knowledge or of some other language factor (e.g., dialect, second language overlay, maturity level). Further, some problems are simply beyond a middle level student's understanding. Major content problems such as insufficient details, unsupported contentions, lack of coherence or unity, and poorly organized paragraphs often fall into this grouping. Students need help in learning these concepts, but this will take time and multiple encounters, not a note at the top of the page about the weakness. Awkward constructions, run-on sentences, dangling or misplaced modifiers, and misused vocabulary terms are common problems at the middle school level, yet even when the underlying concept is explained, many students can neither repair the error nor avoid repeating it.

Some errors actually indicate growth (Hull, 1987). Sentence fragments that are subordinate clauses may occur because middle level students are attempting to use more mature sentence structures.

Teachers need to acknowledge the growth rather than focus on the mistake. Most middle school students do not use participial phrases, so any use of them, even if they are misplaced or dangling, indicates growth. These may deserve instructional attention, either through individual conferences, small group instruction, or whole class mini-lessons, but only after students have developed some confidence in using them. Focusing on the error too soon may cause students to avoid the structure rather than risk making a mistake.

Coping with Errors

Sometimes students care so little about a piece of writing that searching for errors is not worth the effort. However, what is involved when a student really wants to edit the work successfully?

Coping with error actually divides into three parts: *feeling*, *finding*, and *fixing*. To correct a mistake, a writer must first sense that something is amiss. A writer cannot recognize an error if he or she does not feel that a mistake has been made. Even after the writer senses that an error exists, he or she may still be unable to find it. Most writers have had the experience of reading a particular sentence over and over, knowing that something is wrong, but not knowing where the problem lies. Even if a writer can determine what the error is, he or she may still be unable to fix it. A writer may, for example, realize that a sentence contains a nonparallel construction but still not know how to repair the damage.

Developing a sense of error demands that students have a great deal of experience with text. The more they read and write, the more likely they are to develop the necessary radar. Oral reading of their papers may help some students sense the presence of error and identify the mistake. Encouraging them to focus selectively on one part of the process at a time during the writing may help students avoid some mistakes early on or proofread more effectively later.

Having students make lists of their common errors may help them become more sensitive. Another possibility is to have students mark passages in a certain way in the margins (e.g., with an asterisk or a question mark), so that you know that the student sensed but could not find or fix the problem. Another possibility is to recommend that the writer put the piece aside for a while and then come back to it later. Sometimes the problem becomes much easier to recognize after stepping back from the text for a few hours or a day.

Nevertheless, some students are apt to be more sensitive to language than others. Peer editing groups assist students not only in pinpointing their own errors but in detecting them in the work of others. It is also possible to create a class list of common problems and make these a part of group response work. Of course, if several students have similar problems, then a mini-lesson is probably the best approach. This is also the time for a few practice exercises from a handbook, but select these with care. Many textbook exercises focus only on finding the mistake (e.g., "identify which of the following is a fragment"). That is not enough. Using students' work as the basis for instruction is the most effective approach, as long as this can be done without embarrassing the writer, but you can also use illustrations from material that students are currently reading or have read. This is another opportunity to teach grammar terminology in a natural context.

Grammar checkers on computers may help students find some errors, but they also point out some qualities that are not errors at all. Thus, students have to be taught how to use these thoughtfully. To aid students in becoming independent writers, they need to learn to solve their problems successfully on their own. They need access to and knowledge of how to use a variety of references and grammar handbooks to help them learn to fix some common mistakes. Try to have at least a few copies of some student-friendly ones available for reference.

Explaining Errors

If students work in peer editing groups, they will need to be able to explain errors to others. For the most part, students will find a way to do this without much assistance although they often fall back on weak explanations (e.g., "I don't know why, but that's how it's done"). Thus, some modeling is useful. This is precisely the time for teaching language terminology and mechanics. In fact, this is the most effective time to teach these concepts and expect students to develop their understanding as they assist each other in peer groups. Sometimes, however, explaining errors in terms of grammar and syntax may prove to be more confusing than helpful.

Explaining errors is a difficult task for all composition teachers, but especially for beginning teachers. You want students to understand why a problem may have occurred and why it is considered to be a mistake. It may seem easier just to tell students, "Don't ever … ," rather than deal with the ambiguity of language. Although this may be understandable from the teacher's point of view, students eventually have to relearn.

The best approach is to assume the stance of a reader. Tell students how the error creates misinformation, forces you to reread, leads you to believe that the idea is complete when actually it goes on, and so forth. Once the writer sees the problem from the reader's viewpoint, you may then want to categorize or label the problem, noting that it is a dangling modifier or that most writers use a comma before a conjunction in a compound sentence. Students who hear the terms used often in a rather natural way to describe their own writing may grasp grammatical and syntactical concepts more readily than they would if they studied these topics formally using some textbook writer's artificial sentences. Give students the opportunity to re-phrase the explanation in their own words. If they begin to use grammatical terms on their own, so much the better. If they do not, they are still learning the concepts in a way that makes sense to them.

RESPONSE, ASSESSMENT, AND EVALUATION OF WRITING

There are no easy instructions for how to respond to, assess, and evaluate writing. There are some useful guidelines, however. In *A Community of Writers: Teaching Writing in Junior and Senior High Schools*, Zemelman and Daniels (1988) emphasize that the kind of response a teacher provides should match the stage of the writing (see Figure 5.13). At the prewriting stage, for example, students need to be encouraged and supported in their efforts to find good topics and ideas. This is not the time to be critical or to make judgments. When students are still in the process of revising, the teacher needs to respond as a normal reader, noting parts that are unclear and segments that are memorable or vivid. This is not the time to point out mechanical problems or sentence structure difficulties. However, when the paper reaches the publishing stage, the teacher needs to put on the

Responding to Writing as a Process				
STAGE	*Prewrite*	*Draft*	*Revise*	*Edit*
Writer's Focus	Ideas	Fluency	Clarity	Correctness
Kind of Assessment	Observing	Responding	Evaluating	Grading
Teacher Roles	Listener; encourager	Encourager; coach	Coach; expert	Expert; editor
Goal of Feedback	Probe for interests; motivate	Encourage; suggest; teach process	Question; challenge; evaluate	Judge; grade

Adapted from *A Community of Writers: Teaching Writing in the Junior and Senior High School* (p. 223), by S. Zemelman and H. Daniels, 1988, Portsmouth, NH: Heinemann. Copyright 1988 by Heinemann. Adapted with permission.

FIG. 5.13

hat of an editor and judge. However, pinpointing every error in a student's paper is far too time-consuming for the effect it has on student writing. Instead, pick pattern problems. Look for patterns of errors which point to some lack of concept understanding and concentrate on those. Look for opportunities to teach some principle that will help a student eliminate several mistakes simultaneously. Help students see their patterns of problems, not just in one paper but in several, and teach students effective proofreading strategies.

You must expect students to write well-expressed material that meets high standards in terms of both content and mechanics. However, you also need to help students learn when to concentrate on each. Trying to worry about everything all at once produces cognitive overload. Selectively focusing on different aspects of composing at different times reflects what effective writers do and will help less adept writers produce better papers.

Responding to Writing

When you read, how do you react? If you are like most readers, you have a general response based on your personal opinion. When you react to the published work of a professional writer, you should be able to respond in depth and support your comments on the basis of your knowledge of literary quality. However, this kind of response is not particularly helpful to a developing writer. When writing is still under construction, writers need support, encouragement, advice, and suggestions from someone who understands that writing is a complex, mind-bending activity fraught with hurdles. The writer wants and needs an advocate, not a judge. The writer needs someone who can help him or her think through the problems. She or he needs someone who says, "Give it a try and see how it goes."

Student–Teacher Writing Conferences. If you are truly interested in helping students become more proficient writers, you have to become involved in the writing as it proceeds. One of the most effective ways to provide useful responses to student writing is to conduct one-on-one conferences. Atwell, expert middle school educator and author of two editions of *In the Middle* (1987, 1998), used to recommend that teachers meet with writers every day as they work in a writing workshop. She now realizes that most teachers simply cannot manage this. Nevertheless, teachers need to meet regularly with writers in conferences. It is usually better for the teacher to control with whom he or she confers than to open the desk to anyone who wants to come for help. An open desk often means that the same students appear repeatedly, some of whom need reassurance or attention more than writing assistance. Students who really need help may never ask for it.

The most effective conferences are those in which the students do most of the talking. Opening the conference about a piece of writing in progress with a question, such as, "How's it going?" gives the student an opportunity to talk about both writing processes and progress. Through this expression, the student comes to better understand his or her own strengths and weaknesses. Additional questions should prompt writers to reach their own conclusions and find their own solutions (see Activity 5.4). In a one-on-one conference, the teacher acts as both a sounding board and a guide without imposing unduly on the writer's ownership of the discourse. For additional suggestions, see Harris's (1986) *Teaching One-to-One* in the Recommended Readings for this chapter.

Of course, if the student asks for assistance with a particular problem, the teacher should be willing to provide it. Sometimes it is better to just spell a word for a student than to turn the question into a spelling lesson or a lesson in how to use the dictionary. If the student is truly frustrated, it may be better to give him or her a possible solution or a couple of options than to try to guide the student to an answer.

Telling you exactly what to say in a conference to make it work right is not possible. What hits the bull's-eye with one student is likely to antagonize the next. This is the time when knowing your students will prove to be invaluable. However, it is generally best to leave final decisions about the writing in the hands of the writer. Otherwise, students will begin to feel that the paper is more yours than theirs and that they are not doing much except following your instructions, whether they agree or not. However, there is nothing wrong with giving students a model, a demonstration, or an example and then helping the student adapt it to fit the discourse at hand. You are, after all, the teacher and probably the most experienced writer in the room. To withhold your wisdom does not serve students well.

Peer Response Groups Students need to do far more writing than teachers can possibly grade. Not every piece of work needs to be taken to the publishing stage, but much writing deserves the teacher's response so that students know that the teacher cares about what they think. Students do need your aid, but they also need a wider audience to respond to their writing. Furthermore, students need to respond to the writing of others, for a variety of reasons. Peer response groups meet the needs of the writer while providing opportunities for responders to learn in the process.

First, consider the value to the writer. In classrooms with a strong sense of community, peer response group members are sympathetic and supportive. Their standards are usually not as high as those of the teacher, so they are more receptive to work that is hesitant and not yet thought through. They are especially adept at determining how a written piece directed at a peer audience will be received, but they are also good at providing useful information about how some other audiences will respond. More than that, they are quite good at explaining a problem in a way that is understandable to the writer.

Receiving responses from peers can be helpful to writers, but giving those responses may be even more beneficial to the group members. Although the research is not clear on the effects, the indications are that discussions of writing and language in which students engage verbally seem to aid in learning to write (Gere & Abbott, 1985). Thus, peer response groups seem to have as much value for responders as they have for writers. Providing responses requires both careful listening and articulate speaking. Responders get ideas about other discourse to try, other topics to explore, and other techniques to attempt by hearing or reading the work of peers. In addition, responding to writing means engaging in conversations about language and communicating. Unconscious knowledge becomes conscious understanding as students struggle together to define a writing problem and find an acceptable solution. Furthermore, responding to the work of others is a confidence builder. This is an opportunity to act in a responsible way and provide assistance to a classmate.

However, these kinds of values will not be derived from peer response groups unless students are taught how to respond effectively. Criticisms such as, "That's stupid. How could you write something as awful as that?" or something equally rude do far more harm than good. Groups that collectively shrug their shoulders when a writer asks for suggestions about how to improve a paper help neither the writer nor themselves. You also need to protect yourself against having to explain a low grade to a student who exclaims, "But everybody in my group thought it was great!!!"

Students do not always provide useful information to writers. If you want peer response groups to function well, you may need to demonstrate effective response for them. If you ask questions that prompt the writer to explain and explore his or her own thinking, students will learn to do the same in response groups. If you share samples of professional writing to illustrate a concept, students will begin to do this in their groups, too. If you admit that you do not know how to fix a problem and then proceed to work through it with the student using what you know about writing, students will follow suit.

You can enhance the work of peer response groups by structuring their work, too. You can use the fishbowl technique described in chapter 3 to demonstrate effective response group strategies. You can conduct some whole-class sessions or mini-lessons wherein students are asked to respond to anonymous papers (written perhaps by former students or students in another school). Part of this discussion should focus on which comments would be most beneficial to the writer. Early in the year you can have groups focus on just the positives, but demand that they be specific. They cannot just say, "I like it." They have to pinpoint something specific they like—a word, an image, the way the piece is organized, and so on. As the year progresses, have group members state one thing they liked and ask one question. This question need not point out a weakness; it can note a strength. For example, a student may ask a writer, "What made you choose that topic?" or "How did you learn where to put the punctuation in your dialogue?" Later in the year, response group members can offer one suggestion for improvement or one thing they would have tried if they had been the writer. Another possibility is to provide response groups with checklists they must complete and share with the writer. This forces responders to focus on many different facets of the work.

Teaching students how to respond effectively to the writing of others, how to work well together, and how to be constructively critical while still being supportive begins with modeling and demonstrating. For additional information and suggestions for improving the work of response groups, the two books by Spear (1987, 1993) that are listed in the Recommended Readings for this chapter provide excellent guidance. However, you must be patient with your own learning and with peer response groups. If they do not work the way you want them to, be sure that students really do have the knowledge and skills they need to function in such groups. Responding effectively to the writing of others is not a natural talent that is just waiting to burst forth when given the opportunity. Like writing itself, learning to respond must be supported, nurtured, and assessed before the results will be satisfying.

Assessing Writing

One of the conditions of literacy learning identified by Cambourne (1988) is the need for response. Students need feedback on what they write. However, they need to know just as much about what is right as what is wrong. Whether you are responding as a reader or judging as an evaluator, you need to focus first on what the student has achieved, even if this is a small measure of progress. What do you like about this paper? What strikes you as really promising about it? Where has the student really "found the mark" in expressing an idea or creating an image? What is most impressive about the work so far? If students do not see their work through the eyes of a reader, they will have difficulty repeating effective writing techniques.

The strengths that you note in the process of responding are a part of assessment. So are the weaknesses. Assessing has to do with collecting data; evaluating has to do with making sense of the data collected during assessment. Assessing also relates to planning instruction, whereas evaluating relates to determining the effectiveness of instruction after it has taken place. Assessing needs to be a continual process that goes on every day as long as learning is supposed to be happening.

Collecting Data and Keeping Records. Observation and conference notes, informal and formal test results, interest inventories, attitude surveys, anecdotal records, rating scales, checklists, work records, journals, completed papers, self-reflections or self-assessments, portfolios, and other resources can provide useful information about students, their growth, gaps in their knowledge, performance, potential, attitudes, beliefs, and so on. Certainly there is no need to collect all of this information on every student. You will have to make some choices about the kinds of information that will be most helpful to you.

One thing that is quite clear from this list is that the ordinary grade book that generally contains only enough space to record attendance and grades is not sufficient. There are some commercially published record books that provide more flexibility. However, most language arts teachers who collect assessment data find that loose-leaf or spiral notebooks, divided by classes, with at least a page set aside for each student, work better for building a comprehensive picture. Other teachers are experimenting with a variety of computer databases for maintaining records. Once you find the data that are most helpful, you may want to create a summary form that you can duplicate and use during each grading period or for the whole year. However, you will probably want to devise some kind of record-keeping device that shows you the class at a glance. If you maintain individual records on each student on separate pages, you may not realize that an individual has slipped behind.

Processes and Products. Currently, the recommendations for assessing writing focus on obtaining information about more than the products. If learning how to begin and continue a writing task are important skills, then you need to assess writing processes, too (see Activity 5.5). This data collection often involves observing students as they write, conferring with them about their writing and keeping records of these conferences, collecting writing samples under semiformal and formal test conditions, using checklists to show progress over time, and examining collections of student writing rather than examining individual pieces, because one finished product may not be similar to the next. The problem with this approach is that the teacher must keep multiple records and eventually make sense of all of these data.

Evaluating Writing

As was pointed out in chapter 2, evaluation is the process of making sense of all the assessment data. Evaluation used to be a relatively simple, though time-consuming, business. One merely looked over the grades, averaged the numbers or totaled the points, and recorded a grade. All the teacher needed was a grade book and possibly a calculator. For most language arts educators, those days are (or should be) long gone. Frankly, that is just as well, as the final grades often told much more about who came into the class writing effectively and managed to maintain that edge than they told about who learned the most about writing better. Teachers really did not interpret the data they had nor did they look much beyond the separate grades they had already given. Evaluation should take into consideration all of the data collected during assessment, not just the quality of the finished products but the improvement in the processes and the ability to respond to writing effectively.

The problem is that much of the data collected during assessment are descriptive bits of information rather than quantitative ratings. Descriptive data cannot be assigned points nor averaged. These data have to be interpreted. The teacher must rely on professional judgment to make a holistic evaluation of the student as writer. Not surprisingly, teachers often feel reluctant to do this because they worry that their judgment will either lack objectivity or be perceived as lacking objectivity. Evaluating in this manner is especially questionable when the teacher is new to the profession, the grade level, or the school.

Although it may not relieve the tension, you need to know that evaluation of writing has always involved elements of subjectivity. If teachers relied only on objective measures, they would have to reduce writing to quantifiable aspects such as word counts, analyses of sentence structures, numbers of misspelled words, and so on. Although these may be objective measures of certain aspects of writing, they fail to assess much that is considered to be significant. Readers recognize and respond to voice (or lack thereof) in writing, but there is no way to measure it. Teachers know when a paper is well organized (or disorganized), but often these structures are so complicated that explaining them to anyone else would be nearly impossible. A teacher may be able to rate style, but that rating is still just a best guess based on knowledge of discourse. You know when a satirical piece "works" (or fails to do so), but you will be hard put to find any way of measuring satire on a continuum. Teachers want students to write creatively, but no one has yet figured out a way to determine the quality of creativity, although readers recognize it when they see it. Many beginning teachers believe that students should be rewarded for the amount of effort they put forth. But just how do you measure effort without making a subjective judgment? Like it or not, evaluation, whether of writing processes, written products, or some combination of both, demands subjective judgment, although everyone hopes that this will be subjectivity based on professional knowledge.

There are some techniques you can use to maintain a reasonable sense of proportion, though. You can use checklists as you observe. This forces you to look at all students similarly. You can use rating scales as part of your conferences. This, too, forces you to keep your personal opinions in check. You can use rubrics to assign grades to papers. You can have students complete self-ratings and write reflective papers about their learning to help you identify what you might otherwise ignore. You can assign points for completion of tasks, but you must do so thoughtfully in order to avoid assigning grades more on the basis of quantity than quality. Another useful technique is to discuss evaluation with other teachers. Such discussions tend to help everyone involved develop some consistency of judgment and reduce grading idiosyncrasies.

Coping with the Paper Load.   The general public tends to expect language arts teachers to mark every mistake on students' papers. If you do not, you may be accused of not doing your job or of being lazy. There is, however, a significant body of research that verifies that this kind of atomistic marking has little effect on improving the quality of student writing. By the same token, there is a reasonably large body of research that shows that this kind of error correction harms self-esteem and makes students dislike writing. That is not to say that you should never go through papers and mark as many mistakes as you can find. When papers are to be published or displayed outside the classroom, they should be as error-free as possible, for example. However, if you try to do this every time students write, you will quickly find yourself crushed beneath a mountain of papers. You may even decrease the amount of writing that you require just to save yourself from burn-out. *How to Handle the Paper Load* (Stanford, 1979), listed in the Recommended Readings for this chapter, has lots of good ideas, but it also has some of the research data you may want to share with anyone who criticizes you for not editing and grading every paper. Tchudi's (1997) *Alternatives to Grading Student Writing* is another outstanding resource. If nothing else, keep in mind that when you do the editing, you are the only one who is learning much from the lesson. Teachers should be learners, but they should not rob students of the opportunity to learn. If you want students to become self-reliant writers, you should not make them dependent upon you to do their editing for them.

Assigning Grades.   The more feedback you can give while writing is in progress and the more ways you can devise to ensure that papers are well done before you grade them, the easier your life will be. The better the quality, the less time grading takes. Grading written work does take time, but there are some ways to reduce the stress. If your classes are large, you may need to plan instruction so that not all classes write at the same time. Alternatively, you may need to use a variety of forms of feedback rather than always writing responses.

Not every paper that students write should be polished and then evaluated. However, you may still find it necessary to give grades on some papers. There are as many systems for assigning grades to written work as there are teachers. No system is inherently superior, although some are decidedly inferior. Grading work totally on the basis of mechanical accuracy, for example, is not an effective way to help students learn to compose better. Similarly, ignoring mechanics and grading polished pieces solely on the basis of content is unrealistic in the sense that in the real world writers are expected to use conventions with reasonable accuracy. What you will want to develop is a system that helps students both understand what constitutes good writing and improve the quality of what they produce. If students leave the class believing that composition grades depend solely on the teacher's opinion, they probably have not learned much about how to write effectively, but they have learned even less about how to assess and evaluate their own performance (unless, of course, the only basis for grading actually was teacher opinion!).

Although you want to be as objective as possible, you cannot turn yourself into a machine when you grade. There are some strategies you can use to improve the objectivity of your grading, though. Read all of the papers before marking any to get a sense of the overall quality. Do not start with papers from the same class every time, and do not alphabetize the papers before you start to grade. Watch out for your own biases (e.g., preferences for longer papers, typed papers, colorfully decorated papers, mechanically accurate papers). Remember that opinion papers and essay test responses present special challenges; it is very easy to give higher grades automatically to papers with which you agree and those that reflect your own thinking.

One way that you can make composition evaluation less personal while also teaching students something about composition quality is to use rubrics or lists of criteria (see Activity 5.6), which define or describe the aspects of writing that readers value and reflect the weight of those values. If possible, engage students in creating these grading guides so that they know the expectations and use them as yardsticks as they write and respond to writing. Students can also use these lists for self-assessment, and you can use them as the bases of conferences and instruction. Some criteria are general and apply to many discourse modes. Rubrics are usually mode-specific and provide brief descriptions of qualities that identify different levels of performance. It is even possible to develop criteria or rubrics for collections of work, such as portfolios.

One of the most significant values of criteria and rubrics is that students learn what to strive for in writing. They gain a better sense of what it means to be an author by learning what readers seek when they read. Another significant value of criteria and rubrics is that they hold teachers to some kind of standard of evaluation. With such a grading guide, a teacher is less likely to evaluate one paper on the basis of mechanics, another on the basis of content, and another on the basis of voice. We know that teachers tend to give higher grades to longer papers. With a criteria guide or a rubric, teachers may see beyond length and give credit where credit is due.

Above all, students need to know how they will be graded. As much as possible, they need to know this before they begin to write or before they begin to revise the work. Students need to know when mechanics count and when content is more important, if either is to receive more credit than the other. They need to know when clarity is more essential than creativity and when humor is acceptable. If you work with students as they write, they will develop a much better sense of the quality of their work. Grades should not come as a shocking surprise.

A FINAL COMMENT

Although this chapter focuses on teaching writing, the fact that reading and writing support one another cannot be emphasized too strongly. Furthermore, speaking and listening interact with the development of writing. Students who read more tend to write better. Learning to write well can help students improve their reading. Written work is often better if students first have an opportunity to talk about what they are planning to write or what they intend to do next in their writing. Conversing about the process of writing can build an understanding of language use and give students a chance to develop the ability to speak with clarity and confidence. A student who has struggled to write a poem has much greater empathy for what the professional poet has achieved. If students are to learn to write particular types of discourse, they need to read and discuss many examples. If students are asked to write about certain readings, they often develop greater comprehension of the material. Discussion, too, helps build comprehension. Reading, writing, speaking, and listening are all activities of constructing meaning, and each reinforces the others. Furthermore, there are many ways in which writing and viewing can be linked together. Certainly, writing is a part of the planning, creation, and development of many media. Students need to become familiar with the discourse modes which are associated with media, both by reading them and writing them. All in all, writing supports all of the other language arts processes, and the others serve to support writing. As a language arts teacher, you need to make the most of this interdependence and interrelationship by providing an integrated program at the middle school level.

RECOMMENDED READINGS

Atwell, N. (1987). *In the middle: Writing, reading and learning with adolescents.* Portsmouth, NH: Heinemann.

Atwell, N. (1998). *In the middle: New understandings about writing, reading, and learning* (2nd ed.). Portsmouth, NH: Boynton/Cook–Heinemann.

Bromley, K. (1993). *Journaling: Engagements in reading, writing, and thinking.* New York: Scholastic.

Calkins, L. (1986). *The art of teaching writing.* Portsmouth, NH: Heinemann.

Fletcher, R., & Portalupi, J. (1998). *Craft lessons: Teaching writing K–8.* York, ME: Stenhouse.

Goodrich, H. (1996/1997). Understanding rubrics. *Educational Leadership, 54* (4), 14–17.

Graves, D. (1994). *A fresh look at writing.* Portsmouth, NH: Heinemann.

Graves, D., & Sunstein, B. (Eds.) (1992). *Portfolio portraits.* Portsmouth, NH: Heinemann.

Harris, M. (1986). *Teaching one-to-one: The writing conference.* Urbana, IL: National Council of Teachers of English.

Hillocks, G. (1987). Synthesis of research on teaching writing. *Educational Leadership, 44*(8), 71–82.

Judy, S. (1981). *Explorations in the teaching of English* (2nd ed.). New York: Harper & Row.

King, L., & Stovall, D. (1992). *Classroom publishing: A practical guide to enhancing student literacy.* Hillsboro, OR: Blue Heron.

Lane, B. (1993). *After the end: Teaching and learning creative revision.* Portsmouth, NH: Heinemann.

Langer, J. (1998, Fall). Beating the odds: Critical components boost student performance. *English Update, Newsletter From the Center on English Learning and Achievement, 1,* 8.

Moffett, J. (1968). *Teaching the universe of discourse.* Boston: Houghton Mifflin.

Moffett, J. (with Tashlik, P.). (1987). *Active voices II: A writer's reader for grades 7–9.* Upper Montclair, NJ: Boynton/Cook.

Moffett, J., & Wagner, B. (1976) *Student-centered language arts and reading, K–13* (2nd ed.). Boston: Houghton Mifflin.

Purves, A., Jordan, S., & Peltz, J. (Eds.) (1997). *Using portfolios in the English classroom*. Norwood, MA: Christopher-Gordon.

Rothermel, D. (1996). *Starting points: How to set up and run a writing workshop—and much more!* Columbus, OH: National Middle School Association.

Spear, K. (1987). *Sharing writing: Peer response groups in the English class*. Portsmouth, NH: Heinemann.

Spear, K. (1993). *Peer response groups in action: Writing together in secondary schools*. Portsmouth, NH: Boynton/Cook–Heinemann.

Stanford, G. & the Committee on Classroom Practices (1979). *How to handle the paper load (Classroom practices in teaching English 1979–1980)*. Urbana, IL: National Council of Teachers of English.

Tchudi, S. (Ed.). (1997). *Alternatives to grading student writing*. Urbana, IL: National Council of Teachers of English.

Wiedmer, T. (1998). Digital portfolios: Capturing and demonstrating skills and levels of performance. *Phi Delta Kappan, 79*(8), 586–589.

Zemelman, S., & Daniels, H. (1988). *A community of writers: Teaching writing in the junior and senior high school*. Portsmouth, NH: Heinemann.

Writing Activities and Suggestions

- 5.1 Ideas for Teaching Writing Effectively
- 5.2 Writing Strategies Worth Recommending
- 5.3 Writing Assignments That Usually Work
- 5.4 Sample Conference Questions and Responses
- 5.5 Assessing Writing Processes
- 5.6 Criteria of Writing Qualities

Activity 5.1:
Ideas for Teaching Writing Effectively

1. Focus on fluency first by focusing on the familiar. Encourage students to write about what they know best.

2. When students are insecure, try some collaborative writing. Have students work in pairs. Engage the whole class in contributing ideas for a poem or short story. Have a small group create a mystery or science fiction story.

3. Pair writing tasks with concrete activities that students have enjoyed—examining real objects, visiting real places, meeting real people.

4. Use a variety of activities to "prime the pump"—films, field trips, guest speakers, role playing, debates, sports events, television specials, news articles, advice columns, music, sound effects, and so on.

5. Real world tasks are innately motivating—pieces students plan to enter in contests or submit for publication, discourse that will serve a useful purpose in the school or community, communicating with a real person (to them, teachers are not real people), or producing work that will be shared with peers (peers are real people).

6. Incorporate a variety of genres, either assigned or chosen. Most students can find some kind of writing that is satisfying if they have a chance to try several. After all, even professional authors specialize in only a few genres.

7. Allot sufficient time for doing good work and expect excellent results. At the same time, keep in mind that writing is a complex, difficult task that demands a great deal from the writer. No one can expend that much effort all the time.

8. Keep mechanics in their proper perspective. They are important, but only if the content is worthwhile. Mechanically accurate nonsensical drivel is still nonsensical drivel.

9. Vary the length of the writing tasks, but keep in mind that length can be deceiving. Some short tasks demand a great deal of thought; some long papers require far less effort.

10. Be positive, supportive, and encouraging throughout the development of the paper, but when the writer is down to the polishing stage, wear the editor's hat. Expect some errors. Help students see error patterns.

11. Teach students to provide effective feedback to peers and to use this knowledge to become independent evaluators of their own work.
12. Students need honest feedback. If you do not do your best to judge their performance, they will never learn how to assess their own work critically.

Activity 5.2:
Writing Strategies Worth Recommending

Prewriting

1. *Listing.* Make a list of ideas as they occur and then select from among them. Continue adding to the list.
2. *Visually representing* (clustering, webbing, mapping semantically, organizing graphically, and creating idea wheels).

Start with a topic written in the middle of the paper and surrounded by a circle. Out from that draw lines and add whatever other ideas occur. These are also usually circled, and additional lines are drawn out to additional ideas. The visual is done when the writer identifies a topic that he or she wishes to pursue further.

Create a visual that reflects the structure of the discourse being attempted. For example, when the topic follows a chronological sequence or involves a process, try sketching the topic as a flowchart in order to ensure that all parts of the process have been included.

3. *Questioning* (heuristics). Writer asks pertinent questions:
   * What do I want to write about?
   * What do I know?
   * Who should I write about?
   * What purpose will this writing serve?
   * Who is going to read this piece?

K-W-L (Ogle, 1986) is a formal strategy often used to guide a research project:
   Ask, What do I *know* about this topic?
   Then ask, What do I *want* to know about this topic?
   Then, How can I *learn* about this topic?
   At the end of the researching/writing, the individual should be able to answer
   What have I learned about this topic?

Another formal heuristic strategy is known as AAASP:
  Action: What is happening?
  Agent: Who is doing it?
  Agency: How is it being done?
  Scene: Where and when?
  Purpose: Why?

Another is HDWDWW:
  How Does Who Do What and Why?

And then there is the common journalistic strategy known as 5 Ws and 1 H:
  Who? What? When? Where? Why? How?

4. *Writing* (writing to discover a topic).
   • *Free writing*: The writer writes about absolutely anything that comes to mind without pausing to contemplate. He or she continues writing for as long as possible, even if he or she changes the subject or has to write meaningless material (e.g., "I can't think of anything to write").
   • *Timed writing*: This is writing for a specified period of time, usually 5–10 min. The topic may be writer-selected or prompted by the teacher or by students. Writer continues writing for the allotted time, but must stick to the topic given initially although he or she may move further and further from it.
   • *Looping*: The writer freewrites for specified period of time, rereads what he has written, and selects a key word or phrase that sounds interesting. This key word or phrase becomes the focus of the next writing segment. The cycle or loop continues until the writer feels confident that he or she has a topic worth developing.

5. *Creative thinking* (strategies to use when topic is assigned or already selected—most of these strategies do not produce written material that can actually be used in the discourse itself).
   Cubing helps writer create a focus on a topic.
     The writer looks at the topic from six sides (the number of sides in a cube) in order to consider which perspective may be most advantageous or what additional ideas may be worth considering.

Using the selected topic, the writer
   A) describes it
   B) compares it

C) associates it
D) analyzes it
E) applies it
F) argues for or against

SCAMPER helps generate a wide variety of thoughts. Also useful as a revision strategy.

Substitute:	What could you substitute for this topic?
	What might you do instead?
	What would do as well or better?
Combine:	What could you combine?
	What might work well together?
	What could be brought together?
Adapt:	What could be adjusted to suit a purpose or condition?
	How could you make it fit?
Modify:	What could happen if you changed form or quality?
Magnify:	Could you make it larger, heavier, or slower?
Minify:	Could you make it smaller, lighter, or faster?
Put to other uses:	How could you use it for a different purpose?
	What does it suggest?
Eliminate:	What could you subtract or take away?
	What could you do without?
Reverse:	What would you have if you reversed it or turned it around?
Rearrange:	Could you change the parts, order, layout, or sequence?

Synectics: The writer creates the following four kinds of analogies for his or her topic:

A. Personal analogy (If you were the topic, who would you be? What would you think and feel?)
B. Direct analogy (Compare your topic to something you can kick.)
C. Symbolic analogy (Compare your topic to an abstract principle—i.e., something you cannot kick.)
D. Fantasy analogy (Make up a fantasy about your topic.)

6. *Assisted prewriting.* (Requires aid of others.)
   - Cooperative brainstorming in which all ideas are accepted equally and all ideas can be used as springboards to other possibilities.
   - Class discussions and debates.
   - Listening to and/or interacting with a guest speaker.
   - Creating a class composition to which each person can contribute. For example, if students have been studying inventors, the class can create an acrostic poem about an inventor, to which each person contributes one appropriate descriptor.

7. *Experiential strategies* (using personal experiences as the basis for writing).
   A. Viewing—films, videotapes, photographs, diagrams, charts, cartoons, television, real objects.
   B. Creating—drawing, painting, constructing an object.
   C. Participating—creative dramatics, role playing, simulations, games.
   D. Observing—field trips, museum visits, walking tours.
   E. Collecting data—surveys, questionnaires, interviews, field notes.

8. *Personal record keeping*
   - Journals in which they write frequently.
   - Writer's notebooks or portfolios of interesting quotes, settings, incidents, and whatever else seems memorable.
   - List of possible writing topics.
   - Word banks of words associated with mystery stories or lists of special words, such as onomatopoeic words.

9. *Reading.* Extensive reading builds both content knowledge and understanding of discourse structure.

10. *Teacher modeling.* Teacher shares an example of the discourse to be produced—an oral reading of a similar piece or an example written by the teacher. Teacher shares some of his or her personal prewriting strategies and encourages students to share theirs.

11. *Changing genre.* (Use their writing as prewriting.) For example, they change a play they have written into a short story or create a personal opinion essay from a previously written bumper sticker.

Drafting

1. If you usually write in longhand, use a typewriter, word processor, or computer.
2. Use a tape recorder to capture ideas or to practice content before writing it.
3. Use a different writing implement or different kind of paper.
4. Double space on the page so you can make additions and changes later.
5. Start writing in the middle of the piece of discourse. Add the introduction later.
6. Jot notes about ideas in the left margin at approximate locations on the page.
7. Number sentences or paragraphs so they can be renumbered if necessary. Arrows can be used to show rearrangements, too.
8. If you cannot think of a word or phrase, then draw a blank space and go on.
9. Write the conclusion first. Then go back and write the rest.
10. Begin writing with the assumption that you will write at least one more copy of the paper.
11. Reread frequently what has been written. (Good for teacher modeling, too.)
12. If you encounter a block, take a break from the writing or return to prewriting. Talk over what you have so far with someone else. Listeners should try to predict what they can expect to find in the rest of the paper.
13. Reexamine audience and purpose frequently during drafting. If your concept of either changes as you write, you will need to revise later for consistency.
14. Consider shifting genre or point of view if the drafting becomes difficult.
15. Expect to discover something about the topic that you did not realize when you began (i.e., insight, new perspective, different opinion, etc.). This may require redrafting.
16. Start the paper over. Keep what you like and get rid of the rest.
17. Identify some key terms that you want to reemphasize throughout the paper. Highlight or circle them.
18. If your best idea appears late in the drafting, write it out. You can reposition it during revision.
19. If the paper involves chronological order (i.e., steps in a process or narration), use numbers and write the material first in the form of a list or create a sketch or a flowchart.
20. Jot notes in the margins or elsewhere about parts you want to revise, edit, or check later, but do not spend time on making

those changes during drafting unless it may influence the direction of the rest of the writing.

Revising

Adapted from *Discovery to Discourse: The Composing Process* by B. Kirschner & J. Yates, 1983, New York: Macmillan. Copyright 1983 by Macmillan. Adapted with permission.

1. Get some assistance. Talk to someone about the paper. Listen to their questions. Note which part of the paper attracted the most attention. Have someone read the paper to you. Note any points where the person had to reread. Ask someone to read the paper and identify the best part or parts. Have someone read the paper and point out anything that is confusing.

2. Experiment. Change the thesis. Add an opening statement about what the paper is about, who it is meant for, and what the purpose of the paper is. Read each paragraph, matching it to this opening statement. Does everything belong? Summarize the conclusion. Read each paragraph, matching it to the conclusion. Does everything belong? Summarize each paragraph on Post-It notes. Rearrange the order of the notes until a clear sequence emerges. Choose the part you like best. Revise the rest of the paper to focus on this point.

3. Reflect. Read the paper aloud. How does it sound? Does it seem to flow from one idea to the next? Ask yourself questions about the paper as if you were the teacher: What does this mean? Why is this important? How do you know this is true? Why did you start here? Does this really fit? Look for similar words and phrases. Should these ideas be joined rather than separated? Write a cover sheet for the paper explaining what you were trying to do. Check to see if you have achieved your goal. Find the spot where you became interested in your idea. Would this be a better place to start the paper?

4. Visualize. If you drew a diagram of the paper, what would it look like? Is it out of balance anywhere? Tape-record the paper and then listen to it with your eyes closed. What other details can you add? Imagine a reader who has an opposing viewpoint. What can you add or change to help this reader see your perspective? Write a description of the intended audience. Does everything in the paper match this person?

5. Make changes. Expect to make many changes. Add vivid details, examples, illustrations, memories, and experiences. Alter the structure or shift to another discourse mode. Try using a flash-

back or dialogue. Substitute an incident as an introduction. Try a different prewriting strategy to generate more ideas. Add transitions. Remove paragraphs that do not serve a purpose.

6. Recheck focus and purpose. Highlight the key words in the thesis statement. Does everything in the paper fit? Use different colored markers to indicate the mood of the paper. Is there a pattern? Have someone read the first 20 words and then ask them to predict what he or she thinks the rest of the paper will contain. Would you read on if you did not have to? Write the word that best describes how you felt when you wrote the paper. Is this emotion reflected in the paper? Is it what you want the reader to feel? Have you repeated some key words in the paper? Should you do this? Does the title of the paper prepare the reader for what is to come, or does it create curiosity? Is there anything too lengthy, irrelevant, or vague that could be replaced? Is there anything in the paper that is there just because you find it interesting?

7. Recheck for organization. Circle the part of the paper that you think is the most important. How will the reader know that it is primary? If the paper were a painting, would this idea stand out? Reread the introduction. Does this point to any organization of ideas? If so, have you followed this sequence? In a phrase or sentence, summarize the intent of each paragraph. Does each have a clear reason for being in the paper? Does the paper follow any identifiable discourse form? Have you included all of the necessary parts? Reread the last sentence in each paragraph and the first in the following paragraph. Does one idea lead into the next or is there an abrupt shift? Highlight words that show how one idea relates to another. Have you used enough of these or too few? Do you need to add more transitions? Is the tense consistent? Can the reader always be sure of who is speaking in dialogue?

8. Recheck for development. Use two different markers to highlight general statements and concrete details. Which one predominates? What concrete details could you add? Is there any place in the paper where you could show instead of tell? Have you used sensory details? Have someone read the paper and then tell you what they recall. Missing or forgotten parts probably need to be more vivid. Consider using dialogue in the paper. Would facts and figures or quotes from experts add support? Can the reader tell how you know what you have said? Would the ideas be more clear if you added a comparison? Do the ideas fall into categories or classifications? Are these obvious? Are they balanced?

Editing/Proofreading

Suggestions for students adapted from *Discovery to Discourse: The Composing Process* by B. Kirschner & J. Yates, 1988, New York: Macmillan. Copyright 1988 by Macmillan. Adapted with permission.

1. Create a checklist of common problems. Use it as a guide for reviewing your work.

2. Ask someone who is a good editor or proofreader to help you find mistakes. Do not take this person's word unless you agree with him or her.

3. Type or rewrite the paper.

4. Consult a dictionary or handbook.

5. Read the paper aloud.

6. Underline, circle, or use an asterisk to mark anything you need to check before making a final draft.

7. To check spelling, read the paper from the end to the beginning. Point at each word with a pen or pencil.

8. To check capitalization, trace over each with a marker. Be sure you know why each is a capital.

9. To check grammar and syntax, write each sentence in a list form, one underneath the next, or draw heavy slash marks at the end of each sentence. Be sure that each sentence is complete and ends with the proper punctuation. Be sure subjects and verbs agree in each. Rewrite any awkward sentence on separate paper and rephrase until it is smooth. Restate passive sentences to active form. If any sentences contain lists, check for parallel structure.

10. To check usage, circle or highlight pronouns. Do they agree with their antecedents in number? Point to each use of the word *of*. Should any be changed to *have*?

11. To check apostrophes, circle each with red ink. Be sure the apostrophe is needed. Look for all words ending in *s*. Do any show possession? Double check *its* and *it's*.

12. To check other punctuation, use a handbook summary to review. Look for key structures, such as subordinate and coordinate conjunctions, that often require punctuation. Be sure punctuation pairs (i.e., quotation marks and parentheses) are complete.

13. To check style, read the paper aloud. Does it sound like you when you are speaking well? Have you used the most appropriate words? Is the material too wordy? Have you needlessly repeated any words?

Publishing

Preparation of discourse for publication may simply be a matter of creating a legible, tidy copy to read aloud or share with classmates. However, it can also be an elaborate production involving choices of graphics, fonts, layout of text, and so on. Students need to confront a wide variety of challenges associated with publication. The following is a representative list of ways in which students' work can be published.

In school

- bulletin board displays
- class collections for the classroom library
- bound books for school library
- computer disk storage
- cross-grade sharing, verbally and in print
- read work aloud to the class
- read work aloud to a small group
- read work aloud to school as part of daily announcements
- share informally with friends
- print in a school literary magazine
- print in a school newspaper
- print in school yearbook
- include in P.T.A. flyers to be sent home
- include in mailings to parents
- include as part of parent night presentations
- tape-record and add to a listening center
- videotape presentations and add to school library collection
- post in a hallway display case
- create a mobile for displaying student work

Home-related

- share with family
- share with pen pal
- display in the home
- add to home library

Community-related

- send letters to intended audience
- display work in public library or local businesses
- compile booklets for sale at local events
- print in local newspaper
- establish a writer's club for all interested persons
- host a special event for local writers such as a barbecue or picnic
- share with shut-ins, such as those in hospitals and nursing homes

Real-world writing

- college entrance essays
- job application letters
- letters of praise or complaint to companies
- letters to newspaper editor
- church bulletins
- letters to pen pals
- community projects: walking tours, brochures, ads for places or events
- Internet website

Professional publications and competitions

- local newspaper
- *Merlyn's Pen* magazine
- scholastic magazines
- National Council of Teachers of English achievement awards
- Young Author's Conference
- local writing contests
- teacher-written article including student samples

Activity 5.3:
Writing Assignments
That Usually Work

1 **Round-Robin Writing**. To do this, students have to be in groups of five. Each person begins a story by describing a setting. He or she has about 5 minutes to think of a setting and describe it on the paper. When the time is up, each person has to pass his or her paper one person to the right. The next person reads the setting and then describes a main character that fits the setting. Again, each person has about 5 minutes to write. When the time is up, he or she passes the paper one to the right. The next person has to come up with a conflict or a problem that has to be solved. In other words, this person is responsible for creating the antagonist. Again there is time for brief writing before the paper has to be passed. The next person writes a brief rising action section. Basically, he or she has to tell what happens and build the suspense. Then that person passes the paper again. The next person has to add to the rising action and bring the story to the climax point. Then the paper is ready to be returned to the person who started it. That person is responsible for figuring out a suitable ending. The stories often turn out to be more humorous than good, but students write and read and usually enjoy sharing the results. Besides, they learn something about plot structure in the process.

2. **Questions and Answers**. For this one, students have to be in pairs. Each person begins by writing a question. That is the only requirement. As soon as both questions are written, the partners trade papers. Each is to answer the question that has been written as best he or she can, but the writer has to conclude with a new question related to the text that has been written. Partners trade again and continue the process. The trading can go on for several exchanges, as long as the interest holds out.

3. **Story Enders**. Rather than giving students story starters, give them enders. You can even use real lines from short stories (O. Henry and Ambrose Bierce are good sources. The last lines of "The Most Dangerous Game" and "All Summer in a Day" work well if students have not read the stories). Students then have to create the story that leads up to this ending line.

4. **Interactive Stories**. Students can write story starters that are then made available to other students via computer. These students continue the story up to another cliff-hanger point. Then the story is made available to others again. These can continue like soap operas all year long.

5. **Letters to the Editor**. If something is happening in the community that upsets students, let them know they have an outlet for their opinions. They, too, can write letters to the editor of the local newspaper.

6. **Children's Books**. One activity that middle school students find truly engaging is creating books for younger children. It is a good way for them to reexplore some familiar territory without making them feel childish. Good children's books are very difficult and time-consuming to create. You can even develop a unit that focuses on a single author or illustrator (Van Allsburg, Dr. Seuss, and Bunting work well). It may take several weeks for students to produce really good books. If possible, work out a way that they can physically share the books with their intended audience.

7. **Classroom Collections**. These can be mystery stories, poems, or reports on a single topic, but the idea is that each person contributes to the collection. These should be nicely bound so that they can become part of a classroom library.

8. **Alphabet Story Challenge**. This is a very artificial task, so it is probably not a good idea to grade it, but students who like puzzles enjoy this one. The idea is that they have to create a story that has 26 sentences. The first sentence begins with a word that starts with the letter A. Each of the succeeding sentences must begin with the next letter of the alphabet. The story has to have a plot (not 26 people whose names begin with all the letters attending a party, for example). To make the task a bit easier, give students credit if they get all the letters except X and Z. The stories will not be the best in the world, but students will be challenged to use some sentence structures that they do not ordinarily use.

9. **Follow the Leader**. Choose a writer who has a very distinctive style that students will be able to describe. The idea is that they have to use that style to create a new ending for a story, an additional stanza for a poem, another scene for a play, and so on. One interesting way to do this is to find some literature that has a gap in it. Readers have to infer what went on. Students can be asked to write the part that is missing.

10. **The (Potato) Eyes Have It**. This requires some advance preparation on your part. You need a sack of potatoes, enough that you will have one spud for each student. Then, using a marker,

place a small X on one side of each potato. Give each student a potato. They may turn the potato any way they wish, but X always marks the front. The next part of the task is to have each student write a description of the potato. This description is to be so detailed that they could find their potato again even if you put it back in the sack with all the rest. However, they are not to describe the X. When students are done, have them carefully put their potatoes on a large table with the X facing outward. Collect the papers. Shuffle them and redistribute so that no one gets his or her own paper. Each student is to read the description and then locate the potato. When they find the one they are sure is right, they may take it to their seat. Of course, if others tell them they have the wrong potato, they have to return it to the table. This is a terrific exercise in descriptive writing, but it is noisy and chaotic, so be prepared.

11. **Research Pool**. If you run short of time for writing a research paper or if the library is not equipped to handle many students collecting information on different topics, one possibility is to let students select a topic in which most are interested (a few will prefer to go their own way, though) and let them pool their research. A few students can investigate newspaper sources, a few others can check the usual reference books, a few more can investigate specific books on the topic, others can look for sources in audiovisuals or on the computer, for example. Some students can even conduct surveys or interview people. After everyone has collected some data, have a sharing day in which everyone reports what he or she has found. Everybody else takes notes. It is helpful if students can provide bibliographies along with their reports and some printed notes, too. After the sharing is done, each student writes his or her research paper. One of the most interesting outcomes of this approach is that students discover that vastly different products will come out of the same data collection. This gives them some insight into why historians, for example, can look at the same set of facts and reach contradictory conclusions.

12. **Open Journal Testing**. Have students make journal entries as they read material for a unit of literary study. Each entry should contain a summary of the contents, a personal response to the material, and three questions about it. Use student questions to kick off class or small group discussion. At the end of the unit, divide the test into two parts. The first part should be literal recall, including several questions about the who, what, where, when, why, and how of several of the selections. These should be objective questions (i.e., multiple choice, matching, fill-in-the-blanks, and true–false). Once students finish this

part, they turn in their papers and pick up the second part of the test. For this part they may use their journal entries. These questions should be more challenging (short answer or essay). They should ask students to compare and contrast or do more in-depth analysis. Students should have encountered similar questions during class discussion, but on the test they should use different selections than the ones discussed, so that they are not just parroting what was said before. Knowing they can use their journals during the test makes the journal work worthwhile. Students will write a lot, but you will not have to grade a page of it.

Activity 5.4:
Sample Conference Questions and Responses

Openers

- Before I read the paper, can you tell me what you were trying to do in it?
- Tell me about your piece of writing. What do you need help with?
- If I find something that bothers me or that I know is wrong, do you want me to mark it or should I just read it all and tell you what I think?
- Is this still a rough draft, or is it a finished paper? How do you know?
- Would you like a general response, or do you want some specific help?
- Why do you want me to read your paper at this particular time?

Responses and Discussion Starters

- What part do you like best? Why?
- Can you tell me more about this?
- Why did you choose this subject to write about?
- What surprised you when you wrote this paper?
- Why is this important to you?
- What kinds of changes have you made from your last draft?
- How does this draft sound when you read it aloud?
- Underline the part that tells what the draft is about.
- Circle the part that is most exciting.
- What is the most important thing you are trying to say?
- What problems do you have or are you having?
- This is what I liked about it.
- Explain to me how your title fits your paper.
- What do *you* think of what you wrote?
- What do you like best about your paper?
- Is there anything about the paper that bothers you? Why?
- Do you really like this paper? Why or why not?

Pinpointing Possible Problems

- Do you have more than one story or paper in this piece?
- I'm not sure I understand this part.
- Do you have enough information? Too much?
- How did you feel when this happened? Did you write about feelings?
- Are you happy with the beginning and ending?
- What are your action words? Can you add others?
- Did you tell us about something or did you show us by using examples?
- Can you think of a different way to say this? Should you change it?
- Does the beginning grab the reader's attention?

Follow-ups and Closure

- Do you plan to do more with this? If so, what do you intend to do next?
- How does this piece compare with others you have written? Why?
- What do you think you can do to make this piece better?
- What works so well that you'd like to develop it further?

Activity 5.5:
Assessing Writing Processes

As you observe and confer with students about their writing, you may want to make notes about improvements in writing processes. The following items can be used to create a criteria list or checklist that can guide your collection of data. Other items can easily be substituted or added.

Purpose

- The writer clearly states a purpose for each paper.
- The student asks others about the purpose of their writing.
- The writer identifies parts in which the purpose is clear.
- The writer acknowledges that the purpose of a paper is unclear.
- The writer chooses an appropriate purpose.
- The writer is more concerned with communication than grades.

Audience

- The writer identifies an audience for each paper.
- The student asks other writers about their intended audience.
- The writer identifies parts that effectively address audience needs.
- The writer notes segments that fail to address an audience well.
- The writer matches aspects of the piece with the intended audience.
- The writer focuses on making the writing reader-friendly.

Goal Setting

- The writer knows what he or she wants to achieve.
- The writer can focus selectively on various parts of the task.
- The writer adjusts the task to fit the time available.
- The writer chooses an environment that supports his or her writing.
- The writer uses other discourse as a model.
- The writer asks specific questions.
- The writer selects tasks that challenge his or her skills.

Prewriting

- The writer uses a variety of strategies to begin writing.
- The writer returns to prewriting whenever necessary.
- The writer chooses strategies according to the discourse mode.
- The writer maintains a list of possible topics.
- The writer uses many sources to stimulate writing.
- The writer shares prewriting strategies with other students.
- The student recommends that other writers engage in prewriting.

Drafting

- The writer focuses on producing text during drafting.
- The writer expects to write more than one draft of most papers.
- The writer uses a variety of strategies to get words on paper.
- The writer does not necessarily begin with an introduction.
- The student recognizes that others' rough drafts are incomplete.
- The student recommends that others continue drafting when needed.

Revising

- The writer uses a variety of revising strategies.
- The writer experiments with content—mode, organization, development.
- The writer shares his or her rough drafts with others.
- The student volunteers to assist others in revising their work.
- The writer makes good use of suggestions and recommendations.
- The writer asks questions about why as well as how to revise.
- The writer can identify strengths and weaknesses in his or her content.
- The student can describe strengths and weaknesses in others' writing.
- The writer makes substantive changes.

Editing

- The writer uses a variety of strategies to edit work successfully.
- The writer edits independently before seeking assistance from others.
- The writer shares his or her rough drafts with others for editing.
- The writer makes good use of suggestions and corrections.

- The writer asks questions about why as well as how to edit.
- The writer maintains and uses a personal checklist of common errors.
- The student can identify problems and mistakes in others' writing.
- The student can explain how to correct problems and errors.

Publishing

- The writer considers the appearance of the finished piece.
- The writer strives to produce work that has few, if any, errors.
- The writer willingly shares finished work with an audience.
- The writer seeks opportunities to make his or her work available to others.
- The student suggests publication options to other writers.

Self-Reflection

- The writer accurately assesses the quality of his or her writing processes.
- The writer evaluates the quality of his or her written work fairly.
- The writer is aware of his or her own strengths and weaknesses.
- The writer can set goals for self-improvement.

Disposition

- The writer sees him- or herself as a capable writer.
- The writer values writing.
- The writer willingly engages in writing.
- The writer sees writing as a complex but manageable activity.
- The writer sets high standards for his or her own work.
- The writer understands that better writing requires effort and thought.

Activity 5.6:
Criteria Of Writing Qualities

Adapted from *New Connections: An Integrated Approach to Literacy* by Kathy Pike, Rita Compain, and Jean Mumper. Copyright 1997 by permission of Addison Wesley Educational Publishers, Inc. Prprinted with permission.

The following general items can be used for assessing or evaluating the quality of many different written products. The list can also be used as the basis for devising rubrics that match the specific qualities of a particular mode.

Meaning (content)

- Does the writing fulfill the assignment requirements?
- Does the writing communicate something of value or interest?
- Is the topic choice appropriate for the purpose?
- Is content appropriate for the intended audience?

Authorship (quality of information)

- Is the information accurate?
- Is the information documented appropriately?
- Are the distinctions between the author's ideas and those of others clear?
- Is the writer well informed about the topic?

Organization

- Has the writer used a recognizable system of organization?
- Has the writer used sufficient transitions?
- Is the attention to parts of the topic balanced?
- Is the material coherent and unified?

Clarity

- Are all of the ideas expressed clearly?
- Are speakers in dialogue identifiable?
- Have all ideas been sufficiently developed?

Format

- Has the writer selected the proper format for the mode?
- Has the writer followed the format throughout the writing?
- Does the work have a pleasing appearance?

Voice

- Does the writing show a personal touch?
- Does the writing sound as if the writer is speaking?
- When necessary, is the voice objective?

Conventions (use of correct mechanics)

- Is the work free from common mistakes?
- Is the work legible?
- Does the work reflect concern for reader needs?

Teaching Speaking and Performing

Overview

- Final Comments About Speaking and Performing
- Recommended Readings
- Speaking and Performing Activities and Suggestions

CONSIDER THESE QUESTIONS ABOUT SPEAKING AND PERFORMING

1. Why do people speak? What purposes can speech serve? Is there a difference between talking and speaking?
2. What should the goals of an oral curriculum be?
3. What are the speaking skills that students can learn through participating in small group work? What other speaking skills do they need to learn?
4. Can talking and performing help students be better readers and writers? Can talk help some students have a more positive attitude toward school?
5. How can teachers encourage all students to participate in discussions?
6. What speech and theater experiences are appropriate at the middle school level? What preparation do students need before they attempt to perform?
7. What are some of the forms of creative dramatics that can be used in the classroom? What purposes can these serve?
8. What can be done if a student is reluctant to speak?
9. How can speaking and performing be assessed and evaluated?
10. What are some speaking and performing activities that work well at the middle level?

ABOUT SPEAKING AND PERFORMING

Most middle level students are very talkative. They usually enjoy small group work and projects that permit them to interact orally with others. However, faced with the task of presenting an oral report to the class, many develop stomachaches, giggles, and similar maladies associated with embarrassment or even terror.

Adults tend to agree that public speaking is tortuous. Nevertheless, speaking before an audience is part of the real world—in business, community activities, committee meetings, courtrooms, religious gatherings, social affairs, as well as others. People never know these days when someone will confront them with a microphone and request their comments—on the street, at the mall, before a sporting event, in the neighborhood, during a political demonstration, or after an accident, even though they may just be passersby.

Students need to develop their ability to communicate orally with people they know, but they must also learn to speak effectively in a variety of other situations, both planned and impromptu.

PURPOSES ORAL LANGUAGE SERVES

After conducting extensive research on the functions of language, Halliday (1975) identified seven purposes that speaking serves. These are shown in Fig. 6.1.

However, other sources indicate that spoken language can be categorized somewhat differently. The following list of the types of language and their purposes is modified from material contained in *The Essential Guide to Speaking & Listening* (Fidge, 1992):

1. **Personal** language—express personal feelings, opinions, views, concerns, beliefs, and ideas.

Halliday's Model of Language Functions

1. "Gimme!" *the instrumental model* Language is used as a tool to get something of direct benefit to the speaker.
2. "Stop that!" *the regulatory model* Language is used to control another's behavior but not for the direct benefit of the speaker.
3. "What's that?" *the heuristic model* Language is used to find things out: to ask questions, assess answers, and form new questions.
4. "How are you feeling?" *the interactional model* Language is used to build a "weness" between speaker and listener.
5. "I'm scared." *the personal model* Language is used to explore and communicate the speaker's feeling and his or her point of view.
6. "Knock, knock, who's there?" *the imaginative model* Language is used purely for the fun of it, for the "feel" of sounds and for the fun of combining words and ideas, or repeating old ones to amuse or entertain.
7. "It's snowing!" *the representative model* Language is used to represent reality and convey information to others.

From *Language Arts Learning Processes and Teaching Practices* (p. 26), by C. Temple & J. Gillet, 1984, Boston: Little, Brown. *After M. Halliday's Explorations in the Functions of Language*, 1975, London: Edward Arnold. Copyright 1984 by C. Temple and J. Gillet. Reprinted from permission of Addison Wesley Educational Publishers, Inc.

FIG. 6.1

2. **Descriptive** language—describe someone or something, real or imagined, existing in the present or recalled from the past.
3. **Narrative** language—create and tell stories or chronologically sequenced events.
4. **Instructive** language—give instructions or provide directions designed to produce an outcome.
5. **Questioning** language—ask questions in order to obtain information.
6. **Comparative** language—compare two or more objects, people, ideas, or opinions in order to make judgments about them.
7. **Imaginative** language—create and express mental images of people, places, events, and objects.
8. **Predictive** language—predict the possible future.
9. **Interpretative** language—explore meanings, speculate, create hypothetical deductions, and consider inferences.
10. **Persuasive** language—change others' opinions, attitudes, or points of view, or influence the behavior of others in some way.
11. **Explanatory** language—explain, clarify, and support ideas and opinions.
12. **Informative** language—share information with others

In contrast, Barnes (1993), noted expert in speech research, proposed that classroom conversation can be divided into two categories: exploratory talk and presentational talk. Exploratory talk is any use of oral language through which the speaker creates and considers what he or she knows about a topic. As the label implies, exploratory talk is tentative and speculative. It is the kind of conversation in which people engage in order to better understand what they know and to learn from others. Presentational talk, on the other hand, is use of oral language to express what the speaker already knows about a topic. Presentational talk is generally more definite and conclusive. The learning has already taken place; now the information is being related to others. In general, exploratory talk must come before presentational talk; one has to understand a topic before one can state it to others. Barnes said that much learning occurs as students engage in exploratory talk. He argued very persuasively for providing far more opportunities for students to engage in exploratory talk than is commonly the case in classrooms.

Despite the range of possibilities offered by the existing categories and purposes of oral language, which seems to exist, and despite the fact that talking about information and concepts seems to enhance learning, students spend the majority of their time in school listening (Goodlad, 1984). When they do speak, they are usually answering questions. What is more, student responses are generally expected to be presentational rather than exploratory. Teachers tend to ask questions that have a single correct answer; students who answer tentatively, as if they are not sure of their response, may not be rewarded for their exploratory thought. Rewards go to those who already "know" the answers and can state them clearly.

SOME VALUES OF ACADEMIC CONVERSATION

If students are to become proficient speakers, they need opportunities to practice using many categories of oral language in order to achieve a variety of purposes. If you want students to ponder ideas, revise their own thinking, and gain depth of understanding, you need to engage them in exploratory talk—real-world oral experiences (i.e., conversations about books, writing, and educational topics of interest).

One reason for encouraging oral language use in the classroom is related to vocabulary development. People are known to have different though overlapping vocabularies (Lundsteen, 1979). People understand some words when they hear them, but they do not speak them, recognize them in print, or write them. Other people know some words well enough to use in their writing, but they hesitate to use them when they speak. These may be somewhat technical words that sound too pompous or words that are difficult to pronounce. Others are likely to be words that a person cannot use correctly with confidence.

Terms associated with subject areas may fall into this latter category. Students in math class talk easily about adding, subtracting, finding the square root, calculating the tangent and using formulas to find area and circumference. But students in language arts classes often feel as if they will sound too scholarly if they use terms such as *phrase* or *gerund* or even *character development*. They do not seem to mind sounding like a math teacher, but they do not want to sound like an English teacher. Avoiding the use of appropriate terms may also indicate that students are not sure that they understand the concepts. Through verbal participation, encouragement, and expectation, students come to use the terms much more readily and naturally. With use comes understanding. The more times they attempt to use the terms and hear others use them in appropriate and natural contexts, the better their grasp of the concept, which leads to greater confidence. Talking about reading and writing, as well as about speaking, listening, and viewing, gives students the chance to integrate technical vocabulary into their natural speech and to enhance their understanding of concepts.

It has often been said that a person does not truly learn until he or she has taught someone else. There are, of course, many ways to teach, but speaking is one of the most frequently used media. Students who have the opportunity to speak and listen to classmates learn more than they could if they listened only to the teacher. By explaining what they know, they better understand their own knowledge. By listening to others, they learn from them. Through a give-and-take of questions and responses, both speakers and listeners develop clearer understandings (Paratore & McCormack, 1997). If, as the research indicates, direct engagement with the subject matter produces knowledge, then there is every reason to believe that students will learn more if they talk about the subject matter.

Cooperative learning and workshop environments encourage students to use a wider range of oral discourse than is usually the case in teacher-dominated classrooms. However, many teachers are reluctant to use small group work in the classroom because they worry that students will waste too much time. The question that has to be asked, however, is How much time do students waste during other types of instruction? From personal experience, we all know that even if we appear to be listening, we often are not. Some younger students are better at this deception than are others, but what you assume to be on-task silence may just as easily be daydreaming or mental absence. It may be that 5 minutes of oral participation in a small group is more productive than one hour of listening to a teacher explain the same concept.

In a class of 25 students that meets for 50 minutes, each student could only speak for 2 minutes (or 10 minutes a week) if the teacher divided the time evenly and never said anything. In most whole-class discussions, only a small percentage of students participate orally on a regular basis. These are often the students who are the most confident about their speaking ability and their knowledge of the subject matter. Of course, there are strategies teachers can use to avoid inequalities, but many teachers do not use them. Research (e.g., Cazden, 1988; Sadker & Sadker, 1994) shows that teachers are often unaware of how many students do not participate, the imbalance of gender of participants, and the differences in their responses that may be affecting who speaks.

Because of concerns about how peers will react, middle level students may be reticent to contribute orally. Indeed, many middle school teachers are delighted when even one person is willing to volunteer a response. Remaining silent in a large group is relatively easy; remaining mute in a small group is more difficult. In a large group one can remain anonymous and hidden; in a small group neither is possible. If speaking is important to learning and if students learn more when they orally engage in discussion, then you need to use methods that permit and encourage more students to speak in class. Cooperative learning and workshop settings meet this need rather easily. In whole-class situations, you must work harder to make this happen.

IS TALKING ENOUGH?

However, there are reasons to question whether informal conversation, even when it focuses on academics, is sufficient. Allowing and encouraging student talk is certainly better than demanding that students remain silent during most of the school day, but there is sufficient cause to wonder whether practice is enough. Your own experience may even be proof that it is not; although you may speak with assurance when you are among friends, you may find yourself tongue-tied before an audience. Student writing will improve more if some instruction is provided than it will if students simply write more. Increasing the amount of writing is helpful, but through carefully designed writing tasks that receive appropriate and useful feedback, students can make greater gains in writing performance. Assuming that speaking and writing are somewhat similar processes, is it not likely that some formal speaking instruction will be beneficial? Unfortunately, we do not have a definitive answer, particularly at the middle level, but the question hangs heavy.

There is another reason to question whether opening the classroom to student talk is sufficient. Different kinds of speaking situations require different kinds of preparation. At times, impromptu speech is quite appropriate and acceptable to an audience. At other times, extensive planning and rehearsal are required. Factors such as the purpose of the speaking activity, the complexity of the subject matter, and the size and knowledge base of the audience determine the amount of preparation necessary. Simply encouraging students to interact orally on an informal basis with you and their classmates will probably not be enough to prepare them adequately to meet the challenges of more formal speaking and dramatic situations.

THINKING OF SPEAKING AND PERFORMING AS A CONTINUUM

One way to conceptualize speech activities is to think of speaking situations as lying on a continuum spanning from intimate to ceremonial (see Fig. 6.2). *Intimate* speech situations are those in which the speakers know each other so well that words become almost unnecessary. Nonverbal cues and gestures often relay much of the message because the people are so familiar with each other that they know what the other person is thinking. On the other end of the spectrum are *ceremonial* situations, which generally follow strict rules. For example, parts of marriage ceremonies are read aloud so as to ensure that audience expectations and legalities are met. Oral behavior in courtrooms is quite constrained. Initiation ceremonies often follow a script. In these contexts, both the speakers and the audience have very specific expectations, and the boundaries of acceptability are narrow.

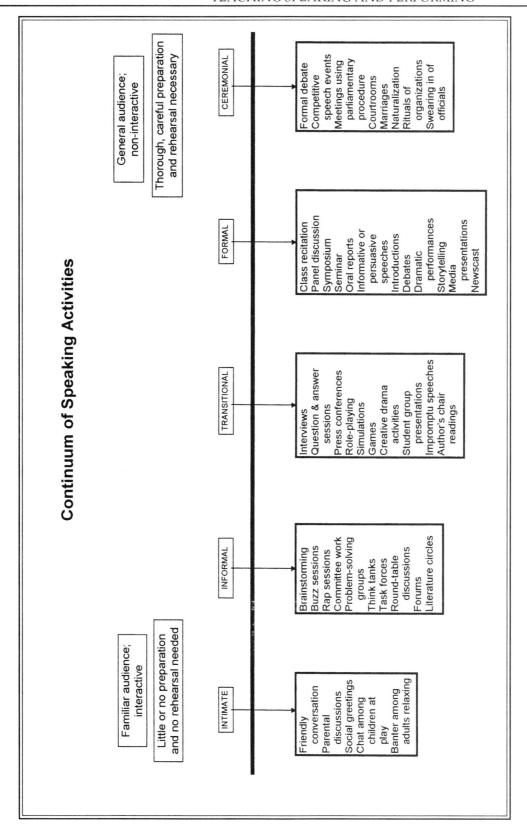

Continuum of Speaking Activities

Familiar audience; interactive

Little or no preparation and no rehearsal needed

General audience; non-interactive

Thorough, careful preparation and rehearsal necessary

INTIMATE

Friendly conversation
Parental discussions
Social greetings
Chat among children at play
Banter among adults relaxing

INFORMAL

Brainstorming
Buzz sessions
Rap sessions
Committee work
Problem-solving groups
Think tanks
Task forces
Round-table discussions
Forums
Literature circles

TRANSITIONAL

Interviews
Question & answer sessions
Press conferences
Role-playing
Simulations
Games
Creative drama activities
Student group presentations
Impromptu speeches
Author's chair readings

FORMAL

Class recitation
Panel discussion
Symposium
Seminar
Oral reports
Informative or persuasive speeches
Introductions
Debates
Dramatic performances
Storytelling
Media presentations
Newscast

CEREMONIAL

Formal debate
Competitive speech events
Meetings using parliamentary procedure
Courtrooms
Marriages
Naturalization
Rituals of organizations
Swearing in of officials

FIG. 6.2

Although students are apt to come to know the intricacies of intimate speech situations from personal experiences, they probably need some introduction to ceremonial situations. Televised courtroom proceedings and legislative sessions provide at least some exposure to these controlled conditions. Taking part in student council or school governance meetings that are conducted according to parliamentary procedure or competing as a member of a debate team may be an excellent introduction to ceremonial speaking contexts. Nevertheless, the area of the continuum that spans from informal to formal situations should probably be of most concern in the language arts classroom.

The activities on this continuum are arranged with two considerations in mind. The first is **preparation**. Informal speaking activities often do not demand that speakers prepare comments in advance, although other kinds of preparation (e.g., reading, study, research, collecting of information, and thinking) may be beneficial. Although it is a sweeping generalization with many exceptions, the more formal the presentation, the greater the need for extensive preparation and rehearsal. Many of the best formal speeches are so well prepared and rehearsed that they appear to be impromptu. The speaker is so polished that he or she does not require notes and yet appears thoroughly prepared and totally at ease. The best formal speakers make the delivery appear deceptively easy and natural. Between these two lie transitional speaking opportunities, which require some preparation but often demand that the speaker respond in an impromptu manner.

The other dimension that governs this continuum is **audience**. When the speech situation is informal, the audience is usually small, familiar, and physically present. In most cases, the audience is able to interact freely with the speaker, and the speaker's content is determined, at least in part, by the nonverbal and verbal cues given by the audience. Toward the other end of the spectrum lie those formal situations in which the audience is much larger and contains many unknown persons who cannot orally interact with the speaker. This audience, as in the case of television and film or videotaped presentations, may not even be physically present at the time the speech is given. In between lie transitional speech activities for which the audience may be of substantial size but often contains many known individuals. In these situations, however, the audience generally does not engage in an oral exchange with the speaker although another speaker may respond or act as a moderator.

Students need to have some experience with a range of speaking activities, from informal to formal. Not only do they need to learn how to prepare appropriately for these different situations, they also need to learn how to meet the needs of various types of audiences.

This, of course, has much in common with learning to write effectively. In addition, students need to learn how to be thoughtful, courteous audience members who respond appropriately to speakers. Thus, speaking activities and listening development make a complementary pair in the classroom.

THE ORAL CURRICULUM

Although the development of speaking skills is generally ignored in literature anthologies and relegated to little more than an isolated chapter or two in language arts textbooks, speaking is one of the skills that language arts teachers are often held responsible for teaching. At the high school level, this responsibility may shift to a speech, drama, or fine arts teacher. At the middle level, these specialists are rare. Middle schools sometimes employ a speech therapist or pathologist whose primary responsibility is the correction of speech impediments such as stuttering and lisping. These people may know a great deal about testing, diagnosing, and remediating speech problems, but they may know very little about teaching the art and skill of speaking publicly and dramatically.

Regardless of whether you encourage it, middle school students will converse informally. However, they may not talk with a wide variety of their peers unless you provide the environment for doing so and structure activities so this is more likely to occur. Without these experiences, students may fail to realize that the kind of speech that is accepted among close friends may be unintelligible or even offensive to other classmates.

Without some instruction, students may fail to understand the significant differences between socializing and working cooperatively to achieve a goal. Socializing often involves determining some sort of hierarchy of acceptance, but goal-oriented groups function most effectively when everyone is accepted as an equal partner in the enterprise. Whether these groups achieve their intended goal depends, at least in part, on how well the members use oral language. Thus, even when the speech situation is informal, students need some instruction about how to behave and contribute. Students working in literature circles or literature response groups need to know some of the different speaking roles that help groups to function smoothly and speech behaviors that impede conversation. They may also need to learn some conflict resolution strategies. Those working in writing response groups need to learn what questions to ask and how to accept and provide constructive criticism. All of these are skills that will be useful throughout life, even when reading and writing are not the topics of conversation.

Similarly, students need assistance in preparing for transitional and formal activities. The kind of instruction that is necessary will depend heavily on the particular activity. The important point to keep in mind is that middle level students may never have been asked to consider consciously what is involved in preparing to speak well. In many respects, teaching students to be effective speakers parallels what they need to know to be effective writers. Most of the factors that constitute the rhetorical problem in writing (i.e., purpose, audience, context, etc.) apply equally in speaking. Students can and should be taught how to consider these factors when preparing to speak.

However, there are other aspects of oral performance that must also be developed. Fluency is one. Volume, pace, pitch, tone, and clarity are others. Using nonverbal signals, gestures, and facial expressions to convey meaning should also be included. Middle level students usually need guidance in how to use notes without reading them or relying on them too heavily. Of course, the content of the speech also deserves a significant amount of instructional attention.

Some districts and states have curricula for speaking. If such sources are available, you should rely on them; however, if you have no other guidelines, one way to plan a program is to use the speech continuum as a guide. Another possibility is to design tasks around Halliday's (1975) list of functions or Fidge's (1992) 12 categories of spoken language presented earlier in this chapter. You may also find the material in Activity 6.3 useful. A curriculum created from any of these resources should provide the variety of experiences that students need.

TEACHING SPEAKING

One of the most important factors to keep in mind about teaching speaking is the goal of participation. Students need to engage in speaking activities, not just talk or read about how to speak. Identifying the characteristics of an effective speaker without trying to be one is of very limited benefit. Creating opportunities for students to interact informally with peers is relatively easy to arrange through cooperative learning and workshops; however, if students are to learn to function in more formal situations, they must have opportunities to speak, both within the classroom and beyond it. They need to participate in speaking activities in which the audience is comprised of people other than their peers. Some of these situations can be created to mesh with existing school events—open houses, parent–teacher conferences that include students, award ceremonies, morning announcements, and all-school convocations (school assemblies). Students can be taught to assume speaking responsibilities at these events.

Other opportunities to speak more formally may have to be designed, although in a classroom that focuses on active learning many such opportunities can grow naturally out of classroom studies or develop as extensions of student interest. Students can create multimedia presentations with accompanying tapes as class projects. They can create and narrate a videotape of the school district that can be shown to new or prospective residents and students. They can speak at school board meetings in favor of or in opposition to some decision being contemplated. Some interdisciplinary projects may lead to students giving presentations before business leaders, community groups, and local and state governmental bodies. On occasion, students have been asked to testify before federal commissions or committees. You may not be able to plan for some of these occurrences, but you can prepare students for them through role playing, just in case an opportunity presents itself.

Public speaking requires attention not only to rhetorical issues but also to physical presentation (i.e., voice, expression, and movement). Other types of speech performance require different skills, some of which stretch beyond the use of oral language into an understanding of various media. What special demands accompany the presentation of a news show, for example? What is the difference between an informative speech and persuasive speech, and what are the values of each? What makes a dramatic reading truly impressive? How do comedians use pauses to enhance humor? Many of these are questions that language arts teachers, especially novices, may not be able to answer readily.

When unfamiliar speaking situations are the focus, it is helpful to keep in mind that middle level students are supposed to be learning. Polished performances, like polished written papers, may be few and far between, with lots of trial-and-error practice in the interim. Students can learn much from their own mistakes and those of classmates if the environment allows for error without permitting anything less than best efforts. Students can be involved in setting speech criteria and in evaluating themselves and their classmates. As is the case with writing, students need feedback about strengths and weaknesses of performances. In this regard, audiotapes and videotapes can be valuable assessment tools that can also be added to student portfolios. The teacher, of course, can learn along with students. For practical information about conducting speaking activities, the O'Keefe (1995) text in the Recommended Readings for this chapter is outstanding.

SPEAKING AS PERFORMANCE

Classroom Discussion

The easiest way to engage students in speaking is through classroom discussion. Peer response groups and literature circles are effective vehicles for active oral participation. However, if you do not wish to use either cooperative learning or a workshop approach as the method of instruction, you can still encourage students to talk about the subject matter. Having students lead discussions is one possibility. If you must lecture for a significant portion of time, you can provide 5-minute interludes periodically when pairs of students alternate in stating in their own words to each other what they have just heard. Doing a "whip-around" on an issue about which nearly everyone wants to talk allows each person to either have a say or pass. You can also increase the frequency of speaking by asking each student to provide an oral update on independent project work or ongoing research that will contribute to a collaborative product created by the whole class.

Oral Reports

Requiring students to present oral reports to the class is a commonly accepted activity meant to aid students in developing speaking skills. However, these assignments often produce negative reactions, in large part because students are aware that most of the audience is uninterested in listening to what they have to say. Hostile or disinterested audiences make all speakers tense; students are no exception. Furthermore, these presentations take an enormous amount of class time. In general, you should think twice about assigning the typical kinds of oral reports, especially those in which students research a topic and then write a report to present to the class. Unless the preparation time is substantial, students will not have assimilated the information well enough to understand it themselves let alone present it coherently and interestingly to people who know nothing about it.

There are some times, however, when oral reports make good sense. If all students contribute to a thematic topic that the class is studying, students are likely to know more about the topic, and the audience is apt to be more receptive. Try to create situations in which listeners really want to know what speakers have to share. Students are quite perceptive about this, so you can offer speaking as an option and let students decide whether their material will appeal to classmates. If speaking is one of several ways in which students can respond to literature, for example, and not everyone is required to give an oral report, the speakers generally feel more confident, and the audience is more attentive. If you want every student to give a speech but you are concerned that listening will bore most of the class, divide the class into small groups for the reports. Instead of listening to 25 or 30 reports, students only listen to 5 or 6. In some cases, you may want to give students the option of tape-recording presentations while allowing those who prefer to present to the class the time to do so. When options are available, keep close records so that you can require oral presentations from each student before the year ends.

Public Speaking

One type of public speaking that generally proves to be effective among middle level students is a demonstration speech. Another similar type is an explanation of a process. These speeches are concrete and hands-on. They give the audience something to watch, and they give the speaker something to do with his or her hands. You can ask students to speak either about something they can already do well or something they can learn to do in a short time. This has to be something they can demonstrate to their classmates. You will need to help students develop good openings and effective conclusions, but you should also help them focus on how to demonstrate the process while talking. Encourage students to use visuals such as posters and handouts in addition to performing the actions. On the whole, students like sharing hobbies, recipes, animal care, sports maneuvers, and creative (and often humorous) approaches to common activities (e.g., how to watch television effortlessly, how to drive parents nuts, how to ask a girl for a date, how to respond to telephone calls asking for donations, etc.). Always have students clear their topics with you beforehand, though.

If they are going to demonstrate how to cook or bake something, students must be reminded that the audience cannot wait for 30 minutes while the product is in the oven. Figuring out how to demonstrate enough but not all of the preparation is an interesting challenge. You also need to remind students that your supply of equipment is limited. If they need appliances, tape recorders, or VCRs, they need to bring their own or let you know well in advance. Also, you will have to remind students repeatedly to rehearse their speeches several times. Thinking about a speech and even planning it on paper is not sufficient. The most common mark of an unrehearsed speech is running far under or over the time limit. Students often have no concept of how long an activity takes if they do not actually practice. Despite some hesitation, mistakes, and shaky hands, these speeches usually work well. Listeners maintain engagement most of the time and are truly appreciative of a good performance.

Furthermore, you learn much about the interests, hobbies, and strengths of some students who may not yet have distinguished themselves in any other way in your classroom.

Oral Book Reports

Another common activity in many classrooms is having students give oral book reports. Language arts teachers want students to speak and to share responses to the literature they read. Oral book reports may seem to be a good combination of goals. However, these reports can be as boring as other kinds of oral reports. After hearing just three or four plot summaries, character descriptions, and opinions of the books, you and student listeners are likely to start wondering just how much longer you can listen. It truly is difficult for students to speak with vibrancy and enthusiasm when presenting factual information about books. You will grow exasperated hearing, "If you want to find out what happens, you'll have to read the book." Every time, you will wonder whether or not the speaker read the ending. One of the major reasons for assigning oral book reports is to determine whether or not the reader read the book, but the speaker's need to withhold certain information in order to motivate the listeners to read conflicts with this goal.

If you wish to have students give some type of oral response to their reading, they should be taught how to present book talks instead. Book talks are designed to inspire listeners to read the books. This is an authentic task, one that you or the school librarian can demonstrate for students. Book talks are not just plot summaries; they are persuasive discourse. Students have to think about what they can do to "sell" their books to their listeners. They must also consider some literary aspects of the text. They can read an excerpt, show something visual, ask questions that pique interest, or link the book to another piece of written discourse, a current movie, or some local event. Book talks give students an opportunity to choose the best method for presenting their books so the activity also involves some creative decision making.

Another possibility, especially for older middle level students, is to have them present critical reviews of books similar in style to the televised movie reviews formerly given by Siskel and Ebert. This is especially good if two students have read the same book. Here again, students must learn how to do this. The best form of instruction is to have students watch videotapes of several movie reviews and discuss the possible ways to organize them. How is each movie introduced? What clips are selected for viewing? Why? What kinds of follow-up comments are given? How do the reviewers handle the situation when the movie did not particularly appeal to them but might appeal to others? How do they bring reviews to a close? Of course, because students will not be able to show clips, they will have to create an alternative—using the book jacket, making their own illustrations, reading some excerpts and so forth.

Linking speaking and literature study is a good idea (see Activity 6.4), but you need to think about assignments from the perspectives of both speakers and listeners. What do you want students to hear? What kind of speaking must occur to prompt the listening response that you want? Search for and try several alternatives. Look for authentic ways that people share information about books verbally, and re-create them. Give students some options rather than requiring that everyone present the same kind of report, even if all students must speak.

Interviews

Many middle level students delight in interviewing others. This is a reasonably familiar mode; they see it on television constantly during news programs, documentaries, and sports broadcasts, although these may not be the highest quality models. Students can interview their peers, teachers, family members, community residents, businesspeople, local politicians, and guest speakers. They can conduct their own telephone interviews. Through teleconferencing, they can interview experts in various fields, and through computer networks, they can interview many different people on-line.

Students need to learn that they must have a purpose for the interview, and they must plan some questions in advance. This keeps everyone on-task and increases efficiency. However, students must also listen closely and ask impromptu follow-up questions that reveal more information. They need to set a time limit and stick to it. When they conduct a formal interview, they must make arrangements to meet the person. That individual is likely to want to know the purpose of the interview and possibly the questions in advance. Students will have to be reminded about common courtesies—arriving on time, dressing appropriately, asking worthwhile questions, not badgering the interviewee, adhering to the time limit, respecting the person's privacy, thanking the interviewee for his or her participation, and so on. Students themselves can probably generate a more complete list of dos and don'ts.

It is a good idea to spend some class time discussing the kinds of questions that work best—worthwhile, open-ended, and related to the topic, for example. It is also a good idea to require that students submit their questions to you for checking before they use them. This can save the student and you some embarrassment. Middle level students have a tendency to ask questions that are much too personal!

You want to do as much as you can to make this a positive experience not only for students but for interviewees as well. This activity is very good for building public relations and support for the schools within the community *if* it is well planned and conducted.

TEACHING DRAMA

English majors tend to think of drama as a literary form to be studied, much as one studies novels or poems. Certainly this is a valid viewpoint, one with which you may agree wholeheartedly. Nevertheless, plays were meant to be seen and heard rather than read. Much of the meaning of a play comes through in the way that lines are delivered and actions are carried out. Although you may not feel that it is or should be your business to develop acting skills among students, the fact is that drama without performance is incomplete. That is not to say that students should read every play aloud from start to finish, nor is it to say that they should perform every play. Much can be gained through viewing the performances of others. Watching videotapes of professional and amateur performances can be quite valuable, but attending a live performance is an experience that many middle level students have never had and will never forget. However, in-class dramatic reading, role playing, storytelling, and performing of scenes add much to both the study of drama and learning to speak well (Wagner, 1998).

If you develop a student-centered program in your classroom, you may find yourself involved in play production, puppetry, readers theater, children's theater, storytelling, or creative dramatics. You may even coach speech or debate teams. However, you may have no professional preparation for teaching any of these. You can learn by reading professional sources, attending workshops, and talking with other teachers who have experience or training. Some helpful sources, such as *Live On Stage!* (Blank and Roberts, 1997) and *Drama as a Way of Knowing* (Heller, 1996), are listed in the Recommended Readings for this chapter. Most of all, you can learn by doing. If you believe that giving students the opportunity to explore the possibilities is more important than either knowing all there is to know beforehand or using your own limitations as an excuse for not taking a risk, then you will accept the challenge to include some dramatic performance work in your classroom. You will make lots of mistakes, but the students will generally be patient because they enjoy the active participation. They will tolerate your shortcomings in exchange for the chance to do something that is a bit out of the ordinary. Furthermore, students may learn something about how to learn by watching you struggle with unfamiliar tasks. They may be more willing to take educational risks if they see you doing it.

Taking on the challenge of moving beyond speaking into performing may seem threatening if you have little or no background in theater. One way to ease your own learning and enhance that of students is to find some experts and invite them into your classroom—a storyteller, a mime, a drama coach, a parent with acting experience, members of an amateur theater group, and so forth. Part of your responsibility as a teacher is to facilitate learning. If you do not have the information that students need, you do have the expertise to go out and find it and make the arrangements to get it into the classroom. If you do not know how, find someone who does.

DRAMA AS PERFORMANCE

Storytelling

Storytelling is an engaging activity that can be used in a variety of ways in conjunction with the study of literature or the writing of narratives, but it is particularly good as part of a unit that includes traditional oral tales. It is one way that students come to understand why different versions of these tales developed. It also helps students understand that storytelling is not just reading a book aloud to young children. The best way to change this perception is to invite a local storyteller into the classroom to give a demonstration and explain how he or she develops a performance. Several books give instructions for storytelling, and some videotapes include demonstrations of how to develop and present stories. It is a good idea for you to be able to demonstrate storytelling for your students, at least eventually.

Middle level students can develop performances and present them at local libraries, child care centers, and elementary schools. This is an excellent speaking experience and a community service that students generally perform with pride. If students are not quite up to storytelling, they can still read books aloud to children. This, too, is a speaking activity. It is also an excellent way to help some remedial readers build their reading skills without being embarrassed about reading children's books.

Puppetry

When teaching puppetry, keep it simple. Sock puppets are easy for students to make, and they can personalize them as they wish. Also, students do not have to coordinate head and arm movements, because sock puppets have only mouths that move. A puppet theater is nice if you have access to one or you can build one, but many commercial ones are too small or need to be placed on a platform that is above the heads of the puppeteers. You can just drape a blanket or sheet over a table to hide the puppeteers and students can maneuver the puppets at table height by sitting or kneeling.

The puppet plays that work best at the middle level contain humor and/or fantasy, although they can have a moral if they are meant for a young audience. Actions need to be broadly portrayed, and the dialogue should reinforce the action, just in case the viewer misses something or the amateur puppeteer cannot quite make the action visible. Keep them short (i.e., 5–10 minutes). Initially, students may have more success with puppets when they compose a commercial or segment within a longer presentation, much as puppet skits are used on *Sesame Street*.

The major problem with puppet plays is that the speakers are hidden, so they must talk very loudly. Actually, this is an advantage in disguise. It forces students to speak up, a common problem at the middle level, and to work on their diction. What students like best about puppet plays is that the puppeteers are heard but not seen. They can attend to their delivery of lines without also having to worry about their own physical appearance on stage.

Creative Dramatics

Creative dramatics can be an excellent introduction to being on stage. It is a way for students to grow comfortable with their own bodies through purposeful movement. The warm-up exercises described in *Theater Games for the Classroom* (Spolin, 1986) work especially well. They actively involve students without creating undue embarrassment. After practicing several warm-ups, you can have students try some pantomimes. If possible, have a guest mime visit the school, give a performance, and then come to the classroom to demonstrate some of the techniques. For days afterward, students will create invisible walls and lean on transparent ledges just for fun. Later you can work on some improvisation and role playing. These are excellent vehicles for introducing some literary concepts—plot development, conflict, character motivation, and setting. Improvisations can be developed into performances by creating a script that uses the best conflicts, events, actions, and dialogue that students discover through experimentation. Students can also role-play parts of stories or novels. You can also have them role-play a situation and use that as an introduction to a new unit or literary selection.

If you want to try some creative dramatics, you need space. This may mean holding class in a more open area or clearing space in the room. I usually tried to do creative dramatics with all of my classes at the same time so that I was not wasting time moving furniture between class periods. Also, students need to know why they are being asked to participate in the warm-up exercises, because some make them feel a bit silly. They need to know that this is natural and somewhat intentional; the point is to release some of their inhibitions so they will feel more comfortable in front of an audience. Warm-ups also force students to focus, something that middle level students often have difficulty doing.

If you include pantomimes, have students perform familiar activities first. However, you will need to forewarn students about the boundaries of acceptability in your classroom. You can even require that they whisper the activity to you before they take the stage. Turn these trials into guessing games in which the audience must figure out what each person is pantomiming. Once students have developed some proficiency at this, you can create typical settings and let students join in one by one as they see a role for themselves. They can be humans, animals, or inanimate objects. A grocery store or restaurant works well as a setting. Movie theaters and the beach are also popular. Usually, the most difficult part of this from the students' viewpoint is remaining in character. However, this can be an advantage as a natural introduction to consistency of character in literature. Once students are comfortable with settings and with ordinary characters performing routine actions, ask students to create conflicts and play them out. This serves as a transition to improvisations.

For improvisations, it is best to limit the number of characters on stage to no more than four. Set the scene and identify one character to appear, but do not create other characters or predict the ending. Students should create these as the improvisation progresses. It is helpful if you assume the role of director so that you can choose who will join the action. As the director you can let the scene play itself out or stop it if it is not developing well. Middle level students have a tendency to improvise violence, and the last thing you want is a mass fight scene. You are apt to find that the minute students add dialogue, physical performance will decline, so you may have to go back and focus on movement again through more warm-ups and pantomimes. In both pantomime and improvisation, debriefing is crucial. During these times you should guide students, particularly the observers, in talking about physical movement, dialogue, and verbal delivery. This helps to emphasize the need for an audience. Nonparticipants quickly realize that they have an important and valuable contribution to make even if they cannot be on stage.

If you expect students to participate in creative dramatics, be prepared and willing to demonstrate and to take part yourself. You will have to monitor, too, but do not ask students to do things that you are not willing to try.

Readers Theater

Readers theater is another effective teaching tool at the middle level. In case you are not familiar with it, readers theater is basically a series of readings that explore a theme or tell a story. There are no sets and few props. Sometimes a few sound effects are added. Some single pieces of literature can be turned into readers theater rather easily. Scripts can also be created by combining excerpts from different sources. The focus of readers theater is on the words and the meaning. Actors usually sit during most of the performance and read from scripts, although they do have to rehearse extensively to get the best expressions. Middle level students like readers theater because they do not have to do much acting, and they do not have to memorize lines. The most difficult part is finding just the right quotations and excerpts and deciding on the order of presentation. In general, readers theater works best when the topic is somewhat introspective. An action novel or plot-heavy short story does not usually set the right tone. Consider framing the script as a kind of debate or conversation in which some readers have parts that express one point of view and others have parts that represent opposing views. This may help students to find suitable material and determine an effective order of presentation. You can also find sample readers theater scripts on the Internet. However, you will probably need to attend some performances of readers theater before you attempt to explain this concept to students or have them try it.

Children's Theater

In general, middle level students find performing children's theater productions very rewarding. There are commercial scripts for children's theater that you can have students perform, but you should consider using these as models and having students create their own plays. To do this, students will have to read literature, make selections, create scripts, rehearse, and give performances. They will have to make all of the decisions. Middle level students like children's theater especially if they have a chance to perform at a local elementary school. The younger students are generally a very appreciative audience, and middle level students are much less intimidated by them; they really feel good about doing something entertaining for those who are not likely to be as critical as peer or adult audiences. The younger ones respond well to the exaggerated action, noise, and movement that is characteristic of children's theater. They like bright costumes and overdone makeup. And middle schoolers are usually glad to oblige.

Play Production

Play production demands an enormous time commitment. It means finding a suitable script, holding auditions, choosing actors, adapting the script, designing and creating sets, having line rehearsals, blocking, having more line rehearsals, advertising, having still more line rehearsals, creating or obtaining costumes, obtaining and applying stage makeup, having dress rehearsals, and finally giving productions. And that is just an outline. Also, this experience usually affects only the few students who are chosen to participate. Many schools choose to perform musicals so that both the language arts and music teachers become involved. Although musicals are very entertaining, most are not known for their dramatic quality. The plots are generally not very complex, the characters tend to be stereotypical, and the dialogue is not particularly memorable. In short, they do not demonstrate what is best about drama. Of greater concern is the matter of language development. Learning the words written by someone else and moving on stage according to a director's decisions demands good memory, but students have few opportunities to make decisions about how to use language more effectively.

You may enthusiastically support the production of a play or musical, especially if it is part of a varied extracurricular program or exploratory curriculum, because the activity encourages leadership, responsibility, and cooperation. Taking part in plays can reveal acting talent and build self-esteem. Whether you approve or not, you may have no choice about assisting with a schoolwide performance if it is a tradition. However, if you have some input, you can suggest that involving students in smaller productions may be more educational. Students can read several plays and choose the scenes they want to perform. Students work in small groups to decide the blocking and how lines should be delivered. Because everyone takes part in some capacity, most of the rehearsals can be included as part of the language arts class work. The final performances can be given during the school day just for others in the school and for those parents who can attend. There may be no sets and no music, but students can wear representative costumes and stage makeup. Scenes can be introduced by a narrator who reads material the actors have written. Certainly this is a far cry from a major musical production, but many more students will be involved, and students are likely to learn much more from this experience.

Another option is to have students write plays themselves. Some of these can be presented at various school events. If not all students can attend the function, consider tape-recording a line reading with added narration so that the production is similar to a radio play, or have students videotape their plays.

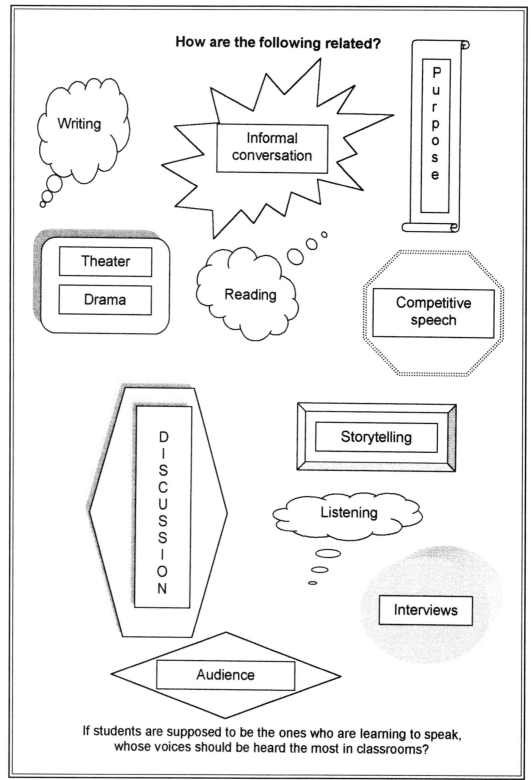

FIG. 6.3

THE RELUCTANT SPEAKER

Whether the speaking situation is informal or formal, whether it relates to dramatic performance or not, some students will be very reluctant to speak aloud. The more supportive the environment, the less likely this will be, but a few students will simply prefer to remain silent much of the time. Others will be too frightened to stand before their peers to give an oral report. What can a teacher do about these students if effective speaking is supposed to be a part of the students' curriculum?

One of the most important factors in considering this question is to know the students well. Some students learn best by listening. They can and do speak effectively when they really have something to contribute, but they much prefer to listen thoughtfully and think about what they are hearing. Often these are the people who are excellent summarizers or ones who can provide a good overview of a group discussion. Thus, they can occasionally be called on to fulfill these oral roles in the classroom.

Some students are simply more shy or retiring. They may lack confidence in the value of their ideas or consider that what others say is much more important or intelligent than anything they have to contribute. In general, these individuals can be drawn out if they work in small groups.

Some students have speech impediments that make them quite hesitant. How to handle this situation depends, in part, on whether the speech problem is one that can be improved through practice or is not apt to change no matter how hard the student tries. In this latter case, tape-recording the performance so that only the teacher listens may be the best choice. Although a few other students in a class may feel that this is unequal treatment, most students are likely to be relieved. They will understand that requiring such a student to perform before the class is apt to be embarrassing for the speaker and stressful for the listeners. Of course, no matter what the impediment, if the student wishes to speak, he or she should be encouraged to do so.

In many classes there may be one or two students who are absolutely paralyzed by the thought of having to speak before an audience. This may be the result of previous experiences that were negative, but some students are simply unable to present a formal speech. One alternative is to rely more heavily on the transitional kinds of speaking activities that tend to be a bit less nerve-racking. Another alternative is to create situations in which speakers work in pairs or small groups to give presentations. With the teacher's assistance, this can be worked out so that the reluctant member contributes and becomes a bit more comfortable about being before an audience without necessarily having to say anything. The idea is to expect these students to participate fully by the end of the year, but that goal should be reached through gradual exposure.

Finally, there are nearly always a few students who are reluctant because they are underprepared or resistant. Often these are the same students who seem to be disinterested in school and appear to be unmotivated, although some students who give this impression whenever the task involves reading and writing are quite receptive to speaking. Inadequate preparation and lack of motivation are problems that stretch far beyond the current assignment. The possibility does exist that speaking and performing may spark a student's enthusiasm, but it may not. The terminally bored student requires a different approach from the one required for students who are capable but lazy. The abused student who has not eaten a good meal in weeks needs different attention from that given to the student who considers school to be completely irrelevant or sees him- or herself as totally incapable of academic success. These individuals need to learn far more than speaking skills. Until the problems that these students bring to the classroom are addressed, no amount of instruction about speaking or performing is likely to have much of an effect.

SOME SPECIAL VALUES OF TEACHING SPEAKING AND PERFORMING

Although Americans tend to think of themselves as verbal people, some cultures are far more reliant on speaking as a part of their lifestyle. For some cultures, oral storytelling is a means of gaining and maintaining status. In others the history of the people is preserved by an oral historian. Students in a global society need to be aware of different cultural attitudes toward speaking and gesturing. What is commonplace in America can be construed as offensive by members of another cultural group. Even when the words are acceptable, the delivery may not be. Teaching speaking can open the door to better cultural awareness and acknowledgment, if not acceptance, of diversity.

Speaking is also a linked to literature through oral tradition tales. One possible way to tie together social studies and language arts is through myths, legends, fairy tales, and folktales. Another possibility is to study speeches given by significant persons. Many English words are of foreign origin. Most of them probably came to us through verbal use. It seems likely that oral language has played a significant role in the development of large cities where one finds ethnic neighborhoods. From several vantage points, speaking is historically and socially significant.

Drama, too, can serve as the medium for developing cultural awareness. Several Asian cultures, for example, have traditional dramatic performances that recount historical events and heroic acts of individuals. Pantomime was used extensively by several Native American peoples to celebrate significant occurrences. Drama can also link with music, not just through musicals but through opera and ballet as well. Focusing on performing opens up many career possibilities that students may not previously have considered. Although they may not find stardom, they may develop a fascination for some of the related industries—costuming, script writing, lighting, sound, set design, special effects, speech writing, and so on. Other students may develop an interest in competitive speaking, Toastmasters, mime, community theater, storytelling, or some other form of public performance.

INTEGRATING SPEAKING AND PERFORMING

Informal speaking should be a normal part of most of your classroom activities. Many of the transitional speech activities listed on the continuum can be linked to other activities such as reading and writing. The results can be presented to classmates and to other classes. Offering students the option to complete a speaking task may be an exciting possibility to the student who envisions him- or herself as an entertainer, politician, or lawyer. Similarly, the student who struggles to read and write successfully may find the chance to speak a welcome relief. You need be the only one who realizes initially that effective speaking often demands good reading comprehension and some of the same skills that are necessary for effective composing (e.g., organization of ideas, sufficient supporting details, audience awareness, and so on).

If you make the most of them, speaking and dramatic activities offer connections to literature and language study, as well as reading and writing, that reinforce or illustrate concepts vividly for middle level students. Both speech and drama provide favorable circumstances for students to engage actively in concrete experiences that help them understand some abstract ideas that are not yet sufficiently clear from verbal explanations and other kinds of examples. This is an opportunity that is too good to miss in the middle level classroom.

Depending on the needs and interests of students, you may wish to teach formal speaking and dramatics as separate units. However, both formal speaking and dramatic tasks can be used as parts of other units, too. For example, if students study a class novel, you can require that they select a follow-up project from a list that includes only speaking and dramatic activities. During other units, you can build in more speaking than is usual. Groups may have to report their progress to the class periodically, for instance.

Speaking and performing are easy to integrate, but they are also easy to ignore. However, there is mounting evidence that having students talk about topics builds knowledge and understanding (e.g., Barnes & Todd, 1995). If you plan to integrate speaking and drama into other units of work, be sure the integration does not translate into little more than a passing nod. Some teachers feel that they are doing an effective job of teaching speaking if they conduct whole-class discussions and require that students present an oral report once a year. Others feel that they have done their duty if they offer speaking activities as options, even though students routinely ignore them. Neither of these provides enough attention to speaking.

ASSESSING AND EVALUATING SPEAKING AND PERFORMING

When you assess reading and writing, you should pay attention to both processes and products. When it comes to informal speaking, the processes and the products seem to occur simultaneously. You can observe the frequency of participation, the clarity with which ideas are expressed, and the quality of the ideas stated. You can also note the variety of speech used—informative statements, questions, expressions of opinion, and so forth. In addition, you can note some things about the effective use of volume, pace, enunciation, pronunciation, expression, and so on. However, these factors are very difficult to observe because of the swiftness of verbal interaction in the whole class and in small groups. One option is to tape-record or videotape the class sessions or small group discussions.

When assessing speaking and performing, you have to be quick. There just is not enough time to write lengthy anecdotal notes. Checklists are much easier to use. They help you focus on a variety of expectations and provide a basis for giving feedback to students. These checklists are also suitable as record-keeping devices, and they can be included in portfolios. However, if you devote a major part of a grading period to speech or drama, you will probably need to assign grades primarily on the basis of performance. This may necessitate more detail than checklists can provide, and students will need more information about the expectations than is usually available on a checklist. Instead, consider using rating scales or rubrics that can be filled out and given to the students. These tools can be designed to describe the various aspects of performance so that students know where they stand currently and what they need to do to improve. The levels of quality can be assigned numeric scores that can be used for calculating final grades.

Most middle level students are rather adept speakers in informal situations. What you need to note are those students who seem to have some difficulty expressing themselves orally so that you can help them set goals for themselves, such as increasing the frequency of contributions, thinking about what they intend to say so they do not ramble, avoiding statements that tend to shut down discussion, and so on. Your instruction should help students understand that some of their speech habits interfere with communication. As part of your assessment, take note of those students whose dialect or usage could cause them to be regarded as less educated or less intelligent by those who are prone to make such judgments. Help these students recognize these language patterns and understand how they can affect some listeners. However, avoid making students so self-conscious that they become reluctant to speak.

When formal speaking is the issue, you can assess some of the processes, because transitional and formal speaking require preparation or rehearsal. You should provide class time for this preparation and observe how students go about it. You can make notes about the strategies they use, and you can assess their improvement over time.

When dramatic performance is a part of the curriculum, you can assess more than speaking if you choose to do so. You can assess such factors as ability to cooperate with others, participation, ability to convey ideas through body movements and facial expressions, willingness to perform for an audience, awareness of audience, meaningful delivery of lines, sufficiency of rehearsal, and so on.

Assessing speech and drama factors (see Activity 6.5) should assist you in planning instruction for the whole class and providing aid to individual students as they develop necessary skills.

On the other hand, when it comes to evaluation, you need to exercise special care. For many middle level students, speaking before peers is frightening. Their performances are likely to reflect this insecurity. Expecting them to give polished speaking or dramatic performances may be asking more than they can produce under pressure. For many, participating in dramatic activities in your classroom may be their first onstage appearances. Thus, in the area of speaking and performing at the middle level, you probably need to focus more on participation than polish, exploration more than perfection, and progress more than mastery. In the long run, your assessment or evaluation may mean little when compared with the authentic response of an audience. Speech should have an impact on the listeners. If you provide opportunities for students to speak in contexts where they can see and hear audience reactions, they will assess and evaluate themselves. However, you can also build in opportunities to reflect on these experiences and bring those self-assessments to the surface for more conscious consideration through discussion.

When speech and drama are a part of the class activities but not the focus of instruction, you may want to note only the positive aspects and give credit for them in calculating the final grade. If it is possible for you to do so, include some supportive statements about performances in reports to parents.

FINAL COMMENTS ABOUT SPEAKING AND PERFORMING

Whether participating in speaking and performing activities leads to "greater" things or not, it should lead to more articulate and confident speech. However, teachers must parallel this with concern for accurate, honest, worthwhile content. Using speech as a vehicle for exploring ethics is certainly possible, given that so much of the oral language that surrounds people is filled with half-truths, misinformation, persuasive gimmicks, and hollow words. You will want students to deliver their words well and to use gestures and body language that convey the intended messages, but you will also want those words to mean something and to reflect critical thinking and logical reasoning. Strive to make sure that students not only speak well but speak truthfully. Consider it your professional responsibility to model not only the best speaking habits but the highest quality of content as well.

And finally, a note about taking the risk to teach something that you yourself do not know much about—the world is full of such things. Students' opportunities to learn should not be limited by a teacher's lack of knowledge.

RECOMMENDED READINGS

Barbieri, M., & Rief, L. (Eds.). (1998). Drama, performance, theater: Means of further inquiry [themed issue]. *Voices from the Middle, 6*(2).

Blank, C., & Roberts, J. (1997). *Live on stage!: Performing arts for middle school.* Palo Alto, CA: Dale Seymour Publications.

Bolton, M. (1989). *Humorous monologues.* New York: Sterling.

Cooper, P. (1985). *Activities for teaching speaking and listening: Grades 7–12.* Annandale, VA: Speech Communication Association.

Coty, S. (1993). Writers all: Drama in the middle. *English Journal, 82* (1), 48–52.

Daniel, A. (1992). *Activities integrating oral communication skills for students grades K–8.* Annandale, VA: Speech Communication Association.

Fidge, L. (1992). *The essential guide to speaking & listening.* Dunstable, England: Folens Limited.

Fleischman, P. (1985). *I am phoenix: Poems for two voices.* New York: Harper & Row.

Fleischman, P. (1988). *Joyful noise: Poems for two voices*. New York: Harper & Row.

Fredericks, A. (1993). *Frantic frogs and other frankly fractured folktales for readers theatre*. Englewood, CO: Teacher Ideas Press.

Gambrell, L., & Almasi, J. (Eds.). (1996). *Lively discussions! Fostering engaged reading*. Newark, DE: International Reading Association.

Hamblin, K. (1978). *Mime: A playbook of silent fantasy*. Garden City, NY: Doubleday.

Heller, P. (1996). *Drama as a way of knowing*. York, ME: Stenhouse.

Latrobe, K., & Laughlin, M. (1989) *Readers theatre for young adults: Scripts and script development*. Englewood, CO: Teacher Ideas Press.

MacDonald, M. (1986). *Twenty tellable tales: Audience participation folktales for the beginning storyteller*. New York: H. W. Wilson Company.

O'Keefe, V. (1995). *Speaking to think, thinking to speak: The importance of talk in the learning process*. Portsmouth, NH: Boynton/Cook–Heinemann.

Paratore, J., & McCormack, R. (Eds.). (1997). *Peer talk in the classroom: Learning from research*. Newark, DE: International Reading Association.

Pierce, K., & Gilles, C. (1993). *Cycles of meaning: Exploring the potential of talk in learning communities*. Portsmouth, NH: Heinemann.

Rothermel, D. (1996). *Starting points: How to set up and run a writing workshop—and much more!* Columbus, OH: National Middle School Association.

Shepard, A. (1994). From script to stage: Tips for readers theatre. *The Reading Teacher, 48*(2), 184–185.

Speech Communication Association. (1994). *Speaking and listening competencies*. Annandale, VA: Author.

Spolin, V. (1986). *Theater games for the classroom: A teacher's handbook*. Evanston, IL: Northwestern University Press.

Townsend, J. (1998). Silent voices: What happens to quiet students during classroom discussions? *English Journal, 87*(2), 72–80.

Trelease, J. (1985). *The read-aloud handbook*. New York: Penguin.

Trousdale, A., Woestehoff, S., & Schwartz, M. (Eds.). (1994). *Give a listen: Stories of storytelling in school*. Urbana, IL: National Council of Teachers of English.

Williams, M. (1987). *Let 'em talk: Oral language activities for the classroom*. Palo Alto, CA: Dale Seymour Publications.

OTHER RESOURCES

National Association for the Preservation
and Perpetuation of Storytelling
P.O. Box 309
Jonesborough, TN 37659
615–753–2171

Readers theater scripts on-line
Readers Theatre Script Service
  P.O. Box 178333
  San Diego, CA 92117
  619–276–1948
  Www.aaronshep.com/rt/RTE.html

Speech Communication Association
  5105 Backlick Rd.
  Annandale, VA 22003

National Association of Dramatic and Speech Arts
  309 Cherokee Drive
  Blacksburg, VA 24060
  703–231–5805

Plays, Inc., Publishers [drama magazine for young people]
  120 Boylston St.
  Boston, MA 02116
  617–423–3157
  www.channel1.com/plays/

Speaking and Performing Activities and Suggestions

Activity 6.1 :
Random Thoughts
on Oral Language

1. Make the activities real and purposeful. For instance, have students give speeches because they have something to share, not because they need to give speeches.
2. Be sure students know what to expect and have the skills they need to proceed. Always plan to teach students how to go about participating in any oral activity. Their perceptions of satisfactory performance may be different from yours. Their past experiences may have been negative. They may never have seen a particular kind of activity before.
3. To generate good discussion, ask the right kinds of questions. Higher order questions that ask students to apply, synthesize, and analyze are the ones that work best. Include only a few recall questions as a prelude to the heart of the discussion. Watch out for personal opinion questions, which may create arguments rather than prompt the sharing of information and logical interpretations.
4. Do not expect students to move easily from small groups to formal speaking. They need to be eased into this. They will be more comfortable at first in front of a larger group if they can speak about things they know quite well.
5. Group presentations, such as panel discussions, give students some confidence about speaking before a group. Have them participate in these kinds of activities before they have to speak alone. Make individual formal speaking an option rather than a requirement for everyone.
6. Because different kinds of oral activities require different sorts of preparation and attention to audience, do not change formats from one extreme to another too often. Doing so may confuse students. On the other hand, variety can stimulate interest and expand skills.
7. Use some oral activities as the basis for helping students learn to ask good questions. The real key to learning is finding the right questions to ask, but students often think that learning is only about answering questions.

8. Teaching students how to be good audience members can give a speaker confidence. Encourage active listening by prompting or even requiring that students ask questions or elaborate on comments in ways that demonstrate that they heard the speaker. Such instruction helps the speaker know what to expect.

9. Have a plan for evaluating oral activities. Often students can help devise a good list of things to look for. Share the plan with students. Keep notes and provide feedback to students frequently.

Activity 6.2:
A Summary Of Oral Activities

A. Discussions and dialogues
  1. Conversation activities
    a. Phone
    b. Explain process
    c. Describe an object
    d. Tell what happened
    e. State and support an opinion
    f. Give directions
  2. Small group discussions
    a. Task talk
      • Brainstorming
      • Consensus building
      • Discussion by panel
      • Group talk
    b. Topic talk
      • Enumeration
      • Comparison
      • Chronology
      • Analysis
      • Illustration
B. Classroom dramatics
  1. Dramatic play
  2. Choral speaking
  3. Mime and improvisation
  4. Role playing and puppetry
  5. Readers theater
  6. Interpretative reading of literature
C. Storytelling
  1. Literary forms
    a. Myths
    b. Legends
    c. Folk and fairy tales
    d. Parables
  2. Tall tales and fish stories
D. Formal speaking
  1. Impromptu speeches
  2. Demonstration speeches

    3. Interviews
    4. Surveys
    5. Announcements
    6. Radio shows and commercials
    7. Formal meetings
    8. Reports
    9. Debates

E. Just for fun
    1. Songs and raps
    2. Poems
    3. Tongue twisters
    4. Jokes, riddles, and puns
    5. Jingles and chants
    6. Sound effects
    7. Guessing games
      a. 20 questions
      b. What's My Line?

Activity 6.3:
Some Ideas

From *Basic Oral Communication Skills: A Program Sequence for Illinois* (*Grades 7–9*), by Illinois State Department of Education, undated, Springfield, IL: Illinois State Board of Education. To explain why these activities were suggested, I have also included their objectives.

1. To demonstrate confidence in their own communication abilities, students can share successful examples, such as convincing a friend to go to a movie, giving a report, or asking questions of a teacher.
2. To understand the concept of choice in decision making and to determine what needs should be met and the outcomes of decisions, students can discuss situations, such as buying a CD, going to a game, studying, or watching TV.
3. To describe the process by which a decision has been made, students can keep a record for a day of all decisions made or keep a record of spending money, and then they can discuss how choices were made.
4. To demonstrate the ability to respond positively to verbal criticism, students can use the feedback of others to improve a speech or written paper.
5. To develop a realistic and positive view of self, students can give a verbal character reference for her- or himself for a job she or he would like.
6. To share self-perceptions with others, students can create a collage about themselves or design coats of arms for their families and explain or describe them to others.
7. To demonstrate a willingness to make decisions, students can participate in role-playing exercises involving decision making or in real decision-making opportunities in class.
8. To begin to test a value system in relation to peers, students can identify 20 things they love to do, compare the list with those of others, and explain choices. Students can also participate in decision-making exercises.
9. To freely express and deal with emotions, students can identify five feelings they have had since they awoke, or they can discuss feelings about class activities that embarrass or cause fear.

10. To develop the ability to initiate conversations with others, students can role-play being a new student in class or school or give impromptu speeches or talk to someone new during the day and report this experience to others.

11. To develop and sustain a line of argument in communicating with others, students can make a pitch to sell a product that each created to a manufacturer or create a verbal ad campaign for a product created by a classmate.

12. To share interests and goals with others, students can give a "Portrait of a Classmate" speech or teach another to do something the speaker does well.

13. To learn to participate in and experience a variety of role behaviors, students can discuss problem situations from different viewpoints in a group for a specified length of time before switching roles and continuing the discussion.

14. To practice following the development of a topic of conversation or discussion, students can start a conversation in a group. Each speaker must add to the previous person's contribution.

15. To develop the skill of summarizing and synthesizing discussions, students can stop at frequent intervals and summarize during discussions or summarize stories and reports.

16. To practice introducing information into discussions, students can stop at various points during group discussions and rephrase what was just said in the form of a question beginning with, "Oh, you meant ... ?"

17. To describe the value of conflict to groups, students can participate in analyses of class courtroom sessions or debates.

18. To improve the ability to express a change of opinion that has resulted from communication, students can discuss current news developments that have changed as the facts have become known, or they can discuss convincing television commercials that proved to be false.

19. To learn to encourage others to participate, students as a class can talk about questioning techniques, reinforcement, and so forth, write down the suggestions, and use their lists while discussing.

20. To learn to use appropriate parliamentary procedure, students can conduct class 1 day a week as an organization, using parliamentary procedure, developing an agenda, and so forth.

21. To identify and respond to the needs and motivations of others, students can conduct a survey of likes and dislikes of food and create a restaurant menu that reflects the results.

22. To begin to differentiate among observations, inferences, and judgments, students can watch a video scene, tell about the

scene, and then identify actual observations, inferences, and judgments.

23. To respond to cultural distinctions and similarities, students can study and orally report on one's own heritage or listen to guest speakers from various cultures and compile a class list of distinctions and similarities.

24. To understand the concept of personal space, students can describe their own rooms or living spaces and discuss why the spaces are or are not large enough. They can discuss situations in which someone invaded their space (e.g., armrest in a movie theater, a chair at the dinner table, lunch table space, etc.). They can conduct experiments to determine when people become uncomfortable with the presence of others.

25. To credit sources used to construct messages, students can include sources in oral messages and ask others to cite their sources.

26. To phrase questions that require unambiguous answers, students can compose questions to use in an interview and discuss open and closed questions.

27. To learn to provide message transitions, students can examine texts of speeches with transitions deleted and practice putting them back.

28. To limit and specify a topic, students can be given a time limit on a speech or create radio and television productions that cannot exceed specific time limits. Given a rough draft of a speech, students can practice deleting extraneous material and narrowing topics.

29. To begin to describe and evaluate their own language usage, students can tape-record themselves and analyze their speech. They can also revise diary entries to fit different audiences, situations, and places.

30. To recognize and adapt to withdrawing forms of physical behavior, students can create videotapes of groups, watch them, and discuss behaviors, or they can keep logs of observations during a day and discuss these.

Activity 6.4: Integrating Speaking and Literature

1. Students can make a mask of a story character using some poster board and a tongue depressor. From behind the mask, they can speak from the character's point of view.

2. Some mystery stories can be effectively re-created as shadow plays. To do this, you need to backlight the stage with a bright light (a lamp without a shade can be used) and hang a sheet between the actors and the audience so that the audience sees only silhouettes.

3. Much literature lends itself well to simulations (these are complicated and time-consuming to set up, so get the students to help design them as well as do them), role playing, mock trials, and debates. One key to success with these is exceptionally good planning. Set up rules and procedures and follow them. For debate, an adapted version in which one side presents, followed by the other side, followed by one rebuttal, and ending with another rebuttal is usually sufficient. In the follow-up, be sure to ask the audience to identify which arguments or statements were the most persuasive and why.

4. Poetry is a "natural" for reading aloud because most of it needs to be heard to be appreciated fully. Believe it or not, there are a few free spirits who really enjoy memorizing and reciting poetry. If your program is flexible, they can have a chance to do this without you requiring that everyone do it. Also there are some absolutely terrific dialogue poems, such as those by Fleischman (1985, 1988) in *Joyful Noise* and *I Am Phoenix* that students enjoy reading aloud after they first decide who is to read which part.

5. Some classic plays have segments of choral reading. Build on this idea by having students add chorus segments to other plays, either published ones or ones they write. During the performance or oral reading of the play, everyone in the audience can serve as a choral reader.

6. Students can choose characters from the literature they have read and create a dialogue among three individuals who proba-

bly have differing viewpoints on an issue. The dialogue must reflect the speech patterns of the characters.

7. Students can re-create literary events in news format and present their version of "The Nightly Literary News."

8. Select a literary work that is available in both print and verbal media forms (i.e., tape recording, film, videotape, stage production, etc.). Have students read the printed version, paying special attention to how they would express dialogue. Compare with the media version.

Activity 6.5:
Assessing Speaking and Performing

The particular qualities you will likely want to assess will vary according to the particular speaking or performing task in which students are involved. Therefore, the following lists of possible aspects are subdivided into categories. However, these are only sample items. Any such lists you use should be adapted to fit your instructional goals.

INFORMAL SPEAKING

1. Participates readily.
2. Helps group initiate discussion.
3. Takes turns and cooperates willingly.
4. Explains thinking.
5. Expresses self fluently.
6. Uses appropriate volume.
7. Asks questions.
8. Speaks with confidence.
9. Encourages others to take part.
10. Respond courteously to others.
11. Listens well to others.
12. Justifies, supports, or elaborates on comments.
13. Comes to discussion prepared.
14. Uses available time well; stays on task.
15. Helps group summarize discussion.
16. Report accurately on group's work.
17. Accurately assesses work of group.
18. Accurately assesses own work in group.

ORAL READING

1. Selects appropriate material.
2. Enunciates clearly.
3. Uses proper pitch and volume.
4. Tries to use pleasant tone.
5. Sets and maintains a pace appropriate to material.
6. Attends to punctuation marks.

7. Pauses at appropriate points.
8. Maintains eye contact with audience.
9. Understands and conveys meaning.
10. Conveys author's mood and intent.
11. Avoids exaggeration that is distracting.
12. Rehearses sufficiently.
13. Varies voice to emphasize meaning or differentiate characters.
14. Uses appropriate gestures.
15. Uses graphics effectively.
16. Introduces reading to focus audience attention.

FORMAL SPEAKING

1. Chooses an appropriate topic.
2. Selects appropriate material to explain or support topic.
3. Informs audience of purpose of speech.
4. Maintains purpose throughout.
5. Meets needs of audience for clarity.
6. Organizes ideas effectively.
7. Opens with something that grabs attention.
8. Uses examples effectively.
9. Uses visuals effectively.
10. Concludes in an identifiable way.
11. Reminds audience periodically of main points or speech structure.
12. Adheres to time limit.
13. Uses notes easily and well.
14. Uses gestures and facial expressions to convey meaning.
15. Maintains eye contact with audience.
16. Appears at ease and confident.
17. Uses appropriate volume, pitch, and tone.
18. Enunciates clearly.
19. Pronounces correctly.
20. Sets and maintains a reasonable pace.
21. Varies volume, pitch, and tone; avoids speaking in a monotone.
22. Rehearses adequately.
23. Self-assesses accurately.

DRAMATIC PERFORMANCE

1. Maintains role in speech and movement.
2. Speaks toward but not to audience.
3. Interacts naturally with other performers.

4. Knows lines or part.
5. Appears at ease and confident.
6. Uses gestures and body language to emphasize meaning.
7. Speaks loudly and distinctly.
8. Uses props or script appropriately.
9. Avoids upstaging other performers.
10. Enters and exits on cue.
11. Remembers blocking details.
12. Rehearses adequately.
13. Pauses appropriately for audience response.
14. Understands and conveys meaning.
15. Cooperates with other performers.
16. Cooperates with performance director.
17. Attends rehearsals regularly and promptly.
18. Stays on task during rehearsals.
19. Demonstrates responsibility and trustworthiness.
20. Takes care of materials, sets, equipment, and props.
21. Can self-assess accurately.

Teaching Listening

Overview

- Consider These Questions
- About Listening
- Listening Processes
- Listening Inhibitors
- Listening Purposes
- Problems of Purpose Mismatch
- Building Listening Skills
- Concluding Cautions About Teaching Listening
- Assessing and Evaluating Listening
- Recommended Readings
- Listening Activities and Suggestions

CONSIDER THESE QUESTIONS ABOUT TEACHING LISTENING

1. How does listening work? What processes are involved? Is there a difference between hearing and listening?
2. For what different purposes do people listen? Do purposes influence how people listen? If so, in what ways?

3. What inhibits listening? What can a person do to offset the effects of listening inhibitors?
4. Students spend most of their time in school listening. Is it enough to practice listening, or must students be taught how to listen? Can students be taught to listen more effectively?
5. Should the language arts teacher be solely responsible for teaching students to listen, or is this every teacher's responsibility?
6. What is active listening? How can it be used in the classroom?
7. How can teachers encourage students to become better listeners?
8. How does listening interact with and support the other language arts?
9. Can effective listening be assessed and evaluated? How? Should it?
10. What are some activities that will help middle level students develop their abilities to listen?

ABOUT LISTENING

Of the traditional language arts, listening has received the least attention (Pinnell & Jaggar, 1991), in part because it is the least observable. How can you tell when someone is really listening? Some students give every visible sign of being fully aware, but they do not have the foggiest notion of what is being said. Other students appear to be distracted or half asleep, but they know precisely what is going on. Some people are better able to listen when only one voice is audible; other people actually find the lack of competing sounds distracting. In effect, it is too quiet for them to listen well.

Assumptions about who is and who is not listening that are based on visual observation alone may be inaccurate. Nevertheless, effective listening is a necessity. Students spend more time in school listening than they do engaging in all of the other language arts combined (Strother, 1987). In reporting conclusions of researchers, Tompkins (1998) stated that among the general population, listening consumes about 50% of our communication time. For those who are auditory learners by nature, these are terrific statistics, but many young people and adults learn best in other ways. It is necessary to adjust instruction to match a variety of learning styles, but it is also necessary to help students develop strategies to make the most of their listening capabilities.

LISTENING PROCESSES

Adults often fault young people for "tuning out." Actually, the ability to disengage from listening is an important one. If people were not able to do this, their brains would be overloaded because they would have to give equal attention to every sound—furnace fans, buzzing lights, stomach growls, shuffling paper, coughing, and on and on, just in the classroom. People would not be able to sort out important sounds if they did not have listening filters. Children learn early not to pay much attention to the words of songs, the dialogue of television actors, commercial announcements, public address messages, and so on. They hear so much verbal garbage in the environment that they tend to tune out voices, and they do this in the classroom, too. Hunsaker (1990) reported that people made effective use of only about 25% of their listening ability. Furthermore, people can listen faster than most speakers can talk, at least twice as fast, in fact (Foulke, 1968). As a result, the brain has a lot of time left over for attending to distractions and for tuning in and out without necessarily missing meaning.

Most teachers assume that listening is a single activity. It either is happening or it is not. However, research indicates that listening is more complex than *on* versus *off*. Listening actually involves four different processes, which demand both physical and mental activity (Jalongo, 1991). As Figure 7.1 shows, one must receive sound before sound can become meaningful. Furthermore, one must pay attention to sounds before meaning can be attached. Then sounds have to be interpreted. Finally, they must be remembered sufficiently to produce a response. To listen well, students have to think. They also have to learn to control these listening processes, much as they must monitor comprehension when they read.

LISTENING INHIBITORS

Learning to control listening processes means, in part, being aware of what can inhibit the processes. Listening effectively can be inhibited by a number of different factors. Some of these are **physical**, some are **environmental**, some are **mental**, and some are **attitudinal**.

A physical disability such as hearing loss or deafness may permanently inhibit or prevent reception of auditory signals, but individuals may also be unable to receive an auditory signal as a result of a temporary condition such as a cold or an earache. Because people who have a permanent or temporary hearing loss often use lipreading and/or interpretations of nonverbal cues (e.g., facial expressions, gestures) to enhance reception of auditory signals, an in-

---

Processes of Listening

Receiving—the physical process of hearing auditory stimuli and, to some extent, seeing related visual cues (i.e., nonverbal communication signals).
> Inhibited by lack of auditory or visual acuity (i.e., cannot hear or see well enough).

Attending—focused perception of selected stimuli which requires effort as well as desire and concerns sifting the significant from the trivial.
> Inhibited by individual's limited attention span, questionable priority system upon which to base selection, and/or lack of motivation to attend.

Assigning Meaning—the mental interpretation or understanding of the auditory stimuli heard and attended to, which is probably accomplished by matching data with existing mental categories (i.e., prior knowledge and schema).
> Inhibited by breakdown in receiving and/or attending; incorrect categorization due to listener's narrow experiences, inadequate vocabulary, etc.; inability to categorize stimuli when needed; and/or strong emotional response in the listener.

Remembering/Responding—storage of auditory stimuli in long-term memory in order to respond (i.e., retell, relate to other experiences, take action, etc.).
> Inhibited by difficulties in one or more of the previous processes, decision to disregard information, or ineffective storage making it difficult or impossible to retrieve.

FIG. 7.1

ability to see the speaker can interfere with receiving auditory messages. Those are all physical inhibitors.

The environment in which listening is supposed to occur can be an inhibitor. If there is a great deal of background noise or if there are visual distractions that compete for attention, listening processes can be hampered. If the setting is not one in which listening is obviously valued and expected, students may not make an attempt to receive messages by listening. To listen well, students must be tuned in. They have to be attending to the act of listening. Some teachers feel that this mental concentration demands physical inactivity. However, attending may not demand the cessation of all other physical movement. Some students can attend well while doing other things. Adults often report that they can actually attend better if they do something else at the same time, usually something rather automatic such as doodling or knitting. Others take notes habitually. Demanding that students be absolutely silent and nearly motionless when listening may be an environmental factor that actually serves to inhibit listening.

Some inhibitors are mental. Students may not be aware of the need to think while they listen. Hearing what is said is not the same as comprehending the message. It is not uncommon to give clear directions that some students immediately disregard or cannot follow. When asked, they will say that they heard the directions and paid attention to them. The problem was not in the receiving or attending; the missing factor was making meaning of the message. For whatever reason, these students inaccurately assigned meaning; they failed to interpret the information correctly and to make sense of it as it was intended. They may have emphasized a word that the speaker did not highlight, or they may have thought of a different definition of a term that has several meanings, or perhaps they drew on a prior experience that misled them.

Listening also involves the process of remembering. Many factors can get in the way of recalling information. The student who hears directions and interprets their meaning accurately may still be unable to follow them if he or she cannot recall all of the steps. Sometimes what a person hears activates memories that are seemingly unrelated. When this occurs, the new information may get stored in the brain with that personal association instead of in a more logical place. Then, when the person wants to recall what was heard, he or she cannot seem to remember it even though the individual knows that he or she heard it and paid attention to it. Thus, listening can be impaired even when one has a positive attitude about the activity.

When negative attitudes exist, listening may be impossible. Students who do not want to listen will not. This may be a factor of their general attitude toward school or the teacher, or it may be the result of their personal feelings of incompetence. Sometimes it is a matter of having what they consider to be more important things on their minds. Sometimes it is just the effects of having a bad day. Sometimes it has much to do with their interest in the topic or subject area. However, it is sometimes a part of their culture or the community in which they live. If their life experiences have convinced them that listening in the classroom is not worthwhile, they probably will not have a positive attitude toward listening just because the teacher says they should. This may be especially true of the student who is in great need of attention. Unless he or she obtains some kind of positive value from the listening experience, be it praise for listening well or recognizable knowledge that is important to him or her, that individual is not apt to engage in listening. The student who seems to have no control over his or her listening processes in a language arts class may be the best listener in a physical education or a vocational technology class. Although that is a simplistic example, attitudinal factors certainly play a significant role in enhancing or inhibiting listening.

All in all, a lot can go wrong when people listen.

LISTENING PURPOSES

As if all the inhibitors to listening were not enough, people may also have difficulty listening because they are not focusing on the right listening purpose at the right time. Wolvin and Coakley (1979, 1985) have identified five different listening purposes (see Fig. 7.2).

Discriminative listening has to do with the ability to sort one sound from another. In the early grades, this has much to do with students learning to use phonics in order to sound out words, but discriminatory listening is also important to adults. Sorting out the sound of a siren, for example, from the other sounds that surround us can be an important survival skill. Students and teachers must be able to distinguish the fire alarm from the tornado signal in school. People also use discriminatory listening when they recognize a familiar voice in a crowd. Discriminatory listening is essential for conversing with people for whom English is a second language or who suffer from one of several kinds of speech difficulties. Unfortunately, people may discredit those speakers rather than recognize that it is their own responsibility to shift into a different listening mode.

Researchers have also reported a kind of listening that they describe as **therapeutic**, although this one could be called *sympathetic* or *empathetic*. When your best friend comes to you with a tale of woe, that friend expects you to listen with emotional understanding. He or she does not want analysis or advice, just a sympathetic ear and a shoulder to lean on. Guidance counselors and therapists must be adept at therapeutic listening. Teachers, too, must develop this ability in order to engage in what is known as *active listening*, which can be a useful tool for dealing with discipline problems and conflict resolution. It is helpful to keep in mind that therapeutic listening cannot occur unless there is a supportive communication climate. All too often people listen critically when they should listen therapeutically. They offer advice or tell people what they think instead of letting the speaker know that they understand. Teens who complain that their parents never listen often mean that adults do not listen with empathy or sympathy.

Although both discriminatory and therapeutic listening are important skills to learn, school settings are usually better designed to focus on the other three listening purposes that researchers have identified. **Efferent (comprehensive)** listening is what most people do most of the time. This is simply listening to comprehend or understand what is heard. **Critical** listening is built on comprehension, but it demands a higher level of thought because it focuses on making judgments. One has to comprehend and then evaluate. **Aesthetic (appreciative)** listening simply refers to the kind of listening people do for enjoyment. Often this is associated with listen-

Summary of Purposes of Listening

Discriminative listening

Definition: Listening to distinguish auditory or visual stimuli

Most appropriately applied: When danger exists or as a necessary condition for comprehension

May involve the skills of:

- Listening to discriminate speech sounds, musical tones, or common environmental sounds
- Developing sensitivity to arguments and language (i.e., recognizing loaded words, fact versus opinion, inductive vs. deductive logic)
- Developing sensitivity to nonverbal communication that accompanies verbal communication
- Ability to compare and contrast
- Decision-making
- Ability to respond with quick physical action

Therapeutic listening

Definition: Listening nonjudgmentally and empathetically, as a sounding board

Most appropriately applied: When the message is personal

May involve the skills of:

- Active listening (reporting back what the speaker hears)
- Avoiding judgmental ego roles typical of all-knowing parents or emotional children
- Resisting the temptation to give advice
- Recognizing the necessity of adopting this role, even though the speaker says heor she wants aid
- Questioning effectively

Efferent (comprehensive) listening

Definition: Listening to understand a message without making a critical judgment

Most appropriately applied: When the message is informative

May involve the skills of:

- Listening for common organizational patterns (e.g., cause and effect or temporal order)
- Distinguishing between factual information and inferences made by the listener
- Listening for links between known and new information
- Listening for various kinds of meaningful connections
- Distinguishing main ideas from supporting points and examples

Critical listening

Definition: Listening not only to understand but to assess, evaluate, or judge

Most appropriately applied: When the message is persuasive or intended
to be polished for public performance, or both
May involve the skills of:
- Detecting faulty and illogical arguments
- Sensitivity to how arguments are structured (e.g., inductively or syllogistically)
- Recognition of loaded words that may cause the listener to apply labels,
stereotypes, and biases without conscious thought
- Judging the credibility of the speaker
- Developing appropriate criteria for judging
- Decision making

Aesthetic (appreciative) listening
Definition: Listening for enjoyment and pleasure
Most appropriately applied: When the message is intended to stimulate
senses and emotions
May involve the skills of:
- Listening to visualize
- Listening for speech rhythms
- Listening for speaker's style
- Listening to interpret character from the dialogue spoken
- Listening to recognize tone and mood
- Recognizing the effect of the speaker's vocal qualities and physical actions
- Recognizing the effect of audience on listener's own responses

FIG. 7.2

ing to music, but in the language arts classroom appreciative
listening relates to enjoying poetry and appreciating powerful and
melodic speaking voices.

PROBLEMS OF PURPOSE MISMATCH

All of these listening purposes are important, but students also need
to know when each purpose should be used. Some teachers are truly
distressed by students who challenge the ideas they have presented.
They expect students to be listening comprehensively rather than critically. On the other hand, some teachers are distressed when students
fail to ask questions that demonstrate that they are looking for holes
and gaps and questionable conclusions. These teachers are expecting
students to listen critically, but students are only listening for comprehension. Some people attend a speech and report it as being awful because the speaker's voice was raspy or the phrases were badly paced.

Other people attending the same speech report it as being excellent because the content was informative, well organized, and supported with relevant examples. The difference between the responses is that the listeners were using different yardsticks to measure the presentation. One group expected to appreciate, whereas the other expected to comprehend. Excellent speakers are able to satisfy both groups of listeners. However, many people who have worthwhile information to share are not good public speakers. Listeners may need to be able to stretch beyond their first impression in these cases in order to focus on a more appropriate listening purpose.

Listeners may also need to be able to set aside their personal biases at times. For example, suppose that you are required to attend a speech being given on a topic that you find personally distasteful or that proposes a position on a controversial subject to which you are opposed. Unless you consciously approach this situation with a comprehensive listening purpose in mind, you are likely to be so critical that you fail to hear some of the main points. You may come away knowing no more about the topic than you did before because you did not set out to learn anything new. Instead, you set out only to find fault and reinforce your own prior convictions. Now, suppose that you are a gifted pianist who attends a concert. You may come away from the performance with the distinct impression that the event was poorly executed, whereas other less critical listeners may feel that the concert was truly enjoyable. The difference is likely to be in the listening. You listened critically, whereas others listened appreciatively. All of these examples illustrate what happens when listening purposes are mismatched with the reality of the situations. Middle school students need assistance in building their skills in using all of these listening purposes, but they also need to know when to use which purpose and the skills associated with each.

BUILDING LISTENING SKILLS

There is very little research that points to what is most effective in teaching students to be better listeners. However, there is general agreement within the profession that listening deserves more instructional attention than it usually receives (Hyslop & Tone, 1988). Directing students to "listen up" or "pay attention" is not enough. Occasionally, students are reminded about certain behaviors that are appropriate during speeches or convocations, or, before going on a field trip to a concert or play, they are given directions about how a good audience member behaves. Teachers who use cooperative learning groups often take some time—but not much—to remind students that listening to other people in the group is necessary as well as courteous. These reminders are certainly better than no emphasis at all, but, for the most part, students are expected to learn to listen better simply by listening. Considering the complaints in adult society about the breakdowns in communication due to ineffective listening, it seems reasonable to conclude that this assumption is not serving students sufficiently well.

Integrating Listening

Teaching a separate unit on listening probably will not improve it. Isolation of skills from a natural context may make the skill more difficult to learn, and skills learned in one situation do not readily transfer to another. Although there are some activities that can be used to engage students in listening and that help them focus attention on listening, integrating listening activities into other units of study and other activities is probably more beneficial. This can be tricky, however, because it increases the likelihood that listening will not receive enough attention. You have to set appropriate goals and plan sufficient time to focus on listening even though your major focus is on some other content or some other processes.

One of the most effective and natural contexts for teaching listening is in conjunction with speaking or dramatic performance. When students are performing for their peers, some discussion of appropriate audience behavior, including listening well, fits easily into the situation. When students introduce their oral presentations, they should provide some information that helps the audience set an appropriate purpose for listening.

Students generally enjoy listening to a well-read story, but they can also be asked to listen for some specific purposes (e.g., details about characters, vivid description, unfamiliar words, etc.). Much poetry needs to be heard to be fully appreciated. For a variety of reasons, including improvement of listening skills, you can have students listen to tapes of short stories and books. If you choose to do this, be aware that text versions vary. If students are to follow along with the tape, you must be certain that the recording duplicates the print they have in hand. Although it is rarely used now, some nonfiction is excellent for listening. Students can be encouraged to listen for purpose, organization, strong voice, and effective style. For additional suggestions and samples, you may find Trelease's (1993) *Read All about It* useful, but Freeman's (1997) *Listen to This: Developing an Ear for Expository* may be a more valuable resource.

Another excellent vehicle for teaching listening is a unit on directions. This can be a social studies unit that looks at geographic directions, a science unit that looks at conducting observations or lab experiments, or a speech unit that includes some demonstration speeches or explanations of processes. It can also be a unit that involves some writing of directions or explanations of how events occur or how an activity should be done. *Directions* is a reasonably broad topic that can be interpreted in several different ways and can include a variety of activities. Among them can be some practice in following verbal directions. This can be turned into a game in which one person gives a direction that the next person must follow. That individual in turn repeats the first direction and then adds another. The third person has to follow both directions in the proper order, and the game continues in this fashion. When someone forgets, the procedure starts again. The traditional children's game Simon Says also fits into this topic and emphasizes effective listening. A unit on directions can also include some focus on game directions that can be given orally. Students can attempt to play the game and then discuss some of the problems they have because of various levels of assigned meaning and remembering. This can be followed by having students create their own games and give oral directions to others for play as a kind of test run of the instructions. On the basis of the results, they can then create a better set of written directions so that other students can play without having to listen and recall. Another activity that students enjoy is asking one person to give to another person directions for creating a sketch. That person must draw according to the directions he or she receives. This activity can also be used in conjunction with a unit on descriptive writing or as part of a short story unit in which setting is studied.

During other units, tape recordings of music can be used to accompany writing and reading. These may be musical compositions that students select because they reflect the pace of the discourse, or they may be pieces the teacher selects in order to set a particular mood or augment the content of the lesson (e.g., music of a particular culture that matches the setting of a story). The primary purpose of this activity is appreciative listening. This idea can be extended so that students select and play accompanying music when they read aloud either their own writing or professionally written discourse that they wish to share with classmates. This also sets the stage for having students choose background music for other types of productions, such as television or radio advertisements, dramatic performances, and computer multimedia projects.

Increasing Awareness of Processes and Purposes

Whether you teach listening as a separate unit, as part of other units, or as part of a reading–writing workshop arrangement, include activities that focus attention on improving the quality of listening processes and broadening the range of listening purposes. Although it is unlikely that students will want to learn all of the intricacies of the listening processes, they may find it interesting to know about the different processes and to discuss how listening can break down. Some students are frustrated by their seeming inability to listen well. They may find it useful to discuss at what point they have the most difficulty. Effective listeners can share some of their techniques for blocking out distractions and for thinking while they listen. The idea here is to make students aware of what they do automatically and to consider ways to break some bad habits they may have developed over the years.

Students can also share what makes listening easier and what makes it more difficult. This information may be beneficial in helping to set some class guidelines for appropriate listening behavior. It can also be used as a problem solver when individuals differ in how they listen best. For example, what can be done if some students listen best when it is quiet and some listen best when there are some other noises? Perhaps a CD player with headphones is the answer. Teachers need to recognize these differences among students if they are to create productive learning environments, but students also need to respect diversity among classmates.

If students are to learn to listen well for different purposes, they need opportunities to do so, but they also need some instruction that helps them use these purposes consciously rather than simply being permitted to use whatever purpose they invoke naturally. Teachers often include listening experiences that are predominately meant to entertain, but they want these experiences to serve as models, so they expect students to listen critically, too. For example, during a unit on oral literature, the teacher may ask a local storyteller to perform as a guest speaker. The teacher's goal for this activity may be to provide students with an effective model of good storytelling techniques. Students, however, are likely to listen appreciatively only and miss the point of the demonstration. At the very least, the teacher should provide some direction about the listening purposes to be used. Follow-up discussion can serve to identify differences in response based on the use of an "inappropriate" purpose. Such discussion can help students recognize how they approach listening tasks and how they miss some important concepts or ideas simply because they are focusing on the wrong purpose. At the middle school level, these need to be emphasized as learning discoveries, not reprimands for poor performance.

To enhance remembering, students can be encouraged to create a scaffold of ideas so that they are not trying to recall isolated bits of information. The more integrated the instruction, the easier it is for students to see skills as part of a web of related ideas. In the classroom, you can try to make sure that any listening activity is linked to the other material being studied. This means, in part, stating the objective for a listening activity to show how it connects with previous and subsequent activities or how the listening activity relates to the topic under study. In this regard, narrative is a strong force. People tend to remember stories and incidents more vividly than they recall expository material. If the material can be related in the form of a story or illustrated through an anecdote, the memory is likely to be much stronger. Also, re-creating the original scenario in which the information was learned may help the listener remember the information. Everyone has said, "Now, where was I when I heard that?" In effect, people are trying to re-create the situation so that they can retrace their memory steps to find the missing link. This is a strategy that can readily be taught to students through demonstration.

As much as possible, you should incorporate listening activities that are worthwhile. That means providing a wider range of opportunities than is often the case in the classroom. Guest speakers and tape recordings are two excellent sources of listening material. A field trip to attend a performance or visit a location where guides or docents are used is also an excellent listening opportunity. Another activity that middle level students generally find very interesting is interviewing another person. This simple idea can be developed into a collection of oral histories, the ethnographic study of a community, or even a collection of data about the culture of the school. Dramatic activities, particularly role playing and improvisation, demand good listening. Debates and simulations encourage students to listen critically, as does evaluating verbal advertisements and political speeches. Even a formal lecture presented by the teacher can be used as the source of listening engagement as well as a practical opportunity for students to develop note-taking skills. In fact, almost any speech activity provides an opportunity for assisting students to develop better listening skills if the teacher takes the time to discuss the matter with students before or after the activity.

Reducing the Effects of Inhibitors

I once supervised a student teacher who was facing the challenge of teaching two hearing-impaired students in the same class. She was directed by the supervising teacher always to speak at the front of the class so that she was visible to these students because both were adept lip-readers. As you can imagine, this was extremely restrictive. The student teacher wondered if this was the only way to cope with the problem, so we brainstormed some alternatives. One was to buddy the students with other students who could pass along any verbal information that was given as the student teacher moved around the room. Another was to do more work in small groups so that these students could communicate with the people in their groups. Another was to put all of the directions on paper for these students. No doubt there are other alternatives, but the important point is that physical inhibitors need not be handled in only one manner. The students themselves can often give you the best hints about effective strategies you can use to assist them in receiving auditory messages.

As for environmental inhibitors, you can begin by setting expectations which emphasize how much you value listening. That means that you have to listen well to students, and you have to ensure that they listen to each other. You can also work with students to create a better setting for listening, one that addresses differing learning styles. Teachers sometimes ask that students clear the top of their desks when they are going to engage in an activity that requires close listening for an extended period of time. It may be better to watch what students do naturally as they listen. Some students will twiddle with pencils, some will sketch, and some will put their heads down. There will be a few who try to finish their homework for another class. Observations of these behaviors provide evidence of listening or lack of it. Other evidence appears in follow-up discussions. You will want to listen closely to the responses that students give and to the questions they ask. Taking these results into consideration, you may recommend certain changes in behavior for the next time the class is to listen, or you may leave well enough alone. Many adults take notes when they listen. It helps them attend and recall. Although not everyone takes notes, adults do not sit straight with their hands folded when they listen. Why should we have such expectations of middle level students?

Of course, if you have a guest speaker, you will need to set the stage in advance. Part of that process is to help students understand that their body language conveys messages to the speaker and that because this person is a guest, they should make him or her feel welcome not only by what they say, but also by what they do. If you choose the speaker well, you can usually monitor behavior with an occasional quiet reminder to individuals. If you can do so, give students who may create distractions the option of completing another task. Because this usually means being separated from the rest of the class, most students will cooperate rather than be isolated.

Mental inhibitors are difficult to control, but there are some strategies that students can learn and you can facilitate. For example, breaking lengthy listening activities into segments and asking students either to write their questions or responses periodically or to share them with a buddy at specific intervals will encourage students to think as they listen. You can make it clear to students that you will not repeat directions but that you will clarify them as necessary. Then you can call on other students to repeat directions you have given. This verifies that your directions were clear and audible. However, it also provides a slightly different vocabulary or emphasis which may help the confused student assign meaning more effectively. Also, try to provide some connections to previous course work or prior experiences so that whatever they are hearing is linked to something familiar.

As is always the case, attitudinal inhibitors are the most difficult to address. There are students who absolutely refuse to listen. The key factor here is to ask why. Some students refuse because they lack confidence. If they do not listen, they do not have to perform. If they do not listen, they cannot be responsible. At least that is what they think. These students need to know that they will be held accountable, but they also need to be assured that they can learn and that they will receive the assistance they need to learn. Some students are preoccupied with trying to satisfy more pressing concerns. They need attention, safety, social acceptance, or confidence, and they are out to get it. Listening just delays gratification for them. Again, the guiding question has to be why. If you can find an answer to that question, you can probably find a solution by creating other circumstances that help them satisfy those other needs. That is not always easy to do, but it generally means that all of their class work—including listening—will improve.

The students that you may find most difficult to work with in the area of listening are those who come from households or community settings in which listening is not valued or where turn-taking behavior is not a part of the culture or customs. These are the students who talk over one another and respect voice volume more than content of discourse. These are also the students who talk through nearly every kind of activity. Although teachers generally find this behavior very distracting, the students see it as normal. At home they talk while family members talk; at the movies they talk throughout the film; with their friends they carry on two or three conversations simultaneously. In some cases, these students are very adept listeners, but much of the time they miss major portions of idea development and connections among thoughts. You may find that individual conferences with these students work wonders, or you may choose to have class discussions about how other students feel about these behaviors. You do need to set expectations and make it clear to students that you expect them to follow the rules, but you may also need to incorporate more speaking activities to provide outlets for these students. Try to remain aware that these behaviors may be part of the students' identity, background, and culture. You will want to help them learn how to increase their listening, but they may not be able to make great gains in a single year.

Day-to-Day Listening Activities

In addition to special activities, there are some techniques that can be used on a regular basis that may enhance listening. Any ordinary speaking activity in the classroom provides an opportunity to reinforce listening improvement. Asking students to rephrase statements in their own words is one of these activities. You can have students rephrase statements made by the teacher or ones made by other students. Sometimes it is helpful to ask students to rephrase questions, too. If you ask a question and a student either cannot provide an answer or provides one that seems to be way off the mark, you can ask the student to say what he or she thought the question was. This may well illustrate that the question itself was not clear or that the listening process broke down at the assigning meaning stage. Teachers can build in illogical statements or misinformation that students must listen for, but this has to be done with some care to make sure that students do not walk out of class believing that what they heard was accurate. Another excellent listening strategy is to ask students to summarize or review the lesson when it is done. This develops several skills simultaneously, including listening, but it also helps the teacher identify ideas that are still fuzzy or incomplete.

CONCLUDING CAUTIONS ABOUT TEACHING LISTENING

When considering how to teach listening more effectively, you should be aware of a couple of cautions. First, avoid listening activities that discourage students from listening. Asking students to share something about a book they have enjoyed, a piece of their own writing they are especially proud of, or a report of a current news event often attracts listening attention, but not if this is an assigned task that everyone has to do. Guest speakers who ramble on and are poorly prepared generally turn students off. Frequent, long lectures will not help students develop better listening skills, nor will listening to one classmate after another present oral reports. Reading text aloud in round-robin fashion also tends to discourage good listening. However, providing opportunities for students to read aloud something that really interests them or strikes them as exceptionally well written prompts the audience, be it the whole class or a small group, to listen more attentively. This may be even more effective if the reader opens with a statement that indicates which purpose for listening is appropriate.

The second caution is related to the first because it, too, may discourage listening. It is easy to slip into a kind of disciplinary mode when it comes to listening. "Charles, are you listening?" "Alice, what did I just say?" "Juan, did you hear me?" "Desiree, you aren't paying attention." It is also easy to embarrass students by calling on them when their attention seems to be wandering. Reprimands about failing to listen generally prompt young students to stay on-task in the elementary grades, but at the middle level these kinds of questions and statements often generate negative responses from students and can lead to hostility and confrontations. If such responses are handled badly, students become even less attentive as the classroom environment takes on an adversarial tone.

One key to teaching effective listening is to give students worthwhile material. Middle level students find staying on-task difficult, particularly when the task seems pointless, irrelevant, and a waste of time. If students are not paying attention, the first question you should ask yourself is whether the content and activities are engaging the students. No matter how important you may think something is, if students do not share that perception, very little improvement in listening is likely to take place. Indeed, very little learning is likely to occur.

ASSESSING AND EVALUATING LISTENING

Assessing and evaluating listening is nearly impossible because it is invisible. You may be able to identify a few students who show evidence of listening well. They nod their heads, frown, or smile at appropriate times. They ask pertinent questions or share relevant examples. They follow instructions promptly and well. However, all of these are only indirect measures. Other students may not demonstrate any observable signs of effective listening, yet they may be quite skillful. You are apt to discover that the student who appears to be totally disconnected from the class work is all too attentive if you make a verbal error. This is the student who delights in pointing out the mistake. Fortunately, there are not many students like this. Some activities that you think will assess listening do not. For example, if you read a story aloud to students and then give them a written quiz on the material, the results may actually measure your oral reading skill or the students' skill in reading the questions more than how well people listened.

Although indirect measures are not foolproof, they are the only tools you will have for assessing and evaluating listening. At least part of the assessment of small group work should include some attention to effective listening. Tape recordings of group interaction can be useful. Another approach is to work with students to create a checklist of behaviors associated with effective listening. This activity will prompt students to think about listening and how to listen well. The checklist can then be prominently displayed to remind students of how to demonstrate that they are listening. It can also be used by the teacher and by students to assess progress and performance.

Whether it involves the use of a checklist or not, the best tool for assessing listening is probably self-assessment. Only students know for sure whether or not they are listening and whether or not they are developing better listening skills. Conferences with students in which they describe their listening processes and problems can be helpful for planning instruction as well as assessing performance. Through self-assessment, students may be able to identify progress that is not evident to you. If they are making a conscientious effort to hone listening skills, they should have the opportunity to make this known and to receive appropriate credit for their growth.

RECOMMENDED READINGS

Blatchford, C. (1997). *Many ways of hearing: 94 multitasked lessons in listening*. Portland, ME: J. Weston Walch.

Brent, R., & Anderson, P. (1993). Developing children's classroom listening strategies. *The Reading Teacher, 47,* 122–126.

Devine, T. (1978). Listening: What do we know after fifty years of theorizing? *Journal of Reading, 21,* 296–304.

Fidge, L. (1992). *The essential guide to speaking and listening.* Dunstable, England: Folens Limited.

Freeman, M. (1997). *Listen to this: Developing an ear for expository.* Gainesville, FL: Maupin-House.

Funk, H., & Funk, G. (1989). Guidelines for developing listening skills. *The Reading Teacher, 42,* 660–663.

Graser, N. (1992). *125 ways to be a better listener.* East Moline, IL: LinguiSystems.

Hennings, D. (1992). *Beyond the read aloud: Learning to read through listening to and reflecting on literature.* Bloomington, IN: Phi Delta Kappa Educational Foundation.

Hunsaker, R. (1990). *Understanding and developing the skills of oral communication: Speaking and listening* (2nd ed.). Englewood, CO: Morton.

Hyslop, N., & Tone, B. (1988). Listening: Are we teaching it, and if so, how? *ERIC/RCS Digest, 3.*

Jalongo, M. (1991). *Strategies for developing children's listening skills* (Fastback #314). Bloomington, IN: Phi Delta Kappa Educational Foundation.

Pinnell, G., & Jaggar, A. (1991). Oral language: Speaking and listening in the classroom. In J. Flood, J. Jensen, D. Lapp, & J. Squire (Eds.), *Handbook of research on teaching the English language arts* (pp. 691–720). New York: Macmillan.

Rixon, S. (1986). *Developing listening skills.* London: Macmillan.

Russell, D., & Russell, E. (1959). *Listening aids through the grades: One hundred ninety listening activities.* New York: Columbia University Teachers College.

Shannon, G. (1994). *Still more stories to solve.* New York: Beech Tree Books.

Sobel, D. (1967). *Two-minute mysteries.* New York: Scholastic.

Sound strategy. (1997, June/July). *Reading TODAY,* p. 8.

Strother, D. (1987). Practical applications of research: On listening. *Phi Delta Kappan, 68,* 625–628.

Trelease, J. (1993). *Read all about it: Great read-aloud stories, poems, and newspaper pieces for preteens and teens.* New York: Penguin.

Underwood, M. (1989). *Teaching listening.* New York: Longman.

Wolvin, A., & Coakley C. (1979). *Listening instruction.* Urbana, IL: ERIC Clearinghouse on Reading and Communication Skills and the Speech Communication Association.

Wolvin, A., & Coakley, C. (1985). *Listening* (2nd ed.). Dubuque, IA: William C. Brown.

OTHER RESOURCES

International Listening Association
366 N. Prior Ave.
St. Paul, MN 55104

Audio Bookshelf (unabridged recordings of some books suitable for middle school)
174 Prescott Hill Road
Northport, ME 04849
1–800–234–1713 (orders)
e-mail: audbkshf@agate.net

The American Audio Prose Library, Inc. (author interviews and readings)
P. O. Box 842
Columbia, MO 65205
1–800–447–2275

Recorded Books, Inc.
270 Skipjack Road
Prince Frederick, MD 20678
1–800–638–1304
www.recordedbooks.com

Radio Spirits, Inc. (cassette and CD versions of old-time radio programs)
Box 2141, Dept. SMO97
Schiller Park, IL 60176
1–800–723–4648

AudioFile (reviews of audiobooks)
   P.O. Box 109
   Portland, ME 04112
   1–800–506–1212

Listening Activities and Suggestions

- 7.1 Suggestions for Supporting Listening
- 7.2 Listening Activities
- 7.3 Listening Checklist

Activity 7.1:
Suggestions for Supporting Listening

- Tape recordings are good sources for listening, as will be audioconferencing when the technology becomes more available. However, middle level students have trouble just listening to a tape or voices. They may even have difficulty concentrating when music is played. Give them something to look at while they listen—some related posters on the wall, some objects they can pass around, the text of the tape, a photograph of the person speaking, and so forth. Another strategy is to give them a few questions to answer as they listen. Have them read the questions before listening. They are not to write while listening, though. Instead, when the tape or conference is done, have them answer only one or two questions in writing. If you want students to listen to a long tape or watch a lengthy videotape, plan to pause at selected points or whenever you notice students getting restless. Ask someone to summarize what has occurred or the main ideas that have been presented. Students can do this in pairs. Then have someone predict what will be next or state any questions that have come to mind that he or she hopes will be answered in the next segment.

- To listen well, students have to be in a receiving and attending mode. Do not try to give directions unless you have everyone's attention and the room is quiet. You need to tell students about this expectation and use some kind of cue that lets them know when you need their ears and minds tuned to you. If you have some students who persistently request repetition of directions, find out why. One way to handle these requests is to institute a procedure at the start of the year in which any student who asks for a repetition of directions is attended to by a student you select. This means that another student gets a special privilege and gets a chance at building self-esteem. It also lets the asker know that he or she will not get your attention with this ploy.

- Many middle level students have not yet learned to listen well to classmates. Set this as an expectation in your classroom. Avoid parroting what students say. If they cannot be heard clearly, then ask them to repeat their comments or questions more loudly. Occasionally you should call on a student to rephrase what a peer has said or clarify it. At other times, redirect a question to a student rather than answer it yourself by saying, "John, what do you think about that?" or "Jane, how would you answer that question?"

- Linguists must develop the ability to hear speech sounds clearly and to distinguish even minor dialectic or pronunciation differences. Although it probably is not wise to set out to make middle level students junior linguists, they can be asked to spend some time listening to the language around them. They can listen for certain kinds of words, such as slang or jargon. They can also listen for polite but basically meaningless phrases, such as "good morning." They can also be asked to try to transcribe some ordinary speech that has been tape-recorded. This should be done in a meaningful context (i.e., a context in which there is a need to record the exact words of the speaker, such as for an oral history project or a transcription of testimony in a mock trial).

Activity 7.2:
Listening Activities

1. Listen to examples of chanting, such as Gregorian chants, sports chants, liturgical chants, and chants used at political or civic rallies. Select poems or other literature that can be chanted effectively. Plan, prepare, rehearse, and present the chant.

2. Moderate a round table discussion by introducing panel members, tossing out the first question, and moving to other questions when the topic shifts. A moderator keeps people on topic, summarizes, and evaluates, but participants are encouraged to respond rather informally to each other.

3. Make tape recordings for others. Listen to the tape before letting others use it.

4. Participate in story theater. As someone reads a story aloud, participants act out the discourse silently.

5. Have students listen to a teacher presentation while a radio and television plays simultaneously so as to improve focusing attention.

6. Have students working in a small group read a script aloud without punctuation or emotion. Then have them read it several times, experimenting with various interpretations. Listeners can provide feedback about which readings are best.

7. Listen to news or sports reporting. Identify examples of facts, opinions, judgments, and well-supported statements.

8. Listen to a debate. Identify the most persuasive arguments.

9. Listen to advertisements for objects, services, or political candidates that include endorsements by individuals. Determine whether these individuals have the credibility to be convincing.

10. Listen to television soap operas or talk shows broadcast on the radio. Discuss the style of the dialogue, especially the image of the person the speech creates.

11. Listen to the constructive criticism offered by peers about a rough draft or the rehearsal of a speech or dramatic performance. Apply the information to polish the paper, speech, or drama.

12. Listen to a musical recording and identify the instruments being played.

13. Take a walking tour inside the school or around the perimeter of the building. Students are to record all the sounds they hear.

They can list the sources or write onomatopoeic words to describe the noises.

14. Have students listen to an oral reading. They are to identify the end punctuation of each sentence. They can use hand gestures to signal each or write each one on paper.

15. Have students watch a videotape of Victor Borge's oral punctuation and then try it themselves while others watch and listen.

16. Give students a diagnostic listening test in which they spell words that are difficult to distinguish (e.g., pin–pen; affect–effect; whether–weather; specific–pacific).

17. Discuss good listening habits. Make a list and turn it into a poster or bulletin board that is accessible to students. Students can share strategies they use to make their listening more effective.

18. Have students set listening goals for themselves.

19. Have students listen to some material read aloud. They signal whenever they hear certain key words or transitions.

20. Read to students a list of directions for performing a common activity. Stop periodically and have students supply the next step.

21. Have students listen to a debate. Then have them make a Venn diagram or T-chart to summarize or graphically illustrate the positions.

22. When reading aloud a continuing story, try to stop at a high point so as to motivate students to listen more attentively the next time. Students can also be asked to predict what they think will happen next.

23. Read a short story or poem aloud but leave off the title or a key word. Ask students to suggest an appropriate title or figure out the missing word.

24. Give students the opportunity to read tall tales aloud to a small group or the class. Listeners must identify the exaggerations. Or let students read humorous material aloud. Listeners identify overstatements, understatements, sarcasm, irony, and so forth.

25. Read mystery stories aloud to students. Listeners should pinpoint clues and examples of foreshadowing. The series by Sobel starting with *Two-Minute Mysteries* (1967) is excellent for this, as is Shannon's *Still More Stories to Solve* (1994).

26. Have students play various kinds of guessing games in which clues are given orally, such as Twenty Questions, Password, or Trivial Pursuit. Mad Gab is especially good for highlighting listening. A modified version of Scategories also works. One student calls out features, such as leaves, bark, and limbs. The first

person who names an appropriate object or animal or whatever fits the category earns a point. If a wrong answer is given, that person must be the next to call out features. Simon Says is another possibility, but it can be extended to include fictional settings, such as a medieval castle, in which actions can be pantomimed (e.g., "Simon says draw your sword; Simon says bow to the queen; Simon says lower the drawbridge; raise the visor on your armor").

27. Students list names of noises, such as swish, gurgle, toot, whistle, chatter, and pop. These are submitted to a speaker who reads the words one at a time. Listeners have to write the word and then name something that makes the noise.

28. Ask students to identify a quality of a character in literature they have read. Then read excerpts from the literature. Have students decide whether or not the excerpt proves that the character has the quality named or proves that the character has another quality.

29. Cut up a printed version of a story. Give each student a part. Have all students read their parts silently. The person who thinks he or she has the opening segment reads it aloud. When that person is done, students have to decide which segment comes next. That person reads and so on.

30. Read aloud a brief poem that is in some way related to literature that students have read. Students try to figure out the piece of literature and the link.

31. Near the end of the year, have students write brief character sketches from stories everyone has read. They read these aloud. Students try to figure out which character is being described.

32. Seat students in a circle. The first person begins by saying, "I went to the mall and I bought—." The next person repeats the initial statement and adds a new item. This continues until someone cannot recall all of the items previously named. This person starts a new sequence. The objective is to continue the sequence all the way around the circle.

33. Begin a story orally, or have a student begin a story orally. At a convenient point, the teller points to someone else who must continue the tale and pass the telling on. The telling stops when listeners hear a teller contradict something already told. This can also be done with pairs of students who pass the telling back and forth.

34. Have students listen to a tape recording of sound effects. Have them list adjectives or onomatopoeic words that describe the sounds.

35. Give students a word and have them pantomime the antonym.

36. Have students listen to tapes of old radio broadcasts. Then have them create their own scripts in the same style (i.e., comedy, mystery, adventure). If they wish, they can use the same main characters.

37. Have students imagine being somewhere specific. They are to list the sounds they would hear if they were in this location. Have them make the sounds. Listeners should react appropriately. They should also identify the setting. For example, students may imagine a zoo. They may then imitate a monkey, an elephant, and a bird. Listeners may point and giggle, show fear, and then smile. Other settings that may work well include amusement parks, golf courses, haunted houses, or sports arenas.

38. To practice following oral directions, have students try origami.

39. Have students listen to political speeches to identify propaganda and advertising techniques or faulty arguments.

40. If possible, have students work with preschool children. Each should keep a log of what he or she hears the children say. These records should be shared, compared, and discussed. Have an expert in the language development of children help students understand what they have observed.

41. Some discussion techniques support effective listening. For example, you can direct students to respond to the previous speaker before making their own comments. They may summarize the previous speaker's point, rephrase it, or question it. Another alternative is to have students build on or elaborate the previous speaker's point before introducing a new thought. Whenever students work in small groups, someone should be responsible for acting as a summarizer and group spokesperson. This responsibility should rotate so that the same people do not always take this role. When possible, these individuals should check the accuracy of their summaries with the group before reporting to the teacher or the class.

42. Require students to listen to peers as they read drafts of their compositions during revising rather than passing papers around and reading them silently. Doing so is beneficial not only as a listening activity but also as a composing one. If students must listen to the papers rather than read them, they are forced to focus on content instead of mechanics.

43. At the conclusion of a guest speaker's presentation, ask students to write questions for the speaker. The guest chooses the most interesting and pertinent ones and answers them. It is a good idea, however, to forewarn students that they will be required to submit questions in writing.

44. Computer software is now available which will read text aloud. Some of these programs are especially helpful to nonnative speakers of English and to those whose speech is heavily accented or occasionally inaccurate. Some of the readings, though, contain errors. Have students listen and view, noting the misreadings that occur and discuss why these happen.

45. Have students view and listen to press conferences on public broadcasting channels and try to pinpoint the central ideas. Their conclusions can then be compared with the various reports that appear in news programs.

46. Have students make tape recordings of brief excerpts from popular television programs. Challenge others to identify speakers. This can also be done with music. Students listen to a very brief segment and then must "name that tune."

47. Certain pieces of music tell a story. One such example is Grofé's *Grand Canyon Suite*. Another is Saint-Saëns' *Danse Macabre*. Have students listen to these works and write the narrative of what happens or describe the setting and images the music invokes.

Activity 7.3:
Listening Checklist

As noted, assessing listening is very difficult. The following are examples of some behaviors that reflect the quality of listening. However, you should consider very carefully whether you are actually assessing listening or some other skill. For example, accurate recall of what was heard may be a measure of listening, but it may be a measure of the student's ability to recall, to summarize, or both. The student may have listened well but still be unable to state the information effectively.

1. Accurately recalls what was heard.
2. Correctly judges the accuracy of what was heard.
3. Actively reduces distractions so as to listen better.
4. Avoids distracting others when they are listening.
5. Looks directly at the speaker.
6. Asks appropriate questions of guest speakers.
7. Accurately summarizes main points.
8. Encourages others to participate in discussion by listening attentively.
9. Brings discussion back on track when participants wander.
10. Disagrees courteously when appropriate.
11. Specifies points of disagreement.
12. Takes notes effectively.
13. Chooses material for sharing verbally from the listener's point of view.
14. Responds to a speaker by using appropriate nonverbal cues.
15. Asks relevant questions.
16. Does not dominate talk; takes turns.
17. Piggybacks on ideas offered by others.
18. Follows directions given orally.
19. Accurately paraphrases messages.
20. Visibly enjoys listening.

8

Teaching Visual Literacy

Overview

- Consider These Questions
- Introductory Comments
- Why Teach Visual Literacy?
- What Should Be Taught
- Some Possible Problems
- Looking Specifically at Viewing
- Looking Specifically at Visually Representing
- Assessing and Evaluating Visual Literacy
- Recommended Readings
- Visual Literacy Activities and Suggestions

CONSIDER THESE QUESTIONS ABOUT TEACHING VISUAL LITERACY

1. What does it mean to view? Is seeing the same as viewing? What does it mean to represent visually? Must one be artistically talented to represent visually?

2. How are viewing and visually representing similar? How are they different?

3. Should language arts teachers be responsible for teaching viewing? Visually representing? Why or why not?

4. What are some similarities between viewing and the other language arts? How can better viewing enhance students' abilities to use other language arts well?

5. What are some similarities between visually representing and the other language arts? How can the ability to represent visually enhance students' understanding of other language arts?

6. How is teaching visual literacy different from using visual aids to improve instruction?

7. What are some key concepts that students need to learn to be effective viewers? What must students know or be able to do in order to represent visually?

8. What are some problems related to teaching visual literacy? How can these be overcome?

9. How can viewing and visually representing be assessed and evaluated? Should they be?

10. What are some viewing activities that may be beneficial? What are some visual representation activities that may be educational?

INTRODUCTORY COMMENTS

That we live in a world filled with visual images is undeniable. To some extent, that has always been true. For as long as humans have used their eyes to perceive the world around them, the sense of sight has been an important asset. However, today's students have, from birth, been immersed in a world of visual images reaching far beyond their immediate surroundings. Through the arts, advertising, television, photography, videotape, film, and, more recently, computer imaging, young people are bombarded by more visions of the real and the imagined than ever before.

What does this fact have to do with the teaching of language arts? Visual literacy, defined here as viewing and visually representing, seems more closely associated with media studies or fine arts than print literacy, linguistics, and literature. It may seem a bit much to add visual literacy to the already crowded language arts curriculum. Perhaps it is, but the growing body of evidence suggests that there are some significant positive effects of teaching both viewing and visually representing (Flood, Heath, and Lapp, 1997). The material in this chapter should be sufficient to stimulate thought and discussion that will eventually lead you to a better understanding of why viewing and visually representing should be incorporated into the middle level language arts program, how both can be included, and the most appropriate extent of inclusion.

WHY TEACH VISUAL LITERACY?

There are several reasons for considering that both viewing and visually representing are not only worthwhile but necessary aspects of a well-designed middle level language arts curriculum. For instance, many people learn most effectively through visual means. Whether the results come from research on learning styles, multiple intelligences, or other sources (e.g., see Messaris, 1997 and Page, 1997), a growing body of evidence highlights the value of incorporating visual aids and activities into classroom instruction. Although it is certainly true that viewing and visually representing cross subject matter lines, most of the language arts processes also bridge such boundaries. Although we know less about how viewing and visually representing function as ways of creating meaning, we do know that both can be used to augment thought. Indeed, some researchers argue that we think by means of images and that memories are stored in the brain as visual representations (Fox, 1994). More importantly, viewing and visually representing are ways of communicating. Because language arts teachers focus on the means and methods of communication, viewing and visually representing fit the goals of instruction. Furthermore, because both viewing and visually representing relate to the use of symbols and metaphors and because language is a symbol system through which people can create and explain metaphors, incorporating these two categories into language arts makes sense.

Using visual aids enhances instruction. Transparencies, photos, videotapes, and concrete objects can act as scaffolds for and motivators of student learning. As a preservice teacher, you have probably been reminded frequently that you should make use of a wide variety of visual materials in the classroom. Many practicing teachers ask students to create visual representations—illustrations, dioramas, collages, posters, bulletin board displays, and dramatic performances—as a means of checking comprehension or of encouraging higher-order thinking, especially application and synthesis. Middle level students often find such activities quite compelling.

Although some students are adept verbal learners who readily succeed when reading, writing, speaking, or listening, other students, described as visual and kinesthetic learners, find other forms of communication much more meaningful. For these students, the use of a wide variety of visuals and objects that can be manipulated makes sound educational sense. Similarly, asking students who have spatial intelligence, kinesthetic intelligence, or both to represent information visually through movement or the construction of a hands-on product allows them to use their strengths to demonstrate language arts knowledge. Thus, the use of viewing and visually representing is one way in which we can differentiate instruction to meet the needs of diverse learners.

Visual activities should be a part of planning effective instruction. Indeed, most teachers should make better use of them as pedagogical methods for helping students understand concepts and attain instructional objectives than they often do (Witkin, 1994). However, using visuals as teaching aids is different from teaching students how to view and visually represent skillfully. If you show a videotape about the author of a young adult novel as a means of introducing the book or motivating students to read, you are using viewing as a teaching method, an alternative means of conveying information. However, if you show the movie version of the novel and ask students to compare the film with the book, then you will be helping students learn to view more critically. In this case, viewing is not just an instructional activity; it is the focus of instruction. Students need opportunities to explore the communicative power and problems associated with visual literacy. Much of the rest of this chapter focuses on how you can take instruction to this next level.

WHAT SHOULD BE TAUGHT

What the Profession Sees as Essential

In chapter 3, you were introduced to the standards for the teaching of English language arts (NCTE & IRA, 1996). Those recommendations are not meant to be restrictive or dictatorial; rather, they are intended to be a springboard for discussing what local standards should be established and a skeletal framework around which more specific standards can be developed. Of these standards the following address the teaching of visual literacy (the numbers preceding each item are those in the original document):

1. Students read a wide range of print and nonprint texts to build an understanding of texts, of themselves, and of the cultures of the United States and the world; to acquire new information; to respond to the needs and demands of society and the workplace; and for personal fulfillment. Among these texts are fiction and nonfiction, classic and contemporary works.

4. Students adjust their use of spoken, written, and visual language (e.g., conventions, style, vocabulary) to communicate effectively with a variety of audiences and for different purposes.

6. Students apply knowledge of language structure, language conventions (e.g., spelling and punctuation), media techniques, figurative language, and genre to create, critique, and discuss print and nonprint texts.

8. Students use a variety of technological and informational resources (e.g., libraries, databases, computer networks, video) to gather and synthesize information and to create and communicate knowledge.

12. Students use spoken, written, and visual language to accomplish their own purposes (e.g., for learning, enjoyment, persuasion, and the exchange of information). (p. 3)

In the fall of 1996, NCTE published a revision of the *Guidelines for the Preparation of Teachers of English Language Arts*. The following list, taken from that document, represents what the profession agrees that teachers should know, be able to do, and believe in order to teach viewing and visually representing effectively. As you peruse this list, keep in mind that these guidelines are not targeted specifically at the middle level teacher (this list has been adapted for presentation here; the numbers preceding each item are those in the original document):

Content Knowledge

7. English language arts teachers should know the processes and elements in the act of composing that are crucial to oral, visual, and written discourse.

Explanation: Oral and written discourse contain like elements and follow processes that teachers need to understand in order to help students develop and extend communication skills. Technology has expanded these processes to include visual discourse through the use of digital media as well as through such traditional media as film, video, photographs, and pictures.

8. English language arts teachers must understand that language and visual images influence thinking and actions.

Explanation: By examining relationships between verbal and visual languages, teachers can help students understand how to distinguish among the purposes of language and how users of language achieve these purposes.

14. English language arts teachers must know the power and the potential of print and nonprint media to understand contempo-

rary culture.

Explanation: Teachers need to be familiar with print and nonprint media and understand how people are influenced by them. They must provide students with the means to appraise the messages they find both in and out of the classroom. Teachers must be able to prepare students to understand the range of media and the negative and positive influences of various media. Teachers should be conversant with new technologies as they develop.

15. English language arts teachers must comprehend that instructional technology can aid, as well as add to, the English language arts curriculum.

Explanation: English language arts teachers need to recognize the potential of media as teaching vehicles. They need to be able to use multiple resources. Of equal importance is the ability to discriminate between valuable media and those that are useless or counterproductive.

Pedagogical Knowledge

3. English language arts teachers should use a variety of materials and media.

Explanation: Teachers need to use a rich variety of print and nonprint materials rather than rely on a single textbook.

7. English language arts teachers should use student creations as a part of the instructional program.

Explanation: Teachers should view student creations as materials valuable for instruction and worthy of recognition by students, teachers, parents, and the community in general.

8. English language arts teachers should incorporate technology.

Explanation: Teachers must be knowledgeable about new developments in technology as well as proficient in applications of technologies already in classroom use. Teachers also need to be able to evaluate the quality and determine appropriate uses of instructional technology.

16. English language arts teachers should build a reading, listening, and viewing community where students respond, interpret, think critically, and contrast ideas with each other.

Explanation: So that reading becomes an interactive process, teachers must be skillful in designing activities that challenge students to step outside themselves and view situations from the perspective of others.

18. English language arts teachers should promote media literacy.

Explanation: Students need to construct meaning through different media, analyze their transactions with media texts, and create their own media texts and performances. Teachers must help students to explore contemporary media as extensions of literature and as entities in and of themselves. They need to understand and be skillful in teaching the possibilities and limitations of media texts.

Attitudes and Beliefs

6. English language arts teachers should willingly encourage students to respond critically to different media and communications technology.

Explanation: Teachers must be willing to use nonprint media to help students grow both in the use of language and in understanding human behavior. To facilitate such growth, teachers should encourage divergent responses to the forms and content of technology and media.

Goals for the Classroom

By creating these standards and guidelines, NCTE and IRA have provided some general views on what the profession sees as important, but when it comes to setting goals for teaching visual literacy in the classroom, you are likely to be on your own. Few schools, districts, or states currently have curricular goals that focus on either viewing or visually representing. In one sense, that may leave you feeling somewhat adrift. In another sense, this lack of predetermined curriculum can be liberating. It gives you the freedom to explore a variety of options and experiment with strategies and activities without feeling pressured to ensure that students reach specified levels of performance or score well on tests of visual literacy. It also gives you the flexibility of incorporating new forms of media as they appear. As an aid in planning, you will find a reference list of visual literacy sources and activities in Activity 8.1.

Modes and Forms

In considering what should be taught in the realms of viewing and visually representing, you should keep in mind that middle level students need to investigate the various modes and forms of print and nonprint media. They also need to begin to consider the structures of such media by comparing print and nonprint sources. How are television news stories organized? How are printed versions organized? How are personal interest stories organized? What are some of the structural differences between newspapers and magazines, and what are some of the differences between these and on-line news sources? Many middle level students may be unaware of the diversity of magazines that exist. What modes of writing can be found in various publications? Why do we have both daily newspapers and weekly newsmagazines? What factors associated with television news reporting influence how that news is reported? Who decides the sequence of items? What are some common patterns that appear? How does this affect viewers or readers? Is it important that television news is linear, whereas newspapers, magazines, and computer sources are controlled by the reader?

It is possible, for example, to consider the narrative mode and to examine the many different ways that chronological order is achieved in both print and nonprint forms. This can begin with an examination of plot structure in short stories, novels, and plays, and then it can move into nonfiction forms and, eventually, into nonprint forms. Are news stories really "stories" in the typical sense? How are they similar to yet different from mystery fiction?

It is also possible to compare various versions of a story as it moves from one medium to another. This can be done with news stories, tracing a single event through both nonprint and print media. This activity highlights the misinformation that often occurs when television reporters try to provide on-the-spot coverage and why the first reports must be recognized as only tentatively factual. A very different approach is to trace a fictional story through the various forms in which it has appeared. One unit appropriate for middle school could focus on *Jumanji*. It should start with an examination of the original children's book by Van Allsburg (1981) and then progress to the novelization (Spelvin, 1995) and the movie. If possible, copies of the screenplay in script form can also be considered. Students can also compare television programs that have spawned novels, such as *Star Trek*. Many middle level students are unaware that some of the movies they have enjoyed appeared first in book form. The key questions in these investigations center on why there are so many forms and how the medium alters the message.

In my own classroom, I found that students learned the most about the strengths and weaknesses of various forms of visual media by producing their own. If nothing else, they discovered just how much time such productions required, how much effort was necessary for rehearsal, how much advanced planning was needed, and how much technical expertise was essential. Production of media demands that students solve many challenging problems. Even a simple puppet play requires that students cooperate, remember details, and learn to perform several activities simultaneously.

Perhaps it is too obvious a statement, but the greater the difference, the more the contrasts become readily apparent. When teachers try to help students understand discourse mode and form by using only printed text, learners often have difficulty seeing these distinctions. However, when the medium changes, the distinctions become more pronounced.

Purpose and Audience

Purpose and intended audience shape written and oral discourse. The same is true of visual discourse. Some visuals are designed to convey information accurately, but others are intended to entertain or persuade, to tell a story, or express personal feelings or opinions. Some are planned to explore new concepts or theories. Some visuals are meant to achieve more than one purpose. Graphs and charts, for example, may convey accurate information, but they can also be used to support a particular viewpoint. Thus, they can be used as a persuasive tool. Comics, cartoons, and caricatures may entertain, but they can also serve persuasive ends. For example, is *Doonesbury* more for entertainment or political and social commentary? Is the series *The Simpsons* merely entertaining, or is it a satirical shaping of attitudes?

Many graphics convey information symbolically. Smiley faces convey a basic kind of emotion, but so do certain colors and gestures. Diagrams, flowcharts, and webs can be drawn to test how ideas may be related. Photos, too, capture more than just a visual image. Were this not so, professional photographers would not need to shoot hundreds of frames to get one usable picture. Students need to learn how to interpret visual information accurately, but they also need to explore the purposes behind the image.

This is also true of audience. Students need to think seriously about how visuals influence them as viewers and as consumers. They need to develop awareness in order to build defenses so that they can see beyond the formulas of television and the glamour of slick magazine covers. To avoid being overwhelmed, they need to know how to focus on what is significant in a visual display or advertisement and to look beneath the surface of a politician's campaign facade.

To read or listen effectively, one must identify a purpose for the activity. Although we do not know all of the specifics, it seems reasonable to assume that there are various audience purposes (i.e., comprehension, critical assessment, appreciation) associated with viewing and visually representing. It is evident that there is a basic level of comprehension associated with viewing. Does the viewer know what he or she is looking at? Although this may seem obvious, it is not always the case. Close-up photographs of common objects can be quite puzzling, and people can watch a television series week after week without becoming cognizant of the stereotypes on which the scripts are built.

Sometimes you view simply to learn the message being conveyed. However, you may also need to view critically, just as you often need to read and listen critically. You need to look beyond the obvious message to the authorship. Is this author or creator an expert in this field? Is there a hidden agenda behind this message? What style of presentation is being used and what is its intent? Is the viewer being manipulated by this visual creator? What has been left out? Why? To what extent does the creator manipulate existing biases of the audience rather than challenge viewers to think about their own attitudes?

Of course, there is also the need to read and listen appreciatively. Similarly, you can view appreciatively as well. Great art, ballet, sculpture, photography, modern dance, and less majestic perfor-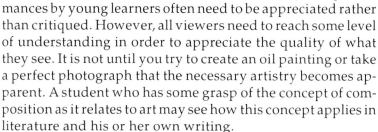mances by young learners often need to be appreciated rather than critiqued. However, all viewers need to reach some level of understanding in order to appreciate the quality of what they see. It is not until you try to create an oil painting or take a perfect photograph that the necessary artistry becomes apparent. A student who has some grasp of the concept of composition as it relates to art may see how this concept applies in literature and his or her own writing.

If reading comprehension involves reading the lines (literal level), reading between the lines (inferential level), and reading beyond the lines (applied level), then it seems probable that viewing may also have three dimensions. Assume that you are watching a television sitcom. To make any sense of it at all, you must comprehend the situation at the literal level. However, to find the humor, you would probably have to recognize and understand the inferences. By contrast, slapstick comedy requires little inferential thought. In general, producers of sitcoms assume that viewers will stop there; they will have been entertained and that will suffice. Indeed, some producers seem to hope that people will not think too much about some of the underlying messages, because they are not very constructive—stereotypical or negative images of sexes or races; children with revolting attitudes toward parents or school; adults who are verbally or physically abusive; the discrediting of honesty, hard work, intelligence, and so on. Some shows, however, are designed with the intent of asking the audience to reach the third or applied level of comprehension. Because many of these messages are implied rather than stated, viewers need to become consciously aware of them and discuss them with others. They need to think about whether these messages accurately represent laudable values.

If students are to become adept receivers and producers of visual information, they need to explore some of what lies behind the pictures and symbols. They need to explore both the purposes of visual representations and the audience factors associated with viewing and visually representing.

SOME POSSIBLE PROBLEMS

Student Attitudes and Expectations

When you think of teaching viewing in the classroom, you may think first of the use of films and videotapes. These visuals can be very useful as sources of content as well as motivational tools for stimulating student interest. However, you may find that students have developed some bad viewing habits over the years. Students may perceive viewing events as pleasurable interludes to which they need not attend closely. The minute the screen flickers, students may slip into a "couch potato" mentality. Sometimes that is fine because you just want students to settle back and enjoy a good story or appreciate a fine dramatic performance. However, you may discover that students consider such events to be the best time to sneak a nap. Even if they remain attentive, they may be startled when they are asked to respond to questions when the viewing is done. "You mean I was supposed to pay attention to this stuff?" They will have seen the visual images, but they may have little if any recollection of them.

If you expect students to view for an educational purpose, you need to set that objective and provide students with the skills they need to do so. Just as you need to provide or encourage students to create prereading questions, you also need to guide students in some pre-viewing activities. Highlighting what is to come, asking students to predict what they think they may see, having them read through a list of questions that will be asked later, outlining the major sections on the chalkboard in advance, or distributing some type of study guide beforehand are strategies that should help students view more effectively. You have to keep in mind that students have been viewing for years, but they probably have not been viewing actively. That is to say, they have probably had little practice in thinking seriously about and questioning what they are watching. If you expect them to do so now, you have to make this event somehow different from going to the movies for recreation.

Furthermore, you need to help students understand how informative visual material differs from entertaining material. Just as students need to approach printed nonfiction with different expectations from those they have for fiction, so too should they approach informative visual material with different expectations. Middle level students will not perk up and pay attention just because you show a videotape or use the overhead projector. There was a time when the use of visuals in the classroom attracted interest automatically. That is no longer true. Students may have to be motivated to attend to visual presentations. Furthermore, they must be taught to assess what they see on an appropriate basis. When the material is meant to be informative, the critical factor by which to judge is whether or not the material succeeds in providing information. All viewers hope that the presentation is enjoyable, but that has to be secondary. Students who come to the viewing of an informative film or video expecting to be entertained are likely to be disappointed. You have to help students learn to set appropriate purposes for their viewing, just as they must for their reading, writing, speaking, and listening.

When students are first introduced to the idea of visual representation, some will be ecstatic. For the first time ever in a language arts classroom they will have the chance to demonstrate what they understand through a comfortable medium. Other students, however, may exhibit reluctance to perform because they feel artistically incompetent. They may prefer words because they understand them. Moreover, they may have succeeded well through the use of print for several years. Asking these students to represent ideas visually can be very threatening.

Visual representation should be a means of opening language arts to a broader audience. It is one way to make the less verbal student feel more welcome and competent. It is also a way for verbal students to explore other avenues of expression. Asking students to represent ideas visually should not be something that makes the class more daunting or risky for any student. The last thing you want to do is to stifle the enthusiasm of linguistically adept students who are already interested in reading and writing. Thus, you need to ensure that students understand the purpose of visually representing. They need to understand that it is a way of demonstrating their thinking in an observable manner. It is not about learning to follow instructions for creating pictures or diagrams, nor is it a way to test their ability to sketch,  draw, paint, or photograph. You need to keep visual representation as an option or an ungraded requirement rather than a test. You also need to give students the opportunity to choose the form of visual representation that works best for them. Furthermore, you need to provide examples that illustrate various ways to represent ideas visually, including the use of abstract symbols rather than actual sketches and the use of photographs rather than original art. Students need to know that it is okay to ask someone else to do the drawing, to trace, to use clip art, or to use pictures cut from magazines. The focus of the activity must be on meaning, not art. At the same time, you need to encourage visually oriented students to use language to explain their visuals. Visual representations need to be viewed as starting points that make thought conscious and visible. Once the thoughts are on paper, they can and should be examined, discussed, debated, and pondered through the use of both spoken and written language.

What About Objectionable Material?

If you want to know what happens when you ask middle level students to draw, just look at the desktops in most classrooms. Those same images—of female and male anatomy, gang symbols, and fictional superheroes, to name only a few—will appear in visual representations. Ask students to bring a photo from home to use for a class activity, and you may be swamped with pictures of people in all sorts of embarrassing situations. If you ask students to bring a magazine from home, do not be surprised when they show up with material that is not sold to minors. If a student brings in a videotape and requests permission to show it to the class, preview it yourself first, no matter how trustworthy you believe the student is.

The fact is that some middle level students are devoted to shock. Even the meekest of students, if given the chance, will do something that disgusts you, his or her parents, or other students. They often gauge the quality of print and nonprint materials by its revulsion value. Horror movies and terror novels are genres that strongly appeal to middle school students.

Incorporating viewing and visually representing into the curriculum does open the door to coping with what you may consider to be objectionable material. You need to set clear guidelines and expectations in this regard. Let students know in advance what the boundaries are, and hold them to those standards.

Although you may not feel like spending time dealing with some of these controversies, the fact is that these are issues that often matter most to students. What is more, they are matters over which adults struggle mightily. What is pornography? How do we maintain the right to free speech when some speech offends others? What symbols are offensive to certain racial or ethnic groups? Why? Should the use of these symbols be unlawful? Is it fair to require students to wear uniforms to school in order to prevent the wearing of symbolic gang apparel? Does this strategy work? These and many other questions are likely to arise. You need to be prepared. It may be that you will prefer to state that such discussions are not appropriate in your classroom and that they should be delayed until students are older. However, you may find it advantageous to consider these questions in private conferences with students. Depending on who you are, the students you have, and the community in which you teach, you may find it best to address these questions openly in class discussion. Within certain guidelines that you establish, you may even find some of these questions to be the grist for research or additional inquiry that extends student understanding of visual representation and its effect on viewers.

Will My Lack of Expertise Embarrass Me?

Many preservice teachers have a fear of exposing their lack of knowledge in the classroom. The general public and your students have the right to expect that you will know your subject matter well and that you will be an adept reader, writer, speaker, and listener.

However, you are human. You will make mistakes, and you cannot possibly know everything. Viewing and visually representing are fairly new areas for language arts teachers. Neither students nor parents are likely to expect that you will have in-depth knowledge of them. Your teaching in these areas will, of necessity, be somewhat tentative and possibly even superficial. However, if you develop an atmosphere of community in your classroom in which you see yourself as a learner as well as a teacher, and students see themselves as both learners and teachers, it is much easier to explore relatively unfamiliar terrain together. You need not be a good artist in order to represent visually. In fact, it may be less intimidating to students if you rely on stick figures and symbolic shapes rather than producing artistic renditions. As a viewer, you have some skills and knowledge that students do not have, simply because you have lived longer. You have seen television change during your lifetime. You have probably seen far more movies than students have. You have looked at more ads, more photographs, more paintings, more dramatic performances, and more cartoons than most students have. You can share those experiences. You can also encourage students who have more expertise or experience with certain forms of viewing to share their knowledge with you and with the class. You may not know much at first, but you will learn. As you learn, your teaching will improve.

LOOKING SPECIFICALLY AT VIEWING

Forms Students Should Explore

It would be wonderful if students at the middle level could explore all of the various forms of viewing. However, as is always the case in schools, you will have to make choices because there simply is not enough time to do it all.

One of the most obvious places to begin is with **simple observation**. Students are often unaware of many facets of their own surroundings. They miss many of the details and they do not recognize the significance of many aspects of their environment. To use a trite metaphor, they may see the forest but not the trees, or they may see only certain trees but not the variety. They need to see both the whole as well as the individual parts. They also need opportunities to view themselves, their school, their community, and their world through "other" eyes by adopting alternative  viewpoints. They must see what is evident, but they should also consider what is hidden. This ability to perceive beyond the obvious is related to making inferences when people read. Observing closely and well relates to writing successful narrative and poetic description. Viewing from other vantage points relates to understanding point of view. In addition, how students view themselves is a crucial factor in self-esteem and self-evaluation. Beginning an exploration of viewing by focusing on what is most important and most familiar to students is an effective starting point.

Related to this, another way to introduce viewing is to study **nonverbal communications**. Although middle level students are often far too aware that certain gestures send messages, particularly obscene ones, they are often oblivious to the fact that other body movements and facial expressions send intentional and unintentional signals to those around them. Facial gestures, arm movements, stance, and clothing all tell a tale. Students can observe nonverbal messages almost anywhere—at the mall, at a religious service, in a traffic jam, at an auction, at the zoo, or at a sporting event, for example. They can make videotapes or take photographs to show the range of messages they observe. You can have students participate in pantomimes to illustrate how nonverbal communication works. Students can compare people of different ages, illustrating the different forms of nonverbal communications used. They can study people of various cultures to determine differences in the use of nonverbal communication. Through a sensitive study of nonverbal communication, students can develop awareness of self and acceptance of others.

One general form of visual media that students should explore is **pictorial media**. This includes a wide variety of specific forms, each of which has its own set of idiosyncrasies—films, videos, photographs, pictures, paintings, storyboards, illustrations, comics, cartoons, and caricatures. All of these forms represent reality, but they vary in the degree to which they do so. They also vary according to the purposes they attempt to serve. Although it is useful to consider pictorial media

collectively and to compare these representations with actual observations, students also need to compare these various pictorial forms with each other. For example, why do some people prefer photographs, whereas others prefer paintings? Why is it taboo in some cultures to take photographs of individuals? What is a storyboard, and how is it used? What are some of the significant differences between film animation and on-location filming? Why is *The Simpsons* animated rather than being done with actors? How is this difference related to comics, cartoons, and caricatures? All of these matters and many more can become the basis for discussion in the middle level language arts classroom.

However, students should also be given the opportunity to use pictorial media to create their own expressions of meaning. Turning a short story into a comic strip, for example, helps students identify the most crucial scenes and consider chronological order. Succinct expression is a necessity when all of the words must fit into a small dialogue bubble. If one wanted to create a collection of humorous photographs, what categories could be devised? Must the labels and captions that accompany the work also be humorous? What labels and captions add to the humor? What is humor, and why is it that not everyone shares the same sense of it? These are some of the kinds of questions that students who are in the process of creating pictorial media must confront. Through examining how professionals in these fields have approached these questions, students will not only create better products, but they will also gain a far more comprehensive understanding of how visual representation influences viewers.

Television is a form of pictorial media, but it is such a pervasive and influential form that it deserves special attention. Like nonverbal communication, television is another part of the familiar world to most middle level students. However, familiarity has not bred contempt. Rather, it has bred insensitivity and a certain apathetic acceptance. You need to help middle school learners take a second look at what is on the tube so they can begin to see what is not obvious. You need to guide them to begin asking questions about the shows they watch:

- On what basis do they choose?
- How much time do they spend watching television?
- How would the programs be different if they were live rather than videotaped? How many different kinds of programs are available?
- For whom are they designed?
- How are the programs structured?
- To what extent are scriptwriters limited by the medium of television (e.g., time slot lengths, commercial interruptions, audience)?
- To what extent do scriptwriters follow formulas? Why?

- How do they manipulate time? What is a segue? What purpose does it serve? How does the camera substitute for the viewer's eyes? Is this an advantage or a limitation that is unfair to the viewer?
- Does the dialogue model effective speech or not? What shows have the most banal dialogue? Why?
- Who are the heroes in the most popular programs? The bad guys? How are women portrayed?
- What impressions do viewers get about various races, religions, and ethnic groups from the programs?
- How realistic are the family situations? The work situations?
- What are some of the underlying messages about behavior that are repeated? What is the purpose of commercials? How much effect does the advertising industry have on programming?
- What are the regulations that affect television? Who are the people who are responsible for what we see?

Although you may not be able to incorporate all of these explorations into the language arts curriculum, you can begin the process of raising questions. Such an exploration can form the basis of a classroom research project because there are so many possible aspects students can investigate, not only through printed sources but through their own collection of primary data, interviews, letters, teleconferences, guest speakers, and so on. The topic also offers opportunities for discussions and even debates. Are the controls of children's programming working? Is there too much violence on television? Who should decide what programs are available? Should there be a better rating system for television? Should television be primarily for entertainment or for education? Students can also discuss and debate some of the conclusions drawn by Healy (1990) in *Endangered Minds*. Public opinion and consumerism shape television, and students need to know just what those forces are and that they are part of that buying public. They need to think about unintended effects, too.

Similarly, students need to take a closer look at other visual forms of **advertising**. They are surrounded by newspaper and magazine ads, billboards, neon signs, posters, junk mail, and banners. Even blimps and semitrailers are emblazoned with advertisements. Students need to think about this inundation. Why do advertisers use nearly every available space for publicity? How would the world be different if billboards featured poetry instead of ads? Why do catalogs have pictures rather than just verbal descriptions, when pictures are much more expensive to print? Could the Postal Service stay in business without bulk mail? Students need to begin to explore some of these issues. Middle level students also need to take a closer look at

various kinds of commercials to determine the propaganda and advertising techniques at work. If students are to become effective voters, they need to be able to recognize bias, persuasive devices, faulty thinking, and manipulation. However, verbal attempts to sway others, such as those used by politicians, are often subtle and difficult to detect. Advertisers are generally more blatant. A study of the strategies used in ads is not only an interesting project for middle level students but an important step toward helping them become more adept at analyzing all forms of persuasion.

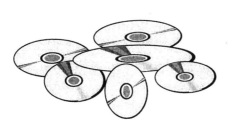

With the rapid growth of **computer technology**, it is difficult to predict the extent to which this visual form will influence American culture, but there is little doubt that computers will change the way we think and communicate. In many ways, this is already a reality. One has to wonder, for example, how young children who watch television commercials in which real objects "morph" into people or animals will learn to distinguish fact from reality. Digital graphics seem to make tall tales not only real, but expected. At this point everyone who has access to the Internet is exploring the possibilities. However, a part of that exploration should include some critical assessment of the visual images on the monitors. All too often, students are just "surfing" around from site to site, looking for the most impressive visual effects. What they are not yet doing is analyzing the information. According to Schrock (1998/1999), "students and teachers need to be able to critically evaluate Web pages for authenticity, applicability, authorship, bias, and usability" (p. 4). Although it seems essential for young people to learn to use computers for a variety of purposes, educators must help students learn how to use them wisely. The middle level is an excellent time to begin or extend critical evaluation of the graphic aspects of digital communication.

Finally, as much as possible, middle level students should be introduced to **live drama**. If you want students to become lifelong lovers of the theater, they need to feel comfortable attending such performances. You can help them learn how to find information about scheduled performances, how to obtain tickets, and how to conduct themselves appropriately during the production. More than that, you can help them understand what to watch for and how to enjoy the production. They need assistance to become aware of the effects of set, special effects, costumes, and makeup. You can also help them notice how a scriptwriter builds in dialogue that helps viewers recognize emotions that may not be visible on stage. When there is no camera to focus the audience's attention selectively, what techniques do actors use to direct the attention of the audience? Students need to know the purpose of a soliloquy and why it is addressed to the audience. By giving them some firsthand experiences, you can help them discover which kinds of drama they prefer and which kinds of performances they like best. Some people prefer theater-in-the-round, for example, whereas others find it distracting. Only by participating as a member of the audience can students come to understand how the behavior and response of the audience can influence the performance. Of course, including the viewing of live drama in the curriculum means that you need to make arrangements for field trips and convince those who control the school budget that these expenditures are worthwhile. All due respect to Shakespeare, but, in this case, the play is not the thing. Middle level students need to grow accustomed to the theater context if they are to acquire a taste for drama.

Skills Students Should Develop

At this point, the skills that students should develop through viewing have not been clearly defined. However, the following list should serve as a starting point for designing viewing experiences:

- viewing to become aware
- viewing to construct meaning
- viewing to understand self and others
- viewing to comprehend information
- viewing to analyze and critique
- viewing to appreciate and enjoy aesthetically

If students are to develop any of the skills listed above, they must first become aware of what they are seeing and construct meaning from the experience. How often do people sit for several hours in front of the television, only to realize later that they cannot recall the names of the programs they watched? Just as people can hear sounds without attending to them, so too can they see images without paying attention to them. We all must use vision selectively. If we tried to attend to everything that is within our visual range, our brains would be on sensory overload all the time. However, all too often we are not even aware that we are not attending to what we are seeing. Students need help in developing the ability to monitor their viewing so that they can better control it purposefully, bringing automatic processes to the conscious level.

Although awareness is primary, constructing meaning is crucial. In order to develop this skill, students need access to many visual forms that address varied audiences and achieve different purposes.

Furthermore, students must be encouraged to respond to viewing in a variety of ways in a risk-free environment that acknowledges the diversity of personal reactions and understandings. Students need to share their responses with others in order to discover that the meanings they construct are not necessarily the same as the meanings others create. Through such investigations, students should learn to identify the purposes of various media and to understand better how those purposes are achieved. Visual symbols are different from text, and text is not reality. Each mode of communication shapes meaning in identifiable ways. Constructing meaning involves being able to sort fact from opinion, truth from propaganda, and logic from fallacy. Students must be able to construct meaning in order to respond, but they must also learn to differentiate between unconscious and conscious responses as well as between emotional and cognitive responses.

Through various kinds of viewing activities, students can be assisted in learning more about themselves and others. They need to see themselves as others see them, especially at the middle level, when they are so concerned about their physical appearance and their social position in respect to their peers. Just as you can build self-awareness through literature, so, too, can you use viewing experiences for the same purpose. Furthermore, through films, videos, photographs, computers, and other visual media, students can gain an awareness of other people and other cultures. A balanced examination of media should assist students in gathering information as well as recognizing stereotypes and other misconceptions that assail them.

We learn much through our sense of sight. However, what we perceive is not always reality. Students can be taught to use viewing as a means of gathering information. Here is a list of examples:

- What can be learned from early photographs of Native Americans?
- What information can be gleaned from pictures of Civil War battlefields?
- Why are films of the Holocaust so much more powerful than the statistics?
- What do graphs, charts, and illustrations tell us more clearly than words alone?
- What do paintings tell viewers about the clothes, habits, beliefs, and lifestyles of people?
- What does television imply about Americans as a nation? Is this information accurate?
- What are the most reliable visual sources, and how do students know that they can trust them?

If students are to use media wisely and well, they must be able to cope with information overload. Indeed, in terms of what is important in the near future, accumulation of information may be far less significant than learning to manage it. With the Internet, gathering information is becoming relatively easy; appraising it, however, is far more difficult.

If students are to make the most of their ability to view, they must also develop the ability to assess and evaluate. This requires higher-order thinking skills. It means making comparisons, sorting fact from half-truth, examining persuasion critically, and drawing logical conclusions based on knowledge and thoughtful reflection. Students need opportunities to analyze, compare, and critique visual media in order to develop a better sense of the appropriate evaluative criteria they need to apply. If they are to make better viewing choices for themselves and for others, they must know something about the qualities that differentiate acceptable from unacceptable, brilliantly arranged from poorly composed, outstanding from typical. Through the development of these critical viewing skills, students can become better consumers of visual media, able to defend themselves against manipulation. They must also develop a clearer sense of how media influences individuals and groups of people, both positively and negatively. To do this, students must be given the opportunity to view from a variety of perspectives. Although looking at events from the standpoint of another is often a challenge for middle level students, this exploration can assist them in moving from concrete, egocentric thinking to abstract, sociocentric thought. Furthermore, it can shed light on literary point of view in printed text while aiding students in understanding visual media.

The development of critical viewing skills can also help students learn to appreciate and enjoy the aesthetic qualities of what they see. Part of the delight of a full life is exposure to the arts. Through viewing activities, you can help students feel comfortable visiting an art gallery or attending a ballet. Here is the opportunity to bring together all that people consider to be the best of the humanities, linking literature, art, music, dance, and other forms of visual media thematically. Drama is not about words on a page, but action on a stage or screen. Through some emphasis on viewing in the classroom, you can help students bridge the gap between language study and life experiences.

How Teachers Are Teaching Viewing

Probably the most common approach used by teachers is a unit on television viewing. Within this unit, teachers often guide students to examine patterns in programming and what these patterns reveal. Why, for example, are there so many news interview programs scheduled on Sunday morning? Why do nearly all of the stations air the evening news in exactly the same time slot and why do they all follow the same sequence of presentation—news, weather, and sports? Many of these units also look at dramatic shows. What is the basic plot of each? How are they similar? Which programs follow a single plot line, and which ones have multiple plots running simultaneously? What techniques are used to help the viewer keep these straight? How are flashbacks handled? Why aren't these used more often? Many of these units include some examination of situation comedies, too. What is humorous about them? What stereotypes are evident? What are the messages that come through? What purpose does each character serve in the program? How are the episodes similar? Most units also include an examination of television advertising. What products are advertised? When? Who is the target audience? What techniques are used to persuade different audiences? Why are the commercials scheduled at nearly the same time on most channels? How have commercials impinged on sporting events? More recently, teachers have included some exploration of the effects of cable television and in-home videotaping. Although teachers design these units differently and focus on different factors, most of the units are intended to help students become more aware of the persuasive nature of television and more critical of both the content and delivery of programs and advertising.

Probably the next most common approach to teaching viewing is a unit or some activities related to advertising. These often include examinations of both the print and nonprint media used for persuasion. Thus, students are often asked to examine not only television and newspaper advertising, but radio ads as well. They usually investigate not only the visual imagery, but the text that accompanies the pictures. Often such units center on teaching students the most common propaganda techniques (e.g., bandwagon, sweeping generalities, testimonial, name-calling) and some prevalent persuasive strategies, such as the use of humor, slogans, and jingles. Some of these units also incorporate a focus on vocabulary by asking students to identify euphemisms and to analyze the connotations and denotations of the words. Another tactic is to look at the text and the visuals for examples of various kinds of figurative language (i.e., similes, metaphors, personification, and other verbal imagery). Pictures are often examined for the use of symbols.

Another rather common approach to teaching viewing is to conduct a study of films, videotapes, or both. Occasionally, middle level students engage in a direct study of films through a brief unit that compares different versions of a story or novel or a series of short films. Sometimes these units lead to the students creating their own videotaped works. These may be documentaries, animated cartoons, claymation films, or photo essays with narration added. Some students produce informative videotapes for younger children, and some produce videotapes that become public relations tools for the school (e.g., an introduction to X Middle School for parents, what's happening at the middle school for the school board, or how to succeed at the middle school for new students).

However, these visual literacy units seem relatively rare. What is much more common is for teachers to build in a few lessons scattered throughout the year whenever the showing of a film or videotape accompanies some other classroom activities. For example, after reading a novel, students view a videotape of it. Then in a follow-up discussion the teacher guides students to pinpoint some of the techniques that were most effective in this production—casting, lighting, sets, costuming, dialogue, and so on. Another frequently used technique is to show a videotape that is somehow similar to a novel or short story students have read. The film may be similar in plot, or it may have the same theme or character motivation. Another option is to show a film that expresses a contrasting viewpoint from the one students have read. Students then search for similarities and differences. These scattered experiences may not have the same impact as a unit, but they have the advantage of being integrated into the rest of the curriculum so that instruction in effective viewing becomes a natural part of the total language arts experience in the classroom.

Although teachers are only beginning to use technology, it is important to point out the expanding world of viewing that has been opened by computers. Through virtual reality, it may be possible for students to attend a Greek tragedy performed in an amphitheater or watch a morality play staged on a wagon somewhere in Europe during the Middle Ages. Students may tour the Globe Theater and watch not only the performance itself but the antics of the audience, from royalty to chimney sweeps. The user will control what he or she sees and in what order. The technology for these creations is already available. Unfortunately, the software is not. But the computer can be used in many other ways as an aid to teaching viewing. Encyclopedias already combine the power not only of text with pictures, but also video clips showing animated versions of processes as well as real events. With a click of the mouse, students can switch to an atlas showing a map related to their topic. They can search CD-ROMs and laser discs for clip art, photographs, sound recordings, and video segments that they can add to their own understanding of an author, a literary time period, a location, or even a language. The truth is that educators have only begun to scratch the surface of how this technology can be used in the classroom to enhance student knowledge. This is especially true of the uses of the Internet. Through these sources, students have access to visual libraries, such as that of the National Archives. They can interview authors, see historical events as they take place, participate in an archaeological dig in real time, and explore places they have read about. What is more, they control the search and use. No doubt, this will mean that teachers will have to help students learn how to search more effectively and judge sources for accuracy. If students find using a school or public library daunting, surely they will find using the world resources of the Internet overwhelming. Teachers will have to work with students to help them locate the best sites and the best routes through these mazes of sources. Certainly students need opportunities for random viewing of what interests them, but they also need to learn how to plan searches to make the most of their on-line time. Teachers can provide the guidance students will need in order to set goals and focus on achieving those aims. Without such a plan, students can wander into dangerous Internet alleys and meander down all sorts of dead-end paths or surf the crests without ever finding the depths. On-line viewing can be informative and mesmerizing, but it is also costly. Students will need help if they are to learn how to make the most of their computer access.

Additional ideas for teaching viewing can be found in Activity 8.2.

LOOKING SPECIFICALLY AT VISUALLY REPRESENTING

Forms Students Should Explore

Students should investigate as many forms of visual representation as they can, but doing so requires access to materials and equipment that may not be available in some schools and classrooms. Further, having students engage in these activities can be extraordinarily time-consuming. What you will be able to incorporate is apt to be dictated by such practicalities. One key factor in making tough choices should be the potential for effect. Although some activities may be intriguing, students may not learn much from them. When students engage in visual representation, they need to be aware of what they are learning through the process. In technical jargon, students need to develop metacognitive awareness while they create representations. They do need to produce visuals, but they also need the time and opportunity to discuss what they are doing, why they are doing it in certain ways, and what they have learned from what they have done. For the sake of both efficiency and effectiveness, you need to make the most of teachable moments as students work through the process of visually representing, no matter what forms they are exploring.

Probably the easiest and cheapest form of visual representation is to engage students in **sketching**. Students can learn to use diagrams as a means of generating ideas for writing and as a way to reconsider their expository text for balance when revising. They can also be taught various graphic organizer forms that they can adapt to better understand material they are reading. Students may prefer to sketch manually or use graphics software. Sketching a story setting or character can aid students in constructing meaning, as well as point out gaps in the text information. Students can also create sketches of missing episodes or alternative endings. Some poetry lends itself well to sketching. In fact, sketching is a very flexible tool that can be used before, during, and after reading and writing. Furthermore, sketches can readily be added to journal work and portfolio collections. At other times, sketches can be done on chart paper, the chalkboard, or transparencies so that the entire class can share in the creation. Much of this sketching should remain in rough draft form because the learning has already been achieved through doing and discussing.

Sometimes, however, it is beneficial to ask students to create more polished **illustrations**. Asking students to illustrate their work or to create illustrations that accompany literature gives students the opportunity to rediscover the natural link between text and pictures (Fig. 8.1). Primary grade children often do not differentiate between these two forms of communication, but as students mature, they tend to leave drawing behind. Given the opportunity, though, many middle level students respond very positively to illustrating their work. They like to add drawings and diagrams to written work, and they seem to enjoy the chance to create illustrations that accompany literary works written by professionals. Through these activities, students can develop a more concrete understanding of symbolism and stereotyping. They also enjoy creating comic strips and cartoons, both of which are far more diffi-

Form of poetry illustration

Various forms of concrete poetry illustrate the natural link between literature and visual illustration. The following shows how a 5 senses poem can include a visual effect:

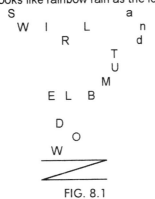

AUTUMN
Autumn is frost-nipped redgold
It smells of maple sugar and spicy pumpkin pie
And tastes of smoky bonfire hot dogs
with gooey marshmallows for dessert
It sounds like a deep sigh of contentment
before it's time to sleep
And it looks like rainbow rain as the leaves

FIG. 8.1

cult to produce than they imagine. Comic strips demand that students effectively summarize material and sort out the main ideas, as well as choose the most significant words for dialogue and narrative comment. Another beneficial activity is to have students create and illustrate their own children's books. However, before students attempt this task, they need to examine a wide variety of such books to see how they are structured, the usual length, the frequency of illustrations, word choice, use of dialogue, plot development, and so on. All of these illustration activities can be significant learning experiences, but the value of that learning depends heavily on the thinking and discussion that occurs along with the creation.

Another reasonably cheap and easy possibility is to incorporate the use of **pictures and photography**. Students can clip pictures from various printed sources or use photographs of their own. If students have access to computers and color printers, they can also obtain pictures from computer software and download them from various sites on the Internet. Whatever the source, by using pictures and photographs to represent visually, students encounter the concepts of point of view, balance, perspective, mood, and theme. Depending on the project itself, they may confront the issues of composition, color coordination, and layout. Many middle level students like to create collages, but without instruction they may conceive of a collage as little more than a pleasing arrangement of pictures on a piece of poster board. You may find it difficult to convince them that an effective collage conveys a visual message and that more than neatness counts. When they produce such pieces in relation to literature, they should be asked to explain how each of the pictures relates to the discourse they have read. Students can create various kinds of scrapbooks and photo collections, replete with tables of contents, chapters, and indexes. Creating such projects can lead to an exploration of humor, satire, and such abstract concepts as freedom, loneliness, or beauty. They can use visuals to create their own bulletin boards to motivate others to read a book they have enjoyed or pique interest in a hobby they have found fascinating. They can also work with pictures and photographs to consider the concept of classification by categories, organizing and reorganizing a collection of visual images in various ways. Furthermore, students can explore the possibilities of creating photojournalistic discourse, as well as explanatory discourse that is dependent on visual images. Students need to recognize that sometimes pictures add nothing except visual appeal, whereas in other texts the print and nonprint forms enhance one another.

Another approach that can be expanded according to the available facilities is the use of **creative dramatics**. Role playing, pantomime, and improvisation can readily be done in the classroom. If one has access to an appropriate space, dramatic performances can be given for other students, parents, and possibly the community. Certainly participation in theater productions is of value to students. Stage performance, however, is something that not every student enjoys. Furthermore, formal productions often center more on aspects such as effective speech, memorization of lines, and remembering where to stand on stage than on the visual impact the actors have on the audience. One alternative is to have students participate in children's theater productions. These usually need to be broadly visual to be appreciated by young children. Another possibility is to make students responsible for directing the play. Having students write the script and then direct other performers demands that they pay close attention to communicating through the visual mode. Yet another possibility is to engage students in in-character storytelling. Students wear some costuming and usually role-play the narrator of the story or one of the characters.

However, visually representing through dramatic activities is more easily done when it is an informal part of regular classroom activities. Asking students to role-play a situation prior to reading about a similar incident can stimulate interest in a story, but asking students to role-play while they are reading or after they have finished a selection gives them a chance to experiment with the visual aspects of the text and to construct meaning in the process. This is also true of improvising and pantomiming. Indeed, pantomiming relies entirely on visual representation.

Although it is more challenging, students can visually represent by creating **videotapes**. Of course, this depends on access to the equipment, but if it is possible to do so, students need to learn to use videotaping effectively to represent their ideas. In some respects, limited access to equipment and low budgets require that students plan better. When there is no equipment available for editing tape, the pressure is on to make every first take final. Students who have to videotape under these constraints quickly realize how much time, effort, money, and technical expertise have to go into television production as well as films and videotapes, although they may not yet understand that professional filming is a nonchronological process. When students create a videotape, they become more familiar with how the camera takes the place of the viewer's eye and the extent to which this manipulates viewer perceptions. Until students actually try this themselves and become aware of all the surrounding sights that are hidden from viewers, this notion of manipulation is very difficult to explain. Another concept that becomes more clear through videotaping is the idea of time manipulation. How can the camera show that time has passed? How do authors of printed texts do this? One significant advantage of videotaping, then, is that it provides a basis for comparing and contrasting. Students can create their own representations of poems and stories and compare the results. They can also compare their work with that of professional filmmakers. Through this process they will not only learn how to represent visually more effectively, but they will also become more adept at evaluating and assessing such representations.

Finally, there is the potential offered by **multimedia presentations**. This used to refer to some combination of visuals, such as slides or transparencies, with taped narration. Now this category includes computer productions that incorporate text, sound, and multiple forms of visuals. Although such productions may appear complicated and difficult to create, the software through which these productions are generated makes them relatively simple to produce (e.g., *Hyperstudio*, *Digital Chisel*, and *Story Space*). Of course, one does need access to computer equipment and appropriate software. With additional hardware, peripherals, and software, as well as access to the Internet and knowledge of HTML or JAVA, much more comprehensive and polished productions can be completed. Students who engage in these presentations must make numerous choices related to visual effect. Not only must they choose the colors and pictures, but they must also decide on the layout, the size of visuals, and the form of transition from one screen to the next. The concept of transitions in writing may become much clearer to the student who notices that visual transitions cannot simply be picked randomly. Creators must also consider where to place text on the screen and how to make it legible. Well chosen music enhances the visual message; thoughtlessly selected noises contradict it. Creators must also decide whether to incorporate video clips or stills, photographs or clip art, freestanding text or text in a dialogue box, and so on. Students quickly learn that video clips eat up an enormous amount of disk space, and photographs also demand many bytes of storage. These also load slower, which may interfere with the communication or disrupt the mood that has been created. Through such experiences, students may come to understand some of the difficulties that face a writer who must select a limited number of photographs to accompany the text and the decisions a newspaper editor must make about which pictures to include. Teachers and students have only begun to experiment with the creation of multimedia presentations, so we can only guess at the kinds of learning that may grow out of this experience. But at this point, multimedia appears to offer much promise in helping students understand the finer points of visually representing. For more information about this topic, consult *Hypermedia as a Student Tool* (Handler, Dana, & Moore, 1995), *Multimedia Projects in Education* (Ivers & Barron, 1998), or *Hyperlearning* (Wilhelm & Friedemann with Erickson, 1998), all of which are listed in the Recommended Readings for this chapter. For an example, see Fig. 8.2.

Skills Students Should Develop

In thinking about the skills necessary for representing visually, many people assume that this should involve artistic skill. Although this is true to some extent, language arts teachers are not typically trained as artists. What you will probably need to focus on is the use of art as a means of communication. The art teacher may find this to be a simplistic or narrow viewpoint, but differentiating between artistic creation and visual representation may help you and students feel more secure. From this perspective, visual representation can be thought of as an aid to understanding and a vehicle for communicating that understanding. A reasonable list of skills would include focusing on visually representing in the following ways:

- as an aid to reading
- as an aid to writing
- as an aid to speaking and listening
- as an aid to thinking and constructing meaning
- as a means of reporting information
- as a basis for evaluating the work of others
- as a means of demonstrating one's own talent

By learning to represent visually, students can develop a stronger motivation to read and the ability to comprehend text more effectively. For example, by participating in role playing before reading, student interest may be stimulated. This activity may also help students identify a purpose for reading and predict possible outcomes. By sketching how text is organized, students more quickly recognize patterns in print. Sketching characters and settings not only increases comprehension but provides a basis for comparing varied responses to text. In addition, visual representation provides an almost limitless list of possible ways to respond to reading and extend one's understanding beyond the text itself.

Visual representation can also aid the writer. It is an effective prewriting device, but it is also a helpful revision strategy. If a student is composing a narrative, a quick sketch of the characters or the setting may prompt the writer to include more details. Sketches made by other students in response to a writer's text may help the writer understand what is missing or misleading. Visually representing the work of professional writers can lead students to recognize the value of certain aspects of style and provide a basis for comparing styles. Furthermore, visual representations themselves can be used as the basis for writing. The only one who fully understands a visual representation is the creator. This sets a real purpose for the writing of explanatory text addressed to an audience that wants and needs to know what the creation means.

Hyperstudio Response to a Novel

Explanation of This Project:

Next

> This project was created by Dr. Sharon Kingen for the purpose of illustrating how computer multimedia could be used in the teaching of literature. Although computer technology and the related use of multimedia have readily found a home in the teaching of science, social studies, and mathematics, they are not yet well-accepted in the English language arts classroom. Many preservice and practicing teachers are unaware of

Sharon Kingen

| Setting | Plants & Animals | facts |

Menu Choices

| Home | Ideas | End |

The ideas choice will suggest other things you might enjoy doing after reading HATCHET.

> In one way, Brian is very lucky. The hatchet, which is the only item he manages to save from the plane, helps him survive. With it he can chop firewood, build a wall to protect his shelter, fashion other

FIG. 8.2

Writing Ideas to Try...

Write a different ending
for HATCHET.

Write a letter to Gary Paulsen
telling him what you liked
about this book. Send it.

Write about an adventure
Brian had that Mr. Paulsen
forgot to tell the reader.

Write a survival
story of your own.

Create the diary Brian would have
written if he had had paper and pen.

Ideas   Menu

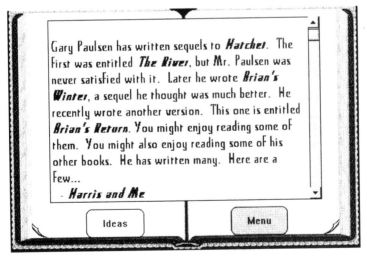

Gary Paulsen has written sequels to *Hatchet*. The
first was entitled *The River*, but Mr. Paulsen was
never satisfied with it. Later he wrote *Brian's
Winter*, a sequel he thought was much better. He
recently wrote another version. This one is entitled
Brian's Return. You might enjoy reading some of
them. You might also enjoy reading some of his
other books. He has written many. Here are a
few...
 - *Harris and Me*

Ideas   Menu

FIG. 8.2 *continued*

Visual representations can also serve as the basis for discussion in which meanings are shared and reconstructed. Speaking to explain a visual is purposeful talk, and others will listen to it. Listening, too, becomes more focused when one is hearing about familiar ideas expressed in new ways and comparing them with his or her own interpretation. Discussion of visual representations also opens the door to sharing techniques. Questions such as, "How did you create the shadows in the picture?" or "How did you get that picture on the computer screen?" or "What gave you the idea for including that object in your drawing?" demand that students explain the processes associated with creating visuals. Students quickly become teachers, sharing the knowledge they have gained with their peers while building their own speaking and listening skills.

Whether or not visually representing supports the development of reading, writing, speaking, and listening, it does seem to aid in thinking. It is a means for constructing individual meaning and expressing that meaning for others. It is also a way to reconsider text from a slightly different perspective, translating it into another form. It also serves as a basis for reflecting on text and on learning. Finally, it helps the learner develop the awareness necessary to become an astute viewer who thinks about what he or she sees and gains knowledge from firsthand experience that can be used to assess and evaluate. Having walked in the shoes of the visual creator, the student is much better equipped to recognize both the strengths and the weaknesses of the work of others.

Although visual representation is an effective means of learning, it is also a valuable tool for reporting information. However, students will need to be able to distinguish between rough draft sketches that explore thinking and polished representations that communicate facts. It is one thing to sketch a diagram of what one thinks the human digestive tract includes and quite another to create a diagram which accurately portrays the system. Role playing what might happen given a certain set of circumstances is not the same as re-creating the events in a story following the reading. Students need to know that the activity of visually representing can serve various purposes. It can enhance thinking, but it can also provide information. The basis for judging the effectiveness of visually representing must be closely aligned with the purpose of the activity and the product.

Students need to become more adept evaluators of visual materials. Although it is important for students to develop the ability to see flaws, it is equally important for students to appreciate the talents of others, whether these others are peers, experienced amateurs, or professionals. Students who have gained hands-on knowledge through the creation of visual representations are more likely to understand the strengths and weaknesses in the work of others than those who have no firsthand experience.

Finally, the opportunity to represent visually should be a means for demonstrating one's own talent. In some cases, this will be an artistic talent. Students who have this ability need to be recognized. Although it is not fair in the language arts classroom to assess all students on the basis of their ability to dramatize, sketch, photograph, or design multimedia presentations, it is fair to give those students who excel in these areas the chance to demonstrate their competence and receive appropriate acknowledgment. Middle level students are hungry for attention, especially peer approval, and many have already discovered that they are not going to develop the athletic talent or the physical beauty that other students are quick to admire. Although situations vary, some middle level students will openly express admiration for skillful sketching or drawing. They are even more envious of those who can create especially compelling videotapes, dioramas, collages, dramatic performances, or multimedia presentations. As much as possible, every student needs to find some part of language arts that is personally satisfying. Visual representation is often just such a niche.

How Teachers Are Teaching Visual Representation

There are several sources listed in the Recommended Readings for this chapter that contain ideas about how to involve students in visual representation. However, the four sources featured below illustrate the potential for learning that can be derived from teaching visual representation, especially at the middle level.

The first example originates from a professional resource book entitled *Visual Tools for Constructing Knowledge* (Hyerle, 1996). This source drew together a number of visualization strategies that proved successful in numerous studies. For the most part, these are strategies for creating visual diagrams of information. For example, the central section of this text described visuals that can aid students in constructing meaning in many different subject areas. One group was identified as *brainstorming webs*. These diagrams, also described in other resources as *semantic maps*, are stylized representations of ideas generated by the learner. These webs generally begin with a topic that appears in the center of the page. From that, arrows are drawn to ideas that are added as the creator thinks of them. The learner can explore the new idea in more depth or go back to the center and find another relationship. These diagrams may be simple, but some are quite complex and show how spin-off ideas relate to one another. Another group, called *task-specific organizers*, contains various examples of diagrams that show how information is organized. These include many of the common kinds of diagrams that show cycles or text structures, such as Venn diagrams, tree charts, or flow charts. This resource has several strengths, not the least of which is a well-stated and supported rationale for the use of visual representation and an extensive number of illustrations of various diagrams accompanied by clear explanations. However, it serves to point out a potential problem in the use of visual diagrams, namely that learning to diagram accurately can be emphasized too strongly. The wise teacher will keep in mind that the visual is only a tool, not the goal of instruction.

The second example comes from a book entitled *Sketching Stories, Stretching Minds* (Whitin, 1996). Using a strategy called *sketch to stretch* (see Activity 8.4), taken from Harste and Short (1988), Whitin, a teacher of seventh graders, describes in detail how students are taught to create visual representations of their reading early in the year. These sketches, which are attempts to capture what readers see as the essence of the material they read, are included in the reader response journals that students maintain. After their initial exposure to this form of response, students are encouraged but not required to use visual representation as the year progresses. These visuals often serve as the basis for discussion in literature circles as well as the source of conversation among students and the teacher. Students may work alone or with peers on these sketches. At times, students create wall or bulletin board displays of their visuals. They may also select some of their sketches for inclusion in their portfolios. If they do so, they must write an essay that explains the sketch and why they have chosen to include it in the portfolio. Although this book is of value because it provides some details about how a teacher may initiate and maintain the use of visual representation in the classroom, of even more interest is the evidence the author provides of gains in student learning that come about through the creation and discussion of the representations. Symbolism is a difficult concept for most middle level students to grasp, but in this book students use symbols readily to create their own meanings and metaphors.

It would be easy to conclude that Whitin's (1996) material cannot readily be applied to a broad spectrum of middle level students because her students were identified as gifted and talented. However, this supposition is denied by Whitin and more substantially verified by the third example, *"You Gotta BE the Book": Teaching Engaged and Reflective Reading with Adolescents* (Wilhelm, 1997). Having worked with middle school learners for many years, Wilhelm became convinced that one of the major reasons that students disliked reading and could not read well was that they did not understand that they were supposed to create meaning when they read. He tested a variety of strategies designed to alter students' understanding of reading processes. One of these strategies was to have successful readers describe what they visualized as they read so that other students would hear about this invisible thinking. He also had students participate in role playing in which they acted out the events about which they were reading. Although many teachers ask students to take part in this kind of activity after they have finished reading a story or novel, Wilhelm found that this worked more effectively as a during-reading activity. He also found that this kind of visual representation was a good way to introduce students to material they would be reading. Having acted out related scenarios before reading the one created by the author, students were better able to fill in gaps and make inferences during the reading. However, Wilhelm also found that role playing was not a panacea. It helped some students engage in reading, but it did not work for all. Through further investigation, he found that some students benefited from drawing sketches associated with their reading. Thus, it appears that visual representation has value for a broad spectrum of students.

The fourth example comes from *Seeking Diversity* (Rief, 1992), a professional resource that is a useful guide to initiating and maintaining a reading–writing workshop. In one chapter, Rief described a collaborative project she conducted with an art teacher and several eighth grade students. After reading some autobiographical works, students created symbolic paintings. Students not only studied how they could represent the essence of each book, but how they could turn these visual images into works of art. This example differs from the previous ones in its focus on product. Rief's students set out to create polished artistic works. This is not just sketching to stretch one's mind and explore thinking, but producing visual art to communicate one's ideas to an audience.

Additional ideas for teaching visually representing can be found in Activity 8.3.

ASSESSING AND EVALUATING VISUAL LITERACY

As tricky as assessing and evaluating most of the language arts is, viewing and visually representing present additional challenges. Certain viewing behaviors can be observed, but assessing the quality of the viewing itself is quite difficult unless students are asked to do something additional, such as write or speak about what they have seen. This indirect assessment is less reliable because you can end up evaluating not the student's ability to view well but his or her ability to write or speak effectively. As for visually representing, assessment and evaluation need to be separated from artistic ability, yet this is challenging. If students are asked to create illustrations for a children's book they have written, for example, it is nearly impossible to ignore artistic quality when evaluating the finished product.

Assessing and evaluating viewing and visually representing will not be easy or clear-cut. However, if assessment is ongoing and involves students, you should be better able to give credit where credit is due. For example, viewing and visually representing seem to be excellent opportunities for having students assess their performances. Asking students to explain their visual products either in writing or aloud not only gives you a window into student thought and a way to examine effort, but it also opens the door to additional and meaningful writing and speaking.

As for visually representing, the most important factor to consider is whether the activity achieved the intended result. In essence, the quality of visual representing must be judged on whether the process assisted the student in achieving the goal of reading, writing, speaking, listening, or viewing more effectively. Therefore, a major portion of the assessment should evolve from student–teacher conferences about the work in progress or from small group or whole-class discussions of the thinking that produced the representations. In terms of assessment and evaluation, the criteria should reflect the expectation. If rough drafting is all that is expected, then the student's work should be judged accordingly. However, at other times, either because of teacher assignment or student's personal choice, a polished piece of work will be the goal. When this is the case and students know the expectation and have some reasonable options about how to complete the task, then some additional criteria should be added to reflect these higher-level expectations. Sample criteria can be found in Activity 8.5.

RECOMMENDED READINGS

Avery, K., Avery, C., & Pace, D. (1998). Bridging the gap: Integrating video and audio cassettes into literature programs. *English Journal, 87*(3), 58–62.

Eisenkraft, S. (1999). A gallery of visual responses: Artwork in the literature classroom. *English Journal, 88*(4), 95–102.

Flood, J., & Lapp, D. (1997/1998). Broadening conceptualizations of literacy: The visual and communicative arts. *The Reading Teacher, 51,* 342–344.

Flood, J., Lapp, D., & Wood, K. (1998). Viewing: The neglected communication process or "when what you see isn't what you get." *The Reading Teacher, 52,* pp. 300–304.

Fox, R. (Ed.). (1994). *Images in language, media, and mind.* Urbana, IL: National Council of Teachers of English.

Francis, C. (1996). Notable novels in the classroom: Helping students to increase their knowledge of language and literature. In A. McClure & J. Kristo (Eds.), *Books that invite talk, wonder, and play* (pp. 78–91). Urbana, IL: National Council of Teachers of English.

Goodwyn, A. (1992). *English teaching and media education*. Philadelphia, PA: Open University Press.

Green, P. (1997). *Teaching viewing*. Palatine, IL: Novel Units.

Handler, M., Dana, A., & Moore, J. (1995). *Hypermedia as a student tool: A guide for teachers*. Englewood, CO: Teacher Ideas Press.

Healy, J. (1990). *Endangered minds: Why children don't think and what we can do about it*. New York: Simon & Schuster.

Hyerle, D. (1996). *Visual tools for constructing knowledge*. Alexandria, VA: Association for Supervision and Curriculum Development.

Ivers, K., & Barron, A. (1998). *Multimedia projects in education: Designing, producing, and assessing*. Englewood, CO: Libraries Unlimited.

Murphy, J., & Tucker, K. (1996). *Stay tuned: Raising media-savvy kids in the age of the channel-surfing couch potato*. New York: Doubleday.

National Council of Teachers of English (1996). *Guidelines for the preparation of teachers of English language arts.* Urbana, IL: National Council of Teachers of English.

Rief, L. (1992). *Seeking diversity: Language arts with adolescents*. Portsmouth, NH: Heinemann.

Rief, L. (1998). *Vision & voice: Extending the literacy spectrum*. Portsmouth, NH: Heinemann.

Rief, L., & Barbieri, M. (Eds.) (1997). Vision and Voice [special issue]. *Voices from the Middle, 4*(3).

Schrock, K. (1998/1999). The ABCs of web site evaluation. *Classroom Connect, 5*(4), 4–6.

Shannon, P. (1995). *Text, lies, and videotape*. Portsmouth, NH: Heinemann.

Whitin, P. (1996). *Sketching stories, stretching minds: Responding visually to literature*. Portsmouth, NH: Heinemann.

Wilhelm, J. (1997). *"You gotta BE the book": Teaching engaged and reflective reading with adolescents*. New York: Teachers College Press.

Wilhelm, J., & Friedemann, P. (with Erickson, J.). (1998). *Hyperlearning: Where projects, inquiry, and technology meet*. York, ME: Stenhouse.

Witkin, M. (1994). A defense of using pop media in the middle school classroom. *English Journal, 83*(1), 30–33.

OTHER RESOURCES

Polaroid Education Program (ideas for using photography in the classroom)
1–800–552–0711

Cable in the Classroom
(classroom guides for using a variety of cable channels)
A&E Television Networks
235 East 45th Street
New York, NY 10017

Films for the Humanities & Sciences
(also has CD-ROMs and videodiscs)
P.O. Box 2053
Princeton, NJ 08543–2053
1–800–257–5126
www.films.com

Filmic Archives
The Cinema Center
PO Box 749
Botsford, CT 06404–0386

Critics' Choice Video
P.O. Box 749
Itasca, IL 60143–0749
1–800–367–7765

Argus Communications (excellent source for posters)
P.O. Box 6000
Allen, TX 75002–1304
1–800–527–4748

Educational Resources (software and technology)
P.O. Box 1900
Elgin, IL 60121–1900
1–800–624–2926
www.edresources.com

Inspiration (graphic organizer software)
Inspiration Software, Inc.
7412 SW Beaverton Hillsdale Highway
Portland, OR 97225
502–297–3004

Hyperstudio (software)
Roger Wagner Publishing Inc.
P.O. Box 710582
Santee, CA 92072–9973

Digital Chisel (software)
Pierian Spring Software
5200 SW Macadam Ave. Suite 250
Portland, OR 97201
1–800–304–4535
www.pierian.com

Visual Literacy Activities and Suggestions

Activity 8.1:
Reference List of Visual Literacy

These lists summarize many of the ideas that have been suggested in the chapter. They should help you plan units or lessons.

VISUAL FORMS

- collages
- dioramas
- schematics
- graphs
- charts
- maps
- diagrams
- sculptures
- paintings
- sketches
- drawings
- pictures
- photographs
- digital images
- pantomimes
- storytellings
- improvisations
- role plays
- dramatic performances
- modern dance

VISUAL MEDIA SOURCES

- films and videotapes
- magazines
- television
- newspapers
- museums
- theaters
- computers

ASSOCIATED ACTIVITIES

- create
- draw
- sketch
- clip
- diagram
- paint
- map
- form
- select
- design
- layout
- photograph
- edit
- analyze
- compare
- contrast
- discuss
- share
- assess
- evaluate
- summarize
- symbolize
- act
- demonstrate
- improvise
- explain
- reflect
- attend
- critique

Activity 8.2:
Opportunities
for Teaching Viewing

Typical In-Class Opportunities

The suggestions in this category are associated with activities that are common in many middle level language arts classrooms.

1. **Visuals to create an environment.** This includes the use of various displays, such as bulletin boards, posters, calendars, wall hangings, plants, and so on. Changing the visual environment stimulates or renews student interest in a topic. Students can choose the visual materials to be displayed or create their own displays. Bulletin boards featuring photos and brief biographies of students add a personal touch. Posters with motivational or humorous messages may brighten a depressing day.

2. **Visuals or objects to stimulate creative writing or speaking.** Students choose a photograph from a magazine and write a character sketch of the person pictured, a dialogue between the people in the photo, a story of the incident, or a description of the event. Irony can be used to produce a humorous piece in which the reader hears not only the dialogue, but the contradictory thoughts of each speaker. Photos can also be used as springboards for role playing in which students generate the dialogue as they go. Real but unfamiliar objects can stimulate some interesting speculations. What is this object? How did it work, or how was it used? Who was the owner?

3. **Newspapers as one source of visual information.** Each edition of a newspaper is a collection of many different visual forms. Furthermore, the newspaper itself, with its narrow columns, represents a unique visual impression. If you can acquire a variety of newspapers from a single day, compare these versions. Students can also use information from the newspaper to create their own graphs or charts. They can, for example, chart movie releases, selected stocks, or weather conditions.

4. **Films, videotapes used as complements.** To make the most of the usual use of films and videotapes, begin by conducting a discussion in which students explore what it means to view ac-

tively. Establish some guidelines as part of this discussion. Help them establish a purpose. If the film or video is a re-creation of a narrative, the most logical activity is to compare the two versions. However, other possibilities can easily be included. Students can be asked to select the single frame of the film that they would choose for the billboard. After viewing, they could quickly give a thumbs-up or thumbs-down rating and a one-line reason similar to those that appear in movie advertisements.

5. **Critical television viewing**. Because current events reported on television sometimes attract so much attention that the planned lesson must be discarded, use this as an opportunity to consider some of the aspects of critical viewing. Have students compare the versions that appear on various channels, for example.

6. **Art in response to literature**. Students can create collages, build dioramas, draw maps of travels, draft blueprints of buildings that play key roles in literary works, sketch settings or characters, diagram plot events, design bulletin boards to advertise books, assemble mobiles representing the highlights of a book, present dramatic versions of key scenes or entire stories, create sculptures or other objects that capture something of significance related to the literature, and so on. Plan for sharing these, possibly in small groups. Another option is to set up a guided tour. Half the class serve as guides, the other half as audience. The audience group can move about the room and listen to the guides explain their work. For the second half of the period, students switch roles.

Design In-Class Opportunities

The following are some suggestions for teaching viewing that are not commonly found in classrooms. These activities require more time and planning.

1. **Photos as collections and writing springboards**. Students can create photobiographies of themselves or their communities. Using pictures from magazines, newspapers, calendars, or the Internet, students can create visual biographies of historical figures or arrange a series of photographs in a narrative form to re-create an event. They can collect photos in thematic albums that also contain appropriate explanatory material. Through thoughtful writing of captions, students can create humorous albums or expository ones similar to children's nonfiction

books. Photographs can also be used as the basis of writing practices or mini-lessons, such as varying the arrangement of details in a description.

2. **Other types of useful films**. One often overlooked source of viewing is the short film, although the running time of 10 to 15 minutes fits nicely into busy schedules. Several are excellent for illustrating certain literary concepts that are difficult to explain, such as irony, symbolism, and theme. Although subtitles can be distracting, some foreign films can be effective devices for helping students better understand cultural differences and similarities. Foreign films without subtitles can be impressive tools for teaching students to be more observant viewers. Can they reconstruct the story even though they cannot understand the language used by the performers? An excellent example is *The Red Balloon*, a nearly silent film that can be used to stimulate discussion about conflicts and writing about the story line.

3. **Reviews to demonstrate critical viewing**. Writing a review is an excellent writing and thinking experience, one that can easily be turned into a real-world task if the local paper is willing to publish student reviews. An extension is to have students create their own versions of televised movie reviews, complete with scenes to support their evaluations.

4. **Better use of television to teach viewing**. In *Endangered Minds: Why Children Don't Think and What We Can Do about It*, Healy (1990) made a strong argument that media are robbing young people of the ability to concentrate, analyze information, and think logically. If students are to be better television consumers, ones who demand better programming, they should engage in some research. They need to watch actively on a regular basis and record their observations. These records can be compared. Selected students can be appointed to a "Television Preview Committee." This committee previews the upcoming week of television programs and reviews and then announces their recommendations to the class.

5. **Visual languages**. Observing and discussing nonverbal communication is worthwhile at the middle level, but many middle level students are fascinated by sign language, codes, ciphers, signs, and symbols. Droodles and other visual puzzles attract student attention. One of the best sources is *Games* magazine.

6. **Interpreting visual information**. Students need opportunities to examine schematics, graphs, charts, maps, and diagrams in order to learn to interpret them accurately. Students can bring in examples of visuals and share them. They can also engage in a treasure hunt of the library, seeking as many different kinds of graphs as they can find. They can create their own collections of

trivia facts using published charts as the basis. They can also use maps to plot a family vacation or use bus, train, ship, and airplane schedules to plan a dream trip. Guest speakers can help them understand various kinds of maps, such as air navigation or topography maps. Students can write interpretations of information derived from maps that show climate, population density, predominant languages or religions, distribution of wealth, and so forth. Historical maps are often fascinating to middle school students. A series of these can show changes over time. Although these media may seem to be more closely related to subjects other than language arts, they are forms of communication that students need to learn to "read." What's more, students need to be aware of geography, cultural factors, and changes in the names of countries in order to understand some literary works.

7. **Viewing the arts and drama**. Students need to have experiences with the visual arts, including drama, to see how others have expressed their visions through dance, sculpture, painting, and other forms commonly associated with the humanities and fine arts. Reproductions of art objects can be used to stimulate interest in an upcoming story about another culture or time period. Reprints can be used as a springboard into the writing of poetry or as the basis for discussing characterization. There are many parallels between artistic creations and literary works; balance, tone, composition, style, unity, and focus are terms shared by artists and authors. Of special note are illustrations in children's books. Looking at children's books for their artistic merit and stylistic traits sheds new light on the material. Drama is meant to be viewed. Students need to learn how to read printed scripts effectively, but they also need to experience drama in its full form by viewing some live productions.

8. **Viewing as a response to literature**. Although designing such activities is difficult, students need opportunities to view as a way to respond to literature. For example, students can find pictures that summarize or parallel the theme or possibly the tone of the selection. They can locate other media that capture their personal response to the text, remind them of the characters, or symbolize character traits. They can select photos to represent the emotions of characters. As a way to reflect on their own reactions, they can choose pictures that show their shifts in attitude as they read or their general feelings about aspects of the text after the reading is done. They can search for some visual form that expresses a contrast to some facet of the literature or that represents some kind of differences that they sensed as

they read. Given some direction about possible options, students can choose to view a film or other medium that is significantly different in order to explore and understand what they have read.

9. **Peer products as viewing opportunities**. Students need to view the visual representations created by other students. In order to evaluate their own productions, students must see what others produce. Visual media created by students need to be displayed in the classroom and in other appropriate locations in the school and the community.

Out-of-Class Opportunities

Beyond the confines of the classroom, the possibilities for viewing become endless. The following list is intended only as a springboard on which to build. The critical factor is to widen students' horizons by helping them discover the many sources of learning that surround them.

1. **Observing around the school and community**. One commonly used activity is a nature walk conducted in and around the school. Even if the area is an urban setting, there is much for students to see if they are asked to look closely. These observations can be turned into descriptions, poems, or story settings, or they can be used for discussing differences between the students' world and the setting of a novel.

2. **Field trips as viewing opportunities**. Field trips are excellent opportunities for helping students become better viewers if teachers take the time to prepare students and set clear learning expectations that students see as relevant and important. Students can visit a photo contest display at the local shopping mall to determine what criteria were used for judging the works. While there, they can record data on nonverbal communication or conduct a survey of shoppers. If another teacher plans the trip, and it focuses on other subject matter, you can still engage students in some comprehensive, critical, or appreciative viewing that they can then use in the language arts classroom as inspiration for additional reading, writing, speaking, or even listening.

3. **Journals and logs of viewing as a homework alternative**. Occasionally, students are dismissed from school because of family vacations or medical problems that require hospitalization. Rather than trying to have students complete the class assignments, they can be asked to keep a journal of their travels or a

log of their experiences. The focus should be on carefully observing the surroundings, people, and events.

4. **Viewing as a family activity**. These activities may be natural conversations about what students' families watch on television or what students see when they attend sporting events. Many family activities, such as going to a play, having dinner out, visiting a museum or park, or attending a family gathering can be the basis for building better viewing skills. If you expect students to be observant, give them opportunities to share those perceptions verbally or use them when they read and write.

Activity 8.3:
Opportunities for Teaching
Visually Representing

Typical In-Class Opportunities

Through the years, teachers have engaged students in many activities of visual representation. The list that follows highlights some activities of visually representing which can be found in many classrooms.

1. **Graphic organizers**. Effective teachers use diagrams and charts to illustrate how ideas connect—semantic webs, story maps, plot outlines, Venn diagrams, and even sentence diagrams. Students can design attribute and K-W-L charts to compare stories and characters as well as guide research. It is even possible for students to keep a running summary of class activities through a wall chart that is maintained throughout the year.

2. **Artistic re-creations**. Students are often given the opportunity to use artistic skills to respond to literature by creating sketches of characters, settings, and selected scenes. For students who are not artistically talented, symbolic representations are one alternative. Another is to encourage students to use magazine pictures, their own photographs, and computer clip art. They can even trace outlines. However, the expectations for these tasks must be clear.

3. **Visual displays of information**. Students can create charts, graphs, bulletin boards, mobiles, or overhead transparencies. Students can also create combinations of visuals and printed text in the form of brochures explaining school policies to parents or student handbooks for new arrivals. These tasks, however, need to be planned, and the finished pieces should be well organized, meaningful, and accurate. Also, they should illustrate various qualities associated with visual appeal. One way to emphasize this is to require that students have all of the data they need on paper before they begin working on a final product. An advantage of this process is that it reinforces the idea of

drafting, revising, and editing, even though the final piece is primarily visual.

4. **Advertising formats**. Having studied various forms of persuasion, students should be well prepared to create their own visual advertisements. These can include posters to encourage better study habits or school behavior, flyers announcing upcoming school events, or book jackets to entice others to read. Another possibility is to have students create bumper stickers as advertisements for their school, grade, or team.

5. **Drama**. Many teachers ask students to act out scenes when they read scripts or to participate in some forms of role playing as a way to open a discussion, examine character motivation, or review literary events. Those who have access to the equipment may involve students in the creation of videotapes. Many middle school students, being hams by nature, thoroughly enjoy these center stage opportunities. Others may need small group experiences to build confidence before performing.

6. **Visual humor**. One activity that generally sparks much interest among middle level students is some study of various forms of visual humor, such as caricatures, cartoons, and comics. Students enjoy these when they are used as bulletin board displays and as part of lessons and units. When students create their own examples, they must consider what humor is. Furthermore, these forms demand succinct language and precise vocabulary. Some require an appreciation for puns and other forms of wordplay.

Design In-Class Opportunities

The suggestions in this category are less common and may require some special equipment or knowledge. Several of them can be used in conjunction with other units of study or as choices for responding to literature.

1. **Creative drama and theater even for the shy**. Charades is one possibility. It can be adapted to fit characters, significant objects, and important events in stories. For the student who does not like to act before an audience but does enjoy drawing, the on-a-roll theater may be a great option. To create this, students need two cardboard centers from paper towel rolls and a long sheet of pin-fed computer paper that matches the height of the rolls. The paper is divided into scenes, each scene is sketched, and the paper is attached to the rolls. Students create a script to accompany each scene. The performance involves rolling the

paper from tube to tube, displaying each scene while the script is read. One more alternative for the shy student is puppetry. Another is shadow theater; all that is required for shadow theater is a sheet, which is then backlit so that the audience sees only the shadows of the actors. Actors who stand behind the sheet cannot see the audience.

2. **Special diagrams**. Students can create floor plans of literary settings. They can create schematics or flow charts to demonstrate their plan for researching a topic or to record their progress as they complete a project. Rief (1992) describes how students create *positive–negative graphs*, which show the highs and lows of their lives. Butler and Liner (1995) describe a similar activity, which they call *Life Maps*. Another variation is Mind Maps (Moffett & Wagner, 1976). The student fills a silhouette of the profile of his or her head with lists of personal interests, concerns, feelings, and whatever else he or she thinks about. Such mind maps can be created for fictional characters, too. Yet another way to represent literary information visually is to create *character pies*. These are simply pie graphs that are divided into as many segments as students choose. The graphs can illustrate the comparative significance of characters in a story or the various personal qualities of a particular character.

3. **Illustrated text**. In these mixtures of printed text and graphics, visual representation is used to clarify or highlight important ideas or supplement printed information. Students can create newspapers and magazines, including appropriate visual materials. Students can design photo essays to report expository information. Another option is to have students create visual representations of the meanings of new vocabulary words. One final possibility in this category is the use of pictorial or concrete poetry, in which the meaning of the words matches the form on the page.

4. **Traditional multimedia presentations**. By combining audiocassettes, overhead transparencies, pictures, video clips, posters, and other visual and auditory sources, as well as real objects relevant to the topic, students can create excellent displays that they can share with classmates and adults, possibly during a language arts fair modeled after science fairs.

5. **Computer visuals**. There is no way to project how students will use computers to create visuals in the near future, let alone the distant future. Presently, students can use various software packets to create not only graphics but combinations of visuals and text. Clip art can be imported from a number of sources. Software, such as *Hyperstudio* or *Digital Chisel*, allows students to add video clips, sound effects, and music to create

high-quality multimedia presentations. The potential of incorporating the Internet is another means of helping students visually represent ideas grows more rapidly than most of us can imagine.

Out-of-Class Opportunities

The following list of possibilities stretch beyond the confines of the individual classroom and some items may serve as the focus of an integrated unit.

1. **Public documents featuring visual materials**. Students can create brochures that may be published by the local chamber of commerce or another public agency. They can write and produce school handbooks with maps for new students and parents. They can cooperate with community groups to create flyers for upcoming activities. They can create maps and handbooks for walking tours of the neighborhood, identifying particular sites of interest, or guidebooks for local points of interest, such as zoos, museums, or sports arenas.

2. **Displays**. If you want the taxpaying public to know about the good things that go on in your classroom, then search for ways to share the positives. Students' work can be created for display in administrative offices, libraries, rest areas, waiting rooms, homeless shelters, and even supermarkets. No doubt students can think of many other suitable locations.

3. **Community resources**. Encourage students to use the skills they are learning about visual representation as they engage in various activities. For instance, young people who participate in 4-H often have to create visual displays of their projects. Other youth groups host meetings and fund-raising events for which visual and written materials can be prepared. Language arts skills can be a source of funds for some organizations. In school, this may take the form of a literary magazine, appropriately illustrated. Outside of school, it may take the form of an informative pamphlet or a monograph that is offered for sale.

Activity 8.4:
A Synopsis of Sketch to Stretch

Sketch to Stretch is a strategy initially described by Harste and Short (1988).

Definition

Sketch to Stretch is a process of reacting to theme, characters and their relationships, conflict, and feelings through sketching symbols, colors, shapes, lines, and textures. Sketch to stretch is not an attempt to re-create settings, characters, or events visually (i.e., to create illustrations or photographs to accompany the text).

Differentiation

Sketching, drawing, and creating artwork in response to literature as a culminating activity is relatively common. This activity is often offered as an option for those students who are artistically talented or who seem to have strength in spatial intelligence. However, these activities often act as a check of comprehension. Students are not encouraged to go beyond the text itself. Instead, they are expected to portray accurately some aspect of the text. The students' products may be graded, and part of the grade may rest on artistic ability or accurately re-creating one (i.e., "the right") interpretation of the text. Details in student work must match the content of the original.

In Sketch to Stretch, the focus is on constructing meaning. By creating symbolic representations, readers come to understand the text and make connections with it beyond literal-level comprehension. Depth of perception and thought, rather than artistic ability, are the bases for assessment. Sketch to Stretch encourages readers to generate varied responses, although they must still be able to explain how these responses emanate from the text itself. Students learn through the process of creating the sketch by thinking about what to include and how to represent it visually, talking about the in-process work, comparing varied responses, and reflecting on different interpretations. Through this process readers revise their own interpretations.

Sketch to Stretch demands that students do the following:

- Move beyond purely emotional (aesthetic) responses. They must be able to explain their sketches. In doing so, they are explaining and defending logically (responding efferently); and
- Revisit the text again and again to reconsider details, interpretations, developing connections that were not evident initially, and evolving perceptions of meaning.

Classroom Applications

Sketch to Stretch can be done before students read a selection, as a way to assess prior knowledge, predict content, set reading purpose, and stimulate interest in reading. However, Sketch to Stretch is generally done during or after reading. Sketches can be rough draft sketches that are

- part of literary response journal work,
- the basis for discussion in literature circles,
- the basis for whole-class discussion, and
- the basis for student–teacher discussions of reading, literature, and learning,

or they can be polished pieces that demonstrate one's understanding of the reading.

When sketches are used as the basis of discussion in literature circles, try using the strategy called *save the last word for me*:

1. A group member puts his or her visual in view of everyone in the group.
2. Members study the sketch and tell the creator what they notice.
3. After each person contributes, the creator explains his or her reasoning.

As an optional extension, have each group nominate one member to share his or her sketch with the entire class.

Whenever sketches are discussed, two questions are key:

1. In what ways has the sketching changed your understanding of the text?
2. In what ways have the sketches you shared enabled you to see something in the story that you did not see before?

Students should sometimes be asked to write explanations of their sketches. Students can use sketching as a prewriting strategy to help them think about what to include in their own work and why. Sketches can be created collaboratively by students working in pairs or small groups. Sketches and verbal explanations of them can be used when students select their own reading material, too. Once students are familiar with sketching to stretch, they can create more elaborate ones for culminating novel projects.

One special adaptation is to have students create pie graphs that use colors, proportional sizes of portions, and relevant symbols to represent certain facets (e.g., emotional attitudes of characters, comparative significance of characters in a story).

Moving beyond literature responses, Sketch to Stretch can be used to capture three things:

- how students view language learning processes,
- how students see their own work in a portfolio, and
- how students visualize their own language growth.

Assessment & grading

Sketches should

- be thoughtful
- be a personal response
- extend ideas in their reading
- demonstrate a clear connection to the content of the story.

If sketches are part of journal work, one possibility is to assign points for each sketch (e.g., 5 pts. for extensive work on a sketch that includes achievement of all of the above-listed goals; 4, 3, 2, or 1 pt. for varying levels of effort and achievement; zero pts. for missing work). Points can be totaled and converted to a journal grade or a portion of the total grade for the grading period.

More elaborate sketches done as culminating novel projects can be graded on the basis of a rubric that is more text-specific but that still focuses on the above-listed goals.

Student self-evaluation should be a part of the grading.

Concluding comment

Sketching is one way, but not the only way, to respond thoughtfully and personally to literature. Initial research indicates that it is a powerful tool, but it is only one of many that a teacher may use. Students need to respond in other ways, too—listing, writing, talking, listening, and creating.

Activity 8.5: Assessing Viewing and Visually Representing

Although you should probably not use all of the items on either of these lists at the same time, items drawn from them can be useful for guiding assessment of either viewing or visually representing.

ASSESSING VIEWING

Is the student attentive while viewing?

Does the student take sufficient time to examine material?

Does the student point out details that might ordinarily be overlooked?

Does the student reveal changes in his or her construction of meaning as a result of viewing?

Can the student identify relationships between or among visual materials and other modes of discourse?

Can the student pinpoint significant differences between or among visual materials and other of forms of communication?

Does the student express connections between his or her experiences and visual re-creations?

Can the student adequately analyze the visual material?

ASSESSING VISUALLY REPRESENTING

Does the work reflect understanding?

Is the work accurate?

Does the work show relationships of ideas?

Does the work achieve its intended goal(s)?

Does the work demonstrate depth of thought?

Is the work as complete as it needs to be?

(The following items can be added when evaluating *polished* visual representations.)

Is the work neatly done?

Is the meaning of the work clear?

Does the work have a purpose, and is that purpose maintained?

Is the content accurate?

Is the work well organized?

Is the work appropriate for the intended audience?

Does the work make the best use of the medium?

Is the work as polished as it should be?

Can the student assess the material and state useful criteria for evaluation?

Does the student choose voluntarily and enthusiastically to view?

Does the student avidly recommend visual materials to others?

Does the student voluntarily use visual materials to demonstrate concepts, support positions, and explain ideas?

Does the student encourage others to express varied responses to the material viewed?

Does the student accept diverse interpretations constructively?

Is the work visually appealing?

Does the work communicate effectively to others?

Part III

Teaching the Content of Language Arts

9

Teaching Literature

Overview

CONSIDER THESE QUESTIONS
ABOUT TEACHING LITERATURE

1. What should be the primary goal of teaching literature?
2. Is there more than one theme in most pieces of literature? How do you know which one is "right"?
3. Who should choose the literature—teacher or students? Why?
4. How can student diversity be addressed through the study of literature?
5. When planning curriculum, in what order should selections be arranged?
6. How many schools or theories of literary criticism can you name? How many can you define? How are these related to teaching at the middle level?
7. Should middle level students be taught literary terms and concepts? If so, which ones? Why?
8. What kinds of questions are likely to prompt the best literary discussion? What are literature circles? Should they be used in middle school?
9. How can you assess literary understanding?
10. What are some effective activities for teaching literary understanding?

TEACHING AND LEARNING ABOUT LITERATURE

To imply, even by omission, that this chapter is a thorough examination of how to teach literature would be grossly negligent. Not only are there entire books about teaching literature in general, but there are single volumes about teaching the works of particular authors, most notably Shakespeare; certain genres, especially the novel and poetry; and certain categories of literary works, such as adolescent fiction and multicultural literature. Use this chapter as an introduction, but explore some of these other resources and read more literature than you are assigned, especially material that will make sense to middle level students and connect them permanently to the habit of reading for pleasure.

LITERARY CONTENT AT THE MIDDLE LEVEL

Reading is a process; literature is content. It is part of what English teachers teach, much as science teachers teach biology and social studies teachers teach American history or geography. At least that is the way literature study has been viewed for quite some time. In fact, some teachers even test students about their knowledge of literary content. Tests may ask them to recall names of main characters, details of setting, facts about authors, or aspects of the historical context that caused a piece of discourse to be produced as it was. Sometimes students must demonstrate their ability to analyze a poem, interpret an essay, or examine the stylistic aspects of a novel.

This kind of analytical approach is certainly one way to conduct the formal study of literature. At the middle level, students need to learn some of the vocabulary for discussing both prose and poetry knowledgeably, and they need some understanding of the concepts to which these terms refer. Although some students could care less about how various kinds of discourse are structured, others find it fascinating to discover that most short stories have similar structures, as do most novels, no matter how long they may be. Moreover, recognizing some of these structures actually aids readers: One can predict more accurately what is coming if one knows how the structuring works. For example, showing students how flashbacks function can help them follow the plot.

On the other hand, too much of a good thing can turn sour for middle level students. Too much analysis can break the material into such small pieces that students quickly become discouraged or bored. Students will lose interest before all of the virtues can be extolled. In the process, they may lose sight of the fact that reading literature should be pleasurable and worthwhile.

What is presented in the remainder of this chapter is intended to make you think about yourself as a literary scholar as well as a teacher of literature. You will be challenged to reconsider some preconceptions you may have. Although this may be a bit unsettling, if you think about these issues now, you will probably be more sure of yourself when you walk into your own classroom.

LITERARY CRITICISM IN THE MIDDLE SCHOOL CLASSROOM

Criticism is often perceived as a negative process through which weaknesses are identified. Literary criticism, however, is a bit different. It may be helpful to think of it as a lens through which the work is viewed. There are many different lenses and each illuminates certain features of a piece of discourse while tending to ignore others. Each school of literary criticism (see Fig. 9.1) has a focus on which responses are based. The work under scrutiny is described, analyzed, or judged on the basis of that focus.

What is most crucial about this concept is that viewing through different lenses produces different conclusions. A feminist reader, for example, may have a very positive response to a text that has a

---

Some Schools of Literary Criticism
Guiding Question: On what basis do we describe,
analyze, and/or judge discourse?

Reader response (impressionist, deconstructionist)—
On the basis of how the work affects the reader
Focus = Audience

Feminist—On the basis of how well the work represents
the female point of view
Focus = Gender

New (practical, formalist, analytical)—On the basis of how well various
aspects of text work to form a unified whole or how well the text
matches the genre characteristics
Focus = Text

Historical/Sociological—On the basis of the extent to which the text
is a product of or accurately represents the historical period or society
out of which it grew
Focus = Context

Biographical—On the basis of other works by the same individual
Focus = Writer

Moral/philosophical—On the basis of whether the work
provides appropriate moral instruction, represents an accepted
philosophical position, or both
Focus = Societal/cultural values

Rhetorical—On the basis of the extent to which the work is an
attempt to persuade the reader
Focus = Writer's purpose/intent

FIG. 9.1

strong female protagonist, whereas a moral/philosophical reader may have the opposite reaction because this female does not represent a traditional role model. A new critic may see a story as wonderful because it exemplifies all of the virtues of short fiction, whereas a biographical critic sees this piece as simply awful because it fails to speak with the same honest voice that marks other works by this same writer.

Although this information about schools of literary criticism is not knowledge that middle level students should study directly, you as a teacher need to be aware of these various schools for several reasons. First, you need to know where you stand personally as a literary critic, because that stance is likely to determine how you view the literature yourself. It can affect which material you select for students to read, the questions you choose for discussion, the responses you expect in written work, and the viewpoints you express verbally and encourage students to voice. It can also influence how you react to student responses. Second, students may use a different lens and respond from a very different point of view, which can take you by surprise. If you know about schools of criticism, you may be better able to accept diverse reactions.

There is another very important reason for being aware of these different schools: No matter what material you choose to use in the classroom, someone, at some point, will question or challenge your judgment. Even if the selection is in an anthology, someone is apt to consider it inappropriate. This is particularly true of much of the material that students find the most enjoyable and thought-provoking. *The Adventures of Huckleberry Finn*, for example, is frequently the cause of strife. Teachers select it for several reasons: because it is a coming-of-age story to which young people respond readily (reader response), because it is a carefully crafted novel that illustrates character development (new/practical), because it was written by an American author of great fame (biographical), or because it shows some of the living conditions, personal relationships, and issues of Twain's time (historical/sociological). Critics, however, judge it as unacceptable because certain language in the novel is offensive to some people and violates current societal standards (moral/philosophical). Others may object because of the stereotypical females (feminist). You may choose to use a particular poem because it is the best known work by a well-respected poet; critics may object because the work advocates some attitude, behavior, or value system that they find deplorable. You may select a work because it speaks eloquently about the diversity of American society; critics may object because the author is homosexual. Although it is generally impossible to please everyone, it is possible to choose with the awareness that not everyone will be looking through your lens. When questions arise, you will have a better understanding of why they have appeared, and you will be better prepared to respond without becoming unduly defensive.

CURRENT LITERARY FOCUS

Middle level students are not likely to care one whit about schools of criticism. For most, there is only one measuring stick: Do I like it? If they like it, it is good; if they do not, it is bad. Rarely will they change their minds once the opinion is formed. They do not care about things like the author being the father of Romanticism, nor do they find sprung rhythm an innovation at which they should marvel. *Moby Dick* is not a classic; it is just a whale of a long book to most of them. In the middle level classroom literary beauty is in the eye of the reader, not in the eye of the teacher, literary scholars, or the educated public.

Some teachers believe that they can teach their favorites in ways that will appeal to middle level students. Some even consider it their duty to do so in the belief that this will raise standards. However, this can lead to watering down the selection so much that the value becomes lost in the transformation. Often it means spoon-feeding the material to students in ways that rob them of the chance to create their own meanings and personal connections with the text. Students become dependent on the teacher for interpretation.

Although you may not be able to teach all of your personal favorites, you can still teach lots of "good stuff" at the middle level. Furthermore, the middle school tendency to judge literature on a personal basis is the perfect medium for using the reader-response school of criticism. At the present time, experts in the field of teaching literature to young students recommend this as the most effective stance for examining literary works. Although you probably should not use this lens exclusively, reader response has the advantage of being primarily concerned with connecting reader and text. Questions associated with reader-response criticism prompt more vigorous class discussions and do not require extensive knowledge of factors with which middle school students may not be familiar (e.g., the author's background, the historical period in which the work was produced, genre characteristics) or those that are much more difficult for students of this age to discern because they are abstract (e.g., persuasive techniques, cultural values, literary movements). However, many of these unknowns can be introduced through reader-response questioning.

In *Language and Reflection*, Gere, *et al.* (1992) identified four types of reader responses, which tend to progress from easy to more difficult. These appear in Fig. 9.2. Each type is marked by certain kinds of key questions that can be asked about most any work of fiction, nonfiction, and some poetry. Other questions (such as the ones that appear in Fig. 9.3) can also be used to prompt a variety of reader responses and explore how readers reacted and why. The use of *why* questions is especially important in helping readers recognize their own basis for making literary decisions. They also help students connect the literature to the realities of human existence, particularly their own lives. Middle level students want to know more about others and understand themselves. Literature explored through reader-response helps them build that understanding. For more details about reader response theory, consult some of the resources listed in the Recommended Readings in this chapter.

Four Types of Reader Responses

Engagement
Write about/state feelings regarding an incident, character, specific section of text, or whole text.
Key question: How do you feel about _____?

Construct-perception
Write about/state perceptions of author's choices of incidents, characters, details, and so forth.
Key question: What effect did the author produce by _____?

Interpretation
Write about/state interpretations of various facets of the work.
Key question: What do you think _____ means?

Evaluation
Write about/state assessments of comparison.
Key question: Compared to _____, how does this rate?

From *Language and Reflection* by Gere *et al*, © 1992. Reprinted by permission of Prentice-Hall, Inc., Upper Saddle River, N.J.

FIG. 9.2

TEACH, TEACH ABOUT, OR TEACH THROUGH?

As you begin to think about how you will teach literature, you need to contemplate three possible goals:

Do you want students to know literature?

Do you want students to know about literature?

Do you want students to learn through literature?

Those may seem to be rephrasings of the same question, but they represent three quite different philosophical positions. Students who *know* literature know the works they have studied. They are familiar with the plots, characters, and settings of particular novels and short stories. They recognize certain poems when they hear lines from them. When they finish studying *Call of the Wild*, for example, they know much about that novel.

By contrast, students who *know about* literature know some of the concepts associated with literature in general. They understand, for instance, what symbolism is and how various authors use it and why. They understand some of the differences between a haiku and a limerick, although they may be unable to recite an example of either from memory. They have some grasp of the total realm of literature rather than knowing individual works intimately.

The final stance concerns having students *learn through* literature. If you want students to understand comprehensive ideas, then you may need to use literature as a vehicle. For example, it is unlikely that students will grasp the concept of human dignity from reading one book, but if they read several, all of which have this same theme, they are likely to better understand this abstraction. Another ap-

---

Twenty Reader Response Questions

1. What character(s) was your favorite? Why?
2. What character(s) did you dislike? Why?
3. Does anyone in this work remind you of anyone you know? Explain.
4. Are you like any character in this work? Explain.
5. If you could be any character in this work, who would you be? Explain.
6. What quality(ies) of which character strikes you as a good characteristic to develop within yourself over the years? Why? How does the character demonstrate the quality?
7. Overall, what kind of a feeling did you have after reading a few paragraphs of this work? Midway? After finishing the work?
8. Do any incidents, ideas, or actions in this work remind you of your own life or something that happened to you? Explain.
9. Do you like this piece of work? Why or why not?
10. Are there any parts of this work that were confusing to you? Which parts? Why do you think you got confused?
11. Do you feel there is an opinion expressed by the author through this work? What is it? How do you know this? Do you agree? Why or why not?
12. Do you think the title of this work is appropriate? Is it significant? Explain. What do you think the title means?
13. Would you change the ending of this story in any way? Tell your ending. Why would you change it?
14. What kind of person do you feel the author is? What makes you feel that way?
15. How did this work make you feel? Explain.
16. Do you share any of the feelings of the characters in this work? Explain.
17. Sometimes works leave you with a feeling that there is more to tell. Did this work do this? What do you think might happen?
18. Would you like to read something else by this author? Why or why not?
19. What do you feel is the most important word, phrase, passage, or paragraph in this work?
20. If you were an English teacher, would you want to share this work with your students? Why or why not?

From "Twenty (Better) Questions", by K. Myers, published in the *English Journal*, (1988) 77(1), pp. 64–65. Used with permission.

FIG. 9.3

proach is to permit students to choose from a selection of books bearing this theme, and provide a variety of opportunities for students to share insights from the different books and become involved in projects that examine the theme from different perspectives. Using this approach, students become familiar with particular texts, and they can discover some concepts about literature, but what they learn the most about is the theme itself. At the middle level this approach ties in nicely with thematic units. One of the advantages of this approach is that it allows for the combining of various genres, and it can show changes over time if literary works from various eras are included. It can also stimulate comparisons when literature from various cultures is brought into the collection. If you want to make literature personally significant to students, then you may need to teach through literature more than you teach it or teach about it.

Your decisions about teaching literature will probably depend on many factors, including your own preferences, the school curriculum and philosophy, the books and supplementary materials available to you, and the community in which you teach. That community includes the other teachers with whom you work. The choices you make, however, should depend most on the students you teach.

CHOOSING LITERATURE

Making decisions about what to include in a literature program is one of the most difficult parts of being a language arts teacher. There is so much that teachers want students to read, and far too little time. Choosing literature means looking at many factors and trying to merge multiple concerns into reasonable compromises. It may mean excluding pieces that are near and dear to you. Sometimes it means deciding to focus on depth rather than breadth. Sometimes it means allotting less time to a novel or short story than you think is necessary. Even if you decide to use a literature anthology, you will probably not cover it all.

Although there are not any surefire techniques for selecting literature to use in the classroom, at least three factors should be considered. The first is the *students*. What appeals to them, what experiences have they already had, what kinds of literary exposure do they need, and what literature is most likely to help them become lifelong readers who enjoy and appreciate literature? The second factor is the *instructional goals*. What do you want students to learn from literature study, what skills do you want them to polish, what concepts do you want them to understand, what attitudes do you want them to develop, how much study will it take before these goals can be achieved, and what is a reasonable time frame for achievement? The third factor is *yourself*. What literature do you feel most confident and enthusiastic about teaching, what literature do you feel compelled to teach for the sake of students even though it is not your first choice, what literature moves you personally, and how much can you include without experiencing guilt over superficial coverage or feeling too rushed?

Little can be said about the latter two factors; these you will have to decide for yourself within the boundaries of whatever curricular frame in which you must work. However, research indicates that middle school students have some preferences that you can use as starting points. Fig. 9.4 shows where middle level students are in their development of literary appreciation. They often prefer to read about characters much like themselves, and they are developing an aesthetic appreciation for well-developed characters who are clearly motivated. Middle schoolers are just beginning to realize that who tells the story is significant. As they move through the middle grades, they become more adept at considering philosophical questions, including themes of universal truths and symbolism. However, it is important to point out that most middle school students are not yet ready to explore these abstractions in depth.

According to Monson and Sebesta (1991), middle school students prefer nonfiction, historical and romantic fiction, and books dealing with adolescence. They also tend to like humorous books and books that involve some adventure. Boys show preferences for nonfiction, science fiction, mystery, adventure, biography, history, animals, and sports. Girls tend to prefer mystery, romance, animals, religion, career stories, comedy, and biography. For nearly all students, contemporary realism is the genre of choice, and they much prefer that the main characters be between the ages of 15 and 19. As for poetry, they prefer poems that have rhyme, rhythm, alliteration, and onomatopoeia, but they do not much care for simile, metaphor, and personification; narrative and humorous poems are good choices, especially if they have romantic and dramatic qualities.

Although it is not an answer to the dilemma of selecting, if you design instruction around themes or genre units, choosing literature becomes easier. If there is some thread of commonality, students will be more likely to see each piece of discourse as a part of a larger picture rather than separate entities (i.e., the next story or poem in the book). However, it is easy to overlook some important selection criteria when you choose thematically. You may want to create a checklist to ensure that you do not skip a literary concept or even a genre when you compile the collection of resources.

SEQUENCING LITERATURE

As shown in Fig. 9.5, there are actually many different ways to sequence literature study.

Growth in Literary Appreciation
(if the reader has lots of positive reading experiences)

K	1	2	3	4	5	6	7	8	9	10	11	12	13	14	15 to adulthood

Into meaning—read to understand story, grasp concept of text, determine why read, develop sufficient skills to read independently (emergent literacy)
<< comprehension >>

Into the book—read for delight, to become unconsciously absorbed, to lose one's self in the book
<< enjoyment >>

Into other places & events—read for vicarious experiences, to learn along with characters about the world
<< plot & setting >>

Into similar people—read about characters who represent or resemble the reader, meet themselves through characters
<< characters & pt. of view >>

Into the world of ideas—read to grapple with philosophical issues, to understand life's mysteries & discover universal truths
<< theme & symbolism >>

Into the writer's skill—read to experience aesthetically the writer's craft, appreciate beauty of language
<<style>>

Adapted from Literature IS by G. Carlsen, 1974, *English Journal*, 63(2), pp. 23–27 and Stages of Growth in Literary Appreciation by M. Early, 1960, *English Journal*, 49(3), pp. 161–167. Copyright 1974 by National Council of Teachers of english. Reprinted with permission.

FIG. 9.4

Options for Sequencing Literature		
• By chronology	• By genre	• By special feature
• By rhetorical technique	• By author	• By topic
	• By theme	• By correlation

FIG. 9.5

Chronology or time order is probably the most common sequence, particularly in survey courses. Although the literature may be of some particular type (e.g., American literature), the literature itself may be presented chronologically. *Genre* is another common means of sequencing with units on novels, short stories, poetry, drama, essays, and so forth, arranged in some logical order. Arrangement by *special feature* includes not only national origin (e.g., British literature) but literary periods as well. This category also includes the Junior Great Books program, in which the material is chosen for its recognized quality and is sequenced so that ideas developed in one discussion are built on in the next. Sequencing literature by *rhetorical technique* is rare. In this approach, composition instruction is the guiding force. Literature is chosen to augment the writing skills that the teacher intends to teach. Thus, the sequence of literature depends on the sequence of composing techniques the teacher wants students to learn.

Another possibility to consider is a sequence of *author studies*. Rarely in schools do students have an opportunity to explore the work of a single author in any depth. This is an unfortunate circumstance because it makes the study of style quite difficult. Unless they can read several works by the same writer, discovering recurrent themes or stylistic features associated with that individual is virtually impossible. Coming to know an author and his or her various works provides insights that cannot grow from chance encounters scattered over several years of schooling. Author studies allow for depth as well as breadth. At the middle level, however, time may force you to limit author studies to one a year.

Another way of sequencing literature is through the use of *topics* or *themes*. The distinction between these two terms is explored more fully in chapter 13. What is of importance here is the idea that the literature is chosen because it addresses a particular subject. The material may include a wide variety of genres and authors, but all of the texts are linked by topic or theme. There are few guidelines for deciding how to sequence these units, although easier ones should probably precede more challenging ones. Units that focus on personal concerns of adolescents probably should be scheduled before units that are more detached from student interests. In the best of all possible worlds, of course, each topical or thematic unit would build on the previous ones. Be aware that anthologies may be divided into what publishers describe as *thematic units*, but closer examination may reveal a hodgepodge of discourse that neither develops the theme well nor presents a variety of perspectives.

The final option for sequencing is by *correlation*. This refers to interdisciplinary units in which the literature is chosen to correlate with what is being studied in other subject areas. Weaving literature into an examination of a theme being explored by a team of students and teachers is quite effective. However, this approach has a serious flaw. The possibility exists that the study of literature can vanish if all of the material is chosen only on the basis of how well it supports and enhances other subject areas. You could find yourself teaching far more social studies, science, math, health, physical education, industrial technology, and so on than literature if correlation is the primary criterion for choice. Literature is worthy of its own niche. Making it a servant to all the other subject areas devalues it. As a member of a team, you will probably want to correlate literature with their units, but at some point they should correlate their curricula with the literature that you choose.

No matter what basis you use for sequencing literature, the most important guideline to remember is meaningfulness. The reason for studying literature in a certain sequence must make sense to students.

ADDRESSING STUDENT DIVERSITY

Preservice teachers often assume, on the basis of their own experiences, that the best way to teach literature is for everyone to read the same text, complete the same activities, and participate in whole-class discussions led by the teacher. However, they wonder how they can address all of the interests, needs, learning styles, and so on in the classroom if everyone is doing the same thing at the same time. They also wonder how they can cope with the fact that some students read much faster than others. These are legitimate concerns for which most teachers do not have a solution. Indeed, practicing middle level teachers say that addressing student academic diversity is one of the topics about which they most need more information (Association of Illinois Middle-Level Schools and the Center for Prevention Research and Development, 1995). Many try to adapt instruction, but only some of these efforts prove satisfactory. Nevertheless, you need to know what the options are. The list in Fig. 9.6 summarizes some of the possible adaptations.

Most of these are discussed more thoroughly elsewhere in this book, but altering group size deserves special attention. Of all the

To Address Student Diversity, you can vary ...	
• The reading material	• The activities
• The presentation	• The time
• The discussion strategies	• The expectations
• The questions	• The group size

FIG. 9.6

options, varying the group size offers the most comprehensive yet flexible plan for adapting and adjusting to meet the needs of individuals. There are primarily three possible group sizes a teacher can use: whole class, small group, and individuals. Within these general frameworks, however, are several approaches based on the work of Small and McLeod (1974).

Whole Class

Whole-class instruction can take the form of **teacher lecture** only. Knowing what you do about the attention spans and diversity of middle school students, this may not seem to be a useful option, but there are times when a whole-class lecture, albeit brief, is the best way to convey information that students need or want. Much of the time, whole-class instruction takes the form of **teacher-led recitation or discussion**. If it is recitation, the teacher asks the questions and students answer. If it is discussion, questions are more open-ended. Also, students may ask questions and interact with each other. In recitations and discussions, there is enough freedom to allow for addressing some student concerns and interests, but not much. The teacher is still in control. **Student-led recitation or discussion** is another possibility (Kletzien & Baloche, 1994; Knoeller, 1994). Although there still may not be a great deal of individualization, having students conduct the class may give some a chance to use their leadership skills, and the questions they create may address some of their classmates' concerns. Reciprocal teaching, as described by Palinscar and Brown (1985), is an example of student-led recitation or discussion.

Moving away from verbal responses to literature, two more possibilities can be added. One is **teacher-designed content-based activities**. Asking students to complete a worksheet about the literature fits into this category. Activities permit students who are less verbal to do more than just listen. However, by maintaining a focus on the content to be learned, such activities may still not address student diversity well. On the other hand, **teacher-designed student-based activities** focus on readers. These tasks connect students and literature. Asking students to do a free write stating their reaction to the literature or to vote for the character they liked best prompts students to express their individuality while retaining the whole-class structure.

Small Groups

No matter how interesting the lecture, recitation, discussion, or activities, whole-class instruction offers limited flexibility. You can vary the assigned reading material, the presentation, the discussion strategies, the questions, and the activities, but you are still likely to fall short of addressing everyone's learning style and interests. However, small group work offers many options. One possibility is **assigned group work without choice**. In this situation, each student is placed in a group that must complete a predetermined unit of work or sequence of activities. The initial task shown in Fig. 3.5 is an example of this controlled assignment. Every group in the class may be completing exactly the same unit, or each group may be completing a different one. For instance, it would be possible to have six groups working simultaneously, each assigned to read and study the same novel or each working with a different book. A slight variation of this is something referred to as *jigsaw learning*. In this plan, each group studies a different part of one topic or theme. Eventually, each group shares what they have studied with the rest of the class so that everyone learns most things about the whole, but only studies one part in depth. Jigsaw learning can also be done within a small group if each group member studies a small part and then all share their parts with the other group members.

Another possibility is **assigned group work with choice**. The students assigned to each group are required to complete certain tasks, but the group also makes some choices cooperatively. They can, for example, choose which project they wish to do. It is even possible for such a group to choose which novel or short stories they wish to read and discuss, as well as how they prefer to demonstrate their learning.

Content-based group work is another alternative. In this case, students are not assigned to a group first; instead, students individually choose a topic of interest. Then groups are formed. Each group is composed of students who have a common interest. For example, in a thematic unit a teacher might offer students a choice of five books. Groups would be formed on the basis of book choice. Depending on how the work is structured, each group might proceed through a sequence of activities designed by the teacher or they might have some control over their own activities, both what they would do and when they would do it.

Need/Interest-based group work is yet another alternative, although this one works best within the general framework of a reading–writing workshop. In this situation, groups form when there is a common need or interest among a small number of students. The group stays together as long as the need or interest continues, and then it dissolves. Sometimes referred to as *floating* groups, these are the kind that meet on a short-term basis to respond to each other's writing (peer response groups) or that gather by their own choosing or by teacher encouragement to discuss a book that they are all reading or a genre in which they are all interested. A teacher may call such a group together in order to provide a mini-lesson on a topic of mutual interest or concern.

Finally, there is the possibility of **free group work**. This would be a cohesive group that stays together for quite some time but works cooperatively to design their own curriculum. This may sound impossible in the middle level classroom, but it is not. If students have a broad set of guidelines, certain general expectations, and materials from which to choose, they can learn in this kind of environment.

Individual

Individual work offers the most flexibility for addressing diverse needs and interests, but it is also the most difficult to implement and maintain. Record keeping is also difficult, but essential. Educators once referred to this as *independent study*, as if it could take only one form. However, there are actually several varieties of individual work. One approach is called **programmed instruction**. This requires some special materials, either commercial or teacher-created. Students work their way through the material at their own pace. All students do the same things, but they do them when they are ready. Usually there are tests associated with this approach. If students are successful, they move on; if they are not, they go back over what they have not yet learned. However, programmed instruction works best when the material is factual. Grammar, usage, and spelling, for example, can be studied through this format. Many computer software programs that focus on writing skills and vocabulary development follow this approach.

Another possibility is **assigned individual work** which means creating a curriculum for each child. Sometimes this has to be done for special education students, but it is not a practical approach for the majority unless you happen to have some very small classes or you are offering a special elective as a part of an exploratory curriculum.

Another option is **individual contracts**. These can be designed in a variety of ways. Some contracts are predetermined by the teacher and spell out exactly what the student is to do. Some contracts are cooperatively designed with the teacher determining some of the requirements and the student choosing others. Some contracts are open; the student designs the entire plan with the teacher's approval. No matter how the contract is set up, each student has a different one, and both the teacher and student agree to fulfill the requirements. Some contracts also include provisions for grading. If the student fulfills all of the requirements, he or she earns an A. Completion of a certain portion earns a B, and so forth.

Although it would be possible to give individuals total charge of their learning, this is the ultimate extreme. However, the possibility of **free individual work** is a reality. In fact, it best describes how a fully implemented reading–writing workshop functions. Individuals decide what they will read and write. They set their own paces. The teacher outlines expectations, confers regularly with individuals to establish goals, observes and assesses progress, provides guidance and instruction as needed, coaches speaking and listening, and in all ways possible facilitates individual student learning. Within this framework, there is some whole-class instruction and some small group work, but most of the class time is set aside for students to read and write according to their own needs, interests, and abilities. However, the teacher also steps in when necessary to encourage higher achievement or require completion of certain tasks. The program is designed to allow students to reach higher levels of performance by giving them as much freedom and responsibility as they can handle, but individuals who need structure can be given daily or weekly requirements. In short, instruction is tailored to meet the needs of each student.

Choosing the Best Option

From a practical standpoint, whole-class instruction is relatively easy for the teacher. Nevertheless, doing this well demands careful planning and preparation on a daily basis in order to keep everyone involved and interested. The major drawback here is that the teacher owns the instruction. The more the curriculum and activities belong to the teacher, the more students are apt to wonder why they have to learn it. Motivation becomes a crucial issue. Small group and individual work demand more from students. They have to be responsible to their classmates and to themselves. They also have to accept some responsibility for their own learning. However, these alternatives are more flexible and offer potential for addressing individual learning styles and adolescent needs. They can reduce some problems often associated with lack of interest and motivation, but they also demand more from the teacher.

LITERATURE DISCUSSIONS

No matter whether you choose to approach the teaching of literature through the use of units of study, the teacher's manual that accompanies the literature anthology, small groups, a reading–writing workshop, or some other instructional design, you will probably want to engage students in discussion of the literature. If you are using some kind of published material, you need to be aware that many of the discussion questions are likely to reflect a new/practical critic perspective, and the questions are apt to be literal level questions or personal opinion. More recent textbooks are better than those published 10 years ago, but the problems continue. Research indicates that American students are generally good at answering basic comprehension questions (who, what, when, where, and how), but they struggle when the questions become more challenging and require that they make inferences from the given information or explain how the information relates to other texts, similar situations, or their personal experiences (Applebee, Langer, & Mullis, 1988). Similarly, when asked to support their personal opinions, student performance leaves much to be desired, possibly because students have not had sufficient practice in doing so.

Effective Questioning

You need to make the effort to use a range of questions in literary discussions. There are many different kinds of questions (see Fig. 9.7). All should be used, but the recommendation is that you avoid relying too heavily on closed, convergent, literal knowledge, and comprehension questions. Experts also recommend that when teachers ask personal-opinion questions, they should require that students explain, elaborate, and support their responses. As much as possible, they should be asked to define their criteria for judging. It is important to ask students for their personal opinions, and you need to respect these as opinions, but as much as possible you should turn them into evaluation-level questions such that students move from a purely emotional reaction to one that has some defensible basis. Also, higher-order questions demand more wait time so that students can think about their answers before responding. Other hints and helps for conducting better discussions can be found in Activity 9.1.

Concerning Kinds of Questions

General

- Closed questions—one and only one answer or a very limited number of correct answers
- Open or open-ended questions—many different and equally acceptable answers, but answers can be supported
- Personal opinion questions—no wrong answers

Critical and Creative Thinking

- Convergent (deductive) questions—one and only one answer or a limited number of correct answers; provokes critical thinking
- Divergent (inductive) questions—many different and equally acceptable answers, often built on answers expressed by others; provokes creative thinking

Reading Comprehension Research

- Literal level question—closed question; answer is found directly on the page
- Interpretative/inferential level question—closed question; answer implied by what is on the page, but it is not printed there. Rather, it is between the lines.
- Applied level question—open-ended question; answer lies beyond the page and draws on both what is read and what reader knows (from previous study or prior personal experience)

Educational Psychology (Bloom's [1956] *Taxonomy of Educational Objectives*)

- Knowledge level question—closed question; requires parroting from text
- Comprehension level question—closed question; requires repeating of answer found in the text, but in own words or another form (i.e., changing a story to a poem while maintaining same meaning)
- Application level question—somewhat open-ended question; requires using the information in some different way or relating an idea to a new situation (e.g., using the moral of a fable to create a new story that illustrates the same moral)
- Analysis level question—somewhat open-ended question; requires that the information be broken into smaller parts or steps
- Synthesis level question—open-ended question; requires information be recombined into new information
- Evaluative level question—open-ended question; requires information be judged or assessed on the basis of some defensible criteria

FIG. 9.7

Literature Circles

Having students control a discussion makes some teachers queasy; others actually design their literature program around this idea. In reading–writing workshops and whole-language classrooms, students are taught to conduct their own discussions. Either the teacher alone or the teacher in collaboration with students sets up guidelines for these conversations, models effective discussion strategies and questions, conducts initial group meetings, and monitors and observes group discussions. Sometimes the teacher provides the questions; sometimes students are required to generate questions beforehand; sometimes the questions simply evolve as the group discusses. Teachers can designate discussion leaders on a rotating basis who are responsible for conducting the small group discussion. Although there are many different ways to structure them, these small groups are generally known as *literature circles*. This is an approach that began in elementary schools and spread to middle schools. It is also in use in a few high school and college classrooms. For more specific details about organizing and managing literature circles, you should review the sources listed in the Recommended Readings for this chapter.

One advantage of literature circles is that they solve the problem of how to deal with multiple texts. It is extremely difficult to conduct a whole-class discussion when students have read three or four different books (or even more). However, students can, with adequate preparation for doing so, conduct these discussions themselves in small groups. Literature circles also have the advantage of increasing the frequency with which individuals participate verbally. In addition, students have an opportunity to explore ideas that are of the most interest to them. They do not have to follow a path of questioning set by the teacher or by the majority of the class.

One disadvantage is that students must be taught to conduct and participate in these kinds of discussions. Also, the teacher must shift from being a conductor to being a facilitator and observer. For some teachers this is not an easy adjustment.

Whether you want to try literature circles or you prefer to conduct whole-class discussions, encourage students to create their own questions for the conversations. Students need to learn to question themselves when they read, but if they never have the chance to create questions, they may never develop this skill. Furthermore, as much as possible, use student questions as part of the discussion. This gives students some ownership of the activity. Student questions often reveal that less experienced readers are puzzled by what seems obvious to competent adult readers. The discussion will seem more relevant if at least some of their questions are used. Sometimes you will have to bend the discussion around a bit to get to some points that you really want them to consider, but if you work with students to help them learn to prepare good questions, you will find that they not only generate some excellent ones, but produce ones that are better than yours.

OTHER RESPONSES TO LITERATURE

In addition to discussion, you are likely to want students to extend and deepen their understanding of what they read by producing some kind of response other than a verbal one. Often this means writing a paper of some sort about the book, story, poem, play, or even the theme. There is a great deal of research evidence to suggest that linking reading and literature study with writing creates opportunities for the development of both realms (e.g., Irwin & Doyle, 1992). Students who write about what they read tend to become more adept readers and to view what they read from the standpoint of an author; students who read tend to become more able writers who can incorporate language learning drawn from their reading. Nevertheless, the read-then-write strategy, *if used habitually,* can quickly diminish the middle level student's enthusiasm for both reading and writing. Students who know that they will be asked to write a paper almost every time they read quickly grow reluctant to begin the reading. However, if students know that once the reading is done they may have a chance to complete a project that interests them, they may anxiously await the chance to read new material.

Students have many different learning styles. One way to take advantage of this diversity and to make literature study more inviting is to offer students a variety of options for responding to literature. One possible base for designing such options is to consider Gardner's (1983, 1991) work on multiple intelligences or Dunn and Dunn's (1999) work on learning styles, as described in chapter 2. For additional ideas, see Activity 9.7.

As noted in chapter 4, the literature students study (as differentiated from what they read independently for pleasure) should probably be material that is at the instructional level of difficulty. That means that students will need some assistance before, during, and after they read. The article by Beach (1987) entitled "Strategic Teaching in Literature," which is listed in the Recommended Readings, is an example of how to use cognitive scaffolding or structuring to assist students in constructing meaning from text. This is a form of guided reading instruction that works well for helping students not only understand what they read, as is the purpose of most guided reading instruction, but appreciate the work as literature, too. Middle level students may need such instructional aids.

GENRES IN THE MIDDLE SCHOOL

Prior to middle school, students usually engage in two kinds of reading. During the primary grades, they read in order to learn how to read. Instruction often focuses on decoding and developing the various cueing systems. By the upper elementary grades they began using reading as a means of learning other information. Instruction often focuses on comprehending the material and developing skills such as identifying main ideas and examining cause-and-effect relationships. However, they may read only from a basal reader throughout most of their elementary years. Although there certainly are exceptions, many students begin middle school without having had any instruction in literature as content. They may not clearly understand some of the most common literary terms—plot, setting, and metaphor, for example. They may not distinguish between fiction and nonfiction. And they may not know what you mean by the terms *novel* or *stanza*. As a middle level teacher, you may have the opportunity to introduce students to the formal study of literature. This is an exciting possibility, but it carries with it much responsibility for making this initial foray a successful one. You will find some especially useful ideas for teaching literary concepts in Activities 9.2 and 9.3.

The Study of Novels

No matter how you decide to teach literature, you will probably want to include some exploration of novels. In fact, because of available resources, this may be the only form of literature you use or the only other form you use in addition to a literature anthology. As part of this study, you may want to introduce certain literary terms and concepts (see Fig. 9.8). If your students have had little prior experience with class study of a full length work, you will probably have to structure this initial experience carefully. This should include some prereading activities that prepare students to begin the reading with enthusiasm and purpose. You will probably want to include some during-reading instruction as well, such as a study guide (see Activity 9.4 for an example) or a graphic organizer showing the development of the plot. Also, ask students to offer some predictions as the reading progresses. No doubt you will want to ask students to describe the characters and discuss how the setting influences the action. Eventually, have students respond to the literature in some fashion, by writing a paper, completing an activity, or doing a project. Analyzing the work to death is not the best way to introduce literature study, but your instruction should probably include some attention to learning certain terms associated with fictional works. Of course, these can just as easily be taught through short stories and applied during novel study.

Be very careful when you choose the literature that you want to teach to everyone. For some students, this may be one of the few books they will ever read. Think carefully about whether this book

Literary Fiction Terms for Middle School

The following list contains literary concepts associated with fiction that most middle school students can learn. This is a good list around which to design curriculum, discussion questions, or both. However, this list should not be used as the basis for testing students on their knowledge of terms, holding them responsible for knowing the terms and definitions without being able to relate them to the literature they read. The intent here is to give students a literary vocabulary that allows them to speak knowledgeably about factors that are generally used to evaluate literary works. An understanding of these concepts needs to be developed over time. It is not a good idea to try to teach all of these terms through any single novel. Indeed, it probably is not a good idea to try to teach all of these terms in any one year.

Plot sequence—Does the plot follow the usual pattern or not?
1. Beginning, introduction, or exposition
2. Inciting moment (conflict begins; protagonist & antagonist meet)
3. Middle, rising action, development, complication, roadblocks (usually 3–5 incidents in which conflict heightens)
4. Climax, high point (conflict reaches peak; outcome becomes evident)
5. Resolution, falling action, or denouement (final outcomes revealed)
    - Is the chronological sequence interrupted by any flashbacks?
    - Is there any evidence of foreshadowing (clues)?
    - Is the structure more episodic than chronological?

Conflict—Which type of conflict produces the major action in the story? Are there any minor conflicts that produce single actions?
- Character versus nature
- Character versus another character
- Character versus society
- Character versus himself

Setting—Is the setting integral to the story or just a backdrop for it?
- Location/space (where does the story take place? Could it occur elsewhere? How much geographic space is covered? How does this affect the story?)
- Weather or climate (important or not?)
- Time (at what time of day does the story begin? Important or not? How much time elapses during the story? How does the author handle jumps in time?)
- Time period (past, present, or future? If historical, what era? If present, how real? If future, how realistic?)

Characters—Which characters fulfill which roles in the story? What is the purpose of each?
- Major character or minor/supporting character
- Protagonist or antagonist; hero or anti-hero?
- Dynamic or static?
- Fully developed (round) or undeveloped (flat)?
- Realistic or not?

continued on next page

Methods of Characterization—How does the author tell the reader about the characters?
- What the character looks like (physical description)
- What the character does (actions)
- What the character says (dialogue)
- What the character thinks and feels (interior or exterior monologue)
- What reactions other characters have to the character (reactions of others)
- Do these methods build a consistent character?
- Has the author provided enough characterization so the reader understands his or her motivation?

Points of view—Does who is telling the story and from what point of view make a difference in the story?
- First-person point of view?
- If third person, is it limited, omniscient, or objective?
- Major character or minor character or observer?
- Reliable or unreliable?
- Consistent or not?

Theme (not a topic and not a moral)—Does the story have a theme or themes? If so, what opinion or attitude about life or behavior is the author trying to express? What aspects of the story create or add to this impression?

Mood—What mood, atmosphere, or feeling surrounds the events in this story? How is this supposed to affect the reader? How does the author create this mood or these moods?

Tone—What attitude does the author have toward the characters and the events in this story? For example, does he/she seem to be sympathetic, non-judgmental, or ridiculing? Is the story meant to be humorous or serious? How do you know?

Style—How would you describe the author's style? Why is this style used? Which of the following stylistic features stand out? (See Activity 9.3)
- Use of dialogue
- Vocabulary or word choice
- Sentence structure
- Use of description
- Figurative language or imagery

Verisimilitude—Does the author create a feeling of reality? If so, how? Is this maintained throughout or do some incidents or characters go beyond acceptable limits? Does this interfere with enjoying the story?

FIG. 9.8

is truly one that everybody should read. At the same time, think about whether reading this book is likely to make students want to read more.

Also, be prepared for the unexpected. I once introduced *When the Legends Die* (Borland, 1963) to a class, expecting to spend the following 2 weeks moving the class gradually through the book. The next day at least five students reported to me that they finished the book. Several more finished it within another couple of days. This created all sorts of problems in discussion because students kept bringing up events that occurred later in the book, ones about which the rest of the class had not yet read. Although it may not be your first choice, you may want to consider the possibility of assigning large chunks or even the whole book rather than breaking it down into small portions. For an example of scaffolding independent study of a novel, see Activity 9.5.

One caution: There are a lot of commercial materials available for teaching novels. Some of them contain helpful suggestions and interesting ideas for projects and activities, but many of them are far too expensive for what they contain. Many are just pages of worksheets ready for duplication. On the other hand, professional periodicals, such as NCTE's *Notes Plus*, contain far more good ideas for the buck, and many are classroom-tested.

The Study of Drama

Although middle level students generally enjoy the study of drama, reading a script can be enormously challenging. Stage or camera directions interrupt the flow of the text. Character description, if it appears at all, is usually provided at the beginning rather than within the script itself. Setting is given only limited attention in many scripts. The vocabulary of stage and camera directions may be unfamiliar and confusing to a reader. Students who are unfamiliar with reading scripts need some assistance just to understand how to approach the task.

Some dramatic terms and concepts appropriate for middle school students are listed in Fig. 9.9. It is worthwhile to study a play in terms of plot, character development, theme, language, and other literary aspects, but students also need to be aware that playwrights must pay particular attention to the medium. A short story writer can visualize him- or herself interacting with one reader at a time; the playwright sees an audience. The poet can assume that the reader may move on to another poem if one is not satisfying, but the playwright's audience is captive. The novelist knows, at least unconsciously, that some readers will ignore the descriptive parts or jump around through the text as they choose, whereas the playwright is

Drama Concepts for Middle School

A study of drama can be fascinating to middle school students if you can take the time to explore various forms and compare them. Historically, drama has been the most accessible of all the literary forms. Common people did not need to know how to read and write to enjoy drama. It was meant for the masses, not the educated elite. To some extent, that situation has changed in the modern era. Although film, videotape, and television versions continue to be readily available, stage performances are less accessible. Thus, students may have had little exposure to some of the best forms of drama while having been virtually drowned in some of the worst.

Literary concepts—See list of literary fiction terms in Fig. 9.8. Most of the same concepts that apply to narrative fiction also apply to drama.

Setting—One of the major differences between stage drama and television or film drama relates to setting. Through editing, the viewer can be moved from one location to another in a wink. Stage drama is far less mobile; scenery cannot be changed in a flash. As a result, stage drama often focuses more on people than events.

Point of view—In drama, the point of view is different. Novelists and short story writers have several choices. Playwrights have fewer options. It is possible to have a narrator, as is the case in *Our Town,* but that is a device which most dramatists avoid. In Greek drama, the chorus often commented on the action and theme. Again, this is a device which is not frequently used now. Most of the time, the point of view is 1st person; that is, each character speaks for him or herself. In a sense, each viewer is the creator of point of view.

Focus—Writers can direct the reader's focus. Similarly, a camera lens can zoom in to highlight significant details, thus eliminating all of the surrounding people and action. In stage drama, words are far more significant because they replace the peering eye of the camera, and everyone remains visible to the audience.

Structure—Students need to learn some things about how drama is structured. What is the significance of the division of the work into acts and scenes? How are one-act plays similar to short stories? What influence do commercials have on the way that television drama is structured? Scripts are structured differently, with lists of characters at the start, followed by some description of setting. After that, the rest of the material is primarily dialogue. Students need to know how to look for these structure elements in scripts in order to read plays effectively.

Vocabulary—Various forms of drama have differing vocabularies. Stage plays contain stage directions that can be very confusing. Film scripts contain camera directions that may be meaningless without a special dictionary or glossary. Students may see these as hindrances, but to the professionals they are essential.

FIG. 9.9

aware that the viewer, locked into the sequence of action as it is presented, can skip nothing (unless the work is on videotape). The dramatist who writes for the stage is limited in time and place and number of characters far more than the television or film script writer. The camera can zoom in to highlight an object or fine motor action of significance. On stage the camera zoom must be replaced with words and visible actions. All students can benefit from some discussion of the limitations that playwrights face and the differences between plays meant for the stage and those designed for the screen. This distinction becomes even more clear if students have the opportunity to write some scripts themselves and try them out by doing an onstage walk-through or videotaping a rough performance. Another possibility is to discuss whether a short story or novel could be transformed into a stage or screenplay and how it might be done.

Teachers often ask students to read plays aloud, and middle level students generally enjoy doing so. However, their oral reading may be painfully inadequate. If you are going to ask students to read plays aloud, then provide some instruction in oral interpretation. Students need to understand that they cannot just pronounce the words accurately; they have to use their voices to carry the intended emotion. For that to happen, they must read the material in advance. If they read a play cold, they may use voice inflections that mislead listeners.

However, in the final analysis, plays were created for viewers, not readers. As much as possible, students need to see performances. This may mean having students perform in class, but it can also mean using videotapes and laser disks. If possible, students should see a live performance.

A Short (But Important) Note About Short Stories

Of all the forms of fiction, you may find short stories to be the most useful in the middle level classroom. Not many short stories have been written primarily for adolescents, although that fact is changing. Gallo, for example, has edited several collections of stories written by popular young adult authors. You may also find collections of works by Cormier and Crutcher especially useful. However, students are often willing to trade the lack of teenage protagonists and contemporary settings for the mystery, adventure, and humor in many short stories. The length, of course, appeals to them, but you also may find this to be a significant advantage. You can introduce a variety of literary techniques, writing styles, and authors in a limited time frame. Students can more easily compare short texts because they can read more selections and recall them well. Reading and discussing novels is important, but short stories fit the middle level student's attention span nicely. They are also an excellent vehicle for introducing more multicultural literature. Many short stories are available in visual and audiotaped versions. Students can transform some stories into scripts that can be tape-recorded in the form of a radio play or performed live. Although the literature curriculum should contain a balance of material, do not skimp on short stories. You will find a list of some recommended titles in Activity 9.6 and options for response in Activity 9.7 near the end of this chapter.

And Then There Is Poetry

Some experts advise against teaching a poetry unit. They recommend that poetry be used constantly throughout the year both in conjunction with other literature and composition as well as for its own sake. They also recommend the oral reading of poetry. This can easily be done by the teacher, but students, too, should be the readers.

This advice seems to be sound, and you may wish to follow it. Certainly poetry can be interspersed, and it adds missing dimensions to thematic units or the study of other literature. Students need to hear poetry read aloud well. If you cannot, then use records and tapes of professional readings. There are also recordings of the poets themselves reading their work, although some of these people are better poets than oral readers. Some students do enjoy sharing poems they like with others, and they will read the material aloud to small groups, although they are much more hesitant about sharing with the whole class. A few take pride in memorizing, but for most this is a chore that makes poetry less appealing. Middle level students delight in the work of Shel Silverstein and Judith Viorst. Jack Prelutsky is a bit too juvenile for them, but they still like some of his work. They really enjoy narrative poems, particularly if they are read with exaggerated drama. They also like some Robert Frost, Emily Dickinson, Langston Hughes, Gwendolyn Brooks, and Maya Angelou, but they will enjoy a wide range of poetry if given the chance to experience it.

Although sharing poetry often is laudable, a poetry unit, if well designed, can be successful. Some of the concepts you may wish to include are shown in Fig. 9.10, along with some poetry forms that are usually successful in the middle level classroom. Other possibilities are included in Activity 9.8. Consider starting with poetry writing. Read some poetry as models for the writing, and have students compose formula poems as a class before they try their own versions. Move through a sequence of poems that starts with some tightly structured forms and progresses to free verse. You may also include some practice activities in which students experiment with poetic devices in their journals. Provide time for them to share their in-process poems informally with classmates and require them to

Poetic Concepts and Forms for Middle School

There is certainly a great deal that one would hope students would eventually learn about poetry, but not everything needs to be taught at the middle level. The following concepts can be effectively introduced:

- **Rhyme and rhyme scheme** (best if illustrated in shorter poems, though. Repetition of rhyme scheme from one stanza to the next puzzles them)
- **Rhythm** (but not the technicalities of meter and feet)
- **Repetition**, (especially in the form of a chorus or refrain)
- **Alliteration** (but assonance and consonance generally fly over the heads of most students)
- **Personification** (students often misunderstand this one initially)
- **Onomatopoeia** (obvious examples work best)
- **Simile** (to distinguish from metaphor, remind students that the word *simile* contains an *l* for the word *like* and an *s* for the word *as*)
- **Metaphor** (if rather obvious)

Students can successfully write poems of the following forms:

A. Formula poems

- *I wish* … or *If I were* … (every line begins with the same phrase)
- Color poem (every line or stanza begins with a color name + *is*, [e.g., yellow is …])
- Contrast poem using *I used to* … /*But now* … (each line or line pair uses these words; can be done as comparative stanzas)
- Description poem (opens with the identification of the topic followed by *is* [e.g., Happiness is …]; each following line describes what the topic is or what something or someone means to the poet)
- Preposition poem (each line begins with a preposition; the last line is usually a kind of revelation of the subject matter)
- Acrostic poem (uses a key word, such as the student's name, written down the page; each line of the poem incorporates the letters in succession)
- Dialogue poem (written for two speakers so that they take turns at times and speak simultaneously at times)
- Take 5 poem (It takes 5 lines to make this poem: the topic; 2 adjectives describing the topic; 3 participles describing what the topic can do; a phrase describing the topic; and a synonym for the topic.)
- Diamente (a poem of 7 lines that shows a contrast or a progressive change. The first 3 lines are the same as those in a Take 5. Line 4 includes 4 nouns; often the first 2 refer to the beginning topic and the second 2 refer to the ending, but this sequence can be more gradual. Lines 5–7 reverse lines 1–3, finishing with the opposite or changed topic, and the poem takes the shape of a diamond when it is finished.)
- 5–senses poem (many variations are possible, but basically this poem opens with an abstract noun, such as *freedom* or *hatred*, followed by the word *is* and then the name of a color. The next four lines tell what the abstract noun *smells*

like, sounds like, tastes like, and *feels like,* using the pronoun *it* to introduce each line. For instance, freedom is red, white, and blue; it sounds like firecrackers booming; it smells like grilled hot dogs and warm apple pie.

B. Free form poems
- Concrete poem (words are shaped to reflect the meaning)
- Found poem (new expression is created from existing text)

C. Syllable- and word-count poems
- Haiku
- Tanka
- Cinquain

D. Rhymed poems
- Couplets
- Clerihews (2 rhymed couplets written about a person)
- Limericks
- Song lyrics
- Narratives

FIG. 9.10

create a booklet of their poems. After they have tried their hand at writing several, engage them in examining some poems together. Select ones that illustrate the poetic techniques students have studied through their writing and that hold particular appeal for middle level students. Encourage students to approach poetry from a problem-solving perspective; consider each poem as a kind of puzzle to be solved, because middle level students generally like mysteries. Emphasize that no single solution is the only "right" one. When they finish, give them time to read the poetry booklets they have created.

Although there are certain poetic concepts that can and probably should be introduced at the middle school level, dissecting poetry is the quickest way to kill interest in the genre. You may wish to introduce concepts as mini-lessons or just as a part of brief responses to poems that you read aloud frequently. Middle level students need not learn all there is to know about these poetic devices or be able to define each of these poetic forms on an exam, but middle school is certainly an appropriate place for introducing poetic vocabulary.

There are lots of good ways to incorporate poetry into the language arts classroom. Verse should be heard, so poems are excellent for practicing speaking and listening for different purposes. Some poems are graphic designs, which can lead into examining other forms of visual art and print techniques. Poetry also links well with music and dance. It adds drama and sensory impressions to historical events. Nature poems that can be linked to science abound, and some poems relate to math. In short, poetry is an enormously versatile form of literature, one that is well suited to interdisciplinary and integrative units. Students need to see poetry not as something stuffy and stilted, but alive with hopes and dreams and the same emotions they feel but may not yet have the words to express.

Last But Not Least: Nonfiction

Nonfiction is all too often ignored, as if it were not literature at all. In general, the term *literature* includes only a small portion of nonfiction—poetry, essays, biographies, autobiographies, and oral tradition tales (i.e., myths, legends, folktales, etc.) although nonfiction actually encompasses a broad range of text. Many students enjoy reading nonfiction material, such as magazines, newspapers, informative articles, "factual" books on topics of personal interest, real diaries, interviews, collections of letters, and so on. If developing a lifelong habit of reading is a primary goal, then there should be a place for nonfiction in the language arts classroom. Much nonfiction may not be literature, but it is certainly discourse, and reading it certainly is or should be a part of becoming a well-informed citizen. Some of the aspects of nonfiction worth exploring at the middle level are shown in Fig. 9.11.

Although it would be nice if teachers in other subject areas used well-written material more readily as part of their curricula (a trend which is gaining ground, particularly at the elementary level and in those schools using a thematic approach), most teachers in other disciplines continue to rely heavily on expository textbooks. Some of these are carefully designed with lots of reading aids to assist students in comprehending; others are simply awful—boring, pedantic, overloaded with facts, and confusingly organized. Students often need reading assistance even when the books are well prepared.

However, students should not be left with the impression that textbooks represent what is good about nonfiction. They need to encounter a wide variety of well-written explanatory and persuasive material as part of their study of literature. As noted in chapter 5, students do not write exposition easily or well. Nor do they compose argumentation with skill. If the only model they read is textbook writing, how can we expect them to write well-crafted exposition and argumentation? Textbooks are intentionally objective, detached, and generally voiceless. If you want students to come to appreciate forceful, impassioned writing that is carefully designed to argue a point, they need to read such discourse. If you want students to create clear but lively explanations that incorporate examples and illustrations, they need to see some of the best examples you can provide. Some excellent guides for using nonfiction in the middle

---

Nonfiction Concepts for Middle School

Give students a chance to explore the wide range of nonfiction material that is available. Many students will be unaware that collections of essays or legends form entire books. Middle level students are often fascinated by unusual books about disasters or weird inventions, collections of maps with explanations, walking tours, actual logs or chronicles of historic events, diaries or collections of letters written by real people, and other book oddities. Even unusual or special-purpose dictionaries interest some students. If possible, make nonfiction texts available for students to browse through, and when appropriate include them in the class work. Give students the opportunity to create similar material, using these as models.

Definition

Students need to know that nonfiction includes a wide range of discourse (i.e., everything that is not considered fiction), but they also need to understand that just because something is considered nonfiction does not mean it is fact. Nonfiction includes all of the following and more:

- Factual material
- Material believed to be or based on fact
- Persuasion, including advertisements
- Folklore, myths, legends, & fairy tales
- Real letters, diaries, logs, & chronicles
- Theories
- Opinions
- Biography & autobiography
- Poetry

Purpose

What often distinguishes fiction from nonfiction is the author's intent or purpose. Fiction is usually meant to entertain. Nonfiction, on the other hand, is usually meant to serve as a record, to inform, or to persuade. Much of it is designed to make the reader think and to help the reader understand or be convinced. Some nonfiction is private–made–public material, such as a diary. The writer may have never meant for it to be published. In that case, readers need to judge the work with that factor in mind. Other nonfiction was written for public use. In that case, the material should be clear and understandable to the intended audience, which may or may not be middle school readers. Although it is nice if nonfiction is interesting to read, judging all nonfiction on that basis is not fair. That is a concept that middle school students find very difficult to accept.

Organization

Fiction is usually arranged chronologically. Some nonfiction is also arranged that way, for example:

- Biographies
- Autobiographies
- Memoirs
- Oral tradition tales (myths, legends, fairy tales, parables, & fables)
- Directions for or descriptions of performing an action or activity
- Diaries & journals
- Logs & chronicles
- Historical texts

continued on next page

However, most nonfiction is arranged in other ways. The most common methods of organization are the following:

- Categories or classifications
- Comparison–contrast
- Cause–and–effect
- Problem–solution

Certain pieces of nonfiction follow formulas. Front-page news stories, for example, present the main ideas first and the rest in descending order of importance. There are many forms of technical writing which also follow prescribed formats.

Uses

Nonfiction serves a variety of purposes. Therefore, it can be used in many different ways by readers. Much fiction is meant to be read from cover to cover. Much nonfiction is not. However, students many need some instruction about using nonfiction material efficiently. They may need reminders about the use of guide words in dictionaries, for example. They may also need some instruction in how to read and interpret graphs, charts, and maps. Without reminders, they may ignore helpful print techniques, such as page divisions, bold print, underlining, and italics. They may not understand some abbreviations or footnote references. They may also need some help using a table of contents or an index.

Management

Much nonfiction material is useful in research. However, when it comes to this activity, middle level students need some carefully scaffolded instruction. Middle level students need help not only in finding information but in learning to manage it well. The following list may be a helpful guide in considering what students need to do when they research:

- Consider what you already know about the topic
- Identify research questions (What else do you want to know?)
- Locate possible sources of information (Is there enough? A variety?)
- Read the material to understand the general concepts (get a general sense of what the experts think about the topic and where the conflicts lie, especially if the topic is controversial)
- Examine each source more carefully, evaluating the quality, accuracy, or appropriateness of the information
- Select the information to use and reread it
- Arrange or organize the information
- Present or report the information, giving credit appropriately

Over the years teachers have developed some strategies for teaching students to do research. Some of these are useful; others are inefficient. With the advent of copy machines and laptop computers, handwritten note cards are basically obsolete. Footnotes have all but vanished, yet some textbooks still teach this style. Be very careful about teaching research strategies that do not make use of current technology and actual practices.

FIG. 9.11

school classroom are *Making Facts Come Alive* (Bamford & Kristo, 1998), *Nonfiction Matters* (Harvey, 1998), and *Eye Openers* and *Eye Openers II* (Kobrin, 1998, 1995).

But there is another reason for including nonfiction in literature study—student interest. Although you may love fiction, some students are far more enthused about exploring nonfiction. That alone is reason enough to make room for nonfiction in the language arts classroom.

YOUNG ADULT LITERATURE

There was a time when fiction and nonfiction for teenage readers could best be described as "adolescent literature." Not only was it written for adolescents, it was juvenile in quality. However, anyone who has read Cormier's (1974) *The Chocolate War* or Crutcher's (1993) *Staying Fat for Sarah Byrnes* knows that adolescent literature has matured. It is not just for kids anymore. In fact, some of it is not for middle level readers either.

Much young adult literature appeals strongly to middle school students because it directly addresses their concerns. The characters could easily be their peers or their older siblings, if not themselves. The settings are contemporary or, at least, believable. The pace is usually rapid, and the reading is generally in the independent range, in part because of the straightforward plot and frequent dialogue. Many short stories written for adolescents examine a variety of cultural issues and societal problems with honesty and sensitivity. Much of the poetry presented in collections for young adults was written by teenagers. Biographies and autobiographies about people who interest teens are more common now. One genre that is nearly missing from young adult literature, however, is drama. There are few plays that have been written and published principally for a young adult audience. But there are hundreds of young adult novels including a wide range of genre and themes—realistic fiction, sports, humor, science fiction, fantasy, survival, race relations, historical fiction, mystery, horror, and more—which are exceedingly popular among teenage readers. Many of these have been transformed into television specials and movies that are now available on videotape.

Unfortunately, some language arts teachers disparage young adult literature. They want nothing to do with it in their classroom, and they adamantly refuse to give students credit for reading this material, even for free reading. Other teachers are quite willing to permit such reading and may even encourage it, as long as it is outside their classroom walls. However, more and more, young adult literature is finding its way into the curriculum. Gradually teachers are discovering that this is material that students will read. What is more, they will read it with enthusiasm. They comprehend it well, and they will discuss it almost endlessly.

Unless you have taken a course that focuses on young adult literature, you may have little knowledge of current titles and authors, except those you may have read when you were younger. Being familiar with some young adult literature will be a tremendous asset in the middle level classroom. One worthwhile personal goal is to read young adult works on a regular basis. See Activity 9.9 for a list of popular and prolific authors. A sample of recommended books appears in Activity 9.10. If you cannot complete a course that focuses on young adult literature while you are an undergraduate, put it on a list of professional development courses that you intend to take later. To keep abreast of new publications, become familiar with the reviews of young adult literature that appear in a variety of sources such as *The Horn Book*, *Book List*, *Children's Literature Review*, the *English Journal*, and the *Journal of Adolescent & Adult Literacy*.

Familiarity with young adult works will be beneficial in the classroom, but you need not feel that you have to know everything about this literature before you begin teaching. If you will give students the chance, they will teach you. Ask them to recommend titles. Give them opportunities to talk about the good books they are reading for pleasure. Have them conduct surveys and interviews about their reading material. Ask them to write journal entries about their favorite books or why they chose the book they are currently reading. Listen as they recommend books to their friends. The school librarian can be a fountain of helpful information, too. Most importantly, do not denigrate young adult literature before you have read the best. You will find this to be time well spent. Do not be surprised if you discover that you absolutely must find a place for young adult material in your literature program.

MULTICULTURAL LITERATURE

Teachers often try to include a wide range of reading material—different genres, different topics, different lengths, and so on—in the hope that somewhere in this variation each student will find something that appeals to him or her. Teachers also try to vary the reading level of the material in order to provide for different skill levels. Some teachers try to offer reading options and let students choose according to their preferences.

One strong motivation for varying reading material is a recognition that the literary canon is predominantly white, male, European, and Protestant (sometimes described in students' terms as "50 dead white guys and Emily Dickinson"). However, American classrooms today are multicultural, multiethnic, multiracial, and multireligious, as well as bigendered. If students are to make connections between the literature they read and the people they are, you need to include literature that both represents a range of humanity and mirrors reader diversity.

Recently published literature anthologies include a wider variety of multicultural literature than older versions. However, some of the selections may be difficult for students to comprehend. Not only will they encounter cultural differences, but they may also confront works written in unfamiliar dialects or texts containing foreign words and phrases. Translated works may include challenging vocabulary and unusual sentence structures. Carefully selected multicultural novels may be more accessible to students than shorter, anthologized pieces. Activity 9.11 contains a bibliography of sources that you may find useful in locating appropriate works for middle level readers.

Several reference books include extensive lists of recommended multicultural literature. However, any book list is out of date the minute it is printed. No doubt there are many recently published books that should be added and by next month there will be even more. Watch the professional resources for recently published books that are receiving high praise, and add them to your personal reading list.

COPING WITH CENSORSHIP

No chapter on teaching literature would be complete without at least acknowledging the rising number of censorship challenges. Despite the fact that educators try to use professional wisdom when selecting material, many parents and community residents find fault with these choices. The choice of literature seems to crystallize the differences in values that American culture encompasses. Although educators may feel responsible for helping students learn about this diversity and accept it as an asset, many people see this as a threat or challenge to the belief system that they wish to instill in their children.

As a teacher, you need to know that almost every piece of literature has, at one time or another, been challenged by someone. If you plan to assign a text to all students, you should know two things about it: (a) why you wish to teach it, and (b) the grounds on which it has been previously challenged. If you choose to teach this particular piece, you are locking yourself into defending it. If you choose to teach about literature or through literature, you can at least substitute some other work or give students some reading options. However, in recent years censors have increasingly demanded that objectionable material be removed from libraries and curriculum. They are no longer concerned with only their child; they see it as their duty or moral obligation to ensure that no child has access to the discourse.

As a teacher, you must work within community standards of acceptability. However, you may find that the community is not in agreement. Further, you may find that you simply cannot stand by and acquiesce to belief systems that are personally or professionally unacceptable. Many school districts have policies concerning making choices of literature. If you choose to teach a work that has not been taught before, you may need to fill out some forms that ask you to justify your choice. This may seem like a burden, but the paperwork may save you from a censorship hassle later. If you have any concerns about a text you are thinking of assigning, talk with the school librarian to see if anyone in the community has ever challenged the material or filed a complaint about it. School librarians usually have lists of challenged books that you can peruse. The American Library Association also has information, and NCTE recently issued a CD-ROM containing rationales for frequently challenged books. Both organizations can also direct you to agencies that maintain records on censorship and offer advice on how to avoid problems. You can also find much information about censored and banned books on the Internet. Discuss your decisions with other teachers and try to gain their support; talk with the principal and keep him or her informed of your plans (no principal likes to be blindsided by parent complaints); talk with some parents informally and try to garner their support as well; keep parents fully informed of your plans and confer with any who have questions. If necessary, label your plan as a pilot study and accept only students who volunteer and whose parents give permission to enroll.

Be prepared to be challenged. Recognize that the parent or group that questions your decision will feel that the best interests of young people are at stake. Many are deeply concerned about the quality of education and want to assist in making improvements. Do not be overly defensive or overreact, but do not ignore the challenge either. Know exactly why you chose the material, and have it in writing. Check to be sure that the challenger has read the text. If he or she has not, ask the person to do so and reschedule a conference. Take the person seriously. Try to understand the other point of view and reach a compromise. If that fails, seek assistance from others.

ASSESSING LITERARY UNDERSTANDING

This section must begin with a deep sigh and a pregnant pause. In a perfect world, it would not be necessary to assess student engagement with literature at all. If the goal of literature study is the development of a lifelong habit of reading and a love affair with literature, the only worthwhile evaluation could not occur until students were long past their years of schooling. However, parents and policymakers are not about to allow teachers to wait that long. You will just have to look at the data you can collect and do your best to interpret it in a professionally responsible way (see Activity 9.12 for a checklist of aspects to assess).

You can test students on some details of the material, their recall of class discussion, and their grasp of literary concepts. However, as is true of most tests, what you really want to measure may not be "testable." Some students who test well will be able to demonstrate that they have learned, but others will not. Paper-and-pencil tests should be only one possible tool that you use for assessing literary understanding. You need to look, too, at the kinds of responses students have to the literature. However, you must exercise special care in examining these responses. It is all too easy to get caught up in assigning grades to responses that do not reflect what students have learned about literature. For example, you can unintentionally grade written responses more on the basis of composition skills than on the basis of what the paper tells about the student's knowledge of literature. Similarly, you can get sidetracked when grading speeches, oral reports, dramatic representations, and even artwork, so that the grade fails to reflect the extent to which the response accurately portrays or links to the literature. You want something that illustrates not only comprehension but depth of understanding. Stating that expectation on a list of grading criteria so that students understand it is nearly impossible. All the same, responses to literature add to the database.

Another factor that should be assessed is discussion. Participation is important, but the quality of comments is equally significant. Keeping records of discussions is cumbersome and time-consuming, though. You can record the frequency of contribution, but making notes about quality in the midst of a lively exchange of ideas can be distracting to you and to students. In some ways this is easier when students work in small groups and conduct their own discussions. That frees you to wander about, listen in on discussions, and make notes. The problem, of course, is that you can only be in one place at a time. Having students write some sort of evaluation of the group's discussion in which they identify the most important and interesting conclusions or suggestions and who contributed them is one alternative. Another is to taperecord some discussions.

However, the best method of determining what students are learning about or through the literature is student–teacher conferences. Without doubt, these are difficult to conduct, particularly at first, and they are even more difficult to schedule. What does the rest of the class do while you interview each student? Even if you talk with each for only 5 minutes, you will need at least three class periods of almost nonstop conferences to assess a class of 25. Practicing teachers will tell you that individual conferencing is one of the most intense kinds of teaching experiences. However, if you can spread these out over a couple of weeks, doing three or four each period, you may be able to withstand the pressure.

The other method, which is still under development, is the use of portfolios. Although the portfolio strategy certainly holds a great deal of promise in terms of telling far more about what students are learning and have learned than any standardized test could ever reveal, teachers do not yet have much experience in evaluating them. As for reading and literature portfolios, most people would say that teachers are still breaking ground. You can collect the material—student reading logs, written papers, pictures of projects, videotapes of discussions and performances, observation notes, diagnostic quizzes, progress tests, reading interest surveys, and so forth, but then what? How do you make sense out of it in some way that will help the student learn more and help you provide better instruction?

If you choose to use portfolios for evaluating either reading and literature or writing, you will have a great deal of data, but you will still have to face the ultimate question: What should the grade be? Portfolios do provide a much better picture of student progress and knowledge, but they do not make grading any easier or less time-consuming. This does not sound very positive, but it is the reality. Then again, grading is never an easy or pleasant task.

No matter what strategies you use to assess literature learning, the key question should be Do students read, and do they read avidly? You can assess their knowledge and you can assess the development of certain skills; you can grade individual pieces or have students create portfolios; you can record the frequency of participation or confer individually with students; but the bottom line must be performance. If students do not read willingly, perhaps even enthusiastically, then they have not yet achieved the primary goal. No matter how well students know literature, how much they know about literature, or how much they learn through literature, if they do not read persistently by choice for pleasure, most of this knowledge will represent wasted effort.

RECOMMENDED READINGS

Abrahamson, R., & Carter, B. (1991). Nonfiction: The missing piece in the middle. *English Journal, 80*(1), 52–58.

Bamford, R., & Kristo, J. (Eds.). (1998). *Making facts come alive: Choosing quality nonfiction literature K–8.* Norwood, MA: Christopher-Gordon Publishers.

Beach, R. (1987). Strategic teaching in literature. In B. Jones, A. Palincsar, D. Ogle, & E. Carr (Eds.), *Strategic teaching and learning: Cognitive instruction in the content areas.* (pp. 135–159). Alexandria, VA: Association for Supervision and Curriculum Development.

Berger, L. (1996). Reader response journals: You make the meaning ... and how. *Journal of Adolescent & Adult Literacy, 39* (5), 380–385.

Burns, B. (1998). Changing the classroom climate with literature circles. *Journal of Adolescent & Adult Literacy, 42*(2), 124–129.

Copeland, J. (1993). *Speaking of poets: Interviews with poets who write for children and young adults.* Urbana, IL: National Council of Teachers of English.

Daniels, H. (1994). *Literature circles: Voice and choice in the student-centered classroom.* York, ME: Stenhouse.

Donelson, K., & Nilsen, A. (1997). *Literature for today's young adults* (5th ed.). New York: Addison Wesley Longman.

Dunning, S., & Stafford, W. (1992). *Getting the knack: 20 poetry writing exercises.* Urbana, IL: National Council of Teachers of English.

Eeds, M., & Wells, D. (1989). Grand conversations: An exploration of meaning construction in literature study groups. *Research in the Teaching of English, 23*(1), 4–29.

Erb, T. (Ed.) (1997). Using literature to enhance reading theme issue. *Middle School Journal, 29*(2), 8–54.

Gallo, D. (Ed.). (1993, Fall). *Literature for teenagers: New books, new approaches* [Issue theme]. *Connecticut English Journal, 22.*

Gambrell, L., & Almasi, J. (1996). *Lively discussions! Fostering engaged reading.* Newark, DE: International Reading Association.

Gilles, C. (1989). Reading, writing, and talking: Using literature study groups. *English Journal, 78*(1), 38–41.

Harvey, S. (1998). *Nonfiction matters: Reading, writing, and research in grades 3–8.* York, ME: Stenhouse.

Hill, B., Johnson, N., & Noe, N. (1995). *Literature circles and response.* Christopher–Gordon.

Hynds, S. (1997). *On the brink: Negotiating literature and life with adolescents.* Newark, DE: International Reading Association.

Kletzien, S., & Baloche, L. (1994). The shifting muffled sound of the pick: Facilitating student-to-student discussion. *Journal of Reading, 37*(7), 540–545.

Knoeller, C. (1994). Negotiating interpretations of text: The role of student-led discussions in understanding literature. *Journal of Reading, 37*(7), 572–580.

Kobrin, B. (1988). *Eyeopeners!* New York: Penguin.

Kobrin, B. (1995). *Eyeopeners II.* New York: Scholastic.

Kooy, M., & Wells, J. (1996). *Reading response logs: Inviting students to explore novels, short stories, plays, poetry, and more.* Portsmouth, NH: Heinemann.

Langer, J. (Ed.). (1992). *Literature instruction, a focus on student response.* Urbana, IL: National Council of Teachers of English.

Lundin, A. (1988). Library literature for teachers. *Language Arts, 65*(3), 335–337.

McTeague, F. (1992). *Shared reading in the middle and high school years.* Portsmouth, NH: Heinemann.

Monseau, V. (1996). *Responding to young adult literature.* Portsmouth, NH: Boynton/Cook–Heinemann.

Padgett, R. (Ed.). (1987) *The teachers & writers handbook of poetic forms.* New York: Teachers and Writers Collaborative.

Petersen, R., & Eeds, M. (1990). *Grand conversations: Literature groups in action.* New York: Scholastic.

Probst, R. (1988). *Response and analysis: Teaching literature in junior and senior high school.* Portsmouth, NH: Boynton/Cook–Heinemann.

Probst, R. (1994). Reader-response theory and the English curriculum. *English Journal, 83*(3), 37–44.

Purves, A., Rogers, T., & Soter, A. (1995). *How porcupines make love III: Readers, texts, cultures in the response-based literature classroom.* White Plains, NY: Longman.

Raphael, T., & McMahon, S. (1994). Book club: An alternative framework for reading instruction. *The Reading Teacher, 48,* 102–116.

Scott, J. (1994). Literature circles in the middle school classroom: Developing reading, responding, and responsibility. *Middle School Journal, 26*(2), 37–41.

Stover, L. (1996). *Young adult literature: The heart of the middle school curriculum.* Portsmouth, NH: Boynton/Cook.

Wiencek, J., & O'Flahavan, J. (1994). From teacher-led to peer discussions about literature: Suggestions for making the shift. *Language Arts, 71,* 488–498.

Wood, M. (1997). *12 multicultural novels: Reading and teaching strategies.* Portland, ME: J. Weston Walch.

Worthy, J., Moorman, M., & Turner, M. (1999). What Johnny likes to read is hard to find in school. *Reading Research Quarterly, 34*(1), 12–27.

Young Adult Library Services Association (YALSA). (1994, October). Top one hundred countdown: Best of the best books for young adults. *Booklist, 9,* 412–416.

OTHER RESOURCES

American Library Association
  50 East Huron Street
  Chicago, IL 60611
  www.recordedbooks.com

Voice of Youth Advocates (VOYA)
Scarecrow Press, Inc.
  4720 Boston Way
  Lanham, MD 20706
  www.scarecrowpress.com

Teaching Literature Activities and Suggestions

- 9.1 Hints and Helps for Conducting Better Discussions

- 9.2 A Sampler of Ideas for Teaching Literacy Concepts

- 9.3 Searching for Style

- 9.4 A Student's Guide to the Study of the Novel

- 9.5 Scaffolding the Reading of a Novel

- 9.6 Recommended Short Stories for Middle School

- 9.7 Short Story Response Options

- 9.8 Poetry Possibilities

- 9.9 Popular and Prolific Authors of Young Adult Fiction

- 9.10 Recommended Young Adult Literature

- 9.11 Multicultural Sources

- 9.12 Checklist for Assessing Literary Understanding

Activity 9.1:
Hints and Helps
for Conducting Better Discussions

1. Preplan some questions that you would like students to consider. You may not have the chance to include all of them, but this preplanning will help you keep the class ontask and focused.

2. Use a mixture of kinds of questions—some literal level, some inferential, and some applied, as well as critical and creative or closed, open-ended, and personal opinion. When the questions require nothing more than literal recall, keep the pace quick, but when the questions require higher-order thinking, allow wait time for students to ponder before answering.

3. Periodically summarize the main ideas that have been stated or implied. At times, you should do this, especially to model the behavior, but students should also be responsible for summarizing. Jotting notes on the chalkboard or an overhead transparency may be helpful.

4. Work to develop a certain line of thinking during the discussion rather than just asking random questions. Provide some structuring comments that help students understand the organization of the conversation. For example, if you want to walk students through the plot, tell them that this is how you want to begin the discussion.

5. Give students the opportunity to participate in designing the discussion. They can be asked to submit questions that they would like to discuss. Sometimes they can be given the option of deciding whether to discuss plot or characters first or whether they want to talk about the beginning or the ending of the selection first. They can also be given the option of discussing the material in a small group before discussing as a whole class. If given proper instruction and adequate motivation to prepare in advance, students can lead discussions, too.

6. Set some rules or establish some guidelines for discussions. If you expect students to converse with others directly, let them know this in advance. If you expect them to raise their hands and wait to be called on, tell them so. If you expect them to listen to the ideas shared by peers, express this goal. Students can be

asked to share ideas about how to make discussions proceed more smoothly if problems arise.

7. Watch out for contradictory behavior. If you prefer to conduct a very orderly discussion that you control, avoid asking questions that are likely to prompt heated debate. If you prefer to call on individuals, then avoid tossing out questions that seem to call for a choral yes or no from the class. Most of all, if you expect students to participate in discussion, do not ask rhetorical questions and do not answer your own questions. If students cannot respond, provide some wait time. If they still cannot respond, rephrase the question. If that does not work, have a student say what he or she thinks you are asking. If that still does not elicit an answer, go on to some other question. You can always come back to the unanswered one later.

8. Adjust the discussion to fit the students. In some classes this means starting with a literal level review of characters and incidents. In other classes such reviews are likely to create boredom. Instead, start with a higher-order question that piques interest. Asking students how the material is related to them personally or what they were reminded of as they read the incidents may be the best way to engage reluctant participants.

9. Before plunging into a discussion, take a few minutes for preparation. This may include asking students to write a response or reread the ones they have already written in their journals. They can also be given a few minutes to glance through the material, looking for something specific such as the climactic point, the most revealing bit of dialogue, or the best descriptive phrase.

10. As much as possible, link ideas that occur in discussion to each other by noting similarities and contrasts. Alert students to contradictions and expect them to point these out whenever they occur. Perhaps more importantly, link ideas from previous discussions to the ones currently being expressed, and expect students to make similar connections. Encourage students to state parallels with other subject matter and other class discussions, too.

Although whole-class, teacher-led discussions have a place in the language arts classroom, the research evidence indicates that students can lead their own discussions. Furthermore, the questions they bring forth often demand more higher-order thinking than those posed in textbooks or by teachers. Although students may not investigate the text broadly, they may discuss in depth. Students must be taught how to discuss and what to examine, but with appropriate facilitation and support from the teacher as well as a clear understanding of the expectations, they can conduct their own grand conversations about literature. If you would like more information about student-led discussions, check out *Lively Discussions! Fostering Engaged Reading* edited by Gambrell and Almasi (1996) or *Literature Circles: Voices and Choice in the Student-Centered Classroom* by Daniels (1994).

Activity 9.2:
A Sampler of Ideas
for Teaching Literary Concepts

Plot Sequence

- Use a graphic organizer that looks like a mountain. Mark the following parts and define each: (a) exposition or introduction (setting); (b) inciting moment (meeting of protagonist and antagonist); (c) rising action as a sequence of events; (d) climax or high point (usually a single incident or even a mental decision that occurs about three-fifths of the way through the text and determines the outcome of the story); (e) falling action/resolution/denouement (students like to pick up a French word in the process). Have students use this diagram to plot the progress of a story or novel they read.

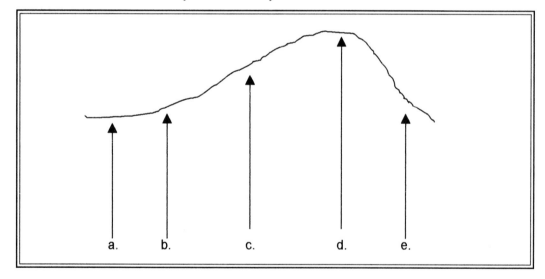

- To examine cause and effect, have students fold a sheet of paper in half lengthwise. Then have them label the left column "Cause" and the right one "Effect." To begin, they must identify an incident that caused something else to happen. They record it on the left. The outcome is listed on the right. Then they move on to find another example of a cause and an effect. Once they have the idea, they try to find examples of situations in which the effect becomes the cause of another event, forming a chain. Finding such chains is a challenge for most middle school students.

- Look for gaps in the plot sequence, especially ones that require students to infer that something important went on ("meanwhile, back at the ranch ... "). Challenge students to fill in the gaps, either by telling orally what went on or by writing the missing part of the text. If they can mimic the rest of the text in the retelling, so much the better.

Setting

- Have students locate real settings on actual maps. This is especially effective if they can trace movements from one location to another and discuss what characters may have experienced between stops. Students can also use computerized atlases and encyclopedias to quickly obtain information about the places. Discussions about differences in time between the story and the information they obtain can be beneficial. If the setting is imaginary, students can create their own maps. They can even re-create the entire setting in the classroom and provide visitors with a walking tour of the locale.

Character Analysis

- Have students create character wheels using paper plates. The character's name goes in the center and each quality of the character as it is discovered in the text is added as a spoke on the wheel. It is a good idea to have students do this in rough draft form first so they know how many spokes they will need in total. These can be decorated and make interesting wall displays. This activity also shows dramatically the difference between round and flat characters.
- Have students make a character map. This looks like a sociogram or web and shows how each character is linked to other characters. If family relationships are involved, a family tree works well.
- If you are dealing with several short stories or novels simultaneously, you may try using a continuum that is based on some quality, such as bravery or sensitivity, to compare characters. Students locate various characters on the continuum, depending on the amount of the quality each character has. These often prompt a good deal of discussion and debate.

Points of View

- To illustrate the idea of point of view, create a still-life arrangement in the center of the classroom and ask all students to sketch it as best they can from their seats. Then have students share their sketches with a partner who was seated at a very different location. Have them discuss what caused the differences in their sketches. Not only will they realize that location had an effect, but they will also acknowledge that artistic skill had an effect. In the literature they read, both the vantage point and the skillfulness of the narrator make a difference in how the story is told.

- To help students sort through various points of view, have them role-play a situation in which a conflict occurs, but set up a screen so that some students can see only part of the action. Then have students tell what they observed, beginning with the people who had a limited perspective, followed by the people who could see all of it. Then have one of the players tell about what he or she was thinking and feeling during the performance. Finally, ask students to tell about the incident as if they had been a scientist viewing it all under a microscope or a bird flying above it all.

Analysis or Summary of Novels

- As an alternative to traditional written or oral book reports, students can create novel cubes. Each side of the cube contains information about one facet of the material. One side, usually the top, is for title, author, and a small illustration; one side is setting; one side is characters; one side is plot; and one side is theme or some other concept. It is important to note that students need to put the information on the cube before it is assembled because it will not be stable enough to write on once it is constructed. When these are done, inform students that the cubes are not dice; they have to be handled gently, not rolled around.

- Another possibility is to have students create mobiles based on their books. These can easily be made using a coat hanger and thread or yarn. Students begin by covering the open frame of the coat hanger with paper and adding the title of the material and the author on both sides. Next, students write information about the material on individual segments of paper—one for plot, another for setting, one for theme, another for tone, and so on. Each is attached to the coat hanger by thread or yarn. The challenge here is to create an aesthetically pleasing arrangement using varying lengths of thread or yarn but one that also balances and makes each of the segments visible. When completed, these can be hung from the ceiling.

Activity 9.3:
Searching for Style

To introduce or review the concept of style, divide students into small groups of approximately three each. Give each group a children's book that contains a narrative (not an alphabet book or a wordless picture book). As much as possible, these books should be chosen because they illustrate effective use of various stylistic qualities. Explain to students that they will be using these books for this activity because the stories are so short that they can be read in just a few minutes (although you may actually hope that this will encourage students to read more children's books on their own or as models for their own writing). Ask that one person in the group read the story aloud as the others follow along. Then give each group a worksheet that contains the questions listed below. Their task is to review the book and to determine the stylistic qualities of this particular author. Once the groups are done, they can be asked to report their findings to the class. (Because you know which qualities students should find, you can guide this sharing of information so that it is not needlessly repetitious.) Discuss how all of this relates to reading other material.

Searching for Style

Directions: On the basis of the book you have examined, jot your answers to the following questions about the author's style. Be prepared to present your results to the class.

1. What kinds of sentences are used (e.g., long or short; easy to read or complicated; statements only or questions, exclamations, and commands; simple only or compound and complex)?
2. What kinds of words are used (e.g., familiar or unusual; easy to understand or difficult; long or short; words with only one meaning or words with several meanings; specific or vague; abstract or concrete; special jargon, dialects, obscene words, etc.)?
3. When you read the material aloud, how did it sound (e.g., like a melody or like noise; like a poem or not; like a slow-moving river, a babbling brook, a waterfall, or waves crashing against the rocks)? What created this impression? Did you have to hurry ahead or slow down at any point? Why? How did the author make this happen?

4. Does the material contain any dialogue? A lot, some, a little, or none? Do the words sound like things real people would say?
5. Is the writing descriptive? Do you see any images when you read the words? Does the material compare one thing to another by using either *like* or *as* (i.e., are similes used)?
6. Does the material contain any symbols? Of what?

On the basis of your findings, write a description of the author's style.

Activity 9.4:
A Student's Guide
to the Study of the Novel

Reading a Novel

Before reading a novel, review the following questions so they may be fresh in your mind during the reading. On completing the novel, respond to the question—either orally or in writing. The answers to all questions must be documented by references to the novel. In written assignments, supply direct quotations and page references to back up your answers.

1. What are the setting and time of the novel? Do these change throughout the story? What reasons are there for change? How effective is the author's use of time and setting?
2. What is the basic plot? Summarize it in a paragraph. Is there a subplot? More than one? What does the subplot contribute to the basic plot?
3. Who are the main characters? What personality traits distinguish them? Are the characters believable? Who are the important minor characters? What purpose do they serve (e.g., to supply humor, to highlight a major character's chief fault, to provide suspense)?
4. What is the basic conflict of the novel? State it in a sentence. List the types of conflict that occur—man versus man, man versus himself, man versus animal, man versus nature, etc.
5. In one sentence state the theme of the novel. A theme says something about a topic; topic and theme are not synonyms.
6. What is the structure of the novel. Is it confusing? How effective is it? If the point of view changes, why does it?
7. What are the major symbols of the novel? For what do they stand? Are they successful devices?
8. What does the title mean? What significant clues does the title give to the meaning of the story? Is the title successfully related to one of the aspects of the novel? Its theme? Plot development? Setting?
9. What is the tone? From what passages in the novel is this deduced? Be especially careful of satirical and ironical tones.

10. What are the main characteristics of the author's style? List the specific devices of the author's technique—sentence length, diction, use of figurative language, and so forth—that distinguish his or her style.

In reporting on a novel, avoid general statements that are true of any work. Support each statement by using data from the novel under analysis. Use the present tense so that the reader experiences the immediacy—the "nowness"—of a novel.

Personal Responses

Now that you have finished reading, you should be able to express an overall reaction to a novel by making a clear statement of your attitude toward it. A novel says different things to different people. That is why a novel may fascinate you, but bore your best friend, move you to tears, and move your friend to laughter. No analysis of a novel is complete without your personal response to it. Here are some considerations to guide you in formulating your response to a novel:

1. Do you agree with the theme? For you, is the statement meaningful? Does it give you an insight into human behavior? Are you more understanding of human nature because of it? Do you feel the theme is a significant one, or a frivolous one?
2. What generalizations does the novel make about life? Do they agree with your personal philosophy? Does your own experience show them to be true or false? Specifically, what personal criticisms do you have of the author's work?
3. Is the plot credible? Is there enough suspense, excitement, and interest to keep you reading? Are you concerned about the outcome of the story?
4. Do you identify with the characters? Are you personally involved with their problems? Does it make a difference to you that the hero is rewarded and the villain punished? At the conclusion of the novel, do you want to know what will happen to the characters in the future?
5. Do you feel the author has written his story as concisely as possible? Has he padded his writing, or dragged out his story by including unnecessary events and characters?
6. Is the outcome of the story logical? Does the nature of the characters determine the outcome, or has the author relied on an outside circumstance to conclude his story?
7. Are the setting and time factors sufficiently limited? Does the story shift so often in space and time that you are confused or ir-

ritated? If actual settings are used, are they factually correct? In a historical setting are the events handled with truth?

8. Does the author's style enrich your reading pleasure by the imaginative use of specific details, interesting images, rich vocabulary, well-turned phrases, variety in sentence structure, and new symbols? Are you annoyed by any stylistic tricks—unusual punctuation, irregular spelling, lack of paragraphing, obscure vocabulary, typography, and so forth?

9. Is the point of view consistent with the development of the novel? Would you have told the story through another person? Does the point of view shift too often? Are you able to tell who is the narrator?

10. Is the conflict of the novel substantial enough to justify the author's writing at such length? Might the conflict be better handled in a short story or a novella? Are there so many conflicts that the main character appears superhuman in order to deal successfully with them? Can you determine the basic conflict of the main character?

11. Is the author's tone readily apparent to you? Is his outrage at a situation, for example, sincere, or is he ironical? Is his agreement an honest one or is he mocking? Is the author straightforward, deliberately misleading, or neutral?

12. Is the story one that stays with you and forces you to think about the characters, the problems, and the solutions to the problems?

13. Is the story realistic—could it have happened this way? Is it contrived? Even a novel of fantasy or science fiction must be believable once the reader has accepted the premise that a story is literally impossible. Does the story seem "natural" in its development? Once you accept the fact that an animal can talk, does the animal talk naturally; does what he says or how he acts appear logical?

Activity 9.5:
Scaffolding the Reading of a Novel

Sometimes when you assign a novel to the class, you will want to break the task into chunks that students complete regularly (e.g., 1 or 2 chapters a night). However, the time may come when you want students to read an entire novel all at once. That is, after all, the kind of habit that students should develop. However, students may still need assistance. One approach you can try is making printed copies of the questions you would ordinarily ask in class discussion available to the students. You can also provide copies of any study guides that you may have used before. Students can then use whatever helps them the most. However, this still may not be enough for some students. The following is a sample handout for teaching one novel, but the directions can be easily modified to fit other works.

Study Helps for *When the Legends Die* (Borland, 1963)

1. Each time you encounter a new character or a new name for a known character, list it either on a separate sheet of paper or the inside front cover of the book (write very small and be brief). Include a page number so you can refer back if you have totally forgotten the character. If and when the character's name reappears later in the book, be sure you can remember who that character is. If you can't, refer to your list. If you still can't remember, refer to the page number you have indicated.

2. To keep the plot events straight, there are several things you can do. If you read slowly and in spurts, keep a record on a separate sheet of paper, but keep the paper in your book. On the record, summarize events very briefly and in your own words. Then, when your reading is interrupted, you can refer back to your notes before beginning to read again. You may also find this record very helpful during discussion. The second method is for those who read more rapidly or in more continuous sittings. After you finish each Part, summarize the major events in chronological order on the book page where the Part begins. For example, after completing Part I, you would summarize what happened in Part 1 on page 1 (where the word *Bessie* appears).

3. One of the most beneficial things you can do during the time you are reading the novel is to discuss what has happened, the

characters, and any other questions you have with a classmate. This can be done during homeroom in the morning, break, lunch, or after school. For a few days, the classroom time will be reserved for reading so that students who do not have another satisfactory place for reading can depend on doing this in the room. If you need to discuss during class, see me and I'll try to make some arrangement on a limited-time basis.

4. As you are reading, ask yourself, "Why?" Why does a character do what he or she does at that time? Why does this event happen at this time? Why does the author state it this way? Why is this an important event, character, or place?

5. If you are having difficulty keeping the locations straight, use the map on the bulletin board or an atlas of your own. Refer to the novel and make comparisons, too.

6. After you finish the novel, be sure you understand what happened, who was involved and who was responsible, where things took place, and so forth. Check back to the novel unit sheet to make sure you understand the terms used there and how each applies to the novel. Don't settle for just one answer if more than one is possible.

7. Use the review material, the guide material, or both to help you before you read, as you read, or after you read. How you use it depends on what method works best for you. Do not, however, let it bog you down. Do not just read so you can answer the questions. This will cause you not to think for yourself as you read. It will also make you enjoy the book much less. The questions are a help, not a major goal. However, if you are confused, don't wait too long to get help.

Activity 9.6:
Recommended Short Stories
for Middle School

"Raymond's Run"—Cambera
"All Summer in a Day"—Bradbury
"The Veldt"—Bradbury
"The Tell-Tale Heart"—Poe
"An Occurrence at Owl Creek Bridge"—Bierce
"Viva New Jersey"—Gonzalez
"One of the Missing"—Bierce
"After You, My Dear Alphonse"—Jackson
"The Red-Headed League"—Doyle
"The Gift of the Magi"—O. Henry
"The Celebrated Jumping Frog of Calaveras County"—Twain
"Rappuccini's Daughter"—Hawthorne
"The Colt"—Stegner
"A Man of Peace"—Williams
"The Voice from the Curious Cube"—Bond
"Charles"—Jackson
"To Build a Fire"—London
"The Necklace"—de Maupassant
"The Lady or the Tiger"—Stockton
"The Monkey's Paw"—Jacobs
"The Banana Tree"—Berry
"The Moustache"—Cormier
"The Ransom of Red Chief"—O. Henry
"Harrison Bergeron"—Vonnegut
"The Sniper"—O'Flaherty
"A Man Who Had No Eyes"—Kantor
"The Open Window"—Saki (Munro)
"Thank You, M'am"—Hughes
"The Most Dangerous Game"—Connell
"It's Such a Beautiful Day"—Asimov
"The White Circle"—Clayton
"A Sound of Thunder"—Bradbury

Activity 9.7:
Short Story Response Options

1. Read at least five short stories by one particular author. Make a Venn diagram that shows the similarities and differences among the stories.
2. Read at least five short stories. Create an attribute chart that compares the narrative structure, characters, and setting of the stories.
3. Read three short stories by different authors. Write an analysis of plot, characterization, setting, and any other factors you wish to include. Include all three stories as illustrations of your points.
4. Copy the climax of a story from the book. Then state in your own words why this point is the climax.
5. Select the most meaningful short story you have read and write a paragraph stating why this story meant a great deal to you.
6. Using an art form of your choice (pen-and-ink drawing, watercolor, painting, sculpture, chalk drawing, etc.), represent an entire story or one portion of a story. For example, you can complete a charcoal sketch of a main character.
7. Rewrite one of the required stories in your own words, but maintain the descriptive quality of the story.
8. In serial cartoon form, retell a short story.
9. Rewrite one of the required stories in script or diary form.
10. Write a 3–5 minute dialogue between two characters from two different stories; the choice of subject matter is yours (for example, the two characters can discuss their reactions to a day at this school—to do this you must put yourself in each character's place—you are not to talk through your own mouth). Rehearse thoroughly. Present this as an oral interpretation in front of the class or on a tape.
11. Write a paper identifying and explaining the theme of at least three short stories you have read.
12. Compile a bibliography of outstanding short stories, short story writers, or both for middle school readers.
13. Research the life or present existence of a particular author. Write a brief paper about him or her.
14. Thoroughly compare two short stories on the basis of narrative structure, characterization, or setting on paper or in poster form.

15. Read an entire collection of short stories by assorted authors. Write a paper telling the reason or reasons these stories were bound together in a single volume.

16. Make black-and-white or color lift transparencies to go along with a rehearsed oral reading of a story.

17. Compose a poem that communicates something about a particular story.

18. Read a novel written by a short story writer that you really like. Write a brief report of this book explaining how it is similar to or different from his or her short stories.

19. Photocopy pictures in books or scan them to a disk. Display them to show the theme of a story or to retell the story from a different point of view. Compose a sound tape to go along with your collection. The tape can include music, lyrics, narration, cuts from famous speeches, and so forth.

20. Use photographs you have taken to illustrate a short story. Use appropriate text or labels and captions with the photographs.

21. Choose a short story you have read and write a one paragraph paper explaining what category the short story belongs in and why. Some categories to consider are the following: adventure, mystery, romance, fictional autobiography, humor, science fiction, memoir, fictional diary, and mood.

22. Make a collage of appropriate materials from newspapers and magazines showing your concept of one of the short stories. Be sure that all included material relates to the story.

23. Complete an art project that visually defines or clarifies theme, symbolism, foreshadowing, flashback, or irony. The artwork should carry the message. Few words, if any, should be included.

24. Choose an object that can be displayed and that symbolizes a particular story. Display it in an appropriate fashion. Include a brief, well-written statement of its relationship to the story.

25. Make overhead transparencies related to the events in a story or to literary techniques used in a story or several stories.

26. Become an expert on the short story writer of your choice: Crutcher, Cormier, O. Henry, Poe, Jackson, Harte, Twain, Bierce, Dahl, Crane, Saroyan, or Thurber, for example. Read at least five stories by that author. Write a paper telling what generalizations you have formulated about the type of writing, kinds of characters, writing style, characterization methods, narrative structure, or themes this author uses repeatedly. Use concrete evidence to support your generalizations. (Biographical information may be helpful, too.)

27. Write a poem about a character, the setting, theme, or plot in one of the stories.
28. Dramatize all or part of an outstanding short story.
29. Select the most exciting section of the most exciting story you read and present a well-rehearsed, expressive oral reading of this section to a small group or the class.
30. Read several stories by the same author. Identify and list at least five literary techniques used very frequently by this particular author. Create a bulletin board display to show your work.
31. Choose a story that can be made into a radio show. Write the script. Get some other students to help you tape-record the various parts and the sound effects.
32. Compile a folder of original work related to one or more of the stories. This can be a book similar to a children's book in which you retell the story in simpler form and include illustrations. Or, it might be a collection of drawings, original or copied poems, pictures, and so forth that represent the story for you. Or, it might be a variety of materials that represent a variety of stories. Include a written explanation.
33. Write several original poems relating to one or more short stories. Include a brief explanation of the collection.
34. Make a collection of poems written by others that relate to one or more short stories. Be sure to include a brief explanation with this project.
35. Select a particularly exciting and interesting story. Practice telling the story with expression. Tell this story to a small group or to the entire class.
36. Write a rap based on one or more short stories.
37. Re-create a story in pantomime. Rehearse. Make a videotape of your presentation.
38. Tape-record selected portions of a short story. Tell the rest in your own words. This must be rehearsed several times and a script written before it can be recorded.
39. Tape-record a story so that other students may listen as they read.
40. Select key quotations from various stories that reflect qualities of the characters. Copy the quotes, illustrate them appropriately, and display.
41. Visually compare the conflicts, themes, individual characters, or mood in one or more short stories.
42. Write an updated version of one of the stories you read. Use modern language (current jargon, words, and phrases). Update the setting if necessary. Illustrate the story appropriately.

43. Create a ballad based on a short story and set it to music. Tape-record your rendition.
44. Create a multimedia project of photos, tapes, transparencies, CD-ROM materials, and so forth based on one or more short stories. Include a script or an explanation.
45. Make a poster, diorama, collage, or other visual that explains conflict, flashback, foreshadowing, imagery, irony, point of view, or symbolism. Be sure to label or title your project. Include examples from stories you have read.
46. Make a poster, diorama, collage, or other visual that expresses the mood, conflict, characters, or theme in one or more of your favorite short stories. Be sure to include a title or label of the story or stories and the element you are portraying.
47. Write a short short story. Before you begin writing, plan the structure and the ending. Your final story will be 3–5 pages in length.
48. Write discussion and quiz questions for one or more stories. Conduct a discussion and give your quiz.
49. Create music to accompany a story. Tape-record it. Play it for a small group who has read the story. Explain how the music enhances the meaning of the story.
50. View a videotape of a short story you have read. Make a list of the similarities and differences you find. Briefly explain whether or not the characters chosen for the roles met your expectations.

The two basic requirements for short story projects are that the finished product must relate to the short stories or to short story concepts and it must be something that can be displayed or shared with others. Evaluation will be on the following bases: (a) attention to detail and neatness, (b) completion on time, (c) originality, (d) use of class time, (e) clarity of relationship to story or stories, and (f) accuracy of information, grasp of literary concepts, or both.

Activity 9.8:
Poetry Possibilities

Here is one suggested sequence for teaching students to write poetry:

1. Explain the poetic form, using a transparency example.
2. Share examples written by children and adults aloud and in printed form.
3. Have students read additional examples in pairs (shared reading).
4. Review the form.
5. Write class collaboration poems.
6. Write individual poems using the writing process.
7. Share completed poems.
8. Have students teach the poetic form to others.

Here is a list of different types of word play related to developing an interest in poetry:

- Riddles written in rhyme,
- Jokes that rely on puns,
- Tom Swifties (playful use of adverbs),
- Creating word pictures (concrete poems), and
- Hink-pinks (rhyming word pairs with definitions).

The following is a list of possible activities to use in conjunction with the study of poems:

- Choral reading (students must make decisions about tempo, rhythm, pitch, and juncture),
- Compiling collections of poems written by others (students must find a common element that holds the collection together; this is also a good way to introduce theme),
- Role-playing narrative or sensory poems,
- Using puppets to act out poems,
- Drawing picture versions of descriptive poems,
- Creating videotaped or multimedia versions of poems,
- Illustrating poems with photographs,

- Selecting music to accompany poetry readings, and
- Finding examples of poetry in common use (e.g., in advertisements).

A poetry unit is an excellent time to introduce the idea of a writer's notebook, in which students record observations, snatches of conversation, quotes from readings, photographs, and anything else that they find interesting about language or experiences.

The following is a list of poems that appeal to middle school students:

"n" by e e cummings

"A tutor who tooted the flute" by C. Wells

"Bells" by Edgar Allan Poe

"The Mosquito" by John Updike

"The Orb Weaver" by Robert Francis

"Narrow Fellow in the Grass" by E. Dickinson

"At Breakfast" by May Swenson

"Two Friends" by David Ignatow

"Arithmetic" by Carl Sandburg

"Sick" by Shel Silverstein

"Eletelephony" by Laura Richards

"Mother Doesn't Want a Dog" by Judith Viorst

"The Cremation of Sam Magee" by Robert Service

"Mummy Slept Late and Daddy Fixed Breakfast" by John Ciardi

"The Highwayman" by Alfred Noyes

"Stopping by Woods on a Snowy Evening" by Robert Frost

"The Eagle" by Lord Tennyson

"Ululation" by Eve Merriam

"Water Picture" by May Swenson

"The Road Not Taken" by Robert Frost

"Ozymandias" by Percy B. Shelley

"Dreams" by Langston Hughes

"The Sniffle" by Ogden Nash

"Cat & the Weather" by May Swenson

"Escape" by Ruth Bachman

"Dreams" by Langston Hughes

"We Real Cool" by Gwendolyn Brooks

"Fences" by Robert Frost

The February 1997 issue of *Voices from the Middle*, (vol. 4, Issue 1), published by NCTE, is a themed issue on poetry that includes an outstanding list of selected resources (pp. 47–49). Also, see M. Myers (1997/1998). Passion for poetry. *Journal of Adolescent & Adult Literacy, 41* (4), 262–271 which contains a model poetry unit.

Activity 9.9:
35 Popular and Prolific Authors of Young Adult Fiction

Alexander, Lloyd (fantasy author)

Avi

Blume, Judy

Bradbury, Ray (science fiction specialist; challenging reading)

Bridgers, Sue Ellen

Cleaver, Vera & Bill

Cooney, Caroline (excellent suspense stories)

Cormier, Robert (some works are for more mature readers)

Crutcher, Chris (writes lots of sports-related material)

Danziger, Paula (books tend to appeal more to females)

Duncan, Lois (suspenseful stories)

Eckert, Allan (writes about nature and history; challenging reading)

Hinton, S. E.

Hobbs, Will (adventure and survival stories)

Kerr, M. E.

Lasky, Katherine (a range of topics, but mainly female protagonists)

LeGuin, Ursula (mostly works of fantasy)

L'Engle, Madeline

Lipsyte, Robert (books tend to appeal more to males)

Lowry, Lois

Mazer, Norma & Harry

McCaffrey, Anne (mostly works of fantasy)

Myers, Walter Dean (focuses on African-American literature)

O'Dell, Scott

Paulsen, Gary

Peck, Richard

Peck, Robert Newton

Peiffer, Susan Beth

Rinaldi, Anne (historical fiction)

Rylant, Cynthia

Soto, Gary (focuses on Hispanic characters)

Spinelli, Jerry (unique characters)

Voight, Cynthia

Yep, Lawrence (focuses on Asian-American literature)

Zindel, Paul

This list is far from complete. Also, adolescent preferences vary widely, and many best-selling authors write material that appeals strongly to young adult readers.

Activity 9.10: Recommended Young Adult Literature

The following list is merely a representative sample of the many outstanding works that appeal to middle level readers. Check for book reviews in language arts periodicals as well as library journals such as *The Horn Book, Booklist,* and *Children's Literature Review.* The Voice of Youth Advocates (VOYA) is an excellent source of information. Since 1994, they have published an annual list of outstanding books for middle school. See the June 1997 and February 1998 issues. (Please note that some of the titles listed below contain controversial material that is more appropriate for more mature readers.)

Novels

The Chocolate War, I Am the Cheese, and *Tunes for Bears to Dance To*—Robert Cormier

Stotan! and *Staying Fat for Sarah Byrnes*—Chris Crutcher

Iceman—Chris Lynch

Face on the Milk Carton and& Driver's Ed—Caroline Cooney

Killing Mr. Griffin and many other titles—Lois Duncan

The Ear, The Eye, and The Arm—Nancy Farmer

Hatchet and *Brian's Winter* plus many others—Gary Paulsen

The Witch of Blackbird Pond—Elizabeth Speare

The Giver and *Devil's Arithmetic*—Lois Lowry

Island of the Blue Dolphins—Scott O'Dell

Out of the Dust—Karen Hesse

The Mixed-Up Files of Mrs. Basil E. Frankweiler—Elizabeth Konigsberg

The Westing Game—Ellen Ruskin

The Ruby and the Smoke and *The Golden Compass*—Phillip Pullman

The Watsons Go to Birmingham—1963—Christopher Curtis

The True Confessions of Charlotte Doyle and *Beyond the Western Sea*—Avi

Dealing with Dragons—Patricia Wrede

The Trouble with Lemons—Daniel Hayes

Maniac Magee and *Crash*—Jerry Spinelli

Annie on My Mind—Nancy Gardner

Fallen Angels—Walter Dean Myers

Moves Make the Man—Bruce Brooks

The Summer of My German Soldier—Bette Greene

Are You There, God? It's Me, Margaret—Judy Blume

Jeremy Thatcher, Dragon Hatcher—Bruce Coville

Beyond the Divide and *True North*—Kathryn Lasky

The Second Bend in the River—Ann Rinaldi

The Ghost Canoe and *Downriver*—Will Hobbs

Summer of the Swans and *The Dark Stairs*—Betsy Byars

Shiloh—Phyllis Reynolds Naylor

Poetry

Reflections on a Gift of Watermelon Pickle—Dunning, Leuders, & Smith (Eds.)

Where the Sidewalk Ends and *Light in the Attic*—Shel Silverstein

Strings: A Gathering of Family Poems—Paul Janeczko

Short Stories

Athletic Shorts—Chris Crutcher

(short stories) any collection of short stories edited by Donald Gallo

Professional Reference

What Do Young Adults Read Next?—compiled by Pam Spencer

Your Reading (frequent editions) published by NCTE

Activity 9.11:
Multicultural Sources

Bibliographies

Barrera, R., Thompson, V., & Dressman, M. and the Committee to Revise the Multicultural Booklist (Eds.). (1997). *Kaleidoscope: A Booklist for grades K–8* (2nd ed.). Urbana, IL: National Council of Teachers of English.

Bishop, R. and the Multicultural Booklist Committee (Ed.). (1994). *Kaleidoscope: A Multicultural Booklist for grades K–8*. Urbana, IL: National Council of Teachers of English.

Frankson, M. (1990). Chicano literature for young adults: An annotated bibliography. *English Journal, 79*(1), 30–38.

Gibbs, S. (1992). In celebration of Black history month: A reading list of suggested books by African American authors. *Notes Plus, 9*(3), 14–15.

McLaughlin, G. (1997). The way to confusion. *English Journal, 86*(6), 70–75. [Native American literature]

Perry, J. (1993). A selected bibliography of multiethnic literature. *Notes Plus, 11*(1), 12–15.

Wilson, C. (1996). Native American children's literature in the U.S.A. *Primary Voices K–6, 4*(3), 26–30.

Related Articles

Dilg, M. (1997). Why I am a multiculturalist: The power of stories told and untold. *English Journal, 86*(6), 64–69.

Vicinus, K. (1993). You don't have to live in the ghetto. *Connecticut English Journal, 22,* (Fall), 95–98.

Related Books

Day, F. (1994). *Multicultural voices in contemporary literature: A resource for teachers.* Portsmouth, NH: Heinemann.

Oliver, E. (1994). *Crossing the mainstream: Multicultural perspectives in teaching literature.* Urbana, IL: National Council of Teachers of English.

Susag, D. (1998). *Roots and branches: A resource of Native American literature—themes, lessons and bibliographies.* Urbana, IL: National Council of Teachers of English.

Activity 9.12: Checklist for Assessing Literary Understanding

The following is a list of some aspects of literary knowledge and behaviors associated with literature study that you might wish to include as part of your plan of assessment. Some of these would need to be adapted, according to the kind of text students were reading.

1. Summarizes reading material accurately.

2. Retells plot of short story, play, novel, or narrative poem.

3. Responds thoughtfully to questions about literary works.

4. Demonstrates awareness of literary features of particular kinds of text (e.g., for short stories—plot, setting, characters, theme; for poetry—rhyme, rhythm, alliteration) in writing and discussion.

5. Draws reasonable conclusions about literary texts.

6. Compares and contrasts characters within a story and between stories.

7. Compares and contrasts authors' styles.

8. Supports opinions when discussing and analyzing texts.

9. Refers to text to support statements made.

10. Relates reading to personal experiences.

11. Takes note of structural and stylistic features of literary texts.

12. Distinguishes among short stories, novels, plays, poetry, and nonfiction.

13. Recognizes popular forms of nonfiction (e.g., autobiography, biography, essay, and informative article)

14. Distinguishes statements of opinion from statements of fact.

15. Recognizes common special genres (e.g., oral literature forms, humorous stories, historical fiction, science fiction, etc.).

16. Assesses the authority of the author.

17. Reads a wide variety of literary forms.

18. Reads for sustained periods of time.

19. Selects literary works of moderate challenge.

20. Uses available resources to locate appropriate literature for independent reading.

21. Has at least one or two favorite authors and some favorite works.

22. Expresses appreciation for quality of literary works, authors' styles, or both.

23. Discusses literature with others eagerly.

24. Shares literature with others informally.

25. Can maintain discussion of literary text without teacher support or supervision.

26. Extends reading through the completion of related projects.

27. Creates effective responses to literature.

28. Uses knowledge gained from reading literature in own writing.

29. Sets goals for additional reading of literary works.

30. On own initiative, states that reading literature is a pleasurable activity.

31. Assesses own understanding of literature accurately.

32. Assesses own enjoyment of literature.

10

Teaching Language

Overview

418

CONSIDER THESE QUESTIONS ABOUT TEACHING LANGUAGE

1. What should be the primary goals of language study in middle schools?
2. Is it important to consider the difference between oral and written language?
3. How many different fields are included in the discipline of linguistics?
4. What is grammar? How is it different from syntax? From usage? Are these distinctions important?
5. At what point in school should the formal study of grammar be introduced?
6. Why are mechanics called *social conventions*? Is this a useful way of thinking about mechanics?
7. What does it mean to teach language in context?
8. What else should be included in language study besides grammar, syntax, usage, and mechanics?
9. How can language study be assessed? Evaluated?
10. What are some language study activities that are effective at the middle level?

ONE VIEW OF TEACHING LANGUAGE

For some obscure reason, literary scholars and linguists seem to reside in different academic worlds, and there is little communication between the two areas. Although it is true that linguists often focus on the spoken word, whereas literature specialists tend to focus on the written word, both are engaged in examining language. It is also true that linguists tend to be more scientific, whereas literature experts tend to view their subject matter as art, not data that can be analyzed objectively. Regardless of whether these factors are the cause for the rift, the gap exists. However, language arts teachers at the middle level usually teach both literature and language study.

Language arts teachers often disagree about pedagogy, but when the issue is language study, the differences are more hotly debated. It is in this arena that researchers and practicing teachers are most widely divided. Because of this controversy, this chapter must begin with some statements about the philosophy that is applied here.

Although literature is often considered the heart and soul of English studies, language can be viewed as the skeletal framework or backbone of the discipline. It is the foundation on which all of the language arts processes rest. It forms the basis of literature. It is the tool people use to communicate most of the ideas that have ever been, are, and will be. When students learn to read, write, speak, and listen, they must also learn the effective use of language. When students study literature, they should also learn how authors use language to make sense of their own experiences, share ideas with readers, and influence how readers view themselves and their world.

The current attitude among researchers and other language arts experts indicates a belief in the power of process alone. They imply that language proficiency will develop naturally if students use the processes (rather than study language directly) (Cambourne, 1988). Although improvement in the use of language can and will occur as students engage in reading, writing, speaking, listening, viewing, and visually representing, this knowledge must be brought to the surface. Students must become consciously aware of their language and how it works. To use the current cognitive terminology, they must become metalinguistically aware. If students are to learn how to control language and use it well to achieve their own purposes, and if they are to understand how others use language to inform and influence them, they must know something about how language works. In short, some language instruction is necessary.

Language study can be interesting, informative, and beneficial, but most teachers would agree that far too much language instruction has been boring, ineffectual, and detached from what matters to students. For many years, teachers believed that teaching students grammar would improve their writing (Weaver, 1996). When researchers discovered little correlation between knowing grammar and writing well (see Hillocks, 1986; Weaver, 1996), they urged that language arts teachers stop teaching grammar and mechanics as separate subjects and focus directly on teaching writing (Braddock, Lloyd-Jones, & Schoer, 1963). From one point of view, they were right; composition instruction had been neglected and sorely needed to receive attention. On the other hand, doing away with the teaching of language directly has not proved to be a solution either. Better ways to link the study of language with composition instruction so that the two support each other, must be developed. In addition, teachers need to find ways to integrate language learning with the study of literature and the development of speaking, listening, and viewing. Further, teachers must provide opportunities for students to examine language as a content area worthy of study. Although there was a time when language study probably had more than its fair share of attention, it now seems to have less than it deserves. Teachers should seek a better balance that will serve students well.

Much of the rest of this chapter is based on these beliefs, but they are debatable. You will have to decide for yourself whether you agree or disagree.

MAKING CHOICES ABOUT LANGUAGE STUDY

Most middle level students consider the study of language to be boring, meaningless drudgery. Class work in language study has often been limited to textbook drills, repetitious exercises, and objective tests. Year after year students start over by studying nouns and verbs. What is in the textbook or handbook may seem to bear little resemblance to the student's own writing and reading. Older students often recall little language study that was of interest or value to them.

The study of language should be a fascinating exploration of what sets us apart as human beings and what relates us as cultures and nationalities (see Fig. 10.1). As much as possible, the study of language should be linked to both the study of literature and composition. As students learn how to read, write, speak, listen, view, and visually represent more effectively, they should be learning how language works. However, students need to know that this is not all there is to linguistic study and that exploring language can be intriguing. Although students must develop better control of language, they should also develop an interest in and an appreciation of language. You can aid in this by promoting the discussion of language and by asking students to examine language as it has been and is used in the real world.

Above all, students need to develop curiosity about language. They also need to develop an attitude of wonder about the marvels that can be achieved through language. Without such an appreciation, students will probably never reach the level of literary appreciation that you, as a language arts teacher, hope they will achieve, nor are they likely to learn to control language in speaking and writing as well as you hope they will.

The key ingredient in the study of language, however, is not the curriculum but the teacher. Effective language arts teachers must be readers, writers, speakers, listeners, and viewers if they are to teach students well. Similarly, if students are to develop a lifelong love affair with language, they need opportunities to work with teachers who find language in all of its myriad forms fascinating. Teachers

Suggested Goals of Language Study
• To stimulate curiosity and wonder
• To develop control of language
• To promote discussion of language
• To examine real language in actual contexts
• To encourage interest and appreciation

FIG. 10.1

who do not question, explore, study, and appreciate language may be insufficiently informed about it and unable to spark student interest (see Fig. 10.2).

The **teacher** is the CRUCIAL INGREDIENT in language study.
The **teacher** must be an avid explorer and student of language, a —
curious
appreciative
sensitive
knowledgeable
participant in language learning.

FIG. 10.2

LANGUAGE PRINCIPLES AND CONCEPTS

The language principles and concepts summarized in Fig. 10.3 may be difficult, if not impossible, for middle level students to comprehend from direct instruction because of the abstractness of the ideas, but you need to understand the significance and implications of these principles and concepts if you are to help students understand why some characteristics that make language so useful also make it complex, manipulative, and deceptive.

For example, language is arbitrary. Infants learn whatever language surrounds them. French children speak French, not because they are innately French, but because they are born into a French-speaking world. Although it might be an easier world in which to communicate if everyone spoke the same language, the variety of languages adds richness to our existence by adding to cultural diversity and identity. Historically, when one country conquered another in war, the winner often forbid the use of the loser's native language. This was one way to attempt to eradicate the identity of the people, demoralize them, and keep them from resisting. Although language is arbitrary, it is also closely associated with who we are as people. Furthermore, because it is arbitrary, it is changeable. Humans created it and humans control it. In addition, because it is arbitrary, not every aspect of language development makes perfect, logical sense.

Language, be it oral or written, is an effective tool, but it has its shortcomings. The flexibility of language makes it a more useful device because it can change as humans change. We can, for example, create new words for inventions and force nouns to become verbs. However, this flexibility also means that language does not remain static. About the time that we figure out what makes a certain liter-

Language Principles and Concepts

1. Language is arbitrary—If this were not so, then all people would automatically speak the same language. No language would be a foreign language. Humans have created language, and they have created languages by making arbitrary choices.

2. Language is flexible—Language can be used in a variety of ways for many purposes. Through it we can express every emotion. Furthermore, we can manipulate it into new forms and develop new uses for it.

3. Language changes over time—If this were not so, then people could not develop new words and get rid of archaic ones. Also, there would be no style changes that reflect the times. There would be no such things as Old English and Middle English. Contemporary English would be the same as the English used by Shakespeare or Hawthorne.

4. Language is systematic—If this were not so, then there would be no patterns and no structure. Each person would have to devise his or her own system which would cause language to be idiosyncratic; people could neither learn language from others nor communicate with others.

5. Language is primarily oral—No society has a written language but no oral language, although the written version sometimes outlasts the oral one. For example, we know something of the way ancient Egyptian was written, but the oral version has not survived. More to the point, young children speak language long before they begin to write it.

6. Language is symbolic—Words represent concepts, but words are not the concepts themselves. Some words have multiple definitions. Some words mean different things to different people. Words often have varied connotations. Because language is symbolic, it can be misunderstood and misinterpreted.

7. Language is a social act—Language is the means people use for communicating ideas, emotions, and values from one person to another. Humans use language to establish and maintain social relations.

8. Language is purposeful—Words are used for a variety of purposes, but their use always serves some kind of purpose, even if people are talking to themselves. At the other extreme, language can be the means by which people express themselves artistically.

9. Language is learned—No child is born with language fully intact. If this were the case, young children would speak as adults do. People are born with the capacity to learn language and to create language, but the language itself must be learned. The language that people learn is the one they hear around them. Most of the language people learn is learned without formal instruction. Further, much of what people know about language is unconscious knowledge. Try this little test. Write the following words in what you consider to be the correct order: *French, the, young, girls, four.* Compare this with what others write. How did you know that that was the correct order? Do you know the rule which governs the order of adjectives? There is actually a set of such guidelines which non-native speakers of English have to learn consciously. If English is your first language, you know the order from experience.

continued on next page

10. Language is enormously complex—Linguists have never devised a complete description of all the possible constructions that speakers of American English use. There are some basic patterns, but there is an infinite number of combinations. Certain constructions defy description. To learn consciously even a major portion of all there is to know about language would take a lifetime. Furthermore, simple rules about language rarely prove to be true. There are far more exceptions than rules.

11. Language both informs and inhibits thought—Having names for things and using language to convey meaning gives us new knowledge. Through language people learn. However, people's thoughts can also be inhibited by lack of language. For example, you probably have about four words for different varieties of snow. The Eskimos, though, have about 27 words for snow because their survival often depends on precise descriptions of it. There was a time when the English word *freedom* simply could not be translated into Russian. The word that came closest in meaning actually meant "chaos." If Americans tried to convince Russians that what they needed was more freedom, it came out sounding as if we were suggesting that they needed more chaos.

FIG. 10.3

ary form acceptable because of the way language is used, someone else develops a new form, causing us to have to rethink everything we thought we knew.

Of all of these language principles and concepts, one that causes much difficulty is the fact that language is symbolic. Middle level students often find coping with multiple meanings of a word confusing. Because language is symbolic, people attach different connotations to words. Real estate agents do not sell houses; they sell homes because most people have a more positive response to the word *home*. On the other hand, if someone says that they live in a home, we may think they live in some kind of institution—a nursing home, a foster home, or an orphanage, perhaps. If words are symbolic, is there any such thing as a "dirty" word, or is the obscenity merely in our own minds? Why is it acceptable to say *excrement* in polite company, and why is *feces* an appropriate term in a medical context, but *shit* is considered neither acceptable nor appropriate?

Language is a social act, but have you ever wondered why we say, "You're welcome," when someone says, "Thank you"? Why is it that we greet people by asking, "How are you?" without expecting them to tell us their actual condition? To what extent is such "meaningless" language acceptable? What purpose does it serve? Not only is language a social act, but it is also a means of determining social class status. We tend to judge people on the basis of how they speak and how they write. In some ways language becomes a hurdle that people must overcome in order to move up the social ladder. There is a current controversy in the United States over whether we should establish English as the only language (Thomma & Cannon, 1995). This would mean discontinuing ESL programs that include teaching students in their native languages while they are learning English. It would probably also mean discontinuing the practice of giving driver's license tests in other languages, providing translators in legal cases, and requiring that people in certain occupations speak a second language. Proponents argue their case as a matter of patriotism and economics; opponents argue that these actions may permanently relegate members of language minorities to the lowest socioeconomic class. No matter which side of this issue is yours, the fact remains that the argument emanates from language principles that produce conflict.

Young children know a great deal about language use (Strickland, 1962), but most are unaware of what they know. Language seems almost as natural as breathing by the time children enter school. By the middle level, students need to begin to explore, at least indirectly, some of these language principles and concepts, bringing this unconscious knowledge to the surface. If language is a part of who we are, then we can learn more about ourselves by studying language.

LINGUISTIC FIELDS OF STUDY

If you are to help students explore language, you need to have some background in the primary fields that comprise linguistics (see Fig. 10.4). Knowing something of the history of the language via *historical linguistics* can help you explain to students why earlier forms of English are so different from modern versions. It can also help you explain some of the curiosities of spelling and pronunciation and how certain phrases came into use, even though the original meaning may have been lost over time.

Many people report that they did not understand how the English language works until they began to study a foreign language. When learners have a basis for comparison, both languages, or even different versions of the same language, become more clear. It is even possible to trace the history of a culture by identifying features of a language. If people are to be able to talk about language, they have to be able to describe it. How does it work? What are its significant features? How does one dialect differ from another and why? How do people use the language? *Comparative and descriptive linguistics* help answer some of these questions. Having speakers of other languages in the classroom opens up many possibilities that you can take advantage of as a language arts teacher.

English is a word order language, so studying the forms and sequencing of words is important. What are the recurrent patterns that

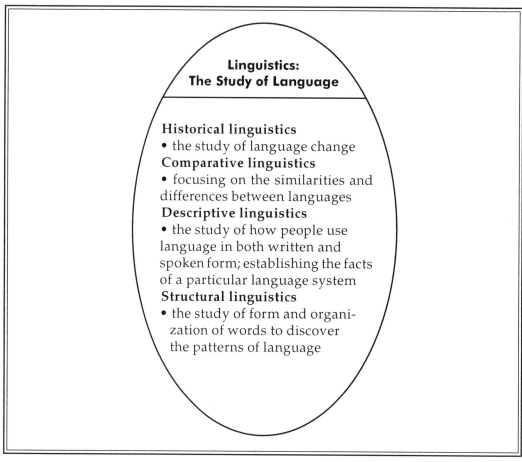

**Linguistics:
The Study of Language**

Historical linguistics
• the study of language change
Comparative linguistics
• focusing on the similarities and
differences between languages
Descriptive linguistics
• the study of how people use
language in both written and
spoken form; establishing the facts
of a particular language system
Structural linguistics
• the study of form and organization of words to discover
the patterns of language

FIG. 10.4

give shape to sentences? How do people alter these structures to
change meaning? What are other salient features of the language
that help us to communicate or that cause miscommunication?
Structural linguistics, which seeks answers to these questions, is an
important part of studying the English language.

In addition to these divisions, linguistics also crosses over into
many other fields of study. Some of these interdisciplinary fields are
shown in Fig. 10.5. The findings from some of these fields, such as
psycholinguistics, have had a direct impact on what is now known
about the teaching and learning of language. Many of the most recent findings that are shaping how teachers plan and conduct instruction come from the growing field of sociolinguistics. As a
teacher, you need a basic grasp of some of this research. However,
middle school students may be totally unaware that any of these
fields of study exist. Most students will not choose linguistics as a career, but as the world grows smaller and more people communicate

Interdisciplinary fields

Anthropological linguistics
The study of language variation and use in relation to the cultural patterns and beliefs of the human race, as investigated using the theories and methods of anthropology.

Applied linguistics
The application of linguistic theories, methods, and findings to the elucidation of language problems that have arisen in other domains. The term is especially used with reference to the field of foreign language learning and teaching, but it applies equally to several other fields, such as stylistics, lexicography, translation , and language planning, as well as to the clinical and educational fields below.

Biological linguistics
The study of the biological conditions for language development and use in human beings, with reference both to the history of language in the human race and to child development.

Clinical linguistics
The application of linguistic theories and methods to the analysis of disorders of spoken, written, or signed language.

Computational linguistics
The study of language using the techniques and concepts of computer science, especially with reference to the problems posed by the fields of machine translation, information retrieval, and artificial intelligence.

Educational linguistics
The application of linguistic theories and methods to the study of the teaching and learning of a language (especially a first language) in schools and other educational settings.

Ethnolinguistics
The study of language in relation to ethnic types and behaviour, especially with reference to the way social interaction proceeds.

Geographical linguistics
The study of the regional distribution of languages and dialects, seen in relation to geographical factors in the environment.

Mathematical linguistics
The study of the mathematical properties of language, using concepts from such fields as algebra, computer science, and statistics.
Neurolinguistics
The study of the neurological basis of language development and use in human beings, especially of the brain's control over the processes of speech and understanding.

continued on next page

Philosophical linguistics

The study of the role of language in the elucidation of philosophical concepts, and of the philosophical status of linguistic theories, methods, and observations.

Psycholinguistics

The study of the relationship between linguistic behaviour and the psychological processes (e.g. memory, attention) thought to underlie it.

Sociolinguistics

The study of the interaction between language and the structure and functioning of society.

Theolinguistics

The study of the language used by biblical scholars, theologians, and others involved in the theory and practice of religious belief.

FIG. 10.5

with those of other cultures and nationalities on a regular basis, some knowledge of language similarities and differences may be a useful tool. Students who are not necessarily interested in the study of language may have an interest in some other field that is related. Helping students become aware of some of these fields may encourage them to develop more interest in linguistics. Other students who already find linguistics fascinating need to know that they can pursue this interest in interdisciplinary ways, linking their linguistic interest to some other field. Exploring these careers by inviting practitioners into the classroom as guest speakers is one way to stimulate interest among students.

LINGUISTICS IN SCHOOL

Although the field of linguistics is quite broad and varied, in most school settings it has remained narrow and pragmatic. This has more to do with the history of education itself than with linguistics, but that would require a chapter of explanation. What often passes for language study in elementary, middle, and high schools usually focuses on four categories: grammar, syntax, usage, and mechanics. Although each of these is a separate entity with particular boundaries, all four are often collectively called *grammar*. This can cause some confusion. For example, the general public sometimes complains that students do not receive enough "grammar" instruction, but this complaint often refers to some perceived lack of usage instruction rather than improvement in the ability to distinguish nouns from verbs or to recognize direct objects.

Nevertheless, much class time is often devoted to the formal study of grammar, despite the research evidence of its ineffectiveness (Hillocks & Smith, 1991; Weaver, 1996). Most of the current textbooks use what is known as *prescriptive grammar* (see Fig. 10.6). Prescriptive grammar makes it seem as if there are certain rules (prescriptions) for how language must function and how language users must speak and write. Prescriptive grammar has a long history of use in schools and is the form of grammar most teachers learned as students. Thus, it is the one they choose to teach because it is the one they know best. Students often like the comfort of rules. When one teaches a prescriptive grammar, one can apply what seems to be objective measures of right and wrong to the way a writer uses language.

By contrast, *descriptive grammars* do not establish rules for language. Rather, they describe how language functions in the real world. Prescriptive grammar tells us that sentence fragments are

---

Two Common School Grammars

Prescriptive (traditional, Latinate) grammar
- Sets up rules for how language should be used
- Prescribes rules, guidelines, and directions
- Attempts to standardize English
- Ignores context, purpose, and audience
- Focuses on eight parts of speech and how they should be used in sentences
- Considers uses of phrases and clauses
- Often involves diagramming

Descriptive grammars
- Describe how language actually is used
- Avoid judgments, rules, and recommendations
- Acknowledge that language changes
- Consider context, purpose, and audience

Structural linguistics
- Focuses on form classes and function words
- Examines sentence patterns

Transformational-generative
- Focuses on phrase structures
- Examines sentence patterns
- Considers transformations

FIG. 10.6

wrong; descriptive grammars simply note that fragments are nonsentences. Prescriptive grammar looks at individual words; descriptive grammars tend to look more at how groups of words work together. During the late 1960s and early 1970s, descriptive grammars, including both structural linguistics and transformational–generative grammar, were taught in schools, but most teachers received little, if any, training in these different ways of looking at language. Both teachers and students found these grammars rather unsettling because they did not provide firm guidelines for use. Parents, too, did not like these grammars, in part because they were unfamiliar, but also because their children were not learning the same regulations they had been taught; parents tended to want their children to learn the same restrictions they had learned, despite the fact that very few of the so-called grammar rules are followed consistently by professional writers and speakers.

Although much of the material in current textbooks is predominantly prescriptive, many include a kind of hybridization of prescriptive and descriptive grammars. Sentence combining, for example, which is associated with descriptive grammars, is frequently inserted among prescriptive definitions and exercises. However, the differences of views are not presented to students. No matter which type of grammar is used, few texts offer a compelling explanation of why linguistic study is worthwhile or important. Not surprisingly, students find the textbooks puzzling, contradictory, and generally irrelevant.

TEACHING GRAMMAR AND SYNTAX

As much as possible, the study of grammar and syntax should be linked to the students' own language use. (For further information about the pros and cons of teaching grammar, consult the sources listed in Activity 10.2). However, some aspects of grammar and syntax can be included as part of the curriculum at the middle level if the focus is on exploration and experimentation. Most students are not likely to fall in love with language as the result of one grammar unit or class, but if you set that as a personal goal, students may surprise you. If you start with the expectation that students will finish the unit or class being able to parse sentences, that is all you will get at best. If you start with a grander purpose in mind, for a few in the class (and maybe even more) it will happen.

Introducing the Study of Structure

Having students open their textbooks to the chapter on nouns is probably not the best way to introduce the study of grammar and syntax.

Consider trying something different, such as starting with some children's books. Ask the students to look at several to see if they can characterize the style of writing that they find in the books. It is likely that during this examination, students will use some grammatical terms. If nothing else, the word *sentence* is apt to occur. Try to get them to define these terms so as to help them develop the sense that part of "doing" grammar is developing a vocabulary for describing language. Then give them excerpts from some other kinds of writing such as news articles and advertisements to see how they characterize these styles of writing. Compare these with the language found in the children's books. Ask them to bring in some material that they themselves select as something they enjoy reading (within the boundaries of what would be acceptable to bring to school, of course), and have them try to characterize the structures of language in these writings. Have them look at their own writing and describe the structures they use frequently. Finally, give them some excerpts from prose writers who use distinctive styles, and ask them to characterize the language they find there. Include some samples that contain dialogue, so that students can talk about some of the differences between oral and written language. Even without the quotation marks, they can probably distinguish between the two, but how? This may lead into some discussion of the differences between spoken and written language. This may also be an excellent time for some initial discussion of dialects and registers, and when people vary their language uses dependent on the situation. In essence, as much as possible, try to begin the study of grammar and syntax by raising students' curiosity about their own speaking, reading, and writing.

Creating and Maintaining Interest

When it comes to teaching grammar and syntax, it is time to pull out every creative activity you can think of that will attract and hold student attention. Consider using some audiovisual material to introduce concepts. You can show portions of the videotape series *The Story of English* (McCrum, Cran, & MacNeil, 1986), some commercial videotapes about grammar, or some relevant slides. Also, consider the possibility of inviting a linguist as a guest speaker to talk about how language is studied and what a linguist does. Another possibility is to invite a professional translator. A local newspaper editor who can speak about the importance of knowing how to use language effectively is another option.

Some humorous things can be done in the name of grammar and syntax study, such as a bulletin board of obnoxious (but not obscene) nouns (or verbs, or whatever) to which students can add. Comic strips often feature some aspect of language use. Students can write puns or formula poems using certain parts of speech. They can write

Tom Swifties, which focus on adverb puns (e.g., "'I can't hit a home run', Tom said foully."). They can create Sniglets (Hall & friends, 1984) for which they must create definitions and identify the parts of speech of their coined words. Mad Libs can be used now and then, too. Students can even create children's books similar to those by Heller (1987).

Grammar can be studied through games. There is a commercial adaptation of Bingo called "Grammar Bingo," a "Grammar Trivial Pursuit," another version called "In Pursuit of Grammar" (Teacher's Discovery), a "Gramopoly" (LinguiSystems, Inc.), as well as others. *Games to Improve Your Child's English* (Hurwitz & Goddard, 1969) and *Inventing and Playing Games in the English Classroom* (Davis & Hollowell, 1977) contain suggestions for other grammar and language games that are easy to create for the classroom. Have students create the materials for these or create the whole game. Students will learn as they work, and you will not spend time on tedium.

Students can also do some kinds of grammar/syntax projects. They can design and create bulletin boards on various parts of speech and sentence constructions. They can write and perform plays in which phrases and clauses have the starring roles as characters. Consider ways to use tape recorders, videotapes, and photographs to study grammar and syntax, particularly for students who are visual learners. Music is another realm that you may want to consider. Students can make up some of their own songs about parts or speech and record them (Remember "Conjunction Junction"?). The more concrete you can make the study of grammar and syntax, the better. Keep an eye out for sources you can use as supplements, and have students watch for them, too. Articles in newspapers sometimes feature grammar and writing. Occasionally there is a special on television that focuses on language.

If you have access to computers, you should have at least one program for drill and practice on grammatical concepts (e.g., *Grammar Games* available from Davidson). If you have access to some test-generating software, students can create their own tests and use them for practice and review. Actually, any good word processing program will work for this. If students have access to a spreadsheet program, they can conduct some research on the frequencies of use of certain parts of speech, sentence parts, or both, and present their results in the form of charts and graphs. It is even possible to do some comparative studies of these frequencies: one author compared with another, one newspaper compared with another, tape-recorded speech taken from student conversation compared with the speech of a television news person, and so forth. Students can probably suggest some even more interesting sources of comparison.

Assuming that you have a textbook or workbook to use, before you ask students to do anything with either, give a diagnostic test to determine more precisely what students know and do not know.

This will give you a good sense of what you need to review lightly and where you really need to begin intensive instruction. Textbook exercises can be useful if you select only those that focus on what students do not yet understand, but repetitious drill can be dulling. Consider finding some ways to disrupt the monotony. Students can work in pairs and tutor each other. Groups can be formed to work together to learn the material and then compete against each other to earn points. Many of the strategies suggested in *Inspiring Active Learning: A Handbook for Teachers* by Harmin (1994) would work really well for these kinds of drill and practice sessions.

To supplement textbook exercises, have students keep some journal records of conversations or some lists of new words they encounter during a typical week. Have them search these records for similarities to the textbook material being studied. Ask them to find the longest sentence they can and discuss how it is structured. Have students look at their work to see how often they use structures such as compound sentences, linking verbs, or infinitive phrases. You can ask them to revise a portion of something they have written so that it contains an appositive or whatever structure you happen to be studying at the time. Discuss the effect that this change has on the meaning. The point is to connect the study of grammar and syntax with their own use of the language. It may not help them write better, but at least they will understand that nouns are something they use every day, not something that only occurs in sentences in their textbook.

The tendency when teaching grammar is to tell and show, but it is also a good idea to question and discover. (For one possible approach, see Activity 10.3.) If you feel comfortable taking the risk, have students give you a sentence that you try to figure out. Make your thinking processes verbal so they can hear how you go about the problem-solving process. The point is not so much to get the right answer, but using good reasons for your choices. Students can then challenge your solution, but they must also verbalize their reasoning. There will probably be some words and structures that you cannot label or explain. Do not hesitate about saying that you do not know or cannot even make a guess; after all, you are not a linguist. If you think a puzzling part is interesting, try to find an answer before the next day, but if you do not have time to research or you are not curious yourself, let it go.

There is no assurance that students will learn the concepts better if you use these strategies, but they may be more attentive.

Teaching the Concepts

Although it may not be an appealing idea, consider requiring that students memorize a list of common prepositions. Let them take the test as many times as necessary, but hold them to this requirement. If this is the only thing you require them to memorize all year and you tell them so, the task may be a bit more palatable. Of course, this will not help students understand what prepositions are or how they function, but it eliminates some confusion when they must label parts of speech.

Research shows that if you want to increase students' syntactical structures so that they write longer, more complex sentences, sentence combining works (Mellon, 1979). There is, however, some speculation that part of the reason sentence combining affects student writing is that it encourages discussion of language. There is also some research to indicate that other activities that prompt discussion of language are of value. These may be better strategies than skill–drill exercises, which tend to focus more on producing right answers. Grammatical terms can easily be introduced into these discussions. The following five activities tend to stimulate such conversation:

1. Sentence combining

   Cued sentences (directions are included for how the sentences are to be combined so that all writers produce similar constructions; especially useful for introducing syntax students do not often use).

   Uncued sentences (lists of kernel sentences which students may combine in a variety of ways and then compare the differences and the shifts in meaning or emphasis that occur).

2. Sentence correction

   Commercial sources (such as *Daily Oral Language*, texts, and workbooks that focus on errors typically found in student writing).

   Teacher-created sources (custom-tailored sentences that focus on recurrent problems or that introduce new skills intended to expand student understanding).

   Student-based sources (sentences taken from students' work and discussed by the class; anonymity is essential!).

3. Sentence patterning

   Students are given a series of similar sentences and they either search for the pattern or are given the pattern. They must produce a sentence that follows the pattern. Another variation is to explore what happens to a sentence when it is transformed (e.g., a statement is turned into a question). *The Art of Styling Sentences* by Waddell, Esch, & Walker (1972) is an excellent reference.

4. Sentence slotting

   Students are given sentences that contain omissions. They must slot in appropriate words or phrases according to the labels.

<u>5. Text re-creation</u>

Students are given a paragraph of text that has been rear-ranged, with one sentence below another in random order. They are to try to re-create the text the way the author wrote it. Sometimes their versions are better than the original. This task becomes more difficult if coherence markers are removed.

Sentence combining seems to be most effective when it is done briefly but on a regular basis, possibly for the first few minutes of each class period. Exercises can be created from students' written work.

Sentence slotting can be more challenging if students are given more specific labels, such as proper noun or action verb. Functions, too, can be inserted (e.g., direct object or adjective phrase). An impossible exercise such as the following can prompt interesting debate:

| _____ | _____ | _____ | _____ |
| adjective | pronoun | verb | adverb |

As much as possible, try to keep students focused on reasoning (e.g., How do you know? What makes you think so? How did you reach that conclusion?) rather than identification (e.g., What part of speech is this word? What is the name of this part of the sentence?). Also, discuss with them the value of this knowledge. Being able to identify an adjective clause is not worth much if they do not also understand that adjective clauses belong in certain places, and if they do not put them there, the sentences become confusing. Have students play around with structures to see where structures fit and where they will not.

In addition to completing exercises and examining their own writing, students can also explore the ways in which authors they respect use language structures. This kind of research leads into an examination of style. Comparisons can also stimulate discussion about audience awareness and writing purpose and how grammar and syntax are used to make these differences. Students may also discover that the authors they favor have quite similar styles or that they like several different styles as long as the characters are young people or the stories are mysterious. This kind of discovery can help them understand that language is only one of several factors that comprise effective writing. Another possibility is to have students experiment with different styles in a writing practice journal or as "test-run" writings. Asking them to write a familiar story in several different ways (e.g., write it for a young reader, change it to a modern setting, include dialogue, shift it from third to first person, etc.) will produce some differences in sentence structure that can be shared and discussed.

For additional information about teaching grammar more effectively, take a look at *Teaching Grammar in Context* and *Lessons to Share*

(Weaver, 1996 & 1998), which are listed in Recommended Readings for this chapter.

Diagramming Sentences

At some point the question of whether or not to teach sentence diagramming is likely to arise. Visual people like graphics. Sentence diagrams may help them see how one part of a sentence relates to another. If it is natural for you to do so and if it seems to aid students, use diagrams to illustrate concepts and show students how to diagram. Allow students to use them if they wish to do so rather than requiring that everyone learn to diagram. Offer diagramming as an option on a test (e.g., either explain how you know that this is an adjective or draw a diagram showing how it relates). Diagramming is useful as a learning tool, but it should not be the goal of instruction.

Other Considerations

Because understanding grammar and syntax is something that develops gradually, you may find that students grasp the concepts more thoroughly if you spread the study of grammar and syntax throughout the year, inserting lessons or short units related to the other work you are doing at the most appropriate times or completing a brief activity on a daily basis, rather than doing all the grammar study at once. Struggling students can fall so far behind in an intensive unit that they simply give up. However, no matter what strategies you use or how well you use them, some middle level students will remain stymied by it all. They may understand nouns and verbs and adjectives, but that may be about the extent of it.

QUESTIONS OF USAGE

The advent of descriptive grammars has raised many unsettling questions about how we use language. Throughout American history, language has been linked to national pride and to social class structure. In the years following the American Revolution, for example, influential individuals made conscious decisions to alter the way in which we spell some words in order to set us apart from the British. This has resulted in two distinct versions of English spellings—American and British—as well as differences in vocabulary.

Language has been one means of entering the middle class. Immigrants coming to America around the turn of the century often prohibited their children from speaking their native language so that they would more quickly assimilate into American life. However, they could not learn just any version of American speech; they had to learn Standard English. Standard English was supposedly the mark of an educated person and one step up the ladder toward achieving the American dream of wealth and power.

Descriptive grammars tend to draw this kind of judgment into question. Is Standard English really any better than any other form, or is this merely evidence of American arrogance, bigotry, and discrimination? Descriptive grammars verify that certain American dialects are not simply substandard speech but actual language variants with their own sets of grammatical structures and systems. If Black English has a legitimate grammatical structure, should students be encouraged to use that variant because it is closely tied to racial heritage, or should its use be discouraged because it marks the speaker as a member of a racial group that has long been oppressed? Is it appropriate to teach students that the language spoken in their own home is "wrong" or unacceptable? Should teachers try to eradicate dialects, or should they value them as marks of cultural or geographic diversity? (For a thorough discussion of Ebonics, see Perry & Delpit, 1998.)

These are not easy questions to answer, and the pendulum of opinion has swung back and forth over the years. Although there is little agreement, the debate has produced a more open acceptance of literature. The works of many multicultural writers who were previously shunned because of the use of dialects or registers other than Standard English are now recognized as significant literary pieces. Some works are even acknowledged as valuable because they serve as a kind of historical record of nonstandard English, regional dialects, or ethnic variants. Nevertheless, many of these works still are challenged by those who say they do not want their children exposed to "substandard" English.

TEACHING USAGE

Middle level students are in the process of discovering who they are, and they are also engaged in finding a social niche for themselves. Their usage is a part of their identity. They come to school with a developed sense of grammar and usage that is still being polished. It may be very close to Standard English, or it may not. Teachers must keep in mind that attempts to change the language students already use may create conflicts in their lives. In some settings, using Standard English rather than street language may prove to be dangerous or even deadly. In some situations, teaching students that the language they use at home is substandard may cause them to reject school or feel more negatively about themselves. On the other hand, denying them access to knowledge can create societal barriers that they may never overcome. One alternative is to help students understand that people use different levels of language at different times and for different purposes. For some students, learning Standard English may be similar to learning a foreign language, one that they use only in certain places and when communicating with certain people.

Middle level students are notorious for being cruel to each other. One of the ways in which they denigrate others is by making fun of their speech. Middle school is a particularly good time to assist students in exploring differences among various groups of people so that they develop respect for one another. At least a part of that exploration can be an examination of different levels, dialects, and variants of language. This can be enhanced through the study of a foreign language. Units of study can be developed in which students examine how language is used in their own community and in the media. Tape recorders and camcorders can be invaluable tools in this research.

Literature, too, can be a source of usage study. The poetry of Langston Hughes, for example, illustrates the power of dialect, whereas the poems of James Whitcomb Riley record a Hoosier idiom that is rapidly vanishing. The narration and dialogue in Peck's (1972) *A Day No Pigs Would Die* convey characterization dramatically. Williams-Garcia's (1995) *Like Sisters on the Homefront* is an excellent source for examining Black English. These texts and many more can be used to initiate discussion of language usage.

There are some audiovisual materials that focus on usage, and some computer programs include usage practice. When teaching grammar, you should concentrate some attention on usage, too. If you cannot teach grammar in the context of writing, the next best practical reason for studying grammar is in order to apply that knowledge in making usage decisions. Knowing when to use the comparative or the superlative form of an adjective demands knowing what an adjective is and which form is which, for example.

Rather than trying to correct every usage error that students make in writing and speaking, select a few and concentrate on these. Choose those that are most apt to be noticed by the general public and ones that are most likely to appear on standardized tests. Teach a mini-lesson on each problem that includes an explanation of why one usage is preferred over another. Use repetition over time to make students aware of the problem. When students misuse a word or phrase, ask them to repeat their statement so as to give them an opportunity to self-correct. If they do not, try to rephrase their statement or question using a preferable form of expression. Offer an acknowledgement or bit of praise when students avoid the problem on their own. For other suggestions for teaching usage, see *The Teaching of English Usage* by Pooley (1974), listed in the Recommended Readings for this chapter.

Few people are skillful enough to avoid usage errors entirely. You probably make some mistakes now and then, too. Tape-record yourself speaking naturally, and listen to your own speech. Make a conscious effort to erase any habitual mistakes. Although you will want to avoid sounding too pedantic when you talk with students and write comments to them, you should serve as a model of effective usage. Use slang and informal expressions infrequently to avoid giving the impression that you are trying to be a buddy or personal friend.

UNDERSTANDING MECHANICS

Grammar, syntax, and usage are all relevant when the focus of attention is either spoken or written language. Mechanics, however, is a separate category, because it relates only to written language. On the other hand, students need to become aware that some mechanics take the place of certain features found in oral communication. When people speak, they use pauses to show thought groups. They also use pitch to show that they are asking a question rather than making a statement. Through volume and stress, people emphasize certain words. They use nonverbal cues to convey meaning. Capitalization and punctuation take the place of some of these speech characteristics, acting as traffic signals, telling the reader when to slow down, pause, stop, proceed quickly, expect a turn, and look ahead for a continuation of the route.

Handbooks tend to give the impression that there are lots of rules and regulations that govern how writers must capitalize, punctuate, and spell, as if some kind of supreme court met and decided how all of this would be done. The fact is that mechanics are social conventions (see Fig. 10.7). No one told people to do so, but as a society we have agreed that we should greet those we know by saying, "Hi," or "Hello." That is a social convention, when *convention* is defined as a widely used or accepted practice. Similarly, no one told people how they should capitalize, punctuate, or spell. In general, those who compile language guidebooks and authoritative sources, such as *The Oxford English Dictionary*, look at how educated people use mechanics and then record that information (although historically a few individuals have taken it upon themselves to make judgments that were not based on how professionals wrote).

It might be much easier to teach students how to use mechanics if there actually were firm and fast rules, but the fact is that what society has agreed to do it can also change. Indeed, the "rules" do change, albeit very gradually. Some people have for quite some time argued in favor of simplifying spelling, substituting *nite* for *night*, for example. There was a time when people would have rejected *nite* as a misspelling. Now, we are more likely to see it as informally acceptable but not the best choice. Journalists tend to omit punctuation that is not absolutely necessary in order to conserve space and avoid errors that can creep in when they work against a deadline. For example, the comma in a series before the conjunction is now often omitted. On the other hand, more and more writers seem to be using a comma before an adverb clause that appears after the main clause in a sentence. As much as you may want to teach students the "rules" of mechanics, you have to realize that most of these are little more than guidelines and that professional writers use their own judgment, particularly about how to punctuate, rather than slavishly following rules.

Learning to use mechanics well means thinking about the message to be conveyed and deciding what needs to be done to make that message clear to the reader. One of the most common kinds of spelling errors that appears in the work of middle level students is misused homonyms. Students often use *its* when they need to use *it's*, or they use *their* for *there*, for example. Rarely do they actually misspell the words, though. Is this truly a spelling mistake or is it a matter of not thinking about the message to be conveyed? If a person chooses to write a piece in stream-of-consciousness, must he or she use quotation marks? Is it ever correct to include a capital letter in the middle of a sentence other than to mark a proper noun or proper adjective (e.g., The question is—Should the letter *S* be capitalized or not)?

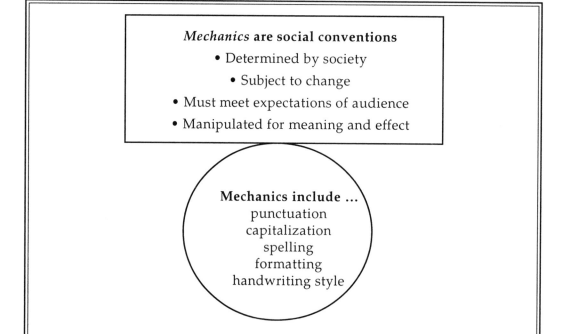

FIG. 10.7

TEACHING MECHANICS

Teaching mechanics effectively means knowing the currently accepted conventions. What is more, you need to be able to use these consistently well yourself, because you will be communicating with other people who may be sticklers about these conventions. Nothing undermines one's professional authority as a language arts teacher more quickly than to send a written note to parents or distribute a handout to other teachers that contains what these readers label as mechanical mistakes. Because you must be a role model for students, the material you write on the board, on transparencies, and on their papers should also be as free of errors as possible. Some middle level students will be quick to point out your mistakes publicly. That is an embarrassment worth avoiding.

There are not enough rules to cover every situation (thank goodness!). Sometimes following the rules is the only way to make the meaning of writing clear, but sometimes writers have options. Middle level students need to learn that as writers they often have to make judgments and decisions about mechanics. Learning to use mechanics well involves learning to think about and make good decisions based primarily on audience need rather than personal preference. Handbooks are useful aids in helping students learn what readers are likely to expect, but they need to realize that in many situations, the final choice has to be decided on the basis of what will best convey the idea clearly.

Experts in the field of composition instruction agree that the most effective way to teach mechanics is to focus on student writing. What do students need to know in order to write a particular piece of discourse well? What kinds of errors appear consistently in their work? What concepts seem hazy or only partially understood? What skills do students have for answering their own questions about mechanics, and what else do they need to learn in order to become independent writers?

When students have revised their written work and are ready to edit the material, mechanics need to be one part of the instructional focus. Students need to learn how to feel that a problem exists and how to find the mistake, but they also need to learn how to fix the error. Checklists or personal lists of common errors are especially useful. Other mechanics can be dealt with most effectively in individual conferences with the teacher, peer response groups, and mini-lessons taught to the whole class or small groups. This is the time for you to make use of a worksheet or some exercise from a handbook. Once the concept has been reviewed in this way, students can immediately apply the idea to their own writing. Studying mechanics in isolation is generally less effective than linking instruction to student writing. Another way to think of this is to focus on applied mechanics rather than looking at mechanics as an academic content area to be studied for its own sake.

If you must teach mechanics formally from a textbook, try to be selective. Quickly review those concepts that students have mastered, and spend more time on the items that cause the most trouble in their writing. At the middle level, that usually means spending much more time on commas than end punctuation, for instance. As much as possible, avoid concentrating on the esoteric. Some rules about capitalization, for example, are rarely used. Teach students to use the handbook as a reference when they encounter these special forms.

One innovative way to conduct a study of mechanics is to have students create their own handbooks. Divide students into pairs and assign each pair one or two topics. Provide several different handbooks they can use for reference. Be prepared to deal with the fact that the books will not agree and that students will be puzzled by this. Use this puzzlement as an opportunity to discuss some of the principles of language, including the fact that language changes over time and that the so-called rules governing mechanics are not static. Have students state the guidelines in their own words and create their own examples. Publish the final booklet and give each student a copy to use as a reference.

WHAT TO DO ABOUT SPELLING

Fig. 10.8 contains a summary of research recommendations concerning the teaching of spelling. Certain forms of instruction increase test scores, but what teachers generally want is for students to spell more accurately when they write. Middle level students may spell words correctly on a test on Monday and misspell some of those same words when they write on Tuesday. In educational jargon, transfer of knowledge from one situation to another is not automatic. Many commercial spelling programs, especially those designed for use at the middle level, require the study of infrequently used words. Student work, on the other hand, often contains misspellings of common words, especially homonyms. Even if spelling study transferred readily to compositions, using a spelling program that does not highlight commonly misspelled words will probably not eliminate the errors that are most bothersome in student writing.

If you have the option, you may consider looking for some spelling material that is designed somewhat differently from most series. Look for a workbook or exercises that focus on words students often misspell in their writing. If possible, find something that contains a diagnostic test that allows you to assign students to complete only those chapters or activities that they really need to complete so they do not waste time reviewing concepts they already understand.

From _SPEL_ _Is a Four-Letter Word_ (Gentry, 1987)

Five general guidelines for creating an effective spelling program (primarily for
students who are not yet fluent, confident writers):
- Teach spelling as part of the whole curriculum, not a separate subject
- Have students write frequently.
- Encourage students to invent spellings for words they may not have learned to
spell (Have them do the best they can at first.)
- De-emphasize correctness, memorization, and mechanics while drafting.
- Respond to writing so that students discover more about spelling.

Procedures that are supported by research (will improve test grades)
- Allot 60 to 75 minutes per week to formal spelling instruction.
- Present the words to be studied in list or column form.
- Give students a pretest to determine which words in the list are unknown.
Have them study these. Administer a post-test.
- Have the students correct their own spelling tests under your direction.
- Teach a systematic technique for studying unknown words (see below).
- Use spelling games to make spelling lessons more fun.

Two systematic techniques for studying words:
Fitzgerald method (more for visual learners)
    1. Look at the word carefully.
    2. Say the word.
    3. With eyes closed, visualize the word.
    4. Cover the word and then write it.
    5. Check the spelling.
    6. If the word is misspelled, repeat steps 1–5.

Horn method (more for auditory learners)
    1. Pronounce each word carefully.
    2. Look carefully at each part of the word as you say it.
    3. Say the letters in sequence.
    4. Attempt to recall how the word looks, and then spell it aloud.
    5. Check this attempt at recall.
    6. Write the word.
    7. Check this spelling attempt.
    8. Repeat the above steps if necessary.

Spelling rules which should be taught:
- Using periods in abbreviations
- Using apostrophes to show possession
- Capitalizing proper names and adjectives
- Adding suffixes (changing y to i, dropping the final silent e, doubling the final
consonant)
- English words do not end in v.
- Q is followed by u in English spelling.

FIG. 10.8 From _SPEL_ _Is a Four-Letter Word_, by R. Gentry, 1987, Markham, ONT: Scholastic Canada Ltd. Copyright 1987 by Richard Gentry. Adapted by permission of the pub-
lisher.

Look for material that is set up so that students can take spelling tests silently. This may be very difficult to find, but some exercises can be adapted to fit this format. This has several advantages. Some good spellers rely on hearing the words during the test, and do not complete the study work. Often teachers use some exaggerated pronunciations that serve as verbal cues when giving tests orally, and adept spellers come to rely heavily on these hints. Teachers are trying to be helpful, but in the long run this practice probably is a disservice to students. If no one pronounces the words, everyone has to study the material to succeed on the tests. Also, if no one must read the words to be spelled for tests, students can study the lists in any order they wish or any order you assign and take the tests whenever they feel prepared to do so. The most significant advantage, however, is that this approach mirrors the way spelling is done when people write. Oral tests in which someone pronounces the words and uses them in made-up sentences is not how writers spell when they compose. Rather, they have a sentence in mind and a word they want to use in it. Then they have to think about how that word is spelled, all on their own. The more your approach to spelling resembles the actual task of composing, the more likely students are to apply their spelling skills when it really counts. It is also helpful if you can locate some spelling material that is or can be adapted to be self-checking so that you do not have to grade the practice exercises yourself or take class time for everyone to check his or her work. Although it may be difficult to find material that has all of these aspects, some supplementary spelling materials and even some commercial spelling texts can be adapted to match many of these features.

Some experts recommend the use of individualized spelling lists. Students record any words they have misspelled in compositions on their lists and then periodically take tests on them (Routman, 1991). If students write large quantities of text and misspell frequently, and if all of their spelling errors are noted, this approach can be useful, but you may find that it creates problems. For example, if you must grade the results, and students are having problems with homonyms, you will not know whether students have written the correct words. Some students will avoid using words they cannot spell in their writing in order to avoid adding them to their spelling lists, and some words that students will be forced to study are ones they are apt to use very infrequently in writing. A few students will spell so well that they will never need to take a test, whereas others will spell so poorly that they will need to study a lengthy list of words after every composition they complete. Although individualized spelling lists sound good in theory, they are quite difficult to manage in reality. However, every student should keep a list of the words he or she commonly misspells and use this as a checklist when they edit.

One alternative for teaching spelling is to use the computer. Some software programs focus on common misspellings, or they can be programmed with word lists comprised of words students misspell when they write. Students can work through these individually. They can take as much or as little time as they need. The computer can keep records of the work being done and the test scores. Also, students should have access to a word processing program with a spell checker. These take note of obvious mistakes, but students still have to determine whether the spelling should be changed. They can also use the "Find" or "Search" command to locate words they frequently misspell.

No matter what else you do about spelling, focus instruction on the words students misspell in their compositions. Look for patterns of error and violations of general principles. Use this information to design and teach mini-lessons that will help the majority of students eradicate their most common mistakes. Have students create mnemonics, similar to those in Suid's (1981) *Demonic Mnemonics*, for remembering how to spell certain words, and have them share these with classmates. Provide time for students to engage in activities that are enjoyable but demand correct spelling. Games such as Hangman and Scrabble as well as crossword puzzles fit these criteria. There are also some computer word games that are suitable.

BUILDING VOCABULARY

The most effective way for students to build vocabulary is through reading. Students who read will encounter words that are initially unfamiliar but that gradually acquire meaning through repeated appearances in text. Vocabulary growth can be enhanced if students list the new words they find in what they read and if their attention is periodically directed to particular words in their reading material. At times, prereading activities should include an introduction to a limited number of vocabulary words that are crucial to the understanding of the material students are about to read. Discussions and activities that occur while the reading is occurring and after it is finished should focus, in part, on the meanings of some key words or phrases.

Another recommended way to study vocabulary is to look at related words or word families. Students can design visual representations of how these words relate. Furthermore, they can look for these words in texts and add these quotes to a bulletin board or word wall. Common prefixes and suffixes can be introduced gradually, but lengthy lists that must be studied intensively generally cause confusion.

The key factor seems to be looking at words in meaningful contexts. Although the practice is relatively common, having students study lists of unrelated and decontextualized words is not effective.

If you ask middle level students to look up words in the dictionary and then use them in sentences, they will write meaningless and inaccurate statements because the dictionary does not provide the nuances of connotation that develop only from hearing and seeing the words used in meaningful ways.

As much as possible, vocabulary study should stimulate interest and curiosity about words. One excellent entry point is through reading and creating puns. Piers Anthony's *Xanth* novels provide a wealth of examples, but books by Lederer, such as *Get Thee to a Punnery* (1988), may be even more beneficial. Kohl's (1981) *The Book of Puzzlements* is another outstanding resource of stimulating questions about vocabulary.

Students can investigate how dictionaries are compiled and examine some special-use dictionaries, such as those designed for crossword puzzle fans, ones that contain only new or obscure words, dictionaries of synonyms and antonyms, and rhyming dictionaries. They can conduct surveys and create their own dictionaries of current slang, or they can listen to old radio broadcasts or newsreels from the 1920s or view videotapes of interviews conducted during the 1960s to identify slang that marked these decades. They can even interview adults about their recollections of these terms. They can also interview people about the jargon associated with particular occupations and examine documents for evidence of these words.

Games and puzzles are especially good for developing vocabulary. Scrabble, Boggle, Scategories, crossword puzzles, anagrams, and many other games, including some word games that are available for computers, make vocabulary study almost painless for middle level students. What is even better is for students to create their own games and puzzles for other students to try. Additional possibilities for motivating interest in vocabulary can be found in Activity 10.4.

OTHER ASPECTS OF LANGUAGE STUDY

Grammar, syntax, usage, and mechanics directly impact how people communicate, and students need to understand how to use these aspects of language well. Furthermore, students need to build their store of words if they are to express themselves clearly and comprehend the messages created by others. However, other areas of language study are beneficial for students. Moreover, these can increase the students' curiosity and sensitivity to language. Focusing on language elements that directly relate to students' own reading, writing, speaking, listening, and viewing and visually representing should take top priority, but if there is time to do so, certain facets of language can be explored because they are interesting and worthwhile. Many of these topics fit nicely into interdisciplinary or integrative units (see Activity 10.5 for inquiry project suggestions), but others are the kinds of unknowns and oddities that pique the attention of middle level learners (Activity 10.6 contains a list of suggested topics).

History and Development

An examination of the history and development of English can be a dry review of dates and events, but it need not be so. For example, students can try their hands at developing various forms of writing similar to pictographs, and they can use rebuses to send messages. They can also compare various alphabets used by different cultures over the years. *Writing* by Lewis (1992) is an excellent source of information and hands-on activities.

When looking just at English, students can examine maps for evidence of various languages being used in particular parts of the country. Just as the United States is multicultural, so is American English. Students who speak other languages can be especially helpful in locating place-names and identifying familiar words that are of foreign origin. Students can examine documents over a period of time to determine when a proper noun such as *Kleenex* moved into the common noun category and investigate the stories behind some interesting words and phrases. History buffs may find it intriguing to study how spelling has changed over the years by looking at copies of original documents that can be obtained from county clerks, the National Archives, the Eastern States Land Office, and other repositories. They can also examine letters written by important historical figures or share ones that are of importance to their own family history. Some students may find it interesting to think about the fact that many diaries, journals, and letters were written by people who never would have believed that their work would eventually be published. Anne Frank's diary is just one example. Personal letters from soldiers in battle, particularly those from the Civil War and Vietnam, ship captains' logs, and slave narratives are additional examples. Some of these documents are the only remaining record of the existence of these people and the events they witnessed.

The relationship between mechanics and the development of printing techniques may fascinate some students. You might begin by sharing *The History of Printmaking*, a book published by Scholastic (1995). The article on punctuation by Lupton (1988), which is listed in the Recommended Readings for this chapter, describes through illustration how changes in the medium of writing prompted changes in capitalization and punctuation over time. Recent growth in the use of computers gives the ordinary writer access to fonts and special printing techniques that were previously available only to publishers. Formatting and layout are becoming increasingly important facets of how we use language. Although handwriting style is probably of declining interest, student curiosity may be piqued by looking at old documents or reproductions that show some of the quirks that were at one time commonplace and the artistry that was once associated with copying manuscripts and handwriting.

Students can survey people about the acceptance of certain changes in punctuation, spelling, or both that have occurred recently, and they can create dictionaries of slang, street language, and contemporary words that have been added to the language within the students' life span. Consider, for example, that *cocktail* has recently been given a new meaning related to the medical treatment of AIDs and cancer.

Although teachers often use literature that is set in a particular period of history as part of an interdisciplinary unit, they generally do not include examples of print and nonprint texts that were actually produced at that time. Few descriptions of such units include suggestions for exploring the status of language at that time, yet this would be an excellent way for students to consider how language has changed through history.

Rhetoric

The American Heritage Dictionary of the English Language (Morris, 1973) defines rhetoric as: "1. The study of the elements used in literature and public speaking, such as content, structure, cadence, and style. 2. The art of prose as distinct from that of poetry. 3. a. Affectation or exaggeration in prose or verse. b. Unsupported or inflated discourse. 4. The art of oratory, especially the persuasive use of language to influence the thoughts and actions of listeners." (1114) Thus, the term *rhetoric* can apply to either written or spoken discourse. Although rhetoric can cover almost all of the concepts that have previously been introduced in relation to the teaching of language in any form, the study of rhetoric usually refers to how writers use language to achieve specific purposes, especially in argumentative or persuasive discourse. For example, rhetoricians look not just at the meaning of content but also why some content was chosen, whereas other content was omitted. They also look at how the arrangement of ideas conveys the intended message. Thus, rhetoric looks at the use of language from a more technical standpoint. Stylistic features, such as those shown in Fig. 10.9, are often considered to be rhetorical features.

If rhetoric is thought of as relating to the use of persuasion, the following topics may be worth exploring in the middle level classroom:

- classical rhetoric
- propaganda techniques
- advertising gimmicks
- faulty arguments

Of all the fields that link literature, composition, and language, rhetoric has the most to offer. Students need to know how language can and is used to manipulate their thinking and how they can use language to persuade. Although people currently tend to consider rhetoric as more closely allied with composition, classical rhetoric included only spoken language. Rhetoricians must be even more alert to how language influences others, more so than literary authors usually are, because the purpose of rhetorical oratory is persuasion.

National test scores indicate that when students write imaginatively, their work is better than when they must explain, support their opinion, or present a persuasive argument (Applebee, Langer, & Mullis, 1988). Although we have no national statistics that verify it, the likelihood seems strong that spoken language abilities parallel writing skills in this regard. From what we know and what we suspect, it seems reasonable to conclude that students need more practice writing and speaking persuasively.

But there are other reasons for believing that students should know some of the basic concepts associated with persuasive language. There are those who believe that our system of democracy

Style	
Sentence structure • Length • Complexity • Variety • Novelty • Purposeful repetition • Rhythm	**Figurative language** • Imagery • Metaphor • Simile • Personification • Onomatopoeia • Idioms
Diction or word choice	
• Connotations • Stereotypes/labels • Slang • Trite expressions • Multisyllabic words • Precise words	• Euphemisms • Gender-sensitive wording • Technical jargon • Archaic words • Words with multiple meanings • Economy of wording

FIG. 10.9

rests on the ability of voters to think critically about the persuasion they hear so as to recognize faulty arguments and propaganda techniques. From another perspective, there is a vast advertising industry dedicated to determining what persuades people, not only to vote for a certain candidate but also to buy a certain product or attend an event. Commercials and advertisements bombard children, teens, and adults. Young children often learn to recognize words such as *McDonald's* long before they can read much else, and they know the words to some commercials better than they know nursery rhymes or fairy tales. Teenagers spend millions of dollars each year on the basis of advertisements.

Middle level students in search of ways to become "one of the crowd" or to do what everyone else is doing are particularly susceptible to the advertising that surrounds them. Searching for an independent identity, they often fall victim to rhetoric espousing causes that they do not fully understand and have not the ability to assess critically. They may have some strong attitudes and beliefs, but no sense of the basis for these pro or con prejudices. Nevertheless, these biases may be strongly associated with how they view themselves.

It is unlikely that most middle level students can relate to a study of the classical rhetoric of the Greeks and syllogistic reasoning may be temporarily out of reach, but they can learn to recognize various kinds of persuasion in their own environment. They can, for example, recognize the difference between emotional and logical appeals. They can examine advertisements, letters to the editor, and other examples of persuasion in search of various propaganda techniques and advertising gimmicks. They can listen to political speeches, promotional messages, and debates over controversial issues in order to pinpoint various kinds of faulty arguments as well as sound reasoning. And they can also create their own examples to demonstrate how these various rhetorical devices are intended to persuade.

These concrete activities introduce persuasive writing. Certainly middle level students should be asked to explore various kinds of written persuasion and argumentation, just as they should engage in exploring a variety of other modes. One of the special values of attempting persuasive writing is that it demands that students focus on the needs of the audience and consider alternative points of view in order to argue successfully. However, keep in mind that this kind of writing is likely to be quite challenging for middle school students. Mastery is unlikely. However, students need to begin to examine and attempt this kind of discourse at the middle level. There are those who argue that one reason students do not write persuasively well is that they do not read this kind of discourse and are not asked to write it frequently. You can fill this void. You can also augment instruction in rhetoric through the use of speaking and listening activities. It is through rhetorical devices that language is used most effectively to manipulate thought and change attitudes. Students deserve to know how language works to achieve these purposes.

LANGUAGE STUDY AND TEACHER KNOWLEDGE

Most language arts experts agree that teachers need to know much more about language than they can possible teach their students. Reading and discussing exceptional works of literature gives you a sound background in literary studies. You may never teach those same works to your students, but your general knowledge of literature should be transferable to the material that matches the developmental level of your students. Oxymorons and unreliable narrators may be concepts that you find intellectually interesting, but middle level students may find them unfathomable. Nevertheless, as a well-educated English major, you should know the technical factors and understand the complex concepts. With this knowledge, you can take students from wherever they are and move them toward the goal of enjoying and appreciating literature within the limits of their current capabilities. However, you do not have to teach them everything you know.

The same concept holds true for language study. You need to know a great deal about language that you will probably never teach directly to students. This understanding will be a useful guide for making curricular decisions, explaining composition errors, and helping students explore the interesting ways in which people communicate (and fail to do so). That does not mean that you need to be a professional linguist, but you do need to have a solid foundation of linguistic background and an appetite for furthering your study of language independently. Middle level students need not be taught everything that can be known about language, but they do need to be introduced to some of the principles and concepts that make language such a useful but frustrating tool, and they need opportunities to discover some of the interesting avenues related to the study of language. The teacher who has strolled along these byways or at least knows that they exist probably has enough knowledge to act as a guide if that teacher is also willing to accept the role of colearner with students. You must be able to use language well yourself, and you must know enough about language to assist your students in developing control over the language they need to use, but you may be less familiar with some of the other aspects of language. Because these are likely to be new routes for most middle level students, your cursory knowledge of these supplementary areas of study is apt to be sufficient if it is accompanied by personal interest, curiosity, and enthusiasm (Sse Fig. 10.10).

General Guidelines for Teaching Language Well

- Build on knowledge students already have about language.
- Recognize that many so-called errors in language use are not mistakes. Students often have good reasons for their usages. Explore them.
- Prepare students for inevitable changes in language.
- Recognize different levels of language. Help students become aware of these and use them appropriately.
- Provide myriad opportunities for students to do all sorts of things with language so that they can explore a wide range of possibilities and purposes.
- Have students use language for meaningful reasons instead of just having them complete exercises.
- Expect relatively slow but gradual progress because students are refining language.
- Depend on students' innate ability to derive linguistic principles from language use in context. Having them use language is probably more beneficial than direct instruction about language, but both are necessary.
- Keep oral language at the center of the language arts classroom. Get students to talk, to respond to talk, and to talk about the language they use and hear.

FIG. 10.10

ASSESSING AND EVALUATING LANGUAGE UNDERSTANDING

Much of what has already been stated about assessing reading, writing, speaking, listening, and viewing and visually representing is actually a statement of how the student's understanding of language should be measured. Part of the assessment and evaluation of writing, for example, should focus on the student's application of grammatical, syntactical, and mechanical guidelines and how well the student fulfills the expectation of the audience for effective use of language. Part of the assessment and evaluation of speaking must be based on language skills. Therefore, no separate checklist is provided in this chapter.

However, the teaching of grammar, syntax, usage, and mechanics is often measured with so-called objective tests. There are several different forms: true–false, multiple choice, labeling, matching, and fill-in-the-blank. If you use this type of testing, you should choose the form that is best for measuring the learning that you set as the goal of instruction. Developing each of these test formats requires some special skills that should be studied in a tests-and-measurements course. If such a class is not part of your program, there are many professional references available that provide detailed information about test design. What follows are some hints and tips that are particularly appropriate for language arts at the middle level.

If the test covers only a small portion of information, a single format may be preferable, but if the test covers more information, you should consider using a combination of formats. However, if you include too many, students will be confused. Students should be informed in advance of the format or formats to be used. The test itself should be legible. The directions should be clear and unambiguous. In general, classroom tests should be designed as knowledge (power) tests rather than speed tests. If students are given too many questions and insufficient time, then the test will measure factors such as reading and recall speed, rather than knowledge of the information. The questions themselves must be carefully designed so that they really do focus on the intended learning. True–false tests may be easy to grade, but students have a 50% chance of getting the correct answer by guessing. Scores on multiple-choice tests are less likely to be the result of guessing, but they are more challenging to create. You have to state the correct answer and then provide at least two incorrect responses that sound plausible. Multiple-choice tests also take up more space, so they require more paper and appear longer to students.

If you choose to give spelling tests orally, have the students number their papers first. Inform them in advance that they should skip any puzzlers and come back to them after all the words have been given. If you do not do this, students will constantly demand more time for each word as it is pronounced. If they skip one but forget to leave a space, and they have no numbers on their papers, they will have no idea later which word they omitted. If you choose to test grammatical knowledge by having students label various parts of speech or mark constructions in specific ways (e.g., circle, underline), consider in advance how you will score multiple wrong answers. For example, if you ask students to circle all of the nouns in sentences, what will you do if the student circles every word? One possibility is to deduct points for each incorrect response, but this can produce a score lower than zero. If you plan to give a fill-in-the-blank test, determine in advance whether you will accept synonyms and descriptive phrases for the terms you are seeking. Students need to know beforehand whether such responses will be accepted.

There are some interesting and revealing adaptations of objective test formats that you may want to try occasionally. For example, on a true–false test students can be asked to explain why each false answer is inaccurate. Multiple-choice tests can include "all of the above," "none of the above," or a blank space that students can fill with the correct answer if it does not appear in the choices. Sometimes it is interesting to ask students to indicate their level of confidence in their answers by using various markings such as pluses, checks, and minus signs (Van Brocklyn, 1988). This is particularly beneficial when the test is part of a longer unit that will continue. Weak confidence levels can indicate concepts that need additional review even though most students respond correctly.

Although objective test formats often do not fit the goals of a language arts classroom, student achievement and school effectiveness is frequently measured by standardized tests that are most often multiple choice. If students are to do well on these tests, they need instruction in test-taking and practice. Although it is sometimes beneficial to use tests to measure comprehension of language arts concepts, most objective tests do not measure higher-order thinking. Other forms of assessment are more useful if that is your goal.

As for more subjective forms of testing, for the most part, short answer questions are more appropriate at the middle level than essay questions. In the elementary grades students are not often asked to write essays, so this demand may be new to them. If you wish to use essay questions, spend time in advance teaching students how to respond to these questions. If you use an essay question, you should know in advance what you expect to find in the responses. Also, keep the questions narrowly focused. Faced with a vague, open-ended question such as "Discuss the symbolism in _____," most middle level students will have no idea of how to compose an answer. Questions that ask them to identify an example and then explain it or that ask them to list several items and then write about one usually produce better responses.

RECOMMENDED READINGS

Artman, J. (1980). *Slanguage: Activities and ideas on the history and nature of language*. Parsippany, NJ: Good Apple.

Bragonier, R.,k & Fisher, D. (1981). *What's what?: A visual glossary of the physical world*. New York: Ballantine Books.

Christenbury, L. (Ed.). (1996). The great debate (again): Teaching grammar and usage [Themed issue]. *English Journal, 85*(7).

Cook, L., & Lodge, H. (Eds.). (1996). *Voices in English classrooms: Honoring diversity and change*. Classroom Practices in Teaching English, Vol. 28. Urbana, IL: National Council of Teachers of English.

Davis, K., & Hollowell, J. (Eds.) (1977). *Inventing and playing games in the English classroom*. Urbana, IL: National Council of Teachers of English.

Dicks, C., & Horsman, P. (1990). Introduction to language: A junior-high unit. *English Journal, 79*(1), 58–61.

Expletives deleted. (1998, May 28), *The Indianapolis News*, pp. D1, D2.

Finegan, E. (1980). *Attitudes toward English usage: The history of a war of words*. New York: Teachers College Press.

Gentry, R. (1987). *SPEL ... is a four letter word*. Portsmouth, NH: Heinemann.

Hall, R., & friends (1984). *Sniglets*. New York: Collier Books.

Harmon, J. (1998). Vocabulary teaching and learning in a seventh-grade literature-based classroom. *Journal of Adolescent & Adult Literacy, 41,* 518–529.

Houlette, F. (1989). Teaching grammar for teachers of writing. In P. Ranieri & L. Wilcox (Eds.), *Through the chrysalis: Source book—II for teachers by teachers.* (pp. 85–94). Muncie, IN: Indiana Writing Project, Ball State University, Indiana Department of Education.

Hurwitz, A., & Goddard, A. (1969). *Games to improve your child's English.* New York: Simon & Schuster.

Kane, S. (1997). Favorite sentences: Grammar in action. *The Reading Teacher, 51,* 70–72.

Killgallon, D. (1997). *Sentence composing for middle school: A worktext on sentence variety and maturity.* Portsmouth, NH: Boynton/Cook–Heinemann.

Kohl, H. (1981). *A book of puzzlements: Play and invention with language.* New York: Schocken Books.

Lederer, R. (1987). *Anguished English: An anthology of accidental assaults upon our language.* Charleston, SC: Wyrick & Company.

Lederer, R. (1988). *Get thee to a punnery.* Charleston, SC: Wyrick & Company.

Lederer, R. (1990). *The play of words: Fun & games for language lovers.* New York: Pocket Books.

Lewis, A. (1992). *Writing: A fact and fun book.* Reading, MA: Addison-Wesley.

Lupton, E. (1988). Period styles: A punctuated history. *Teachers and Writers Collaborative Newsletter 20*(1), 7–11.

McCrum, R., Cran, W., & MacNeil, R. (1986). *The story of English.* New York: Elizabeth Sifton Books—Viking.

Noguchi, R. (1991). *Grammar and the teaching of writing: Limits and possibilities.* Urbana, IL: National Council of Teachers of English.

Perry, T., & Delpit, L. (Eds.) (1998). *The real Ebonics debate: Power, language, and the education of African-American children.* Boston, MA: Beacon Press.

Pooley, R. (1974). *The teaching of English Usage.* Urbana, IL: National Council of Teachers of English.

Rosencrans, G. (1998). *The spelling book: Teaching children how to spell, not what to spell.* Newark, DE: International Reading Association.

Routman, R. (1991). *Invitations: Changing as teachers and learners K–12.* Portsmouth, NH: Heinemann.

Scholastic (1995). *The history of printmaking.* New York: Scholastic.

Simmons, J., & Baines, L. (1998). *Language study in middle school, high school, and beyond: Views on enhancing the study of language.* Newark, DE: International Reading Association.

Southard, B., & Muller, A. (1993). Blame it on Twain: Reading American dialects in *The Adventures of Huckleberry Finn. Journal of Reading 36*(8), 630–634.

Suid, M. (1981). *Demonic Mnemonics: 800 spelling tricks for 800 tricky words.* Belmont, CA: Pitman Learning.

Thomas, L. & Tchudi, S. (1999). *The english language: An owner's manual.* Boston, MA: Allynard Bacon.

Thomma, S., & Cannon, A. (September 17, 1995). Speaking the language. *The Indianapolis Star*, pp. D1, D4.

Waddell, M., Esch, R., & Walker R. (1972). *The art of styling sentences: 20 patterns to success*. Woodbury, NY: Barron's Educational Series.

Weaver, C. (1996). *Teaching grammar in context*. Portsmouth, NH: Boynton/Cook–Heinemann.

Weaver, C. (Ed.) (1998). *Lessons to share: On teaching grammar in context*. Portsmouth, NH: Boynton/Cook–Heinemann.

OTHER RESOURCES

Grammar Games
Davidson & Associates, Inc.
   P.O. Box 2961
   Torrance, CA 90509
   1–800–545–7677

Gramopoly
LinguiSystems, Inc.
   3100 4th Avenue
   East Moline, IL 61244–9700
   1–800–776–4332

In Pursuit of Grammar
Teacher's Discovery
   English Division
   2741 Paldan Drive
   Auburn Hills, MI 48326
   1–800–583–6454

Teaching Language Activities and Suggestions

Activity 10.1:
General Points About Teaching
Grammar, Usage, and Mechanics

1. Learning grammar is a metalinguistic task. Students know much about grammar in terms of how to use the language, but they are not aware of how they do this or how they learned. Grammar study helps bring this knowledge to the conscious level.

2. Introduce terms, but do not expect mastery of terms or concepts quickly.

3. Use students' work to teach language as much as possible.

4. Teach grammar, usage, and mechanics by means of mini-lessons on the basis of group need. Coordinate with literature study by looking at where words go in sentences and how longer sentences are built. Design activities that guide students to search for patterns and manipulate sentences and sentence parts in certain ways (e.g., forming various transformations). See if students can create generalizations based on what they produce.

5. Design language study activities to get at specific problems students are having or growth you hope to see from them. Do not try to teach them in one year all the grammar, usage, or mechanics you know to .

6. Teach grammar because it is fascinating and because it can alert kids to language possibilities and give them confidence and control over language. However, recognize that grammar study does not improve writing quality, nor does it cause students to think more analytically.

7. People use the term *grammar* loosely. Parents often say they want more grammar taught, but what they really mean is usage or mechanics. Sometimes the errors to which they refer are ones commonly made by even the parents themselves.

8. Grammatical structures in speaking generally outpace their use in writing. However, beginning at the upper elementary level and continuing into middle school, students encounter structures in their reading which they rarely hear and do not use when they speak. This can present reading comprehension

problems and tangled syntax when students try to imitate what they are reading when they write.

9. English is a word order language. If this were not so, patterns would not exist. Students need to begin to understand this factor of word order. This may be a particularly important concept to students whose native language is not English.

10. The teaching of grammar should stimulate students' curiosity about how language works. Help them discover some of the principles. Encourage them to ask questions, experiment, and seek ways to find answers. Handbooks can be very useful for student reference. Teach them how to use them for this purpose.

11. Usage has to do with the social acceptability of language, not with matters of always right and always wrong. It is very important to keep in mind that usage is situation-dependent. Levels of usage exist. Standard English may be like English as a second language to some students. It is a choice, but it is a powerful one that students should know how and when to select.

12. To study usage, have students study varieties objectively. An objective study of dialects can be very enlightening.

13. To encourage the use of Standard English, use some non-threatening situations—choral reading, oral reading of nondialect plays, stories, poems, and oral language games. Students need to hear standard usage first. The teacher must act as a model, but he or she must also be able to shift levels of usage as needed.

14. Expect a rebound effect when you teach mechanics. Whenever you teach a particular concept, expect students to overuse and misuse it for a while. A lesson on run-on sentences is likely to increase the number of fragments. A lesson on commas may produce sprinklings of commas everywhere.

15. To teach mechanics, keep the following in mind:
    - Ignore random errors unless they mark serious weaknesses in basic skills.
    - Look for error patterns in students' work and teach lessons only on these.
    - Focus on what is most necessary and what students can understand now.
    - Mechanical errors are very difficult to locate in one's own work.
    - Some "errors" actually signal growth and attempts at new skills.
    - Whenever students try something new in writing, mechanical problems are likely to increase.
    - Checklists of mechanics, either in student portfolios or posted somewhere in the room, can be helpful.

Activity 10.2:
Formal Teaching of Grammar:
The Pros and Cons Bibliography

The following sources present the conflicting evidence and opinions concerning the usefulness of teaching grammar formally. The majority argue against traditional prescriptive grammar. Additional support in favor of teaching grammar is available from NCTE's Assembly for the Teaching of English Grammar which publishes a newsletter, *Syntax in the Schools*. For additional articles, see the November 1996 issue of *English Journal*.

Braddock, R., Lloyd-Jones, R., & Schoer, L. (1963). *Research in written composition*. Champaign, IL: National Council of Teachers of English.

Elbow, P. (1973). *Writing without teachers*. New York: Oxford University Press.

Elley, W., Barham, I., Lamb, H., & Wylie, M. (1976). The role of grammar in a secondary school English curriculum. *Research in the Teaching of English, 10*, 5–21.

Fraser, I., & Hodson, L. (1978). Twenty-one kicks at the grammar horse. *English Journal, 67*, 49–53.

Glatthorn, A. (1988). What schools should teach in the English language arts. *Educational Leadership, 46*(1), 44–50.

Haley-James, S. (Ed.) (1981). *Perspectives on writing in grades 1–8*. Urbana, IL: National Council of Teachers of English.

Hillocks, G. (1986). *Research on written composition: New directions for teaching*. Urbana, IL: ERIC Clearinghouse on Reading and Communication Skills.

Kolln, M. (1981). Closing the book on alchemy. *College Composition and Communication, 32*(2), 139–151.

Maxwell, R., & Meiser, M. (1993). *Teaching English in middle and secondary schools*. New York: Macmillan. [Chapters 7 and 8 are especially applicable]

Milner, J., & Milner, L. (1993). *Bridging English*. New York: Merrill.

Noyce, R., & Christie, J. (1983). Effects of an integrated approach to grammar instruction on third graders' reading and writing. *Elementary School Journal, 84*, 63–69.

Sanborn, J. (1986). Grammar: Good wine before its time. *English Journal, 75*(3), 72–80.

Sherwin, J. (1969). *Four problems in teaching English: A critique of research*. Scranton, PA: International Textbook.

Streed, J. (1993). Labeling for form and function. *English Journal, 82*(5), 85–87.

Tompkins, G. (1994). *Teaching writing: Balancing process and product* (2nd ed., pp. 345–350). New York: Merrill.

Vavra, E. (1993). Welcome to the shoe store? *English Journal, 82*(5), 81–84.

Wall, D. (1971). The state of grammar in the state of Iowa. *English Journal, 60*(8), 1127–1130.

Warner, A. (1993). If the shoe no longer fits, wear it anyway? *English Journal, 82*(5), 76–80

Activity 10.3:
Researching Grammatical Concepts

Directions: Assign students to one of four groups—nouns, verbs, adjectives, or adverbs. Give each student an attribute chart similar to the one shown in Fig. 10.11. The group must fill out the column they have been assigned, but the other columns will be completed later. Students examine grammar handbooks, dictionaries, and other resources to find the information they need. After the groups have finished, they put their information on transparencies and report to the rest of the class. Students fill out their own charts on the basis of these reports.

Explanation of attributes: Students should state a definition of the term in their own words. *Special varieties* includes categories such as *common* and *proper* for nouns and comparative forms for adjectives. *Physical features* refers to any visible marker that indicates the part of speech. For example, nouns become plural with the addition of an -*s* or -*es*. On the other hand, a third person singular verb is often marked by an -*s*. *Other properties* include singular and plural, tense, and comparison. *Location* has to do with where in the phrase or sentence that part of speech was most frequently found. Nouns, of course, can be almost anywhere, but adjectives appear most often in only two places, near a noun and somewhere after a linking verb. One of the most distinguishing features of many adverbs is mobility; a single adverb can appear in almost any location in a sentence. *Function* refers to the purpose the word serves. Nouns, for instance, can function as subjects, direct objects, indirect objects, objects of prepositions, and predicate nominatives. *Frame* is a blank that the part of speech often fills. Common nouns, for instance, can follow *a* or *an*, so the frame for a common noun is simply *a/an*_____. Verbs work with *have*, *had*, and *has*. Adjectives go with *very*. Adverbs move around, so the frame for them is _____ he _____ *walked*_____. If the word fits in all three places, it is probably an adverb although not all adverbs work this way (e.g., most intensifiers such as *too* and *very* won't fit, which is part of the reason structural linguists argue that they belong in a class by themselves). These frames are far from foolproof, but they often aid students when they are having trouble with identification.

Additional possibilities: An alternative is to give students the blank chart and then have them fill in the parts as a kind of review at the end of each section of study. They can then share these to make sure that everyone is on target. They can also use their charts as a reference when they take a test.

One of the reasons this seems to work well is that it forces students to make direct comparisons among these 4 parts of speech. They cannot just "do" nouns and then forget about them when they move on to verbs. Also, it points out that the function words (prepositions, conjunctions, and interjections) do not work the same as the form words (nouns, verbs, adjectives, and adverbs). They cannot be charted this way. Fortunately, there are far fewer of them.

Pronouns deserve some special attention. They can be charted, but some of the information is a repeat of what can be stated about nouns. However, they do not fit the same frame as nouns, and they do not have the same physical features. Pronouns are less numerous, so they are a bit easier to detect, but there are many special varieties of them. Furthermore, the misuse of pronouns accounts for an enormous proportion of the usage errors that people make, and acceptable usage of pronouns is always shifting. This makes pronouns particularly difficult to teach.

Attribute	Nouns	Verbs	Adjectives	Adverbs
Definition				
Special varieties				
Physical features				
Other properties				
Location in sentence or phrase				
Function				
Frame				

FIG. 10.11

Activity 10.4: Motivational Activities for Vocabulary Study

1. Have students look specifically at-"nyms" (antonyms, homonyms, synonyms, acronyms, and pseudonyms). They can also look at-"fixes" (prefixes and suffixes).
2. Conduct a treasure hunt in which students are to find words in their reading and writing that fit into a word family.
3. Have students search for examples of puns, create examples of puns, or both (comic strips are a great source).
4. Display posters of word oddities, such as palindromes and oxymorons, and have students produce similar displays using examples they find or create.
5. Have students become linguistic field researchers who look at and listen to their own language and the language of the people they encounter.
6. Have students conduct surveys and administer questionnaires about the way words are used. They can graph and write interpretations of results.
7. Have students interview people about the changes they have noticed in the way language is used.
8. Students can create their own dictionaries of local lingo, handbooks for surviving linguistically in their communities, and guidebooks that include their own rating scales of places, music, concerts, movies, television shows, and so forth (all of these require that students write clear definitions).
9. Use games and puzzles as often as possible. Some of the old favorites such as Hangman, Scrabble, and Twenty Questions work really well, but there are also newer commercial ones such as Pictionary that develop vocabulary. Creating vocabulary games can be an effective homework assignment.
10. Involve the use of computers. There are several vocabulary programs that students can use, such as ones that give them practice on analogies.
11. Students can create bulletin board displays that focus on particular kinds of words, word families, origins of words and phrases, or unusual words. Students can participate in word

contests, too, such as finding the longest word used in a novel or the longest list of names of colors of paint.

12. Give students one of the diagrams from Bragonier & Fisher's (1981) *What's What? A Visual Glossary of the Physical World* after removing all the labels. See how many of the proper terms they can find for each part of the object.

Activity 10.5:
Language Study–
Inquiry Questions
and Interdisciplinary Links

1. How is it possible that American infants learn to speak English, whereas Chinese infants learn Chinese, and French infants learn French? Is language innate? If so, how is it possible that a child of American parents who is born in Mexico may learn both Spanish and English? (Link to cultural studies.)

2. Are all languages based on an alphabet? Are all alphabets composed of letters? How are some languages related to art? (Link to cultural studies or art.)

3. How many different kinds of dictionaries exist? What are the different purposes they serve? How many different companies publish general reference dictionaries? How are they different? Why do some people buy one dictionary but not another? (Link to human behavior, marketing, or economics.)

4. How do we acquire spoken language? Is this process unique for each infant, or are there some patterns of development? (Link to a unit on human development and perhaps involve observing young children.)

5. How has language changed because of the development of moveble type? How has language changed with the advent of media? How will language change with the advent of the computer and instant worldwide communication? (Link to history, vocational exploration, future studies.)

6. Why do words shift and change, come and go? Has this always been the case with language? Is this the case with other languages, too? (Link to cultural studies.)

7. What does a map of the United States tell us about language development in this country? How did all of the states, rivers, cities, and landmarks get their names? (Link to American history or geography.)

8. A unit on cultures of the world can culminate in the creation of a map that shows what languages are spoken in various countries and an explanation of how this occurred (e.g., the effects of colonization on language). Students can also investigate

through the Internet what linguistic groups or dialects are spoken in various countries and whether these mark various social classes, present problems in communication, or both.

9. To what extent does the community in which the language user resides affect how he or she uses language? Does language bear any relationship to religion?

10. More affluent mothers interact with their children, asking questions and expecting answers. Thus, the way they communicate actually encourages their children to use language. Lower SES mothers tend to give directives to their children. They do not engage in conversations with them. Thus, their children often have less practice in using language. What can middle school students do to "correct" this situation? (Link to community action, sociology, family life.)

11. In science, many of the terms can be confusing. Students could research the origin of some of these terms, which may lead to an investigation of Latin, but it may also lead to reading biographies of famous people or historical accounts of scientific discoveries.

Activity 10.6:
Possible Topics of Language Study

1. Stereotypes and labels
2. Euphemisms
3. Connotations and denotations
4. Propaganda techniques
5. Persuasive devices
6. Cliches and trite expressions
7. Idioms
8. Sexist language
9. Dialects
10. Jargon
11. Slang
12. Levels of usage
13. Levels of semantic abstraction
14. Various methods of communicating used by other creatures (e.g., insects)
15. Other symbol systems: baseball signals, sign language, codes, math, and so on
16. Communicating through media: dance, art, photography, mime, and so on
17. Development of writing: pictographs, ideographs, logographs, rebus writing
18. Development of the English alphabet; for comparison, look at Cherokee and Japanese syllabaries, Hebrew writing, or Roman and Greek alphabets
19. Language families that have produced current languages
20. Old English, Middle English, & Early Modern English
21. How dictionaries are compiled
22. Special reference books about words: thesauri, dictionaries of new words, poor speller's dictionaries, crossword puzzle dictionaries, slang dictionaries (be careful with these!), and rhyming dictionaries
23. Words borrowed from other languages
24. Coined and created words and word histories
25. Comparing current British English with American English

11

Teaching Media

Overview

CONSIDER THESE QUESTIONS ABOUT TEACHING MEDIA

1. With everything else to be taught, must the language arts teacher also teach media? Is it not enough to teach the processes of viewing and visually representing?

2. What must students learn about media? What do they already know? Why is this knowledge important?

3. Should media studies be a separate unit or class, or should knowledge of media be integrated into other language arts studies?

4. Why have media studies not been a traditional part of the language arts curriculum? Why are they more important now?

5. Is using media in the classroom sufficient? What is the difference between viewing media and studying it?

6. What are the various forms of media? How can they be categorized? On what basis can you start to plan media instruction?

7. How technical should media study be at the middle level? What goals are appropriate for these students?

8. If you enjoy media, but you do not know much about it, what can you do to build your own content knowledge?

9. How can media understanding be effectively assessed and evaluated?

10. What are some activities that would help students develop a better understanding of media?

MUST I TEACH MEDIA?

According to the NCTE/IRA standards (1996), the answer to that question is "Yes, if you are a teacher of English language arts." Four of the standards for English language arts recently issued by NCTE/IRA included statements of what students are supposed to be taught in regard to media (statements are adapted here, but numbers are those in the original):

4. Students adjust their use of ... visual language to communicate effectively with a variety of audiences and for different purposes.

6. Students apply knowledge of ... media techniques ... to create, critique, and discuss print and nonprint texts.

8. Students use a variety of technological and informational resources (e.g., libraries, databases, computer networks, video) to gather and synthesize information and to create and communicate knowledge.

12. Students use ... visual language to accomplish their own purposes (e.g., for learning, enjoyment, persuasion, and the exchange of information). (p. 3)

In order to achieve these goals, teachers need knowledge, skills, and positive attitudes. Thus, the NCTE has established the following recommendations for preparing teachers (adapted from NCTE, 1996):

Teachers of English language arts need to know the following:

- How to evaluate, select, and use an array of instructional materials and equipment that can help students perform instructional tasks, as well as understand and respond to what they are studying.
- How nonprint and nonverbal media differ from print and verbal media (e.g., how television and computers differ from print media).

Not only must you know how to teach *through* various media, but you must also know how and what to teach *about* them.

Teachers of English language arts must be able to do the following:

- Guide students toward enjoyment and critical understanding of nonprint forms by helping students understand the techniques and objectives of the producers of nonprint forms, as well as perceive the effects of nonprint media on consumers. Teachers must also be able to guide students in preparing nonprint products.
- Help students make appropriate use of computers and other emerging technologies to improve their learning and performance, including the use of word processing, current computer software, and other emerging technological innovations.

You must have the knowledge and skills to use nonprint forms in your instruction and teach students about them, but you must also have expertise to produce nonprint forms as well as teach others to do so.

Teachers of English language arts need to develop the following attitudes in relation to media:

- A willingness to respond critically to all the different media of communication.
- A willingness to encourage students to respond critically by allowing and encouraging divergent responses to promote each student's critical thinking abilities.

This means that you must use nonprint media in your own teaching, but you must also draw upon students' experiences with media outside the classroom.

This is a rather tall order even for many experienced teachers. Certainly these are high expectations for preservice teachers. Even if technology were not continuing to explode, these demands would probably seem to be overwhelming, but when one considers the rapid rate of computer access to all sorts of information and constant upgrades in equipment and software, the task seems daunting. On the other hand, many of you have been watching television, viewing music videos, renting videotapes, and experimenting with computers for several years. In fact, this media wonderland may seem more familiar to you than it does to practicing teachers, and your students are likely to know even more about it than you do.

LOOKING BACK

Fifty years ago, teaching media in the English classroom, if it occurred at all, generally meant teaching a newspaper unit. Depending on the community, the curriculum might also have included a lesson or two on how to answer the phone courteously and how to behave appropriately when attending a public performance. Commercial movies were, for the most part, considered light entertainment and not a proper subject for academic study, except perhaps by people in the fine arts areas. In some communities, movies were labeled as frivolous trash or even the work of the devil; religious leaders often admonished youth to avoid movie houses. Drive-in theaters, called "passion pits" in the 1950s, were believed to be a major cause of teenage pregnancy and a general decline in morality. When Elvis Presley first appeared on television, cameras had to remain focused above his waist so that the audience would not be offended by his physical gyrations. The viewing of an educational movie in school was a rare event, a diversion that was cause for student celebration, even if the films were pedantic, boring, and colorless. Radio, of course, was around, but it, too, received little attention in the English classroom.

CURRENT STATUS

Today people are surrounded by entertaining and educational media, both commercial and public, and have come to realize that these media have a strong impact on how people communicate. Media often influence how people spend money, for whom they vote, how they perceive world events, and what they believe about many significant issues. In short, media shape people's thinking. At the same time these changes have taken place, the curricula of schools have broadened. Every subject area has added more content matter to its core body of knowledge. The teaching of English has shifted from a study of literature and grammar to a study of communication in all of its forms. Dividing lines that once separated language arts from speech, journalism, and the fine arts have blurred, even though the complexity of each of these areas demands specialized training.

Stage and screen performances delve into people's worst nightmares, assault them with realities they prefer to ignore, confront them with futuristic visions of chaos, and share with them the grace and honor of humanity. With the flick of the remote control, television shows people, up close and personal, the horrors of war and terrorism, the beauties of nature, the make-believe world of soap operas, the excitement of a fast-paced sporting event, and the sordid lives of dysfunctional people who willingly bare their souls to a talk show host, a live audience, and millions of unseen faces beyond the camera. People are bombarded by news from the world, the nation, the state, the cities, and even the local communities. Desktop computers take us to the nearby university library, to the databanks of the National Aeronautics and Space Administration (NASA), and onto the terminals of strangers around the world. With the punch of a few telephone buttons, a salesperson can conduct everyday business from his or her car or an airplane flying miles above Earth. And the list goes on.

In all of this maze of media communication, what is the English teacher's responsibility? Media cross many boundaries—electronics, information processing, computer programming, mechanics, desktop publishing, set design, photography, jurisprudence, acting, journalism, business economics, psychology, and so on. What are the useful limits for planning instruction? How do you decide what students must know and be able to do when the subject is media? What are the most effective methods for helping students learn both to produce and consume as well as to critique and appreciate media?

Although there is a great deal of controversy surrounding the teaching of the traditional language arts processes and content, not much surrounds the teaching of media simply because very little is known about how to do it well, although Flood, Heath, & Lapp (1997) demonstrate that the knowledge base is growing rapidly. What is controversial is the idea itself—that language arts teachers must now deal with teaching media. Yet to be answered is the question of whether media study should focus on the processes (i.e., How does one become an effective viewer, consumer, user, and producer of media?) or on the content (i.e., How do various media function, How do these media affect people and their thinking, What are appropriate criteria for evaluating media?). However, it seems logical to assume that knowing how to use media well entails at least some basic knowledge of how media function. Thus, content and process knowledge are tentatively viewed as complementary.

Although this seems to be a reasonable assumption, the fact is that the language arts profession has not yet come to grips with many of the fundamental questions related to the teaching and learning of media. Considering the speed with which technology is expanding, it is little wonder that teachers find themselves far behind, insufficiently informed, and questionably prepared to meet the challenge that faces them. However, ignoring the matter is not a solution. The students in today's classrooms must be assisted in learning how to cope in this age of information technology. Although you may wish that others who know more would come along to provide media instruction, you need to accept that the primary function of media is communication, and at the moment language arts teachers are the closest approximation that most middle schools have to an expert in this vast field. Most of those who teach are all too aware of their limitations, but teachers are effective learners. This is indeed a field of study that all teachers should investigate because media affects everyone.

DEVELOPING A PLAN FOR INSTRUCTION

As long as media continue to develop and change, what you do in the classroom will have to be considered work-in-progress. This fluidity and ambiguity is likely to characterize the careers of all who are just beginning to teach. No doubt there will be recommendations, standards, guidelines, and suggestions issued frequently. Some of these will help to clarify what can and should be done in the English classroom in relation to the study of media. At the moment, however, few guidelines exist.

Using what is known about effective instruction in general, you can assume that hands-on experiences are probably more valuable than a detached academic study of media. You can also assume that integrating the study of media with other language arts is probably better than studying it separately. Further, you can hypothesize that the best place to start is with what students already know and that your best direction is to help students bring that knowledge to the surface, explore it, and extend it. Considering that this is an area in which many language arts teachers feel poorly prepared, the perspective of teacher-as-learner within the classroom community makes much sense.

One thing you will have to guard against, however, is the natural tendency to pretend that you are teaching media when all you are doing is using them. Viewing and visually representing are useful processes, but the curriculum must also include opportunities for discussing and evaluating media as forms of communication. Showing a film in class is certainly making use of one medium, but students need to explore film as a genre, discuss its effects, and evaluate its impact, not just review the contents. If they are to develop media skills, students must spend some time examining the techniques of the actors, the scriptwriters, and the camera operators. As a starting point, some common terms associated with filming are included in Activity 11.1 .

Viewing is not enough. Consider, for example, that people view thousands of ads, yet they cannot assess the claims or identify the advertising strategies that manipulate them. They may have seen hundreds of television news reports, but they may have little sense of the potential biases in them, and they are not cognizant of the amount of choice that goes into planning each report. How many people have come to accept unconsciously that all the important news that occurs daily fits a 30-minute time allotment? How many people feel satisfied that they know all the facts about an incident after hearing a 10-second review? Studying media means learning to find information, question, analyze, and evaluate. Using media as an instructional tool is beneficial, but it is not the same as studying media as a means of communication.

TRIMMING THE IDEA TO SIZE

What is media? How can you get some sense of this vast and varied field so that you can begin to make some choices and decisions about what to teach and how to teach it? No doubt there are many ways to categorize media. You may think about *purpose* as a defining feature and group accordingly. Another possibility is to categorize by *intended audience* (e.g., young consumer, college graduate, head of household, child, etc.). You can also think about groupings created on the basis of *creators* (e.g., journalists vs. artists vs. scholars). Indeed, pondering how to categorize various forms of media will probably help you and your students see media from unusual perspectives.

However, for this book, a relatively familiar system is used. As Fig. 11.1 shows, the media have been grouped primarily according to the senses that are stimulated. However, two special categories have been added—electronic and nonliterary print. At this point the electronic grouping contains only one entry: computers. Certainly the computer belongs in the study of media, but it deserves to be listed as a separate topic because of its multisensory potential and because of the number of different subcategories that can be associated with it. Furthermore, computers encompass all of the other forms of media because they can be used to either access those other forms or create them.

You may question the notion of nonliterary print and wonder why it is included here. From one perspective, all printed material is literary simply because it is printed. However, *literary* is often associated

---

Forms of Media

Nonliterary print
- Books
  - Informative
  - Self-help
  - Instruction manuals
  - Comics
  - Reference works
- Newspapers
- News magazines
- Popular magazines
- Trade publications
- Brochures, fliers, posters and announcements
- Fax
- Historic documents
- Letters
- Diaries, journals, and logs

Aural only
- Radio
  - Commercial
  - Public
  - Citizens band and short-wave
- Scanners
- Telephones and teleconferencing
- Audiotapes
- Recorded music

Visual only
- Pictures and photographs
- Works of fine arts
- Performing arts
- Realia
- Transparencies
- Chalkboards

Visual and aural combined
- Screen plays
  - Film
  - Television
  - Video
- Live performances
  - Musical
  - Drama
- Television
  - Commercial
  - Public
  - Instructional
  - News source
- Videotapes
  - Informative
  - Entertainment
  - Interactive
  - Laserdiscs

Electronic
- Computers
  - Software
  - Hardware
  - E-mail
  - Databases
  - Visuals
  - Multimedia
  - Games
  - Instruction
  - Simulations
  - Reference data
  - Reference sources
  - On-line chats
  - Internet
  - World Wide Web
  - Word processing
  - Advertisements
  - Shopping

FIG. 11.1

with literature. Literary scholars, for example, usually exclude the study of nonfiction sources other than biographies, autobiographies, and essays. Instead, they focus attention on the traditional forms of literature—plays, novels, poems, and short stories. Even substantial works of nonfiction have a difficult time finding a home under the sheltering label of literary works. Many other forms of printed material do not even pretend to be literary; reference works, for example, serve a distinctly different purpose and do not deserve to be judged according to the aesthetic standards by which literary discourse is evaluated. Printed forms of advertising serve yet another purpose, one far more closely related to visual and auditory versions of persuasion than to the persuasive techniques used by novelists, poets, and playwrights. According to *Webster's II New Riverside Dictionary* (1984), media are "a means of communicating information or ideas" (p. 438). Certainly these nonliterary print forms satisfy the necessary conditions.

FINDING A FOCUS

As Fig. 11.1 shows, the term *media* covers a lot of territory! How much is enough? Where is the best place to start? First, you should keep in mind that your students are in the middle grades. For the most part, that means that an introductory exploration of media will be sufficient. This could be as simple as surveying students about the media they encounter regularly and discussing their preferences. Another exploratory activity is to have students create simple rubrics with which to evaluate films, television or radio programs, or nonliterary print sources. They can invite guest speakers, write reviews, conduct interviews, and administer questionnaires. They can select and read informative material about media and share their findings in informal groups. In essence, start with what students already know or are interested in learning.

Considering that most preservice teachers have a limited background in media studies, it is also reasonable to consider beginning with those forms of media that you know best, if only from the standpoint of personal interest. If you are a film buff, you can share that joy with students. If you are an avid television viewer, you may prefer to begin there. Perhaps you prefer public radio. If so, you have an excellent opportunity to share something new as many middle level students are unfamiliar with this medium. However, you should also give students the opportunity to share their own preferences and teach you and other students about media they have discovered on their own.

Media study needs to focus on communication. Although you and some students may develop an interest in technical aspects of particular forms of media, that should probably not be your goal of instruction. This is, after all, a language arts class, not an art, photography, or computer programming course.

One of my personal experiences should serve as an illustration to you of what not to do. As part of a program of exploratory minicourses, I once offered a film study class to middle level students. Enrollment was heavy, indicating that students had much interest in the topic. Those who chose to participate watched a number of short films, many of which were representative samples of art film genres. These were not at all what students expected to view. Several of the films contained absolutely no dialogue, and many had a strong theme but little action or what students would identify as plot. Many were heavily symbolic or abstract. In short, students thought these were some of the weirdest films they had ever seen, and they had great difficulty making any sense of them. Using these kinds of films was only my first mistake, though. My second was using them to introduce students to various film techniques—camera angles, lighting, manipulation of time, point of view, flashback, and so on. Looking at film from a technical or artistic standpoint was totally foreign to my students. I learned far more from this minicourse than did students. Most importantly, I learned not to offer it again.

Students can benefit from studying media directly, but the instruction needs to match the students' experiences. Such study needs to occur in a meaningful context rather than being isolated from other language arts learning. A mix of feature length films with some familiar plots, videotapes of some young adult novels and short stories, and a few short films that illustrate some special techniques is a better design. Another alternative is to compare novels and short stories with feature length and short films. Yet another option is to engage students in examining parallel versions of print and nonprint texts. Original novels can be compared with versions that appear as stage plays, television movies, and novelizations. A list of young adult novels available on videotape appears in Activity 11.2.

Although it is important for students to examine media from the standpoint of users and consumers, students also need the perspective of being producers and creators. Media production offers many excellent career opportunities (see Activity 11.3 for a list of possibilities), and middle level students are in the process of considering what occupations might suit them best. The middle school is an important time for discovering hidden talents and undiscovered strengths. This can be particularly important to the student who has already decided that he or she does not have and cannot learn the skills typically associated with academic success. Finding through exploration that one has potential to achieve success through the eye of a camera or behind a microphone or before a computer keyboard may be the difference between giving up and giving school another chance.

SOME INSTRUCTIONAL POSSIBILITIES

Resources included on the list of Recommended Readings for this chapter provide details about some units and activities that are of interest to middle level students. Additional suggestions can be found in Activity 11.4. The following suggestions are intended as prompts to assist you in creating your own media study activities and units.

Nonliterary Print

Students need a well-balanced diet of varied discourse forms and genres, including nonliterary print forms. You need to welcome these writings into your classroom, make them a part of your classroom library, suggest good titles for students to read independently, and provide time for students to discuss these works. Students can create their own versions of nonliterary print forms, too. As they study other content, they can create their own reference books or make collections of information they have discovered about a theme. These can include maps, diagrams, and other visual media, as well as printed instructions and informative articles. They can even publish their own instruction manuals or self-help books after examining and discussing a variety of models.

Although they are probably unaware of it, students are surrounded by history. Through microforms they can examine newspapers that reported significant events when they occurred. They can also examine old letters, diaries, journals, and logs written by people of historic significance as well as those written by the general populace, people not so much different from themselves. These resources can add much to the study of literature, but they can also make students aware that what is current will be history, and that they, too, can be a part of documenting what may be invaluable to people in the future. Media provide a means of recording both the significant and the mundane, but the value may not be apparent until years or even decades later.

In a more contemporary vein, students need to learn how to use a fax machine. Part of this instruction should include some examination of the most appropriate time to use this form of communication (i.e., when one needs to share a brief document speedily). Students also need to learn how to prepare documents for transmission, in-cluding the necessity of clearly identifying the recipient and being succinct so as to control costs. However, this instruction will be more effective and sensible if students are engaged in activities in which faxing is a natural part of their study. For example, they can order materials or request information pertaining to a topic they are researching. They can take part in a pen pal program in which letters are exchanged via fax at least once.

Aural-Only Media

Most middle level students are familiar with certain radio stations, and they may also be more familiar with current recorded music than you are, but that does not mean that they know much about aural media. They may never have listened to a broadcast of a dramatic performance or a mystery show. For example, despite his popularity, most middle level students are not acquainted with Garrison Keillor's work. Although they may have heard some call-in programs, they may not have listened to political commentators, debates, or interviews. They may even be unaware that some stations broadcast in languages other than English.

Some middle level students will not have had the opportunity to hear scanners, marine radio, citizens' band (CB) radio, or ham radio. Nevertheless, these forms of communication are significant, especially in times of emergency. Scanners provide useful information about threatening weather as well as allowing people to overhear the communications of fire, police, and emergency medical personnel. Those who use CB radios regularly speak a lingo that is both colorful and unintelligible to others. Indeed, some of the language is not suitable for middle level students. Nevertheless, it is worthwhile for students to know that CB operators also provide information to other travelers, including details about traffic jams, road construction, and dangerous drivers. In times of war and natural disasters such as floods and hurricanes, ham radio operators are often the only ones who can successfully maintain communication. Some students may be fascinated by the use of Morse code. Others may be drawn to the fact that they can communicate with people around the world at virtually no cost. Although they may never have occasion to use them, some knowledge of how airplane and marine radios function could save their lives.

Some parents will tell you that middle level students know far more about telephones than anyone should. They may even report a fear that their children will have to be surgically separated from the receiver. For many young people the telephone is the medium for 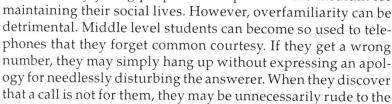 maintaining their social lives. However, overfamiliarity can be detrimental. Middle level students can become so used to telephones that they forget common courtesy. If they get a wrong number, they may simply hang up without expressing an apology for needlessly disturbing the answerer. When they discover that a call is not for them, they may be unnecessarily rude to the caller. On the other hand, students need to know how to cope with telemarketers so that they cannot be duped into providing information that can be misused, such as credit card numbers. For their own safety, middle level students need to be given some tips for responding to unfamiliar or anonymous callers and obscene remarks. They also need to know that making prank calls and other misuses of the telephone can place them in judicial jeopardy. Most students will have been taught how to place an emergency call, but they may need some reminders. No doubt many will have seen television broadcasts that include replays of emergency calls filled with garbled voices, screams, and hysterical statements. Discussions of these can be used to highlight the need for calmness, clarity, and effective speech. Some knowledge of how the 911 system functions and the costs that are incurred may be useful in eliminating unnecessary runs by emergency personnel.

In addition, students need the opportunity to consider how other telephone communication is conducted. For example, students need to be familiar with how cellular and digital phones and pagers work. They also need some knowledge of some basic telephone services such as call-waiting and call-forwarding. Voice mail systems can be both confusing and frustrating unless one is familiar with how these tools function. Participating in teleconferencing requires some skills that are unique to the situation. When people are not in visual contact, how do you know when it is your turn to speak? Is a moderator helpful? How must you speak to be clearly heard? How can you express ideas succinctly so that others have a chance to respond? What has to be done in advance to make the most of the on-line time? Considering the time difference across the country and around the world, when can teleconferences be scheduled? Although teleconferences can be difficult to arrange, students need the opportunity to become familiar with this medium. That is not likely to occur unless they take part in such conferences.

Finally in regard to aural media, students need to know that many books are now being recorded on tape. These are especially good for use when traveling, exercising, doing household chores, or at most any time when students may otherwise be listening to cassette tapes. Although recorded books will not appeal to everyone, they can add much to the background of the student who has a learning disability that inhibits comprehension of printed text or the student who has a visual impairment. Those who are auditory learners may also find that audiotapes of books are easier to comprehend. There is a wide range of quality available. Some versions are abridged. Some include background music, whereas others do not. Some texts are read by professional speakers; others are read by individuals who speak in a monotone. Some readings are dramatic; others are flat. Sometimes the text and speaker are well matched; sometimes they are not. Students need the chance to listen to some recorded books and determine what kind of reading they prefer and how to judge before buying. Additionally, excerpts from tapes can be played in the classroom to stimulate interest in reading or listening to selected books.

Visual-Only Media

It is quite possible that you will find some budding amateur photographers among your middle level students. Given access to a camera, many students will become immediately engaged; others may become surprisingly shy. The first instinct of many middle schoolers is to take snapshots of friends, especially humorous views. As is often the case with a new "toy," middle level students probably will not use good judgment, taking too many pictures of nothing significant and running out of film at the critical moment. Having some information about effective photography and some clear purposes for using a camera may prevent wasted film, time, and money. Keep in mind, however, that good results usually require much practice. Professionals take many shots, even when photographing experienced models under ideal conditions. Some terms and guidelines for teaching photography are included in Activity 11.5.

Photography can be a very effective tool for teaching point of view. It can also link with a study of history, geography, or culture if students have a chance to hear or read about the adventures of news and nature photographers. Both *National Geographic* and *Smithsonian* magazines are excellent sources of pictures and related articles. Through the Internet, students can converse with photographers as well as examine some of their work.

Old photographs highlight the value of nonprint media as historical records. Students can share photos of their childhood, previous residences, and vacation sites as part of an autobiography project. If any are available, they can also share pictures of ancestors as an addition to a family history unit. They can create a pictorial history of the school or community. However, students need to move beyond the familiar to fully appreciate the historical value of visual media. A single photo of Holocaust victims may be chilling, but a collection of such pictures has far greater impact. When one has to choose the few pictures that can be included in a history textbook, nonfiction book, or informative article, what criteria has to be used? What do we know about Native Americans from the photos we have? What do we know about Ellis Island and immigrants from visual images?

Would we feel differently about the Civil War if Matthew Brady had not recorded the aftermath of the battles? Do we think differently about earlier wars because there are no pictures? What biases are evident in the sketches and paintings of Christopher Columbus? To what extent is our thinking shaped by these artists' renditions?

A study of visual-only media, especially the fine and performing arts, opens up numerous possibilities for interdisciplinary teaching. How, for example, has sculpture changed throughout history? What messages are sent by gargoyles on church cornices? What does religious imagery convey to the viewer, and how have these images changed over the centuries? What forces—economic, political, and social—have affected both the medium and the message? Many similar questions can be asked about painting and dance. Architecture, too, can be a subject of investigation. What do modern buildings communicate to viewers? Why have other civilizations chosen particular forms of dwellings? Certainly many factors are involved, but the shape, size, and construction of buildings communicate messages to others.

There is virtually no end to the possibilities presented by real objects that can be seen, touched, and used. Students can investigate how these objects are produced, why they were created, how one goes about patenting a new design, and so on. Something as seemingly simple as a golf ball is actually a very complex gadget that has been developed, redesigned, and perfected over decades. But the signifi- cance of objects also resides in the direct or implied messages they send. What, for example, do the trappings of modern American life say about what we value? Many functional objects also carry artistic designs and language. What do these tell us about the people who created them? We may know little about some ancient civilizations, but their artifacts tell part of the story if we know how to read the objects and images uncovered by archaeologists. We can even talk about learning to read the earth as do geologists and paleontologists and learning to read the human body as do doctors. Researching the history, development, and meaning of objects can draw on student interest while revealing the prevalence of communication.

Closer to the classroom, students can be taught to communicate effectively through ordinary visual media, including transparencies and the chalkboard. They can also learn to create visuals via computer. Developing these images requires skill in summarizing and stating succinctly. Students can also explore some unusual ways to use these media. More importantly, they can ponder the value of each. Teachers are often chided for continuing to use the chalkboard when other media are available. Transparencies, however, have to be prepared in advance. Projection requires a screen and equipment.

Although it may be an old tool, the chalkboard is still readily available, easy to use, and flexible. There is a good time to use transparencies and computer-generated images, and students need to know about these options, but there are also times for using more traditional devices, even paper, pencil, markers, and poster board, as well as the chalkboard.

Visual and Aural Combined Media

Chapter 8 of this book includes many ideas for incorporating visual and aural combined media into the classroom. Learning to view and represent visually by seeing screenplays, live performances, and television programs and participating in producing these forms should lead students to investigate some of the critical elements that differentiates each. What may be of additional value is a more intensive examination of actual scripts and systematic comparisons of different versions. This is the time to explore, for example, some of the reasons for script form and some of the technical vocabulary associated with different kinds of productions. How is a made-for-television movie different from a film? What exactly is a docudrama? Why do some ads for or introductions to television programs highlight that a live audience is present when the acting takes place? This may also be a good time to look at the career opportunities of media, as well as the economics. Some television programs include lengthy lists of executives, producers, and editors as well as actors, camera people, sound technicians, and so on. What do all of those people do? Who pays their salaries? What impact does this have on the contents of the programs? What are the average wages of these people? Do they have benefits and job security? How do they get their jobs? How does one learn to be a professional actor or stage performer? What does one have to do to become a stand-up comedian or a talk show host? Obviously, the study of visual and aural forms offers many opportunities for conducting research, writing letters to obtain information, interviewing in-person or on-line, and using a variety of language arts processes while learning media content.

The extent to which distance learning will influence instruction at the middle level is as yet unknown, but it is having an impact on  the curricula and programs in many high schools. As the technology advances and spreads, it seems possible that specialty programming will become available to middle schools, too. There have been hints of this in some of the science programs available through NASA and various museums around the country. Perhaps students should be involved in shaping the direction of this movement and in determining whether or not it should be a part of their studies. Often these decisions are made by school boards and teachers, but no one asks students for their input. Adults spend much time and effort examining and weighing the options, considering the expenses and the potential benefits. Here is a real-world task in which students can engage and an opportunity for them to take responsibility for making an important decision. Although it is difficult to project the directions that distance learning may take, it does seem possible that students will have many more opportunities to take part in this kind of instruction. Would it be possible, for example, for a student to earn a GED degree while still in middle school? Could young students enroll and successfully complete high school classes offered via television? If they are capable of performing successfully at these levels, should they be prevented from taking part because of their age? If appropriately designed distance learning classes are offered to middle level students, what new skills will they need in order to make the most of this instructional approach? Clearly, there are many questions and few answers surrounding distance learning, but this is an area of media about which all teachers should be well informed.

Electronic Media

The current emphasis in electronic media is on use. Most teachers have only begun to look at ways they can incorporate computers into their curricula and instruction. Teachers can use computers for maintaining student records, producing reports, and generating lesson plans. With links to the Internet, teachers have access to an almost limitless number of sites where they can obtain information, peruse teaching ideas, and chat with other teachers. There are also many ways that students can use computers. They can create and maintain databases, use word processing programs for writing, send e-mail to other students nearby or around the world, create multimedia presentations, conduct research that may include downloading copies of original documents and photographs, participate in games and simulations designed to build skills, interview specialists, chat with people who have similar interests, and much more. However, students must also learn to use electronic media wisely. To do so, they must have the chance to take a step back and think about how computers are influencing the way we communicate. This includes considering such factors as copyright infringement and fair use. It also includes matters of ethics. What language is appropriate on-line? Should certain sites be off-limits to children? Should some content be entirely excluded from access? Who should decide?

Although it is certainly true that the Internet opens an almost limitless number of doors to information, a modem is not a one-way device. Whenever one is on-line accessing information, one is also accessible. Middle level students need to recognize that they are vulnerable. Without intending to do so, they can invite unwanted attention and develop potentially harmful on-line relationships. Unfortunately, too many young people think that the computer offers them the opportunity to role-play. They think they can remain anonymous while communicating in the guise of an older person. Teachers, as well as parents, can help students understand that this kind of game is dangerous.

At the same time, students need to explore other effects of the anonymity that computers allow. One serious problem is judging the validity of authorship. Thousands of sites provide data with little, if any, information about the source. If one is looking for recommended young adult literature, for example, a search will reveal not only those sites that have been created by authors and librarians and other experts in the field, but sites that are designed to lead students into reading particularly violent or even pornographic material. The search is also likely to reveal several sites created by young people reporting on books they have enjoyed. Students will have a difficult time evaluating computer sources. Although more and more managers of reputable sites are including information that allows the user to sort the valid from the personal or persuasive, middle level students will need much guidance in looking for and recognizing the value of these verifications. The article by Schrock (1998/1999) in the Recommended Readings for this chapter is an excellent list of criteria for evaluating websites.

One other aspect of electronic media that students should consider is the evaluation of both software and hardware. This, too, can be an excellent way to engage students in research. How many different kinds of computers currently exist? On what criteria are they rated? What do all of the descriptive terms mean? As ironic as it may seem, an entire publishing industry that focuses on computers has sprung up. One of the largest sections in many bookstores is dedicated to print information about computers, how to use popular programs, and how to write computer programs. In addition, there are many periodicals that focus on popular computers, programs, and even games. Students need to know that these exist. They also need to know how to judge them for possible purchase. Similarly, they need the opportunity to evaluate a broad array of software so that they learn how to make good decisions about which ones are worth the money. Computers are wonderful devices, but like all tools, they have their limitations. Anyone who has tried to read a novel on-line can probably vouch for the fact that having the book in hand is a more satisfying experience.

However, if one cannot obtain the book in print form, an on-line version is certainly better than not being able to read the text at all. Despite the apparent advantages of word processing, some people find that pen and paper or an old typewriter is more conducive to writing well. Teachers can assist in helping students make the most of the power of computers while also helping them understand that productive use of electronic media requires the ability to think critically and make good decisions. The ability to communicate should not depend on whether the electrical power is out or the server is down.

THE IMPORTANCE OF INTEGRATING MEDIA

Although it is possible to study media separately and even to study various forms individually, this approach seems much more appropriate for mature students than those at the middle level. It is important to integrate the use of a wide variety of media into the study of language arts because students can develop their own language skills while consuming and producing media. Viewing a film or acting out scenes can enhance understanding of literature. Appreciation of drama is better developed from attending performances than from reading scripts. Media can easily be used in conjunction with writing. However, in addition to consumption and production, students also need the opportunity to examine some aspects of media more closely. This can still be done even if media study is integrated into the rest of the curriculum. It will not happen, though, unless you make a conscious effort to develop certain lines of thinking. Occasional questions about media techniques, criteria for evaluation, and relevant vocabulary are potentially helpful, but these are probably not enough. If students are to develop some sense of the communicative power of media, then some class time needs to be allotted for this focus. Looking at one script is probably not enough to help students develop a comprehensive understanding of what scripts are and why they are formatted in a unique manner. Rather, they need repeated exposure over time and the chance to examine a variety of scripts with some opportunity to make comparisons and draw conclusions. The same is true of media forms. To ensure that this occurs, you need to choose one or two media study goals for the year, consider how to realize these goals in several units, and focus on achieving those goals during the instruction. If you consciously plan to integrate media study, you are far more likely to make it happen than if you just have a vague sense that you will try.

ASSESSING AND EVALUATING MEDIA UNDERSTANDING

The best measure of literary understanding is continued reading of quality material throughout one's life. Similarly, the best measure of media understanding is the thoughtful selection and creation of media to meet one's needs. Media can be used to enhance society and the quality of life, but it can also be used to manipulate unethically and entice immorally. Your success in teaching media content should be assessed by how well your students eventually consume and produce media. Of course, that is not the yardstick that you will be able to use in calculating a student's grade. Nevertheless, it is the ultimate goal on which your sights probably should be fixed.

What you will have to settle for in the meantime is whatever data you can accumulate about the student's current level of understanding, incomplete as it may be. A sample list of criteria is included in 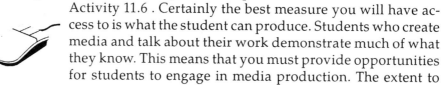 Activity 11.6 . Certainly the best measure you will have access to is what the student can produce. Students who create media and talk about their work demonstrate much of what they know. This means that you must provide opportunities for students to engage in media production. The extent to which this is possible will depend, at least in part, on available equipment and funding. As advantageous as media production may be, there may be so many barriers that both you and students become frustrated. If students do not have access to good equipment or sufficient time to learn to use it well, you must adjust your expectations accordingly. Indeed, you may want to think twice about requiring that students create media if you know that the circumstances will prevent them from producing their best work. Sometimes teachers think that a little experience is better than none, but students may conclude that if shoddy work is acceptable on this task, it is acceptable on the rest.

If media production is not possible or not likely to be successful, then you may have to settle for indirect measures. These can include observations of students' selections of media, use of equipment, voluntary attendance at performances, use of media as part of other presentations, and verbal comments offered during discussions. To some extent it is also possible to test students' understanding of media. Although it is not a good idea to teach vocabulary in isolation, student knowledge of media terms can be assessed. That is not to say that you should teach students the parts of a camera and then test them on these labels. If they do not have a chance to use the camera, knowing the parts is not of much value. However, if they have access to the equipment and can take some photographs, they should also be able to define some common terms associated with photography. On the other hand, having them write directions for taking good pictures is apt to tell you more about what they know than will a vocabulary quiz.

RECOMMENDED READINGS

Bone, J., & Johnson, R. (1997). *Understanding the film: An introduction to film appreciation* (5th ed.). Lincolnwood, IL: NTC Publishing Group.

Bordwell, D., & Thompson, K. (1986). *Film art: An introduction* (2nd ed.). New York: Knopf.

Christenbury, L. (Ed.) (1998). Media literacy [themed issue]. *English Journal, 87*(1).

Costanzo, W. (1992). *Reading the movies: Twelve great films on video and how to teach them.* Urbana, IL: National Council of Teachers of English.

Giannetti, L., & Eyman, S. (1991). *Flashback: A brief history of film* (2nd ed.). Englewood Cliffs, NJ: Prentice-Hall.

Goodwyn, A. (1992). *English teaching and media education.* Philadelphia, PA: Open University Press.

Healy, J. (1990). *Endangered minds: Why children don't think and what we can do about it.* New York: Simon & Schuster.

Lester, P. (Ed.) (1996). *Images that injure: Pictorial stereotypes in the media.* Westport, CT: Praeger Publishing.

Roblyer, M., Edwards, J., & Havriluk, M. (1997). *Integrating educational technology into teaching.* Upper Saddle River, NJ: Merrill–Prentice Hall.

Schrock, K. (1998/1999). The ABCs of web site evaluation. *Classroom Connect, 5*(4), 4–6.

Teasley, A., & Wilder, A. (1997). *Reel conversations: Reading films with young adults.* Portsmouth, NH: Heinemann–Boynton/Cook.

Thoman, E. (1998). Media literacy: A guided tour of selected resources for teaching. *English Journal, 87*(1), 34–37.

Teaching Media Activities and Suggestions

- 11.1 Learning the Language of Film
- 11.2 Adolescent Literature on Video
- 11.3 Media Careers
- 11.4 Media Study Tasks and Projects
- 11.5 Photo Vocabulary and Photography Hints
- 11.6 Some Qualities of Media Understanding

Activity 11.1:
Learning the Language of Film

Common Terms Associated with Filming

Close-up—camera shot in which a single object fills most of the screen.

Establishing shot—opening view that identifies setting and spatial relationships.

Extreme close-up—camera shot in which a portion of an object fills the screen.

Eye level—camera angle showing what a character would see. Also called point-of-view or first-person shot.

High angle—camera high above looks down on character or location.

Long shot—a distance view, making the subject seem smaller.

Low angle—camera is below and looks up at character or location.

Medium shot—camera shot in which an object is of moderate size.

Pan—camera moves horizontally right or left.

Slow motion—a special effect in which more frames per second are shot, but when viewed at normal speed, the action seems to occur slowly.

Tilt—camera moves vertically from up or down.

Tracking or dolly shot—camera moves horizontally along with subject.

Zoom—camera focus changes from distant to close-up (zoom in) or the reverse (zoom out).

Common Terms Associated with Film Transitions

Cut—abrupt scene change or shift in time.

Dissolve—a transition in which one scene gradually replaces another.

Fade—lighting of screen changes from dark to light (fade in) or the reverse (fade out).

Wipe—line passes across screen replacing old image with new one.

Common Terms Associated with Sound Production

Dead track—portion of film which has no sound.

Sound links—repetitious use of sound as a cue to link characters or action.

Soundtrack—portion of the film where sound is recorded or the musical score from a film recorded on tape or disk.

Dubbing—adding sound to visuals or replacing one voice on a soundtrack for another to correct errors or substitute another language.

Voiceover—added narration, commentary, or interior monologue when character is not speaking dialogue.

Activity 11.2:
Adolescent Literature on Video

Many books that were written for or appeal to middle level students have been filmed and are available on videotape. They can be used in conjunction with the study of the novels (e.g., What are the similarities and differences between the versions? Why was this novel appropriate for filming whereas others are not? How does the camera eye alter the viewer's perception, and was this different from the author's intention?), used as part of thematic units, or studied separately as examples of filming techniques.

Across Five Aprils

Bless the Beasts and Children

Born Free

Brian's Song

Bridge to Terabithia

Call of the Wild

The Cat Ate My Gymsuit

Charly

The Chocolate War

The Chosen

Diary of Anne Frank

Fahrenheit 451

The Hobbit

Island of the Blue Dolphins

Jacob Have I Loved

Julie of the Wolves

Light in the Forest

Little Women

Lord of the Flies

Lord of the Rings

The Miracle Worker

My Brother Sam Is Dead

My Side of the Mountain

Old Yeller

The Outsiders

The Red Badge of Courage

Roll of Thunder, Hear My Cry

Scorpions

The Secret Garden

A Separate Peace

Shane

Shiloh

Sign of the Beaver

Sing Down the Moon

Sounder

Treasure Island

20,000 Leagues Under the Sea

Where the Red Fern Grows

Activity 11.3:
Media Careers

Middle school is a perfect time to introduce students to a wide variety of career options. The careers and activities associated with media production and distribution are enormous. The following list should provide a starting point for student research or for considering possible guest speakers who can describe their responsibilities and discuss the interesting and challenging aspects of their occupations. Although students may not choose a career in media, some of these tasks can be done voluntarily (i.e., in a community theater or local history museum) or are compelling hobbies (e.g., using a ham radio, amateur photography).

Graphic Artist	Museum Director
Commercial Artist	Docent
Software Designer	Curator
Cartoonist	Radio Announcer
Film Producer	Talk Show Host
Film Editor	Professional Reader
Sound Technician	Radio Operator
Camera Operator	Emergency Call Technician
Equipment Repair Person	Stagehand
Musician	Prompter
Actor	Teleprompter Operator
Stand-in	Speech Writer
Extra	Advertising Copywriter
Set Designer	Playwright
Makeup Artist	Computer Consultant
Photographer	Programmer
Writer	Systems Analyst
Printer	Game Designer
Editor	Researcher
Journalist	Web Page Designer
News Commentator	Word Processor Typist
Photo Restorer	Salesperson
Consultant	Advertising Executive
Movie Theater Manager	Critic

Through guest speakers and field trips associated with the classroom study of viewing, visual representation, and media, students can be introduced to some of these career and avocation possibilities.

Activity 11.4:
Media Study Tasks and Projects

Play It Again, Sam

Students may compare some classic children's stories, such as *Peter Pan* or *The Wizard of Oz*, with the film versions. This could be extended to include variations such as the movie *Hook* and the musical *The Wiz*. Many classic short stories have been re-created in visual form, some more than once, providing an opportunity for students to compare multiple film versions with the original. Students can consider the different ways that authors and screenwriters shift scenes, guide readers and viewers through flashbacks, or show forward leaps in time. Bierce's "An Occurrence at Owl Creek Bridge" is excellent for looking at how an author manipulates time and how that is captured on film. Students can contrast the original version of *Jurassic Park* (Crichton, 1997) with the movie and the novelization, for example. Or they can compare the movie *Jumani* to the novelization by Spelvin (1995) and then to the original children's book by Van Allsburg (1981). More than identifying the differences, though, students need to contemplate why changes occur. Why, for example, are the film endings of *Sounder* and *The Chocolate War* different from the books? Why did the television producers or scriptwriters decide that Cooney's (1990) *Face on the Milk Carton* could not stand alone without adding its sequel, *Whatever Happened to Janie* (Cooney, 1994)?

In the Reference Section

Rather than writing reports about research on a theme, students can use the information they have gleaned to develop informative articles; these articles can then be bound together to form a book that other students can read and use as a source. As part of interdisciplinary or integrated studies, students can publish their own instruction manuals or self-help books.

Media Humor

One topic that sparks interest among middle level students is a unit on humor. As part of that unit, students can study the history and evolution of comic books. A guest speaker who is a knowledgeable collector can be invited to discuss with the class the qualities that make comic books valuable. A cartoonist can be invited to speak to the class about the origin of humorous ideas, the factors that make certain comics appealing, and the difficulties of producing humorous works on a daily basis. With this background, students can produce their own joke books, collections of humorous essays, comic strips, and comic books.

The Ordinary as History

Students need to be aware that what is commonplace to them now could easily become historically significant. As mundane as it may seem, what they had for breakfast may be a detail of great interest to a historian, archaeologist, or scientist sometime in the future. Recording the ordinary is worth doing. One concrete way to approach this is through the creation of a time capsule. Another alternative is to have students begin a personal scrapbook that includes observations about their daily lives. Although students will not realize it at the time, such a record of one's life can become an heirloom. To prove the point, students can visit a local courthouse and view documents dating back to the establishment of the county. For a small fee, students can obtain copies of military records describing service in the Revolutionary War, ship passenger lists of their immigrant ancestors, court records of important trials, and land records that verify migration routes and patterns. They can collect data about the historic buildings and landmarks in their vicinity and study abandoned cemeteries in the area. They can also study visual information related to historical periods—drawings, sketches, paintings, and photographs—and compare them with ones that document their own region or town.

Media and Mystery

A unit on mystery stories can be enhanced through the use of tape recordings of classic radio broadcasts. Once students hear such performances, they can create their own modern versions, including dramatic voicing, sound effects, and music that creates a particular mood.

On the Phone

Teleconferencing is an excellent way to interview authors, obtain information about distant places, communicate with scientists working at remote sites, and confer with experts about a theme the class is studying. Initially, the class may choose a few individuals to act as spokespersons while others listen and write additional questions that are passed to the speakers. However, all students should eventually have the opportunity to converse on-line.

On the Tube

In addition to perusing commercial television, students can also be asked to research cable and public broadcasting channels. Students need to view some congressional hearings, watch both conservative and liberal talk shows, and view informative programs. Some broadcasters provide free materials and lesson plans to teachers, and programs can be taped (within the legal limits) for educational use. The school librarian or media technician will probably have information about the possibilities, schedules of programs, packets of materials, and so forth.

Chalk Talk

Use colored chalk to create a sequence of scenes on the chalkboard from a novel students are reading or one that is being read to them. If you have artistic talent, you can do this yourself. If you do not, a student or faculty member may be willing to help. Try sketching a scene in advance to motivate interest in upcoming reading. Students can use sidewalk chalk to advertise books, stimulate interest in themes, and promote school events. This writing tool can also be used to present intriguing word puzzles or doodles so that students start each day by viewing an engaging question on the way into the building.

What Is Art?

Investigate how various persons define art, including artists themselves, museums, and legal groups. What works of art were previously banned but are now accepted? What books have been banned? Are any of these works in the school or public library? Is their use restricted? On what basis? Ultimately, what is the difference between art and pornography?

Truth or Consequences

Investigate laws and regulations and voluntary standards that govern the media. What are the laws and regulations pertaining to copyrighted material? Research ad claims. Are they always true? What is omitted? What is misleading?

Newsworthy? Who Decides?

Compare various news sources—television, radio, and newspapers—on a given day or in relation to a particular story. Who reported the story or what stories were given top billing? Which sources were most informative? Complete? Did the use of visuals compensate for words? How are news agencies using computers to increase their coverage?

Media and Money

Compare prices for various kinds of media services (e.g., cellular phone, cable television, satellite television, computer hardware). Create a spreadsheet that summarizes the services and costs. Reach some conclusions about which are the best buys.

Media Advertising

Use various forms of media advertising to detect common propaganda and persuasion techniques. Students can also make comparisons. For example, billboards and bumper stickers are similar in succinctness, but very different in size. How do advertisers make the best use of both media? What are some of the central differences between television and radio ads? Students can also look at various magazines directed at significantly different audiences to see examples of adapted appeals. Another interesting possibility is to look at how advertisements change over time. Old newspapers on microfilm are an excellent source of ads for comparison. What do these changes in ads reveal about changes in American culture? Another option is to have students investigate the marketing industry associated with advertising in the media. Who makes the decisions about which ads to use? How do ad agencies decide which appeals work best? How much does it cost to advertise on television? When are the rates highest? What makes the best advertising slogan and logo?

Activity 11.5:
Photo Vocabulary
and Photography Hints

Vocabulary
Parts of the camera
- shutter
- aperture
- battery pack
- lens
- focusing ring
- flash (built-in or attachment)
- frame counter
- aperture setting
- winder
- viewfinder

Facts about film
- speed
- light
- paper grain
- flash
- care of

Artistic Aspects
- lights and shadows
- focus
- distance
- composition
- background
- balance

Hints
1. Be sure that the film is the proper speed for the conditions.
2. Be sure that the film is loaded properly in the camera.
3. Double check all settings to match the film and lighting.
4. Be sure that the lens is properly attached.
5. Use the viewfinder to check for proper distance from the subject.
6. Use the viewfinder to check for a complimentary background. Consider changing the camera angle if the background clashes.
7. Use the viewfinder to check for shadows that will obscure details.
8. Use the viewfinder to check for your own shadow in the photo.
9. Do not face the sun unless you have special equipment for this.
10. Be sure that your fingers are not visible in the shot.
11. Hold the camera steady. Use both hands.
12. If the shot is crucial and you can do so, take two just to be sure.
13. Try using different angles rather than always straight ahead at eye level.
14. Ask subjects to remove apparel such as sunglasses and hats that hide features.
15. Be patient. Wait for the right shot.

Activity 11.6:
Some Qualities
of Media Understanding

Because of the variety of media forms, a list of technical knowledge would be much too lengthy for inclusion here. However, there are some general qualities or characteristics that can be considered when assessing media understanding, including the following:

- Chooses to use media for learning
- Chooses appropriate media for communicating ideas
- Ensures that media productions are polished
- Differentiates among similar forms of media
- Uses correct terms when conversing about media
- Evaluates media on the basis of appropriate criteria
- Recognizes the different purposes of various media
- Communicates ideas clearly through the use of media
- Expresses interest in media
- Voluntarily participates in media production
- Voluntarily participates in media use for enjoyment
- Recognizes when media is intended to manipulate
- Effectively evaluates validity of media sources
- Takes care of equipment
- Shows concern about the costs of media equipment and production
- Uses a variety of media forms
- Expresses appreciation for effective media produced by others
- Voluntarily compares and contrasts various media

Part IV

Connecting Teaching and Learning

12

Integrating the Language Arts

Overview

- Consider These Questions
- Putting the Pieces Together
- Integrated Language Arts Units
- Thematic Units in Language Arts
- Inquiry Learning in Language Arts
- Reading–Writing Workshop Approaches
- Using Computers in Language Arts
- What Do I Do with the Textbooks?
- Recommended Readings

CONSIDER THESE QUESTIONS ABOUT INTEGRATING THE LANGUAGE ARTS

1. What does it mean to integrate language arts? Is this the same as interdisciplinary or integrative teaching?
2. Is integrated language arts instruction developmentally appropriate for middle school students? What needs does it address? Could these be addressed in other ways equally well?

3. Is it easier to teach aspects of language arts separately, concentrating on one at a time? What are the disadvantages of this kind of separation?

4. If you put all of the content and processes together, how can you be sure that you do not leave out something important?

5. What would a model integrated unit look like? Could it be based on a literary genre? A process such as writing? A content area of language arts?

6. How is a thematic unit different from an integrated unit? Similar? Is it possible to teach a thematic unit that integrates all of the language arts processes and content?

7. What is inquiry learning? How is it different from other forms of integrated language arts instruction?

8. What is a reading–writing workshop approach? What must you do to make this approach successful if you choose to use it?

9. What are some ways that you can integrate the use of computers into the first language arts classes you teach? What are some future possibilities?

10. If you integrate instruction, can you still make use of the textbooks your students are required to purchase or rent? Should you? If so, how?

PUTTING THE PIECES TOGETHER

Middle level educators argue forcefully that all subject areas should be integrated, a topic that is explored in depth in the next chapter. However, many schools have not yet developed a fully integrated curriculum. Even in schools where teams plan interdisciplinary or integrated units, some time is usually allotted for individual teachers to focus on their own content areas. This chapter explains some of the different approaches that a language arts middle level teacher can use in his or her own classroom when teaching apart from a team.

In chapters 4–8 you encountered some of the most current information about how to teach the language arts processes effectively. In chapters 9–11 you studied ideas about teaching the content of language arts appropriately at the middle level. It would be possible to teach these processes and content areas separately. Some teachers do. They teach punctuation, for example, by following the explanations and exercises from a textbook, as if punctuation has no relationship to the writing students do. Some of their class time is set aside for teaching literature. Students read the works, answer questions, listen to lectures and explications, and take tests over what they have studied. However, they may not participate in any speaking or viewing activities or use the literature as a basis for learning how to read or write more effectively or examine how the authors use language to achieve their goals.

Although this kind of separate-skills, isolated-content instruction is relatively common in some schools, it is not the type of teaching and learning that researchers and professional language arts educators recommend. Rather, they urge that language arts be taught in an integrated manner. Even when language arts is taught separately from other disciplines, students should engage in many language arts processes and study the various content areas almost simultaneously. Within any integrated framework, though, effective teachers still apply the best knowledge available about teaching language arts processes and content. For example, even if writing is integrated with other activities, teachers continue to help students understand that writing is a process, and they encourage students to set a purpose for their writing and write for authentic audiences. They also seek ways to ensure that students write a wide variety of discourse modes.

There are several different ways of integrating the study of language arts. The material in this chapter briefly describes several of the most popular forms. As you read and think about these, keep in mind all that you have already learned about teaching processes and content and how these ideas fit into these integrated models. Think, too, about what you have learned about middle level students, and consider how these approaches address the intellectual, physical, social, emotional, and moral needs of young adolescents.

INTEGRATED LANGUAGE ARTS UNITS

Integrated language arts units are designed to incorporate the teaching and learning of several language arts processes and content areas. Such units usually include goals and objectives for learning some processes associated with reading, writing, speaking, listening, and viewing and visually representing. They may also include goals and objectives pertaining to one or more of the content areas. However, in these units, all of these ideas are tied together. The skeletal descriptions that follow, all of which are based on units that have been used successfully in middle level classrooms, illustrate how integrated units can be designed.

A Model Integrated Short Story Unit

This unit begins with a motivational activity in which students read silently or view a videotape of a particularly compelling yet somewhat puzzling short story. For viewing, "An Occurrence at Owl Creek Bridge" by Bierce works well. For reading, "The Voice from the Curious Cube" by Bond is a good choice. Discussion about the story follows, focusing on asking students to create a preliminary definition of what a short story is. Students spend the next two days exploring various resources that contain information about the qualities and characteristics of short stories and taking notes. These resources include printed material as well as videotapes and CD-ROMs that provide information about plot, setting, characters, point of view, irony, and other literary concepts associated with short stories. The next class day is set aside for sharing the results of the research so that all students have a useful collection of notes to which they can refer.

The next part of the unit, which is also the longest, requires that students read and discuss three short stories and listen to a fourth. The purpose of this segment is to give students an opportunity to explore how authors use the various characteristics of short stories in different ways. Students are given a list of 12 to 15 short stories from which to choose. They are also given a list of stories that are available on audiocassettes for listening. They may read and listen in any order. As soon as they finish reading or listening to one story, they write a 3-sentence summary of the story and submit it to the teacher. When the directions for this part of the unit are given, the teacher, using a write-aloud technique and the overhead projector, demonstrates how to compose such a summary using the initial selection as the basis. If the student has listened to a story and the summary is acceptable (i.e., verifies that the student has understood the text), the student is given credit for completing the listening task. If the student has read a story and the summary is acceptable (i.e., verifies that the student is likely to do well on the quiz), the student takes a quiz on the story. The quiz includes nine objective (literal and inferential level) questions plus one short essay question that focuses on one of the literary concepts covered in their notes. If the summary is not acceptable, the student is directed to talk with someone else who has read the story and then resubmit the summary, after which he or she may take the quiz if the revised summary is satisfactory. After completing the quiz, the student uses the chalkboard to sign up for a discussion group on the story. As soon as four students have completed the preliminary work and signed up, the group obtains the list of discussion questions from a file folder, reports to the teacher their intention to discuss, and meets to talk about the story. Each set of discussion questions is based on Bloom's (1956) *Taxonomy of Cognitive Objectives* so that the questions progress from knowledge to comprehension to application and on to analysis, synthesis, and evaluation. In addition, the questions focus on the literary concepts under study. Students are encouraged to use their notes during the discussion, to refer back to the text to support their points, and to discuss with the group any of their own questions in addition to those provided.

Near the end of the unit, students select a literary response project from a provided list that includes the option of designing their own task. These projects include options for reading, writing, speaking, listening, viewing, or visually representing. In addition, the teacher conducts some whole-class discussions about the stories and the literary concepts during the days set aside for project work. Students take a unit test. The culminating activity is the presentation of their projects. Speaking projects are presented either to the whole class or to small groups, depending on the number being given. Writings and visual representations are briefly explained and then displayed on the bulletin board. Other projects are briefly explained to the class and discussed in more depth with the teacher.

A Model Integrated Descriptive Writing Unit

This unit focuses on writing, but incorporates reading, speaking, listening, and viewing as models for students to explore. Several days before the unit begins, the teacher creates an interesting visual exhibit for one wall of the classroom and puts it on display but does not call attention to it. To introduce the unit, the teacher gives each student a packet of activities. The first activity asks students to make a list of everything displayed on the exhibit wall of the classroom without looking at it. Then they look and add to the list. The point of this activity is to highlight the value of observing closely. The second activity is The (Potato) Eyes Have It, which is described in Activity 5.3 in this book. The point of this activity is to highlight the value of describing in detail. Students are then instructed to work through the activities in the packet, some of which are required and some of which are optional although all students are required to complete at least two optional activities. The required activities include listening to a cassette tape of nature sounds and writing as many descriptive details as the writer can that come to mind from the listening. Another of the required activities involves viewing either a collection of detailed pictures or a videotape that contains a sequence of images designed to stimulate various senses. These can be digital photos displayed on computer. For this task students fill in a chart that is divided into sight, sound, touch, taste, and smell categories. Another required activity asks students to bring to class a piece of wrapped candy or a piece of fruit such as an apple or orange. Students describe the appearance, feel, smell, sound, and (most interesting to them) taste of the item. Another of the required activities directs students to read a brief personal experience narrative or a character sketch, taking note of the descriptive detail that is incorporated. The optional activities include a wide variety of tasks drawn from a number of published resources and teacher-created materials. One of these tasks has students write an obituary for a piece of trash, such as a discarded soft drink can or a banana peel. Another engages students in creating a travel brochure for their home area as if it were a vacation spot. Students have the option of describing themselves as an animal or combination of zoo creatures, or they can describe their rooms at home with a focus on how the room reflects or contradicts their personality. Another task leads them through some steps designed to produce a thoughtful character sketch of a person they admire. Yet another engages them in writing several examples of similes and metaphors leading to the creation of a metaphor poem. There is also one that involves them in writing a personal experience narrative about attending an event that stimulates the senses, such as a movie, a sporting event, a concert, or a dinner party.

Throughout the unit, students keep all of their writings in folders or portfolios. All of the required and optional tasks are considered to be rough drafts and writing experiments. Students are encouraged to assist each other informally and share their writing as they go. The teacher moves around the room to monitor student participation, answer and ask questions, and support the writers. A brief portion of time is set aside at the end of each class period for students to talk about the tasks they have worked on (this often encourages hesitant students to attempt a task they thought was too difficult), any successful writing strategies they have discovered, or excerpts from their writing. However, all of this work is considered to be prewriting. The teacher periodically checks a list of completed work that each student maintains, now and then encouraging an individual to do more on a particular task or view it from another angle.

The final portion of the unit is a whole-class writing task. Students are asked to create a fictional beast for a story they might like to write. This can be an especially beautiful, ugly, threatening, or cuddly creature. They are given a list of criteria to guide their thinking that includes questions about the creature: What does it look like? Smell like? Sound like? Where does it live? What does it eat? How does it spend its time? What are its likes and dislikes? If it talks, what does it say? At the same time that students are writing descriptions of their beasts, they are also to draw a picture or combine parts of photographs from magazines to create a visual image of it. In addition, they are to highlight the interesting quirks of their creatures by providing labels and captions along with the drawing. During this portion of the unit, students are placed into assigned groups. Within the groups students are to share their writing and drawing as it develops to get responses from group members. When they are ready to do so, they share their written drafts orally and discuss the best way to organize their details. They also discuss effective beginnings and endings and make sure that each writer in the group has incorporated a variety of sensory details and used especially descriptive words and phrases. A day is set aside when each group member must bring in a polished rough draft for the rest of the group to read and edit. Shortly thereafter, each student is to submit his or her final draft along with the visual representation.

Each of the papers is mounted on construction paper with the picture as the last page. All of the papers are displayed on the bulletin board. This gives students from other classes a chance to see what their peers created. A few days later, after students have had some time to peruse the papers, the teacher asks the classes to pinpoint the parts of the written papers that they consider to be best. After some verbal sharing of ideas, students are asked to write their praises so they can be passed on to writers in other classes. The written comments are collected and distributed to the appropriate writers along with the teacher's written response to each work. If a grade is necessary, it can be attached to this response. The grade may reflect the content of the writing folder or portfolio as well as the description of the beast.

A Model Integrated Poetry Unit

This unit is divided into two basic parts. The first part focuses on poetry writing, the second on poetry reading. However, the two parts support each other. The initial activity in this unit is designed to stimulate interest in poetry and break down any negative attitudes that students may bring with them. Students are not informed in advance of the topic of the unit. Instead, they are shown an overhead transparency that contains several visual word puzzles, sometimes known as Wacky Wordies or Pundles (Nash & Nash, 1979). Examples appear in Fig. 12.1.

After spending some time solving roughly 20 to 25 puzzles on the transparency, students are asked to flip through their literature anthology and stop on any page where a poem appears, but they are not to read the material. The teacher then asks students to explain how

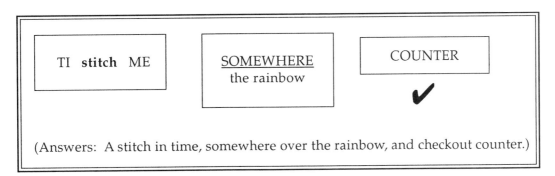

Fig. 12.1

they knew that the material was a poem just by looking. Students are also asked to think about how poems are like the word puzzles.

With that introduction, students are informed that the next unit of study will be a poetry unit. Students are encouraged to share their reactions to that statement. Usually the responses are mixed, but all are accepted. If there is much hostility, the teacher may make some encouraging comments about the fact that this unit may be more interesting than they think. To prove the point, students are shown a series of hink pink puzzles (also known as rhyme time or wordy gurdy puzzles), which are definitions that lead to pairs of rhyming words. Each puzzle includes the number of syllables in each word and the number of letters, as in these examples:

A tiny sphere = _____ / ____ (1 syllable)
Answer: small ball

A thin bird = _____ / _____ (2 syllables)
Answer: narrow sparrow

Enthralled by a cut = _____ / _____ (4 syllables)
Answer: laceration fascination

Students are challenged to create their own puzzles by first writing a pair of rhyming words (the easy part) and then creating the definition (much harder). After they have produced three or four, a few students are appointed to go to the board and write their puzzles. As soon as a member of the audience knows an answer, he or she may go to the board, fill in the spaces, and then write a new puzzle. (Students often enjoy this activity so much that they continue to put these puzzles on the chalkboard voluntarily throughout the remainder of the unit.) This activity introduces the poetic technique of rhyme. Using these pairs as end rhymes, students are shown, through a write-aloud demonstration, how to compose couplets. After that, students move on to creating limericks by first hearing several examples read aloud and then writing their own by filling a grid as shown in Fig. 12.2. As soon as students have some confidence in their work, they are encouraged to experiment with the form by adding more syllables at the beginning or end of lines.

The next part of the unit involves the use of formula poems. Students are given directions for writing a particular poetry form, such as a Take 5 (see the description in Fig. 9.10). After introducing the form, the teacher shares some examples. Then, working as a class, students create a collaborative poem. Students are expected to copy the formula and the class creation before attempting to write their own. A similar procedure is used for writing a pyramid poem, a diamente, and a five-senses poem. The students are then introduced

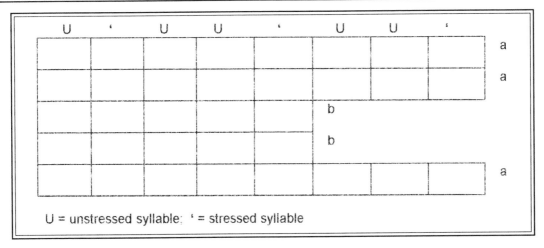

U = unstressed syllable; ' = stressed syllable

FIG. 12.2

to a colors poem, which has no particular form. Although the teacher shares examples of colors poems, there is no class poem created because there is no formula.

Throughout these activities, students are reminded that they must keep all of their attempts in their writing portfolio. The reason for this direction becomes clear when the teacher explains the next part of the poetry writing, which is the development of poetry booklets. Students are given a list of requirements. This list includes the work they have already done (i.e., samples of hink pinks, couplets, and limericks, as well as the five other poetry forms). Thus, part of the content of their books is already done, although students are encouraged to write several more examples and poems and then select their best ones for their polished booklets. In addition, they are to include work on a series of assignments that involve producing examples of rhythms, onomatopoeia, alliteration, personification, simile, and metaphor. For rhythms, they are to create couplets of various lengths and look for patterns of stress in the lines; for onomatopoeia, students must listen to an audiocassette of sound effects and write echo words; for alliterations, students must write and then read aloud to a partner a series of tongue twisters; for personification, they are to read a sample poem and then find and copy an example of personification; for similes, students are given several stems that they must complete; and for metaphor, students read a metaphor poem and then write a description of a familiar person as a metaphor. They are also to complete two additional assignments from several choices. The assignment choices include a wide range of tasks, but most focus on having students explore by reading, discussing, or reciting poetry, and by visually representing, especially in the form of concrete or pictorial poems.

After students have had an opportunity in class to complete the tasks and to share their work informally with classmates in order to obtain suggestions for revision and editing, students are instructed to complete their books outside of class using whatever fonts, colors, images, or other visually appealing devices they choose. However, their book must contain a table of contents matched to page numbers where the various products appear.

While students are finishing their books at home, the second part of the unit is launched in class. Students are given a printed collection of carefully selected poems. Many of the poems are somewhat puzzling by nature, such as some of e. e. cumming's work, Dickinson's "Narrow Fellow in the Grass," and rhyming riddles. Other poems have been modified slightly. For example, the titles of some poems have been removed or a key word has been blacked out. Other poems are included because they illustrate the major poetic devices under study. The collection also includes a number of sensory poems that highlight descriptive phrasing and imagery as well as examples of various poetic forms, such as haiku, tanka, ballads, narrative, and concrete poems. Students working as a whole class and in small groups read, contemplate, and discuss as many of the poems as time permits. Usually the teacher selects certain poems to highlight, but he or she gives students the opportunity to choose others they have questions about or would like to discuss. If possible, the teacher plays a recording of the ballad or a professional reading the narrative poem. As an alternative, a polished speaker can visit the class to recite. This part of the unit concludes with a test that not only reviews the poetic techniques as they apply to sample poems, but asks students to select the better version of a formula poem and support their choice. The final task on the test is to explicate briefly a poem they have never seen but one that is about teenagers and their characteristics.

The final two days of the unit are reserved for perusing the finished poetry books. Students do this somewhat informally, in that they may choose with whom to share their books. Usually they are sufficiently proud of their material to share it willingly with several classmates, although they may refuse to share with those they do not trust. The books are then given to the teacher (who has already seen much of the work as it developed during class although many of the books will contain new entries that students composed on their own). These are evaluated on the basis of completeness, following directions, word choice, grasp of concepts, mechanics, and polished appearance of the finished product.

Fig. 12.3 summarizes the contents of the three integrated units presented here. Each of these units has a somewhat different plan of organization, although each begins with some task that grabs student attention and ends with an activity that provides closure. Each incorporates reading, writing, speaking, listening, and viewing and visu-

Summary of integration of short story, descriptive writing, & poetry unit

Activity	Short story unit	Poetry unit	Descriptive writing unit
Reading	• Short stories • Packet directions • Quiz and test questions • Discussion questions • Concept information • Project work (options)	• Professional poems in packet • Students' poems • Directions, assignment cards, and test	• Professional models • Assignments in packet • Students' booklets
Writing	• Plot summaries • Essay answers • Project work (options)	• Poems • Definitions of terms • Table of contents in booklet	• List of phrases • Responses to required tasks in packet • Polished description
Speaking	• In small group discussions • In pairs to clarify comprehension • Project work (options)	• In small group discussion • In whole-class discussion • In informal sharing • Reading poems aloud to partner	• In small revising groups • In whole-class discussion • In informal peer discussion
Listening	• To taped story • In small group discussion • To audiovisual narration about concepts	• In small group discussion • In whole-class discussion • To oral reading of poems • To sound effects tape	• In small group discussion • To audiotape of sounds • To whole-class sharing
Viewing and visually representing	• Audiovisual introductory story • Project work of other students • Project work (options)	• Formula and concrete poems • Posters about poetic techniques • Examining books of other students	• Creating visual for final paper • Viewing visuals created by others • Examining photos

FIG. 12.3

ally representing. Students have opportunities to work alone, in pairs or small groups, and with the whole class. They also have some options about content or tasks, and they have some freedom to decide the order in which they will do the work. All three of the units make use of literature, and most include some focus on language study. Although students are sometimes tested on their knowledge of concepts, they also demonstrate their understanding in other ways.

THEMATIC UNITS IN LANGUAGE ARTS

Another way to integrate language arts instruction is through the use of thematic units. Because interdisciplinary and fully integrated units usually focus on themes, more will be said about this approach in chapter 13, but it is possible to create such units solely for the language arts classroom. The intent of a thematic unit is to aid students in coming to understand the theme itself. In order to do so, students must engage in the use of language arts processes by using content materials associated with the theme.

The most common kind of thematic unit focuses on literature that presents the central topic, often from several points of view. For example, if the theme were *intolerance*, students might read and discuss one or more novels that illustrate various forms of bigotry—racial, ethnic, religious, political, sexual, and so on. They would also read other material about the topic—poems, short stories, essays, nonfiction books, biographical sketches, speeches, and so forth. In addition, they might view related films or videotapes, interview public officials, search for information on the Internet, collect examples from newspaper reports, role-play conflict resolution techniques, create scripts for readers theater productions about intolerance, design posters warning others against stereotypical thinking, listen to speeches presented by representatives of intolerant groups so as to identify the faulty arguments used, collect data and conduct a debate about censorship, and so on. At the end of the unit, students would probably complete some kind of project or create a display of their work. They should know more about reading, writing, speaking, listening, and viewing and visually representing than they did when the unit started. They should also know more about literature, language, or media. However, they should be experts on the theme they have studied.

A Model of a Thematic Unit

This unit focuses on pursuasive language, the idea that language can manipulate people. Although it uses one language arts content area as the springboard, the unit is designed to make students more aware of how language affects them. It is not an objective study of language from a linguistic stance. Although students may learn some linguistic terminology along the way, they should end the unit with an understanding of the need to protect one's self against language misuse. Also, this unit demonstrates how to incorporate a jigsaw learning approach.

The initiating event of this unit is a diagnostic test that focuses on tricky language. Students are told that this is a diagnostic test and that they should do their best even though no grade will be given. The test may begin with some choices. Students can be asked to choose between hamburger steak or salisbury steak for dinner. They can be asked whether they would prefer to be described as piggish or porcine. They could choose between purchasing a lipstick labeled "purple" or one labeled "ripe plum." Some brain teasers that focus on tricky wording can also be used, such as the one about how much dirt can a person dig from a hole that is a certain height and depth or the one that asks in which country the survivors of a plane crash would be buried. As much as possible, the teacher should present the questions with as much dignity and seriousness as possible. This is a good test to give orally so that students cannot read over the questions and spoil the fun too early. If students do not catch on before the test is done, have them grade their own papers and give them a second chance to discover how they have been tricked.

The next part of the unit is to introduce students to some of the slippery language devices that can be used to manipulate and persuade people. For this unit the topics include signs and symbols, denotations and connotations, euphemisms, stereotypes and labels, propaganda and advertising techniques, and faulty arguments. If possible, the teacher can use an informative videotape that introduces these concepts. If none is available, the teacher can introduce these devices through the use of visuals, quotations, advertisements, taped excerpts from political speeches, and even cartoons and comic strips. The purpose of this part of the unit is to provide an overview of the concepts. Students should finish this part of the unit with some general sense of how each topic fits into the theme.

The major portion of the unit is completed in small groups. Because these groups will work together for several days, the members should be selected rather carefully so that each group includes a range of talents. Each of the groups is assigned to study one of the six devices in-depth. To guide the work, each group is given a packet of tasks. Each packet includes at least five required assignments and several optional activities. Although the required ones are tailored to fit the particular subtopic, there is some consistency among these requirements. Each group is required to research their language aspect by reading and taking notes from several of the sources listed in their packet. Each group is required to create some kind of visual display about their subtopic—bulletin board, overhead transparencies, a poster, and so on. Each group is also required to examine carefully some visual source of information, such as a commercial poster about stereotypes, photographs of signs, advertisements, political bumper stickers, and so forth. Each group is required to put together a booklet of information about their subtopic that explains to classmates the work they have done during the unit. Finally, each group is required to prepare and present a one-period lesson in which they teach the classmates as much as possible about their subtopic. The other tasks in each packet engage students in exploring their device in-depth. By completing these tasks, students learn more about their topic, but they also create more material for their booklets and generate more ideas for ways to teach their classmates. Throughout the unit, the teacher must guide each group to consider what they will want to present, how they will want to do this, and who will be responsible for what part of the preparation. As the presentations draw near, the teacher also needs to encourage groups to rehearse so that they will meet but not exceed the time limit. This is also the time for reviewing good speaking techniques. One of the requirements is that everyone in the group must speak before the class, although the time need not be equally divided. Similarly, each member of the group must complete a reasonable share of the booklet writing. Before the presentations begin, students are informed that they will be tested over the six devices that groups have studied. On the day before presentations begin, all booklets are to be submitted. The teacher checks these rather quickly overnight or makes a photocopy of each so that they can be available for checkout the day that presentations begin. Students who are absent when a presentation is given by another group have checkout priority, but any student can take a booklet home overnight to review a subtopic that is unclear.

Each of the groups gives its presentation. At the end of each, students may ask the group questions. This is also a good time for the teacher to correct any misconceptions, clarify fuzzy ideas, and fill in gaps left by the group. When all the presentations are finished, students spend a day reviewing for the test, which focuses equally on the six devices and how each can manipulate, mislead, or persuade. Also, each student completes a self-assessment of his or her work during the unit (this often provides information about extra work, dysfunctional group members, and effective learning that may not have been apparent during class sessions). Grades for this unit are based on the test, the booklet, the presentation, effective use of class time, group participation, and individual performance.

Whether you teach separate skills units (e.g., a unit on punctuation, a unit on giving speeches, a unit on one novel) or implement integrated or thematic units in your classroom, it is a good idea to include more than one unit in each grading period. If you include only one, students' grades may vary radically from one grading period to the next. Students and parents tend to look for consistent or improving performance. Significant changes in grades can be difficult to explain and defend. If you include more than one topic of study in each marking period, students have a better chance of at least ending up with a satisfactory average that is more likely to be similar to grades earned previously.

INQUIRY LEARNING IN LANGUAGE ARTS

Inquiry learning is a relatively recent development in instructional approaches. It differs from both integrated and thematic instruction in that it is less structured. In inquiry learning, the teacher can try to ensure that students will engage in a number of different language arts processes and learn more about language arts content areas, but this is not always possible. Furthermore, although inquiry learning demands a significant amount of preparation, instruction cannot be planned extensively in advance. Rather, the teacher must respond and plan while students are engaged in study.

Inquiry learning can be thematic or nonthematic. It can also be done individually or in a small group. The key factor that sets it apart is that it begins with a question or a series of questions that interest the student or group. Students identify a question they wish to investigate, a problem they wish to try to solve, or a topic they wish to investigate, which leads to a project they would like to complete. As much as possible, this should be an important question that has no known answer, a real problem that has no accepted solution, or an authentic project that provides a useful service or produces a valuable outcome. The rest of the unit is a search for answers. Often this search leads to other questions that generate a new cycle of inquiry.

It is possible to initiate an inquiry unit by asking students about topics they would like to explore. If all the members of a class can agree on a particular topic, then everyone moves in the same direction. However, if there are differences of preference, the class may be divided into two or more groups. Another option is to begin with a topic that students are supposed to encounter, according to the curriculum guide. Suppose, for example, that middle level students are supposed to study point-of-view or poetry forms. It would be possible to use either as the topic for inquiry. Students would create questions that they want to pursue, such as How many points of view exist, Which point of view is used most often in literature, Where can poems be found, or How are new poetry forms created?

Once the topic and the guiding questions are identified, the inquiry begins. What is unpredictable about this approach is the outcome. One never can accurately predict where any line of inquiry will lead a student or a group. Furthermore, it is nearly impossible to ensure that students will engage in a variety of language arts processes in the natural course of inquiry. Thus, the teacher must be able and willing to make suggestions, recommendations, and even assignments so that students achieve a wider range of goals and build skills in a number of areas.

The more the inquiry topic emanates from the student's interests, the more likely it is that the student will read, write, speak, listen, and view and visually represent in order to gather information and share it with others. However, because these investigations proceed in unpredictable ways, the teacher may have to establish some minimum requirements and think innovatively to create opportunities for incorporating the learning of language arts skills and concepts. Much of the instruction must occur at the "teachable moment" while students work, and much of it must be done individually or in small groups. Although inquiry process instruction offers many possibilities, students can become so involved in gathering knowledge that they fail to learn some of the language arts processes well. The teacher must often search for ways to slip this instruction in, rather than planning for it in advance.

However, inquiry learning mirrors the way in which adults behave. Doctors, scientists, business professionals, and people in many other fields must conduct research that usually begins with a question. They do not set out to learn language arts processes, although they often use a variety of communication modes as they seek an answer. In effect, inquiry learning is a simulation of and practice for real-world investigations. In some cases, the inquiries are very real. Students can, for example, study community problems and recommend solutions to the proper authorities. They can examine social issues and take positive actions, such as setting up a conflict-resolution team or arranging for a school program on youth gangs. Although younger students need to have some explicit instruction about language arts learning added to their inquiries, they can still conduct studies and focus most of their attention on finding answers to their significant questions.

READING–WRITING WORKSHOP APPROACHES

Reading–writing workshops are strongly endorsed by many language arts educators and those who support the middle school philosophy. Anyone who is or plans to be engaged in teaching middle level language arts should be familiar with Atwell's *In the Middle: New Understandings About Writing, Reading, and Learning* (1998) or her earlier *In the Middle: Writing, Reading and Learning With Adolescents* (1987), which is generally considered the seminal work on this methodology. Another work of significance is Rief's (1992) *Seeking Diversity*, which describes one middle school teacher's adaptation of Atwell's model. Several other resource books provide descriptions and suggestions for implementing reading–writing workshops in middle level classrooms, including *Just Teach Me, Mrs. K.* by Krogness (1995), *Rooms to Grow* by Butler and Liner (1995), and *There's Room for Me Here: Literacy Workshop in the Middle School* by Allen and Gonzalez (1998). Numerous journal articles about instituting and maintaining workshops have appeared in professional journals as well, particularly *English Journal*, *Voices in the Middle*, and *The Middle School Journal*. Of all the approaches, the reading–writing workshop has received the most attention in recent years, in part because this approach addresses many of the developmental and motivational needs of middle grades students.

Nevertheless, many teachers are reluctant to attempt workshops, primarily because this approach is significantly different from traditional teacher-directed methods. Implementing a workshop approach involves creating an environment that is much more student-centered, constructivist, and individualized. Teachers in these settings must have extensive knowledge of reading materials that appeal to middle level students as well as broad and deep knowledge of writing strategies and skills. Furthermore, they must be comfortable in the role of guide, facilitator, and learning partner. They must also be able and willing to teach students how to take responsibility for their own learning.

The primary goal of this form of instruction is to create confident and enthusiastic readers and writers. The premise on which the workshop rests is that students who like to read and write will do so. Through practice that occurs in a supportive environment that includes whatever instruction the individual needs, reading and writing skills will improve. When this approach is used, students primarily do two things: They read and they write. In addition, they talk about their reading and writing with the teacher and other students. They also listen to others talk about reading and writing.

What makes the workshop distinctly different is that for the most part students choose what they read and write, although they may occasionally participate in some shared reading, either with a small group or the whole class. In general, students discuss their reading and writing in small groups that they control. They follow some guidelines and models, but they decide when and with whom to discuss, and they generally determine the questions to answer or the type of response they need. Writing tasks are usually extensions of the reading or self-selected. Rarely does the teacher assign writing tasks, although students may be required to satisfy a broad set of minimums. In most workshops, students compile portfolios that may include written papers, surveys, idea lists, records of activities, reading logs, literary responses, journal entries, self-assessments, teacher notes and comments, and possibly photos, videotapes, or audiocassettes of their work. Assessment and evaluation are ongoing and cooperative. The teacher observes, makes anecdotal records, and collects other data continuously. These forms of assessment are used to diagnose student strengths and weaknesses so as to plan for instruction. Evaluation is holistic, individualized, and based on progress. Usually the teacher and student confer about grades. Objective tests and graded assignments are rare.

Another key feature of reading–writing workshops is peer response groups. These may be designed somewhat formally and meet on a regular basis to discuss literature (e.g., literature circles) or share writing (e.g., revising and editing groups). In other workshop settings, groups are fluid. They meet as needed whenever students want to discuss what they are reading or writing, remain together until the tasks are done, and then disband.

Direct instruction is provided mainly in two forms—mini-lessons and conferences. Atwell (1987) described four kinds of mini-lessons: procedures, craft, strategies, and conventions. Procedural lessons focus on how the workshop functions and what students are expected to do. Most of these lessons are taught at the beginning of the year, although they may be used whenever procedures need to be changed or reaffirmed. Craft lessons provide information about techniques, styles, genres, authors, and literary works. Strategy mini-lessons may include teacher demonstrations of reading and writing strategies, in the form of think-alouds, or explanations of aspects of reading and writing processes. Mini-lessons on conventions include examples and instruction about spelling, capitalization, punctuation, syntax, usage, and other language factors that create problems in student writing or that authors use in unique ways. The mini-lesson topics are selected on the basis of student need or the teacher's desire to introduce a new concept. Some mini-lessons are taught to the whole class, some to a small group, and some to individuals during conferences. Atwell initially described mini-lessons as teacher presentations lasting for no more than 10 minutes, but she now believes that they should be more interactive and may extend well beyond the 10-minute limit (Atwell, 1998). Individual conferences with students may serve a number of different purposes—motivation, personal attention, assessment, evaluation—but some conferences focus on providing the instructional assistance students need while they are reading and writing.

In addition to reading–writing time, mini-lessons, and conferences, the reading–writing workshop often includes some provision for student sharing. In some classrooms, this occurs in the form of Atwell's (1987) status-of-the-class report, which marks the beginning of each session. In about 3 minutes, going around the class, students report how they will be using their time during the workshop. The teacher jots notes about each student's plan. Although the primary purpose of this activity is to monitor student progress and keep records of their work, these announcements also inform other students of the task each individual is doing. Many teachers set aside the final minutes of each class session so that students can meet as a class to hear book reviews and recommendations, reading and writing strategies students are using successfully, things they have discovered about literature, papers they have polished, and tasks they think they might like to try next. This sharing time serves a triple purpose of stimulating and informing other students, giving individual speakers center stage for a few moments, and keeping the teacher better informed. Other teachers do not plan a formal sharing time, but they encourage students to talk about their work informally with other students and display the finished products of their learning.

Although professional language arts educators recommend the use of the workshop approach for teaching both reading and writing, many teachers have elected to use this approach for teaching only one or the other, but not both. The more common choice is a writing workshop, such as that described by Rothermel (1996).

USING COMPUTERS IN LANGUAGE ARTS

At present, computers are simply one of several technology tools teachers use to supplement or augment their instruction. In many classrooms computer use is limited to either remediation or enrichment. Of course, how one is able to use computers in the classroom depends on access to both software and hardware as well as the teacher's flexibility, creativity, and willingness to investigate the potential that computers offer. In some classrooms the use of computers is limited to what may be termed "skill and drill." Students use software that is little more than reprinted workbooks or colorfully animated practice exercises. Others, such as *Electronic Bookshelf* and *The Accelerated Reader*, consist of objective tests that the computer can quickly score and store. The defining quality is that the student produces nothing original; he or she simply presses a key or two or fills the space with a word or phrase. Although there is a place for this computer use, it does not take full advantage of the computer's capabilities, nor does it aid students in developing a full range of communication skills.

Computers As Research Tools

At the very least, students should use computers as research tools. Even if there is no access to the Internet available, students need to learn to use electronic dictionaries, encyclopedias, and other reference works. Consider the value, for example, of ESL students having access to talking dictionaries that can provide pronunciations over and over. A student who begins an investigation of a topic and wishes to pursue a particular line of inquiry need not waste time digging through three or four weighty encyclopedia volumes. With a click of the mouse button, the user has access to all the rest of the entries. What is more, the researcher may also have access to video clips, animated demonstrations, verbal explanations, and sounds, all of which aid the visual and auditory learner, as well as those who are generally satisfied with the printed word. If students are to be effective learners as adults, they must begin to develop digital research skills early.

Although most of these are designed for older students, CD-ROMs are available that focus on the works of American poets and selected authors such as Shakespeare, Twain, and Poe. Other disks introduce the user to drama, poetry, or short stories. Although these reference works do not provide for student creativity, the user does control the material to be examined and the order of viewing. The student may choose to combine text with relevant photographs as well as immediately accessible explanations, definitions, and critical reviews. In some instances, the student also has access to sound, motion, or both. Students can, for example, choose to take a guided tour through the Globe Theater. These disks contain far more content than can economically be published on paper, and they are much more portable than a printed collection of literature.

Several interactive children's books are currently available, including Van Allsburg's *The Polar Express* (Houghton Mifflin Interactive). Young children can read the text for themselves, hear it read to them in its entirety or select the specific words to be pronounced. In addition, they can point to almost anything on the screen and obtain a reaction. This may be just an animated motion that entertains the viewer, but it may be an identification of a character, a definition of a word, some background information about an object, or an explanation of the character's motivation. Similar materials for older readers have not yet appeared, but they are certainly feasible. Some poetry, for example, could be illustrated and presented in an interactive format that would allow the reader to access prereading questions during reading activities and after reading responses. The disk could also provide a glossary, explanations of allusions, commentaries, appropriate photographs, information about poetry and poets, and even video clips of polished speakers or the poets themselves reciting the works. Of course, it is possible that this kind of resource tool will be found more commonly on the Internet than on CD-ROM, but the concept is already a reality in material designed for younger students. Of the books listed in the Recommended Readings for this chapter, *Using Computers to Teach Literature: A Teacher's Guide* by Jody and Saccardi (1998) contains a treasure trove of ideas for teaching students of all ages.

Computing to Enhance Student Productivity

One may wonder why using computers appears in this chapter among the approaches for integrating language arts. Although it is true that most of the skill–drill and testing packages do not ask students to read and write much text, many other programs require that students both read and write extensively. Other programs give students access to sound, and some allow students to add their own speech to the material they are creating. They can also add clip art and photographs to make their products more visually appealing, and many pieces of software engage students in viewing. In many respects, some of the best computer resources are excellent examples of what can be achieved when all of the language arts are put to use simultaneously.

Students need the opportunity to explore computer potentials for supporting and enhancing their own productivity (see Roblyer, Edwards, & Harriluk, 1997). For example, students need to become proficient in the use of at least one word processing program. They should also learn to create a database for storing their own information and making it available to others.

In addition to general productivity software, more specialized resources are gradually becoming available. Although the choice is still rather limited for middle school language arts, more should become available in the near future. One program that is now available as shareware supports students throughout the writing process. This program, called *Write Environment,* incorporates much of the current research on the teaching of writing by providing on-line, user-controlled assistance as students engage in prewriting, revising, and editing. Other writing programs aid students in creating a particular genre, such as *Storybook Weaver* (MECC/The Learning Company), which focuses on narratives, and *Write, Camera, Action* (Broderbund), which focuses on scriptwriting.

If students have access to desktop publishing software, they can produce their own magazines, newspapers, greeting cards, brochures, and other professional-looking documents. If they have access to multimedia software, they can produce reports and responses to literary works that combine visuals, sounds, and text. Even some skill–drill software offers opportunities for students to create their own additions. For example, *Crossword Wizard* from Cogix includes many crossword puzzles for students to solve, but it also has an option through which the user can create his or her own crossword puzzle. Other pieces of software lend themselves well to an integrative curriculum. Many of these are designed around themes such as preservation of the environment. *Destination: Rain Forest* (Edmark) is an example of one such problem-solving software program that engages users in a variety of activities, including some language arts tasks.

Language Arts in Computer Labs

Planning and conducting instruction in a computer lab demands a somewhat different approach, one that is similar in many ways to the reading–writing workshop. In this environment, the teacher must devise ways to introduce students to the equipment and expectations. The teacher must also know how to make it possible for students to use a network and a server or other software sources. This may include learning to use a special projection device in order to demonstrate computer use. In addition, the teacher will need to feel comfortable functioning in the role of monitor, guide, and consultant. Much of the instruction in a computer lab must be conducted one-on-one. However, the teacher will also need to consider how to accommodate the students' need for peer interaction, particularly in the middle grades. This may mean that at times students should work with a learning partner even if there are enough computers for each student in the class. Furthermore, the teacher will need to consider what kinds of tasks make the most of the available software. It may be possible for students to use the computer to complete the same kinds of tasks that appear in a grammar handbook or a spelling workbook, but is that a wise use of the technology?

Some of a teacher's favorite assignments may no longer fit in a computerized environment. On the other hand, the computer opens up a vast array of possibilities. For example, a class of students working with the teacher's assistance could design a database of recommended readings that could then be used by other students as a guide for selecting independent reading materials. It would even be possible to create a page on the World Wide Web and make the database accessible to others around the world. Taking part in such a project would involve students in a number of language arts processes while also engaging them in a consideration of how to evaluate literature. Students would have to read, write, speak, listen, and possibly represent visually to create the homepage. For additional ideas and directions, see Leu and Leu (1999) in the list of Recommended Readings for this chapter.

Even when the task is more familiar, such as the writing of a short report, the expectations may need to change if students complete the composition on the computer. It is reasonable, for example, to expect that students who have access to spell checking will use it and that students who can easily experiment with various methods of organizing text will revise extensively. If the task demands support from sources, it is reasonable to expect that students who can search from their terminals will include more references than they would if they were limited to the resources in the school library. However, this presents some problems. Students may need to be taught additional citation forms. If they are to use the Internet wisely, they must be taught how to conduct searches efficiently and how to evaluate the quality of sources. Copying material from the encyclopedia is far easier when students have access to computers. The problem of cut-and-paste research papers, not to mention papers that are for sale on the Internet, demand that teachers reconsider assigning the typical expository report if their students use computers extensively.

The Future of Instructional Computing

At present, most teachers are searching for ways to mesh what they have been doing with the possibilities that computers offer. They see the computer as another way to make what they already do more effective, much as they use overhead projectors and VCRs to add a visual dimension to their repertoire of teaching strategies. However, in the near future, language arts teachers may actually design classroom instruction around the use of the computer. In some settings this has already occurred. For example, many composition courses at the college level feature computing. Some courses are even being taught in the form of distance learning classes conducted through the use of interactive video transmitted via satellite as well as computer e-mail. Other courses are being conducted entirely on the Internet. Although these experiments tend to bring to mind the image of every student attending school by staying at home and logging onto a network, most educators seem to agree that this is probably not a realistic view of the future of education. Learning is, in part, a social activity. To learn well people need to interact with other human beings. Of course, computer users can interact with others now, but much is lost when the communication is limited to print on the screen. What is more, the slow speed of the exchanges may not appeal to middle level learners. Computers can be linked through video, but the technology is not yet polished enough for teachers to feel confident about relying on it. If and when these cutting-edge developments become commonplace, teaching may require a significantly different set of skills and knowledge. Meanwhile, teachers need to seek ways to make the most of the available hardware and software.

At this point, predicting precisely what you will need to know in order to use computers successfully and well in the middle level language arts classroom is impossible. Nevertheless, if you have not already done so, you need to learn to use whatever computer resources you currently have available. It is likely that you will not encounter exactly the same setup of hardware, software, network arrangements, Internet access, and e-mail system that you presently use once you are teaching, but if you understand how one system operates, you will find it relatively easy to adjust to another system. In addition to becoming familiar with a variety of utilities and general reference programs, you need to peruse a number of different software programs designed for use in schools, and you need to think about how you can incorporate them into your teaching. Keep in mind that computer use often stimulates student interest. An otherwise unmotivated student may be willing to study if it means having a chance to use the computer. Consider also the kinds of tasks and projects that can be possible if you have access to paint and multimedia programs, video hardware and software, the Internet, digital cameras, satellite reception, and so on. Think also about how you can make the most of a single computer in the classroom, weekly access to a computer lab, and unlimited access to such a lab. Each of these alternatives demands an adjustment in your teaching approach. At the very least, you must be knowledgeable enough to respond to interview questions and have some preconceived thoughts about how you would like to use computers in your classroom. Hiring officials will want to know, and you need a response.

WHAT DO I DO WITH THE TEXTBOOKS?

When I accepted my first teaching position, my students did not have any textbooks. The department had some classroom sets of various books that I could use, but my students were not required to buy or rent any, and I was not required to use any specific texts. Although I did not realize it at the time, this one factor probably shaped my thinking about teaching and learning more than any other. I could plan instruction from scratch. I was not bound by anyone else's idea about what I was supposed to teach or in what order I was supposed to teach it. Of course, the lack of texts meant that I had to search for material to use, make lots of choices, and create my own activities. However, for the most part, I think this was a better system because I had to rely on my students to define their needs.

Some of you would probably find this no-text situation as empowering as I did, but some of you may feel that you need the support of a textbook, at least to help you get started. Either way, you need to be aware that a textbook can be a useful tool, but it can also be a limitation. Unless you are careful, the textbook can define the curriculum, and that curriculum may be quite irrelevant to the students in your classroom. In some schools and some systems, textbooks are used to control teachers. Administrators may use them as a measure of teaching effectiveness, as may parents. Other teachers may use them as a device for forcing colleagues to cover specific content so that they do not have to teach it themselves. Students can become reliant on the textbook, so much so that when you try to do something that is not in the text, students may be puzzled, astonished, or even resistant. Even more problematic, however, is that textbooks tend to isolate rather than integrate the language arts, although some of the most recently published texts attempt to address this concern.

Many different textbooks exist for use in middle level language arts classrooms—literature anthologies, basal readers, grammar handbooks, spelling books, language or language arts texts, and even handwriting books. Literature anthologies are much like your college anthologies, although they often contain more questions, activities, and assignments. Middle school basal readers are usually continuations of various series used in the elementary schools that focus on reading skills. Students read a brief piece of discourse and then practice some related reading skills, such as pinpointing main ideas or identifying cause-and-effect relationships. Some basal readers come with workbooks or sets of black-lined masters of exercises. Publishers of literature and reading material for middle school students have recently begun to issue thematic unit collections. These are relatively thin booklets that contain a variety of material and activities related to one topic. Some publishers allow you to choose several of these from a range of themes and then bind your selections together into a single volume. Grammar handbooks contain definitions of terms, examples, and exercises. Although these are usually meant to be used as handbooks, in the sense that students should refer to them when they are having difficulty, many teachers march students through them page by page. Many of these handbooks come with supplementary material—workbooks, black-lined masters for duplication, transparencies, and even computer software. Spelling books usually contain weekly lists of words. Most of these lists focus on certain spelling rules or patterns, or they include words that are somehow related (e.g., all are homonyms or foreign words). Interestingly, there always seem to be just enough lessons in these books to match the number of weeks in most school schedules. Language books often cover the gamut. They may have some chapters on writing, some on grammar, some on punctuation, some on spelling, some on effective speaking, and possibly one on listening. Other chapters may cover a variety of topics—history of the language, dialects, research or library skills, advertising techniques, creative dramatics, and almost anything else that is remotely related to language arts. What you may quickly notice about most of these texts is that there seems to be little logic to the sequence of topics, and there is more to cover than time permits.

In addition to several of these books, you may find that you are expected to use some kind of vocabulary building material and possibly even some critical thinking or problem-solving exercises. If the stack of texts for language arts is taller than the students, you may want to question seriously whether this is a school in which you want to teach. Textbooks are useful instructional tools, but they alone do not teach. Sometimes school boards mandate the use of texts without carefully considering that two or more are already in use in the language arts classroom or that the books do not match the approaches used by most of the teachers. This may indicate that the administration and the teachers are not communicating very effectively or that the board wants to dictate the curriculum and methodology.

Textbooks are expensive, a fact that may force you into thinking that you really should follow the books, particularly after teachers expend much time and energy choosing them. Nevertheless, when textbooks are used, they should support the instruction that you design. Although you may not consider it appropriate to do so initially, you should eventually feel free to ignore some of the material in textbooks, substitute other material, create your own sequence, and in other ways tailor the texts to suit your instructional goals. You should even become confident enough to determine that students do not need to use a particular text at all. The best way to approach textbooks is to either ignore them or use them as little as possible until you know your students. After that you can select the text material that is most important for them to use, and you can decide whether that use should involve the whole class, selected students, or individuals. You may even decide to involve students in making selection decisions. Some of the content in anthologies and teaching suggestions in the teachers manuals are excellent. There is no reason to reject textbooks or teaching resources outright. Peruse these sources carefully and glean from them what is best, but use them wisely to serve the needs of your students.

Finally, as soon as possible, become involved in textbook selection. Usually this means that you should volunteer to serve on a committee that decides which textbooks will be used at each grade level. In a small school, you may have to serve on such a committee, but in larger schools and districts that have many middle schools, this committee may be drawn from several faculties. When it is time to adopt various kinds of textbooks, publishers send examination copies for committee members to peruse. This is an excellent opportunity for you to look at the variety of materials, sequences, and activities that these books represent. This can give you lots of teaching ideas, even if the committee selects a text that you do not prefer. Service on this kind of committee gives you a chance to share ideas with other teachers, too. If you question the district or school policies about reliance on texts, participation on this kind of committee, a curriculum task force, or other policy committee can give you a chance to voice questions about these practices and suggest alternatives.

RECOMMENDED READINGS

Allen, J., & Gonzalez, K. (1998). *There's room for me here: Literacy workshop in the middle school.* York, ME: Stenhouse.

Atwell, N. (1998). *In the middle: New understandings about writing, reading, and learning* (2nd ed.). Portsmouth, NH: Boynton/Cook–Heinemann.

Burkhardt, R. (1994). *The inquiry process: Student-centered learning.* Logan, IA: Perfection Learning.

Butler, D., & Liner, T. (1995). *Rooms to grow: Natural language arts in the middle school.* Durham, NC: Carolina Academic Press.

Carter, B. (1996). The library connection: Young adult literature on the world wide web. *The ALAN Review, 23*(2), 46–83.

Claggett, F., Reid, L., & Vinz, R. (1996). *Learning the landscape: Inquiry-based activities for comprehending and composing.* Portsmouth, NH: Boynton/Cook–Heinemann.

Forte, I., & Schurr, S. (1996). *Integrating instruction in language arts: Strategies, activities, projects, tools, and techniques.* Nashville, TN: Incentive Publications.

Handler, M., Dana, A., & Moore, J. (1995). *Hypermedia as a student tool: A guide for teachers.* Englewood, CO: Teacher Ideas Press.

Harte-Hewin, L., & Wells, J. (1992). *Read it in the classroom! Organizing an interactive language arts program grades 4–9.* Portsmouth, NH: Heinemann.

Jody, M., & Saccardi, M. (1998). *Using computers to teach literature: A teacher's guide.* Urbana, IL: National Council of Teachers of English.

Krogness, M. (1995). *Just teach me, Mrs. K: Talking, reading, and writing with resistant adolescent learners.* Portsmouth, NH: Heinemann.

Leu, D., & Leu, D. (1999). *Teaching with the Internet: Lessons from the classroom.* Norwood, MA: Christopher-Gordon.

Mitchell, D., & Young, L. (1997). Creating thematic units. *English Journal, 86*(5), 80–85.

Morris, E. (1998). *The book lover's guide to the internet.* New York: Fawcett Columbine.

Morrow, L., Smith, J., & Wilkinson, L. (Eds.). (1994). *Integrated language arts: Controversy to consensus.* Boston, MA: Allyn and Bacon.

Moss, J. (1994). *Using literature in the middle grades: A thematic approach.* Norwood, MA: Christopher-Gordon.

Rief, L. (1992). *Seeking diversity: Language arts with adolescents.* Portsmouth, NH: Heinemann.

Roblyer, M., Edwards, J., & Havriluk, M. (1997). *Integrating educational technology into teaching.* Upper Saddle River, NJ: Merrill–Prentice-Hall.

Rothermel, D. (1996). *Starting points: How to set up and run a writing workshop—and much more!* Columbus, OH: National Middle School Association.

Routman, R. (1991). *Invitations: Changing as teachers and learners K–12.* Portsmouth, NH: Heinemann.

Sheppard, R., & Stratton, B. (1993). *Reflections on becoming: Fifteen literature-based units for the young adolescent.* Columbus, OH: National Middle School Association.

Wiener, R., & Cohen, J. (1997). *Literacy portfolios: Using assessment to guide instruction.* Upper Saddle River, NJ: Merrill–Prentice-Hall.

OTHER RESOURCES

Destination: Rain Forest
Edmark
  P.O. Box 97021
  Redmond, WA 98073–9721

The Polar Express
Houghton-Mifflin Interactive
  120 Beacon St.
  Somerville, MA 02143
  www.hminet.com
  617–503–4888

Electronic Bookshelf
  5276 S. Country Road 700 W.
  Drawer C
  Frankfort, IN 40641–8113
  1–800–EBS–READ

Accelerated Reader
Advantage Learning Systems, Inc.
  P.O. Box 8036
  Wisconsin Rapids, WI 54495–8036
  1–800–338–4204
  www.advlearn.com

Storybook Weaver
MECC/The Learning Company, Inc.
  One Athenaeum St.
  Cambridge, MA 02477
  614–494–1200
  Cust serv@learningco.com

Write, Camera, Action
Broderbund
  500 Redwood Blvd.
  Novato, CA 94948–6121

Write Environment
Www.writeenvironment.com

Some Useful Internet Sites

K–12 Internet Resources (http://www.informns.k12.mn.us)

Cyberkids magazine (http://www.mtlake.com/cyberkids)

Internet in the Classroom (http://www.schnet.edu.au)

U.S. Department of Education (http://www.ed.gov)

The Children's Literature Web Guide
(http://www.ucalgary.ca/~dkbrown/index.html)

Ask the Author (http://www.ipi.org/youth/AskAuthor/)

Getting kids involved in literature (http://mgfx.com/kidlit)

On-Line English Grammar Clinic (http://www.edunet.com/english/grammar/index.html)

Vocabulary puzzles and games (http://syndicate.com)

Literary magazine for ages 8–13 (http://www.stonsoup.com)

Inkspot for Young Writers
(http://www.inkspot.com/~ohi/inkspot/young.html)

International WWW Schools Registry
(http://web66.coled.umn.edu/schools.html)

Teachers Helping Teachers
(http://www.pacificnet.net/~mandel/)

Eric lesson plans (http://ericir.syr.edu/Virtual)

Teaching units in secondary language arts
(http://www.ed.psu.edu/k–12/units)

National Council of Teachers of English teacher talk
(http://ncte.org/chat)

13

Interdisciplinary and Integrative Teaching

Overview

- Consider These Questions
- Interdisciplinary and Integrative Teaching: What Are the Options?
- Why Do This?
- Generating Themes
- Developing Units
- Community Service Projects
- Getting Started and Maintaining Momentum
- Practical Issues
- Integrating Technology
- Assessing and Evaluating Integrated Learning
- Recommended Readings

534

CONSIDER THESE QUESTIONS ABOUT INTERDISCIPLINARY AND INTEGRATIVE TEACHING

1. What are the differences among integrating the language arts, interdisciplinary teaching, and integrative instruction?
2. Are interdisciplinary and integrative instruction the same or different? In what ways?
3. Integrated instruction sounds complicated. Why is it worth the extra effort?
4. What is the difference between a topic and a theme? Which is better as a basis for integrated units? What are some successful ideas?
5. What do you need to consider to develop good integrated units? How can you ensure that students learn language arts while studying these units?
6. What are community service projects, and how are they related to integrated teaching?
7. How can you get started teaching integrated units?
8. What are some practical matters that may hamper efforts to implement integrated units? How can these hurdles be overcome?
9. How can computer technology best be used in integrated instruction?
10. How can you assess and evaluate integrated learning?

INTERDISCIPLINARY AND INTEGRATIVE TEACHING: WHAT ARE THE OPTIONS?

Chapter 12 provided a variety of options for integrating the various language arts processes and content areas. However, the NMSA (1995) strongly supports the integration of curriculum across subject matter boundaries. Such integrated units are usually planned and conducted by teams of teachers who share the same group of students. You may find yourself in a school where teaching teams are committed to developing integrated units, but you may find that curriculum integration is a goal that the faculty is not moving swiftly to achieve.

The forms of cross-curricular integration that are now in use may accurately be described as *diverse*. Beane (1997) argued forcefully for combining content so thoroughly that one cannot distinguish a language arts class from a math or social studies class, but many faculties are combining subject matter on a much more limited basis.

One form of team instruction that has existed for many years is often identified as a *core* program or a *humanities* class. Usually this approach involves two or three teachers who share the same students and the same classroom space. Two or three subject areas are combined (e.g., language arts and social studies, or mathematics and science). In a core or humanities program, the curriculum is often almost completely integrated, to the extent that it is difficult to tell where one content area ends and another begins.

Teachers who are just beginning to move toward integrated instruction often conduct what is sometimes described as *parallel* or *reinforcement* teaching. Two or more teachers, usually from the so-called academic areas, teach a unit in tandem. They may resequence lessons or rearrange topics they have taught in prior years so that students encounter similar material in two or more classes. For example, a science teacher and a math teacher may teach a unit on the metric system simultaneously. A language arts teacher may have students study *Shades of Gray,* a novel by Reed (1989) about the effects of the Civil War, while students are studying this historical period in social studies. In both classes the same skills and content are reinforced, but students are quite aware that one class is language arts and the other social studies. Although parallel or reinforcement teaching is interdisciplinary, each content area remains distinct.

Complementary team teaching usually involves teachers from several areas who share the same students. These teachers work together to select a common topic, theme, or issue that will be studied for a limited time (e.g., a two-week unit). Often the teachers set some goals as a group, but each teacher usually designs his or her classroom activities. Complementary teaching crosses subject matter boundaries, but again each subject area can be easily recognized. Students can readily distinguish between language arts class and math class, for example, even though in both classes they are studying how symbol systems have developed or the prevalence of patterns in everyday life.

A more complicated form of team instruction is sometimes labeled *webbed* teaching. Teachers from most or all areas who share the same students choose a topic. Often this is a topic directly related to one of the subject areas, such as pollution (science), the Industrial Revolution (social studies), the stock market (mathematics), or mass media (language arts). Once the topic is selected, teachers create a semantic web of related teaching ideas, and they work very closely to identify the concepts and skills that students are to learn. These units generally focus on content knowledge that students are expected to master. Projects and activities are created cooperatively by the teachers, who may also redesign their schedules to provide some time blocks that are longer than the usual class periods. Webbed teaching highlights the strong links among the subject areas, and the class activities readily cross discipline boundaries so that the lines of demarcation blur. Students no longer study science or language arts; instead, they study the content itself, using science and language arts skills.

The ultimate version of teamed instruction is *integrative* teaching. All teachers from all areas who share the same group of students work together. In integrative teaching, the theme, issue, or problem is one that develops from student interests and concerns. Working in conjunction with students, teachers design projects that focus on the theme. Because the classroom activities are usually involved and complex, block scheduling is used. When the instruction is fully integrated, the goals of all the disciplines are interwoven within the unit so that students can no longer distinguish one subject from another. Students may choose, for example, to study the effects of urban development on the natural resources in their area. As they collect and test water samples, record observations, peruse old maps of the region, interview residents, photograph construction sites, attend zoning board hearings, and take part in a variety of other activities, they use all of their language arts and social studies skills, scientific knowledge, mathematical processes, knowledge of health, artistic abilities, and so on.

No matter which form of cross-disciplinary, integrated instruction is used, you must be aware of a potential pitfall. You must make sure that language arts is actually taught as well as used. Language arts should not be reduced simply to a service role (i.e., a means for learning other content) without an identity and purpose of its own. A well-planned interdisciplinary or integrative unit will still achieve specific language arts goals and objectives.

WHY DO THIS?

As you may imagine, integrated instruction is difficult to plan, conduct, and assess. Even parallel and complementary teaching demand more time and effort than teaching in isolation. The task becomes even more challenging when more teachers are involved and the subject areas are more closely linked. The more the divisions between subject areas blur, the more a teacher must provide instruction in disciplines other than his or her specialty. In fact, the NMSA has recommended that all who plan to teach at the middle level should complete more than one content major in college in order to be prepared for this challenge (NMSA, 1996; see also McEwin & Dickinson, 1995).

There are, however, several reasons for striving to create an integrated curriculum. To begin, it is authentic. It is the way people behave and learn in the real world. Scientists must read and write and calculate. Business managers use skills from many academic disciplines simultaneously. Young children learn language without studying it directly. Rather, their learning is embedded in everyday activities. Similarly, integrated instruction uses the human capacity to construct meaning from complex and interwoven events and endeavors. It is more coherent and meaningful to students because it builds bridges among the subject areas. When teachers work in isolation, they may be unaware of what students are studying in other classes. Without realizing that they are doing so, they may repeat or even contradict each other. Integrated instruction has the potential for being more efficient because there is less repetition but more concentrated reinforcement. Teachers and students who have participated in integrated instruction report that it enhances student motivation, stimulates curiosity, and prompts higher-order thinking. Integrated instruction can increase flexibility through the use of varied groupings and differentiated activities that match each student's rate of learning growth. Because of the diversity of projects and activities, students can make better use of their particular learning styles and strengths. Integrated instruction encourages teachers to share both content and pedagogical knowledge. In effect, teachers teach each other as well as teaching students. Many teachers say that this kind of professional development stimulates their own curiosity and rekindles their enthusiasm for teaching. Because the learning is hands-on, integrated instruction offers opportunities for teachers to demonstrate and model learning processes. When teachers work together, they can make better use of resources and facilities. Finally, integrated instruction encourages cooperation and collaboration among all who are involved.

It certainly appears that integrated instruction has many values, but possibilities are not realities. Whether this kind of instruction will be more educational than other forms of learning depends on many factors. This is a very different kind of teaching and learning, one that demands much from both teachers and students. First attempts may not be as successful as you may hope.

GENERATING THEMES

For the purpose of clarity in this book, topics are defined as single words or noun phrases that identify a subject for study, such as *war*, *animals*, *team sports*, or *friendship*. Themes identify a topic, but they also express a point of view about that topic. "War is hell," for example, is a theme, as is "the value of sports in America," as both express an opinion. Even the phrase "the controversy over endangered animals" expresses the idea that there are valid arguments on both sides of the issue. "Friendships, fleeting and forever" points out a direction that can guide instruction whereas the topic *friendship* can include just about anything.

Although many thematic units are designed around single words or phrases, you may find that units are more manageable if the theme is phrased as a question (e.g., How many forms of discrimination exist? or Is there more violence today than in the past?). Starting with a question, such as What is humor? or Who lives in my home state? can give direction to the unit and guide student inquiry. A unit developed around a question such as Why must we save the rain forests? would be quite different from a unit that evolves from the question Should we save the rain forests? A topic such as "communication" or even "modern communication" offers many possibilities, but little direction. However, if this topic were developed into a thematic statement, such as "communication overload in today's world" or "the future of communication," teachers and students would have some boundaries, but they will also have many alternatives from which to choose. A topic such as "murder and mayhem" may attract much student interest, but it may also produce some undesirable areas of investigation. However, if the topic were restated as a theme, such as "crime: past and present" or "the detrimental effects of murder and mayhem," the unit should encourage students to treat the topic more objectively or maturely, rather than seeking the inflammatory or repugnant. Along the same line, Tomlinson (1998) recommended the use of concepts and principles as the basis for integrated units, because she believed that concept-based study is more powerful in terms of the learning it generates. Good themes indicate what it is that students are supposed to learn. Well-designed units build understanding of a thematic concept. By the time students finish a unit, they should be able to demonstrate their grasp of the theme and its related concepts.

Themes can be generated from many sources. A sample of possible themes appears in Fig. 13.1. Broad topics, such as *patterns and probability*, generally offer more possibilities for integrating all of the subject areas naturally. Other possible topics, such as *justice and equality*, are a bit more narrow.

DEVELOPING UNITS

According to Strubbe (1990), students who have taken part in interdisciplinary learning report that successful units include the following characteristics:

- relevant topics,
- clear goals and objectives,

Unit Theme Possibilities

Seeing possibilities by making new connections
Justice and equality—same or different?
Fact, fiction, & fantasy—Where are the boundaries?
The more things change, the more they stay the same (constants & changes)
Weird and wonderful—looking at human behavior
Life in the future—better or worse?
People as symbol makers (symbol systems and their meanings)
Life is filled with mysteries and surprises
Telling the whole truth—the history of———(state, town, city, etc.)
Actions, reactions, and interactions—how things work
Looking at the business world—pros and cons
Is conflict always bad?
Solving ecological problems
Dinosaurs—past and present
Struggle against or live in harmony with nature?
What can we learn from whales and other sea creatures?
The effects of technology—Where have we been and where are we going?
Biases and discrimination—Is just a little too much?
What is a good neighbor?
Perplexing and purposeful patterns and parallels
Cultural diversity—friends and foes
Learning a lesson or two from insects
Interesting questions
National parks—the tension between use and preservation
Feet speak—What is important about shoes?
Are all deserts dry?
The Renaissance and why it happened
People worth knowing (biography)
Why do people create? Inventions and the people behind them
Environment is a matter of perspective
Communications—problems & solutions
Seeing yourself—what makes you unique?
Language and languages—words, symbols, and actions
Finding and evaluating information
Choices—making the most of opportunities
Generations—sex, health, & genetics
Taking a stand—believers and beliefs
Adventures and adventurers—When is it worth taking a risk?
Cemetery study—views of death and dying
Careers—Can you be anything you want to be?
Across time and space—linking past, present, and future
Friendships—tried and true
Problems—solved and unresolved
Is it a small world after all?
Read all about it—how media influence people

FIG. 13.1

- variety in topics, activities, and groupings,
- choice of topics, projects, and groupings,
- adequate time,
- focus on processes, products, or both,
- field trips,
- group cooperation,
- sharing, and
- community involvement.

In *Interdisciplinary Inquiry in Teaching and Learning*, Martinello and Cook (1994) suggested the following guidelines for designing theme studies:

1.) Select a theme.

2.) Develop a web of related ideas and activities.

3.) Form questions to guide student inquiry.

4.) Identify concepts; formulate generalizations. (What will students learn?)

5.) Check against accepted standards for curriculum.

6.) Map the general sequence. (Sketch a general time line.)

7.) Use resources to explore questions. (Are enough resources available?)

8.) Develop ideas for learning-activity clusters. (How can activities be grouped most effectively?)

9.) Identify content and process objectives.

10.) Design learning activities.

11.) Choose culminating projects.

12.) Organize specific scope and sequence; check for integrity and coherence. (Will the unit achieve the goals? Does one learning activity lead to the next? Will students have the skills they need to succeed?)

13.) Decide on record keeping, reporting, and ongoing assessment.

Although these guidelines are useful, the list seems a bit overwhelming. Following all of these instructions may lead to a unit that is so tightly structured that little room remains for building on student interest and incorporating the flexibility necessary to keep students engaged. Consider using this list at first, but as you and your students become more familiar with integrated units, you may want to involve students in planning them. Students can help select the theme, develop the web of related ideas, and formulate questions. They can even categorize the ideas to create clusters, as well as suggest learning activities and culminating projects. They can also assume some of the responsibility for keeping records, reporting progress, and assessing their performance.

COMMUNITY SERVICE PROJECTS

Attention has recently been turned toward the potential values of engaging students in community service projects. Although the programs are controversial, some high schools now require that students perform voluntary service within the local community before they can graduate. The interest in such projects has also risen in many middle schools across the country (e.g., see Erb, 1996). Developmentally, middle level students are interested in social concerns—pollution, the homeless, violence, abortion, animal rights, pornography, and so on. They often have opinions about political issues, censorship, the use of drugs, cheating, shoplifting, and other topics that concern their parents and the adults around them. Many students take part in civic activities, and others join religious and social organizations that engage in service work. Others feel the desire to do something positive to improve the world or their community, but they have no outlet for taking action.

Teachers who have created integrated units of instruction often find that students select themes related to global and local matters of concern. When this occurs, including some kind of community service project is a natural addition. A unit on pollution, for example, may include cleaning a section of highway or waterway, clearing an unsightly vacant lot, planting trees at a local playground, or organizing a recycling center. A unit on growing up and growing old may include regular visits to a home for the elderly, assisting in a geriatric ward in the local hospital, volunteering at a day care center, or collecting oral histories of elderly residents and compiling them into a book that is added to the public library collection. Depending on the unit topic, students can attend meetings of various organizations, such as Students Against Drunk Driving (SADD), a local historical society, Planned Parenthood, or friends of a museum or zoo, just to see what these groups do. They can take part in building a Habitat for Humanity home. Through the Internet, they can investigate the background and current activities of various activist groups, although this should be done with parental permission and accompanied with discussion of the pros and cons of the positions taken.

Many middle level students have a need to be heard and noticed. Others question their self-worth and wonder what niche in society they can fill and what they can do to be of use. Some find it difficult to be accepted by their peers. Engaging in community service projects or taking part in global efforts such as the United Nations Children's Fund (UNICEF) or the American Red Cross may help middle level students feel important. They need to know that they can make a difference now. You can help them by looking for ways to introduce voluntary service projects within the school curriculum. Integrated instruction often opens the doors to civic participation and involvement that can last a lifetime.

GETTING STARTED AND MAINTAINING MOMENTUM

If you are assigned to a team of teachers, you may find that not all are interested in integrating instruction. Being the "new kid on the block," you may not feel that you can or should assume a leadership role at first. As much as you may want to participate in interdisciplinary or integrative teaching, you may have to be patient. The best way to begin is to find those who are willing to participate, even if that is just one other person on your team. If there are no teams or no one on your team is willing to collaborate, locate others in the building who are. Work with them to plan something that can be done as an extracurricular project or an exploratory course. Consider the possibility of cooperatively planning a unit for future use and then requesting reassignment to another team so that the unit can be attempted. Even if you never have the opportunity to implement the unit, you and the other faculty members will benefit from the communication and sharing that is involved in planning.

Start small. If integrated instruction is not high on the priority list in the school, do not force it on others. Integrate within your own classroom. Try to develop some units that parallel or complement what other team members are doing, even if they are not willing to reciprocate. If you can collaborate with other team members, then set a goal to plan one relatively brief unit to be used near the end of the year or implemented the following year. Expand gradually to find your limits as well as the limits of your team members and students. Integrated learning can be exciting, but it can also be quite stressful for both teachers and students. Do not overdo it.

If other faculty are willing to try some integrated instruction, select a broad theme that naturally fits the subject areas involved. That way teachers will not have to step out of their content comfort zones so far that they feel uneasy. Avoid stretching a subject area just to make it fit the theme. If the teachers feel that they are wasting valuable time teaching the theme when they need to be teaching more of their content, their enthusiasm for integrated instruction will diminish. As much as possible, start with the easiest and most sensible approach and activities. Keep in mind that students, too, may have to be eased into this different kind of learning.

The first unit needs to be planned with extraordinary care. Consider in advance all of the possible things that can go wrong and revise the plan to avoid these pitfalls. Arrange to continue meeting as a team on a regular basis after the unit is under way. Some of this time should be set aside for assessing how the unit is progressing and what must be done to keep the work on track and moving ahead. Sufficient time must be set aside for learning the unit material. Similarly, sufficient time must be provided for teacher learning. Expect to make mistakes. Be flexible. Evaluate what you do carefully and thoroughly, but do not wait until the unit is finished before assessing.

As you plan and teach the unit, communicate with other faculty, staff, and administrators. They need to know what you are doing, but they may also be able to provide suggestions and materials that will be useful to you and students. Look beyond the school walls for resources. There may be people in the local community who have special expertise that they will gladly share if asked. Local libraries, museums, civic groups, and businesses may provide books, guidance, artifacts, volunteers, or monetary support. Keep parents informed, too. Positive public relations may reveal additional resources, but more importantly, positive support from parents can make the unit run much more smoothly.

PRACTICAL ISSUES

Curriculum integration has many potential benefits, but all teachers work within the context of practical considerations that may limit the degree of integration that is possible.

Timing

If the district will be opening a new school the next year and several faculty members will be transferring, then this is probably not the right time for attempting integrated learning. If a significant number of faculty members will be retiring soon, they are apt to be reluctant to attempt a new way of teaching. If the school is overcrowded and understaffed to the extent that everyone is already overextended, teachers will not have enough time or energy to devote to effective planning and communication until the staffing situation is resolved. If this is the year that the school or district is undergoing state-mandated changes or an accreditation examination, then integrating instruction may need to be delayed. Teachers never have enough time, but if they feel that curriculum integration is too much to bear with all the other obligations they have to fulfill, integrated teaching will not succeed.

Not only must teachers have the time for planning, but they must also have a schedule that makes it possible for all the participants to meet on a regular basis. Some teams meet every day; others meet once a week. Some teams vary the frequency of team meetings depending on need. They may meet frequently during the initial planning stages, less frequently when they are collecting materials and designing activities, and then more frequently while the unit is in progress. A common planning time is the best situation, but some teams must meet before or after school or during lunch. However, in many schools, teachers have assigned duties, family responsibilities, or coaching activities that make such meetings impossible. One alternative is to use e-mail, but this may not produce as rich an interchange of ideas as face-to-face meetings. If there is no time when participants can meet to plan, integrating the curriculum will be difficult if not impossible.

Integrated instruction does have a significant time advantage, though. Through shared responsibility, integrated instruction offers the chance to create learning opportunities that most teachers find too complicated or time-consuming to tackle on their own. When instruction is separated by disciplines, many teachers are reluctant to plan a field trip, for example, because it would interrupt the work of other teachers, as few field trips can be completed in a single class period. Teachers often feel that field trips take too much time and energy—garnering support from the administration, arranging transportation, obtaining parent permission, contacting the site to purchase tickets and schedule the visit, convincing other teachers to assist as chaperons, preparing students to conduct themselves appropriately, and so on. However, when the responsibilities can be shared among team members, arranging field trips does not seem so daunting. In fact, some teams conduct extended field trips with middle level students that involve traveling, camping, canoeing, and even archaeological excavating.

Whether the event is a field trip, a guest speaker, or a performing group, the team needs to collaborate to ensure that the arrangements are complete and do not conflict with the plans of others. Scheduling a visit by a mime troupe the same day that the band instructor intends to conduct the final rehearsal for an evening performance is not a good way to win the support of other faculty members.

Curriculum Mandates

Teachers have the responsibility of ensuring that students meet the requirements set forth by the state and the local district. Sometimes these goals and objectives are broad and flexible; sometimes they are narrow and rigid. Sometimes the goals and objectives in the various subject areas can easily be interwoven; sometimes they cannot. If, for example, the state requires that students must study state government and pass a competency test before they begin high school or if students have an opportunity to complete an algebra course for high school credit while still enrolled in middle school, curriculum integration may be difficult to achieve. One alternative is to exclude the subject matter area that cannot be changed. Another possibility is to design one or more units around the content of the inflexible discipline. Nevertheless, unless the goals and objectives in several content areas link naturally, curriculum integration will be quite challenging to plan.

Grouping of Students

Another practical issue concerns grouping students. The complex projects and activities usually associated with curriculum integration demand that students have some skills and knowledge, as well as some capacity for working with others and learning independently. If students have only experienced teacher-directed instruction previously, they must be taught how to learn in small groups and on their own. When classes include a heterogeneous mix of students, peers can teach each other. However, if one or more classes contain a high concentration of students who are unmotivated and lack skills, which is often the case when students are tracked, projects and activities will probably need to be modified. All in all, homogeneous grouping by ability makes integrated instruction more difficult. Furthermore, teachers need to consider carefully how to group students effectively within the classrooms. Integrated instruction can be designed to provide opportunities for teachers to work with small groups while other students engage in activities independently under the guidance of faculty team members. However, these arrangements must be carefully coordinated. If they are not, two or more teachers may plan to meet with particular students at the same time. Not only will students be frustrated by this conflict, but not enough teachers will be available to monitor and assist the rest of the class.

Conflicting Teaching Strategies

Yet another practical issue that must be considered is instructional strategies. Teaching teams must think seriously about their organization and management procedures so as to avoid contradictions. If one teacher allows students to move about the classroom freely, whereas another controls movement, students may find themselves in a perpetual quandary if these two teachers share instructional space. Teachers may need to reach compromises about these differences in advance. Varying instructional strategies helps to maintain student interest and enthusiasm, but too much variety during integrated instruction can be frustrating for students, especially when they are tackling projects that demand concentrated effort and time. The team will need to reserve some blocks of uninterrupted time for students to work. Additionally, the team will need to coordinate their plans to avoid duplication of strategies. For example, guest speakers or formal lectures should not be scheduled on the same day in several classes. Student presentations should not occur day after day, period after period, at the end of a unit. Similarly, students should not be required to read silently in class after class.

Space

Space can be a problem. At times it can be advantageous for all students on a team to meet for some special activity, such as the appearance of a guest speaker. Whether this is possible may depend on whether there is sufficient and appropriate space for the event. Although it may be more efficient to show a movie to all of the students at once, it may not be wise to do so if the only available space is a cafeteria that has lots of windows without drapes or a commons area that has a skylight. Some schools have open learning spaces that permit the combining of one or more classes, but most do not. If the classrooms in which students on a team meet are scattered throughout the building, coordinating integrated learning is more challenging. Even when classrooms of student teams are closely grouped, the tendency to isolate one discipline from another persists.

Space can also be a problem when students engage in projects and productions that evolve over several days. Most classrooms do not have adequate storage for such works-in-progress. Unless the faculty team plans carefully, teachers can find themselves awash in visual projects, cameras, art supplies, unlabeled tapes, and all sorts of other learning materials. This can create other problems—theft, intentional and accidental damage, lost or misplaced items, and so on. To avoid these kinds of difficulties, the faculty team must plan in advance and create some systems for storing materials and keeping records of equipment. It may even be necessary to set aside one classroom just for storage.

In other ways, though, integrated instruction may be more efficient. The team may decide, for instance, to have each student maintain a single portfolio for the unit rather than keeping one for each subject matter class. This can save space and avoid needless duplication.

Evaluation and Reporting Procedures

Although there are other practical issues that can be a hindrance to curriculum integration in particular schools, one that seems to affect many teachers who contemplate the shift is evaluation. In most schools, evaluation systems are designed around separate subjects. Report cards, for example, usually provide space for a grade in each discipline. Participation in extracurricular activities may hinge on the average of a student's grades. Parents expect to see some indication of how well the child is performing in each subject.

However, once the curriculum is integrated, these forms and expectations no longer fit the reality. When students are studying a theme using skills from all of the disciplines simultaneously, it is virtually impossible to separate one area from another so as to assign grades. Assessment must be based primarily on authentic performances and projects that demonstrate what the students have learned rather than on paper-and-pencil tests that can be graded numerically and then averaged to produce a percentage or an equivalent letter grade. Even when the reporting system can be adjusted to fit the integration of curriculum, the team of teachers must determine how student work will be assessed and evaluated. They must also collaborate to design an effective set of record-keeping procedures that all team members can implement and share. The more complete the integration, the more closely the teaching team must work to decide what will be assessed and evaluated.

In addition, the team will have to determine the criteria for evaluating the work. As much as teachers like to think that they grade objectively and consistently, research shows that this is not so. Some teachers focus on individual progress; others tend to compare students in a class to each other. Some teachers focus on mechanics in written work; whereas others focus on content or give equal weight to both. Rubrics and checklists can be helpful tools for assessing and evaluating student work, but reaching agreement on the contents of these tools may be difficult.

However, discussions of how to assess and evaluate students can be enlightening. They can even change the way teachers grade when they are not participating in an integrated unit. They may, for example, rely less heavily on tests and quizzes. They may also be more explicit about their expectations. As painful as the process of shared evaluation may be, it can be quite beneficial in the long run, especially for students.

INTEGRATING TECHNOLOGY

In addition to integrating the subject areas, you will also need to consider how you can use technology to link content and processes. One of the benefits of integrated instruction is that students can devote some time to researching the available sources that relate to the theme. You should not be the one to locate all of the materials and resources; instead, turn this task over to the students. In their search, they may find some visuals, recordings, tapes, and Internet sites, as well as books and people that can be shared with classmates in interesting ways. When they find such items, they can create classroom displays, add to a list of Internet sites worth visiting, use a variety of audiovisual equipment to produce multimedia reports, arrange a teleconference, evaluate various forms of media, and discover connections between topics that were not readily apparent to them at first. Given the time, equipment, and opportunity, students will find innovative ways to incorporate technology. They can share their learning with classmates and teachers, so that all learn more about how to find, assess, and use the many forms of technology that are available.

ASSESSING AND EVALUATING INTEGRATED LEARNING

As noted previously, integrated instruction deserves integrated assessment and evaluation. Teaching teams must cooperate closely to decide what to assess, how to maintain records of observations, which criteria to use for assessing student work, and how to reach agreement about evaluating each student's learning. Although it is not advisable to attempt to break integrated learning into separate disciplines so as to grade each individually, it is also not advisable to assign a single composite score for an integrated unit. That is to say, it is not a good idea to report to the student that he or she earned a B grade on a 3-week integrated unit. If the unit is fully integrated, this would mean that the student earned a B in every course for a portion of the grading period. This kind of scheme could be disastrous if the student performed poorly and the unit encompassed all or most of a grading period. A single, overall grade does little to help the student understand his strengths and weaknesses, and it does not help parents understand the basis for the grade or the criteria for performance.

As an alternative, students can maintain portfolios. Students can be informed in advance of which tasks will be graded and on what basis. At the end of the unit, have students present their portfolios for grading and meet with a faculty member to review their progress. The teacher and student can share their impressions and cooperatively determine an overall grade to be reported in conjunction with grades in other subject areas if the reporting policy of the district requires such grades. If possible, conferences with parents should also be held. If these can be arranged, they should be student-directed so that the students have an opportunity to explain how the grades were determined and what strengths and weaknesses were identified during the unit.

Although there are few models for assessing and evaluating integrated instruction, one factor does deserve some special attention. In the excitement and initial confusion of exploring the possibilities of curriculum integration, you must keep in mind the learning goals and objectives that are important for students to achieve. Just as students may thoroughly enjoy playing a video game without necessarily learning anything from the experience, so too may they participate avidly in an integrated unit without gaining any educational ground. In the midst of exploration and discovery, it will still be your task as the language arts expert to ensure that students continue to grow in their ability to read, write, speak, listen, view, and visually represent. It will also be your duty to make sure that students develop a broader and deeper understanding of literature, language, and media no matter what the unit theme is. Although the learning may be deeply embedded within the activities, projects, and performances, you must still do your best to tease out evidence of improvement in skills and understanding of concepts. In the final analysis, the success or failure of an integrated unit must be determined on the basis of student learning. If there is little or no evidence that students are more capable, better informed, and more enthused about learning when a unit is done, then you must think quite seriously about the value of the unit before repeating it.

RECOMMENDED READINGS

Bannister, B. (1994). *Ready-to-use thematic activities.* West Nyack, NY: The Center for Applied Research in Education.

Beane, J. (1997). *Curriculum integration: Designing the core of democratic education.* New York: Teachers College Press.

Chatton, B., & Hepler, S. (1996). Linking literature and language use through thematic units. In A. McClure & J. Kristo (Eds.), *Books that invite talk, wonder, and play* (pp. 189–205). Urbana, IL: National Council of Teachers of English.

Christenbury, L. (Ed.). (1997). Interdisciplinary English [themed issue]. *English Journal, 86*(7).

Combs, D. (1997). Using alternative assessment to provide options for student success. *Middle School Journal, 29*(1), 3–8.

Erb, T. (Ed.). (1996). Connecting kids to communities [themed issue]. *Middle School Journal, 28*(2).

Erb, T. (Ed.). (1998). Curriculum reform: Disciplinary, interdisciplinary, & integrated [themed issue]. *Middle School Journal, 30*(2).

Five, C., & Dionisio, M. (1996). *Bridging the gap: Integrating curriculum in upper elementary and middle schools.* Portsmouth, NH: Heinemann.

Gutloff, K. (Ed.). (1996). *Integrated thematic teaching.* West Haven, CT: National Educational Association Professional Library.

Jacobs, H. (Ed.). (1989). *Interdisciplinary curriculum: Design and implementation.* Alexandria, VA: Association for Supervision and Curriculum Development.

Lounsbury, J. (Ed.). (1992). *Connecting the curriculum through interdisciplinary instruction.* Columbus, OH: National Middle School Association.

Manning, M., Manning, G., & Long, R. (1994). *Theme immersion: Inquiry-based curriculum in elementary and middle schools.* Portsmouth, NH: Heinemann.

Martinello, M., & Cook, G. (1994). *Interdisciplinary inquiry in teaching and learning.* New York: Macmillan.

Maurer, R. (1994). *Designing interdisciplinary curriculum in middle, junior high, and high schools.* Boston: Allyn & Bacon.

Meinbach, A., Rothlein, L., & Fredericks, A. (1995). *The complete guide to thematic units: Creating the integrated curriculum.* Norwood, MA: Christopher-Gordon.

Pace, G. (Ed.). (1995). *Whole learning in the middle school: Evolution and transition.* Norwood, MA: Christopher-Gordon.

Siu-Runyan, Y., & Faircloth, C. V. (Eds.). (1995). *Beyond separate subjects: Integrative learning at the middle level.* Norwood, MA: Christopher-Gordon.

Stevenson, C., & Carr, J. (Eds.). (1993). *Integrated studies in the middle grades: "Dancing through walls."* New York: Teachers College Press.

Strubbe, M. (1990). Are interdisciplinary units worthwhile? Ask students. *Middle School Journal, 21,* 36–38.

Strube, P. (1993). *Theme studies: A practical guide.* New York: Scholastic.

Tchudi, S., & Lafer, S. (1996). *The interdisciplinary teacher's handbook: Integrated teaching across the curriculum.* Portsmouth, NH: Boynton/Cook–Heinemann.

Tomlinson, C. (1998). For integration and differentiation choose concepts over topics. *Middle School Journal, 30*(2), 3–8.

Usnick, V., & McCarthy, J. (1998). Turning adolescents onto mathematics through literature. *Middle School Journal, 29*(4), 50–54.

OTHER RESOURCES

Classroom Connect
  431 Madrid Avenue
  Torrance, CA 90501–1430
  1–800–638–1639
  www.classroom.com
  (high-quality resources for teaching language arts, thematic units, and integrated curriculum using the Internet)

14

Integrating into the Teaching Profession

Overview

- Consider These Questions
- Becoming a Professional Educator
- The Importance of Self-Reflection
- Continued Professional Development
- Teacher as Researcher
- Contributing to the Profession
- Working With Administrators, Faculty, and Staff
- Developing Positive Relationships with Parents and Other Caregivers
- Tests, Assessments, Grading, and Report Cards
- Avoiding Undue Stress and Burnout
- To Teach Well You Must Also Live Well
- Recommended Readings

CONSIDER THESE QUESTIONS ABOUT INTEGRATING INTO THE TEACHING PROFESSION

1. Besides applying what you have learned in this book, what else can you do to become a professional middle school teacher?
2. What is self-reflection? How can it help you to improve your teaching?
3. What are some ways that you can continue to grow during your teaching career? Is it a good idea to start an advanced degree immediately?
4. If you have questions about which approach works best, should you conduct your own research project to test your theories? If so, how can you go about doing that?
5. Why should you consider joining professional organizations? How else can you contribute to the profession? Should you?
6. How can you work effectively with administrators? Other teachers? The staff in your building?
7. How can you enlist the aid of parents? Should you? How should you handle parent conferences?
8. What can you do to make tests, assessments, grading, and reporting grades more effective and less stressful?
9. With all that must be done, how can you avoid needless stress and burnout? How can you maintain a positive frame of mind?
10. How can you balance your professional responsibilities and your personal life?

BECOMING A PROFESSIONAL EDUCATOR

At the beginning of this book, you looked at middle school students as the most important factor in planning and conducting instruction. Then you explored much that is known about teaching the processes and content of language arts at the middle level. The previous two chapters focused on how to bring all of these elements together to form an integrated whole. However, that integration will not be complete without you. You will build the bridges that connect students and language arts in meaningful ways. However, to achieve that end, you, too, must actively strive to connect yourself to continued learning while you teach. I have never heard anyone say that they became a teacher with the intention of being mediocre. Nevertheless, many teachers fail to excel. If you want to rise to the status of Professional Educator, then you must set high standards for your continuing growth and development. The information in this chapter will help you to achieve that goal.

THE IMPORTANCE OF SELF-REFLECTION

As you progress through your college preparation, you will probably begin to question yourself and wonder whether you are truly meant to be a teacher. This kind of self-doubt seems to be a normal part of the process. No matter what the course of study in college, as graduation nears, many students have second thoughts about the future. At the same time, you will probably feel a strong urge to get into your own classroom and try all that you have learned. You may be quite anxious to try on the mantle of "teacher" to see how it fits. The closer you come to finishing your program, the more likely you are to feel somewhat constrained by classroom instructors, clinical field experience supervisors, and other mentors. Although this conflict between self-doubt and the desire for autonomy may cause you to feel somewhat unsettled or even irritable, these two emotions can be powerful forces to aid you in your development after you complete your primary preparation.

Effective teachers are risk-takers. They continually search for the best ways to meet the needs of all of their students. They are unwilling to settle for less. They never lose their desire to try different things in their classrooms. They continually question what they do. When a lesson or unit goes well, they ask themselves why. Then they use that knowledge when they plan the next lesson or unit. Sometimes the cause is just serendipity, but most of the time a thoughtful teacher can identify certain factors that produced an especially good learning experience. Re-creating those factors is apt to produce another positive experience.

Examining your teaching performance so as to improve is an essential skill that you need to develop before you begin full-time teaching. To use professional jargon, you need to become a *reflective practitioner*. This is an individual who applies professional knowledge of teaching and learning to analyze his or her own teaching, assesses the results objectively, and uses that knowledge to improve performance. In addition, a reflective practitioner identifies his or her strengths and weaknesses in order to make the most of positive attributes while strengthening weaker ones. This is also the type of person who asks questions about teaching and learning and who actively seeks answers by using a number of resources well and conducting in-school research.

Plan Thoughtfully and Thoroughly

There are several techniques that you can use now to enhance your ability to reflect on your own teaching performance. One simple technique is to have a well-developed lesson plan in hand before you teach. The process of creating this plan should help you think about your teaching and student learning before it takes place. However, having the plan to review later can be equally beneficial. It will help you recall details and identify causes of problems to avoid in the future.

Engage in Professional Conversations

Another excellent possibility is conversing with teachers. This includes clinical supervisors, but other teachers can be quite insightful. During student teaching, you may find that peers who are also in the field are the most sympathetic and supportive. If you cannot meet with them, use the telephone, computer, or both to maintain contact. Consider communicating with previous college instructors who can help you think through your questions. In fact, it is probably a good idea to ask for assistance from several others so that you obtain a variety of perspectives. Most teachers readily give advice to student teachers, although not all of it will be useful. Once you begin full-time teaching, you may find it difficult or uncomfortable to ask for aid, so use every opportunity you have while you are still considered a student.

Maintain a Teaching Journal

Another excellent device for reflecting is a teaching journal. In it you can record incidents, responses, your thoughts and feelings, questions, hypotheses, and relevant information. Although maintaining such a journal requires some time, this activity forces you both to analyze and to synthesize your thoughts. It also prompts you to recall information from your college course work that now makes more sense to you. What is especially valuable about a teaching journal is the record of progress that it provides. Reading back through the entries made over several weeks of teaching will help you gain a more holistic perspective of your growth. It may also help you identify trends of productive or negative thought that may be developing. A teaching journal is quite useful during student teaching. By reviewing the entries made during the past days before meeting with your visiting supervisor, you can isolate particular questions or concerns that need to be discussed in conference. Selected entries from your teaching journal that highlight your ability to reflect effectively on your performance can also be impressive additions to a teaching portfolio.

Use Technology to Self-Assess

Probably the best source on which to base reflection is a collection of videotapes of your teaching. Audiotapes are also useful, but you need to see yourself as students do in order to become cognizant of some kinds of behaviors and interactions that are occurring. Experienced teachers are often unaware that they actually create certain difficulties until they view tapes of their teaching. They may, for example, be oblivious to the fact that they respond differently to the male students in their classroom or that they only look at certain students during discussions. They may not realize that they monitor only a few areas of the room visually and ignore other areas. The first time you see yourself on tape, you are likely to feel somewhat embarrassed and even disappointed. You will probably notice all of your flaws. However, you need to repeat this activity often enough so that you are able to move beyond examining yourself. The key is to focus on students and how your performance affects them. Videotapes of your performance provide an excellent source for discussing your teaching with others. Also, you will want to select your best or edit several teaching episodes to create a tape that you can add to your professional portfolio. Furthermore, should you choose to apply for national board certification sometime in the future, you will have practice in the part of this process that requires you to videotape and critique yourself.

Some of these forms of reflection may be required by your supervisors or instructors. If they are not, you would be wise to try them on your own. During student teaching you should experiment with a variety of reflective techniques to determine which works best for you. Once in your own classroom, you may find yourself involved in an induction process that includes observations by a mentor teacher, a team leader, or an administrator. Their comments, questions, and advice should assist you in thinking about your performance, but you should not rely solely on their judgment because they cannot be in your classroom every day. Although their recommendations must be taken quite seriously, you must take the initiative to conduct your own analytical reflection.

CONTINUED PROFESSIONAL DEVELOPMENT

There is always more to learn about teaching. Once you have succeeded in obtaining a contract, you should take some time to celebrate. However, you will also want to begin preparing for opening day. This will be an exciting time, but it is likely to be somewhat frightening, too. There will be much to learn and much to do. For a while, probably most of the first year, your attention will need to be focused on the task at hand—learning school policies and procedures, becoming familiar with curricula and books, making friends with other faculty members, arranging and decorating your classroom, and getting to know your students. Most schools are complex systems, and you need some time to feel comfortable with all of the twists and quirks of the context. You may also be involved in moving to a new area and making a number of changes in your personal life. All in all, it will be exciting but hectic.

Your teaching experiences will doubtless present you with some challenges that will raise questions. Initially, you will do the best you can to find an answer or a suitable solution to a problem, but in moments of contemplation you are likely to wonder whether you made the best decision. Although further investigation may need to wait until you have completed at least your first year of teaching, when questions begin to arise you should develop a plan that will help you grow and develop professionally. What you have studied in this book is a synthesis of some of the most current information about what works in the middle level classroom, but by the time this book is published, other data will have become available. More still will be published while you are involved in your first year of teaching. It is not easy to remain well informed about education, but this is a necessity if you are to reach beyond mediocrity in the classroom.

Read Professional Literature

One of the most convenient ways to keep yourself professionally sharp is to read. The following periodicals are those most likely to contain useful suggestions about improving middle level language arts instruction:

- *English Journal, Voices in the Middle, and Language Arts* (NCTE)
- *Middle School Journal and Middle Ground* (NMSA)
- *Journal of Adolescent & Adult Literacy* (IRA)
- *Childhood Education* (Association for Childhood Education International)
- *Phi Delta Kappan* (Phi Delta Kappa)
- *Educational Leadership* (Association for Supervision and Curriculum Development)
- *Kappa Delta Pi Record* (Kappa Delta Pi)
- *Education Week* (Editorial Projects in Education, Inc.)
- *Education Digest* (Prakken Publications, Inc.)

For current research, the following journals and newsletters are quite useful:

- *Research in the Teaching of English* (NCTE)
- *Reading Research Quarterly* (IRA)
- *Research in Middle Level Education Quarterly* (NMSA)

- *Review of Educational Research* (American Educational Research Assn.)
- *English Update* (Center on English Learning & Achievement)

While you have ready access to these and others that you may find valuable in your college or university library, take the time to peruse some recent issues to ascertain the kinds of articles and ideas contained in each publication. (As you are examining some of these periodicals, take a look at the February issue of *Educational Leadership*, [Scherer, 1998] which contains a number of articles that address concerns of beginning teachers.)

Choose one or two of these publications that are most appealing and make plans to subscribe once you are gainfully employed. Be aware also that some school districts have small professional libraries for their teachers. Some of these publications may be available there.

Many professional organizations, such as NCTE, IRA, and NMSA, publish resource books for teachers. Several publishers also produce books about teaching and learning. A list appears at the end of this chapter. Consider contacting some of them and requesting to be added to their catalog mailing list so that you can keep abreast of recent publications that you may find useful.

Set Goals for Future Professional Growth

Reading current periodicals and books is one way to continue to grow professionally, but there are several others. If you can do so, you should set some goals for yourself. Many teachers report that developing the portfolio and completing other tasks that are required for certification by the National Board for Professional Teaching Standards changes their lives as teachers. Another goal you can set is that of participating in a summer institute conducted by an affiliate of the National Writing Project. However, to participate in these programs, you must have taught successfully for 3 or more years. Another option to consider for the future is enrollment in one of the summer programs offered by the National Endowment for the Humanities.

A part of your professional development plan should include some formal study. If you focus only on your own classroom, school, or district, your perspective will be quite narrow. Problems and issues need to be seen within the context of a broader viewpoint, and you need to rub against new research and recommendations. Unless you move beyond the boundaries of your own terrain, you can feel quite isolated. Continuing your formal education by enrolling in a university course at least occasionally is an asset to your career.

Whether you decide to pursue an advanced degree will depend on a number of factors, such as licensing requirements, availability of courses, scheduling, time, and costs. School systems often pay higher salaries to those who complete additional degrees, although few districts provide monetary support while the study is in progress. Sabbatical leaves for professional development at the K–12 level are rare, but a few districts offer this opportunity after several years of teaching. Whatever the situation, you should set a goal to continue to enroll in courses on a regular basis. If you want to work toward an advanced degree, search for a program that includes or allows you to take classes that are relevant and interesting. If you can do so, you may find it beneficial to take a course or two at several institutions before choosing a degree program. Also, because your career is likely to change as you gain experience, you may not want to begin a formal sequence until you are sure of your professional goals. Although you may not think it so now, you may eventually discover that you really want to focus on technology or gifted and talented education or special education. After teaching for a while, you may find that you really do not want to move into school administration after all. Although it is not wise to delay formal study for too long, rushing into a degree program quickly may not be advisable either.

Attend Conferences and Workshops

Graduate study should be a part of a long-term plan, but there is much that you can do in the meantime. If possible, you should try to attend some workshops or conferences. Many professional organizations host lengthy annual conferences. Most of these are held at different locations each year, so watch for ones near you. NCTE holds its major conference in mid-November and a smaller spring conference in April. The IRA conducts its main conference in early May. The National Middle School Conference, which is one of the largest in the country, occurs in early November. In addition, state affiliates of these organizations host conferences at other times during the year. Many state humanities councils, departments of instruction, and local colleges and universities sponsor one- or two-day conferences and seminars that focus on special topics such as teaching reading, children's and young adult literature, storytelling, and so forth. Many of these conferences and workshops are announced in *Education Week*.

Numerous educational consultants conduct workshops and seminars throughout the year. You can find advertisements for these in professional and popular press periodicals. Once your name appears on some educational mailing lists, ads for them are likely to appear in your mailbox. Some of these programs are excellent; others are worthless and expensive. Before signing up, check with colleagues who may have attended previously. You may also want to peruse articles written by the consultant or speaker to see if he or she is likely to address your particular interests and concerns.

Your school or district may provide some professional development, although they may use the terms "staff development" or "in-service training." In some instances, you may be required to attend these presentations. Other participation may be optional. One advantage of these offerings is that most will be free of charge to you. However, many of these are "hit-and-run" programs. A speaker is hired to give a presentation or conduct a workshop. The person hits the participants with a mountain of information in an hour or two and then runs off to the next site or back to a university office.

Take Part in a Local Study Group

According to the Indiana Education Policy Center (1996), if professional development is to have an impact on your teaching, it should focus on topics that are of interest to you. Also, it should be of significant duration (i.e., several days or even weeks), and there should be some kind of ongoing support from presenters or participants. Short-term events, such as half-day in-service programs or guest speakers, may introduce you to some interesting concepts, but unless you then inquire further and study independently, your teaching is not apt to be affected. If you are given options for participating, take advantage of school-based professional development that promises to be the most beneficial to you.

One option that is currently available in some districts is participation in a study group. Such groups are usually organized by teachers themselves, and participants choose the activities and schedule. Study groups often focus on very narrow topics such as how to improve the teaching of spelling in the district or how to make peer response groups more effective. In other locales, groups of teachers have formed book clubs. They meet on a regular basis, sometimes outside of school or during lunch, to discuss their pleasure reading. If a study group or book club is available, take advantage of the opportunity. Although you probably should not do so until you have been teaching for a while, you may consider establishing a study group or book club yourself if none exists where you teach. Some of the resources listed in the Recommended Readings for this chapter offer suggestions for establishing both of these groups. Also, the NCTE has packets available on certain topics to support study group investigations.

Engage in Local Service

There may also be some special activities or committee work in your school or district that can help you grow professionally. Some teaching teams devote part of their meeting time to sharing professional reading, reporting on ideas obtained at conferences, and describing effective strategies they have developed in their classrooms. Textbook selection committees, reaccreditation groups, curricular task forces, and special committees on topics such as revising reporting procedures can be professionally stimulating, or they can be boring formalities. Some schools and districts are overloaded with extracurricular responsibilities that teachers are expected to perform. You should do your fair share of service, but if this participation is not personally enlightening, you may want to limit the time you devote to these extra duties and find other ways of continuing your professional growth.

TEACHER AS RESEARCHER

After you have been teaching for a while, some particularly perplexing and recurrent problems will come to your attention. These may be matters that you approach from a number of angles without finding a satisfying solution. At this point, you should consider the possibility of conducting some formal research in your own classroom. Although this may sound daunting, it really is not. Basically it is just an organized and logical way to try to solve a problem. In a nutshell, action or classroom research includes the following steps:

1. Identify a concern.
2. Review the professional literature to see what others have found.
3. Propose a solution (hypothesis: If I do x, y will be the result).
4. Design a course of action to test your theory.
5. Collect data while carrying out the plan.
6. Analyze the results.
7. Reach conclusions.

Of course, you can do this just for yourself, but with a bit more attention to detail and some time devoted to writing, you can share your findings with others by submitting your description for publication. Another option is to make your results accessible on the Internet. *Teachers are researchers: Reflection and action* (Patterson, Santa, Short, & Smith, 1993), which is listed in the Recommended Readings for this chapter, is an excellent guide for beginning researchers.

CONTRIBUTING TO THE PROFESSION

Your first priority must be your students. You have a responsibility to be the best teacher possible, and that includes continuing to grow professionally through study, discussion, and various other means. However, you also have a duty to contribute to the profession. As much as possible, you should seek opportunities to help all teachers become more effective, and you should find ways to make teaching a more satisfying career. Unfortunately, many teachers do not see participating in and contributing to the profession as a part of their job description. They may applaud the efforts of other faculty who select textbooks or negotiate contracts but never volunteer to serve on committees. They may read articles in professional journals avidly but never write for publication. They may attend conferences but never assist in the planning or prepare a presentation.

Membership in one or more professional groups is an important way to participate in and demonstrate support for the activities of the organization. At the beginning of your career, a limited level of involvement is reasonable. However, as you gain experience, you should think seriously about more active participation. One of the easiest entries is to take part in the activities of local affiliates or chapters of professional organizations. Become acquainted with leaders of these groups and offer to help. You can also join special interest groups and take an active role in their programs. NCTE has a number of commissions and standing committees that need practicing teachers as members in order to be effective. Other organizations have similar groups that welcome the expertise that experienced teachers can share. Addresses of several of these are listed at the end of this chapter. Another possibility is to join a chat group on the Internet in which teachers share their best ideas and answer questions posed by others.

There are many other ways in which you can contribute to the profession. You can write about an effective unit or activity and submit it for publication. Or you can volunteer to serve on a review panel for a professional journal. You can propose and, if chosen, give presentations at conferences. Within your own school, you can serve on or even chair various committees and work groups. You can volunteer to be a mentor to a new teacher or a clinical supervisor for a student teacher. You can conduct an in-service program for other faculty.

All of these contributions are valuable, not only to the profession but to you as an individual. Through active participation you learn about yourself and about teaching. Moreover, you develop your own skills. However, there is one additional contribution that you can make to the profession that may be even more important than any of the others: You can be an informed advocate who is willing to express yourself publicly. American education has borne the brunt of much criticism recently. The media is quick to highlight flaws, but reticent to showcase strengths. Rarely do the news writers know the research or the stance of professionals, and many of their reports are filled with myths and misinformation. All too often teachers respond with silence. They do not write letters to the editor to point out inaccuracies in reports, nor do they contact local news media about laudable programs and events taking place in their classrooms. They do not attend legislative sessions or contact elected officials to express their professional views. They do not attend school board meetings on a regular basis. They do not seek students who have the academic talent and personality traits that make them excellent candidates for a career in teaching and encourage them to investigate this vocation. All too frequently, teachers are the worst critics of the profession. They openly fault teachers in other subject areas or at lower grade levels. They verbally express dissatisfaction with the teaching methods of others, showing an intolerance for the instructional diversity that gives the profession strength and vitality. You can be different. Through active participation and vocal support, you can take a leadership role in making teaching better.

WORKING WITH ADMINISTRATORS, FACULTY, AND STAFF

The Principal

The building principal can be your best friend or your worst enemy. Obviously, the former is far superior to the latter. If you have the option when choosing a job, you should give some thought to whether the principal is an individual with whom you can work. Indeed, you should consider carefully whether the tone of the school and the attitude toward students matches your own philosophy. If you prefer a teacher-dominated classroom that is tightly controlled, then find a school where that is the context, even if you must look outside the public school system. You may be happier in an alternative school or possibly a military school. If, on the other hand, you are excited about the middle school philosophy, and you are anxious to participate in team teaching, integrated curricula, and all the other aspects of developmentally appropriate instruction, then search for a principal who expresses support for the concept and can show evidence of progress toward this goal. Watch out for the principal who espouses a middle school philosophy but who comments about lack of faculty support. This is apt to be a school in conflict. If you are committed to using a reading–writing workshop approach, you need to look for a school that is somewhat flexible and a principal who supports innovative instruction. You may not be able to establish a workshop in a school that is dominated by textbooks, required reading, competition, and grades. If there is one, a student handbook may tell you more about the school's philosophy than any other document.

The extent to which the principal influences you may depend on whether he or she is focused on business matters or the instructional program. Some principals see themselves as instructional leaders; others do not. Some principals want to know everything that goes on in their schools; others only want to know about potential problems. You will need to walk gently at first until you have a clearer sense of how the principal sees her or his role. An assistant principal, dean of students, or guidance counselor may prove to be more helpful to you. Be aware, too, that other faculty in the building may hold some administrative power or have the ear of the building administrators. These individuals may have an official title, such as department chair or lead teacher, or they may not have any special designation.

Other Faculty

In *Schoolteacher* (1975), Lortie described the many ways in which school faculties socialize new teachers. Some groups of practicing teachers welcome new teachers and delight in hearing about recent trends in education. They look forward to the opportunity to learn from as well as guide novices. However, many practicing teachers want new teachers to copy them. There is a certain kind of ego satisfaction in finding a kindred spirit, someone who shares beliefs and teaches similarly. Imitation, after all, is a form of flattery. In some instances, new teachers are told rather directly to forget what they have learned in their teacher education courses because that is not the way things are done in this school. Hopefully, that will not be the case in your school, but you need to be forewarned of the possibility.

You should also be aware that you may be walking into a setting where there are conflicting factions. The faculty may be divided over some issue, such as a change in policy, deciding how to allocate funds, or whether a new gymnasium is necessary. Each side may attempt to win you over to its point of view. From the outside a school may seem peaceful and congenial, but once you join the faculty you may discover that there is much divisiveness over time, money, schedules, committee assignments, extracurricular duties, and power. Some of these struggles revolve around matters that are relatively insignificant in an educational sense. Sometimes the issues are more about personality clashes than teaching and learning. However, some disputes can affect the quality of education.

As a new teacher, your best posture is that of listener and observer. Be friendly and ask questions, but avoid giving opinions too readily.

If you have a mentor, work as closely with this person as he or she will permit, but look for other members of the faculty to whom you can relate. If you are assigned to a teaching team, be willing to follow their lead for a while. Do your best to be a congenial, contributing member. If you are invited to take part in social activities, do so. If possible, invite some members of the faculty to your residence, or take some to lunch. Although it would be better if teachers did not gossip, other members of the faculty may have some of the same students who are assigned to your class, and they may make comments to students that can make your job easier or more difficult. As a new person, you can easily become entangled in some complex interpersonal situations. However, if you retain a professional stance, you may avoid these problems. Until you know the faculty members well, it is probably wise to keep your professional life separated from your personal life.

School Staff

Many individuals are necessary to the effective functioning of a school. From the bus drivers to the cafeteria aides and from the speech therapist to the social worker, all those who have contact with students play a part in setting the tone of the school. Lack of respect can be contagious.

One person who is very important to you is the school librarian. You should make a special effort to develop a positive working relationship with this person. Another individual who can be very helpful is the guidance counselor. He or she often knows the history of problem students better than others in the school. This person may also know family members and home situations. Sometimes it is a good idea to check with the counselor before calling a student's home. The school nurse is another member of the staff who has information that you may find helpful. She or he may be aware of medical conditions, prescription medications, hearing and vision problems, and other physical challenges that affect student learning and behavior. The nurse is also the person who will help you learn what you must do if you have a student who is HIV positive and what you should do if you suspect that a student has head lice. This person may also be the best informed about absenteeism patterns. In some states, if a teacher recommends that a child have a vision test, the school district may be charged for the cost of the examination. The school nurse should be able to tell you whether this or any other similar policies that could create problems apply in your school

There are two groups of people in the building who can make your life much easier or much more difficult: the school secretaries and the custodians who are in charge of your area. Secretaries and receptionists are often in charge of many teaching supplies that you will need—chalk, erasers, photocopy paper, grade books, and so on. They often have access to the intercom system and can decide whether to interrupt your class. They can warn you that an angry parent is about to visit or let this arrival come as a surprise. All in all, these are people that you want on your team. You also need to get to know the custodians who take care of your room and office space. Custodians can do things that are very irritating. They can, for example, rearrange the desks in your classroom every day. They can throw away student folders or projects that are left out intentionally or accidentally. They can wash your chalkboard even though you mark what you wish to save, or they can refuse to wash your boards unless you first erase everything. Take a few minutes to get to know these people. Find out if there is anything that you can do to make their work easier, such as having students put chairs on top of desks at the end of the day. Ask what you should do if you want the room arrangement left as it is or if you want information on the chalkboard to remain overnight. Be careful about telling custodians how you want things done. Spending the day or night cleaning up after middle school students is not fun. If you can make the custodians' lives a little easier, do it. All of this may seem unnecessary until a student throws up in your classroom and you do not even know who to send for to come and clean the area. This is not a good time to get acquainted.

DEVELOPING POSITIVE RELATIONSHIPS WITH PARENTS AND OTHER CAREGIVERS

Perhaps the most important advice about working with adults who care for students is to avoid making any assumptions. If you picture a mother and father when you think of parents, you may be in for a shock. Many students live in single-parent households. Some reside with older siblings. Grandparents or more distant relatives care for others. Families may be complex collections of stepchildren and half-brothers and half-sisters. Some children are adopted and others are wards of the state under guardianship. Names can be tricky, too. You cannot assume, for example, that the parents of John Jones are Mr. and Mrs. Jones. John may be the son of Mrs. Jones, who is now Mrs. Smith. Children in one household may have several different surnames. What is more, the school records may not show the most recent names of the adult or adults in the home. Do not assume that the student who appears to be Asian-American has Asian-American parents, and do not be surprised if an African-American student arrives for a conference with White parents. The better you know your students, the less apt you are to be caught off guard and to commit a blunder that may offend both the student and the adults.

The remainder of this section will use the term "parents" with the understanding that this label refers to all who are the legally responsible adults in the lives of middle level students, whether these are relatives, guardians, foster or adoptive parents, or other caregivers.

Assessing the Climate

There is much research to verify that students do better in school when parents are actively involved in the education of their children. Parents and teachers need to be partners. They need to communicate openly and often, and that communication must be a two-way exchange, not just from school to home. When you are seeking employment, you need to ask about parent involvement. Are parents welcome in the schools and classrooms? Do they attend open houses and parent conferences? Do they volunteer to assist? Do they take part in decision-making? Is there an active parent–teacher organization? What is the school doing to encourage parent participation? What does the school do to accommodate working parents?

If you find yourself in a school where parents are actively involved, count yourself lucky. At times you may find parental scrutiny bothersome, especially when they challenge your methods, grades, or reading selections, but this is far better than teaching where parents are intentionally excluded, choose to remain uninvolved, or cannot take part because of their many other responsibilities. If parents are not a presence in the school or district, this situation should be addressed by the entire faculty and the administrators, particularly if the school is intent on implementing a middle school philosophy. Widespread lack of parent involvement is not a problem that you can solve on your own. However, it is an issue that a teaching team can tackle.

Improving Parental Involvement

Let's assume, however, that you are the only person who is concerned about lack of parental involvement. What can you do to improve the situation? You may want to start by exploring why parents remain aloof. Perhaps they have previously been denied access to teachers. Perhaps they themselves found school frustrating and hostile when they were students. Perhaps they cannot communicate in English. Perhaps they believe that they only need to visit if there is a problem. It is possible that the community assumes that if a parent goes to the school, his or her child must be in trouble. Perhaps parents are simply overwhelmed by the demands of their own lives, to the point that they have neither the time nor the energy for taking part in school activities. Once you have a clearer sense of why parents do not take part, you may find it easier to choose options that are likely to succeed.

Parents sometimes report that they would like to be involved, but they do not know when or how. This can be puzzling to school personnel who know that announcements are sent home regularly. However, there is the issue of adult literacy. Some parents may not be able to read the announcements. Others may toss them out along with the junk mail. Also, some parents are transient or homeless. Often communications from the school are hand-carried by students, but this can be ineffective. Middle level students are notorious for losing things, and many are not above throwing away messages addressed to parents. Announcements of open houses and invitations to parent conferences that are supposed to be carried home by students may never arrive there. In fact, parents may not see report cards, unsatisfactory progress reports, and other school documents.

Although you should probably check with administrators before doing this, you may consider making some home visits, just to introduce yourself and invite parents to work with you. You can try to locate three or four parents who would be willing to meet with you as a kind of advisory council to discuss ways of involving more parents. You may also try phoning parents just to introduce yourself and answer any questions they may have. You may also want to inform parents about when to expect report cards. This may seem like a suggestion that will demand an inordinate amount of time, but in some schools teachers are required to phone parents frequently. Students can create a newsletter about class or team activities to be shared with parents. If most students take part in creating this document, and it is something they are proud of, they are more likely to show it to parents. You may also consider sending home praise memos or smilegrams that call attention to something the student has done well. These can be especially effective if parents have never heard from the school except when a problem has occurred.

It is of some value to note that attempts to involve parents in school programs and activities may not be to students' liking. From their perspective, it is advantageous to keep home and school apart and parents uninformed. After all, if parents do not know what homework is assigned, they cannot pressure their children to complete the work. If parents are unaware that their child is not completing tasks, the child will have to bear the consequences only when report cards are issued rather than more often. Thus, if you begin to involve parents, some students are apt to be unhappy with you, but the results should be worth the trouble. Of course, it helps if the tasks students are to do outside of school are interesting and worthwhile. They may even be projects that involve parents. One possibility is to require that students interview adults. They can, for example, create a family tree or ask about the parents' recollections of recent historical events. Students can also be required to read to parents for a brief period of time each evening. Parents would have to sign a form each day verifying that the task was completed, but you may need to double-check to make sure that students are not forging a parent's signature.

Many middle level schools regularly schedule parent conferences. If yours does not, you can try to hold some anyway. If you have an advisee group, start with them. Consider conducting some of these meetings before school or on Saturday to accommodate parents' schedules. When you meet with parents, try to focus on what students can do, instead of what they cannot. As much as possible, inform parents of these strengths. All too often parents hear only negatives. Have some suggestions for parents about what they can do at home to assist their child in improving. If you can arrange it, have students participate in or even conduct these conferences. This is an excellent time for students to show off work that is displayed in the classroom and explain materials in their portfolios. Although this idea may sound far-fetched, in some middle level schools student-conducted conferences are the norm.

A Note of Caution

Some cautions must be stated in regard to working with parents. It is important to keep them informed and to garner their support. They need to feel that they are welcome in the school. However, parents can be unpredictable. It is not beyond the realm of possibility that you may be confronted with a parent who is drunk, high on drugs, physically or verbally abusive, or violent. Wisdom dictates that you should not meet with parents that you do not know unless others will be in the building. If you suspect that the conference may be difficult, ask another faculty member to join you. If the parent is angry or out of control, end the meeting politely but firmly, and tell the parent that you will contact him or her about rescheduling at a later time. Similarly, do not schedule a conference if you are angry or frustrated. Venting by listing all of the student's misbehaviors, poor performances, negative attitudes, and insufficient work habits is apt to make a bad matter worse. It makes parents defensive and convinces them that you do not like their child. Finally, be aware that if you must report to a parent that his or her child is not meeting expectations, you may prompt an incidence of physical or verbal abuse that could be harmful to the child and destroy any hope of establishing a more positive rapport with the student. Choose your words carefully. Search for solutions by asking the parent for assistance. Be sure that the parent leaves the conference with some specific suggestions about how to assist the child. It may even be advisable to avoid involving the parent and to attempt an in-school solution rather than put the child at risk.

Most parents want the best for their children. Indeed, the reason many have no time to be involved in their child's education may well be that they are struggling to provide for their children as best they can. Their parents may not have been good models, and they may not be aware that their involvement can have a significant impact. Do not expect parents to go out of their way to participate although you may have to extend yourself in order to draw them in. Furthermore, you may need to provide some instruction so that parents can assist their children. In essence, if you want to create a positive partnership with parents, you may need to engage in some adult education along with instructing young adolescents.

TESTS, ASSESSMENTS, GRADING, AND REPORT CARDS

Students often believe that they are the only ones who are stressed out by evaluation, but you will discover that testing and giving grades produce high levels of anxiety for teachers, too. Although it is not a fair measure, teachers often feel that student grades are a yardstick for assessing teacher performance. If students do well on a test, the teacher tends to feel some self-gratification. If students do poorly, the teacher may chastise him- or herself for not teaching more effectively or slip into a negative mindset about students.

No test will reveal all that students have learned. Tasks that are designed to produce demonstrations of skills may highlight only part of the total picture. As a professional, you must be cognizant of the flaws in various forms of testing, including standardized tests, so that you can help students and parents understand the values and limitations of tests and assessments. You must acquire knowledge about any standardized tests that are given so that you can accurately interpret the results.

Initially, creating classroom tests and performance assessments will be very difficult. You may expect too little at first, but you are more likely to expect a higher level of performance from middle level students than they can produce. Unless you are careful, your tests are apt to be too long and your assessments too complicated. Writing clear directions and unambiguous questions can be a struggle. Until you have some experience with the diversity of performance that exists among middle level students, you are apt to feel unsure of how to measure student learning. Thus you will find yourself wondering what is reasonable to include when you create checklists, scales, and rubrics.

Despite the difficulty, grading individual pieces of work may be less problematic than determining how to fit all of the pieces together into a single grade for the period. This is particularly true if you are using a portfolio system or a collection of performance assessments. Although collecting data based on observations does provide a more complete picture of student learning, this kind of "kid-watching" requires skills that you may not as yet have perfected. Furthermore, you will still have to figure out how to incorporate this information into a grade. No matter how objective and accurate you try to be, you will probably find that some students who do not deserve high grades earn them and some students deserve better grades than they actually earn.

In many districts the major tool of communication between the school and parents is the report card. Although this is unfortunate, it may be the reality in your school. This means that you need to pay close attention to what you report about student work. Report cards are private records, but they can become public documents in legal cases. Your grade book can also be called into court, as can any other records that are known to exist, including anecdotal records and teaching journals. The best approach is to record only factual information and observable data. Professional hypotheses and questions may also be included, but it is best to keep personal comments and subjective thoughts out of print.

Know What Is Expected of You

Although it is impossible to give specific advice about assessment and evaluation, there are some general guidelines that may prove to be beneficial. First, you need to know what is expected of you. How often are grades given? In many places the interval is 6 weeks, but others issue reports every 9 weeks. Is there a report form that must be completed, and what does it include? Some schools have a single form, one per student, but others have multiple forms. In some schools, teachers only give a single grade, but in others the language arts teachers give grades in different subskills. For example, they may be required to give a spelling grade, a reading grade, or both separate from a language arts grade. Another possibility is that teachers are required to complete a checklist of behaviors, write comments about each student's performance, or both. You will have to adjust your teaching plans to match the reporting system that exists, and you need to know as much as possible about that system before the school year begins. Many schools are now using computerized grading systems. If that is the case in your school, you need to know how this system works. For example, if you intend to weight some grades, you need to know whether the system will accommodate this. You may find that you need to record scores separately and calculate averages before entering them in the computer. For example, if you are required to give spelling tests each week, students may end each term with more grades in spelling than any other area. Unless the grades are weighted or spelling is entered as a single average score, the student's end-of-term grade may reflect far more about spelling than about the rest of his or her work.

Be Consistent With Other Faculty

As much as possible, you should try to be consistent with other faculty. If you have a mentor teacher, you should probably consult this person about how teachers in the building usually grade the students and what he or she considers reasonable to expect. If most of the teachers rely on objective tests, then you should probably include some of these in your planning, even if this strategy does not match your philosophy. Although a mix of objective tests and performance assessments is probably better than using only one or the other anyway, as a beginning teacher you may find that using both gives you a sense of security about the validity of grades you assign on compositions and other subjective tasks. It is a good idea to try to give grades that are somewhat similar to those given by other faculty. If yours are significantly higher or lower, you may find yourself having to defend your grades. Of course, you should be able to do this, but if you can avoid challenges, you will save yourself time and stress.

Inform Students

Students need to know how their work will be evaluated and graded. They need to know what kinds of tests you will be giving, what kinds of tasks they will be asked to complete, and what other aspects of their performance will be included in their grades. They do not, however, have to know all of that on the first day of school. Middle level students need this information while they are working on the assignments and preparing to demonstrate their skills and knowledge. If possible, involve students in designing checklists, scales, and rubrics, as this is one way to enhance achievement.

If you are going to give a test, try to develop it before the unit begins. At least part of your instruction should be designed to help students do well on the test. That does not mean that you give them the answers in advance, but it does mean that you give them a chance to practice the skills they are to demonstrate. Also, give yourself plenty of time to create the final version of the test. This is not something that can be dashed off at the last minute. Furthermore, allow some flexibility in the grading in case you find that a question misled students. Unless you include only literal-level or factual questions, you are apt to include at least one question that is unclear or ambiguous the first time you give any test.

You will also need to give some thought to the grading of homework. Of course, this will depend on the frequency and type of homework that you assign. Some teachers require that students use time outside of class for independent reading. They may then require that students report that reading in some fashion or discuss it with other students. Other teachers require that students complete computerized quizzes about their reading. Others require projects. Each of these requirements calls for a slightly different system of record keeping. On the other hand, some teachers rely heavily on paper-and-pencil tasks as homework. Often these are supposed to demand that students practice skills studied in the classroom. They can easily be marked and a score derived, but should practice be graded? Or should practice be the time when one can learn from mistakes without being penalized? If practices are graded, what is the difference between practice and performance? On the other hand, what do you do about the student who does no homework but scores well on tests? Should you demand that students complete tasks that ask them to practice skills they already have? These are decisions that you need to ponder before you hear the inevitable, "Will this be graded?"

Allow Adequate Time

Although there is never enough time for grading, assessing, and reporting, do the best you can to set aside adequate time for these activities. Calculating grades for 150 or so students takes far more time than you may think, even if you use a point system or simply average the scores. Filling in checklists and writing comments is extremely time-consuming. Initially you will probably need to use several hours outside of school for preparing grades and reports, but this time demand should decrease as you gain experience and revise your record-keeping system.

AVOIDING UNDUE STRESS AND BURNOUT

Yes, you must teach. Yes, you must continue your professional development. Yes, you should contribute to the profession. Yes, you must work effectively with adults as well as students. However, doing all of that seems to be a sure prescription for stress and eventual burnout. How can one teach and have a life, too? That is a good question. Unfortunately, too many outstanding teachers fail to find a satisfactory answer, but many others manage to balance their professional and personal lives successfully. These are the people who set goals for themselves and find opportunities for improving. They do not engage in activities that are unproductive and self-defeating. They find ways to network with others who have similar attitudes and interests. Most importantly, they maintain a positive outlook. They believe in themselves and their students. When things in their own classrooms are not going as well as they would like, they do not complain or cast blame on students, parents, or administrators; instead, they search for ways to make their teaching more effective, even if it means using strategies that are different. At the same time, they try to leave worries and problems at the school doorstep rather than carrying this emotional baggage home day after day. They establish priorities, including time for relaxation and doing whatever they find enjoyable—hobbies, visits to interesting places, family outings, immersion in the latest best-seller or whatever else provides a release from tension and breaks patterns of stress. They also organize their time to ensure that they take part in activities that are personally satisfying.

As a teacher, you will find that stress is unavoidable, but it can be managed. Precisely how you approach the problem depends on your level of tolerance and your lifestyle. Initially you will have to cut some corners and make some compromises with which you probably will not be happy. It is important, though, to give yourself the time to learn and the leeway to make mistakes without feeling too guilty. There will be perfect classes and even perfect days. There may even be some perfect weeks, but there will also be lessons you will wish you had not tried, incidents that you will wish to forget, and words you will wish you had never said.

It is important to do your best to educate every student, and it is natural to worry about those you have difficulty reaching, but you have to retain some perspective. Visualize your classroom and identify all of the ones who are responding well and who are excited about learning. Give yourself a pat on the back for having said the right things. Think about all of the parents who did not call to complain.

If you feel yourself drowning, then you should seek professional aid. Other teachers may be able to help, especially those with whom you have established a positive rapport, but if this is not enough to get you through a temporary period of anxiety, consider enrolling in a stress-management class or workshop. You may even need to consult a counselor or psychiatrist. Although you may be reluctant to seek assistance, you must keep in mind that if you are suffering from excessive stress, you are not performing well in the classroom. You may not be your best self in your private life either.

TO TEACH WELL YOU MUST ALSO LIVE WELL

Teaching is stressful. There is always more to do than is humanly possible. Teaching will absorb as much time as you devote to it and demand even more. If you are to be a productive, effective teacher, you must take care of yourself, mentally and physically. Family and friends are essential to your well-being. Vacations or some time to yourself must be a part of your life. Exercise, eat well-balanced meals, sleep well, and attend to medical problems promptly. As important as it is, there is more to life than teaching. Taking care of yourself is important. To teach and learn well, you must be well. There is no point in using all of your strength and energy for the students you have now if you will have nothing left for the ones who will be in your classroom next semester or next year or in 20 years.

RECOMMENDED READINGS

Birchak, B., Connor, C., Crawford, K., Kahn, L., Kaser, S., Turner, S., & Short, K. (1998). *Teacher study groups: Building community through dialogue and reflection*. Urbana, IL: National Council of Teachers of English.

Branscombe, N., Goswami, D., & Schwartz, J. (Eds.). (1992). *Students teaching, teachers learning*. Portsmouth, NH: Boynton/Cook–Heinemann.

Brown, R. (1993). *Schools of thought: How the politics of literacy shape thinking in the classroom*. San Francisco: Jossey-Bass.

Glatthorn, A., & Fox, L. (1996). *Quality teaching through professional development*. Thousand Oaks, CA: Corwin Press.

Hayes, I. (Ed.) (1998). *Great beginnings: Reflections and advice for new English language arts teachers and the people who mentor them*. Urbana, IL: National Council of Teachers of English.

Hubbard, R., & Power, B. (1999). *Living the questions: A guide for teacher–researchers*. York, ME: Stenhouse Publishers.

Indiana Education Policy Center. (1996). *Learning together: Professional development for better schools*. Bloomington, IN: Author.

Mayher, J. (1990). *Uncommon sense: Theoretical practice in language education*. Portsmouth, NH: Boynton/Cook–Heinemann.

Myers, J., & Monson, L. (1992). *Involving families in middle level education*. Columbus, OH: National Middle School Association.

National Middle School Association. (nd). Classroom connections: Parent–teacher conferences. Columbus, OH: Author.

Newkirk, T. (Ed.). (1992). *Workshop by and for teachers 4: The teacher as researcher*. Portsmouth, NH: Heinemann.

Patterson, L., Santa, C., Short, K., & Smith, K. (Eds.). (1993). *Teachers are researchers: Reflection and action*. Newark, DE: International Reading Association.

Routman, R. (1996). *Literacy at the crossroads: Critical talk about reading, writing and other teaching dilemmas*. Portsmouth, NH: Heinemann.

Scherer, M. (Ed.). (1998). Strengthening the teaching profession [themed issue]. *Educational Leadership, 55*(5).

Scherer, M. (Ed.). (1998). Engaging parents and the community in schools [themed issue]. *Educational Leadership, 55*(8).

Wells, M. C. (1996). *Literacies lost: When students move from a progressive middle school to a traditional high school.* New York: Teachers College Press.

OTHER RESOURCES

Professional Organizations and Groups

National Council of Teachers of English
1111 West Kenyon Road
Urbana, IL 61801–1096
217–328–3870
www.ncte.org

International Reading Association
800 Barksdale Road
PO Box 8139
Newark, DE 19714–8139
302–731–1600
www.reading.org

National Middle School Association
2600 Corporate Exchange Drive
Suite 370
Columbus, OH 43231–1672
1–800–528–NMSA
www.nmsa.org

National Writing Project
University of California
5511 Tolman Hall, #1670
Berkeley, CA 94720–1670
510–642–0963
www-gse.berkeley.edu/Research/NWP/nwp.html

American Federation of Teachers
555 New Jersey Avenue, NW
Washington, DC 200101
202–879–4400
http://www.aft.org

National Education Association
  1201 16th Street, NW
  Washington, DC 20036
  202–833–4000
  http://www.nea.org

Professional Development Sources

Association for Supervision and Curriculum Development
  1250 N. Pitt St.
  Alexandria, VA 22314–1453
  1–800–933–2723
  www.ascd.org

Center for Applied Research in Education
  110 Brookhill Drive
  West Nyack, NY 10995–0002
  http://www.phdirect.com

Christopher-Gordon Publishers
  1502 Providence Highway
  Suite #12
  Norwood, MA: 02062–4643
  1–800–934–8322

Heinemann (book ordering)
  88 Post Road West
  P.O. Box 5007
  Westport, CT 06881
  1–800–793–2154
  www.heinemann.com

Lawrence Erlbaum Associates, Inc.
  10 Industrial Ave.
  Mahwah, NJ 07430–2262
  201–236–9500

The LPD Video Journal of Education (videotapes about teaching for teachers and staff development. They also conduct workshops and institutes.)
  8686 South 1300 East
  Sandy, UT 84094
  1–800–572–1153
  www.videojournal.com

Richard C. Owen Publishers, Inc.
Rockefeller Center
Box 819
New York, NY 10185

Perfection Learning Corporation
(posters, games, transparencies, etc.)
1000 N 2nd Ave.
Logan, IA 51546
1–800–831–4190

Stenhouse Publishers (book orders only)
P.O. Box 1929
Columbus, OH 43216–1929
1–800–988–9812
www.stenhouse.com

Teacher Ideas Press
Libraries Unlimited, Inc.
P. O. Box 6633
Englewood, CO 80155–6633
1–800–237–6124
www.lu.com/tip

Teacher's Discovery (almost anything related to language arts)
Attention: English Department
2741 Paldan Drive
Auburn Hills, MI 48326
1–800–583–6454

Textbooks and Teaching Resources

Allyn & Bacon
Department 894
160 Gould Street
Needham Heights, MA 02494
1–800–278–3525
www.abacon.com

Harcourt Brace & Jovanovich
School Publishers
6277 Sea Harbor Drive
Orlando, FL 32887
407–345–3800

Holt, Rinehart and Winston
    6277 Sea Harbor Drive
    Orlando, FL 32887–0001
    1–800–225–5425
    www.hrw.com

Houghton Mifflin
    181 Ballardvale St.
    P.O. Box 7050
    Wilmington, MA 01887

Macmillan
    345 Park Avenue South
    New York, NY 10010–1707
    http://www.macmillan.com

Prentice-Hall
School Division
    1 Lake Street
    Upper Saddle River, NJ 07458
    1–800–848–9500

Random House
    201 E. 50th St.
    New York, NY 10022
    www.randomhouse.com/acmart

Scholastic
    555 Broadway
    New York, NY 10012

Sundance (paperback books for middle school)
    234 Taylor St.
    Box 1326
    Littleton, MA 01460
    1–800–343–8204
    www.sundancepub.com

References

Adams, D., & Cerqui, C. (1989). *Effective vocabulary instruction.* Kirkland, WA: Reading Resources.

Adams, M. (1990). *Beginning to read: Thinking and learning about print.* Cambridge, MA: MIT Press.

Allen, J. (1999). *Words, words, words: Teaching vocabulary in grades 4–12.* York, ME: Stenhouse.

Allen, J., & Gonzalez, K. (1998). *There's room for me here: Literacy workshop in the middle school.* York, ME: Stenhouse.

Almasi, J. (1996). A new view of discussion. In L. Gambrell & J. Almasi (Eds.), *Lively discussions! Fostering engaged reading* (pp. 2–24). Newark, DE: International Reading Association.

Alvermann, D., Hinchman, K., Moore, D., Phelps, S., & Waff, D. (Eds.). (1998). *Reconceptualizing the literacies in adolescents' lives.* Mahwah, NJ: Lawrence Erlbaum Associates.

American Association of University Women Education Foundation (1999). *Gender Gaps: Where schools still fail our children.* New York: Marlowe & Company.

Ames, C. (1992). Achievement goals and the classroom motivational climate. In D. Schunk & J. Meece (Eds.), *Student perceptions in the classroom* (pp. 327–348). Hillsdale, NJ: Lawrence Erlbaum Associates.

Applebee, A., Langer, J., & Mullis, I. (1988). *Who reads best? Factors related to reading achievement in grades 3, 7, and 11.* Princeton, NJ: Educational Testing Service.

Archer, J. (1998, November 18). States anteing up supplements to teachers certified by Board. *Education Week, 18*(12), 1, 12.

Association of Illinois Middle-Level Schools and the Center for Prevention Research and Development. Top staff development needs cited by middle grades teachers. Cited in *Middle Ground* (Spring, 1995, p. 3). Columbus, OH: National Middle School Association.

Atwell, N. (1987). *In the middle: Writing, reading and learning with adolescents.* Portsmouth, NH: Heinemann.

Atwell, N. (1998). *In the middle: New understandings about writing, reading, and learning* (2nd ed.). Portsmouth, NH: Boynton/Cook–Heinemann.

Baines, L. (1998). From tripod to cosmos: A new metaphor for the language arts. *English Journal, 87*(2), 24–35.

Bamford, R., & Kristo, J. (Eds.). (1998). *Making facts come alive: Choosing quality nonfiction literature K–8.* Norwood, MA: Christopher-Gordon.

Barnes, D. (1993). Supporting exploratory talk for learning. In K. Pierce & C. Gilles (Eds.), *Cycles of meaning: Exploring the potential of talk in learning communities* (pp. 17–34). Portsmouth, NH: Heinemann.

Barnes, D., & Todd, F. (1995). *Communication and learning revisited: Making meaning through talk.* Portsmouth, NH: Boynton/Cook–Heinemann.

Beach, R. (1987). Strategic teaching in literature. In B. Jones, A. Palincsar, D. Ogle, & E. Carr (Eds.), *Strategic teaching and learning: Cognitive instruction in the content areas* (pp. 135–159). Alexandria, VA: Association for Supervision and Curriculum Development.

Beach, R. (1993). *A teacher's introduction to reader-response theories.* Urbana, IL: National Council of Teachers of English.

Beane, J. (1997). *Curriculum integration: Designing the core of democratic education.* New York: Teachers College Press.

Beers, K., & Samuels, B. (Eds.). (1998). *Into focus: Understanding and creating middle school readers.* Norwood, MA: Christopher-Gordon.

Benjamin, F., & Irwin-Devitis, L. (1998). Censoring girls' choices: Continued gender bias in English language arts classrooms. *English Journal, 87*(2), 64–67.

Bereiter, C., & Scardamalia, M. (1987). *The psychology of written composition.* Hillsdale, NJ: Lawrence Erlbaum Associates.

Berkley Books (1984). *Webster's II new riverside dictionary.* New York: Author.

Betts, E. (1946). *Foundations of reading instruction.* New York: American Book Company.

Blank, C., & Roberts, J. (1997). *Live on stage!: Performing arts for middle school.* Palo Alto, CA: Dale Seymour.

Bloom, B. (Ed.). (1956). *Taxonomy of educational objectives: The classification of educational goals.* New York: David McKay.

Bonvillain, N. (1997). *Language, culture, and communication: The meaning of messages* (2nd ed.). Upper Saddle River, NJ: Prentice-Hall.

Borland, H. (1963). *When the legends die.* New York: Bantam.

Braddock, R., Lloyd-Jones, R., & Schoer, L. (1963). *Research in written composition.* Urbana, IL: National Council of Teachers of English.

Bragonier, R., & Fisher, D. (1981). *What's what?: A visual glossary of the physical world.* New York: Ballantine Books.

Brazee, E. (1997). Curriculum for whom? In J. Irvin (Ed.), *What current research says to the middle level practitioner* (pp. 187–201). Columbus, OH: National Middle School Association.

Britton, J., Burgess, T., Martin, M., McLeod, A., & Rosen, H. (1975). *The development of writing abilities (11–18).* London: Macmillan.

Butler, D., & Liner, T. (1995). *Rooms to grow: Natural language arts in the middle school*. Durham, NC: Carolina Academic Press.

Caine, R., & Caine, G. (1994). *Making connections: Teaching and the human brain*. Reading, MA: Addison-Wesley.

Calkins L. (1986). *The art of teaching writing*. Portsmouth, NH: Heinemann.

Cambourne, B. (1988). *The whole story: Natural learning and the acquisition of literacy in the classroom*. Auckland, New Zealand: Ashton Scholastic.

Canter, L., & Canter, M. (1976). *Assertive discipline: A take-charge approach for today's educator*. Seal Beach, CA: Canter and Associates.

Carlsen, R. (1974). Literature IS. *English Journal, 63*(2), 23–27.

Carnegie Council on Adolescent Development (1989). *Turning points: Preparing American youth for the 21st century*. New York: Carnegie Corporation of New York.

Cazden, C. (1988). *Classroom discourse: The language of teaching and learning*. Portsmouth, NH: Heinemann.

Chall, J., & Curtis, M. (1991). Children at risk. In J. Flood, J. Jensen, D. Lapp, & J. Squire (Eds.), *Handbook of research on teaching the English language arts* (pp. 349–355). New York: Macmillan.

Cohen, E. (1986). *Designing groupwork: Strategies for the heterogeneous classroom*. New York: Teachers College Press.

Coles, G. (1998). *Reading lessons: The debate over literacy*. New York: Hill & Wang.

Cooney, C. (1990). *The face on the milk carton*. New York: Laurel-Leaf.

Cooney, C. (1994). *Whatever happened to Janie?* New York: Laurel-Leaf.

Cormier, R, (1974). *The chocolate war*. New York: Laurel-Leaf.

Crichton, M. (1997). *Jurassic park*. New York: Ballantine.

Crutcher, C. (1993). *Staying fat for Sarah Byrnes*. New York: Laurel-Leaf.

Crystal, D. (1987). *The Cambridge encyclopedia of language*. New York: Cambridge University Press.

Curwin, R., & Mendler, A. (1988). *Discipline with dignity*. Alexandria, VA: Association for Supervision and Curriculum Development.

Dahl, K., & Farnan, N. (1998). *Children's writing: Perspectives from research*. Newark, DE: International Reading Association and Chicago, IL: National Reading Conference.

Daniels, H. (1994). *Literature circles: Voice and choice in the student-centered classroom*. York, ME: Stenhouse.

Daniels, H., & Bizar, M. (1998). *Methods that matter: Six structures for best practice classrooms*. York, ME: Stenhouse.

Davis, K., & Hollowell, J. (Eds.). (1977). *Inventing and playing games in the English classroom*. Urbana, IL: National Council of Teachers of English.

Delpit, L. (1995). *Other people's children: Cultural conflict in the classroom*. New York: The New Press.

Dixon-Krauss, L. (1996). *Vygotsky in the classroom: Mediated literacy instruction and assessment*. White Plains, NY: Longman.

Dunn, R., & Dunn, K. (1999). *The complete guide to learning styles*. Needham, MA: Allyn & Bacon.

Early, M. (1960). Stages of growth in literary appreciation. *English Journal, 49*(3), 161–167.

Eeds, M., & Wells, D. (1989). Grand conversations: An exploration of meaning construction in literature study groups. *Research in the Teaching of English, 23*(1), 4–29.

Ellis, A., & Fouts, J. (1997). *Research on educational innovations.* (2nd ed.). Larchmont, NY: Eye on Education.

Emig, J. (1971). *The composing processes of twelfth graders* (Report No. 13 of NCTE Committee on Research). Urbana, IL: National Council of Teachers of English.

Epstein, J. (1988). Effective schools or effective students: Dealing with diversity. In R. Haskins & D. MacRae (Eds.), *Policies for America's public schools: Teacher equity indicators.* Norwood, NJ: Ablex.

Epstein, J. (1989). Family structures and student motivation: A developmental perspective. In C. Ames & R. Ames (Eds.), *Research on motivation in education* (Vol. 3, pp. 259–295). New York: Academic Press.

Erb, T. (Ed.). (1996). Connecting kids to communities [themed issue]. *Middle School Journal, 28*(2).

Ernst, K. (1972). *Games students play (and what to do about them).* Millbrae, CA: Celestial Arts.

Fidge, L. (1992). *The essential guide to speaking and listening.* Dunstable, England: Folens Limited.

Finders, M. (1997). *Just girls.* New York: Teachers College Press.

Fleischman, P. (1985). *I am phoenix: Poems for two voices.* New York: Harper & Row.

Fleischman, P. (1988). *Joyful noise: Poems for two voices.* New York: Harper & Row.

Fletcher, R., & Portalupi, J. (1998). *Craft lessons: Teaching writing K–8.* York, ME: Stenhouse.

Flood, J., Heath, S., & Lapp, D. (1997). *Handbook of research on teaching literacy through the communicative and visual arts.* Newark, DE: International Reading Association.

Flower, L., & Hayes, J. (1980). The dynamics of composing: Making plans and juggling constraints. In L. Gregg & E. Steinberg (Eds.), *Cognitive processes in writing* (pp. 31–50). Hillsdale, NJ: Lawrence Erlbaum Associates.

Foulke, E. (1968). Listening comprehension as a function of word rate. *Journal of Communication, 18,* 198–206.

Fox, R. (1994). Image studies: An interdisciplinary view. In R. Fox (Ed.), *Images in language, media, and mind* (pp. 3–20). Urbana, IL: National Council of Teachers of English.

Freeman, M. (1997). *Listen to this: Developing an ear for expository.* Gainesville, FL: Maupin-House.

Frymier, J. (1985). *Motivation to learn.* West Lafayette, IN: Kappa Delta Pi Press.

Gambrell, L., & Almasi, J. (Eds.). (1996). *Lively discussions! Fostering engaged reading.* Newark, DE: International Reading Association.

Gardner, H. (1983). *Frames of mind: A theory of multiple intelligences.* New York: Basic Books.

Gardner, H. (1991). *The unschooled mind: How children think and how schools should teach.* New York: Basic Books.

Gentry, R. (1987). *SPEL ... is a four-letter word*. Portsmouth, NH: Heinemann.

Gere, A., & Abbott, R. (1985). *Talking about writing: The language of writing groups. Research in the Teaching of English*, 19, 362–381.

Gere, A., Fairbanks, C., Howes, A., Roop, L., & Schaafsma, D. (1992). *Language and reflection: An integrated approach to teaching English*. New York: Macmillan.

Glasser, W. (1990). *The quality school*. New York: HarperCollins.

Glasser, W. (1997). A new look at school failure and school success. *Phi Delta Kappan*, 78, 597–602.

Goldstein, A., & Carr, P. (1996). *Can students benefit from process writing?* (NAEP facts, 1. Report No. NCES–96–845. ED 395 320). Washington, DC: U.S. Department of Education, National Center for Education Statistics.

Goleman, D. (1995). *Emotional intelligence*. New York: Bantam.

Goodlad, J. (1984). *A place called school*. New York: McGraw-Hill.

Goodman, Y., Watson, D., & Burke, C. (1987). *Reading miscue inventory: Alternative procedures*. Katonah, NY: Richard C. Owen.

Gordon, T. (1974). *TET: Teacher effectiveness training*. New York: Wyden.

Graves, D. (1994). *A fresh look at writing*. Portsmouth, NH: Heinemann.

Haberman, M. (1995). *Star teachers of children in poverty*. West Lafayette, IN: Kappa Delta Pi.

Hall, R., & friends (1984). *Sniglets*. New York: Collier Books.

Halliday, M. (1975). *Explorations in the function of language*. London: Edward Arnold.

Halliday, M., & Hasan, R. (1976). *Cohesion in English*. London: Longman.

Handler, M., Dana, A., & Moore, J. (1995). *Hypermedia as a student tool: A guide for teachers*. Englewood, CO: Teacher Ideas Press.

Harmin, M. (1994). *Inspiring active learning: A handbook for teachers*. Alexandria, VA: Association for Supervision and Curriculum Development.

Harris, M. (1986). *Teaching one-to-one: The writing conference*. Urbana, IL: National Council of Teachers of English.

Harste, J., Short, K. (with Burke, C.). (1988). *Creating classrooms for authors: The reading–writing connection*. Portsmouth, NH: Heinemann.

Harvey, S. (1998). *Nonfiction matters: Reading, writing, and research in grades 3–8*. York, ME: Stenhouse.

Healy, J. (1990). *Endangered minds: Why children don't think and what we can do about it*. New York: Simon & Schuster.

Heller, P. (1996). *Drama as a way of knowing*. York, ME: Stenhouse.

Heller, R. (1987). *A cache of jewels and other collective nouns*. New York: Grosset & Dunlap.

Hill, D. (1998, January 14). On Assignment: English spoken here. *Education Week*, 17(18), 42–46

Hillocks, G., Jr. (1986). *Research on written composition*. Urbana, IL: National Council of Teachers of English.

Hillocks, G., & Smith, M. (1991). *Grammar and usage*. In J. Flood, J. Jensen, D. Lapp, & J. Squire (Eds.), *Handbook of research on teaching the English language arts* (pp. 591–603). New York: Macmillan.

Hoffman, J. (1979). The intra-act procedure for critical reading. *Journal of Reading*, 22, 605–608.

Holdaway, D. (1979). *The foundations of literacy.* Portsmouth, NH: Heinemann.

Hull, G. (1987). Constructing taxonomies for error (or can stray dogs be mermaids?). In T. Enos (Ed.), *A sourcebook for basic writing teachers* (pp. 231–244). New York: Random House.

Hunsaker, R. (1990). *Understanding and developing the skills of oral communication: Speaking and listening* (2nd ed.). Englewood, CO: Morton.

Hurwitz, A., & Goddard, A. (1969). *Games to improve your child's English.* New York: Simon & Schuster.

Hyerle, D. (1996). *Visual tools for constructing knowledge.* Alexandria, VA: Association for Supervision and Curriculum Development.

Hyslop, N., & Tone, B. (1988). Listening: Are we teaching it, and if so, how? *ERIC/RCS Digest,* (3). ERIC Clearinghouse on Reading and Communication Skills.

Illinois State Department of Education (n.d.). *Basic oral communication skills: A program sequence for Illinois.* Springfield, IL: Illinois State Board of Education.

Indiana Education Policy Center. (1996). *Learning together: Professional development for better schools.* Bloomington, IN: Author.

Irvin, J. (1998). *Reading and the middle school student: Strategies to enhance literacy* (2nd ed.). Boston: Allyn & Bacon.

Irwin, J., & Doyle, M. (1992). *Reading/writing connections: Learning from research.* Newark, DE: International Reading Association.

Ivers, K., & Barron, A. (1998). *Multimedia projects in education: Designing, producing, and assessing.* Englewood, CO: Libraries Unlimited.

Jalongo, M. (1991). *Strategies for developing children's listening skills* (Fastback No. 314). Bloomington, IN: Phi Delta Kappa Educational Foundation.

Jensen, E. (1998). *Teaching with the brain in mind.* Alexandria, VA: Association for Supervision and Curriculum Development.

Jody, M., & Saccardi, M. (1998). *Using computers to teach literature: A teacher's guide.* Urbana, IL: National Council of Teachers of English.

Johnson, D., Johnson, R., Holubec, E., & Roy, P. (1991). *Cooperation in the classroom.* Edina, MN: Interaction Book Company.

Judy, S. (1981). *Explorations in the teaching of English* (2nd ed.). New York: Harper & Row.

Kingen, S. (1994). When middle school students compose: An examination of processes and products. *Research in Middle Level Education, 18*(1), 83–103.

Kirschner, B., & Yates, J. (1983). *Discovery to discourse: The composing process.* New York: Macmillan.

Kletzien, S., & Baloche, L. (1994). The shifting muffled sound of the pick: Facilitating student-to-student discussion. *Journal of Reading, 37,* 540–545.

Knoeller, C. (1994). Negotiating interpretations of text: The role of student-led discussions in understanding literature. *Journal of Reading, 37,* 572–580.

Kobrin, B. (1988). *Eyeopeners!* New York: Penguin Books.

Kobrin, B. (1995). *Eyeopeners II.* New York: Scholastic.

Kohl, H. (1981). *A book of puzzlements: Play and invention with language.* New York: Schocken Books.

Kohn, A. (1993). *Punished by rewards: The trouble with gold stars, incentive plans, A's, praise, and other bribes*. Boston: Houghton Mifflin.

Krogness, M. (1995). *Just teach me, Mrs. K: Talking, reading, and writing with resistant adolescent learners*. Portsmouth, NH: Heinemann.

Langer, J. (1998, Fall). Beating the odds: Critical components boost student performance. *English Update, Newsletter from the Center on English Learning & Achievement*, 1, 8.

Lederer, R. (1988). *Get thee to a punnery*. Charleston, SC: Wyrick & Company.

Leu, D., & Leu, D. (1999). *Teaching with the Internet: Lessons from the classroom*. Norwood, MA: Christopher-Gordon.

Lewis, A. (1992). *Writing: A fact and fun book*. Reading, MA: Addison-Wesley.

Lipsitz, J., Jackson, A., & Austin, L. (1997). What works in middle-grades school reform. *Phi Delta Kappan, 78*, 517–556.

Lortie, D. (1975). *Schoolteacher: A sociological study*. Chicago: University of Chicago Press.

Lowry, L. (1989). *Number the stars*. New York: Dell.

Lundsteen, S. (1979). *Listening: Its impact at all levels on reading and the other language arts*. Urbana, IL: ERIC Clearinghouse on Reading and Communication Skills and the National Council of Teachers of English.

Lupton, E. (1988). Period styles: A punctuated history. *Teachers and Writers Collaborative Newsletter 20*(1), 7–11.

Manning, M. (1993). *Developmentally appropriate middle level schools*. Wheaton, MD: Association for Childhood Education International.

Manzo, A. (1975). Guided reading procedure. *Journal of Reading, 18*, 287–291.

Martinello, M., & Cook, G. (1994). *Interdisciplinary inquiry in teaching and learning*. New York: Macmillan.

Maslow, A. (1943). A theory of human motivation. *Psychological Review, 50*, 370–396.

Mayher, J. (1990). *Uncommon sense: Theoretical practice in language education*. Portsmouth, NH: Boynton/Cook-Heinemann.

McCarthy, B. (1987). *The 4MAT system: Teaching to learning styles with right/left mode techniques*. Barrington, IL: Excel.

McCrum, R., Cran, W., & MacNeil, R. (1986). *The story of English*. New York: Elizabeth Sifton Books–Viking.

McEwin, C. & Dickinson, T. (1995). *The professional preparation of middle level teachers: Profiles of successful programs*. Columbus, OH: National Middle School Association.

Mellon, J. (1979). Issues in the theory and practice of sentence combining: A twenty year perspective. In D. Daiker, A. Kerek, & M. Morenberg (Eds.), *Sentence combining and the teaching of writing* (pp. 1–38). Conway, AR: University of Akron and University of Central Arkansas.

Messaris, P. (1997). Visual intelligence and analogical thinking. In J. Flood, S. Heath, & D. Lapp (Eds.), *Handbook of research on teaching literacy through the communicative and visual arts* (pp. 48–54). New York: Macmillan.

Mizelle, N. (1997). Enhancing young adolescents' motivation for literacy learning. *Middle School Journal, 28*(3), 16–25.

Moffett, J. (1968). *Teaching the universe of discourse*. Boston: Houghton Mifflin.

Moffett, J., & Wagner, B. (1976) *Student-centered language arts and reading, K–13* (2nd ed.). Boston: Houghton Mifflin.

Moffett, J. (with Tashlik, P.). (1987). *Active voices II: A writer's reader for grades 7–9*. Upper Montclair, NJ: Boynton/Cook.

Monson, D., & Sebesta, S. (1991). Reading preferences. In J. Flood, J. Jensen, D. Lapp, & J. Squire (Eds.), *Handbook of research on teaching the English language arts* (pp. 664–673). New York: Macmillan.

Mooney, M. (1990). *Reading, to, with, and by children*. Katonah, NY: Richard C. Owen.

Morris, W. (Ed.). (1973). *American heritage dictionary of the English language*. New York: American Heritabe and Boston: Houghton Mifflin.

Myers, I. (1962). *Introduction to type*. Palo Alto, CA: Consulting Psychologists Press.

Myers, K. (1988). Twenty (better) questions. *English Journal, 77*(1), 64–65.

Nash, B., & Nash, G. (1979). *Pundles*. New York: The Stonesong Press.

National Board for Professional Teaching Standards (1994). *Early adolescence/English language arts standards*. Detroit, MI: Author.

National Council of Teachers of English (1996). *Guidelines for the preparation of teachers of English language arts*. Urbana, IL: Author.

National Council of Teachers of English and the International Reading Association. (1996). *Standards for the English language arts*. Urbana, IL and Newark, DE: Author.

National Middle School Association (1995). *This we believe: Developmentally responsive middle level schools*. Columbus, OH: Author.

National Middle School Association. (1996). *National Middle School Association/NCATE-approved teacher preparation curriculum guidelines.*Columbus, OH: Author.

Oakes, J. (1985). *Keeping track: How schools structure inequality*. New Haven, CT: Yale University Press.

Ogden, E., & Germinario, V. (1994). *The nation's best schools, blueprint for excellence.* (vols. 1–2). Lancaster, PA: Technomic Publishing.

Ogle, D. (1986). K-W-L: A teaching model that develops active reading of expository text. *The Reading Teacher 39*, 564–670.

O'Keefe, V. (1995). *Speaking to think, thinking to speak: The importance of talk in the learning process*. Portsmouth, NH: Boynton/Cook-Heinemann.

Opitz, M., & Rasinski, T. (1998). *Good-bye round robin: 25 effective oral reading strategies*. Portsmouth, NH: Heinemann.

Page, G. (1997). Visual intelligence and spatial aptitudes. In J. Flood, S. Heath, & D. Lapp (Eds.), *Handbook of research on literacy through the communicative and visual arts* (pp. 55–61). New York: Macmillan.

Palinscar, A., & Brown, A. (1985). Reciprocal teaching: Activities to promote "reading with your mind." In T. Harris & E. Cooper (Eds.), *Reading, thinking, and concept development*, (pp. 147–159). New York: The College Board.

Pappas, C., & Pettegrew, B. (1998). The role of genre in the psycholinguistic guessing game of reading. *Language Arts, 75*, 36–44.

Paratore, J., & McCormack, R. (Eds.). (1997). *Peer talk in the classroom: Learning from research*. Newark, DE: International Reading Association.

Patterson, L., Santa, C., Short, K., & Smith, K. (Eds.). (1993). *Teachers are researchers: Reflection and action*. Newark, DE: International Reading Association.

Pearson, D. (Ed.) (1984). *Handbook of reading research*. New York: Longman.

Peck, R. (1972). *A day no pigs would die*. New York: Random House.

Perry, T., & Delpit, L. (Eds.). (1998). *The real Ebonics debate: Power, language, and the education of African-American children*. Boston, MA: Beacon Press.

Pianko, S. (1979). A description of the composing processes of college freshman writers. *Research in the Teaching of English, 13*, 5–22.

Pike, K., Compain, R., & Mumper, J. (1997). *New connections: An integrated approach to literacy* (2nd ed.). New York: Addison Wesley Longman.

Pikulski, J. (1991). The transition years: middle school. In J. Flood, J. Jensen, D. Lapp, & J. Squire (Eds.), *Handbook of research on teaching the English language arts* (pp. 303–319). New York: Macmillan.

Pinnell, G., & Jaggar, A. (1991). Oral language: Speaking and listening in the classroom. In J. Flood, J. Jensen, D. Lapp, & J. Squire (Eds.), *Handbook of research on teaching the English language arts* (pp. 691–720). New York: Macmillan.

Pooley, R. (1974). *The teaching of English usage*. Urbana, IL: National Council of Teachers of English.

Raffini, J. (1996). *150 ways to increase intrinsic motivation in the classroom*. Boston: Allyn & Bacon.

Reed, C. (1989). *Shades of gray*. New York: Avon Books.

Ridley, D. S., McCombs, B., & Taylor, K. (1994). Walking the talk: Fostering self-regulated learning in the classroom. *Middle School Journal, 26*(2), 52–57.

Rief, L. (1992). *Seeking diversity: Language arts with adolescents*. Portsmouth, NH: Heinemann.

Rimm, S. (1986). *Underachievement syndrome: Causes and cures*. Watertown, WI: Apple.

Roblyer, M., Edwards, J., & Havriluk, M. (1997). *Integrating educational technology into teaching*. Upper Saddle River, NJ: Merrill-Prentice Hall.

Rosenblatt, L. (1938). *Literature as exploration*. New York: Appleton-Century.

Rosenblatt, L. (1978). *The reader, the text, and the poem: The transactional theory of the literary work*. Carbondale, IL: Southern Illinois University Press.

Rothermel, D. (1996). *Starting points: How to set up and run a writing workshop—and much more!* Columbus, OH: National Middle School Association.

Routman, R. (1991). *Invitations: Changing as teachers and learners K–12*. Portsmouth, NH: Heinemann.

Sadker, M., & Sadker, D. (1994). *Failing at fairness: How America's schools cheat girls*. New York: Scribner's.

Scales, P. (1996). *Boxed in and bored: How middle schools continue to fail young adolescents—and what good middle schools do right*. Minneapolis, MN: Search Institute.

Scherer, M. (Ed.). (1998). Strengthening the teaching profession [themed issue]. *Educational Leadership, 55*(5).

Schmidt, P. (1994, September 28). Idea of "gender gap" in schools under attack. *Education Week, 14*(4), 1, 16.

Scholastic (1995). *The history of printmaking*. New York: Author.

Schrock, K. (1998/1999). The ABCs of web site evaluation. *Classroom Connect, 5*(4), 4–6.

Shannon, G. (1994). *Still more stories to solve: Fourteen folktales from around the world*. New York: Beech Tree Books.

Slavin, R. (1983). *Cooperative learning*. New York: Longman.

Small, R., & McLeod, A. (1974). Promoting individualization in English. *English Education, 5,* 84–89.

Smith, F. (1997). *Reading without nonsense* (3rd ed.). New York: Teachers College, Columbia University.

Sobel, D. (1967). *Two-minute mysteries*. New York: Scholastic.

Spear, K. (1987). *Sharing writing: Peer response groups in the English class*. Portsmouth, NH: Heinemann.

Spear, K. (1993). *Peer response groups in action: Writing together in secondary schools*. Portsmouth, NH: Boynton/Cook–Heinemann.

Spelvin, G. (1995). *Jumanji*. New York: Scholastic.

Spolin, V. (1986). *Theater games for the classroom: A teacher's handbook*. Evanston, IL: Northwestern University Press.

Stanford, G. (Chair). (1979). *Handling the paper load* (Classroom Practices Series). Urbana, IL: National Council of Teachers of English.

Stauffer, R. (1980). *The language experience approach to the teaching of reading* (2nd ed.). New York: Harper & Row.

Stevenson, C. (1998). *Teaching ten to fourteen year olds*. (2nd ed.). New York: Longman.

Strickland, R. (1962). The language of elementary school children: Its relationship to the language of reading textbooks and the quality of reading of selected children. *Bulletin of the School of Education, Indiana University, 38*(4).

Strickland, D., Dillon R., Funkhouser, L., Glick, M., & Rogers, C. (1989). Research currents: Classroom dialogue during literature response groups. *Language Arts, 66,* 192–200.

Strother, D. (1987). Practical applications of research: On listening. *Phi Delta Kappan, 68,* 625–628.

Strubbe, M. (1990). Are interdisciplinary units worthwhile? Ask students. *Middle School Journal, 21*(2), 36–38.

Styslinger, M. (1999). Mars and Venus in my classroom: Men go to their caves and women talk during peer revision. *English Journal, 88*(3), 50–56.

Suid, M. (1981). *Demonic mnemonics: 800 spelling tricks for 800 tricky words*. Belmont, CA: Pitman Learning.

Tchudi, S. (Ed.). (1997). *Alternatives to grading student writing*. Urbana, IL: National Council of Teachers of English.

Temple, C., & Gillet, J. (1984). *Language arts: Learning processes and teaching practices*. Boston, MA: Little, Brown and Company.

Thomma, S., & Cannon, A. (September 17, 1995). Speaking the language. *The Indianapolis Star*, pp. D1, D4.

Tomlinson, C. (1998). For integration and differentiation choose concepts over topics. *Middle School Journal, 30*(2), 3–8.

Tompkins, G. (1987). *Language arts: Content and teaching strategies* (4th ed.). Upper Saddle River, NJ: Prentice-Hall, Inc.

Topping, K., & Whiteley, M. (1990). Participation evaluation of parent-tutored and peer-tutored projects in reading. *Educational Research, 32*, 14–27.

Trelease, J. (1993). *Read all about it: Great read-aloud stories, poems, and newspaper pieces for preteens and teens.* New York: Penguin.

Vacca, R., & Vacca, J. (1989). *Content area reading* (3rd ed.). Glenvew, IL: Scott, Foresman.

Van Allsburg, C. (1981). *Jumanji.* Boston: Houghton Mifflin.

Van Brocklyn, R. (1988). The candor test. *Curriculum Review, 27* (5), 12–13.

Vars, G. (1997). Effects of integrative curriculum and instruction. In J. Irvin (Ed.), *What current research says to the middle level practitioner* (pp. 179–186). Columbus, OH: National Middle School Association.

Vygotsky, L. (1978). *Mind in society: The development of higher psychological processes.* Cambridge, MA: Harvard University Press.

Waddell, M., Esch, R., & Walker R. (1972). *The art of styling sentences: 20 patterns to success.* Woodbury, NY: Barron's Educational Series.

Wagner, B. (1998). *Educational drama and language arts: What research shows.* Portsmouth, NH: Heinemann.

Weaver, C. (1994). *Reading process and practice: From socio-psycholinguistics to whole language* (2nd ed.). Portsmouth, NH: Heinemann.

Weaver, C. (1996). *Teaching Grammar in Context.* Portsmouth, NH: Boynton/Cook–Heinemann.

Weaver, C. (Ed.). (1998). *Lessons to share: On teaching grammar in context.* Portsmouth, NH: Boynton/Cook–Heinemann.

Weitzman, D. (1974). Break the ice with 5 squares. *Learning, 2*(9), 32–37.

Wheelock, A. (1992). *Crossing the tracks: How "untracking" can save America's schools.* New York: New Press.

Whitin, P. (1996). *Sketching stories, stretching minds: Responding visually to literature.* Portsmouth, NH: Heinemann.

Wiedmer, T. (1998). Digital portfolios: capturing and demonstrating skills and levels of performance. *Phi Delta Kappan, 79*(8), 586–589.

Wilhelm, J. (1997). *You gotta BE the book: Teaching engaged and reflective reading with adolescents.* New York: Teachers College Press.

Wilhelm, J., & Friedemann, P. (with Erickson, J.). (1998). *Hyperlearning: Where projects, inquiry, and technology meet.* York, ME: Stenhouse.

Williams-Garcia, R. (1995). *Like sisters on the homefront.* New York: Puffin.

Witkin, M. (1994). A defense of using pop media in the middle school classroom. *English Journal, 83*(1), 30–33.

Wolvin, A., & Coakley C. (1979). *Listening instruction.* Urbana, IL: ERIC Clearinghouse on Reading and Communication Skills and the Speech Communication Association.

Wolvin, A., & Coakley, C. (1985). *Listening* (2nd ed.). Dubuque, IA: William C. Brown.

Wood, K., Lapp, D, & Flood, J. (1992). *Guiding readers through text: A review of study guides.* Newark, DE: International Reading Association.

Yopp, H., & Yopp, R. (1996). *Literature-based reading activities* (2nd ed.). Boston: Allyn & Bacon.

Zemelman, S., & Daniels, H. (1988). *A community of writers: Teaching writing in the junior and senior high school*. Portsmouth, NH: Heinemann.

Zemelman, S., Daniels, H., & Hyde, A. (1998). *Best practice: New standards for teaching and learning in America's schools* (2nd ed.). Portsmouth, NH: Heinemann.

Author Index

Subject Index